D0575749

DISCARDED

UNIVERSITY OF WINNIPEG
PORTAGE & BALMORAL
WINNIPEG, MAN.   R3B 2E9
CANADA

The Chronicler of Barsetshire

PR
5686
S88
1988

The Chronicler
of Barsetshire

A LIFE OF ANTHONY TROLLOPE

R. H. Super

The University of Michigan Press
Ann Arbor

Copyright © by the University of Michigan 1988
All rights reserved
Published in the United States of America by
The University of Michigan Press
Manufactured in the United States of America

1991   1990   1989   4   3   2

Library of Congress Cataloging-in-Publication Data

Super, R. H. (Robert Henry), 1914–
   The chronicler of Barsetshire : a life of Anthony Trollope / R.H.
Super.
      p.   cm.
   Bibliography: p.
   Includes index.
   ISBN 0-472-10102-1 (alk. paper)
   1. Trollope, Anthony, 1815–1882—Biography.   2. Novelists,
English—19th century—Biography.   I. Title.
PR5686.S88 1988
823'.8—dc19
   [B]   88-14100
                                                        CIP

For Rebecca

Preface

Nearly two hundred years ago a very well-known biography opened with the words: "To write the life of him who excelled all mankind in writing the lives of others . . . is an arduous, and may be reckoned in me a presumptuous task." If I might substitute for the "lives of others" the words "his own life," I should express my sense of the present undertaking. Trollope's is one of the best of all autobiographies, and has so dominated our thinking about him that any narrator of his life is faced with the dilemma of how to deal with that book. Indeed, it may be said that *An Autobiography* has heretofore largely precluded any serious attempt at writing his life; only his earliest biographer, T. H. S. Escott, has declared his independence of it, and he was a personal friend who published in 1913. (Escott's personal acquaintance with Trollope and his knowledge of the literary circles in which Trollope moved make his biography a most valuable source of information that will not be entirely superseded.) Michael Sadleir's was not a life but "a Commentary"; the work of Lucy and Richard Stebbins was an account not of Anthony but of a whole "writing family." It does show a substantial amount of original research and is dominated by a strong dose of Freudian psychology, according to which Plantagenet Palliser and Lady Glencora are unconscious portraits of Trollope's father and mother. James Pope-Hennessy's *Trollope: A Biography* is good reading, with especially attractive descriptions of the Irish countryside Trollope knew; he has read all the novels and integrates them with the biographical facts, but for these facts he depends almost entirely on *An Autobiography*. He is somewhat obsessed with Trollope's presumed infatuation with the young Bostonian woman Kate Field, whose father he confuses with the publisher James T. Fields (as does Lord Snow) and whose face and figure he discerns behind many of Trollope's heroines.

In the present work, I have attempted to escape the shadow of *An Autobiography* by constructing my narrative essentially independently of it, though I have frequently turned to it for an indication of how the events of his life appeared to Trollope in retrospect from the point of view of his early sixties. His is not an authoritative record of events put down as they actually occurred, and where my story differs from *An Autobiography* it may be assumed that the evidence is on the side of the present narrative.

I hope that I have escaped the worst aspects of Trollope's recipe for writing biography—a recipe he himself used in his *Thackeray* and *Lord Palmerston:* "Scrape together a few facts, . . . indulge in some fiction, . . . tell a few anecdotes, and then . . . call [the] book a biography."[1] The present work may be much more liable to the objection that it is too involved with detail, too caught up in what has been called "the historian's fascination with the obstinate idiosyncrasy of the particular."[2] A book of this sort has many functions, not always easily compatible. It is a narrative, the story of the life of an interesting, versatile, significant man; the details themselves, one hopes, are interesting and revealing, "those little unremembered acts," as Wordsworth called them. But it is also to the reader a source of accurate information, and accuracy implies detail and precision. Because it depends entirely on surviving evidence known to the writer, it may in unknown ways distort the proportions of the life; the preservation of letters, for example, is so much a matter of chance that large bodies of significant correspondence may have vanished, leaving no clue even to what they dealt with or by whom they were written. Many close friends of Trollope's have doubtless left no reminiscences. Archives are more impersonal and undiscriminating (if they survive wars and "troubles"), but only a few Trollope scholars have had the patience to explore archival materials. Were it not for the novels, there would be little reason for a life of Trollope, but the handling of them in a biography presents problems: I have tried to view them always in relation to other events in the author's life, and while the reader will want to have some information about their subjects, some sense of their flavor, he must look elsewhere for detailed literary criticism. Fortunately there are many books of such criticism.

By far the most important source of our knowledge of Trollope is the two-volume edition of his *Letters* by N. John Hall, an exemplary piece of scholarship superbly annotated, not with obvious comments but with recondite, yet illuminating information that is the fruit of abstruse research. This edition is only the chief of Professor Hall's many valuable contributions to the study and reputation of Trollope. He is now himself writing a biography that will appear at much the same time as the present book; more than a century after Trollope's death there is ample room for two such works. Professor Hall has never failed in his generosity in answering my questions; his concern is the integrity of the scholarly ideal, not jealousy of personal reputation.

Modern scholarship on Trollope owes perhaps its greatest debt to Michael Sadleir—novelist, publisher, bibliographer, book collector, and biographer. His *Trollope: A Commentary*, first published in 1927 and revised twenty years later, is, however, precisely what its title suggests, a commentary within a biographical framework, not a biography. It is lively in style and as imaginative in its interpretation of Trollope's character and motives as if it were a novel, yet for the events of Trollope's life it depends very largely on *An Autobiography*. Where Sadleir has discovered unpublished letters, as in the files of the publishing houses of Longman and Smith, Elder, he interrupts his narrative to give us a rudimentary edition of the correspondence. The first one-third of the book is an analysis of the mid-Victorian era and a not very accurate account of Mrs. Frances Trollope's life, especially her adventures in America (where Anthony did not accompany her). It is a pioneering work, but if only because a pioneer cannot do everything it is now entirely obsolete. More valuable, and infinitely more painstaking, is Sadleir's *Trollope: A Bibliography* (1928; with *Addenda and Corrigenda* from 1934). It is, however, a book designed for collectors, not for scholars, with by far the greatest amount of space devoted to first editions in book form—the form that was circulated through the lending libraries—and an almost back-of-the-hand dismissal of those later editions which Trollope's readers actually bought. It is also regrettably slovenly in attention to those minutiae to which one might expect a bibliographer to be especially attentive—transcriptions of title pages, dates of publication, etc. (Lance O. Tingay's privately printed little book, *The Trollope Collector* [1985], is a very meticulous listing of all Trollope editions that does much to remedy Sadleir's incompleteness.)

It is perhaps Sadleir's very experience as a publisher that was of greatest disservice to him, for a practical publisher is very different from a historian of publishing. Again and again in both *Commentary* and *Bibliography* Sadleir is led into believing that because, from his own experience, things may well have happened in a certain way, they necessarily *did* happen in that way; he habitually states as fact matters for which he has no evidence and about which, as modern research brings out the evidence, the truth turns out to be quite different. In at least one matter he is our only source of information—his transcripts of Trollope's correspondence with Longman, of which the originals were destroyed by fire—and there even his dating of letters can be shown, in some cases, to be inconsistent with the evidence of Trollope's current travel diaries or of other incontrovertible sources of information. For example, he misdates by a year the correspondence dealing with *The New Zealander*. It must be said with some firmness that no statement made by Sadleir can be accepted without positive confirmation from some other source.

His greatest contribution to modern scholarship is as a collector. He knew Trollope's son Henry, and either purchased from him or obtained other purchasers for vast amounts of material from Anthony's carefully preserved papers, including the travel diaries mentioned above (now in the library of Princeton University) and, perhaps most important, Anthony's records of his contracts with publishers and his diaries of the actual writing of his works (now in the Bodleian Library, Oxford). Sadleir's hand can be traced in almost every collection of Trollope manuscripts; for nearly every error perpetrated in his books he has provided the evidence for correcting it in the primary materials he so strenuously collected.

C. P. Snow's *Trollope: His Life and Art* (1975) is chiefly valuable as a picture book: its well over a hundred illustrations give a remarkable visual image of Trollope and his age. The two chapters on "Trollope's Art" are the shrewd observations of a skillful novelist, but the account of Trollope's life is essentially a summary of *An Autobiography*, supplemented at times from Sadleir's *Commentary*, and with a surprisingly casual attitude toward facts. One book that is the result of infinite pains and wonderful enthusiasm is the *Guide to Trollope* published by Winifred Gregory Gerould and James Thayer Gerould in 1948. Names, places, plots are all there in alphabetical order, with laudable completeness.

At long last, thanks to the efforts of Professor Hall and, more recently, to the very moderately priced editions from Dover Publications, all Trollope's novels and most of his other books are currently available to the purchaser. But very little has been done to set right the almost incredibly slovenly texts with which the reader is faced. P. D. Edwards has added a long list of variant readings from manuscript and early editions to a photo-facsimile of the first edition of *He Knew He Was Right*; whoever wants to take his pen and correct the text thus has the materials at hand. Robert H. Taylor has collated the manuscript and the magazine version with the first edition of *The American Senator* and published a list of nearly 250 variants.[3] Many years ago with wonderful perversity Frederick Page and Michael Sadleir printed *An Autobiography* from the manuscript, thereby restoring blunders of fact that Henry Trollope had corrected in seeing the first edition of the book through the press (errors such as the year in which *The Warden* was conceived), and they appended their multitude of textual variants classified in a useless and unintelligible manner. My own edition of *Marion Fay* aims at giving an authoritative reading text, based on the manuscript and corrected where necessary from early editions; it does not list textual variants on the ground that it would be preposterous to suppose that a novel reader should be made to pay for setting such things in type. (The complete textual variants are available from the editor, should individuals or libraries request them.)

Of Trollope's forty-seven novels, thirty-six survive in manuscript so far as is now known (*Framley Parsonage* only in the last ten of its sixteen installments in the *Cornhill Magazine*). Most of the missing manuscripts are the early ones; of the novels later than *Framley Parsonage*, only *Brown, Jones, and Robinson*, *Linda Tressel*, *The Golden Lion of Granpere*, and *Is He Popenjoy?* are not now known in manuscript. In addition, we have the manuscripts of *North America, Australia and New Zealand, An Autobiography, South Africa,* and *The Life of Cicero.* It would be a real service to make accurate texts of these works available at a reasonable price—and a reasonable price cannot be achieved by that school which makes editing an end in itself, rather than the production of a more perfect piece of literature. Unfortunately, not every scholar is an accurate editor; fortunately, on the other hand, an editor seldom learns of his own blunders.

The present book is the product of the Victorian seminar at the University of Michigan. It was set in motion when Dr. Ronald Gordon, assigned to scrutinize the techniques of a modern literary biography, demonstrated conclusively the scholarly inadequacy of all existing lives of Trollope. Other students from that seminar have completed dissertations or published books on subjects relevant to the study of Trollope: Patricia Thomas Srebrnik on the publisher Alexander Strahan, Judith Wittosch Malcolm on *St. Pauls Magazine*, Donna Wessel-Walker on the *Contemporary Review*, David Arnett on the *Fortnightly Review* under John Morley. Whitney Hoth, my teaching assistant, spent hours browsing the library shelves for references to Trollope among the memoirs published by the Victorians. Colleagues, collectors, and librarians everywhere have been uniformly helpful; ours is a cooperative profession. Especially deserving mention is Nigel Cross, archivist at the Royal Literary Fund. Such as it is, this book is the work of many hands.

I must express my personal gratitude to my friend and colleague Professor James Gindin, who from the moment, a decade ago, when I mentioned that I might embark on this project, has been constant in his encouragement, and who, with his broad and detailed knowledge of nineteenth- and twentieth-century fiction, has spared me (and my readers) countless blunders by his meticulous reading of my manuscript. Nor can I forgo this final opportunity to praise the director of the University of Michigan Press, Walter E. Sears, and his entire staff, with whom I have worked with the greatest pleasure and satisfaction for many years. Both author and readers owe a great debt to the arduous labors of Christina L. Milton and Christina Postema, who edited the work for the press.

Shortly before her death, George Eliot remarked to Tom Trollope's wife, "Biographies generally are a disease of English literature," and Anthony Trollope seems to have agreed with her.[4] It is a sobering thought for one whose scholarly career began many years ago with a biography of Walter Savage Landor and now ends with another work in the same genre.

Contents

Illustrations

15. **Cover for the monthly parts of** *The Way We Live Now* (1874–75).
    Black on blue background, signed "J.B." and engraved by H. Linton.
16. **"Siege of the Deck Cabin," June, 1878.** Drawing by Mrs. Hugh
    Blackburn for Trollope's *How the "Mastiffs" Went to Iceland.* The occasion
    was an attempt to expel the cigar-smoking male from the ladies' lounge.
    John Burns, chairman of the Cunard Steamship Company, wields the
    rope's end; his brother James Cleland Burns empties the pail of water.

Photographs courtesy of: James and Rosemary Farquharson (no. 6); Trustees of
the Boston Public Library, Kate Field Collection (jacket and nos. 1, 2, 5, 8);
Harvard University Museums (nos. 3, 4, 7, 9); Parrish Collection, Princeton
University Library (no. 2); University of Michigan Library (nos. 10–16).

Chapter I

1815–34

There are no longer any houses on Keppel Street in London. The street itself has been sadly truncated by the massive structure of the London University Senate House, which cuts it off from its former access to the west side of Russell Square. Even Russell Square is changing beyond recognition from the comfortable professional homes in which Thackeray's Sedleys and Osbornes lived. A few steps from where Keppel Street used to join the square, the house in which the great chancery barrister Sir Samuel Romilly cut his throat in 1818 (to Byron's delight)[1] still stands, but looks as though it cannot hold out much longer against the concrete masses of the university. And yet at the end of the last century the region had changed so little from its pre-Waterloo days that Thomas Adolphus Trollope, visiting it near the end of his long life, found the sweets shop he patronized as a boy still selling its wares, with the same family name on the sign.[2] "Keppel Street cannot be called fashionable, and Russell Square is not much affected by the nobility," Trollope tells us when Lady Anna's mother takes lodgings there. Mr. Prendergast, the solicitor in *Castle Richmond*, "was one of those old-fashioned people who think that a spacious substantial house in Bloomsbury Square [near Keppel Street], at a rent of a hundred and twenty pounds a year, is better worth having than a narrow, lath and plaster ill-built tenement at nearly double the price out westward of the parks. A quite new man is necessarily afraid of such a locality as Bloomsbury Square, for he has no chance of getting anyone into his house if he do not live westward. . . . But Mr. Prendergast was well enough known to his old friends to be allowed to live where he pleased." In Charley Tudor's novelette *Crinoline and Macassar*, the couple was married in Bloomsbury Church (where Anthony had been baptized) and took lodgings in Alfred Place, off Store Street and only a few steps from Keppel Street.[3]

At No. 27 Keppel Street in 1803 a young War Office clerk named Henry Milton set up housekeeping with his two older sisters, Mary and Frances. The three were children of the Reverend William Milton, vicar of Heckfield, Hampshire, close to Reading. William in turn was the son of a Bristol saddler, but had gone to Winchester and St. John's College, Oxford, then had become a fellow of New College; Heckfield was a New College living. His first wife, Mary Gresley, the mother of the three children, had died when they were small, and he had remarried; the second wife was affectionately regarded by her stepchildren and had no children of her own.[4] William Milton, though something of a scholar, was also an amateur engineer; he had published a pamphlet on redesigning the docks of Bristol and was soon to publish another on *The Danger of Travelling in Stage-Coaches* (1810), the object of which was to call attention to a patent coach of his own invention which was far less subject to the danger of upsetting than the ordinary coach: luggage, instead of being carried on top, was stored in a compartment beneath the coach to lower the center of gravity, and the four principal wheels were seconded by four slightly smaller "idle wheels" mounted just inside them so that they could take over in an instant should a principal wheel break or fall off. The conception seems like a good one, and Milton published testimonials to its effectiveness from the users of the two coaches built to his design by a Reading firm and placed in service. Nevertheless, it does not seem to have caught on.

Henry Milton was about nineteen years old when he took his clerkship, and he remained with the War Office until his death in 1850. He was an intelligent and kind young man who, in the months immediately following Waterloo, went, like so many Englishmen, to Paris; his special errand was to see the works of art Napoleon had plundered for the Louvre and to write a description of them for the British public. Indeed, while he was there in September, he watched the Venetian horses being removed from the triumphal arch near the Louvre and the Flemish paintings being taken from their frames to be returned to their homes to the north. His book ranged beyond paintings and sculpture to architecture and the theater: Talma and Mlle. Mars filled him with enthusiasm, the latter "an inimitable, a perfect actress." Sixty years later the nephew who was born just before Waterloo described the same Mlle. Mars as one of the greatest actresses he had ever seen. Henry Milton's was the earliest of an impressive number of travel books to be written by members of his family. A very few years later he took under his wing the widow and young son of another War Office clerk from near Reading, and the son, John Lucas, became one of the most fashionable portrait painters of the mid-century; his portrait of Henry Milton would hang in the Royal Academy exhibition of 1830. (Henry's complete baldness is a foreshadowing of a prominent characteristic of his nephew.)[5]

Among the callers on the household in Keppel Street was a promising young chancery barrister about ten years older than Milton, and like him the son of a clergyman. Thomas Anthony Trollope, born in 1774, was also a Wykehamist and still held his fellowship at New College, Oxford (he was obliged to resign it, and its stipend of £200 per annum, when he married). "I do not think that a greater curse can fall upon a

highly-educated man than a gift of a permanent fellowship unaccom-
panied by work," his novelist son told a Liverpool audience in 1870.
Thomas Anthony took his B.C.L. from Oxford in 1801, was admitted to
the bar from the Middle Temple on May 11, 1804, and transferred to
Lincoln's Inn on December 12, 1806; his chambers there were in the Old
Square. His father, also Thomas Anthony (though he generally dropped
the "Thomas"), was the youngest son of a Lincolnshire baronet and held
the Hertfordshire rectory of Cottered and the nearby vicarage of Rushden
until his death on June 3, 1806, at the age of seventy-two. The reverend
Anthony had married the second daughter of the wealthiest man in the
parish, Adolphus Meetkerke of "Julians."[6] The dynastic inclinations of
the Meetkerkes were perhaps indicated by the fact that there had always
been an Adolphus Meetkerke since Sir Adolphus had come over from his
home near Bruges to represent the revolting United Provinces of the
Netherlands at the court of Queen Elizabeth I and had taken up his
residence in London. Penelope Meetkerke Trollope's only brother, Adolphus, however, though married, was childless, and as the years passed it
seemed more and more likely that his magnificent estates would pass into
the male line of the cadet branch of the Trollopes.[7]

On May 23, 1809, Frances Milton, then twenty-nine, married the
younger Thomas Anthony Trollope at her father's church at Heckfield.
The couple set up housekeeping at No. 16 Keppel Street, a house Thomas
Anthony owned only a few doors from the one in which Frances had been
courted. There four sons and one daughter were born in the next six years:
Thomas Adolphus, whose middle name indicated the Meetkerke expectations (1810), Henry (1811), Arthur William (1812), Emily (born and
died 1813), and Anthony (born April 24, 1815); all save Emily were
baptized at the church of St. George's, Bloomsbury. Two more daughters,
Cecilia Frances and a second Emily, were baptized, after the move to
Harrow-on-the-Hill, in 1817 and 1818. Of the seven children, only three
lived to be more than twenty-five and one of these, Cecilia, died at thirty-
two.[8]

For the two oldest boys life seems to have been rather pleasant: they
were good companions for each other, and could wander at large in the
city; they customarily walked over to meet their father and accompany
him home from his chambers in the evening. Though Thomas Anthony
was scarcely a prosperous lawyer and the housekeeping was frugal, it
would not have occurred to him to be without a servant dressed in the
Trollope livery (just as Anthony's stationery later in life was adorned with
the Trollope crest). At dinner, there were no dinner napkins to be seen,
but "they were perhaps less needed by clean-shaven chins and lips," wrote
Thomas Adolphus philosophically many years later, thinking of his own
and Anthony's facial adornments. Frances seems to have been a lively

hostess (despite the demands of the nursery) and life was on the whole most agreeable. She loved flowers and managed to have a tiny garden behind the house.[9] Mrs. Furnival, wife of the lawyer in *Orley Farm,* remembered the early days of her marriage in Keppel Street as the happiest of her life.[10] There was a private day school at No. 1 Keppel Street kept by a Dr. Lloyd, which the children of their family friends the Merivales from Red Lion Square attended (the young Merivales' mother was a Drury, daughter of the late headmaster of Harrow School and sister of one of the current masters there),[11] but the Trollope boys were taught, it seems, by their father, probably for reasons of economy. Anthony was his mother's favorite; "we used to consider [him] the Benjamin," Tom recalled.[12]

૨&

Anthony, however, can have had no memory of Keppel Street. About the time he was born, his father, partly to augment an inadequate law income through investment in agriculture, perhaps also from a taste for rural living, resolved to move his family to Harrow, about ten miles from London. He took an extended lease on some farmland south of Harrow Park from the principal landowner of Harrow, the second Lord Northwick, and built a rather fine house which they called "Julians."* They moved sometime between May 18, 1815, when Anthony was baptized in London, and February 19, 1817, when William Milton came over to baptize Cecilia in the Harrow parish church; probably the move was close to the former date. Naturally the Trollopes rented a pew (at five shillings a year) in the parish church, of which the strongly evangelical John William Cunningham was vicar.[13]

There was a secondary economic reason for the move to Harrow: the charter of Harrow School provided that sons of all residents in the parish might attend without charge, "on the Foundation." Anthony later commented that the free schooling was less of a boon to parents than to landlords, for the cost of property in Harrow was increased in proportion to the advantage.[14] Nevertheless, the Trollope family was by no means the only one to make such a move: Shelley's widow Mary took a house there to gain an education for her son Percy Florence, and later in the century Matthew Arnold and the father of Walter Leaf (future translator of Homer) did likewise. It was always intended that the Trollope boys should go to Winchester if they could win scholarships, but Harrow

---

*It is commonly assumed that the house was named with an eye to that of Uncle Adolphus Meetkerke, but in fact that part of Thomas Anthony's leasehold was known as "Julian Field" before he took it, and the name survives in Harrow.

would serve to prepare them and to start them on their way, and Tom and Henry were entered in the autumn or winter of 1818. Tom certainly, and probably Henry also, were private pupils of Mark Drury, who was so stout that he had to have a huge chair fitted to his size. One day a boy put some cobbler's wax on the seat of the chair, but luckily Drury saw it in time and did not sit down; the prank may have suggested Anthony's famous pre-scription to the novelist for sticking to his chair. [15]

There may still have been some of the pleasant visits to Heckfield that Tom describes in his memoirs, but Grandfather Milton died on July 12, 1824, when Anthony was only nine. [16] The difference between Anthony's recollections in *An Autobiography* and the generally brighter picture of the family that appears in his brother's memoirs can be attributed in large part to the difference in age between the two: Tom could remember the relatively happy days that Anthony had not known, and was sufficiently older when disaster struck so that he suffered far less—indeed, could do his part to keep things right. Soon after the move to Harrow the first catastrophe occurred to the hopes of Thomas Anthony: the childless Aunt Meetkerke died on July 22, 1817, and on October 8 of the next year sixty-four-year-old Uncle Adolphus took a second, much younger wife. A younger Adolphus was born in due course, and the prospect of the great inheritance vanished. Family memories make much of Thomas Anthony's shattered hopes, and may reflect the world of illusions in which he customarily lived, for he would never have seen the inheritance in any case: Uncle Adolphus outlived him by nearly six years. Many years later the family association was renewed when Cecilia Meetkerke, second wife of the interloping Adolphus and an aspiring poetess, approached Anthony for advice on her literary career and became a contributor to *St. Pauls Magazine*. When Anthony died, she wrote two articles of recollections of him for the magazines. [17]

҉

True to their destinies, Tom and Henry went to Winchester when they reached the age of ten, in 1820 and 1821, leaving Arthur and Anthony at home with the girls. Both entered Harrow School early in the spring of 1823: "Trollope, sen." and "Trollope, jun." are on a list of the school for April 9 of that year, among the "unplaced" students (i.e., those too young for the third form). The intention was, not that they should proceed through Harrow, but that they should acquire sufficient learning to win scholarships at Winchester. Anthony was then not quite eight years old. For three terms he was "lag" of the school, an unpleasant-sounding designation that meant simply that he was the bottom boy, largely on account of age. [18] In July, 1824, Arthur died, and Anthony was left to trudge off to the school by himself, nearly a mile up the hill. Most of the miserable picture he paints of his Harrow years is drawn from this early period. All testimony is to the effect that "home boarders" were not merely snubbed but persecuted and chased with stones on their way home. The formidable Dr. George Butler, subsequently dean of Peterborough, was then headmaster, and Anthony recalled that on one occasion he was humiliatingly accosted by Butler, who wondered that a lad with so dirty a face could possibly be a pupil at the school. "He had perhaps never seen my face before," Trollope remarked, implying that a flogging headmaster was far better acquainted with the other end of the little animal. [19] The mature Trollope is merely repeating a schoolboy joke, but the humiliation over the public reprimand was real and lasting. "Tho' [Butler] was very severe to little boys, he was a very inefficient master—and the school went on declining till he resigned—he was altogether unable to keep the head boys in order, and rather feared them, than was feared by them," Trollope wrote a decade later. [20]

Henry Trollope left Winchester in September, 1826, but Tom prospered there and by 1825 was a prefect, or head of one of the dormitories. Anthony early in that year was removed from Harrow School and placed under another member of the Drury family (Arthur) in a tutoring school at Sunbury (on the Thames, near Hampton). Here he found himself "more nearly on terms of equality with other boys than at any other period during my very prolonged school-days." Nevertheless, when he wrote his autobiography, he recalled chiefly that he had once been accused, with three other boys, of perpetrating "some nameless horror" of which, since it was unnamed, he could not prove his innocence. Each lad had to copy out a sermon as punishment, and Anthony's was longest, but what hurt most, even in his later years, was the thought that the other three boys, "the curled darlings of the school," would never have chosen him as their associate in crime. Drury later half confessed that his condemnation might have been wrong, but Anthony was too shy to press further in establishing his innocence. [21] The home of Mrs. Woodward and her three daughters, heroines of *The Three Clerks,* is placed "just on the outskirts of the village [of Hampton], on the side of it farthest from town" (chap. iii), and on one occasion, as a token tribute to his school days, he sends her and one daughter to Sunbury to dine (chap. xxxvii). Though Trollope in his maturity seems to have been nothing of an oarsman, the novel reflects his schoolboyish delight in boating on the Thames.

At Sunbury he made sufficient advances in his learning to be placed on the list of Winchester scholars in the autumn of 1826, though not very high on the list. A place became available for him the following spring, and in April, 1827, his mother wrote to Tom that the young lad was filled with excitement at the prospect of being in his older brother's chamber there; Anthony was admitted on April 14.[22] Tom regarded the government of the school (as regards ordinary discipline) by the older boys, or prefects, as the perfect form of government, and of course Dr. Thomas Arnold, himself a Wykehamist, adopted it at Rugby with great success a decade or so later. Much of the actual teaching of the younger boys was in fact at the hands of the older lads: Anthony was Tom's pupil, and Tom's theory of teaching included frequent salutary application of a big stick. It is not uncommon for an older brother to have high ideals for a younger one, and Tom's idealism doubtless sprang from pride and affection; as for his method, he learned his theories of discipline from his elders, both at home and at school. Though the brothers loved each other dearly in later life, Anthony was not so happy as he had hoped to be with their relations at school. Nor was Tom the only obstacle to his delight. "It was just possible to obtain five scourgings in one day," he tells us, "and . . . I obtained them all." Tom assures us that there is a certain exaggeration here. It was indeed possible to have five floggings—on a bare bottom—in one day, but the extent of the bareness was rigorously controlled by protocol: two boys unbuttoned the victim's braces and separated the trousers from the shirt by precisely the width of a crown coin (about two and a half inches), and the master then administered three perfunctory strokes with a lash of a design peculiar to Winchester, with four strands that floated so wildly they seldom struck the bare skin at all. The punishment was so commonplace as to entail no humiliation, and was of quite a different order from punishments or rebuffs at the hands of fellow students. "Fagging"—the treatment of the younger boys as slaves of the older—was far worse at Winchester than at Harrow. But there were more "scholars" (free students) at Winchester than the "home boarders" at Harrow, and they were less looked down upon.[23] (Nonetheless, in later life Anthony referred to himself as a "charity boy" at Winchester.)[24]

Life at the college was very Spartan. "Beer was the only beverage provided,—or indeed permitted,—for breakfast, dinner, or supper." Tea was held in such disrepute as a luxury that if a master on inspection found teacups or a teapot among a boy's possessions he insisted that they be broken to bits at once. The substance of the diet was mutton, passed out daily in pound lumps called "dispars" (unequal divisions) since they were sometimes good leg of mutton, sometimes fat from the sheep's breast. There were no plates, no knives or forks; the older boys secured for themselves wooden trenchers, but there were not enough of these to go round to the younger lads. There was an outdoor conduit for washing in cold water, but hot water was so difficult to procure that the very meticulous washed their feet once a week, the less meticulous once a quarter. All the lads wore long black cloth gowns that became unspeakably filthy.[25]

There was one unforeseeable consequence both for Anthony and for

English literature that came from his schooling at Winchester. The college and the cathedral are adjacent and closely linked, and though Anthony many years later said he had never lived in a cathedral town and had no acquaintance with a cathedral chapter, he in fact spent three years in the shadow of Winchester cathedral and worshipped there or in the chapel (by his own account) as often as three times a day.[26] Moreover, his schoolboy rambles must often have taken him along the river to St. Cross Hospital, an endowed charity for aged men that bears more than casual resemblance to Hiram's Hospital of *The Warden.* If a visit to Salisbury nearly thirty years later was the immediate stimulus for the first of the Barchester novels, the books are saturated with the memories of the twelve-to-fifteen-year-old schoolboy. Francis Arabin, the triumphant champion of *Barchester Towers,* had been schooled at Winchester. Florian Jones of *The Landleaguers* was to have gone to Winchester, but the money ran out; his older brother Frank went to the Queen's College, Galway, but "would have been better trained to meet the world had circumstances enabled him to be sent to a public school in England." Arthur Wilkinson, of *The Bertrams,* was (like Tom and Anthony) a scholar at Winchester, and when he did not get a New College scholarship went, like Tom, to another Oxford college. But George Bertram was a commoner at Winchester, and he got the scholarship at Trinity College, Oxford, that Anthony missed. "He . . . received the best education which England could give him."[27] One of Anthony's schoolfellows at Winchester was the future Liberal politician Robert Lowe (later Viscount Sherbrooke), who was a commoner there from 1825 to June, 1829. A quarter of a century after Trollope's death, his biographer T. H. S. Escott remarked that "Lowe was for many years the one politician in the front rank with whom Trollope had real intimacy." One wonders how true this statement is.[28]

ﾈ▲

Meanwhile the farming at Harrow did not prosper, and neither did the law practice in London. (Agriculture throughout England fell on hard times just then.) In 1823 Thomas Anthony published *A Treatise on the Mortgage of Ships, as Affected by the Registry Acts,* respectfully dedicated to the prime minister, the Earl of Liverpool, but the learning there exhibited did not sufficiently enhance the demands for his legal talents. Many years later Anthony contrasted the relative security of his own civil service career with the disappointments of "briefless barristers, without business, hoping through hopeless years till hope was over."[29] There was a serious economic slump beginning in 1825 which so affected the moneyed classes as to produce a marked falling off in the number of students at the public schools. At Harrow, for example, there were 214 boys at the beginning of

1826, and only 127 by Christmas of 1828. The number of free scholars (townspeople) rose to seventeen in 1825.[30] As early as the beginning of 1820 Thomas Anthony had written to Lord Northwick (in a hand very much like the mature hand of Anthony) that his health was such that he was thinking of giving up the house he had built and returning to town, keeping the nearby farmhouse for the family vacations. Instead, the farmhouse (a fine enough one which indeed Thomas Anthony substantially enlarged) became the permanent home of the family; it still stands and bears the name of "Julian Hill." Millais used it as a model for his picture of Orley Farm.*[31]

It soon enough became necessary to give up even the comfortable farmhouse. Thomas Anthony took some additional farmland at Harrow Weald, to the north, and, leasing out Julian Hill, moved to the old farmhouse there, perhaps in the late summer or early autumn of 1827. This was a good deal farther from the school and a good deal less comfortable.[32] Very soon thereafter, Mrs. Trollope, impelled partly by the hope of reducing their expenditures by sojourning abroad, partly by newfound enthusiasm for social reform, and partly by the wish to remove her daughters from the increasingly disruptive displays of their father's tempestuous rages, took Henry and the girls to America. With them went the French language tutor who was living in their Harrow household, the young artist Auguste Hervieu.†[33]

The journey to America is a saga which may be told rather briefly, since Anthony was left behind. In early 1822, Mrs. Trollope had met, through her brother Henry, the strikingly tall and earnest-looking young Scotswoman Frances Wright, a wealthy orphan then about twenty-seven years old, who was taking the radical social thinkers of London by storm. She was doubtless the first advocate of women's rights Anthony encountered. On her return to Paris her staunch republican principles led her to attach herself to the grandfatherly General Lafayette; she persuaded him to adopt herself and her younger sister in order to avoid scandal from the closeness of her attachment. When in September, 1823, Thomas Anthony and Mrs. Trollope went to Paris, she introduced them to Lafayette, who invited them to visit him at his country estate, La Grange. Less than two

---

*Some time after Trollope's novel appeared, the house was used as a private school; the proprietor, recognizing the house in the picture, christened his school "Orley Farm." Orley Farm School still exists, but it is no longer in that house. It should be added that the Orley Farm of the novel is not in Harrow, but in Essex, east of London.

†A good many years later Trollope recalled "a line of poetry, learnt in my earliest youth, and which I believe to have emanated from a sentimental Frenchman, a man of genius, with whom my parents were acquainted . . . :

Are you go?—Is you gone?—Am I left?—Vera well!

Now the whole business of a farewell is contained in that line."[34]

years later, in 1825, Frances Wright showed her devotion to the cause of
the American slaves by founding a colony for some of them on 2,000 acres
of land she bought at Nashoba, in the wilderness along the Wolf River
about fourteen miles east of Memphis, Tennessee. Slaves were purchased
and given their freedom, and a socialistic community of blacks and whites
was to be organized. Miss Wright was as firmly set against another form
of slavery, that of married couples to each other: she was not irrevocably
opposed to marriage in itself, but was vehemently against any restriction
of movement, and raised something of a storm of criticism when she
urged a young man in New York to come as a schoolteacher to Nashoba,
leaving his wife behind to fend for herself.[35] In October, 1827, on a visit
to England, she stopped at Harrow to see the Trollopes, and apparently
made her Tennessee Utopia so attractive that Frances Trollope resolved to
go out with her on her next voyage. Her decision to go was made firm
only five days before they departed, when Thomas Anthony gave his
consent. Hervieu went along as a teacher-to-be in the community school
at Nashoba. On November 4, 1827, the party sailed for New Orleans.
Tom and Anthony of course remained at Winchester.[36]

On the voyage out Frances Wright wrote a pamphlet setting forth
her ideals for the Nashoba community in the hope of recruiting members.
But Nashoba was a disastrous disappointment, no less for Frances Wright
than for Frances Trollope. Nothing could disguise the poverty of the place
or its privations; there was neither a community nor a promise of one.
There was no sign of a school for Hervieu to teach or the Trollope children
to attend. Nashoba was not very far geographically from the site of Martin
Chuzzlewit's Eden, and not very unlike it; Eden in fact may owe something to Dickens's later conversation with Mrs. Trollope.[37] And so
Frances Trollope took her daughters and Hervieu up the Mississippi and
Ohio rivers to Cincinnati; very soon after their departure Frances Wright
disbanded her Nashoba settlement and joined Robert Dale Owen at his
recently acquired community of New Harmony, in Indiana, where Henry
Trollope also stopped.[38] On March 14, 1828, Frances Trollope wrote to
her "beloved boys" at Winchester about all the disappointments her
family had encountered, and in due course the boys heard also from Henry
of the large amount of manual work he had to do at New Harmony in
proportion to the very small amount of education he was receiving. He
soon rejoined his family in Cincinnati.[39]

In that city, Mrs. Trollope first associated herself with the Western
Museum, a collection of curios to which she added novel displays (with
Hervieu's help) such as reconstructed scenes from Dante's *Inferno*, presided
over by a gigantic and terrifying Lucifer, or a fog-filled room in which an
"oracle" answered (in several languages) questions from patrons; the voice
was Henry's. Hervieu managed to support them by painting and giving

lessons; Henry's attempt to secure pupils for tuition in Latin was unsuccessful.[40] Then, with considerable ingenuity, Mrs. Trollope conceived the notion of erecting a building which would provide both culture and entertainment for the community: it would have a variety of shops and boutiques on the main floor, with a refreshment hall and gallery for paintings; on the next, a ballroom and concert hall, and atop the structure a large dome in which might be placed a "panorama" of some historic event. The whole design had the sort of Moresco-Turkish flavor that certain American fraternal orders have been fond of. It was to stand high above the river, and to command a fine view of the valley. The financing was to come from the money she had inherited from her father, and Thomas Anthony and Tom were summoned for their help (Tom had now completed his schooling).[41]

In September, they sailed for New York, traveling steerage in a sail-powered passenger vessel that made the crossing in thirty-eight days; not surprisingly it was a miserable voyage. In Cincinnati the prospect seemed bright enough to warrant commissioning contractors to construct the building. Thomas Anthony and Tom remained for some three months, then sailed for England from New York on February 5, 1829, and reached Harrow Weald early in March.[42] Anthony continued at Winchester; how he had spent his lonely holidays we do not know, but it must be remembered that he was not without close relatives in England of whom he was fond. He recalls that on another occasion he spent his summer holidays living in his father's chambers at Lincoln's Inn. "There was often difficulty about the holidays,—as to what should be done with me. On this occasion my amusement consisted in wandering about among those old deserted buildings, and in reading Shakespeare out of a bi-columned edition, which is still among my books. It was not that I had chosen Shakespeare, but that there was nothing else to read."[43] In October, young Tom matriculated at St. Alban Hall, Oxford; his was not an easy career there, made worse by his father's financial difficulties and temperamental quirks, in consequence of which latter Tom was shifted to Magdalen Hall (now Hertford College); he took his B.A. in 1835.[44]

During the spring of 1829 more and more frantic letters arrived from Cincinnati, as Mrs. Trollope heard nothing from her husband. Thomas Anthony had agreed to purchase goods for sale in his wife's shop in the bazaar, and actually laid out £2,000 upon them, but they were ill chosen, and in any case by the time the shipment reached Cincinnati Mrs. Trollope had run out of money, the creditors had closed in, and the shipment was seized: not one penny of its value went to her. Her bright prospects collapsed entirely. Henry returned to England, and showed up at the Harrow Weald farmhouse on April 19, 1830, after a voyage on a freighter from New York to Liverpool. That autumn he entered Caius College,

Cambridge, but dropped out a year later when the money was exhausted.[45]

Mrs. Trollope left Cincinnati, traveled eastward with her daughters to stay with a friend in Washington, and wrote from there to Tom in the summer of 1830: "My poor dear Anthony will have outgrown our recollection! Tell him not to outgrow his affection for us. No day passes,—hardly an hour—without our talking of you all. I hope a letter from your father is on the way." As she sought new means of supporting her family, Mrs. Trollope now hit upon the one that was to succeed—one that required no capital, but needed the lively mind she had already shown. She began to write a book, a book about America. Hervieu would do the illustrations, sketches of the people and scenes they had encountered.[46]

In his autobiography Trollope speaks of the humiliation of being told at Winchester that his modest allowance of spending money was no longer being paid by his father. Shortly after mid-July, 1830, he left the college and in January, 1831, reentered Harrow, walking the three miles of muddy winter road between Harrow Weald and the school twice each morning and twice each afternoon.

Whereas in 1823 he had been the youngest boy in the school, he was now older and bigger than most boys in his form (though he never reached six feet in height). His size at least kept him from the abuse he had suffered before.[47] On one occasion that autumn he established himself by a combat in the fighting-ground with a new (but not young) boy named James Lewis; when they were separated after nearly an hour by one of the masters, William Mills,* Lewis was so badly battered that he had to be sent home, and he did not return to Harrow. Living as he did with only one parent and that a negligent one, Anthony was "the most slovenly and dirty boy I ever met," not only in person and dress, but also in his work: "His exercises were a mass of blots and smudges," as William Gregory of Coole Park, near Gort in Galway, recalled; yet Gregory rather liked him. Though rude and uncouth, "I thought him an honest, brave fellow. He was no sneak. His faults were external; all the rest of him was right enough." (Many years later, Gregory's widow was to befriend William Butler Yeats at Coole Park.) Gregory was first drawn to Trollope when a Latin poetry prize he was especially eager to win, and for which his verses were in fact adjudged the best, was withdrawn from him because of a

---

*Trollope later wrote, "I used always to stick up for Mills—I don't know why—for he is a weak, quarrelsome, conceited ass—not to speak of his absolute vulgarity and ignorance. He has always a most laughable mode of keeping up his dignity, and walks with his nose ludicrously in the air. . . . He used constantly to make bad puns on the boys' names." This last trick must have been especially unpleasant for Anthony.[48]

technical infraction of the rules; Anthony was sympathetic and consoling. Still, there was the social stigma of the home boarder, and the additional rumor that the lad's father, "old Trollope," had been outlawed, so that it was the duty of every loyal subject of the king to shoot him on sight. Thomas Henry Baylis, later a judge, was himself a home boarder and Anthony used to call for him on the way to school; he, like Gregory, sat next to Anthony in the sixth form.[49]

An Autobiography rightly remarks that Harrow had the reputation of giving out more prizes than any other school in its day; at least one of them came to Anthony. Frederick George Brabazon Ponsonby, heir to the Irish earldom of Bessborough, recalled later that he took extraordinary pains with an English essay in the hope of winning one competition, and was told by the headmaster (no longer Butler, but Charles Thomas Longley, future archbishop of Canterbury), "You did well, but, you see, Trollope writes better English than you do at present."[50] (Note the name "Brabazon," which Trollope used in *The Claverings*. Toogood and Clutterbuck, Broughton, Sowerby, Mogg, Round, and Vesey, which appear in his novels, were also Harrow names while he was there, and Mildmay and Daubeny were Winchester names.)[51] "[Dr. Longley, master of the sixth form,] very rarely,—almost never,—called upon me, who was certain to fail," Trollope recalled thirty years later. "When I failed, what could he do? What he did do was to undergo a look of irrepressible, unutterable misery at the disgrace which I brought upon his sixth form, and bid me sit down with a voice of woe! How well I remember his face when he was thus woful! How I reverenced him and loved him,—though he could never have loved me! And I love him and reverence him now." Trollope seldom indicated real-life counterparts for his fictional characters, but his preliminary sketch for *The Way We Live Now* identifies the admirable bishop of Elmham in that book with "Old Longley."[52] In his present three and a half terms at the school, Trollope made regular progress from the "Shell" (an intermediate class under the supervision of Mills) through the fifth and sixth forms, and in his last term he was a monitor. Following the school tradition, he scratched his name on the door frame of the west cupboard of the headmaster's desk in the fourth-form room, where it may still be seen.[53]

Among the pupils at Harrow with Trollope were a nephew of Wordsworth, a son of Shelley, and an heir to the Byron peerage, as well as the future Roman Catholic archbishop of Westminster, Henry Edward Manning. These are not names that figure in his biography. But the succession of Merivales, the sons of the London friends of Trollope's parents, do figure. Charles, the second son, left Harrow in 1824 and naturally Anthony did not know him well there, but they were often closely associated in later life. Nearer in age and in friendship at the school was the fifth son, John Lewis Merivale, who left Harrow in 1832. Another of Trollope's schoolfellows was A. J. Beresford Hope, later proprietor of the *Saturday Review,* who for many years sat with Trollope on the General Committee of the Royal Literary Fund. When in 1846 Mrs. Trollope met Frederick William Faber, the hymn writer and disciple of Newman, he recalled having been at Harrow with Anthony, and recalled also that though Cunningham gave him his earliest religious thoughts, "he always had a sort of misgiving that he occasionally talked nonsense." Like Anthony, Faber had been an enthusiastic admirer of Harrow's own poet, Byron.[54]

At Harrow the schooling was almost entirely classical, with strong emphasis on memorization; Charles Merivale said he memorized the whole of Lucan's *Pharsalia* while walking about the countryside there, and Charles Wordsworth was required to learn from thirty to ninety lines of Juvenal by heart every day.[55] Despite Lord Bessborough's account, the writing of English was quite neglected—or at least it had been so before Longley took over. Moreover, Trollope later asserted that neither at Harrow nor at Winchester had he ever been *taught* Latin: the boys were expected to work it up for themselves and the classroom periods were entirely devoted to hearing them recite what they had prepared.[56] In any case, Trollope throughout his life retained an enthusiasm for the classics; parallel to his career as novelist, and from beginning to end, there ran the career of writer on Roman history, from his significant articles on Charles Merivale's *History of the Romans under the Empire* in the *Dublin University Magazine* of 1851 and 1856 to his digest of Caesar's *Commentaries* in 1870 and his excellent two-volume life of Cicero in 1880. Of the famous beginning of Cicero's third oration against Catiline, he remarked: "Whether it be from the awe which has come down to me from my earliest years, mixed perhaps with something of dread for the great pedagogue who first made the words to sound grandly in my ears, or whether true critical judgment has since approved to me the real weight of the words, they certainly do contain for my intelligence an expression of almost divine indignation." To the end of his life Trollope was quoting Horace's Latin familiarly.[57]

The mark of Harrow is shown too in Trollope's admiration of Lord Palmerston, one of her most distinguished sons, whose life he published in 1882:

> He had all that could be done for him, both for good and evil, by a thoroughly English education of the first class. He could fight and would fight as long as he could stand; but as conqueror he could be thoroughly generous. He could work, requiring no rest, but only

some change of employment. He shot, he hunted, he raced, he danced. But he seems to have cared for the niceties of erudition neither in classics nor in philosophy. He was a man who from the first was determined to do the best he could with himself; and he did it with a healthy energy, never despairing, never expecting too much, never being in a hurry, but always ready to seize the good thing when it came.

In *Orley Farm,* the amiable young Peregrine Orme was educated at Harrow, but the unpleasant Lucius Mason was educated privately and showed "a conceit which public school education would not have created."[58] Both Mark Robarts and Lord Lufton in *Framley Parsonage* were Harrovians. And so also was young Frank Gresham, the hero of *Doctor Thorne.*

ʒ•

"I had read Shakespeare and Byron and Scott, and could talk about them," Trollope remarked in some apology for his poor showing in penmanship and arithmetic when he entered the employ of the Post Office in 1834, and his *alter ego* Johnny Eames of *The Small House at Allington* "could read and understand Shakespeare. He knew much,—by far too much,—of Byron's poetry by heart."[59] In fact, before he left Harrow Trollope was showing a lively interest in the literature of his native country. About 1830 he began keeping a journal, in which he wrote for some ten years, but which he destroyed in 1870 because it seemed evidence of early wasted hours—though it "had habituated me to the rapid use of pen and ink, and taught me how to express myself with facility." If his actual journal was like Johnny Eames's, it showed him to have been "a deep critic, often writing down his criticisms in a lengthy journal which he kept. He could write quickly, and with understanding." (*The Small House* was published a few years before Trollope went back and looked, with disillusion, at his own journals.)[60] The family group, when reunited at Julian Hill in October, 1832, started a kind of periodical, the *Magpie,* consisting of manuscript essays mounted in a scrapbook and then read aloud to the other "Magpies," who included, besides the Trollopes, their neighbor Mrs. Grant and at least one of the Drurys. Henry Trollope was the rigorous editor. Though the scrapbook survived in the possession of Tom Trollope's widow to the end of the century, it has now disappeared and we have no indication of Anthony's part in it.*[61] But his most

---

*The *Magpie* seems to have been somewhat like *The Fox How Magazine,* which the family of Dr. Thomas Arnold produced; one senses that such an enterprise was not unusual in a literate family.

impressive surviving taskwork is his commentary in the margins and the blank pages of a little copy of Burke's *Philosophical Enquiry into the Origins of Our Ideas of the Sublime and the Beautiful,* which is inscribed on the flyleaf, "Harrow. Sep. 1833." It was not a school text; he must have read it for sheer intellectual pleasure. And his comments—a running debate with Burke or an amplification of Burke's examples—show a homely common sense, a familiarity with the books Burke cites, and a reasonable facility even with Greek. "All men . . . concur in calling sweetness pleasant, and sourness and bitterness unpleasant," asserted Burke. "No," retorted Trollope. "There are those to whom the taste of vinegar is not unpleasant, & there [are] those to whom honey is unpleasant." "I do not like figs," he asserted elsewhere, "& yet it is nothing peculiar or unique to dislike figs." He caught Burke in an erroneous reference to Locke's *Essay on Human Understanding.* On the relation between grief and pleasure, he firmly disagreed with Burke: "Grief is not pain, any more than joy is pleasure. The one is the effect & the other the cause. . . . [A man] does not love grief, he cannot; grief is essentially an unpleasant & therefore unamiable sensation. Grief & melancholy may be widely different—the one is the romance of the other. A man may be fond of the romance of grief . . . but it is the romance he likes. NO ONE CAN LIKE GRIEF." When Burke found that the sublime need not reside only in large objects, for "serpents and poisonous animals of almost all kinds . . . are considered as objects of terror," Trollope snorted, "You cannot say a wasp has any thing sublime about it." The book was apparently one of those slipped through the fence when the bailiffs a year later took possession of Julian Hill, for it passed on to Trollope's son and still survives.[62]

The young man who completed his schooling just as the bailiffs descended was not a dunce, not uneducated, not indeed notably unhappy with his life: he had lively interests and the foundation for substantial intellectual accomplishment—and he was proud to be a Harrovian and a Wykehamist.

In the May number of the *Cornhill* for 1860, a writer who signed himself "Paterfamilias" (but who was widely known to be Trollope's friend Matthew James Higgins, "Jacob Omnium") touched off a pamphlet and journalistic debate by sharply pointing out that education at the large, wealthy public schools, and at Eton in particular, was woefully poor, largely because of the irresponsibility of the masters and governors. A consequence of the revelations was the appointment on July 18, 1861, of the Clarendon Commission, charged with inquiring into all aspects of the work of the nine most distinguished public schools. Matthew Arnold, himself a Wykehamist and Rugbeian, joined the debate with *A French Eton* in 1863–64. The publication of the commission's report in 1864 led to Trollope's article on "Public Schools" in the *Fortnightly* for October 1,

1865—an essay filled with reminiscences of his own experiences at Winchester and Harrow. Here, a decade before beginning to write *An Autobiography,* he remarked, "We look back at it all with affection." "Whilst there we made our friendships. There we learned to be honest, true, and brave." There, in fact, the English gentleman was formed: "The son of the squire of the parish and the son of the parson are placed together at the same school, are educated in the same way, enjoy an equal footing, so that in after life they meet together with mutual sympathy, and on an absolute equality as gentlemen,—though the school education of one has cost three times the sum expended on the other. This is what the old endowments do for us, and their inestimable benefit, let us hope, we may preserve." He was writing as one who had been educated "on the foundation"—free of tuition charges—at two of England's most expensive schools.[63]

Chapter II

1831–40

Mrs. Trollope and her daughters returned to Harrow from America on August 5, 1831, and found the amenities of the house at Harrow Weald in a disastrous state.* Tom was "lying in a comfortless garret, without a pillow under his poor aching head"; indeed, "Not one of our five children has a pillow for his head," she chided her husband. "God knows what will become of us all," she told her friend Julia Garnett Pertz. "Tom is doing very well at Oxford—Henry and Anthony are perfectly without destination—they are both excellent scholars—but latin and greek are very *unmarketable*. We are living at a miserable house on the Harrow Weald farm—my pretty cottage Julian is let—my dear children are *all* devoted to me—I never saw more attached or affectionate children—This is my greatest comfort." By November 25 she was able to boast that Anthony had just got a prize at Harrow.[1]

Luckily there was the two-volume manuscript of *The Domestic Manners of the Americans*. The publisher's reader, Captain Basil Hall, was so warm in his praise of it, and spoke so enthusiastically about it in London literary circles, that she had a reputation even before the book appeared; publication was held back until after his review appeared in the *Quarterly*. "Why did she not bring it to me?" asked London's leading publisher, John Murray, who had read the review copy more than a month before publication. "It will sell like wildfire!" And within a few weeks after its publication on March 19, 1832, Murray had her to dinner in London, "a most splendid entertainment." John Gibson Lockhart, editor of the *Quarterly,* and John Wilson Croker, one of his principal contributors, Mrs. Lockhart, Captain Hall, Walter Savage Landor, "and half a dozen more [were there], all lions. . . . I was abundantly complimented."[2] Even more important, the book brought her money with which she could move to rectify in some part her husband's negligence, and her success in finding a public encouraged her to begin the writing of a novel, *The Refugee in America,* for which by July, 1832, her publisher gave her £400.[3]

---

*The getting home was not easy. "I wrote to Mr. Trollope and told him that for my dear girls' sake I was *determined* upon returning to England—and that if he was unable to furnish me with the means, I would apply to his family for them. *This* brought eighty pounds—and here we are."

When the lease on Julian Hill terminated on September 25, she moved the family back, paid half a year's rent and taxes in advance, bought new furniture (including pillows), and a cow.[4]

Even before the move from Harrow Weald, Mrs. Trollope brightened up the family's social life considerably (at least while she was with them, for on several occasions she and Cecilia spent some months in lodgings in London, so that she could move in the literary circles there).* She "was one of those people who carry sunshine with them," Tom wrote. Immediately after her return from America, the vicar of the parish, John William Cunningham, brought Dr. Longley over to meet her. Herman Merivale, from London, called with "a halo of pretty Drury cousins round him."[5] Anthony and Tom were much together on Tom's holidays from Oxford, once having a combat with singlesticks that Tom had brought home from London, in which Anthony showed himself superior in quickness and adroitness, and in bearing pain also. On another occasion they walked fourteen miles or more to Vauxhall Gardens, the London amusement park, to see some fireworks and festivities. They had only enough money—a shilling apiece—to pay the entrance fee, and so they could afford nothing to eat, but Anthony danced from about nine in the evening to one in the morning, and then they walked home.

There is universal agreement in the various family reminiscences that Thomas Anthony had an uncontrollable temper, not improved by perpetual headaches and dyspepsia. For this latter he took mammoth doses of calomel, a mercury compound that instead of bringing relief actually was slowly poisoning him.[6] (It was in common use well into the present century for the relief of stomach disorders, but has now entirely disappeared from the pharmacopoeia as far too dangerous.) Nothing succeeded, in his profession or his farming. But he found an occupation about the time of his wife's return, one that kept him busy for the short remainder of his life—the writing of an *Encyclopaedia Ecclesiastica*. "He really seems quite another being" with this occupation, she wrote to a friend, "and so am I too, in consequence."[7] The undertaking was prodigious—an alphabetical compendium of ecclesiastical terms, explanations of Christian rites and ceremonies, accounts of all Christian denominations from the earliest ages, and descriptions of the religious orders. That one man should think of doing it by himself is almost inconceivable, yet its usefulness would be

---

*She had, indeed, delighted in literary society long before she became an authoress. On February 11, 1822, she, Thomas Anthony, and Frances Wright called on the Merivales in London to meet the distinguished Italian writer Ugo Foscolo. John Herman Merivale recorded that she came "in her deepest blue stockings," but "the 'Siddonian glances' which [Edmund] Kean detected the other night in Mrs. Trollope were entirely thrown away on Foscolo, who shrugged up his shoulders and observed that she was *very blue*."

exceedingly great. By February, 1832, the publisher Murray had seen the first part of the manuscript and his reader much approved of it. By the beginning of 1834 the first volume, a handsome quarto covering the letters *A* through *F,* was published, with seven full-page illustrations of religious habits by Hervieu. The articles, ranging from brevity to an extent of several pages each, are lucid and free of pedantry, and the work is most impressive. But Thomas Anthony lived to do no more of it. It was undoubtedly his father's model for ambitious scholarship that led Anthony at some time early in his career (probably in his twenties) to draw up a ten-page plan for a monumental history of world literature.

There was also brief hope of an appointment for Thomas Anthony to a London magistracy, and Adolphus Meetkerke addressed a letter to the home secretary, Lord Melbourne, upon this hope. Melbourne himself replied cordially to Thomas Anthony's application: "The answer did not appear to me to be favourable," Mrs. Trollope wrote to Tom, but characteristically "Your father . . . says that he *has no doubt* that Lord M. intended to intimate that he should have the office." Mrs. Trollope's judgment was the more correct.[8]

❧

During the spring of 1833, the influenza struck with vigor, and the remedies were worse than the disease. Henry had fourteen leeches applied to him; Anthony was bled until he fainted; Hervieu was so disoriented by his medication that he was found wandering in the fields in delirium—indeed no member of the household escaped.[9] But Mrs. Trollope was determined to gather materials for another book of travels, and by June 1 she and Henry and Hervieu were on their way to Belgium. Mrs. Fauche, the wife of the British consul at Ostend, was an old friend of hers, and the travelers spent some days as guests there. (Twenty-eight years later a son of the Fauche family served as intermediary in an attempt to secure Anthony as nominal editor of *Temple Bar,* one of the magazines that had started up in the vintage year of 1860 that also produced the *Cornhill.* Anthony declined the offer.)[10]

Mrs. Trollope and her companions went on into Germany, and Thomas Anthony joined them in Hamburg. By the end of the year they were back in England. John Murray agreed to publish the book and she was setting her notes in order.[11] But there had been one other object in her tour: she was convinced that the family resources would no longer permit their living in Harrow, and fixed upon the charming Belgian city of Bruges as their future home—cheaper than England, and yet easily accessible by channel steamer. Mrs. Fauche assisted the family to find a dwelling, the Château d'Hondt, a short distance outside the city on the west side, near St. Peter's Gate. Mrs. Trollope told Tom of the plan: "We are, in truth, arrived at the *corner* I have so often talked about, and if we can but turn it, things must be better with us than we have seen them for years. £250 in a cheap country, with my own management, and the hope of gaining more by my own means, your, and Henry's, cannot be called a dreary prospect."[12] It was settled that Thomas Anthony should cross to Belgium on April 18, 1834, and Mrs. Trollope, Henry, and the girls should follow a week or so later.

The change, however, was not so easy; though the future seemed brighter, the past had by no means been cleared away. Young Anthony, who ended his Harrow schooling in March in the uncertain anticipation of the move, was suddenly instructed to drive his father to London and put him on the Ostend boat.[13] By the time he got back to Harrow, the house was in the hands of the sheriff's officers: Lord Northwick had ordered all the Trollopes' property seized in payment of debts, and had Thomas Anthony not made his escape, he might have been imprisoned. The hospitable next-door neighbors, Colonel Grant and his family, helped them smuggle as much as they could through the fence, and gave them all a home for several weeks. Lord Northwick was by no means a popular landlord, and sympathy was all on the side of the Trollopes. From their earliest days at Harrow, Anthony tells us, "we all regarded [him] as a cormorant who was eating us up."[14] It must have been with real satisfaction (however private) that Anthony twenty-seven years later, in an essay on "The National Gallery," expressed with some emphasis the view that a painting of "The Infancy of Jupiter" attributed to Giulio Romano and purchased for the gallery from Lord Northwick's estate for £920 had been overpriced, was a very poor thing, and indeed was in all probability not Giulio's at all. "I confess, I wish we had our money back again."[15]

❧

The generosity of the neighbors was heartwarming. The Trollopes had the hospitality of the Grants, but other friends came forward with similar offers, and the vicar paid a long visit to Mrs. Trollope and offered a home for her daughters in his house. Cunningham was a marked Evangelical in his doctrines, and no favorite of Mrs. Trollope's (who as early as 1822 had written, but not published, a satire against him for his refusal to allow Byron to set up a memorial tablet to his natural daughter, Allegra, when she was buried in the Harrow church).* He was "a man almost wor-

---

*The nominal sticking point was that Byron wanted her described on the tablet as "daughter of G. G. Lord Byron," whereas she was well known not to be the daughter of Byron's wife; such acknowledgment of illegitimate paternity might be regarded as encouragement to immorality. Cunningham had in fact named one of his daughters (born 1817) Louisa Byron Cunningham. Anthony about this time copied out his mother's satire and made comments on its felicities and infelicities.

shipped by the low church party at Harrow, very unpopular with the gentry, and much feared by the poor," Trollope wrote two or three years later; "a most despicable hypocrite—a gentleman like man with very pleasing manners and a sweet voice. I used to talk to Cunningham a good deal at one time, and recall he always used to be very civil to me, but he is a cringing hypocrite and a most confounded liar, and would give his eyes to be a bishop."[16] He is sometimes said to be the model for Mrs. Trollope's Vicar of Wrexhill, though that picture is probably too cruel to represent her judgment of him; he certainly is akin to her son's Obadiah Slope, Samuel Prong, and Jeremiah Maguire.[17] Cunningham too had his difficulties with Lord Northwick, from whom the advowson had been purchased for him in 1811. For many years he lived in a large house near the tollgate on the London road, not far from the house Thomas Anthony had built, but his income from tithes was far less than Northwick had promised and by November 22, 1833, he wrote in agony to his lordship: "I appeal as a Clergyman with eleven children whose circumstances have lately driven him from the house he has inhabited for 19 years, to a high and honorable English nobleman without a family; and I feel that, in that capacity, I may expect more from your Lordship than in any other." He got little satisfaction, but the house into which he moved his family was "Julians," Thomas Anthony's mansion; he still lived there, so far as Trollope knew, when Millais went down to Harrow to sketch "Julian Hill" as Orley Farm in December, 1860.[18]

ॐ

None of the Trollope sons could have expected a university education without substantial financial assistance. Tom had an exhibition from Winchester to Oxford, and Henry a sizarship at Cambridge (though Henry quickly dropped out). But Anthony never got an exhibition from Harrow, nor did his attempt to get a scholarship at Trinity College, Oxford, succeed. It was just as well: with nothing at all to supplement such a grant he "would have ended in debt and ignominy," he rightly tells us, with an eye to Henry's fate at Cambridge. And so, with the family fortunes in total collapse, he accompanied them to Bruges; he crossed with Cecilia about the middle of May. His mother, meanwhile, warned by the doctor that the climate of Ostend and Bruges would be fatal to Henry's weak lungs, hurriedly took him to stay with her cousin Fanny Bent in Devonshire.[19] Fanny Bent was dearly loved by the Trollope family; Tom, in his account of her life at Exeter, makes her sound very much the prototype of his brother's spinster lady from that city, Miss Jemima Stanbury in *He Knew He Was Right* (a character of whom Anthony was especially fond).[20] After some final negotiations with Lord Northwick and the constables, Mrs. Trollope and Emily joined the others at the Château d'Hondt. And the lonely Henry begged, and obtained, permission to join them about the middle of July. The doctor at Bruges bluntly named his ailment—consumption, not "a delicate chest"—and Mrs. Trollope was faced with the double occupation of nursing a dying patient and writing her novels. Through the kindness of a friend, she was able financially to fullfil Henry's wish for one more look at London: they and Emily in September took temporary lodgings in Northumberland Street, Marylebone. After three weeks they returned to Bruges, and now Cecilia was sent to live with her uncle Henry Milton at Fulham, in the hope of shielding her from the infection of Henry's disease.[21]

Meanwhile Anthony took a post as classics "usher" (instructor) in a school conducted at Brussels by the Reverend William Drury, son of Harrow's Mark Drury and brother of the headmaster of the preparatory school Anthony had attended at Sunbury. (Both Mark and William "were obliged to run away from their creditors at Harrow," Anthony tells us, and had already found the same refuge in Belgium the Trollopes were finding.) Anthony gives as the reason for his taking this post the fact that "there came from some quarter an offer to me of a commission in an Austrian cavalry regiment," for the acceptance of which he should have to know German and French, and so he arranged to exchange his services as teacher for instruction in those languages.[22] There is a certain improbability in the story as told,* but in any case his stint as teacher lasted only about six weeks.

The secretary to the Post Office in London (the permanent head of all British postal services, working under the nominal supervision of a postmaster general who was a member of the political party in power) was a Bristol man, Sir Francis Freeling; one of his sons, G. H. Freeling, was his assistant secretary, and another, Clayton Freeling, also a civil servant, was married to a dear friend of Mrs. Trollope's. And so Mrs. Freeling bestirred herself on behalf of her friend's nineteen-year-old son. About the middle of October young Frederick Diggle, after an unsatisfactory career of some two and a half years as junior clerk in the office of the secretary to the Post Office, was permitted to resign in order to avoid dismissal. On the twenty-eighth Tom Trollope learned in London that G. H. Freeling was prepared to offer the vacant post to Anthony. Anthony sped to London, was interviewed at the General Post Office in St. Martin's-le-Grand, and was asked to demonstrate the legibility of his handwriting;

---

*Nevertheless his mother had a wide circle of friends and was industrious in helping her sons find employment, so that she may indeed have known an Austrian with sufficient influence to obtain such a commission; after her visit to Vienna in 1836 she certainly had such connections.[23]

when he failed miserably he was told to copy a passage carefully at home and bring it back next day. He chose a passage of Gibbon's history, but was never asked to show it. A threatened examination in arithmetic did not take place. On November 4 his appointment was routinely approved by the postmaster general. "Mr. Trollope has been well educated and will be subject to the usual probation as to competency," wrote Sir Francis.[24] Twenty-six years later Trollope told a large audience of Post Office employees and their families that the Civil Service was a profession young men seldom chose; it was chosen for them by impecunious parents "because an early income was desirable."[25]

&

Anthony first took up his residence in London with his brother Tom, who was supporting himself by tutoring private pupils in Latin and Greek. Their lodgings in Little Marlborough Street were kept by a tailor and his mother, "a queer house . . . [which] stood in its own court, by which it was separated from the street." They were good lodgings, though the tailor's mother laid down the rules for her tenants' conduct with great firmness. No trace of the house survives, but it cannot have been very different from that in nearby Great Marlborough Street where Phineas Finn lodged with the radical legal copyist Jacob Bunce.[26] Little more than a month after Anthony began his work at the Post Office, word came that young Henry Trollope had died at the Château d'Hondt on December 23. Cecilia had moved from her uncle's house to that of Lady Milman (mother of Henry Hart Milman, future dean of St. Paul's) at Pinner near Harrow; Tom went to fetch her, and they reached Bruges a day or two after the funeral.[27] Tom remained until the first week in April; Anthony apparently could not get leave to go. Poor Henry—his whole life had been a search for something to do, but every career he tried to prepare himself for proved not to his taste or not within his abilities. Throughout his life he displayed a remarkable (if transient) interest in all sorts of schemes and adventures; he loved travel, and he loved his family. But at least from the time he went to Cincinnati he was clearly doomed by a disease in those days both common and incurable. His father's quarrels with him for his lack of steadfastness came close to breaking up the home altogether.[28] And now he was gone.

Tom did not again live in London, and so early in 1835 Anthony moved to lodgings of his own at No. 22 Northumberland Street, Marylebone. No doubt these were the same lodgings his mother, Emily, and Henry had stayed in on Henry's last visit to London the preceding September. They looked out on the brick wall and rear entrance of the

Marylebone workhouse;* they were the lodgings from which the Reverend Joseph Emilius slipped out to murder Bonteen in *Phineas Redux*.[29] In late February and early March Mrs. Trollope was in London and there made an agreement with the publisher Richard Bentley for a book about Paris; the rest of the family remained in Bruges.[30] She was now committed to a career of writing; her travel books and novels would henceforth be the sole source of income for herself, her husband, and her daughters.

≷

The working day at the Post Office was from ten to four, and a stern order of slightly later date that survives in the archives suggests that the junior clerks were then too accustomed to spend their first hour eating their breakfast instead of doing the required copying.[31] For copying was their business—copying documents, copying letters into the minute books. Perhaps it was thought that they might learn the business that way. Sir Francis Freeling, whose secretaryship went back to the last decade of the eighteenth century, soon became too ill to perform his duties regularly, and he died a little more than eighteen months after Trollope's appointment. "How well can I remember the terror created within me by the air of outraged dignity with which a certain fine old gentleman, now long since gone, could rub his hands slowly, one on the other, and look up to the ceiling, slightly shaking his head, as though lost in the contemplation of my iniquities! I would become sick in my stomach, and feel as though my ankles had been broken," Trollope recalled thirty years later. "And yet the old man showed me signs of almost affectionate kindness, writing to me with his own hand more than once from his death-bed."

Freeling was succeeded by Lt. Col. William Leader Maberly, whose first commission in the army dated from a few months before Waterloo and who went on half pay at his present rank in 1832. He was something of a martinet, and Trollope asserts that the two were constantly at odds, but the slight evidence of the records suggests that he was on the whole well disposed toward Anthony. Edmund Yates, who began his service at the General Post Office thirteen years after Trollope, described Maberly as "a big, heavily-built, elderly man" whose "chief characteristic was . . . indifference," though he could be "uncommonly unpleasant some-

---

*Northumberland Street is now Luxborough Street, and the workhouse has been replaced by the new buildings of the London Polytechnic. In December, 1839, young Charles Dickens moved into a house at No. 1 Devonshire Terrace, at the corner of Marylebone High Street and the New Road (Marylebone Road)—only a few steps from Trollope's lodgings on Northumberland Street and not much farther from those he later shared with his mother on York Street in 1839.

times."[32] He became the model for Sir Boreas Bodkin, secretary to the Post Office in *Marion Fay* (nicknamed "Aeolus," god of the winds)—"a violent and imperious martinet, but not in the main ill-natured" (chap. vii). The Civil Service provided Trollope with subjects for *The Three Clerks* and *The Small House at Allington* as well as *Marion Fay,* and one senses that even *An Autobiography* shares their slightly fictitious exaggeration.

❧

The most difficult aspect of this new life was not the work, but the leisure. Only two years before his retirement, Trollope commented that the Civil Service commissioners' grave concern for the moral character of their applicants was misapplied. "Many a young clerk [with a good character] became bad in character under the auspices of the Service. Many a lad placed alone in London, with six hours' work to be done in a day and with no amusements provided for his evenings, has gone in shivers on the rocks of Metropolitan life. Many more will continue to do so till parents confess the necessity of providing recreation as well as that of providing work."[33]

He speaks of enjoying long expeditions on foot in the country with friends, chief of whom were his Harrow contemporary John Merivale and his fellow collegian at Winchester Walter Awdry (who had also been at Magdalen Hall, Oxford, with Tom). Their rules included not spending more than five shillings a day, and never paying for any conveyance; they got as far as Southampton on one occasion, but chiefly remained within the home counties of Bucks and Herts. Since Anthony's initial stipend was £90 a year, even five shillings was slightly beyond his average daily income.[34]

Other sociability included card playing after lunch in one of the rooms of the Post Office building assigned for the use of whichever clerk was detailed to spend the night on the premises, or suppers and card parties at night with the lucky sorters in charge of foreign mails, who had free lodgings in the building; tobacco, cards, and spirits rather than tea were the order of the day. If he wished to avoid these parties, he could always dine alone. One story he tells is of a young woman in the country who invited him down to dinner. On his arrival, she proposed that they get married and, as a gentleman, he found himself unable positively to say no, though he slipped away within half an hour without his dinner. There followed an avalanche of passionate letters from her, without response from him. Then one day her mother burst into the clerks' room in the Post Office where he was at work with six or seven others, "having a large basket on her arm and an immense bonnet on her head," and demanded, for all to hear, "Anthony Trollope, when are you going to marry my daughter?" Charley Tudor had a similar visitor to his office in *The Three Clerks*.[35]

Another plight in which he claims to have found himself occurs even more frequently in the novels—the ever-compounding debts to a money-lender. As he remembered it, a promissory note for £12 to a tailor was turned over to a broker in "a little street near Mecklenburgh Square" (where Samuel Crocker, the Post Office clerk in *Marion Fay*, lived); that and a £4 advance from the man grew, through repeated renewals, to above £200, substantially more than twice his annual salary. Like the mother from the country, but far more frequently, the man sought out Anthony in the clerks' room and urged him to pay up punctually.[36]

೭೩

The necessity of acting as messenger boy on behalf of his mother in her dealings with her London publisher gave him early opportunity to inquire whether Bentley could assist him to place some "lucubrations of my own" in some periodical. "My object of course is that of turning my time to any account that I am able." But it was another fourteen years before his first recorded appearance in a periodical, and by that time his first novel had been published. Even before his own approach to Bentley, his mother had asked John Murray if he could manage to employ Anthony in some evening occupation such as proofreading. "He is a good scholar, and . . . has very good abilities." This proposal also seems to have come to nothing. Tom was already publishing articles in the periodicals, anonymously, and was being paid for them.[37]

One early notebook at least Anthony did not destroy later in life—a two-volume "commonplace book" labeled "Private" and dated August, 1835.[38] It is divided into alphabetical sections, and contains twenty-three entries from *A* to *P*. Fourteen are merely names and dates of authors (Italian, Portuguese, Spanish, French) with sources of information about them (most often Sismondi and A. W. Schlegel); the other nine are more extended comments on books, authors, and (in one case) rules of conduct. Three entries are dated: Bulwer (December 19, 1840), Johnson's Life of Cowley (November 18, 1840) and the first epistle of Pope's *Essay on Man* (August 29, 1836). One book he discusses was published in 1841.

Most interesting, as a prelude to the doctrine he later advocated for other writers as well as himself, is the entry headed "Order—Method—":

> I am myself in all the pursuits (God help them) & practices of my life most disorderly & unmethodical—& the injury which this failing has occasioned is so near as this to utter ruin that I can but set up

myself as an example to others. . . . The first impression which a
parent should fix on the mind of a child, is I think love of order—It
is the reins by which all virtues are kept in their proper places—&
the vices, with whom the virtues run in one team, are controlled—

Order is especially important in religion, in studies, in accounts, diet,
and cleanliness. Only the first and third are discussed. "The hero who says
that he worships his Creator in the fields & his God in the streams—really
knows that he will not undergo the trouble of worshipping him at all."
"In accounts again—a man entering life wd. make no bad bargain in
dividing half his last shilling to buying a red book with blue perpen-
dicular lines—Those blue lines so hated by the young gentry of small
fortunes, would fill themselves with figures on the right sheet, were they
properly attended to in every monetary transaction—"

His discussion of Bulwer quickly leads to self-criticism: "When
reading, I long to be writing—& attempting to write, I become weary of
the labor, & do nothing; I am not contented with mediocrity—want the
perseverance to accomplish superiority, & therefore fall into utter inferiority." Bulwer's novels at least make Anthony think—"think how
wrong he is in his ideas on life & human nature—how false his philosophy
is, & to what little purpose he has worked his brain." And yet he is the
most energetic and poetic of novelists "since Scott's palmy days." Only
Galt and Lockhart (Trollope names *Adam Blair*) can be called Bulwer's
modern superiors. As for G. P. R. James's three-volume *Corse de Leon*
(1841), it "consists of an improbable string of adventures very badly put
forth in bad writing." "I trust this will be [the] last of the modern
adventurous class of novels I shall be tempted to read—for nothing gives
me so great an idea of wasting my time—no not even idleness and castle
building." He has heard that George Sand is an immoral writer, but he
finds that the first volume of her *L'Uscoque* (1838), the only thing of hers
he has read, contains nothing "which the most careful mother need fear to
put into the hands of her daughter. . . . It makes vice ugly & virtue
beautiful"—a standard to which again and again in his later criticism he
holds up the modern novel.

He carries on a long debate with Pope's *Essay*, largely drawing upon
an earlier reading. "Some three years ago . . . [I] fancied I understood
it—perhaps I did but I can hardly do so now—Since that time by
idleness—dissipation—& riot of my mind I have lost in a measure the
power of thinking and reflecting." He does, nevertheless, deliver himself
at some length, and wittily. Pope is "a sort of metaphysical Calvinist—a
rational predestinarian—man is with him nothing— . . . a tool used by
some power—a puppet . . . of the workings of a system—And I fleece
my brother that the chain of a preordained system might not be broken."

Anthony suggests he should not have chosen so popular, so deep, so powerful a poem at which "to cast my blunted—wingless shafts—but I suppose I have done what was intended in writing this—I should be content for whatever is, is right!" Johnson's Life of Cowley persuaded him that he shall "not take up much time in reading Cowley—or his fellows." "A poet who is more learned than enthusiastic & more witty than sublime or pathetic, is not to my taste."

There are indications as well that he plans an essay on "the excellencies and defects of the modern English [drama]—as displayed in" plays by Fanny Kemble, Sheridan Knowles, Henry Taylor, Joanna Baillie, and Thomas Noon Talfourd. And most interesting is his sketch of a play he thinks might be written on the usurpation of Henry IV and Richard's death, a play that fills the gap left by Shakespeare's failure to deal precisely with the moment of the usurpation and the motives of Henry's supporters. "I think every poem should have some prevailing sentiment—in this it should be the [beauty] of liberty—& the difficulty of ascertaining in what state Liberty is to be best enjoined."

There survives also from this period a plan to write single-handed a history of world literature.[39] He devotes himself largely to a discussion of methodology, but the model of his father's *Encyclopaedia* is clear from his plan to publish the work in a series of volumes:

> I do not think the reading necessar[y] for the whole—or the greatest portion, need be finished before the 1st. part of such a work went to press—A Vol. or two might be published at a time—& might be completed without much more study than that necessary to the particulars of the first ages of Literature—which would from their distance—from the paucity of subjects—from the immense deal that has been written on them, & from my stile of education, be to me the easiest portion of the work—

The student from Harrow and Winchester is not modest about what he has learned.

These surviving notes augment and perhaps somewhat correct the account Trollope later gives of his intellectual interests at this time. The reference to "castle building" confirms his description of the antecedents of his novel writing. "I was always going about with some castle in the air firmly built within my mind. . . . For weeks, for months, if I remember rightly, from year to year, I would carry on the same tale, binding myself down to certain laws, to certain proportions, and proprieties, and unities. Nothing impossible was ever introduced,—nor even anything which, from outward circumstances, would seem to be violently improbable. I myself was of course my own hero." Only when, after some years, he learned to discard himself as hero could he actually construct a novel.

Meanwhile, he did read and study, practiced until he could read Latin and French comfortably, and became an enthusiastic admirer of the great poets. His comment in these notes that he found Johnson's judgment of Cowley fairer than many of his other judgments is the opposite side of the (doubtless exaggerated) story in the *Autobiography* that he threw the *Lives of the Poets* out of the window because Johnson spoke slightingly of "Lycidas."

Drama was his first ambition; it seemed beyond him, "but I thought it possible that I might write a novel. I had resolved very early that in that shape must the attempt be made" to find occupation for himself with pens and paper.[40] His career was no chance product of youthful daydreaming, but the fruit of a young man's serious study and reflection.

Chapter III

1835–42

While at Bruges Tom received news that he was likely to be appointed an assistant master at King Edward's Grammar School, Birmingham; he hastened thither at the beginning of April, 1835, only to learn that the appointment, though almost certainly his, had been postponed. He stayed for a time in mid-April with Anthony in London, and then took his degree at Oxford on April 29.[1]

With the Birmingham appointment still deferred, Tom joined his parents and sisters in Paris, where they had gone both to gather materials for Mrs. Trollope's book and in the hope of finding a medical specialist who could mend Thomas Anthony's clearly deteriorating health. As so often was the case, the doctor could only shake his head sadly, prophesy no immediate crisis, and offer no remedy. The family's sojourn in Paris was only a little more than a month; then they all returned to Bruges. Another visit by Tom to Birmingham in early October revealed only further postponement of the appointment, and he spent another evening with Anthony in London on the way back to Bruges. There Thomas Anthony died on October 23, and was buried two days later near his son Henry. He had grown progressively worse since the journey to Paris, but apparently the illness was never diagnosed or treated. He was sixty-one years old.[2]

Thomas Anthony's death was only the second loss of the three Frances Trollope and her family were to suffer in the space of fourteen months. The business of settling the estate took her to London, but so too did Emily's condition, for she was obviously declining rapidly with tuberculosis. The doctor advised that she spend the winter in England, and Mrs. Trollope at once sought out a house there, sending instructions to Tom and Cecilia to pack up the family's belongings and give up the Château d'Hondt. She found and leased "a pleasant house with a good garden on the common at Hadley, near Barnet," north of London, into which she and Emily moved at the beginning of the new year, 1836. Hadley had been the home of Thackeray's grandfather, and the rector of the church when the Trollopes moved there, the Reverend Mr. Thackeray, was a distant cousin of the novelist.[3] The house which Mrs. Trollope described as her "pretty cottage" was doubtless larger than that term implies, since one Christmas she had eight house guests in addition to her family. In this cottage Emily died on February 12, with Anthony at her bedside, and she was buried in the churchyard up against the east end of the church. She was a month short of her eighteenth birthday. Tom was still in Bruges, but Cecilia, who had come to London, was staying once again with Lady Milman at Pinner. It fell to Anthony to notify Tom ("It is all over! Poor Emily breathed her last this morning. She died without any pain, and without a struggle.") and to bring Cecilia back from Pinner, as Tom had done when Henry died.[4] More than twenty years later Anthony set the scene for *The Bertrams* at Hadley Cross, and as he described the ringing of the church bells for his heroine's wedding he added: "I know full well the tone with which they toll when the soul is ushered to its last long rest. I have stood in that green churchyard when earth has been laid to earth, ashes to ashes, dust to dust—the ashes and the dust that were loved so well."[5] Tom and Anthony appeared immune, but the shadow of tuberculosis hung over Cecilia, despite her happy years of love and marriage, until she too died of the disease thirteen years later. When Trollope near the end of his life devised the story of *Marion Fay,* he was recalling the pain of his own family's experience. "Oh! consumption, thou scourge of England's beauty! how many mothers, gasping with ill-suppressed fears, have listened to such words as these"—the doctor's verdict that there was no organic disease, as yet—"have listened and then hoped; listened again and hoped again with fainter hopes; have listened again, and then hoped no more," he wrote in *The Three Clerks* (chap. xxx), where young Katie's symptoms and the remedies prescribed (rum and milk and cod-liver oil, and a winter at Torquay on the south coast of England) showed the fearful helplessness of the doctors in the face of the disease. But Katie did not have tuberculosis, and again Trollope was recalling his brother's and his sisters' perpetual optimism when he wrote: "Katie was . . . positive that her own illness would be fatal—a symptom which might have confirmed those who watched her in their opinion that her disease was not consumption" (chap. xlii).

In the summer of 1836 Mrs. Trollope, Tom, Hervieu, and several others assembled at Anthony's lodgings, then set off in the early evening on the night coach for Dover, the first leg of a journey to Vienna which was to be the subject of her next travel book, *Vienna and the Austrians*. She was abroad this time for nearly a year, but Tom was summoned to England in the dead of winter to take up, at last, the Birmingham appointment. His salary was £200 a year, more than twice Anthony's.[6]

છ

Anthony was "getting into continual hot water, for not doing his work at the Post Office," wrote his brother later, of the early part of 1835. "He was, I take it, a very bad office clerk."[7] Certainly the official records show that he frequently displeased his superiors. On a Saturday in December, 1838, while he was on night duty, he failed to copy and then forward important letters to the railway companies involving some significant and immediate change in their arrangements for postal service. "I am by no means satisfied" with his explanation, wrote the assistant secretary. "I have observed with much regret an habitual carelessness on the part of this Officer in the performance of his duties." And so the postmaster general, acting on his recommendation, wrote: "Let Mr. Trollope be suspended *from pay* for one week, and let him be most seriously warned that unless there is great alteration in his attention to his duties, I shall be under the necessity of removing him from the service."[8] Four months later, he overstayed a weekend leave of absence by half a day and was threatened again with loss of pay; on this occasion his explanation was found satisfactory and there was no penalty. But in May, 1839, he had fallen so far behind in his work that Maberly recommended he be obliged to stay in the office two extra hours a day until the arrear was cleared off, and that he lose his seniority for the next vacancy to which he might be promoted. "Mr. Trollope is without excuse, as he has good abilities & as this neglect, which has undoubtedly brought the Dep[t] into discredit (for some of the Cases are most gross) is entirely produced by the want of proper attention to his duty." The postmaster general concurred: "I hope it may be a warning to him to be more attentive & regular for the future."[9] In November, 1840, when the junior clerks to a man were found remiss about following instructions for reporting expenditures to the accountant general, Trollope was especially remiss.[10] Despite these memoranda, Trollope (at least when he grew older) remembered the discipline of the office as incredibly lax. He told the story of one junior clerk called before his superior and confronted with copies of letters he had entered in the minute book the preceding day. "If you can read *one line* of this, I shan't dismiss you," said the superior. Alas, the unfortunate lad could not—he had merely scrawled on the page in pretense of copying, and so he was dismissed.[11] More than one chapter of *Marion Fay* is set among the clerks in the secretary's office as Trollope remembered it from his youth.

One of Trollope's fellow clerks, five years his senior in the service and two years his senior in age, was John Tilley,[12] who frequently accompanied Anthony to Hadley to visit his family. Like the Post Office clerk George Roden in *Marion Fay*, who also accompanied his friend to the family home in a village north of London, Tilley fell in love with his friend's sister. At the end of 1838 he was appointed surveyor (district supervisor of the mails) for the Northern District of England, and on February 11, 1839, was married to Cecilia Trollope in St. Mary's Church, Bryanston Square, by the Reverend T. F. Dibdin, a well-known biblio-

phile and (in the judgment of Tom Trollope) a notably bad preacher who
delivered "with much gesticulation, emphasis, and grimace the most
trashy sermon[s] I have ever heard; words—words—words without a
shadow of an idea in them." Mrs. Trollope, Tom, and Anthony were
there, and so were some of the Grants as bridesmaids, the Milton cousins,
other close friends, and at least one clerk from the Post Office, J. H.
Newman, who in time himself became a surveyor.[13] After the ceremony,
Mrs. Trollope accompanied the Grants to their home at Hayes, and
returned to London by train the next day—her first railway journey. Her
new son-in-law, she told a friend, was "indeed a very admirable person,
and all the minor matters of income, house, and so forth are quite as I
could wish, so that I feel that *that* part of my business on earth has been
very well accomplished.[14]

By the time of the wedding Mrs. Trollope had given up the cottage
at Hadley and moved to London (June, 1838), "a change which both
Anthony's occupation and mine renders very desirable. . . . Four hours
out of every day is too much for Anthony to pass in, or on, a coach, which
is what he now does—and moreover I find the necessity of seeing London
people, whether for business or pleasure recurs too frequently for conve-
nience or economy." When it was that Anthony had given up his lodgings
in town to live with his mother in Hadley is not clear. But when she
moved to No. 20 York Street, in the parish where the wedding took
place, he accompanied her. (The new residence was not very far from
where he had lived on Northumberland Street, and not far either from the
house he would take in Montagu Square after his retirement from the Post
Office.) Very soon after the move, the *Times* reported her as lying dan-
gerously ill at the house of Henry Milton.[15] Tom now gave up his post in
Birmingham, and after a short journey to Manchester with his mother to
gather material on factory conditions for her novel *Michael Armstrong*
Tom, with a contract for three hundred guineas in hand, went to Brittany
to write a couple volumes on that region; Hervieu went along to do the
illustrations. From this time on Tom devoted himself to a career of
writing, like the rest of the family—writing histories, novels, newspaper
columns—and to accompanying his mother on her travels.[16]

❧

In late July she and Tom visited Cecilia and John Tilley at Penrith, in the
Lake District near Ullswater.[17] Mrs. Trollope fell in love with her
daughter's home: "Nothing can be prettier. [Her] windows look out upon
the pretty Lake mountains, which . . . are beautiful in no ordinary degree from the boldness of outline, and the great variety of picturesque
combination which they display." Anthony's duties kept him fixed in

London, but his mother did not forget him. His annual leave from the Post Office was due in December, and she had made him a promise that she would take him to Paris. It is "perhaps the only opportunity he may have of seeing la belle ville." Little did she foresee his future, or perceive the inheritance of "travelling delights" that was in his blood.[18] His mother's social life in Paris was most active; "her visiting list was a roll-call of the most illustrious personages . . . , native and foreign," and Anthony greatly enjoyed "going to so many good parties," she reported. His visit was for only a month or so; she and Tom stayed until May 30, 1840. Apparently the York Street lodgings had been given up, for Anthony was now staying a short distance away at No. 3 Wyndham Street (the street on which Lady Anna's mother lived before her move to Keppel Street).[19]

When they got back to London they found, to their shocked surprise, that Anthony was deathly ill; his symptoms were asthmatic, but the doctors could neither determine the cause nor prescribe a remedy. Having lived through a similar experience in Thomas Anthony's last illness, Mrs. Trollope was desperate: "Day by day I lose hope."[20] She called in Dr. John Elliotson, whom she had first met a little more than a year earlier and who had treated her during the illness of June–July of the preceding year.[21] (Thackeray too was treated by Elliotson, in 1849, and dedicated *Pendennis* to him out of gratitude.) Elliotson, formerly on the staff of University College Hospital, had become devoted to therapeutic hypnosis, and brought with him on his visits two young sisters named Okey, aged about thirteen and fourteen, who had supersensory powers and could predict the imminent death of a patient by mysterious visions. Fortunately, on none of their many visits to Anthony's bedside were they moved to foretell his doom, and he recovered. By curious coincidence, one of them became a maid in his household at Waltham Cross some twenty or more years later.[22] His sick leave extended from mid-May to September 4, during which time a temporary clerk was engaged to perform his duties in the secretary's office. By autumn he was well enough to pay a flying visit to the Tilleys and his mother in Cumberland.[23]

While he was in London, Anthony could serve as his mother's agent with the publishers, picking up and dropping off proofs and collecting payments, and she instructed friends who might not be current with her movements to address her in his care, at the General Post Office.[24] And so it perhaps seemed of less concern to her now to be at the center of things; in any case, Penrith was so lovely that by June, 1840, she determined to leave London, bought "a field in a very beautiful situation overlooking the ruins of Brougham Castle and the confluence of the Eden with the Lowther, and proceeded to build a house on the higher part of it." Most of the time the Cumberland house was under construction his mother and Tom were on the Continent (April, 1841 to February or March, 1842), paying their first visit to Italy. Not until July 23, 1842, did they move into their new house, "Carlton Hill."[25] By that time Anthony had been for ten months stationed in Ireland.

ప

By 1841 Anthony's salary had reached £140 a year, and promised soon to rise to £180. London, however, was expensive, and in any case the way to promotion was to move out of the headquarters office and into the field. Tilley, as a surveyor, was already making £300 plus generous travel allowances of a guinea a day and eightpence a mile on the road. In the summer of 1841 word came that there would be a vacancy as a surveyor's clerk in western Ireland. With a strong sense that at age twenty-six he was going nowhere in London, and with the firm conviction that Maberly would be glad to be rid of him, Anthony requested the transfer even though the starting salary was only £100; the travel allowances (fifteen shillings a day and sixpence a mile in Ireland) were the crucial considerations initially, as well as the much lower living expenses in Ireland. The appointment was made on July 29.[26]

To clear up his debts and pay the expense of moving, he borrowed £200 from "a dear old cousin, our family lawyer," John Young, who "looked upon me with pitying eyes,—shaking his head."[27] (The sadly shaking head is the one image that dominates Trollope's later recollections of his elders and superiors of those days.) His annual income, once he moved to Ireland, rose immediately to over £300.[28]

He was granted a fortnight's leave of absence at the end of August to prepare for the move. But his departure from St. Martin's-le-Grand was not without incident. On the eve of his going he had a violent quarrel in the office with a fellow clerk, Adolphus Shelley (not of the poet's kin), and used such violent and insulting language toward him as to draw a reprimand from Maberly, and he was required by the postmaster general to write a letter of apology to Shelley. "Any refusal on his part to give it will be at his peril." The letter of apology was written and met with Maberly's and the postmaster general's approval.[29] There was another matter hanging over his head. An Irish bank note for £3 had been improperly enclosed in a newspaper for transmission by post at the printed paper rate; it was discovered, confiscated, and sent to the secretary's office where it fell to Trollope to record it and keep it secure. The bank note, unfortunately, disappeared. When some months later it still had not been found, Maberly on October 13 recommended that he be required to make good the loss. In this instance Trollope's explanation of his part in the matter was held to excuse him, and he was relieved of the necessity of repaying the money.[30] It is not impossible that this episode was linked to the story he tells in his *Autobiography:*

> On one occasion, in the performance of my duty, I had put a private letter containing bank-notes on the Secretary's table,—which letter I had duly opened, as it was not marked private. The letter was seen by the Colonel, but had not been moved by him when he left his room. On his return it was gone. In the meantime I had returned to the room, again in the performance of some duty. When the letter was missed I was sent for, and there I found the Colonel much moved about his letter, and a certain chief clerk, who, with a long face, was making suggestions as to the probable fate of the money. "The letter has been taken," said the Colonel, turning to me angrily, "and, by G——! there has been nobody in the room but you and I." As he spoke, he thundered his fist down upon the table. "Then," said I, "by G——! you have taken it." And I also thundered my fist down;—but, accidentally, not upon the table. There was there a standing movable desk, at which, I presume, it was the Colonel's habit to write, and on this movable desk was a large bottle full of ink. My fist unfortunately came on the desk, and the ink at once flew up, covering the Colonel's face and shirt-front. Then it was a sight to see that senior clerk, as he seized a quire of blotting-paper, and rushed to the aid of his superior officer, striving to mop up the ink; and a sight also to see the Colonel, in his agony, hit right out through the blotting-paper at that senior clerk's unoffending stomach. At that moment there came in the Colonel's private secretary, with the letter and the money, and I was desired to go back to my own room. This was an incident not much in my favour, though I do not know that it did me special harm.

As for the irregularity of enclosing correspondence in a newspaper, "Who can make a widow understand that she should not communicate with her boy in the colonies under the dishonest cover of a newspaper?" he asked in one of his novels.[31]

∼

Trollope was assigned to assist the surveyor of the Central District of Ireland, James Drought—no doubt kinsman to the Sir Orlando Drought who caused the downfall of the Duke of Omnium's government in *The Prime Minister*. (Drought was a somewhat cantankerous man who was several times rebuked by Maberly for the "intemperate" language of his reports.)[32] He landed in Dublin on September 15, spent the night at a dirty hotel, and (mindful of the reputation of his new countrymen) ordered some whiskey punch after dinner. The whiskey did little to relieve his loneliness in a country where he did not know a soul—or hardly a soul. It was a more sophisticated Trollope who some years later advised a young surveyor's clerk, "Do not be too economical. You should always live at the hotels as a gentleman. It will pay best in the long run." Next morning he called on the secretary to the Irish Post Office and learned that Maberly had sent a letter of warning that young Trollope was thoroughly unreliable; "but I shall judge you by your own merits," the secretary said. (There is no record of such a letter from Maberly in the Post Office archives.) On the nineteenth he reached Banagher, a town on the River Shannon almost exactly in the center of Ireland, which was to be his headquarters.[33]

"From the day on which I set my foot in Ireland all these [past] evils went away from me. Since that time who has had a happier life than mine?" Trollope remarked in his *Autobiography*. He had an almost instant moment of triumph. Within a fortnight of his arrival he was sent out to look into the accounts of the postmaster of Oranmore, a town on Galway Bay. Trollope first made the man show him how the accounts were required to be kept, then found him to owe a substantial amount and recommended that he be dismissed as an incorrigible defaulter. Dismissed he was on November 1 and later was found to have been even further in arrears than at first supposed. To be sure, Trollope had his twinge of regret at the drastic action: "He had been a very useful man to me. I never had any further difficulty in the matter."[34]

The neighborhood of Banagher and Limerick to this day is alive with the legend of the "Colleen Bawn," a beautiful peasant girl drowned in the Shannon when her husband wished to take a wife more suited to his social class. The story is told in Gerald Griffin's novel, *The Collegians* (1829), which Trollope was fresh from reading when he moved to Ireland. Though a somewhat similar event actually occurred in the region in 1819, and the husband and his accomplice were hanged, it was the Griffin novel that created the legend; in it the young husband was named Hardress Cregan and his accomplice Danny Mann, and the fiction was set in the late eighteenth century. Wandering about the countryside there, Trollope fell in with a priest, and began speculating where Hardress committed "that foulest of murders. What a scene! what passion, what character, what skill I find in that novel!" "Hardress?" said the priest, and facing Trollope laid his hands on his shoulders. "Hardress was my first cousin, and I stood on the scaffold when he was hung." No doubt the priest kept a straight face as he said this; Anthony certainly told the story seriously to Mrs. Juliet Pollock twenty-seven years later, for she was moved to horror and sympathy at Anthony's unfortunate remark. Needless to say, Hardress Cregan

THE
UNIVERSITY OF WINNIPEG
PORTAGE & BALMORAL
WINNIPEG, MAN.   R3B 2E9
CANADA

was a fictional character, and in the fiction he was transported, not hanged. Works like *The Collegians,* however, did help set the tone a few years later for Trollope's pictures of Irish life in his first novels. Fortunately, he did not try to imitate the overwrought ingenuity of Griffin's style.[35]

From July 9 to August 2, 1842, Trollope's duties took him to the seaside resort of Kingstown, outside Dublin. There he made the acquaintance of Edward Heseltine, Rotherham agent of the Sheffield and Rotherham Banking Company, and his wife and daughters. Rotherham was a market town of about 8,000 inhabitants six miles distant from Sheffield, which then had a population of over 110,000; it shared some of Sheffield's industry but still had strong contacts with the country and had also a strong sense of its own identity. Its church dated from the reign of Edward IV (fifteenth century). The bank offices were in an imposing old house on the High Street, and the manager and his family lived above them; legend had it that both Mary Queen of Scots and Charles I had stayed the night in that house when traveling as prisoners toward London. One of Heseltine's junior clerks recalled many years later how the manager sunned himself daily on fine days, "with his blue coat and gilt buttons, a chevalier of the old school." ("Another antique figure was the Earl of Effingham, [with his] flesh coloured pantaloons, shoes, and buckles"; Trollope borrowed the name Effingham for one of his more attractive heroines.) Heseltine was, as befitted his position, one of the town's leading citizens and a director of the Sheffield and Rotherham Railway, opened in 1838. He had a hobby of collecting armor.[36]

Clearly Kingstown was attractive. Trollope returned there for a fortnight's holiday in mid-August, then quickly applied for a two-week extension of his leave and it was granted. Heseltine's fourth daughter, the twenty-two-year-old Rose, and he seemed to know at once that they were meant for each other.[37] Trollope once mentioned the difficulty facing a novelist who attempts to describe the scene of a proposal of marriage, an event in which he is likely to have participated but once and never otherwise observed. Nevertheless,

> The absolute words and acts of one such scene did once come to the author's knowledge. The couple were by no means plebeian, or below the proper standard of high bearing and high breeding; they were a handsome pair, living among educated people, sufficiently given to mental pursuits, and in every way what a pair of polite lovers ought to be. The all-important conversation passed in this wise. The site of the passionate scene was the seashore, on which they were walking, in autumn.

Gentleman. "Well, Miss ———, the long and the short of it is this: here I am; you can take me or leave me."

Lady—scratching a gutter on the sand with her parasol, so as to allow a little salt water to run out of one hole into another. "Of course, I know that's all nonsense."

Gentleman. "Nonsense! By Jove, it isn't nonsense at all: come, Jane; here I am: come, at any rate you can say something."

Lady. "Yes, I suppose I can say something."

Gentleman. "Well, which is it to be; take me or leave me?"

Lady—very slowly, and with a voice perhaps hardly articulate, carrying on, at the same time, her engineering works on a wider scale. "Well, I don't exactly want to leave you."

And so the matter was settled: settled with much propriety and satisfaction; and both the lady and gentleman would have thought, had they ever thought about the matter at all, that this, the sweetest moment of their lives, had been graced by all the poetry by which such moments ought to be hallowed.[38]

Our only pictures of Rose are of later date, but we have one hint about her appearance: "The sweetest, softest, tenderest, truest eyes which a woman can carry in her head are green in colour!"[39] She was a good deal shorter than Anthony.

❧

The latter part of his leave Anthony used for a quick visit to the new house at Penrith, and Tom returned to Ireland with him. Tom found him a very different man from what he had been in London, and they tramped together over the mountains above Killary Harbor on the far west coast, one of the loveliest spots in Ireland. Anthony's chief, Drought, was a master of foxhounds and spent the greater part of his time in the field; Anthony "stood high in his good graces by virtue of simply having taken the whole work and affairs of the postal district on his own shoulders." And out of the circumstance sprang one of Anthony's greatest passions in life: he bought a horse, and rode to the hounds. From that time until the sad moment nearly forty years later when he found himself too old for so strenuous a sport, he followed the hounds "with a persistent energy," and allowed himself the pleasure also of introducing a hunting scene into nearly every one of his novels.[40] Sometimes the scenes are narrated objectively, though often with anecdotes from his own or a friend's experience; once in a while, as with the literary gentleman Pollock in *Can You Forgive Her?* he places himself, thinly disguised, on the scene. There most of the huntsmen had gone down into the country the night before the hunt, and spent the evening playing whist and drinking hard, but Pollock had done three hours of writing by candlelight before he left his home at 7:45 in order to catch the 8:30 A.M. train from Euston (chap. xvii).

What did Anthony look like in those days? There are no photographs until about twenty years later. He and his brothers were always very stocky, but was he yet as heavy as he later became? His eyesight must certainly have required spectacles. When did he first grow a beard? Certainly before the beginning of 1858, when he wrote in *Doctor Thorne,* in the ironic voice of Frank Gresham: " 'All I require is a relay of napkins for every course;' and he went to work [on his soup], covering [his beard] with every spoonful, as men with beards always do" (chapt xxxv). We do not know when he became bald.

About forty miles west of Banagher was the fine estate of Trollope's fellow Harrovian, William Gregory, at Coole Park.* Trollope became a frequent visitor there, and from Gregory learned a good deal about the conditions of landlord and tenant on the Irish estates; Gregory was intelligent, sympathetic to his tenants, and his family had lived in Ireland since the era of Cromwell. About the time of Trollope's transfer to that country Gregory was elected to the Parliament at Westminster as member for Dublin, at a cost of £9,000 (including the purchase of 1,500 votes at £3 a head). He was active in the debates over government relief of the famine a few years later, and undoubtedly influenced Trollope's thinking on the subject. His house was commonly full of guests; here Trollope met the Irish novelist Charles Lever. Like Lord Ballindine in *The Kellys,* Gregory was an enthusiast for horse racing, and once won £5,000 on the Derby.[41] Trollope's assertion that his life at school had been miserably lonely must be modified in the light of his subsequent active friendships with old schoolfellows.

---

*Yeats's friend became Gregory's second wife nearly two years after Trollope's death, and Yeats came to know her more than a decade later, so that there is no evidence Yeats knew of Trollope's friendship with Gregory. But Yeats enjoyed Trollope's novels: he "declared *Ulysses* to be a mad book, . . . and finally was unable to finish it so that he found himself reading Trollope instead."

Chapter IV

1843–51

There are two exultant marginal notes in the early pages of Trollope's travel diaries. Opposite September 15–24, 1843, is "Began my first novel"; near June 9, 1844, "married."

On September 5, 1843, Anthony left Banagher for a month's stay at Drumsna, on the River Shannon somewhat more than fifty miles to the north, "where the postmaster had come to some sorrow about his money." There John Merivale came to stay with him for a few days, and resuming their London pleasures they walked out into the country; near the village of Headfort they turned through a deserted gateway, followed a grass-grown road and came to the modern ruins of a country house. Such ruins are by no means uncommon in Ireland, but they always tease the imagination, and Anthony and Merivale began suggesting to each other the causes for the house's abandonment. At last Anthony had a subject for a novel; "While I was still among the ruined walls and decayed beams I fabricated the plot of *The Macdermots of Ballycloran*."[1]

The writing by no means followed the strict schedule he later practiced, and he does not seem even to have made a calendar of his progress as he was later to do so regularly. "It was only now and then that I found either time or energy for a few pages." By the date of his marriage (June 11, 1844) he had completed only a third of the whole.[2] And then, somehow, he mislaid the manuscript. Fortunately it was quickly recovered, and his mother (to whom he had spoken about the novel when he and Rose went to see her at Penrith after the wedding) wrote, through Rose, to encourage him to finish it, though she prudently added that he must not neglect his official duties in order to do so.[3] A year later the novel was done; again Mrs. Trollope was visiting at Penrith,* again Anthony and Rose visited there, and this time she undertook on her way through London to try to place the manuscript with a publisher.

She chose Thomas Cautley Newby, a modest publisher in the neighborhood of Cavendish Square who managed to squeeze a small profit from

---

*Mrs. Trollope and Tom gave up their own house at Penrith and went out to Italy on September 1, 1843; Florence became their permanent home, and they returned to England only occasionally.[4]

bringing out books by unknown authors or authors not likely to sell well enough to attract the more "respectable" members of the trade. It was a publisher of precisely this sort with whom she herself had made her beginning.[5] Newby was rather generally looked down on, and somewhat suspected of sharp practices, but a man who within the space of less than ten months in 1847 introduced to the world the first novels of Anthony Trollope and Emily Brontë (*Wuthering Heights*) may be said to have performed a useful function. At least some of his authors found it pleasant to take refuge from the London cold in the snug and warm office, in his house, to chat with him and with the kind, nice, capable "woman of business," Miss Springett, who made up his entire staff.[6] He would advance all the cost of publication, and when he had reimbursed himself from sales would divide the subsequent profits evenly with the author; if the sales fell short of the expenses he absorbed the loss. He estimated that *The Macdermots* in the usual three-volume form priced at a guinea and a half would meet expenses with the sale of about 190 copies, and thereafter the profit to be divided would be about one pound threepence a copy. He sent Trollope a publishing agreement for signature on September 15, with the expectation of publishing an edition of 400 copies by February, 1846.[7]

The advantage of such an arrangement to an impecunious author is obvious; the disadvantage is that a publisher working on so slim a margin cannot always command the capital he needs; it is probably for this reason that there was no sign of the book on the proposed date. On her annual visit to London in the summer of 1846, Mrs. Trollope stopped to make inquiry of Newby and got from him "a most wretched account of the novel market. . . . He thinks [the book] very cleverly written, but . . . Irish stories are very unpopular."[8] Newby printed the work in his own establishment, and it is hard to imagine a shoddier piece of work. It was finally advertised in mid-March, 1847, but even in this it was unfortunate, for the advertisement on several occasions attributed the book to "Mrs. Trollope," and drew a public rebuke from one of her regular publishers.[9] The three-volume edition was reissued with a new title page after June, 1848, to take advantage of the timing of Trollope's next novel, *The Kellys,* but it quickly dropped from the market; Trollope received no share of the profits from it. His regular publisher of later years, Chapman and Hall, republished it in one volume in February, 1861, and it remained in print throughout the author's life. Trollope claimed never to have seen a review of it, but in fact it was duly noticed in the weekly literary journals, generally favorably.[10] More than once his relationship with Mrs. Trollope was mentioned. One reviewer noted a likeness to the Irish novels of Maria Edgeworth, who was indeed still living in Edgeworthstown, within Trollope's postal district; he mentioned her living there in *The Macdermots*.

&

Of Trollope's two-year courtship we know nothing beyond what may be inferred from the passage in *Doctor Thorne*. He and Rose can have seen very little of each other after their first meeting. But on May 10, 1844, his application for a month's leave of absence was approved; on Tuesday, June 11, they were married at the parish church of Rotherham. The newspaper described him only as "son of the celebrated authoress." When Trollope began his *Autobiography* in the latter part of 1875, Rose jotted down memoranda, year by year, of their life together, beginning:

> 1844. Married 11.th June. (hurrah) Went to the lakes and Penrith— first met your mother, Cecilia Tom & John Tilley—To Ireland in July. at Kingstown. To Bannagher—driven into the Shannon canal. [11]

Rose of course wrote to her mother-in-law from Ireland, reporting that she was carrying in her luggage a large number of books to read, and a subscription to a library; she got an affectionate reply. [12] The Tilleys had by this time purchased the house Mrs. Trollope had built near Penrith, and Rose and Anthony were guests there again the next summer. [13] We never hear of their visiting Rotherham, but they must have done so.

The transfer of Stephen Maberly, surveyor's clerk for Northern Ireland, to London brought instant applications from Trollope and from the clerk for Southern Ireland to be transferred to the vacant position, with its headquarters in Dublin. The other clerk had seniority, and so Trollope and Rose took the second best—their transfer to the Southern District was authorized on August 27. Thus "I left the west of Ireland and the hunting surveyor, and joined another in the south," James Kendrick, who became a good friend. [14] They lived first at Cork, and then (after March, 1845) at Clonmel, in Tipperary, which became Trollope's headquarters. Here his sons Henry Merivale and Frederic James Anthony were born (March 13, 1846, and September 27, 1847); Henry was the name of Trollope's deceased brother and of his uncle Henry Milton, and Frederic was named after Rose's younger brother. Henry's godparents were John Merivale, his uncle Thomas Adolphus, and his grandmother Frances Trollope; Fred's were James Kendrick (from whom he got one of his names), John Tilley, and Isabella Heseltine. [15] Clonmel was a town of some size on the Suir, with some fine old buildings, and was a famous sporting center, the headquarters of the Tipperary foxhounds.

Trollope's was not an occupation that made marriage easy. Occasionally he was able to settle in one place (with Rose) for a period—at Cork for September–February, 1844–45; then in temporary charge of the post offices at Miltown Malbay on the west coast from March to mid-June, 1845; at Kilkenny in October and at Fermoy for most of November–February, 1845–46. But there was also much traveling: from May 9 to September 21, 1846, for example, a few weeks after the birth of his first son, he was in a different town nearly every night. His most strenuous efforts went to shifting the postal services from the mail coaches to the rapidly expanding Irish railways.[16] (When Trollope moved to Mallow, he tells us in *Castle Richmond*, "the Great Southern and Western Railway was not . . . open so far as Mallow, and the journey from Dublin was long and tedious" [chap. xix].)

When the Irish districts were redivided to provide a fourth surveyor in February, 1848, Trollope at first requested and was granted a transfer that would permit him to remain in Clonmel (now made a part of the new South Midland District), but he remained in the Southern District with Kendrick when both were permitted to retain their headquarters at Clonmel until they could at their leisure dispose of their houses and move their families. Late in that year the Trollopes moved to Mallow, in County Cork, where they took a house and where the hunting was, if anything, even better.[17] Just as *The Macdermots* and *The Kellys* were largely set in Trollope's first district, so *Castle Richmond* a decade later takes place chiefly in his new one in County Cork.

ॐ

Though we have no record of when he began his next novel, Trollope probably did not wait until he saw *The Macdermots* in print; he was certainly at work on the new novel by May, 1847.[18] By October 16 all but sixty pages (the last three chapters) of *The Kellys and the O'Kellys* was completed, and Trollope this time determined to approach his mother's publishers, and firmly determined also that he wanted the book purchased by the publisher outright, not brought out on half-profits. Richard Bentley agreed to look at it, but within a month told Trollope that he would not publish it.[19] The manuscript then went to another of her publishers, Henry Colburn, from whom word came late in March that he would bring it out on a half-profits basis, and this offer Trollope reluctantly accepted. Colburn forwarded a copy of the publishing agreement for signature on March 30, 1848. "My present impression is that, considering the Work is illustrative of Irish Society, it should appear as soon as it could be printed. . . . I will use my best exertions for its success."[20] It is worth noticing that the agreement provided that the sale was to be determined and the account wound up within three months of the date of publication. The full title (almost certainly on Colburn's advice)* was *The Kellys and the O'Kellys, or, Landlords and Tenants. A Tale of Irish Life.* By June 22, this "New Irish Novel" was advertised as "just ready in 3 vols." in the *Times.*[22] Like *The Macdermots* it had its share of reviews in the weeklies, and Henry Chorley, who treated both books in the *Athenaeum* with respect, preferred *The Kellys* for its humor.[23] The review in the *Times,* Trollope learned, had been in some measure "bespoke" by a friend in London over dinner at his club with one of the editors, and exciting though a review there was to a young author, he determined never again to have any dealings, if he could help it, with a critic on his own behalf. It was, indeed, not quite so brutal a review as he remembered it; in one short paragraph came the pronouncement that "There is a native humour and a bold reality in the delineation of the characters" which make the book "substantial," combined with a "predilection for the ruder manifestations of Irish life, taken rough as they come," which makes it "coarse."[24]

As good as his word (or nearly so), Colburn forwarded his accounting as of mid-October, with the assurance that the regular sale was now over and more than half an edition of 375 copies would have to be remaindered. The loss to date was £63 10s. 1½d. Trollope wrote on Colburn's accompanying letter, "Kellys & OKellys Account. Oh!!" This letter, much of which Trollope published in *An Autobiography,* said: "The greatest efforts have been used, but in vain. . . . It appears clear to me that although in consequence of the great number of novels that are published, the sale of each, with some few exceptions, must be small, yet, it is evident that readers do not like Novels on Irish subjects so well as on others. Thus you will perceive, it is impossible for me to give any encouragement to you to proceed in novel writing." Lady Lytton had once amused the Trollope family by calling Colburn "an embodied shiver"! "I [did not] doubt the wisdom of the advice, . . . though I never thought of obeying it," commented Trollope—who by that time had nearly finished a third novel.[25] Like *The Macdermots, The Kellys* was republished in one volume by Chapman and Hall about 1859 and in that form remained in print.

❧

"Thady," said old Macdermot, as he sat eating stirabout and thick milk, over a great turf fire, one morning about the beginning of October, "Thady, will you be getting the money out of them born divils this turn, and they owing it, some two, some three years this November, bad cess to thim for tenants! Thady, I say," shouted, or

---

* "I eschew the fashion of double names for a book," said Trollope.[21]

rather screamed, the old man, as his son continued silently eating his breakfast, "Thady, I say, have they the money, at all at all, any of them, or is it stubborn they are? there's Flannelly and Keegan with their d——d papers and bills and costs; will you be making out the £142.7*s*.6*d*. before Christmas for the hell-hounds; or it's them'll be masters in Ballycloran; then let the boys see the landlord they'll have over them, that time." (Chap. iii)

This scarcely sounds like the opening scene of a Trollope novel, and readers who come to *The Macdermots of Ballycloran* after reading his better known tales will find themselves on unfamiliar ground. It is indeed an "Irish novel," with a great deal of dialect and a certain amount of conventional caricature. "'I am cowld within me, and divil a word I'll spake, till I've dhriv it out of me with the sperrits,' and he poured the glass of whiskey down his throat, as though he was pouring it into a pitcher" (chap. ix). Only a fictional Irishman could present his side to an opponent in a duel in such a way as to endure a painful, though not serious, bullet wound "under the tails of his coat"—and the duel is entirely irrelevant to the story, introduced only for the farce (chap. xxviii). Among the books in Father John McGrath's library are the works of St. Chrysostom and novels like *Nicholas Nickleby* and *Charles O'Malley*. Trollope, as we have seen, knew the author of the latter, Charles Lever, at William Gregory's Coole Park. Works like *Harry Lorrequer* and *Charles O'Malley* (both published before Trollope came to Ireland) certainly had their impact on *The Macdermots,* and so too did the novels of William Carleton, whose *Tales of Ireland* Trollope compared to Edward Ramsay's pictures of Scottish life. The Irishman of fiction was reinforced by Trollope's own observation in the course of his rides to set up mail routes and his pleasure tramps through the countryside; a Dublin lady who knew him at this time said that "his close looking into the commonest objects of his daily life always reminded her of a woman in a shop examining the materials for a new dress." Perhaps the most Trollopian aspect of the work is his fine sense of people in a place. It "is a good novel, and worth reading by any one who wishes to understand what Irish life was before the potato disease, the famine, and the Encumbered Estates Bill," he tells us.[26]

"I do not know that I ever made [a plot] so good,—or, at any rate, one so susceptible of pathos."[27] Pathos was of course built into the story from the moment of its origin, with its feeling for the decay of the owners of the house from moderate prosperity to poverty and extinction, "a sad monument to the memory of the Macdermot family," as Trollope calls it (chap. xxxvi). The Macdermots were gentry of an ancient Irish line who had come on bad times as the tenants were less and less able to pay their rents to the sympathetic indigenous landlords. By the time the story opens, there is little enough visibly to separate the Macdermots from the peasants, but the latter are always aware of the social distinction and proud to acknowledge it: a fugitive Thady Macdermot taking refuge in a poverty-stricken hovel is nevertheless brought bits of meat when his hosts eat nothing but potatoes. The servant Biddy was to have been bridesmaid at a village wedding, and had found herself a huge cap to signal her part in the ceremony, but when Feemy Macdermot arrives the priest insists that Feemy take precedence (chaps. xxiii, xii). Much of the pathos, however, is melodramatic. A revenue officer seduces the daughter of the house; her brother beats the officer's brains out with a shillelagh to frustrate their elopement and is hanged for the murder, while the girl dies of what Trollope calls "premature parturition" (chap. xxxiii), with her seducer's name on her lips. A moneylender forecloses on the property, but his agent Keegan has his foot hacked off by a group of tenants armed with an ax, and is left to die or not as luck may provide. Trollope's mature art includes remarkably sensitive exploration of the minds of his characters, but he had no experience with the mind of the criminal facing execution, and Thady's reflections have something of the false note of Fagin's reflections in his prison cell.

"I am aware that I broke down in the telling, not having yet studied the art."[28] There was some conscious artifice, certainly. "The first foot Keegan puts on Ballycloran, he shall leave there by G—d," said one of the tenants early in the novel (chap. iv); by the end of the novel Keegan has done precisely that. "It's warning you want yourself, Captain dear," said another of the lower-class characters; "but if you a'nt quiet enough before Christmas, it's odd, that's all" (chap. xii). By Christmas the Captain had had his skull beaten in. But these foreshadowings are easy to miss; what one remembers is such long, rather slow-moving passages as the steeplechase and its accompanying festivities at Carrick-on-Shannon: the very kind of digression Trollope was later to excel in is here more than a bit tedious. Throughout his career, Trollope loved legal conflicts in his novels, and the trial of Thady Macdermot for murder is the first of Trollope's many courtroom trials. But the very long chapter of conversation between Father John McGrath and the Dublin barrister O'Malley as they plan Thady's defense is sheer pedantry, almost as if the ghost of Thomas Anthony were lecturing to students on the practice of his profession. The trial itself repeats much of that conversation, and is dragged out by an account of the trials of other, unrelated, cases at the same assizes. (Lawyers Allewinde and O'Laugher, incidentally, are the only examples in the book of the use of "label names," a Thackerayan practice Trollope later became very fond of.) The revisions Trollope made for the one-volume edition of 1861 were done partly to reduce the length, but are relevant to his concept of narrative art as well: he cut out the chapters describing Father McGrath's journey to Dublin and his discussion with lawyer O'Malley (vol. 2, chaps. ii–iii) as well as the final chapter, which in the original rounded out the framework of the narrative by returning to the abandoned house at Ballycloran after all the events had worked themselves out.[29] The final sentence of the novel now became: "The shops were closed during the whole day; but it was many days before the melancholy which attended the execution of Thady Macdermot wore away from the little town of Carrick on Shannon." The novel justly has its admirers, but it does little to prepare the reader for its author's greater achievements.

In October, 1843, Daniel O'Connell, "the Liberator," called a mass meeting at Clontarf on behalf of repeal of the Act of Union that more than a generation earlier had deprived Ireland of her own parliament. The government proclaimed the meeting an illegal assembly, and though O'Connell then canceled it, he, his son, and half a dozen others were indicted and tried in Dublin on a long bill of complaints early in 1844. All but one were convicted, though the verdict was ultimately overthrown by the Law Lords in London. The trial provides a chronological framework for *The Kellys and the O'Kellys,* of which the opening scene is in the crowd outside the Four Courts on the eleventh day of the trial, and the final episode is a wedding late in May or early in June, 1844, after the verdict of the packed jury had been reached.

It is a story of a very different kind from *The Macdermots.* Frank O'Kelly, twenty-six-year-old third Viscount Ballindine, is in love with an heiress who has £20,000 in her own right (a sum increased to £100,000 by the death of her brother early in the story), but her guardian is determined to prevent her bestowing the money on a horse-racing wastrel like the Viscount. A very distant relative of Ballindine's, Martin Kelly (all the Kellys, Blakes, and Dillons are related to all others of the same name), is a tenant on Ballindine's land in County Mayo, the poorest county in Ireland; he is the son of a widow who keeps an inn and a grocery shop in Dunmore,* and he is in love with Anastasia Lynch, who has £400 a year in her own right but whose brother Barry, desperately in debt, will stop at nothing to prevent their marriage. Martin is of common stock; the Lynches had attempted to set themselves above the common by sending Barry to the same English public school Lord Ballindine went to. At the end of the novel the obstacles to both marriages are overcome and the weddings are celebrated.

This is clearly the kind of fiction Trollope was ultimately going to master, and readers of his later novels will feel very much at home with this one. Little things have changed from *The Macdermots:* there are, for example, a good many dated epistles from one character to another

---

*The town of Ballindine was in the Central Postal District of Ireland, and Trollope's official duties at least once took him to Dunmore, near the border of Galway and Mayo.

through which we can mark the progress of the story, whereas letters are very rare indeed in *The Macdermots,* and only vaguely dated. There is a literal authenticity about the scenes of the story—street names, hotel names, the canal boat from Dublin to the west which may indeed have taken Trollope on his first journey from Dublin to Banagher. Here is the first of the hunting scenes that Trollope was so fond of. The Reverend George Armstrong with his nine children (his was the only Protestant family in his parish, so that he might claim literal paternity of every child in his congregation) was a foreshadowing of the Reverend Mr. Quiverful of Barchester, poorer than Quiverful but more cheerful. The Countess of Cashel is one of those incompetent, worrying women (not unlike Jane Austen's Mrs. Bennet) for whom life is always too much. Though plagued with an unsatisfactory cook, she is obliged to organize a large house party on the spur of the moment: "What are we to do? What can have become of all the cooks?—I'm sure there used to be cooks enough when I was first married." And then to balance the guest list: "I don't know any young men. . . . I remember, years ago, there always used to be too many of them, and I don't know where they're all gone to. At any rate, when they do come, there'll be nothing for them to eat" (chap. xxix). Lord Kilcullen did not mind proposing to an heiress whom he would make "miserable for life, by uniting her to a spendthrift, a *roué,* and a gambler—such was the natural lot of women in the higher ranks of life—" but he was too honorable to wish to rob her of her money (chap. xxx).

Brutality is not unknown in Trollope's later novels—*Doctor Thorne* begins with a young *roué's* having his brains bashed out by the irate brother of a seduced girl—but the brutality is much reduced from the level of *The Macdermots.* In *The Kellys* the one brute, Barry Lynch, who conspires unsuccessfully to bribe the doctor to let (or help) his sister die, is somewhat reminiscent of Dickens's recent Jonas Chuzzlewit. Throughout the whole novel one senses Trollope's love for Ireland, and especially his advocacy of the religious toleration which, indeed, he tells us elsewhere he generally found there; his sharpest satire is directed at the clergyman O'Joscelyn, "a most ultra and even furious Protestant" who regarded Oxford (Newman's Oxford) as "a Jesuitical seminary, devoted to the secret propagation of the Romish falsehood," and whose folly comes out sharply in his conversation with the tolerant, sweetly disposed Armstrong (chap. xxxviii). This book is among that half of Trollope's novels that have been kept in print up to our own day. Arnold Bennett, some seventy-five years later, found it "consistently excellent. . . . The characterization is admirable, strong, true, and sober."[30]

❧

The postal surveyor was responsible for every aspect of the service in his district, including the supervision of deliveries and of postmasters and their offices, and investigation into complaints and suggesting improvements. Of course much of the work fell to the surveyor's clerk, or assistant. Trollope delighted to tell anecdotes of his experience, sometimes no doubt with more concern for a good story than for the literal truth. One of these is related by Tom Trollope, who heard from his brother so many stories that he felt himself competent to write a book of "Memoirs of a Post Office Surveyor" (though of course he never did so). The tale is of a dishonest postmaster in the southwest of Ireland, and the moral is that a cheat can always be foiled by superior wit and decisive action. On a visit of inspection Trollope had noticed that the man carefully locked a large desk in the office. Two evenings later, word reached Trollope that a letter of some value was missing; the man's behavior had been suspicious. On the instant Trollope hired a horse and rode to the distant office. Rousing the postmaster in the small hours, he strode into the office and demanded that the desk be opened. Unfortunately, said the postmaster, the key had been lost for some months. Trollope kicked open the desk and (of course) found the missing letter.[31] A parallel tale is in fact confirmed by the newspapers of the day. In 1848 complaints came in of letters and cash lost from the mails that passed through Tralee, and so Trollope wrote a letter from a fictitious father in Newcastle (Limerick) enclosing a marked sovereign to a fictitious daughter in Ardfert, had it sealed in the bag at Newcastle on September 18, then sped to Ardfert to await its arrival. The bag had to be opened at Tralee as a distributing center, and the letters consigned to other bags; when the proper bag reached Ardfert Trollope's letter was not in it. And so he hastened to Tralee, where, accompanied by a constable with a search warrant, he found the marked sovereign in the purse of Mary O'Reilly, assistant to the postmaster. As a witness at her trial on July 26, 1849, Trollope was subjected to cross-examination by the future leader of the Home Rule party in the House of Commons, Isaac Butt, who turned the questioning into a silly debate with Trollope about the location of the mark he had placed on the coin—"under the neck on the head" (i.e., on the obverse side of the coin); "under the neck on the head" is anatomically impossible, said Butt, and the two wrangled in high good humor. Butt called attention to Trollope's reflections on Irish courts and barristers in *The Macdermots*.[32] Perhaps this episode may be seen as an anticipation of Chaffanbrass's cross-examination of the novelist Bouncer at the trial of Phineas Finn; it was certainly behind Trollope's description of the liveliness of the Irish assizes in *Castle Richmond*.[33]

Not always was Trollope's firm line triumphant. In December, 1848, Colonel Maberly was obliged to draw the attention of the postmaster general to a quarrel Trollope got himself involved in with a mail guard named Conolly, whom Trollope had tried to bar from the post office at Fermoy; there was an explosion of some magnitude between the men and each made written accusations against the other. Maberly tried to temporize by cautioning Conolly that superior officers must on all occasions be treated "with becoming deference & respect," and by warning Trollope to be careful in his conduct toward his inferiors so as "not to give rise to these unpleasant charges against him." Trollope was imprudent enough to remonstrate against the warning and was told bluntly that in the secretary's view he had been quite simply wrong in his conduct toward Conolly.[34]

More amiable is the story of a country squire in County Cavan who wrote letter after irate letter to the officials to express a grievance with the postal service. Though the man did not live in Trollope's district, he was asked to look into the matter, and arrived at the house in an open jaunting cart just at dusk in the middle of a snowstorm. The door was opened by a butler, but the squire came bustling up, saw the very wet young clerk, and ordered some brandy and water—very hot—to be brought at once. Before Trollope knew what was happening he was shown to a bedroom and told that he must spend the night. Dinner was altogether too pleasant a social occasion for his host to allow any discussion of business, and after dinner the daughter sang in the drawing room while Trollope listened and the host dozed in his armchiair. Breakfast also gave no opportunity for discussion, and Trollope was sent off with the simple explanation from his host that "Here I sit all the day,—with nothing to do; and I like writing letters." Trollope reported to his superiors that the man's complaints had been satisfied; there were no more letters, and Trollope mildly regretted that he had deprived the man of his occupation.[35]

&

The Ireland of *The Macdermots* was poverty-stricken, but worse was to come: famine. "Early in the autumn of 1846, the disease fell upon the potato gardens like a dark mantle; before the end of September entire fields were black, and the air was infected with the unwholesome odour of the blight; before the end of October it was known that the whole food of the country was gone. . . . The hand of Providence fell upon the country utterly unawares and unprepared."[36] "There was a form of face which came upon the sufferers [from the famine] when their state of misery was far advanced, and which was a sure sign that their last stage of misery was nearly run. The mouth would fall and seem to hang, the lips at the two ends of the mouth would be dragged down, and the lower parts of the cheeks would fall as though they had been dragged and pulled. There were no signs of acute agony when this phasis of countenance was to be seen, none of the horrid symptoms of gnawing hunger by which one generally supposes that famine is accompanied. The look is one of apathy, desolation, and death. When custom had made these signs easily legible, the poor doomed wretch was known with certainty. 'It's no use in life meddling with him; he's gone,' said a lady to me in the far west of the south of Ireland, while the poor boy, whose doom was thus spoken, stood by listening. . . . I found that her reading was correct."[37]

Horrible as the famine was, however, there was a great deal of exaggeration in the reports printed in the newspapers, both Irish and English. "The air was said to be polluted by unburied corpses; . . . descriptions were given of streets and lanes in which bodies lay for days where the starved wretches had last sunk; and . . . districts were named in which the cabins were fabled to contain more dead than living tenants." Yet "I never saw a dead body lying exposed in the open air, either in a town or in the country. . . . The whole period was spent by me in passing from one place to another in the south and west of Ireland. I visited at the worst periods those places which were most afflicted; and if corpses, lying exposed, unheeded, and in heaps, were to be seen, no man's eye would have been oftener offended in that way than mine."[38]

Nor was there the violence which might have been expected, and indeed was reported. "I only remember one instance in which the bakers' shops were attacked; and in that instance the work was done by those who were undergoing no real suffering. At Clonmel in Tipperary the bread was one morning stripped away from the bakers' shops; but at that time, and in that place, there was nothing approaching to famine. The fault of the people was apathy."[39] Even the "Smith O'Brien rows" that Rose remembered as she thought back over her life with Anthony were much exaggerated in the *Times* accounts, "describing the movements of rebels in towns, of which the inhabitants of those towns had heard nothing; and it was frequently only on receipt of that paper that ladies learnt that they have been moving about in the midst of an armed insurrection!"[40] People, however, "were beginning to believe that there would never be a bit more to eat in the land, and that the time for hope and energy was gone. . . . The only thing regarded was a sufficiency of food to keep body and soul together. . . . It was this feeling [of despair] that made a residence in Ireland at that period so very sad."[41]

It was with these observations fresh in his memory that Trollope in June, 1849, read in the *Times* a series of long letters signed "S.G.O." (Sidney Godolphin Osborn), critical of the government's inadequate and inappropriate measures for the relief of Ireland. Trollope quickly responded to these with a letter to the *Examiner*, published, after some weeks' delay, on August 25 over the signature "A.T." This is the earliest of Trollope's contributions to periodicals and foreshadows many an essay on the political issues of the day; when, nearly twenty years later, he became editor of a journal himself, one of his requirements was that his magazine regularly engage itself in political questions, though not in a partisan manner. [42] Having thus seen himself in print, on his next visit to London in February, 1850, he presented himself at the home of the *Examiner*'s editor John Forster in Lincoln's Inn Fields to propose a series of letters in defense of the government's measures for Irish relief, based on his own close observation of the country. Forster (later the biographer of Dickens and Landor) agreed to entertain the idea, and from March 30 to June 15 half a dozen letters on "The Real State [or "Real Condition"] of Ireland" appeared in the *Examiner,* in addition to a short note on the relation of poverty to crime in that country. Forster did not, however, conceive that he had agreed to pay for the letters, and Trollope carried his sense of the imposition for many years. [43] The thrust of the letters, which are lucid and unemotional, was that the government's response to the famine had been "prompt, wise, and beneficent; and . . . the efforts of those who managed the poor were, as a rule, unremitting, honest, impartial, and successful." [44]

❧

Less than two months after their summer visit to Penrith in 1847, and while they were rambling pleasantly about Germany, Tom and Mrs. Trollope got word from John Tilley that the doctors had ordered Cecilia to spend two years in Italy for her health. She joined them in Florence at the end of September. But her Florentine doctor, though at first encouraging, decided that her lungs would not endure a winter in Florence, and so all three moved on to Rome. The change did her no good; it was clear that she too was dying of tuberculosis, and as she longed to be reunited with her husband and her five children, she returned to England in May of 1848. [45] A few months later the assistant secretary to the Post Office (Colonel Maberly's immediate subordinate) died. The postmaster general, the Marquis of Clanricarde, "who in a matter of patronage was not scrupulous" (as Trollope said), with a remarkable display of affability toward Thackeray's friend Lady Blessington, raised Thackeray's hope of obtaining the post, but bowed to pressure from the postal establishment. "It may be said that had Thackeray succeeded in that attempt he would surely have ruined himself," Trollope commented. [46] (Curiously enough, Trollope has been taken to task for this statement, as if the second-highest administrative office in the postal system required no experience; both common sense and Trollope's pride in the service were properly offended by the notion of patronage appointing an amateur, however good as a novelist and however warmly regarded by Trollope himself.) On September 29, John Tilley, with nearly twenty years of experience as clerk in the secretary's office and as surveyor, was appointed assistant secretary. [47] Six months later (April 4, 1849), Cecilia died at her new home in Allen

Place, Kensington. Her mother had spent the preceding month with her, once again (now nearly seventy years of age) watching at the bedside of a dying member of the family. Anthony had seen Cecilia only a few weeks earlier when he went to London to take her little daughter Edith home to live with Rose and himself in Ireland, and had carried away with him the image of "her patience, her trusting confidence in the fate that awaits her, and her tender thoughtfulness for every one," but he was unable to return for the funeral on April 10. "God bless you my dear John—I sometimes feel I led you into more sorrow than happiness in taking you to Hadley," he wrote to Tilley. Within a year, three of Cecilia's children died.[48]

"Bring mama over here." And so, although delayed by an illness that beset Mrs. Trollope soon after Cecilia's death, Tilley accompanied her to Mallow in the latter part of July, and they all went to the Lakes of Killarney, walked through the Gap of Dunloe, and listened to the echoes which then, as now, were started by the bugler. "Anthony and his excellent little wife are as happy as possible," was Mrs. Trollope's verdict, and Rose's later recollections of those days confirm the judgment. About August 12 she went back to England, having planned with Anthony and Rose another visit to the Irish lakes the next summer, in the company of Tom and his new wife Theodosia. But this plan was abandoned in due course for reasons of economy.[49] When Tilley, early in 1850, married his first wife's cousin, Mary Anne Partington (whose mother was Thomas Anthony's sister), Edith Tilley went back to live in Kensington once more. "The chance of losing her at any moment after we had become fond of her, was the only drawback to the pleasure of taking her," Anthony wrote to his mother.[50] Mrs. Trollope, meanwhile, had suffered another loss when her brother Henry died on January 16, 1850, at the house in West Brompton he had named "Heckfield Lodge."[51]

❧

In the same letter in which Colburn told Trollope he could give him no encouragement to proceed in novel writing—indeed in the very next sentence—he wrote, "As however I understand you have nearly finished the novel of La Vendée, perhaps you will favor me with a sight of it when convenient." The conjunction of the two sentences, as Trollope later remarked, "was not strictly logical," but he had nothing to lose by accepting the invitation.[52] It was no doubt Tom who had mentioned the book to Colburn in the course of transacting business for his mother; Anthony tells us that Tom negotiated the contract, but Tom was in Italy when the contract was actually signed. Almost fifteen months later Anthony sent the completed manuscript to Colburn, who on February 15, 1850, agreed to print 500 copies, and promised to pay Trollope £20 at once, £30 more if 350 copies were sold within six months of publication, and yet another £50 if the sale reached 450 copies in that period. The book was published promptly, and once again Anthony was unlucky in the publisher's advertisement—"by T. Adolphus Trollope, Esq."[53] (This from the very publisher who had protested Newby's error in advertising *The Macdermots*.) He received nothing beyond his initial £20, but for the first time authorship had paid him. The book was republished in one volume in 1874 and was in print when Trollope died. This was the first of his novels in which he gave titles to his chapters; hitherto they had merely been numbered. (Chapter titles were then supplied in later editions of the two earlier novels.)

To someone born two months before the Battle of Waterloo, the events of the twenty-six years between the fall of the Bastille in 1789 and the final defeat of Napoleon must have had an immediacy, even though not a matter of memory; the world young Anthony gradually became aware of was a world untangling itself from the confusions of revolutionary and Napoleonic Europe. Not until Anthony was fifteen did the last of the brothers of the guillotined Louis XVI cease to reign in Paris. For Anthony's parents, of course, the entire revolution was a matter of memory: Thomas Anthony was fifteen, Frances was nine when the Bastille was stormed. Anthony was eight when his parents were guests of Lafayette at La Grange—the Lafayette who had become leader of the National Guard immediately after the Bastille fell. Bertrand Barère, one of the most bloodthirsty of the villains of the Terror, survived until 1841, and the publication of his *Memoirs* drew the full thunders of Macaulay's rhetoric for nearly a third of an issue of the *Edinburgh Review* in 1844: "Barère approached nearer than any person mentioned in history or fiction, whether man or devil, to the idea of consummate and universal depravity." "Barère had not a single virtue, nor even the semblance of one."[54] Both Barère and Lafayette were characters in Trollope's new novel. In another context, Trollope in 1872 remarked, "The history of the French Revolution is to us as the history of our own times." And indeed the revolution was closer to him in 1849 than World War I is to us, yet World War I seems to many today a contemporary rather than a historical occurrence.

Moreover, the events of those days were kept alive for Trollope's generation by such spectacular works as Carlyle's *French Revolution* (1837) and Sir Archibald Alison's infinitely longer and more tedious multi-volume *History of Europe from the Commencement of the French Revolution in 1789 to the Restoration of the Bourbons in 1815* (1833–42). That era was popular in contemporary fiction: a large portion of *Vanity Fair* (1847–48) takes place before the Battle of Waterloo (which is of course a significant

event in the novel).* Sir Walter Scott had whetted the British taste for
historical fiction, and was throughout Trollope's life one of his favorite
novelists. Scott's successors in that genre, G. P. R. James and William
Harrison Ainsworth, were in full career as Trollope turned to his third
novel.

He had read with pleasure "the delightful Memoirs of Madame de
Larochejaquelin," translated by Sir Walter Scott in 1826, which gave him
an intimate and moving account of the revolt of the people of La Vendée,
an agricultural district along the Loire, against the revolutionary government. Here was a story he could use, and in incorporating it into his novel
he hoped "that the historical details of the Vendean War have not been
greatly misrepresented . . . and that a tolerably correct view is given of
the general facts of the revolt." (*La Vendée*, I, iii) He supplemented his
historical data from Alison's *History*, which itself at this point (chap. xii)
depended heavily on Mme. de Larochejaquelin, and in at least one instance he acknowledged a debt to Lamartine's *Girondists*. Most of his
characters were real people, including his two heroes, de Lescure and
Henri de Larochejaquelin; the authoress of the *Memoirs* was wife (then
widow) of the former and subsequently (outside the scope of the novel)
married the younger brother of the latter. A few characters were invented,
including the too melodramatic Adolphe Denot, who went mad for love
of the equally fictitious sister of Henri. A remark Trollope made nearly
thirty years later gives some clue to what he thought he might be achiev-
ing: "Among historians who [is] so often read as Macaulay,—who is
inaccurate, but whose style is charming? Who so readable as Herodotus,
who tells us tales? What so unreadable as Allison [*sic*] who tells us
facts?"[55]

The novel failed, but not primarily because historical fiction was
falling into disfavor. Nine years later Dickens's *Tale of Two Cities*, also set
in revolutionary France, was a spectacular success that retains its popularity today. Trollope's own analysis in *An Autobiography* is essentially
true: "The story is certainly inferior to those which had gone before;—
chiefly because I knew accurately the life of people in Ireland, and knew,
in truth, nothing of life in *La Vendée* country, and also because the facts of
the present time came more within the limits of my powers of story-
telling than those of past years."[56] Though he himself had not been in the
Vendée, his brother Tom, with their mother's assistance, had published
his *Summer in Brittany* and *Summer in Western France*, which would have

---

*It is curious that Emily Brontë very carefully set the events of *Wuthering Heights*
(1847) in the years 1802–3, well before her own birth in 1818. There is no hint in her
novel of the world-shaking events of those years.

given Anthony some feeling for the region. But the real failure is stylistic. There is the pseudo-Shakespearean dialect: "Hold thine unmannerly, loutish, stupid tongue, wilt thou, thou dolt!" (I, 191). And, between lovers, "I know not that mine eyes are turned oftener on him than on others." "Nay, Marie, dear Marie, I did but joke." (I, 147–48). Besides that there is the silly-sophisticated dialect he was later to put into the mouths of characters like Archie Clavering: " 'That's nonsense, you know,' growled the corporal; 'you must come, you know, and as well first as last' " (I, 34). Four pages are given to an elegantly rhetorical sermon meant to stir the peasants to action, and even the peasant mother of the postillion Cathelineau delivers her patriotic sentiments in elaborately rhetorical form (I, 211–15; III, 159). The more experienced Trollope would hardly have fallen into such language. And the novel reader usually wishes to follow the career of one or two characters in whom an interest is developed, whereas in *La Vendée* one follows a mass of characters through a mass of events.

As he was still casting about for a direction for his writing, he attempted another work in a different genre, but set at about the same historical moment as *La Vendée*. It is a dramatic comedy called *The Noble Jilt,* which takes place in Bruges immediately after the revolutionary French troops under Dumouriez defeated the ruling Austrians at Jemappes on November 6, 1792. But the historical setting is of no consequence to the story, nor is there any sense that Trollope knew or cared anything about the setting in Bruges, though of course he had once lived there. It is a comedy without wit, without character, without incident. The dialogue is written partly in utterly flaccid blank verse, partly in prose, and both are repetitive and empty. Not a single scene shows conflict; the one significant reversal, the heroine's change of heart back to her betrothed, is scarcely motivated by any event. Trollope had always held drama in greater esteem than prose fiction,* and it is of course not inconceivable—as one knows from examples as diverse as Fielding and Galsworthy—that an author should succeed in both novel and drama. Trollope did not.

An old friend of Mrs. Trollope's was George Bartley, long-time manager of Covent Garden Theatre and well known as an actor of comedy (his favorite role was Falstaff). Anthony polished and refined his manuscript and sent it to Bartley for a judgment. The reply was dated June 18, 1851, courteous but firm: "Had I been still a manager, 'The Noble Jilt' is not a play I could have recommended for production. . . . You ask me for my honest impressions—and I have too much regard & respect for your

---

*Precisely at this time (December, 1850, to December, 1853) Trollope was reading strenuously in his copy of the folio edition of the plays of Beaumont and Fletcher.

excellent & highly gifted mother, and all her family, not to give them candidly as they are." Trollope went no further.[57]

But thirteen years later he transformed the plot of the play into a contemporary English setting for the novel *Can You Forgive Her?* And then, having succeeded thus far, he was able to jest about his work by sending Lady Eustace and her friends to see *The Noble Jilt* at the Haymarket Theatre; it was "from the hand of a very eminent author," and the gossip from the leading actors was that no person could play it so as to obtain the sympathy of the audience. Lizzie's friends pronounced it a failure, the critics were divided, and it had a run of only four or five dozen consecutive performances.[58]

Another literary venture also failed. The publisher John Murray was bringing out a series of *Handbooks for Travellers* that were the equivalent of the more modern Baedekers, and he had at this time no such guide to Ireland. With good reason Trollope thought himself very well acquainted with that country. He began to write a *Handbook* for Ireland, and with a fair specimen of the work (Dublin, Killarney, and the route between) he journeyed to London in February, 1850, to show it to Murray. Murray, who was one of Mrs. Trollope's publishers, took the manuscript with the promise to look at it. After nine months Trollope wrote angrily for a decision and his manuscript was returned to him still unopened.[59] Murray's first *Handbook for Travellers in Ireland* (anonymous) was published in 1864.

Meanwhile Anthony published (anonymously, as was the policy of the journal) a long article in the *Dublin University Magazine* (May, 1851) on the first two volumes of his old friend Charles Merivale's *History of the Romans under the Empire*, "the best review of the work which has appeared," Merivale told him. His highest praise initially is bestowed on Merivale's style: "It is in no way peculiar. . . . [The reader] will be . . . neither struck by the splendid fluency of a Macaulay, nor harassed by the involved obscurity of a Grote. . . . The elaborate brilliancy of a rhetorician [like Gibbon] distracts the attention from the matter written to the mode of writing, and ultimately fatigues the reader." In a second article, on volumes 3–5 of the work (July, 1856), however, there are specific criticisms of style that illustrate Trollope's own ideals. "The greatest fault" Trollope could find in the substance of the books was that Merivale "is too prone to have a hero. . . . We [have] never read a novel in which the chief character [is] kept so systematically, so constantly in view. Caesar is always present in Mr. Merivale's pages [in the first two volumes], and always in action." And yet Trollope himself a year earlier told Tom, "I should be inclined to say that Caesar was the greatest man who ever lived."[60] The two articles are essentially narrative accounts of the period of history to which Trollope later in his career was to devote his books on Caesar and on Cicero. The second of the articles brought him seven guineas, after he had protested the lack of any payment for the first.[61]

The Great Exhibition of 1851 was to have been a meeting place for the Trollopes of Ireland and the Trollopes of Italy, but the latter changed their minds. Anthony and Rose were in London on a month's leave from postal duties in May and June; Rose indeed won a bronze medal for an embroidered screen.[62] Then Tom's curiosity about the exhibition was whetted by the reports that reached him in Italy, including Tilley's enthusiastic accounts, and he made a flying trip to London in September. By then Anthony, Rose, and little Harry were living in Exeter, where Tom visited them.[63] The residence at Exeter was unforeseen, the beginning of a two-year special assignment to the postal districts of the West of England and Wales.

Chapter V

1851–55

In 1857 Trollope wrote a lively seven-page history of the Post Office in Ireland, for the postmaster general's report to Parliament.[1] It is anecdotal, amusing in its instances of eighteenth-century casualness about patronage, but ending with a serious boast about the efficiency of the service by the middle of the nineteenth century. The English and Irish postal services were amalgamated in 1830, four years before Trollope entered the service at St. Martin's-le-Grand, and "in no part of the United Kingdom has more been done for the welfare of the people by the use of railways for carrying mails and by the penny postage system than in Ireland. . . . There were [in 1784] posts six days a week on only four lines of road; letters to all other places being conveyed only twice or thrice a week. Now there are daily posts to almost every village; and I know of but one important town that has not *two* daily mails both with London and Dublin." When Herbert Fitzgerald set out from Castle Richmond to see his lawyer in London, his agent on that day wrote to the lawyer, and "this letter, not having slept on the road as Herbert did in Dublin, and having been conveyed with that lightning rapidity for which the British post-office has ever been remarkable—and especially that portion of it which has reference to the sister island,—was in Mr. Prendergast's pocket when Herbert dined with him."[2]

Mail coaches were introduced in England in 1784, and were adopted in Ireland six years later. These gradually spread over the main routes, but the branch routes were served by the local postmasters, left to arrange things as they wished (usually adopting the means which would give them the highest profit). Ireland had one distinct advantage, however, in the services of the Italian-born but naturalized Charles Bianconi, who set up an ever-expanding network of horse-drawn passenger vehicles, carefully plotting his routes to take in the greatest number of towns and villages with the least possible expenditure of miles. When he started carrying the mails as well as passengers on these cars, he was obliged to bargain with the individual postmasters; after the amalgamation of the postal services in 1830 he contracted directly with the postmaster general, and by 1848 owned 1,400 horses and covered 3,800 miles daily. About the time Trollope got to Ireland the railways came in; they gradually supplanted the mail coaches and in many instances also Bianconi's cars. But Bianconi adjusted his arrangements, withdrew to the remoter districts, and when Trollope wrote his historical sketch still had a flourishing business that covered 2,250 miles a day and owned 1,000 horses. "No living man has worked more than he has for the benefit of the sister kingdom," said Trollope. This was the changing world in which Trollope and his colleagues had to work, and Trollope's gratitude to Bianconi was not merely for his significance in delivering the mails but also for showing him, practically, how to plan routes. Trollope was a frequent guest at Bianconi's country house, "Silver Spring," near Clonmel.[3]

Trollope's pride was both in the service to which he belonged and in his personal achievement. Two years earlier he had testified before a parliamentary select committee on Irish postal arrangements—testimony that required four days and was exceedingly detailed; he insisted on giving every bit of what he had to say, even when the questioner seemed eager to move on, and he was somewhat cantankerous in his insistence. "I do not think any other officer has local knowledge of the whole district except myself; I have local knowledge over the whole of Ireland. By chance [of employment] it has happened that I have been through the whole country." The secretary to the Post Office explained how a surveyor (or his assistant) worked: "First of all the surveyor determines what would be the extent of a walk which a man can reasonably be expected to perform in a day;* and he arranges the walk so as to include as many villages and hamlets as he can. Then he proceeds to ascertain the number of letters addressed in a week to those several villages and hamlets; and if the numbered reckoned at a penny each be sufficient to cover the additional expense thrown upon the department, by establishing the particular post, the Postmaster-general grants it."[4] This, then, was the task Trollope was performing in the Southern District of Ireland.

❧

There were, meanwhile, significant changes at St. Martin's-le-Grand. In the first third of the century the postage charge for letters depended both on their weight (or the number of sheets of paper used) and on the distance they were to be conveyed; the charges were commonly collected from the recipient. In 1840 Rowland Hill, seconded to the Post Office as an officer of the Treasury on limited term appointment, effected the establishment of the penny post—a uniform rate for letters no matter how far within the kingdom they were going—and invented the adhesive postage stamp as a convenient means of prepaying the charge. When his limited term expired, he was without employment. Friends in the Whig party created for

---

*Sixteen to eighteen miles was the figure arrived at.

him in November, 1846, the anomalous post of "Secretary to the Postmaster General" at a salary of £1,200, while Colonel Maberly remained "Secretary to the Post Office" at £2,000 a year. It was left for the two to adjust their domains as best they might. Certainly the situation was uncomfortable; Hill, however, was not one to make it easier, and tried energetically to use his political influence to have Maberly retired, or transferred, or induced to resign by the offer of full salary by way of pension.[5]

An important part of Hill's mission of reform was the extension of rural postal deliveries, and he was impressed with Trollope's work. On July 21, 1851, he wrote to the postmaster general: "The prompt and satisfactory completion of the revision of the Rural Posts in Mr. Kendrick's district is very creditable to Mr. Trollope to whom the duty was entrusted, . . . and I beg to recommend that the advantage of his assistance be afforded to one of the English Surveyors in the performance of the similar duties." Trollope's effectiveness is evidence of his energy: he himself walked the routes to discover what might be expected of the carriers, or, more often and more expeditiously, went over them on horseback. "It was the ambition of my life to cover the country with rural letter-carriers." On August 1, 1851, he sailed from Cork to Bristol to take up his new duties.[6]

He was assigned first to the surveyor for Western England. By early December his superior in Southern Ireland urgently requested his return, but he remained in Ireland only from December 21 to the following March 11; so valuable was his work on the rural routes that when those for Western England were completed he was assigned to do the same task for South Wales. Despite further urgent appeals from the surveyor of his Irish district, Maberly found him most useful in Wales; moreover, "I believe he was led to expect that his services would be continued here for some time longer, & if therefore he would be inconvenienced by the change, he is entitled to every indulgence."[7] He never returned to the Southern District of Ireland. His detailed reports on the revision of rural posts out of Dawlish and Teignmouth in October, 1851, survive, and minutes putting into effect his recommendations for Stratford-on-Avon, Stroud, Banbury, Tetbury, Woodstock, Poole, Stourbridge, Bromsgrove, Worcester, and Hereford from February 26 to November 2, 1853, give some indication of how busy he kept.[8] The postmaster general was gratified to observe that in the districts of the revised posts "every House, however remote, is included in some free delivery," and Trollope himself said that he visited nearly every house—certainly every house of importance—in Devonshire, Cornwall, much of Dorset, Somerset, part of Oxfordshire, Wiltshire, Gloucestershire, Worcestershire, Herefordshire, Monmouthshire, and the six southern counties of Wales. His zeal for the service was reinforced by the wish to augment his income with as large an allowance for mileage as possible, and in the winter he could arrange his routes to take in all the most interesting hunts of the region.[9]

The rural posts figure frequently in the novels. The Marquis of Brotherton scornfully commented on his brother's propensity for walking: "He ought to have been a country letter-carrier. He would have been as punctual as the sun, and has quite all the necessary intellect."[10] The folks at Nuncombe Putney had less punctual service.

> The post used to come into Nuncombe Putney at about eight in the morning, carried thither by a wooden-legged man who rode a donkey. There is a general understanding that the wooden-legged men in country parishes should be employed as postmen, owing to the great steadiness of demeanour which a wooden leg is generally found to produce. . . . The one-legged man who rode his donkey into Nuncombe Putney would reach his post-office not above half an hour after his proper time; but he was very slow in stumping round the village, and seldom reached the Clock House much before ten.

Those who lived "beyond the beat of the wooden-legged postman" were obliged to "call at the post-office for their letters." And then there was poor Mrs. Crump the postmistress, who had been visited by an inspector shortly before Lily Dale undertook to ask her to send the Dales' letters up to the house early.

> "Oh, letters! Drat them for letters. I wish there weren't no sich things. There was a man here yesterday with his imperence. I don't know where he come from—down from Lun'on, I b'lieve: and this was wrong, and that was wrong, and everything was wrong: and then he said he'd have me discharged the sarvice. . . . Discharged the sarvice! Tuppence farden a day. So I told 'un to discharge hisself, and take all the old bundles and things away upon his shoulders. Letters indeed! What business have they with post-missuses, if they cannot pay 'em better nor tuppence farden a day?[11]

Trollope meanwhile was beginning to feel discontent with his slow progress up the Civil Service ladder. His second cousin, Sir John Trollope, offered to use his political influence. "But I ought not to want any private interest. The more I see the way the post-office work is done, the more aggrieved I feel at not receiving the promotion I have a right to expect," he wrote to his brother. "However, . . . I can't fancy any one being much happier than I am,—or having less in the world to complain of. It often strikes me how wonderfully well I have fallen on my feet." When the superintendent of the Mail Coach Office in London died, Trollope applied to the postmaster general, Lord Hardwicke, for the position. Sir John

Trollope wrote to urge the appointment, and Tilley, eager that he should have it, called on the postmaster general at home to solicit his support. Hill too conceived that Trollope deserved promotion and would fill the office well. But Maberly appointed the senior person already in the Mail Coach Office. Hill's conflict with Maberly shows all too plainly in Hill's memoranda on the matter; sensitive, jealous, suspicious, he feared Trollope and Tilley were plotting against him and at the same time believed they had aroused Maberly's anger by supporting Hill's reforms. As for the Mail Coach Office, it was abolished in an administrative reorganization less than two years later. And at about the same time (April, 1854), Maberly transferred from the Post Office to the Board of Audit. [12]

Trollope was so long in England that he moved his family with him, first to Exeter, then Bristol, Carmarthen, Gloucester, Cheltenham, and Worcester. Exeter and Cheltenham figure significantly in his novels, the former in *He Knew He Was Right* and *Kept in the Dark,* the latter in *The American Senator* and *Mr. Scarborough's Family*. At Cheltenham (1852–53) they took lodgings in the Paragon (the home of Miss Todd in *The Bertrams* and *Miss Mackenzie,* in both of which novels Cheltenham is called "Littlebath"), and the boys went to school. On one occasion, about June 8, 1852, when his mission carried him to Budleigh Salterton, he called on a Winchester College contemporary, the Reverend Hay Sweet Escott, and there met the lad who was to become his first biographer. "Boy, help me on with my coat," was the only memorable remark the lad could record. [13]

A few months before Trollope went to Western England the inhabitants of Jersey (which was in the Western English District) had submitted a formal memorial on their postal service to the postmaster general; in response, and as part of his special assignment, Trollope was sent to the Channel Islands from November 4–24, 1851. With his usual vigor he made his report in seventeen days—a detailed reorganization of the postmen's routes, with the establishment of two horse posts for carrying mail from St. Helier to the outlying portions of Jersey (formerly carried entirely on foot), and with provisions for more frequent delivery of letters internally, so that services were no longer keyed solely to the three weekly boats from England. Every item of cost and time was carefully calculated. The report was approved and the reorganization effected. There were difficulties in the execution; one of the sorters, for example, was a very old man who had been slow enough at best and who could not get used to the new routes. Letters of complaint came in, and few letters of commendation. But postal arrangements never do elicit praise, Trollope replied. "People injured complain, but those who are benefitted rarely express gratification. If the horse posts were now taken away, the loss would probably be much felt."[14]

One part of Trollope's report, however, brought nothing but enthusiasm.

> There is at present no receiving office in St. Heliers, and persons living in the distant parts of the town have to send nearly a mile to the principal office. I believe that a plan has obtained in France of fitting up letter boxes in posts fixed at the road side, and it may perhaps be thought adviseable to try the operation of this system in St. Heliers—postage stamps are sold in every street, and therefore all that is wanted is a safe receptacle for letters, which shall be cleared on the morning of the London Mails, and at such other times as may be requisite. Iron posts suited for the purpose may be erected at the corners of streets in such situations as may be desirable, or probably it may be found to be more serviceable to fix iron letter boxes about five feet from the ground, wherever permanently built walls, fit for the purpose can be found, and I think that the public may safely be invited to use such boxes for depositing their letters.

The recommendation was endorsed by John Tilley, sketches were made, an iron founder commissioned, and seven freestanding boxes were cast, four for Jersey and three for Guernsey, at a cost of £7 each. In due course posters appeared announcing to the public that the roadside letter boxes would be opened on November 23, 1852, with collections twice daily except Sunday. Within a fortnight reports came in that the inhabitants wanted more of them, especially in the rural districts. One of the boxes originally set up proved too small for the demand, and a larger design was evolved. A fifth box was set up in Jersey less than a year after the first four, and this one, with the rector's consent, was let into the wall of the rector's garden.

Formerly, letters could be deposited only at post offices; the use of letter boxes supposed a uniform rate of postage for letters and prepayment of postage by the sender. The establishment of the penny post and the invention of the adhesive postage stamp provided the necessary conditions. Now letters could be dropped in by senders and picked up for dispatch at hours when the post offices would be closed. By the middle of the decade roadside letter boxes had spread all over the kingdom, and the number of new ones was proudly reported each year to the House of Commons by the postmaster general (actually, of course, by Rowland Hill, the secretary).[15] Though Trollope did not invent the pillar-box (having taken the idea from France, as he said), his simple suggestion has had an impact on the lives of everyone for more than a century. His report and his mission to the Channel Islands were especially commended by his superiors. "Mr. Trollope appears to have given much attention to the subject and your lordship may perhaps think it right to inform him that you are much satisfied with the manner in which it has been treated," Tilley diplomatically suggested to Lord Clanricarde, the postmaster general. [16]

The letter boxes became so popular that influential citizens began to clamor for their erection near their homes, and one part of the secretary's duties came to be answering such requests as were addressed to him personally by people who could claim an acquaintance with him. In May, 1865, for example, John Everett Millais, who lived at No. 7 Cromwell Place, London, asked Tilley to set up a pillar-box in his neighborhood; the box he requested still stands on the corner of Cromwell Place and Cromwell Road, perhaps a partial reward for his having illustrated the novels of the secretary's brother-in-law. [17]

It was with self-depreciating irony, therefore, that Trollope described the conservative stubbornness of Miss Jemima Stanbury of Exeter in *He Knew He Was Right:*

> As for the iron pillar boxes which had been erected of late years for the receipt of letters, one of which—a most hateful thing to her,— stood almost close to her own hall door, she had not the faintest belief that any letter put into one of them would ever reach its destination. She could not understand why people should not walk with their letters to a respectable post office instead of chucking them into an iron stump—as she called it,—out in the middle of the street with nobody to look after it. Positive orders had been given that no letter from her house should ever be put into the iron post. (Chap. viii)

୨ଈ

The two years in Western England were "two of the happiest years of my life," Trollope said, but his official duties "so completely absorbed my time that I was able to write nothing." They did not prevent his reading the newspapers. [18]

In that era of reform, all sorts of scandals were being unearthed in the hope of their being permanently abolished. The Church of England was undergoing change at the hands of the legislature—change which it resisted as strongly as it could. And one abuse that kept showing up everywhere was the abuse of ancient charitable endowments under the governance (in many instances) of the bishops themselves. At Rochester the headmaster of the cathedral school, Robert Whiston, disclosed that though the income from the endowment had increased greatly, it was not being used to provide the free schooling for needy boys or the scholarships at the universities that the statutes of the endowment required, but was being appropriated by the dean and chapter of the cathedral. He published a long pamphlet on his findings in 1849, and this led to legal proceedings from July, 1851, to October, 1852, which were kept constantly in the public eye by the columns of the *Times*. There were similar misappropriations of funds at Dulwich College, in South London. Closer to Trollope's heart, no doubt, was the case of St. Cross Hospital, Winchester, an endowed charity for the maintenance of indigent old men which even in 1819 Keats had called "a charity greatly abused." The master of the hospital was the Reverend Francis North, appointed to the post by his father, the bishop of Winchester, in 1808, when he was about thirty-five years old. He remained in that post until he was forced to resign in 1855 (having in the meanwhile inherited the title of Earl of Guilford); he was, therefore, master while Trollope was at Winchester College. The income from the endowments was payable to the master, and from it he was obliged to maintain decently fifteen old men, to provide clothing, board, lodging, and an allowance of £6 5s. a year each. The rents and the like were sufficient to provide him with between £2,000 and £3,000 a year for himself. He performed no services; indeed, he was seldom in residence, and his duties were performed by subordinates whom he paid at a minimum rate. But it was not only his management of St. Cross that was in question: it was his holding various profitable appointments in the diocese by the favor of his father, and his being a flagrant pluralist, receiving the income from a number of parishes so widely separated that he could not be expected to serve them himself, and having therefore hired curates to do the work at a fraction of what he himself received for it. The affairs of St. Cross achieved public notoriety by the summer of 1849, when a suit was brought in the Court of Chancery by the attorney general, whose attention had been called to it by a clergyman who was resident in a parish that contributed to St. Cross. On August 1, 1853, judgment was delivered against the Earl, he was obliged to repay certain monies, and a new scheme for the administration of the hospital was established.[19]

These, then, were the matters that were in Trollope's mind when his work took him to Salisbury, and there, one May evening in 1852, as he wandered about the purlieus of the cathedral, he conceived the story of *The Warden*.[20] Both his grandfathers had been clergymen, and one of them, William Milton, had been a pluralist; while he was rector of Stapleton, near Bristol, he was appointed to the dual livings of Heckfield and Mattingly, near Reading, in 1774, but he did not move permanently to Heckfield until 1801.[21] Trollope, therefore, was not by disposition ready to view the clergy as monstrous in their greed, and the loveliness of the setting at Salisbury would have melted the hardest heart. He conceived the problem as a dilemma: the church possessed "certain funds and endowments which had been intended for charitable purposes, but which had been allowed to become incomes for idle Church dignitaries," and yet "the severity of the newspapers towards the recipients of such incomes" was undeserved and unscrupulous. "When a man is appointed to a place, it is natural that he should accept the income allotted to that place without much inquiry. It is seldom that he will be the first to find out that his services are overpaid." The Earl of Guilford's defense was that he had done his duty scrupulously, even generously, and had merely accepted the perquisites as they came down to him with his position, even as they had been accepted by his predecessors. Then, within a few weeks of Trollope's moment of inspiration in Salisbury, Dickens's *Household Words* on June 12, 1852, published a vigorously sarcastic anonymous article about the treatment of the pensioners at a similar charity in London, the Charterhouse.[22]

It was more than a year before Trollope began to write *The Warden* (initially entitled *The Precentor*) on July 29, 1853, at Tenbury, in Worcestershire. A fortunate relief from his strenuous work in the Southwest District of England, in the form of appointment as surveyor of his own district in the northern counties of Ireland, enabled him to carry out his resolution to set apart regular segments of time from his official work to do his writing. But the task of taking up a new district, making himself familiar with the postal arrangements there and with "the characters and peculiarities of the postmasters and their clerks" prevented his pushing ahead with his book until the end of 1853.[23] Early in October, 1854, he sent the manuscript to the important London publisher William Longman, to whom he had been introduced by John Merivale. The publisher's reader, Joseph Cauvin, gave a prompt and enthusiastic report, and Longman forwarded to him a contract dated October 24, 1854. Once again, it was on the system of equal division of profits after expenses had been met. "I had no reason to love 'half profits,' but I was very anxious to have my book published, and I acceded."[24] This time the first edition came to a thousand copies. It appeared about January 5, 1855,[25] "there were notices of it in the press, and I could discover that people around me knew that I had written a book." When six months later he received his first annual accounting, more than a third of the copies had been sold, and his share of the first year's profits was a check for £9 1s. 2d. Proudly he gave the money to Rose as a gift.[26]

ॐ

The journey from central Ireland to Barchester has taken about ten writing years; now at last we meet Archdeacon Grantly and Mr. Harding, as striking and remarkable on first acquaintance as they remained to the end. A few months before his death, Trollope visited Wells and Glastonbury in Somerset and there affirmed that though the town of Barchester was

Winchester, where he had gone to school, and the notion of Hiram's Hospital was taken from St. Cross, the country of Barsetshire was Somerset.[27] There is some confirmation in the fact that in *The Warden* the trains from Barchester to London come in to Paddington Station,[28] as they would do from Somerset but not from Winchester or Salisbury. Some dozen years later Trollope told a correspondent that Ullathorne, the mansion in *Barchester Towers,* was somewhat modeled on Montacute House, near Yeovil in Somersetshire. And Sadleir notes that the description of Archdeacon Grantly's church at Plumstead Episcopi tallies in every particular with the parish church of Huish Episcopi in Somerset.[29]

   The Warden is a novel almost without incident. A zealous reformer discovers that far more of John Hiram's endowment for indigent old men goes to pay Mr. Harding's stipend as warden than to support the twelve pensioners, and he places the matter in the hands of a firm of solicitors. The bishop, relying on the aggressive advice of his son the archdeacon, engages the attorney general to defend the diocese and the warden. Harding, on reflection, decides that he cannot justify his position and goes to London to inform the attorney general that he is resigning the wardenship; at the same time the reformer, John Bold, also withdraws from his legal proceedings out of love for Harding's daughter Eleanor, whom he marries. There are many "scenes" in the novel, but the single piece of action is Harding's journey to town, followed by the archdeacon, and his visit there serves more to give a view of contemporary London through the eyes of a naïve provincial clergyman than to advance the plot. With Harding, for example, we hear part of a debate in the House of Commons, visit a routine service in Westminster Abbey, and eat dinner in a low-class steak house in the Strand. It has been said with some truth that *The Warden* is scarcely more of a unified, plotted work of fiction than the papers about Sir Roger de Coverley in Addison's and Steele's *Spectator.* There are, indeed, independent essays embedded in the book, some quite long like the chapter on the *Times* (xiv: "Mount Olympus"), others shorter like the sketch of the warden's tea party, with its mock heroic battle lines and its Popeian card game dominated by the archdeacon (chap. vi). The warden himself is something of a caricature, as he perpetually fingers and bows his imaginary cello, and the archdeacon's sons are introduced purely to ridicule three live bishops of the Church of England, Charles James Blomfield of London, Henry Phillpotts of Exeter, and Samuel Wilberforce of Oxford (chaps. viii, xii). (Contrast the satiric figure of Henry here with the same person as the admirable suitor of Grace Crawley in *Last Chronicle.*) Most striking is the chapter (xv) in which Trollope imagines how Dickens and Carlyle might have dealt with the abuses of ecclesiastical endowments. *Bleak House,* concerned with the reform of the chancery courts, was coming out in parts as Trollope was meditating *The Warden,* and so he imagines the Dickens-like novelist "Mr. Popular Sentiment" bringing out in parts a new novel called *The Almshouse*. In our day, he says, "ridicule is found to be more convincing than argument, imaginary agonies touch more than true sorrows, and monthly novels convince, when learned quartos fail to do so. If the world is to be set right, the work will be done by shilling numbers. . . . Mr. Sentiment is certainly a very powerful man, and perhaps not the less so that his good poor people are so very good; his hard rich people so very hard; and the genuinely honest so very honest" (chap. xv). Trollope had been an admirer of Carlyle, but recently he had bought the collection of Carlyle's *Latter Day Pamphlets*, and told his mother that he looked on his eight shillings as money thrown away. "To me it appears that the grain of sense is so smothered up in a sack of the sheerest trash, that the former is valueless. . . . He has one idea,—a hatred of spoken and acted falsehood; and on that he harps through the whole eight pamphlets."[30] At some moment in his peregrinations on behalf of the Post Office, Trollope hit upon his name for the character who would personate Carlyle, "Doctor Pessimist Anticant," and jotted it inside the cover of his travel diary lest he forget it. The parody of Carlyle in Anticant's pamphlet on the Hiram's Hospital case (chap. xv) is a brilliant demonstration of Trollope's ear for eccentricities of style.

The book, then, is less a novel than a collection of essays and virtuoso pieces grouped around a single social problem, joined by a thin thread of narrative. Whether it would have survived without its sequel is not easy to say. But the sequel did come, and *The Warden* is still read and loved. Clearly Trollope enjoyed himself with the names he made up, especially for the Barchester parishes—Plumstead Episcopi, Crabtree Canonicorum, Crabtree Parva, Eiderdown, Goosegorge, Stogpingum.

There are echoes of the author's own experience. The leader of the pensioners petitioning for redress, Abel Handy, had been permanently crippled in a fall from the scaffolding during the renovation of Barchester Cathedral (chap. ii), precisely as the Trollope family's old friend Dr. George Nott had been injured while supervising the restoration of Winchester Cathedral. (If Anthony, as he affirmed, had never met an archdeacon, he did know this gaitered Winchester prebendary from infancy.)[31] It is hard to believe that Trollope went out of his way to demonstrate his own oft-boasted ineptness with arithmetic, but he effectively does so at the outset when he tells us that Harding added twopence a day to the pittance of each of the twelve bedesmen, "making a sum of sixty-two pounds eleven shillings and fourpence, which he was to pay out of his own pocket" (chap. i). It is not clear what he meant by this, but it is clear that the figure cannot be divided by twelve. Trollope's literary education, on the other hand, clearly has not been neglected—his is the highly sophisticated, allusive style of a person who loves books.

Chapter VI

1853–57

No doubt one reason for the delay between that moment of conception at Salisbury and the beginning of the writing of *The Warden* was the six-week journey Trollope and Rose made from April 19 to May 31, 1853. It was their first visit to the Continent together, and her recollections of the little incidents on the journey reflect something of the excitement of the occasion. John Tilley was with them. They crossed France by rail to Chalon-sur-Saône (having spent one night in Paris), took a canal boat to Lyon, coached to Chambéry, crossed the Mt. Cenis Pass and spent a night in Turin. Then on to Genoa, partly by rail and partly by omnibus coach; there Tom met them, scolding because their arrival was four hours late. After two days in Genoa they posted to Pisa via Spezia, and had a row with the driver when they started. There were some lovely weeks in Florence, where they first saw Tom's two-month-old daughter Beatrice, then they returned via Lake Maggiore and the St. Gotthard Pass (which they crossed partly by diligence and partly by sledge when their places were taken from them by two Germans), through Lucerne, Basel, Mannheim, down the Rhine to Cologne, then on to Antwerp, Ostend, and home. Though Rose does not mention the fact, the last leg of their journey must have taken them through Bruges. Rose especially enjoyed the hospitality of her lively mother-in-law in Florence. "She took me about everywhere, and explained everything to me. And she made me happy by a present of an Italian silk dress. She also gave me a Roman mosaic brooch, which had been a present to her from Princess Metternich during her stay in Vienna. It is a perfect gem." She gave regular weekly evening receptions, "attended by some of the pleasantest English residents in Florence; and she always had her own special whist-table. I thought her the most charming old lady who ever existed. . . . I do not think she had a mean thought in her composition."[1]

On their return, Trollope was prepared to resume his work in South Wales, but Patrick Urquhart, who had been surveyor of the Northern District of Ireland for more than forty years, was ill and Trollope was urgently needed to supply his place; he was made acting surveyor on August 18 and took up his duties by the end of the month, with headquarters first at Armagh, then at Belfast. For a year he was in some uncertainty as to his future—it seemed clear that Urquhart would have to retire, but it was not equally clear that Trollope would get the permanent appointment. He even found it necessary to cancel a second journey to Italy which he and Rose had planned for May, 1854. But at last, on October 9 of that year he became officially surveyor for the Northern District. As for the stipend, it gave him initially little advantage (as clerk he made £150, as surveyor £240, but the travel allowances were on a different basis and he could no longer claim the mileage that had been so profitable to him); within a year, however, an entirely new salary scale raised his base pay to £700 (twice the pay of a surveyor's clerk on the new scale).*[2] More than salary was involved in the promotion, however: he was now a senior official, useful in helping to make important administrative decisions for the postal service and in investigating overseas arrangements, no longer the subordinate who had to toil up and down the countryside. Though he had been commended officially more than once by his superiors, this was his first tangible step toward the top, and his correspondence with his mother and brother at the time shows the extent of his anxiety until the matter was settled.

There was one amusing episode while he was acting surveyor. Young Livesay Maberly, a kinsman of Colonel Maberly's and one of three Maberlys on the Irish postal establishment, had proved himself monstrously incompetent as surveyor's clerk in the Northern District, and Trollope was called upon for his observation. The Colonel himself declined to express any opinion, but the potential for embarrassment was still great. Then came the word that Colonel Maberly was being transferred out of the Post Office, and Livesay was instantly demoted. He was not, however, dismissed (would that he had been): a dozen years later he was cited in the Irish Post Office minutes for bringing false charges against a superior officer.[4]

What Trollope really wanted was an appointment on the English establishment, even though money went further in Ireland, so that he reckoned his £700 to be the equivalent of about £800 at home. Failing England, he much preferred Dublin to Belfast for his headquarters— "preferring on the whole papistical to presbyterian tendencies." And so he quickly sought, and received, permission to move his headquarters to Dublin at the beginning of 1855. Harry had been at school in Cork, then both boys went to school in or near Belfast, but after the move to Dublin they were sent to Exeter.[5] It is said, on what authority is not clear, that in Belfast the family lived first near the Queen's College and the post office in Custom House Square, then at Whiteabbey, whence he rode his horse to work along the sands via Whitehouse and Greencastle. There were those

---

*Almost the first thing he did when the new salary went into effect was to reckon the income tax on it—£44 6s. 8d.[3]

earlier in the present century who heard that their grandparents recalled Trollope's great black beard waving in the wind as he rode to work. In the suburbs of Dublin they took a fine house at No. 5 Seaview Terrace, Donnybrook.[6]

❧

One event about this time has left no trace in the correspondence or in Rose's autobiographical notes. Her father had been manager of the Rotherham bank since about 1828, when it was part of a private partnership; it became a joint stock company in 1836. He was, as we have seen, a distinguished citizen of the town, and was also a man firmly disposed to do as he pleased. He had a good deal of discretion in the making of loans from his branch, and when his directors by 1850 became apprehensive that he was making commercial loans on insufficient security, he ignored their cautionary instructions. By the beginning of 1853 his health was failing and his competence was impaired, so that retirement was very strongly urged upon him and he was promised an annual pension of £200 (perhaps about half his salary). He retired at the end of 1853 and began a series of peregrinations to various health resorts in the company of his wife.

Almost at the moment his cashier at the bank succeeded to the managership, large deficits were discovered in the accounts locally and with the London agents, so that the pension was stopped until the matter was cleared up: it was through his having attempted to draw the first quarterly pension payment by check that his whereabouts were traced, first to Torquay, then to Plymouth, then to Gainsborough in Lincolnshire. The bank engaged a detective to keep him in sight.

Heseltine repeatedly promised to return to Rotherham and, with the help of the books, to explain what had happened, but his mind was clearly confused (as two of the bank's directors who went to see him confirmed). The directors moved slowly, but would not promise to abstain from legal proceedings, and so in February, 1855, he put himself beyond their reach by moving to Le Havre, where he died on September 15. The deficits were found to have existed for well over a decade, and in at least one case were apparently caused by his having several times credited nonexistent repayments to the account of an unstable firm to which he had insisted on making loans despite the directors' instructions. Since the firm manufactured railway cars and Heseltine was interested in the Sheffield and Rotherham Railway, he may have been moved in this instance by a business friendship. It was never perfectly ascertained what the total deficiency was, probably well over £4,000. A request for a widow's pension on Mrs. Heseltine's behalf was peremptorily refused. There is no indication that Heseltine gained personally from the irregularities, and insufficiently secured loans of even greater magnitude have been revealed in the banking world of our own day.[7] But whether or not Rose and Anthony knew of the hounds on her father's trail, his health and wanderings must have caused her some anxiety. Even his death is not mentioned in any surviving correspondence, nor does Rose write of seeing him (if she did) on the journey she and Anthony took in May of 1855, when they crossed to Boulogne and traveled to Basel.

≥●

The Continental journey of May 3 to June 13, 1855, was the one postponed from the preceding September because of the uncertainty of Trollope's appointment to the surveyorship. Mrs. Trollope had visited London when Anthony and Rose could not come to Italy in the early autumn of 1854, and there fell under the spell of Daniel Home, the medium (Browning's "Mr. Sludge"); Rose was puzzled that a woman of such strong common sense should have fallen victim to such absurdities, "but her imagination and romance got the upper hand." In October, 1855, Home was her guest (and Tom's) for a month, and there were séances nearly every evening at the Villino Trollope. Luckily the Brownings did not return from London to Florence until a few days after Home's departure.[8]

Once again Tilley accompanied Anthony and Rose. This time they went from Paris to Dijon by rail, then took a carriage and sledges over the Jura to Geneva. An expedition to Chamonix was curtailed by deep snow and they had to return to Geneva; en route they lost their luggage (whether it was recovered Rose does not say). They then went to Martigny, crossed the Simplon by sledges, and passed through Milan and Verona to Venice, where Tom and his mother were waiting. The journey from Milan to Verona was rather impromptu: they were dining at their hotel when they decided to catch the six o'clock train and telegraphed the hotel keeper in Verona for rooms. The telegraph was then new and very expensive; when they reached Verona they were astonished to find the proprietor and a supporting staff awaiting them at the railway station: it was the first telegram he had ever received, and he was sure they must be a very grand party indeed. After a fortnight of delightful sightseeing in Venice, the five of them went north through the Dolomites to the Brenner Pass. There the men left on a mountain expedition; Rose and her mother-in-law took a coach. At the top of the pass the coach stopped for lunch at an inn, but on the pretext that it was a religious fast day they were served only some thin soup and a small trout. An Austrian soldier at the next table, exempt from fasting as a wounded man on sick leave, was served a platter of smoking cutlets; these he divided and presented the half to Mrs. Trollope as "his mother." "Had it been correct," Rose said as she told the story, "I should like to have kissed that Austrian gentleman." The parties met in Innsbruck, then Tom and his mother went directly to Paris, while Rose and Anthony posted via Kreuzbad and Munich and rejoined them in Paris to see the exhibition and return to London. It was Mrs. Trollope's final visit to her native country.[9]

Immediately on his return Trollope was faced with a special assignment for the Post Office. A parliamentary select committee had been set up to investigate the postal arrangements for most of Southern and Southwestern Ireland, a territory Trollope had formerly known well; now he was asked to bring himself up to date on the region and testify as the department's expert. His leave of absence ended on June 13; from the fourteenth to the twenty-fifth he was traveling about in Southern Ireland while Rose was settling into the house at Donnybrook, and from June 26 to August 1 he was in London. His testimony before the committee, given on July 16, 20, 23, and 27, has already been alluded to.[10]

Inasmuch as the very existence of the select committee was a challenge to the Post Office, the designation of Trollope as their witness was a sign of great confidence in him. Tilley was eager to have his services acknowledged, procured a statement from the Treasury official in charge of the committee's arrangements to the effect that Trollope had "exhibited great knowledge and efficiency as an Officer of the Department," and then drafted a letter of commendation for the signature of the postmaster general.[11]

Tilley was not always on Trollope's side, however. In February, 1856, Trollope fell ill in Derry and was confined to bed there for a week. Since he was then away from his headquarters he applied for his per diem travel allowance for the period of his illness as well as for the remainder of his tour, but Tilley disallowed that portion of the application on the ground that a man who is in bed, ill, is "not then actively engaged in the service of the Department."[12]

≈

Once *The Warden* was on its way to publication, Trollope set to work on two sequels more or less concurrently; one was of course *Barchester Towers,* the other a book unknown until its publication from his manuscript in 1972.[13] *The New Zealander* was a collection of thirteen essays (plus introduction and conclusion) descriptive of British institutions, art, and society. In October, 1840, Macaulay had reviewed Leopold von Ranke's *History of the Popes* in the *Edinburgh Review.* Contemplating the incomparable antiquity of the Roman Catholic Church and its flourishing present, its prospects for the future, he remarked: "She was great and respected before the Saxon had set foot on Britain. . . . And she may still exist in undiminished vigour when some traveller from New Zealand shall, in the midst of a vast solitude, take his stand on a broken arch of London Bridge to sketch the ruins of St. Paul's." Was English society in fact doomed? Trollope speculated. The past achievements of the nation have left an indelible mark on mankind; when the New Zealander does visit the ruins of London, he will be speaking the English language. But at the present moment there are such manifest signs of corruption in every aspect of life that the doom may be imminent. "If we are or can make ourselves an honest people, there may be hope that not in our time, nor that of our children or children's children, not in that of many coming ages, will the flag of which we are so proud have to lower itself before that of any nation which may float hither either from the East or from the West. But if this is not so, and cannot become so, why should we even wish that the power of England should endure?" (p. 12). He chose as his epigraph a line of verse he used later in more than one of his novels, the first of them *Barchester Towers:* "It's gude to be honest and true."[14] Though the style is not notably Carlylean except in its too often high-pitched hortatory tone, the theme is not unlike the one Trollope attributed to the *Latter Day Pamphlets:* "a hatred of spoken and acted falsehood."[15]

The most obsessive of Trollope's castigations of dishonesty is that of the newspapers, to which he devotes one of his longest essays, and it is here that the link with *The Warden* is apparent. What in fact we have in the book is the expression of certain ideas that were to be thematic in many of his novels: the chapters on trade and on the Civil Service (both now missing) were developed in *Brown, Jones, and Robinson* and *The Three Clerks,* and passages that survive in the manuscript are later lifted bodily into *The Three Clerks* and *Doctor Thorne* (the latter on election frauds). One recognizes Trollope's constant dislike of the evangelical clergymen and of lawyers. As the modern editor of the work remarks, in very many instances "this work presents an early treatment of themes to which Trollope constantly returned in his fiction."[16]

And yet the book is for the most part very tedious and often obtuse. The publisher's reader observed that Trollope writes "in such a loose, illogical and rhapsodical way that I regret to say I would advise you not to publish the work on any terms." It is "a most feeble imitation" of the *Latter Day Pamphlets.*[17] Here, early in his career, we are presented with the striking paradox about Trollope's intellect: he can handle with remarkable delicacy and sympathy social concepts as they work upon the lives of his fictional characters, yet in essays and lectures may treat the same concepts quite obtusely. Who that reads of Clara Amedroz's humiliation in *The Belton Estate,* caused entirely by her legal disabilities as a woman, can imagine that Trollope's blunt answer to the question of women's social and legal inequalities is: "When the men can bear the babies, then the sexes may be equals"? Lawyers, he believes, are devoted to letting criminals go free whereas sensible men would instantly lock up the criminals. True, but is the accused man in fact guilty of the crime that brings him before the court? Did the man who was hanged actually commit the murder? In a novel he did so, if the novelist wants it that way; in life, the question must be determined by proofs.

Not long after Trollope's death a reviewer of his *Autobiography* quoted the opinion of Frederick Greenwood, former editor of the *Pall Mall Gazette* (a newspaper for which Trollope wrote), "that Mr. Trollope was not an able political writer, and hardly ever touched a political question so as to throw any fresh light upon it."[18] Half a century later the most influential modern pioneer of Trollope studies, Michael Sadleir, remarked: "He possessed an intuitive understanding of individual human nature which no other English novelist can rival, and a command of easy flexible language exactly suited to the expression of ever-changing human moods. But he was uncertain as a reasoner and insensitive to ideas, . . . because in default of critical instinct he relied on practical good sense."[19]

The liveliest essay in *The New Zealander* is the one on society, with its warm appreciation of the pictures drawn by Pepys, Fanny Burney, Jane Austen, and his mother's good friend Mary Russell Mitford. His description of social gatherings is as amusing in the essay as it can become in the novels. His discussion of English literature contains its surprises: his list of the eighteen greatest authors from Spenser to his own day includes five from his own century: Scott, Byron, Southey, Sir Henry Taylor, and Tennyson, but not Wordsworth or Keats. (Browning's *Men and Women*, on which his reputation built its most solid foundation, was too recent for Trollope to take into account.) But the essay quickly meanders off into condemnation (once again) of the newspapers and ridicule of cheap novels sold at railway stations.

The New Zealander was written at hot speed, and often with an eye to the latest event reported in the daily press. The swindler John Sadleir committed suicide on February 16, 1856; his death is mentioned in the "Conclusion," written about March 9. On March 27 Trollope sent the manuscript to Longman with the request that he make a prompt decision about publication. "There are some reasons incident to the MS. itself which will make it desirable that it should be published soon."[20] The verdict of Longman's reader was quick and decisive, and Trollope never again mentioned the venture—neither in surviving correspondence nor in *An Autobiography*.

≈

The Warden had not been before the public more than six weeks when Trollope informed Longman that he had already written about one-third of a new novel that should form a second part of that story; indeed, he said, he had designed *The Warden* with the intention of writing a sequel.[21] If so, the sequel originally planned must have been much shorter than the *Barchester Towers* we know, for he intended to finish it in about two months, whereas *Barchester Towers* took him more than six months. In fact, the only sequel implicit in *The Warden* is the filling up of the wardenship; when he laid the scheme aside for more than year, that theme had amplified itself greatly through the introduction of two magnificent new characters, Mrs. Proudie and Mr. Slope, who would be in conflict over the appointment, and around these figures grew up a whole cathedral chapter, so that instead of the starkness of *The Warden*'s relatively few characters we have the richness and abundance of Trollope's most famous novel.

For the first time (so far as we know) he kept a precise record of his daily production. When he began the record on May 12, 1856, he had already written 85 pages; he completed the book on November 9, in 1,108 manuscript pages.[22] It was the longest novel he had published thus far, though it was quickly surpassed by its half-dozen successors. His daily stint ranged from one to twelve manuscript pages; usually it came to eight or nine. And there were ninety-six working days in the period, against eighty-six days on which he wrote nothing. He told his mother about his progress, and she replied on July 8: "The degree of activity of which I have been wont to boast [in myself] . . . [is] positive *idleness* when compared to what you manifest. Tom and I agree in thinking that you exceed in this respect any individual that we have ever known or heard of—and I am proud of being your mother—as well for this reason as for sundry others." She had set him the model he adopted for the rest of his writing career, of getting up early in the morning and doing an uninterrupted stint before the day's regular work began.[23] And there was an aspect of modern technology that speeded up his composing—now that he could use the railway for his transportation instead of the horse, he had a portable desk designed and did his writing as he traveled. "My only objection to the practice came from the appearance of literary ostentation, to which I felt myself subject when going to work before four or five fellow-passengers. But I got used to it." There was domestic assistance as well: writing on a train must be done in pencil, and Rose then copied the entire manuscript in ink before it could go to the publisher.[24]

Longman's reader Joseph Cauvin, who had already passed enthusiastic judgment on *The Warden* and condemned *The New Zealander,* was puzzled by the new work. Some of it was up to the best writing of contemporary novelists, some was repulsive in its vulgarity and exaggeration; chapters like those on Mrs. Proudie's reception (in which part of her dress is accidentally torn off) and Slope's making love to the Signora might even be unfit for publication. Trollope was embarrassed: "Nothing would be more painful to me than to be considered an indecent writer." Of course the Signora is "indifferent to all moralities and decent behavior, [but] the vice [is] not made attractive." Tilley, being in London, was empowered to alter whatever seemed to him offensive.[25] In the end, Trollope complied with nearly all the reader's objections as to specific passages that seemed "too warm." The epithet "foul-breathing" was dropped from the description of Mr. Slope in the proofs and the burly chancellor's "fat stomach" was altered to "deep chest." On one other matter, Trollope held his ground: Longman wished the title to read ". . . or, The Female Bishop," and Trollope replied, "I do not like a second title nor the one you name. I do not wish the bishop male or female to be considered the chief character in the book."[26]

Longman, moreover, was uncertain whether the novel in three volumes would pay for itself, and here too Trollope remained firm: he could write a new book that would be shorter, but "no book originally written in three [volumes] can be judiciously . . . reduced [to two]." Moreover, he insisted on receiving £100 in advance, and he wished a terminal date to be placed on the contract. The agreement for *The Warden* provided for the same profit-sharing on all editions Longmans wished to publish during the life of the copyright; thus "the author is left without the power of republishing in an after time when your interest in the work shall have ceased." There was a compromise: he got his £100 in advance, but they retained the right of all future publication, and that right made a slight difficulty when the collected "Chronicles of Barsetshire" were published two decades later.[27] Longmans produced the book rapidly; 750 copies of the three-volume edition were published at a nominal price of a guinea and a half on May 8, 1857; 200 copies were bought by Mudie's Library, and by the end of June publication costs were fully recovered, including the advance. When a one-volume edition came out at five shillings in early April, 1858, sales were brisk and Trollope's annual income from the book averaged over £65 for some years to come.[28]

Complaints about Trollope's "immorality" were to raise themselves occasionally in connection with later works also, though the modern reader can only be bewildered by the charge. No reader today would wish the Signora to be changed or omitted from the novel, and as a modern novelist has remarked, her portrait "is a shrewd, mature study of a thoroughly shady woman with a really disreputable past. . . . Trollope, a man of the world, knew what the Vesey-Neronis were really like and what the precise circumstances of their Pasts had been."[29] With this knowledge Trollope had ventured to say of Madeline's marriage to a captain in the papal guard, "When the moment [for marrying him] came, she probably had no alternative," and that "six months afterwards she arrived at her father's house a cripple, and a mother."[30]

The novel closely reflects the conditions of England in its day. It does not have the precise calendar that Trollope devised for the events of some of his later novels; the year is always "185——" and the only time a day of the week is identified with a day of the month is in a letter dated "Monday morning, 20th August, 185——," which would be 1855, about a year before he wrote the passage; he probably meant nothing by it. Yet the Crimean War is in the background, and the doctrines of Utilitarianism, of the new men who are "carrying out new measures and casting away the useless rubbish of past centuries," threaten the peace of old Barchester. The legal reforms governing the Church of England are in every cleric's mind, from the summoning home from Italy of Dr. Stanhope, after twelve years of absence from his duties, to the reduced salary of the new dean. The conflicting doctrines and practices of the Evangelicals and the Tractarians are at the center of the plot. (In one instance the Evangelical arguments affected Trollope professionally: though Mrs. Proudie and Mr. Slope may not have stopped the trains from running to Barchester on the Sabbath, the Post Office was under constant pressure to cease Sunday deliveries and even Sunday handling of mails on the trains.)[31] His detailed awareness of events and of life around him is remarkable; one wonders sometimes how he learned so much, so accurately.

Trollope is especially interested in the Tractarian background of Mr. Arabin, who (Trollope ironically uses the language of the conservative high and dry churchman) "at one point in his career . . . all but toppled over into the cesspool of Rome." Two of Trollope's contemporaries at Harrow had done so, Henry Edward Manning and Frederick William Faber. Their names he does not mention; he does mention "the great Newman," who in later years became one of the most ardent readers of his novels. The oft-repeated statement that Trollope portrayed his clergymen not in their religious aspect but simply as human beings in a clerical milieu is somewhat misleading. There is a great deal of religion in *Barchester Towers*—religious doctrine, religious emotion; and Trollope seems to understand the theological implications of the doctrines. What he does do is show that, man being a political animal, religious doctrines and emotions have their political aspects. As the Signora remarked when she prepared to conquer the clerical world by her beauty at Mrs. Proudie's reception, "Parsons, I suppose, are much the same as other men if you strip them of their black coats" (chap. x).

There is a remarkable increase in self-confidence in Trollope's writing, and a wonderful liveliness of mind; we would know without his having told us so that "in the writing of *Barchester Towers* I took great delight."[32] The delight shows through in the frequent allusions to the epics of Greece and Rome and of Milton, in the mock-heroic tone in which so many scenes are cast; the language of Shakespeare's tragedies is echoed everywhere, but not seriously. His delight shows in such ironic comments as his remark that when Mrs. Proudie left the scene of her defeat in the bishop's study, she "did not forget to shut the door after her"; as Mr. Slope's preparing to call on the Signora by dabbing on "a soupçon of not unnecessary scent"; as "Doubting himself was Mr. Harding's weakness. It is not, however, the usual fault of his order." Trollope's frequent dialogue with his reader is meant to show an insight into human nature or to explain his theory of fiction. He does not disdain "plot" in the sense of interrelated and properly motivated action, and *Barchester Towers* has an excellent plot; he does disdain the artificial plots of the contemporary sensation novels that depend for success on suspense, not authenticity of character, novels in which the reader, on reflection, perceives that the novelist has not played him fair but has withheld information. Plot, he tells us in *An Autobiography,* is the vehicle for a "picture of common life enlivened by humour and sweetened by pathos," "crowded with real portraits . . . of created personages impregnated with traits of character which are known," and such a vehicle is absolutely necessary.[33] *Barchester Towers* is Trollope's most popular novel, a genuine masterpiece. It is a serious understatement for him to call it "one of those novels which do not die quite at once, which live and are read for perhaps a quarter of a century."[34] One admirer of the new novel was the anonymous reviewer in the *Westminster Review,* a beginning novelist who later became closely associated with Trollope through their common connection with the publishing house of Chapman and Hall: George Meredith.[35]

When the Archdeacon visited the bedside of Dean Trefoil after his apoplectic stroke, he "looked on the distorted face of his old friend with solemn but yet eager scrutinizing eye, as though he said in his heart 'and so some day it will probably be with me.'"[36] Trollope might have said this in his own heart, had he foreseen his fate a quarter of a century hence.

ॐ

Something of Trollope's boisterous conviviality comes out in a fragment of correspondence with his old London friend John Merivale, who consulted him about the organization of a dining club to be called "The Goose and Glee," that would meet periodically in a tavern in South London. He threw himself heartily into the drafting of the rules and the devising of a motto that should make punning sense in both Latin and English. He was eager to get to London to share in the festivities, though he had some ground for concern. The tavern had recently become modern to the extent of constructing a second-story room that projected out from the walls of the building, for use as a toilet, but though that construction made obsolete a by-law prohibiting members from urinating into a chamber pot in the banqueting hall, Trollope was afraid the supporting props were not strong enough for his bulk and that if he used the new room he might be plunged to the street in an undignified disarray. One of the club's officers who saw the correspondence noted that the letter should be preserved: Trollope was a rising novelist whose autograph would rank in value with those of Dickens and Thackeray.[37] Trollope's enthusiasm led him to include several meetings of a similar club, "The Goose and Gridiron," in the novel *Brown, Jones, and Robinson,* not at all to the improvement of the book. He tells us that there had been a Goose and Glee Club in Barchester, though by the time of *Last Chronicle* it had disbanded (chap. xlii).

Ten days after signing the publishing agreement for *Barchester Towers* on February 5, 1857, Trollope began his next novel, and his pen fairly sped. It is clear from the early chapters that he was writing in high spirits, from the Macaulayesque opening sentence onward: "All the English world knows that branch of the Civil Service which is popularly called the Weights and Measures." The Civil Service had recently attracted a good deal of attention, with the publication as a government blue book of a long recommendation for its reform written by Sir Charles Trevelyan and Sir Stafford Northcote,* together with a series of invited comments on their proposals by other more or less informed public figures, including Benjamin Jowett. Their basic assumption was that the civil servants were disastrously incompetent, ignorant, idle, and indeed preternaturally prone to bad health; the remedy was clearly a rigorous qualifying examination that would admit only the best. Twelve half-days of written papers and an oral examination were proposed, which should test the candidates' knowledge of "history, jurisprudence, political economy, modern languages, political and physical geography, and other matters, besides the staple of classics and mathematics." This, exclaimed Trollope in an anonymous review of the blue book in the *Dublin University Magazine* for October, 1855, this in an examination to be given to seventeen year olds![38] The authors of the proposals are looking in the wrong direction: no one will submit to such study and such examination merely for the sake of winning a place, if the place be not attractive. The Civil Service is in fact the only government service in which the top officials do not rise from the ranks: bishops have been parish priests, generals have been lieutenants, admirals have been midshipmen, but the heads of the various branches of the Civil Service (including Trollope's own superiors, Colonel Maberly and Rowland Hill) have been placed in their posts by

---

*Sir Charles Trevelyan, whom Trollope did not yet know personally, figures as Sir Gregory Hardlines in *The Three Clerks,* and Sir Stafford Northcote's name suggested that of Sir Warwick Westend in the novel.

patronage. (Hence his real horror when he learned that there had been some thought of making Thackeray assistant secretary to the Post Office, through the influence of Lady Blessington.) The only way to improve the quality of the civil servants was to offer a career that would attract and reward the best men.

One of the two chapters named in the table of contents of *The New Zealander,* but not to be found in the surviving manuscript of that work, is "The Civil Service." It may well be that this segment has been preserved almost verbatim in the highly rhetorical chapter by that title in *The Three Clerks;* nothing in the chapter alludes in any way to the story of the novel, and it was dropped after the first edition (where it appeared between the present chaps. xxvii and xxviii).

It was not only in this chapter, however, that *The Three Clerks* was an extension of the impulse that produced *The New Zealander.* The sad moral state of England is the theme of the book—the dishonest tergiversations of Sir Robert Peel were no different from the roguery of a swindler like John Sadleir, who had been singled out in *The New Zealander* as evidence that "falsehood, dishonesty, pretences, subterfuges" were no longer odious in people's eyes.[39] The thoroughly corrupt Undecimus Scott is highly esteemed in the London political society of *The Three Clerks,* and his sophistication deceives and ultimately ruins one of the heroes. Election bribery is scourged in both books, as are the commercial aims of the City, "where every heart is eaten up by an accursed famishing after gold." The corruption of the legal profession is made clear by the names of Alaric Tudor's solicitor, Mr. Gitemthruet, and his counsel, Mr. Chaffanbrass ("banter and brazenness"); the hollow prejudices of the clergy by the sermons of the Reverend Mr. Everscreech (whose name appears in *The New Zealander* as well).[40] Mr. Everscreech is the product of the necessities of his order: "How often does it come to pass that the man who will work is seen begging his bread?" asked Trollope. "We may almost say never— unless, indeed, he be a clergyman."[41] In some of its aspects, *The Three Clerks* is a Swiftian satire, repeating the ideas of *The New Zealander.* There is no Trollope novel that has a higher proportion of label names, and label names that are wildly improbable: Sir Gregory Hardlines, Fidus Neverbend, Whip Vigil, Captain Cuttwater, Sir Jibb Boom, or the candidates for the Civil Service examination, Uppinall, A. Minusex, Alphabet Precis. One passage, indeed, the comparison between the question period in Parliament and the sport of badger-baiting, is taken verbatim from *The New Zealander.*[42]

But *The Three Clerks* is also a very moving story of three young men starting out in life, and their fates. Some parts of it we recognize as Trollope's own account of his early career in the Post Office. It is commonly assumed that any story told in *An Autobiography* is confirmed by having been told of Charley Tudor in *The Three Clerks,* but it might be questioned if a story first told as fiction can establish a fact of Trollope's life: perhaps there is an element of fiction in both accounts. There is heartwarming emotion in the novel, and lively high comedy as well, as when the transition from girlhood to young womanhood is signaled by the frocks coming down below the drawers, instead of the drawers coming down below the frocks (see illus. 12).[43]

In *The Three Clerks,* moreover, Trollope identifies the world of fiction to which he wants to belong. Dickens's attack on the Civil Service through the Circumlocution Office in *Little Dorrit* had drawn a response from Trollope in a letter to the editor of the *Athenaeum,*[44] so that it was natural that *Little Dorrit* should be alluded to at the beginning of *The Three Clerks* and in the chapter on "The Civil Service," but both Mrs. Gamp of *Martin Chuzzlewit* and Bill Sikes of *Oliver Twist* also figure in the novel; indeed, degrees of villainy are debated as between Sikes and Sir Richard Varney of Scott's *Kenilworth.* (At about the same time Trollope quoted "Barkis is willing," from *David Copperfield,* in *Brown, Jones, and Robinson.*) And the sponging house on Cursitor Street in which Charley Tudor was confined would be familiar to readers of *Vanity Fair,* in which Rawdon Crawley enjoyed the same hospitality.[45] Thackeray praised *The Three Clerks* to Frederick Locker-Lampson soon after its publication, and Locker agreed with him. Trollope himself regarded it as "the best novel I had as yet written."[46]

Far less successful is another, shorter novel that also had its origin in *The New Zealander.* Another chapter named in the table of contents of that book, but no longer surviving, is "Trade." The instant *The Three Clerks* was completed Trollope began what he conceived of as a Christmas novel, *The Struggles of Brown, Jones, and Robinson; by one of the Firm.* "It will be intended as a hit at the present system of advertising, but will, of course, be in the guise of a tale," he told Longman on July 15, 1857; he intended it to be about two-thirds as long as *The Warden,* but in the end the two are almost exactly the same length.[47] He worked on it for two weeks from August 24, then laid it aside when he broke off from the house of Longman; he resumed it in June, 1858, left it off again, and completed it from June 24 to August 3 of 1861 when he had found a publisher.[48] Just as Carlyle's writing had influenced *The New Zealander,* so too here the symbol in *Past and Present* of the tall wooden hat on a cart as the model of modern advertising is used to represent the dilemma of the shopkeeper.[49] Echoing "the greatest philosopher of the age," the character from whose point of view the story is told exclaims: "Ah, me, what an age is this in which we live! Deceit, deceit, deceit;—it is all deceit!"[50] But if deceit prevails, it does so because the public wishes to be deceived; if advertising makes false claims, these can be justified by the greed of a clientele that wants bargains that would cheat honest tradesmen.

The names "Brown, Jones, and Robinson" are a commonplace expression for any three ordinary people; Trollope had already used them for three Civil Service clerks in the preceding novel.[51] Here he attempts to endow them with some personality, as they set up a haberdashery shop in Bishopgate, in the City, dedicated to the principles that credit is better than capital, that publicity is more important than quality. The venture fails, but the bankruptcy sale is so successful as to leave the proponent of these principles convinced that next time he will succeed. The satire on advertising and false business practices is witty in its irony, and strikes an echo in the mind of a modern newspaper reader. But the "tale" in which the irony is embedded never takes itself seriously or wins our sympathy as does the tale of *The Three Clerks.*

Although the book remained uncompleted and unpublished for several years, it was always present in Trollope's mind during that interval. As he said somewhat wistfully in *An Autobiography,* "I attempted a style for which I certainly was not qualified, and to which I never again had recourse. It was meant to be funny, was full of slang, and was intended as a satire on the ways of trade. Still I think that there is some good fun in it, but I have heard no one else express such an opinion."[52]

ૐ

Trollope surpassed his own expectations in the speed with which he wrote *The Three Clerks:* when he began it on February 15, he aimed to complete it by October 31, but the task was finished on August 18. And this despite an occasional short interval of no production, as when he scrawled on his writing schedule late in February, "Bad foot." Three days later he inquired of Longman on what terms he would publish it, with a strong hint that this time he wanted more money. When Longman offered the same £100 advance he had given for *Barchester Towers,* Trollope replied, "I fear it will hardly be worth while for you to have the MS read."*[53] He and Rose were about to take their third Continental journey together, on a six-week leave that began on September 5. He therefore stopped in London, where he called first on his mother's current publishers, Hurst and Blackett, successors to Henry Colburn, but was unable to find anyone at their office except a foreman with whom he was unwilling to leave the manu-

---

*In the course of his negotiations with Longman over *Barchester Towers,* Trollope had written, "You allege very truly and with great kindness that a change of publisher will be prejudicial to my interests as an author. [But if the book is not worth suitable payment,] I have no interest to prejudice," and in that case he will take back the manuscript even though "I shall be sorry to be deprived of the value of your name on my title-page." In *An Autobiography* he improved upon this reply: "I did think much of Messrs. Longman's name, but I liked it best at the bottom of a cheque."[54]

script. And so he took it to another of his mother's publishers, Richard Bentley, with the offer to sell the copyright for £250. By the time the leave of absence was up, Bentley had accepted the terms and forwarded the agreement. Trollope could not resist letting Longman know that in fact Bentley was paying even more than he had asked of Longman.[55] The book was published about November 26, but with the date "1858." This was Trollope's first outright sale of his copyright, and though the book brought him no further income, he was pleased to see it kept in print throughout his life; indeed, after the firm of Bentley was purchased by Macmillan at the end of the century, the book remained in print with the new publishers.

Rose's recollections of the journey are full of little adventures. They crossed to Boulogne, took the rail to Basel and then went on to Schaffhausen, Zurich, Ragaz, Thusis, and across the Splügen to Chiavenna, Como, and Milan. The conductor of the train out of Basel took them for disguised prisoners; the kindly landlady at Thusis gave Rose a belt; the hotels were all full at Milan. The rail took them to Verona, the diligence to Bologna and across the Apennines. Tom met them and escorted them to Florence, where they spent three weeks. Anthony's mother they found much changed and broken, not caring for her afternoon drive, indifferent even to her rubber of whist. She had now published her last novel, *Paris and London*. On their return journey Anthony and Rose went up the coast to Genoa, on to Turin, and crossed the Mt. Cenis Pass at night, this time part of the way by rail. They crossed Lac Bourget by steamer (presumably having stopped at that favorite watering place of the British, Aix les Bains), went on to Paris and Versailles, reached the London Bridge Hotel on October 17, and were back in Donnybrook a day later. On the twentieth Trollope began to write *Doctor Thorne*.[56]

Chapter VII

1858–60

The years 1858–60 marked a most significant turning point for Trollope.
Heretofore he had been a relatively obscure member of the Irish postal
establishment, who wrote occasional novels that he took from door to door
in search of a publisher. His daily life in Ireland must have had strong
characteristic resemblances to his later life, but our knowledge of it has
been the merest skeleton. Though he visited Ireland shortly before his
death and then saw some of his former friends, we know almost none of
his Irish acquaintances even by name.

Nothing shows quite so clearly as Trollope's career how very important it was for an author to live in England—indeed to live in or near
London. By the end of this two-year period he was a trusted higher official
in the British postal establishment, close to the headquarters, and readily
called upon for missions abroad or for advice on setting things right at
home. And he was a professional writer, with a publisher of his own, a
regular method of writing, and a conviction that, though he worked
vigorously at his postal tasks, his real career was as an author. A few years
later he wrote a rather remarkable letter to G. H. Lewes, whose son was
applying for a clerkship at the General Post Office:

> Do not let him begin life with any idea that his profession is inferior
> to others. . . . In the Civil Service, now a days, exertion will give a
> man a decent gentleman's income not late in life, if it be accom-
> panied by intellects not below par. I do not know that more can be
> said of any profession except that in others there are great prizes. To
> compensate this the Civil Service allows a man, who has in him the
> capacity for getting prizes, to look for them elsewhere. A govern-
> ment clerk, who is not wedded to pleasure, may follow any pursuit
> without detriment to his public utility.

He goes on to mention literary men in the government service: Henry
Reeve, editor of the *Edinburgh Review,* himself, and some others less well
known;[1] he might have added Matthew Arnold. In Trollope's case, his
Post Office work actually played into his authorship: his missions abroad
produced his travel books and articles, as well as a series of short stories
based on his observations of life in foreign countries, and gave substance
for some of his novels. At the same time, his market as a writer was

increased through the sale of his works to the magazines and through the decision of his publisher to emulate Dickens and Thackeray in the publication of his novels in parts.

The first step in his entry into the world of professional writers (if one excepts the obvious first step of writing and marketing his first novel) came when he stopped briefly in London in January, 1858, to find a publisher for *Doctor Thorne,* on which he had been working for about three months. Naturally he approached Bentley first, and Bentley agreed, in conversation, to pay £400 as Trollope asked. Then Bentley made a foolish mistake: he wrote to Trollope a few hours later to say that he had miscalculated his sale of *The Three Clerks,* and that he could offer no more than £300. (His "calculation" illustrates once more what great weight was placed on the initial sale of a book: *The Three Clerks* had been on the market only two months when he wrote this.) Trollope immediately called on his older brother's publisher, Edward Chapman of Chapman and Hall, and concluded with him an agreement for the larger sum. By the time of Trollope's death, Chapman and Hall had published twenty-two novels of his, four travel books, two collections of short stories, three small collections of sketches of English life, and a biography of Cicero. Bentley was quick to realize his blunder: three days after that first note, he added £150 to his offer (contingent upon sales), but Trollope had already left London and Bentley got his answer three months later: the manuscript was to be published by Chapman late in May. Bentley tried again the next year, but he had lost his fish: "I should not at all object to your midwifery for a new book. But as long as Mr. Chapman will give me what I ask him for my goods, of course I shall continue to sell them to him."[2]

·

When the need arose for the Post Office to send an experienced man through the Mediterranean to Alexandria and Suez, and one of the senior English surveyors begged off the assignment, Trollope was chosen. Slightly more than a month later he was on his way. After horrible seasickness on the Channel, he met Tom and took the time to visit the cathedral at Chartres. The glass windows there, he told Rose, are "the finest in the world, . . . magnificent!" They would have to go there together some day. He also smoked a cigar with Tom to prepare himself for his diplomatic conferences over the oriental hookah or narghile. He almost makes it sound as if this were his first cigar, and it may indeed have been so, for he had been brought up in a home where tobacco was forbidden; his mother very early spoke of her "unhappy Tobacco-phobia." However that may be, he soon became a heavy smoker. He went to Marseilles on February 2, embarked immediately by packet for Malta and on to Alexandria, following the pattern of the mails. In Alexandria, which he reached on February 10,[3] he had two missions. One seems rather simple: might bags be used for the shipment of mails through Egypt to India, or must the letters continue to be sealed in iron boxes as they then were? Bags would be easier on the camels, but, Trollope reported, they would be subject to great friction on the camel's back and, more telling, each camel in a train of eighty or ninety had his own driver, armed with a knife and eager to rip open a mail bag. Let there be no change until the railway was completed. But the latest model of boxes (wooden rather than iron) was decidedly worse than its predecessor: they popped open easily and closed with difficulty. At least, no more of those! Once the railway from Alexandria to Suez should be completed, bags might be used on the mails that went by sea from Southampton; those that traveled overland through France to Marseilles might still require the security of iron boxes (though on second thought perhaps not, for though they travel through France they are always accompanied by an Englishman). As it turned out, though no one had told Trollope, the great obstacle to bags was the quarantine regulations; once these were changed to permit bags to go through without being emptied, iron boxes became extinct.[4]

The second mission was by far the more important: arranging a new agreement with the Egyptian government for the transfer between Alexandria and Suez of the mails bound to or from India and Australia, an agreement needed both because of the construction of the new railway between those cities and because of the abolition of the East India Company, with which the current agreement had been signed. Trollope carefully measured the time consumed in every step of the operation (including the normal speed of a camel until the final link of the railway should be finished), and with some vigor insisted that the interest of the mails took priority over other, sometimes conflicting, interests. The steamship company wanted delays for what they pretended was the comfort of the passengers; the Egyptian Transit Administration, represented in the negotiations by Nubar Bey, wanted wider margins of time for the performance of its contracted work and was suspected of being under the thumb of the steamship company.* But Trollope held to his point that the mails should be aboard ship at one port no more than twenty-four hours after the arrival of the ship at the other port. Because English mails congested

---

*Nubar Bey, a newcomer on the Egyptian scene, was an Armenian Christian who rose to the premiership of Egypt in the latter part of the nineteenth century. More than two decades later he recalled his dealings with Trollope, whom he found pleasant, conversational, but in his dealings about the treaty very peremptory and not at all a diplomatist. Trollope had made no secret, Nubar said, that he thought Nubar's motive was chiefly to oblige the Peninsular and Oriental Steamship Company.[5]

the transit system by arriving at Alexandria simultaneously from South-ampton and Marseilles, he agreed that the shipping schedules should be changed to space the arrivals. In the negotiations he was well supported by the British consul general at Alexandria. By February 23 a draft treaty had been prepared and approved by the viceroy. Trollope was then free to make a ten-day visit (March 13–23) to the Holy Land. He was homeward bound by April 4, and the actual agreement was signed by the Egyptians in June. There was a bit of crowing in a letter to Frederic Hill, Rowland's brother and assistant secretary:

> I believe that one should never give way in any thing to an Oriental. Nubar Bey, who now that the treaty is signed declares that there will be no difficulty in carrying it out, assured me at least a dozen times, that if the Viceroy insisted on his signing such an agreement he would at once abandon his office, seeing that the work to which he would be bound would be absolutely impracticable! That was the method he took to carry out the views of the Steamship Company's Agent.

In his annual report on the Post Office for 1859, the postmaster general praised Trollope by name for his accomplishment.[6]

His work was not finished, however, with the Alexandrian negotia-tions: his instructions also directed him to look into the management of the Post Office in Malta. He spent a week there (April 9–15), then reported that even making allowance for the natural inefficiency of the Maltese, the office was overstaffed. But his sympathy for the lower orders of civil servants comes out in his recommendation that no one be dis-missed; let the next vacancy not be filled, and let the money freed thereby be used to increase the salaries of the other clerks. Also, their regular hours of work were needlessly long, considering that they were often called on at irregular and inconvenient hours when the mail packets arrived. And there was, in Trollope's view, an unnecessary amount of record keeping and busywork.[7]

His recommendations were approved and acted upon promptly in London. And now, having almost completed his mission, he took a six-day holiday in the south of Spain between boats at Gibraltar. There were still four days in which he could make a study of the Gibraltar Post Office comparable to the one he had made at Malta. He reached London on May 10.

ે♦

Throughout the journey he worked regularly on *Doctor Thorne;* "I must do 5 of my pages daily, or I cannot accomplish my task," he told Rose, to whom fell the duty of making a fair copy, inserting his afterthoughts, and reporting to him how many pages her fair copy came to. She had certain editorial tasks as well: "You must of course be careful about the reading, and also alter any words which seem to be too often repeated."[8] He completed the task on March 31 at Alexandria, and next day began *The Bertrams*.

This first of Trollope's postal missions abroad produced no travel book, but many pages of the new novel were reflections of his experiences in the East. He was still on his voyage home when he described George Bertram's visit to the Holy Land, beginning with his ride from Jaffa to Jerusalem:

> There is something enticing to an Englishman in the idea of riding off through the desert with a pistol girt about his waist, a portmanteau strapped on one horse before him, and an only attendant seated on another behind him. There is a *soupçon* of danger in the journey just sufficient to give it excitement; and then it is so un-English, oriental, and inconvenient; so opposed to the accustomed haste and comfort of a railway; so out of his hitherto beaten way of life, that he is delighted to get into the saddle. But it may be a question whether he is not generally more delighted to get out of it; particularly if that saddle be a Turkish one. . . .
>
> One rides up to the gate [of Jerusalem] feeling that one is still in the desert; and yet a moment more, with the permission of those very dirty-looking Turkish soldiers at the gate, will place one in the city. . . . The dirty Turkish soldiers do not even look at you, and you soon become pleasantly aware that you are beyond the region of passports.

The visit to the Church of the Holy Sepulchre on the last Sunday in Lent was a memorable experience:

> No one who has not seen it, and none, indeed, who have not seen it at Easter-time, can fully realize all the absurdity which it contains and all the devotion which it occasions. Bertram was first carried to the five different churches which have crowded themselves together under the same roof. The Greeks have by far the best of it. Their shrine is gaudy and glittering, and their temple is large and in some degree imposing. The Latins, whom we call Roman Catholics, are much less handsomely lodged, and their tinsel is by far more dingy. The Greeks, too, possess the hole in which stood—so they say—the cross of Our Saviour; while the Latins are obliged to put up with the sites on which the two thieves were crucified. Then the church of the Armenians, for which you have to descend almost into the bowels of

the earth, is still less grand in its pretensions, is more sombre, more dark, more dirty; but it is as the nave of St. Peter's when compared to the poor wooden-cased altar of the Abyssinians, or the dark unfurnished gloomy cave in which the Syrian Christians worship, so dark that the eye cannot at first discover its only ornament—a small ill-made figure of the crucified Redeemer. . . .

Five or six times Bertram had attempted to get into the Tabernacle of the Holy Sepulchre; but so great had been the rush of pilgrims, that he had hitherto failed. At last his dragoman espied a lull, and went again to the battle. To get into the little outside chapel, which forms, as it were, a vestibule to the cell of the sepulchre, and from which on Easter Saturday issue the miraculous flames, was a thing to be achieved by moderate patience. His close contiguity to Candiotes and Copts, to Armenians and Abyssinians was not agreeable to our hero, for the contiguity was very close, and Christians of these nations are not very cleanly. But this was nothing to the task of entering the sanctum sanctorum. To this there is but one aperture, and that is but four feet high; men entering it go in head foremost, and those retreating come out in the other direction; and as it is impossible that two should pass, and as two or three are always trying to come out, and ten or twelve equally anxious to get in, the struggle to an Englishman is disagreeably warm, though to an Oriental it is probably matter of interesting excitement.

But for his dragoman, Bertram would never have succeeded. He, however, so pulled and hauled these anxious devotees, so thrust in those who endeavoured to come out, and clawed back those who strove to get in, that the passage became for a moment clear, and our hero, having bent low his head, found himself standing with his hand on the marble slab of the tomb.

Those who were there around him seemed to be the outcasts of the world, exactly those whom he would have objected to meet, un-armed, on the roads of Greece or among the hills of Armenia; cut-throat-looking wretches, with close-shaven heads, dirty beards, and angry eyes; men clothed in skins, or huge skin-like-looking cloaks, filthy, foul, alive with vermin, reeking with garlic,—abominable to an Englishman. There was about them a certain dignity of demeanour, a natural aptitude to carry themselves with ease, and even a not impure taste for colour among their dirt. But these Christians of the Russian Church hardly appeared to him to be brothers of his own creed. . . .

"Why do those Turks sit there?" said Bertram as he left the building. [Both Egypt and the Holy Land were under Turkish rule when Trollope visited them.] Why indeed? It was strange to see five or six stately Turks, strict children of the Prophet doubtless, sitting there within the door of this temple dedicated to the Nazarene God, sitting there and looking as though they of all men had the most right so to sit, and were most at home in so sitting; nay, they had a divan there, were drinking coffee there out of little double cups, as is the manner of these people; were not smoking, certainly, as is their manner also in all other places.

"Dem guard de keys," said the dragoman.

"Guard the keys!"

"Yes, yes; open de lock, and not let de Christian fight."

So it is. In such manner is proper, fitting, peaceable conduct maintained within the thrice Christian walls of the Church of the Holy Sepulchre. (Chap. vi)

At the end of the novel its two heroes journey across France and the Mediterranean for no other apparent reason than to give their author an excuse to write a long chapter (xxxviii) describing the sights of Cairo, a visit to the Pyramids and a detailed description of the weekly Friday ceremonials of the college of dervishes, with their frantic dance that ended with one of the participants violently and repeatedly dashing his head against the wall. "They were no mock blows, but serious, heavy raps, as from a small battering ram." After three such raps, each apparently vigorous enough to be fatal, the man's devotions were restrained, so that he might batter himself another day.

Wilkinson and Bertram returned to England on "that gallant first-class steamer, the 'Cagliari,'" on which, it may be assumed, Trollope had sailed.[9] Other experiences from his mission appear in the short stories he collected as *Tales of All Countries*.

Doctor Thorne was published about May 20, only ten days after his return to England. Trollope tells us that the plot had been sketched for him by his brother Tom on that last visit to Florence—the only instance in which he had turned to a source other than his own brain for the thread of a story.[10] How much Tom supplied one cannot of course tell. Essentially, the story is of a laboring man who shattered with a cudgel the skull of his sister's gentleman seducer. He paid the penalty of a prison term for the manslaughter, his sister married a former suitor and went abroad, and the infant daughter born of the seduction was adopted and brought up by the brother of the murdered man, a doctor. The murderer, after his release, showed his genius as a construction engineer, made a fortune, won a baronetcy, and settled near the doctor, whose patient he became, knowing nothing of the fate of the illegitimate daughter or of her adoption by the doctor. He died, a victim of the same brandy that had led him to commit the murder, and bequeathed his fortune to his sister's eldest child—the doctor's niece and ward, as it turned out, who then could marry the handsome son of an impoverished gentleman of ancient family in the neighborhood.

The novel is the third of the Barchester series, but very unlike its predecessors. The clerics figure hardly at all; Mrs. Proudie makes only a token appearance. There is a good deal more about the county families, and especially the Duke of Omnium, the Earl de Courcy, and Mr. Gresham, names that became more important in Trollope's later political novels. It should be remarked that neither the Barchester series nor the so-called parliamentary novels are, in their entirety, sequential in the sense that, for example, *Barchester Towers* is a sequel to *The Warden* and carries on the story where the earlier novel leaves off. Some of the novels are closely related to each other in their narratives, but others (like *Doctor Thorne* and *The Small House at Allington* of the Barchester group, *The Eustace Diamonds* of the parliamentary series) are attached largely through geography and the recurrence of a few characters. As has been remarked, some of the parliamentary characters make their first appearances in the earlier series; other characters from the parliamentary group, like Glencora, Duchess of Omnium, and Violet, Lady Chiltern, appear in *The American Senator,* which belongs to no group. Mr. Chaffanbrass practices his forensic art in *The Three Clerks, Orley Farm,* and *Phineas Redux,* although otherwise the characters of these novels do not overlap. The Beargarden Club, threatened with dissolution in *The Way We Live Now,* staggers along its somewhat disreputable way through *The Duke's Children,* with some of the original Beargardeners still present—Dolly Longestaffe and lords Nidderdale and Grasslough. Henry James once remarked upon Trollope's "practice of carrying certain persons from one story to another—a practice which he may be said to have inherited from Thackeray."[11] James was gentle about it; the *Saturday Review* was less so: "If the present fashion continues, and the heroes of one novel reappear so constantly in the next, readers will begin to hope that funerals, and not marriages, may in future be made the finale in which all romances terminate," said its reviewer of *Framley Parsonage,* and cited the author of *The Newcomes* as another guilty party.[12] Not only is *The Newcomes* a sequel to *Pendennis,* but in it Colonel Dobbin, of *Vanity Fair,* is a guest of Colonel Newcome, and even Becky Sharp is heard of, offstage—"her who wrote the hymns, you know, and goes to Mr. Honeyman's chapel."[13] Moss of Cursitor Street, who entertained Rawdon Crawley in his sponging house, moved westward some three quarters of a mile in the intervening years, and became Moss of Wardour Street in *The Newcomes.*

Doctor Thorne sold about 700 copies in its first month and attracted the notice of the reviewers, one of whom published a long collective article on Trollope's four most recent books, on the whole very admiring.[14] Trollope now felt, he tells us, "a confident standing with the publishers" that "made me know that I had achieved my object. If I wrote a novel, I could certainly sell it."[15] It is at this point in *An Autobiography* that he tells us how rigorously he scheduled his work—"so many pages a week," on the average about forty. "And as a page is an ambiguous term, my page has been made to contain 250 words; and as words, if not watched, will have a tendency to straggle, I have had every word counted as I went."[16] This may be the best-known passage of *An Autobiography*. But it must not be taken literally. His writing diaries survive, and the manuscripts of about two-thirds of his novels. The uniformity of his page of manuscript depended, not on counting words, but on his always using paper of the same size, so that, even though (as it does) the number of lines per page varied and also the number of words, the average was fairly consistent and easily calculable, just as is the work of a modern typist who always uses paper of the same size. And the diaries show a wide range of number of pages written in a day: a working day produced from one to nine pages of *Doctor Thorne,* and during the composition of the book there were 104 working days to 59 idle ones.[17] The oft-repeated boast had a strong element of fiction: Trollope was by no means so mechanical as he makes himself appear. Still, it is no mean achievement to have written a novel of 225,000 words in five and a half months.

ᶻ🐦

Rose met her husband in London on his return from the Mediterranean, and together they went to Ollerton, in Sherwood Forest, not far from Rose's former home near Sheffield and only a mile or two from Rufford Park, which gave its name to one of the principal characters in *The American Senator*. The holiday journey continued to York, Edinburgh, Dunkeld, Perth, Blair Atholl, and Inverness in northern Scotland.[18] Rose returned to Ireland but Trollope remained in Glasgow for two weeks in the middle of June,

> to revise the Glasgow Post Office. I almost forget now what it was that I had to do there, but I know that I walked all over the city with the letter-carriers, going up to the top flats of the houses, as the men would have declared me incompetent to judge the extent of their labours had I not trudged every step with them. It was midsummer, and wearier work I never performed. The men would grumble, and then I would think how it would be with them if they had to go home afterwards and write a love-scene. But the love-scenes written in Glasgow, all belonging to *The Bertrams,* are not good.[19]

He was at home for three weeks early in July, then returned to Scotland on duty until mid-September.[20] On some of his exploratory walks in

Glasgow he was accompanied by the Reverend R. S. Oldham of St. Mary's Episcopal Church (later dean of Glasgow), who visited with him some of the worst slums of the city, and was moved to establish day and Sunday schools and mission chapels that survived well into the present century.[21]

Brown, Jones, and Robinson was still unpublished, and Edward Chapman declined it after mature deliberation: "I should not like to do it without your name & at the same time I feel convinced that it is better that your name should be withheld, for there is a strong impression abroad that you are writing too rapidly for your permanent fame."[22] He was echoing the *Saturday Review*'s judgment a few days earlier: "Those who care for the interests of literature, and wish to see Mr. Trollope take the position to which he is unquestionably capable of rising, cannot but feel a considerable degree of uneasiness at the rapid multiplication of his progeny."[23]

Trollope's district saw little enough of its surveyor in 1858, for on November 2 he went to London to receive instructions for another mission abroad, and two weeks later sailed for the West Indies.[24] Two of the proposed three volumes of *The Bertrams* were in Chapman's hands by that time (Chapman having contracted to pay £400 for the entire copyright for three years and half the copyright thereafter); on shipboard Trollope wrote steadily so that when he reached St. Thomas in the Virgin Islands on December 2 he could send seven more chapters. His confidence in the postal service was such that he expected proofs to reach him on a schedule that would enable him to send them back corrected, with the remainder of the manuscript, to reach Chapman by the middle of February. "Then the remainder can be corrected by Mr. Tilley." With some pride he wrote at the top of his working calendar for the novel, "Begun in Egypt, and written on the Mediterranean—in Malta, Gibraltar, England, Ireland, Scotland and finished in the West Indies" on January 17, 1859. The novel was published about March 8, while Trollope was still abroad.[25]

❧

Though *The Bertrams,* like most of Trollope's novels, was available to readers for the rest of the nineteenth century in an inexpensive single volume after the three-volume edition had exhausted itself in the lending libraries, it was not one of those novels reprinted in the twentieth century until the 1980s; it has been easy, therefore, to dismiss the work altogether. In fact, it is very sensitive and moving, a story of pride and promise, mistaken aims and ultimately modest contentment. Young George Bertram, after a brilliant career at Oxford, was at a loss for a profession. He had no money of his own, and though he was apparently the closest living relative of the very wealthy uncle after whom he had been named, there was no guarantee that the money would come to him on his uncle's death. The old man was crotchety and crusty; he was fond of young George but would not let himself be imposed upon in the determination of his bequests. And young George would not be so mercenary as to play up to him for his wealth. "There's only one decent career for a man in England—politics and Parliament," he said to his fellow Oxonian, the slightly older Henry Harcourt. But this was a slow process for someone without money. "A man, at any rate, may write a book without any electors." "Yes, but not have it read. The author who does any good must be elected by suffrages at least as honestly obtained as those of a member of Parliament" (chap. ii).

By way of putting off a decision, Bertram went out to the Near East in search of a father he had not seen for many years. Sir Lionel Bertram was an army officer attached to the diplomatic service abroad, a charming ne'er-do-well always short of funds, tiding himself over by "borrowing" (even, when they met, from his son), and with an eye out for an unmarried woman with undoubted wealth whom he might flatter into marriage. In Palestine George fell in with a group of English travelers that included an elderly Miss Todd, a middle-aged Miss Baker, and the latter's niece Caroline Waddington, an angel, a goddess, perfect in every feature, tall but not unfemininely so, whose "head stood nobly on her shoulders, giving to her bust that ease and grace of which sculptors are so fond, and of which tight-laced stays are so utterly subversive." "But perhaps the most wonderful grace about her was her walk. 'Vera incessu patuit Dea'" (chap. ix). Caroline Waddington and George quickly fell in love with each other, and when George pursued the acquaintance after their return to England they became engaged. She turned out to be the "ward" of old Uncle George Bertram (actually his granddaughter, offshoot of a brief marriage of which young George had never heard). She had high ambitions: "She would never marry . . . without love; but . . . in her catalogue of human blisses love in a cottage was not entered. . . . She knew that no figure in the world could be made without means, [and] her own fortune was small" (chap. x).

As he looked at the holy places, walking from Bethany to the Mount of Olives and Jerusalem, one part after another of the Gospel narrative echoed in his mind, and he determined to become a clergyman. Both Caroline and Sir Lionel counseled against it—Sir Lionel because a country vicar's pay was so small, Caroline because the ordinary country parson's life was so lacking in nobility. "They are generally fond of eating, very cautious about their money, untidy in their own house, and apt to go to sleep after dinner." Though she said of herself, "It is useless for a woman to think of her future; she can do so little towards planning it, or bringing about her plans," she clearly had no intention of "becoming a respectable vicaress" (chap. x). And so by the time he returned to London, George resolved upon the law, took chambers in the Middle Temple and began reading under one of the most distinguished chancery barristers of the day. But Caroline declined to marry him until there was an assured income, as much to avoid future misery for him as for herself. Though they both were in love and regarded themselves as firmly engaged, the postponement shattered his resolution; he stopped his legal studies and even published, anonymously, a little book called *The Romance of Scripture,* denying the literal truth of many Scriptural statements. He had introduced Harcourt to Caroline—Harcourt, now a member of Parliament and a rising figure in government. Caroline made the mistake of consulting Harcourt about her engagement, and showed him an angry letter from Bertram in response to her insistence on a postponement. Bertram demanded an apology for her breach of confidence, but she was too proud to apologize and the match was broken off. Uncle George offered to bequeath his nephew any sum he might choose to name if he would return to his purpose of marrying her, but in his turn young George was too proud to accept.

And so two people completely in love with each other were parted by a mistaken sense of honor and by their unwillingness to concede any point to each other. Caroline married Harcourt, now Sir Henry and solicitor general, and lived with him, lovelessly, in a large fashionable house in Belgravia. In time she found the loveless marriage unbearable and left him to take refuge with her grandfather. Sir Henry's political fortunes declined, his expenses mounted, and when Uncle George died, leaving his wealth to establish "The Bertram College" for the education of the children of London fishmongers, Harcourt committed suicide. George resumed the study of law, and five years later he and Caroline married; the novel ends with their "living together very quietly, very soberly, but yet happily." Despite this close, the novel bears few of the marks of the typical Trollope novel in which hero and heroine are confidently destined for each other from the beginning, and is remarkably sensitive to the fluctuations of the human spirit, to the willful pride of people who are nevertheless honorable and loving.

It constantly reflects the politics and the ideas of the forties—Peel's repeal of the Corn Laws, Palmerston's racehorses, Louis Philippe's final years as citizen king of France, the publication of Strauss's *Life of Jesus* and Dean Stanley's writings on the Holy Land, and the novels of Marryat and Dickens (there are specific allusions to *Peter Simple* [1834], *Martin Chuzzlewit* [1843–44], and *Bleak House* [1852–53]). Trollope's own life is evident, not only in the setting of old George Bertram's home in Hadley and Caroline Waddington's in Cheltenham (which Trollope rechristened "Littlebath").[26] George's scholarship at Trinity College, Oxford, was one for which Anthony had stood unsuccessfully. There was at the outset a familiar condemnation of competitive examinations for Civil Service positions, and there is a small discourse on the advantages and disadvantages of receiving the morning's letters in time for the breakfast table: one is glad to have something to talk about, but "One would fain receive [some] letters in private" (chap. xxv). The novel contains no hunting scene, but an amusing chapter (xxii) is devoted to another of Trollope's favorite sports, whist. In Miss Todd's room were assembled Miss Ruff, Lady Ruth Revoke, Lady Longspade, Miss Finesse, Mrs. King Garded, and the Fuzzybells. Miss Ruff was an ardent player and a stern critic, whose severity was made more striking by the fixity of her glass eye. When Lady Ruth put her thirteenth trump on her partner Miss Ruff's thirteenth heart, the explosion was awesome. "I wish she had a glass tongue as well," said Lady Ruth, "because then perhaps she'd break it." John Henry Newman regarded the novel as "decidedly the most powerful thing of [Trollope's] that I have read—tragic, instructive, humiliating"—though when he came to the third volume, he found it "a dreadful fall off." "We confess that we like this new tale better than any that Mr. Trollope has written," said the *Saturday Review*. *The Bertrams* was the first Trollope novel to be published in the English language edition of Bernhard Tauchnitz of Leipzig (1859); six years later, while he was working on *War and Peace,* Tolstoy in Russia read it and was filled with awe at Trollope's talent, however different from his own. Tauchnitz published in all fifteen of Trollope's novels (in addition to two travel books, *An Autobiography,* and a collection of short stories), and Tolstoy owned eleven of them.[27]

As early as 1855 the government had resolved to make all colonial post offices except for military stations like Malta and Gibraltar independent of the General Post Office in London and to place them under local control. But the legislatures in Jamaica and British Guiana had been reluctant to authorize the transfer, partly at least because the local postal officials saw their positions threatened and therefore somewhat disingenuously represented to the colonial legislatures that the change would greatly increase the burden of cost locally. On his mission to the West Indies, Trollope thus had to negotiate with the political powers in both places. The packet services, of course, remained under the control of London, and it appeared that they were neither so speedy nor so inexpensive as they should have been, so that Trollope had also to study every detail of the shipping arrangements. Next, the transfer of mails across the Isthmus of Panama (or alternatively across Central America at some other point) for the west coast of America (especially British Columbia) and even, perhaps, for

Australia and New Zealand, had to be examined at close range in order to secure the most advantageous arrangement. And the Spanish islands of Cuba and Puerto Rico had to be persuaded to reduce their charges for local forwarding of mail sent from the United Kingdom. On November 16 he "started in great force" from London (to use Tilley's words), and next day sailed from Southampton on the steamship *Atrato*, armed with a very long letter of instructions in which Frederic Hill, the assistant secretary in charge of the packet services, authorized him to travel almost at will throughout the Caribbean area as he might find need.[28]

At St. Thomas he left the *Atrato* and traveled to Jamaica aboard a smaller vessel, the *Derwent,* which reached Kingston on December 6. The postal arrangements at Jamaica presented problems that in the end could be resolved only by a broad hint that Her Majesty's government would give up the administration of the posts there whether or not the local government was prepared to assume it. The legislature's fear that the postal administration, if local, would be subject to jobbery on the part of the governor was held by Trollope to be no concern of the home government, and the local surveyor's estimate of the financial loss to Jamaica if the British ceased their subsidy was shown by Trollope to be largely the fiction of a man who was going to lose his position when the change was effected. Nevertheless Trollope traveled the post routes on the island and suggested certain economies that would help balance the account. His final letter from Jamaica was dated January 22, 1859.[29]

Two days later he boarded the sailing brig *Linwood* for the south coast of Cuba, having been assured that there would be great saving of time if he traveled by sea only to Cienfuegos and then overland to Havana. But he and his advisers had reckoned without the wind: "We have been becalmed half the time since, and I shall lose more time than I shall gain," he wrote to his mother from the vessel on the twenty-seventh. "I believe that in these days a man should never be tempted to leave the steamboats." Nevertheless, he had another reason for undertaking the voyage over this route: to see whether, when the railway under construction between Cienfuegos and Havana was completed, it might be more economical to send the mails there from Jamaica instead of sailing round to the north coast of Cuba.[30]

From Cuba he went back to St. Thomas, then on the route along the Windward Islands to Barbados, St. Vincent, Grenada, Trinidad, and British Guiana, then again to St. Thomas aboard "that most horrid of all steam-vessels, the *Prince*," to take another vessel for Santa Martha (in New Granada, or Colombia), Cartagena, and Aspinwall or Colon. A part of his instructions had been to prod the postmaster at Demerara, a veteran in the service who had grown very slack about remitting the public money that came into his hand, and to report upon the postmistress at Grenada, "who has occasioned a great deal of trouble to the London office by the manner in which she has performed her duties, and who has shewn very slight signs of improvement."[31]

The negotiations in Panama were twofold: an attempt to persuade the authorities of New Granada (which then possessed Panama) to abrogate the tax they were levying on all British transit mails and an attempt to arrive at a less costly contract with the Panama Railroad Company for the conveyance. The shortest way to handle the former problem was to follow the example of the United States and simply refuse to pay the tax, since the government of New Granada was too remote and too weak to enforce the payment. But there was some need to retain their goodwill, and Trollope learned from the local government officials that a substantial reduction could be at once negotiated. By the end of December a new treaty was signed in London. As for the railway company, the expenses of their operation were such that Trollope found their charges not excessive; nevertheless he did obtain from them a reiteration of a previous offer to transport all mails, regardless of weight, for a flat annual fee, should the volume warrant entering into such an arrangement.[32]

The British man-of-war *Vixen* then took him up the Pacific to Costa Rica, to inspect the route of a proposed canal across Central America; he himself crossed, under the most primitive conditions, to Greytown (San Juan del Norte), where he was picked up by the *Trent* and returned to Colon. He remained skeptical about the feasibility of a canal, though undoubtedly the route through the Nicaraguan lakes and the San Juan River of Costa Rica was the best. But "all mankind has heard much of M. Lesseps and his [proposed] Suez canal. . . . I have a very strong opinion that such a canal will not and cannot be made," and the eloquence of other French projectors in Central America left him unconvinced. Trollope was sensitive to the prospect for change in the entire region; he knew, for example, of Yankee territorial greed and the decay of the Spanish empire, and even expressed the opinion that it would perhaps be best if Cuba should become an American possession. But he had no way of knowing that the United States was on the brink of a civil war, that the *Trent* was to figure in the international crisis that had all America and Britain by the ears the next time he visited the States, or that the American frigate *Merrimac,* aboard which he was a guest at Panama, was to become the mainstay of the Confederate fleet and, sheathed in iron, was to fight a famous battle in Hampton Roads with the little cheesebox *Monitor.*[33]

At San José Trollope attempted to see the British envoy extraordinary, Sir William Ouseley, and sent his card by a servant to Sir William's secretary, whose response, loud enough to be heard, was, "Oh, tell Mr. Trollope to go to the devil. It's much too hot to see anyone!" Trollope was soon taking over the secretary's living quarters, and the man, William

Webb Follet Synge, became a lifelong friend. Indeed, the friendship between the Trollope family and Synge's family endured for at least three generations. Synge's sons spent their holidays at Waltham House, and the eldest, Bob, amused Anthony once by refusing a banana at dinner: "At school that's the cheapest grub we can buy." Both he and his mother were attentive to Rose in her old age.[34]

The boldest and most significant of Trollope's recommendations was not made until his return to London. "In these latitudes the respectable, comfortable, well-to-do route from every place to every other place is via the little Danish island of St. Thomas . . . —or [was so] when this was written," he said in *The West Indies,* with an eye to the change he hoped to effect. "The Royal Mail Steam Packet Company dispense all their branches from that favoured spot." Trollope's report of July 16 was to recommend making Jamaica the center of distribution instead of St. Thomas. Thus the mails would travel a greater part of their way to their ultimate destination on the faster transatlantic vessels, there would be no longer a multiplying of distances by conveying mails from St. Thomas to Jamaica, Havana, and Panama on vessels traveling nearly parallel courses as far as Jamaica, the transfer point would be on British soil, to the greater prosperity of the Jamaicans, and the large contingent of Englishmen engaged in handling the mails would be removed from, "as I believe it to be, the most pestilential harbour in the West Indies." "As far as I have been able to learn, the harbour of St. Thomas—not the island on shore— is more subject to yellow fever than any other thickly inhabited spot in the West Indies. The officers employed in the intercolonial service of the company are all sent out as very young men, and the service is one to them of much danger." St. Thomas would be reduced to a coaling station, and while coal was being taken on, the mails for the nearby Windward Islands and Demerara (British Guiana) could be transferred to a smaller vessel. The whole of Trollope's report on this matter shows that he had spent his voyage outward not merely finishing *The Bertrams* but also talking to the officers of his ship about such technical matters as the effect of prevailing winds on the speed of vessels of different sizes, the condition of navigable passages between islands, and the location of suitable alternate harbors. His meticulous calculation indicated a saving of 3,300 miles a month over the packet company's plan, or (at the rate at which mileage was calculated) more than £15,000 a year. When the packet company's representatives in London demurred at his proposals, Trollope went into even greater detail, and urged an appeal to the Admiralty, whose hydrographer replied: "I entirely concur in Mr. Trollope's proposal and recommend that it be carried into effect as early as sufficient notice of the changes can be given." The Treasury also concurred in a preference for Jamaica as the central station in the West Indies.

The packet company prevailed, presumably because they feared their commercial interests would suffer from the change, but the weight of Trollope's demonstration hung over them in the performance of their mail services, with the threat that if their own scheme for acceleration did not prove satisfactory, they would find the change forced upon them. The postmaster general's next annual report fairly glowed with pride in Trollope's achievement, "although a landsman"![35]

⁂

A month in Jamaica, with the prospect of extensive but still undefined further ramblings, prompted Trollope on January 11 to propose to Chapman a volume of travels in those parts, price £250, manuscript to be ready no later than October 31 for Christmas publication. Chapman accepted, and Tom Trollope signed the agreement on his brother's behalf on April 19.[36] At last the younger son of Mrs. Trollope was writing a travel book.

The West Indies and the Spanish Main is an engaging volume, mingling serious and thoughtful sociological discussion with amusing personal anecdote and impetuous indignation against those incompetents who had increased his hardships on the journey. He began the writing while becalmed aboard the *Linwood* between Jamaica and Cuba, and the opening sentences are a most eloquent echo of the Ancient Mariner's outcry against the calm and the heat. We learn a good deal about Trollope himself. He journeyed by rail across Panama with "the ordinary kit of a travelling Englishman—a portmanteau, bag, desk, and hat-box." He customarily left his keys and his money everywhere, and seldom found time to lock his portmanteau, yet he was never robbed. He was by now expert in judging cigars, and nowhere had discovered better than those pressed upon him by the captain of the port of Cienfuegos, in Cuba. He had now attained a full 210 pounds. And with some amusement he gives the description of himself on the passport he obtained from the Spanish consul in Jamaica for his travel to Cuba: stature, tall ("Never before this have I obtained in a passport any more dignified description of my body than robust"); eyes, blue; eyebrows and hair, chestnut ("Any but a Spaniard would have declared that as to hair, I was bald"); color, healthy; beard, luxuriant ("If I have any personal vanity, it is wrapped up in my beard. It is a fine, manly article of dandyism, that wears well in all climates, and does not cost much, even when new").[37]

The principal sociological problem he had to comment on was the effect of the emancipation of slaves in the British colonies in 1833 and the abolition in 1846 of the tariff protection of colonial products in the British market, two measures which combined to destroy a great many of the sugar plantations and to leave much valuable land idle or at the mercy of squatters. Slavery had even more recently been abolished in some other of the Caribbean countries, and Trollope ventured to prophesy (in 1859) the abolition of slavery even in the United States, though not probably in his own time.[38] Although firm in his conviction that slavery was intolerable, he can find no solution to the problem of casting hundreds of thousands of penniless human beings upon the world with no provision for their support. And inevitably there is a good deal of discussion of racial characteristics from the point of view of a man who had never before seen the whites in an overwhelming numerical minority. He himself, with some justification, attributed the vitality of his book to the fact that it was written without notes, day by day as the experience was fresh. And "on the whole, I regard [it] as the best book that has come from my pen."[39]

From the West Indies he went on to Bermuda aboard the steamer *Delta* and then once more by sailing vessel, the brig *Henrietta,* to New York (a voyage marked in his travel diaries "Alas! alas! alas"). There had once been some thought that Rose might join him there, but that plan came to nothing, probably because there was too little time left to make her voyage worth while. After three nights in New York he made a quick journey to Niagara (where he donned the usual tourist oilskins and was thoroughly soaked in the walk behind the falls), then he went on to Montreal, and returned to New York City by way of Saratoga Springs, a dull town in which he spent a single night. There were four more nights in New York before he sailed on June 23 aboard the Cunarder *Africa* for Liverpool, which he reached on July 3. He was home in Dublin the next day.[40]

By this time he had another project under way—*Tales of All Countries.* "Each refers to or is intended to be redolent of some different country—but they apply only to localities with which I am myself conversant." While he was in New York he presented the idea to Harper and Brothers with a view to publication in *Harper's New Monthly Magazine;* the first two stories were in their hands, and their payment of £40 had reached him, by September 1. He also offered to sell them advance sheets of his forthcoming book on the West Indies; they declined, then later purchased the advance sheets from his London publishers at Harper's own price.[41]

The *Tales* were Trollope's first venture into the form of the short story, and sought to combine the appeal of a travel book with that of fiction. Some are mere anecdotes, which Trollope professed to have been based upon his own experience, like "The O'Conors of Castle Conor" (set in County Mayo, Ireland), "Relics of General Chassé" (in Antwerp), and "John Bull on the Guadalquivir" (in and near Seville). Others had what might be called a plot: "Miss Sarah Jack, of Spanish Town, Jamaica," "The Courtship of Susan Bell" (at Saratoga Springs), "An Unprotected Female at the Pyramids" (at Cairo; an "unprotected female" is a tourist traveling by herself, but predatory in her search for a husband), "The Chateau of Prince Polignac" (at Le Puy, in south-central France), and "La Mère Bauche" (at the little Pyreneean spa of Vernet-les-Bains). The last, indeed, presents much the same situation as *Doctor Thorne*: a young man falls in love with an orphan girl befriended by his mother; she opposes their marriage, and when in this instance the young man yields to his mother the girl, forced into marriage with an unattractive older man, leaps to her death from a high cliff.

⁂

The summer of 1859 was exceedingly busy. Trollope had only a week at home before he set out for London to write his reports on the West Indies, and while there he arranged his transfer to the Eastern District of England, whose surveyor was retiring. The new appointment did not become official until January 10, 1860, but he lost no time in finding a house within his new district. On August 2 he announced to Rose, in high-spirited, pseudo-Elizabethan language, that she was now "ye. ladie of Waltham House in ye. Countie of Herts"—at Waltham Cross, just on the boundaries of Essex and Middlesex and not far from the house at Hadley which his mother and two sisters first took on their return from Bruges in 1836. It was easily accessible by rail, fourteen miles from the Shoreditch Station in London. He concluded his letter to her: "In ye. mean time I am with all true love and affection your ladieships devoted servant and husband."[42] Rose seems so obscure in contrast with her ebullient and well-known husband, but their relationship was always affectionate and good humored, and she was very present to his mind when he was away from home. His books occasionally contain little messages for her: "I never kept any lady waiting before—except my wife," he remarked in *The West Indies*.[43]

During his sojourn in England he was asked to observe at first hand a system of "restricted sorting" of the mail in Glasgow, Liverpool, and Manchester, with a view to introducing it in Dublin. But his literary enterprises also kept him busy. On August 2 he signed an agreement with Chapman to publish a new three-volume novel, *Castle Richmond*, which he began to write two days later; the manuscript was to be delivered by the end of March. For £600 they would purchase all rights for three years, and would own half the copyright thereafter. (The witness to Chapman's signature on this agreement was named Sowerby; Trollope used the name later in the year in *Framley Parsonage*.)[44] And of course there was the proofreading of *The West Indies* for publication in late October. The growing permanence of his place in literature was shown by the appearance of cheap editions of his novels: *The Three Clerks* from Bentley in March, and from Chapman and Hall *Doctor Thorne* also in March, *The Kellys* in November, *The Macdermots* early in 1860, and *The Bertrams* in May, 1860. A one-volume cheap edition of *Barchester Towers* appeared from Longmans in early April, 1858, and a companion edition of *The Warden* three years later. In August, 1859, Trollope sold the Continental rights to this pair of novels to Bernhard Tauchnitz of Leipzig.[45]

He took a much-needed six-week leave of absence from September 7 to October 20 to travel with Tilley and Rose to the south of France, on what, from the variety and spectacular interest of the places they visited, must have been the most exciting of their tours thus far. He now took Rose to Chartres, as he had promised, to Bourges, and to Clermont-Ferrand (where Tom met them). In Le Puy she was impressed by the mammoth metal statue of the Virgin atop one of the volcanic rock spires (one could ascend steps within and peer out from the top; it was a predecessor of the French-made Statue of Liberty). At Nîmes they saw the Roman amphitheater and the nearby Pont du Gard. Then they took the railway to Perpignan, at the east end of the Pyrenees, and the diligence to Vernet-les-Baines, the setting for "La Mère Bauche." Rose later recalled that at Bourg-Madame Tom and Tilley crossed into Spain and tried to get beds at Puigcerdá, where they danced in the kitchen. There was a spectacular ride over the mountains to Ax-les-Thermes, then on to the medieval city of Foix (where Tom left them), to Luz (where Tilley was ill, and Anthony had to go by himself to the Cirque de Gavarnie, in which the legendary hero Roland had kicked out a massive breach in the cliff and where Browning a few years after their visit conceived the scheme for *The Ring and the Book*), to Cauterets (which Tennyson celebrated in a poem) and the nearby Lake of Gaube (which Swinburne hymned). They took in the resorts on the Bay of Biscay (including San Sebastian, in Spain), then went northward through Angoulême, Tours, and Amiens, and back to England.[46]

Early in October the publishing house of Smith, Elder announced the prospective publication, beginning with the new year, of a new shilling monthly periodical, "edited by Mr. W. M. Thackeray, who will be a regular Contributor to its pages, and with whom will be associated some of the most Eminent Writers of the day."[47] It took only about two weeks of deliberation before Trollope wrote to Thackeray from Dublin, offering to write for the new periodical and proposing the *Tales of All Countries* for publication, perhaps in alternate months with *Harper's* in New York, who did not wish to publish the stories more frequently than once every two months. Five of them were now written, and by way of exploring Thackeray's rate of pay he mentioned that Harper gave him £2 a page, or £20 for a ten-page story. The first reply to his letter came, not from Thackeray but from the publisher George Smith, accepting the idea of short stories at £2 a page (though remarking that a page of the new magazine was only one-half the size of a page of *Harper's,* so that the rate was in fact doubled). "We should however much prefer a continuous story to extend through [384 pages] of the Magazine, which would be equivalent to the bulk of an ordinary three volume novel, and for the entire copyright of which we should be happy to pay you One Thousand pounds." Then came Thackeray's most flattering letter of October 28, expressing delight at Trollope's offer of help and the hope that the *Cornhill Magazine* would get from him a novel as much to Thackeray's taste as *The Three Clerks.* "The Chapmans [who were also Thackeray's publishers], if they are the honest men I take them to be, I've no doubt have told you with what sincere liking your works have been read by yours very faithfully, W. M. Thackeray." Less than five months earlier the *Times,* in a laudatory review that occupied more than two full columns, had proclaimed that Mudie, the "majestic" proprietor of Britain's largest lending library, "knows that at the present moment one writer in England is paramount above all others, and his name is Trollope." Smith's and Thackeray's reception of his proposal, therefore, was perhaps predictable.[48]

These letters brought Trollope instantly to London by overnight boat of November 2–3. Naturally his first impulse was to use the novel he already had one-third complete, *Castle Richmond,* and the Chapmans gave their consent. But Smith demurred at an Irish story and urged something on the church, "as though it were my peculiar subject." The agreement was signed on November 3; the book would be published in sixteen installments, the first of which was due on December 1, and pro rata payments were to be made monthly as the manuscript was supplied. Trollope must have had some intuition of what Smith would want, for he wrote the first seven pages of *Framley Parsonage* on the journey from Dublin to London. He continued the writing on the return journey to Dublin, and scarcely paused until the book was half finished by December 23. Then (on January 2) he resumed *Castle Richmond* and met his deadline of the end of March.[49]

Novels at mid-century were not infrequently issued serially in monthly paperbound parts at a shilling (as with most of Dickens's and Thackeray's) or in the numbers of a magazine (as with *Oliver Twist* and *A Tale of Two Cities*) prior to publication in clothbound volumes. An important aspect of the *Cornhill* was to give each month as much of a novel as was customarily published in a separate part, but to include a great deal more of literary interest in the same monthly issue, all for a shilling. The same idea had occurred to Macmillan, who brought out the first number of his shilling *Macmillan's Magazine* two months before the first number of the *Cornhill,* and ran as the serial Thomas Hughes's *Tom Brown at Oxford.* (Smith had approached Hughes as editor for the *Cornhill* before he engaged Thackeray, but Hughes declined.)[50] The sensational success of the *Cornhill* came from lavish payments that could command the best contributors and from the excellent taste and business sense of George Smith, who in fact did the greater part of the editor's work himself. And Trollope's contribution to that success was affirmed in a remark Smith made to Frederic Chapman the following July, "that if Ainsworth got [Trollope] to write a story for Bentley's Miscellany and he reduced the price to one shilling it would be fatal to the Cornhill Mag."[51]

For all his confidence in his ability to write to a schedule, Trollope was aware that there were certain risks in permitting the early part of a novel to be published before the end was written. Not only might some misfortune intervene to prevent work on the conclusion, but "an artist should keep in his hand the power of fitting the beginning of his work to the end," should some unforeseen shift occur in the course of the narrative. The advantage of his having pride of place at the beginning of the new magazine led him to run these risks, "but I have never broken [my rule] since," he claimed in *An Autobiography*[52]—a boast that was not true when he made it in 1876, and that was overtaken by a sad irony at the end of his life. *Orley Farm, Small House, Can You Forgive Her?* and *Belton Estate* all began serial publication before their writing was completed.

Framley Parsonage was Trollope's first attempt at serial publication, and made him aware also of a new requirement: "The author . . . should not allow himself to be tedious in any single point. . . . He cannot afford to have many pages skipped over out of the few which are to meet the reader's eye at the same time. Who can imagine the first half of the first volume of *Waverley* coming out in shilling numbers?" Working according to this conviction, he boasted that "in this novel there is no very weak part,—no long succession of dull pages."[53] His remark may reflect his sensitivity to the *Athenaeum's* review of *The Bertrams,* which, though on the whole favorable, complained of its occasional diffuseness and long-windedness.[54]

In the year 1859 Trollope's income from writing, with only two installments of *Framley Parsonage* paid for and of course none of *Castle Richmond,* was more than £1,000; for the first time literature brought him more money than the Post Office.[55] The shift is significant.

ᦂ

Castle Richmond is a tale of innocence and decency under attack from villainy and blackmail. The Irish setting, as Trollope frankly acknowledged, "is in these days considered almost as unattractive as historical incident;* but, nevertheless, I will make the attempt" (chap. i). The story has a single plot. An apparently respectable and prosperous widower named Talbot with a very young son moved into a Dorsetshire parish soon after the battle of Waterloo and within three months married the eldest daughter of an impoverished local clergyman; two months later the man bolted, leaving behind a mass of debts and the little boy. A sister of the runaway husband was found, and she undertook to take the child into her home. The abandoned wife's father, learning that the man had been seen in Paris, crossed the Channel to seek him out, and was able to satisfy himself that the man had been killed in a gambling-house brawl. In due course the clergyman's daughter married a young Irish baronet, Sir Thomas Fitzgerald, who took her to his large estate, Castle Richmond, in County Cork near Mallow and Kanturk. At the time of the story's beginning, the winter of 1846–47, Sir Thomas and Lady Fitzgerald had a son, Herbert, recently graduated from Oxford, and two daughters. (This date was two years before Trollope himself moved to Mallow.) Nearby lived the widowed Countess of Desmond with her sixteen-year-old daughter Lady Clara and her thirteen-year-old son, the present Earl, who, despite the great poverty of the Desmonds, was a schoolboy at Eton. Lady Clara was loved by a Fitzgerald cousin, Owen, and by Herbert of Castle Richmond, to whom she became engaged with her mother's encouragement; for the Countess the engagement was prudential, as promising a much-needed source of income, but for Lady Clara it was a match engendered by admiration and love.

Then there appeared on the scene a father and son who were in fact Lady Fitzgerald's former husband and her stepson, the once-abandoned infant. Working in secrecy, so that she learned nothing about it, they threatened Sir Thomas with exposure as not in fact the real husband of his lady, so that his three children were illegitimate and the entailed estate as well as the baronetcy would pass on his death to the cousin, Owen Fitzgerald. The blackmailers so hounded Sir Thomas as to drive him to an early grave; their story came out, preparations were made by the family to turn the estate over to the new Sir Owen, and Herbert began the study of law in London. But at this point it was revealed that Talbot's "sister," the woman who had brought up his son when he decamped, was in fact the first woman he married after becoming a widower: his bigamous marriage to the Dorsetshire clergyman's daughter was invalid and her marriage to Sir Thomas was legitimate. All these things, as revealed, "will be plain to

---

*Recalling what Hurst and Blackett's foreman had told him half a dozen years earlier: "Your historical novel, sir, is not worth the paper it's written on," or, indeed, "is not worth a damn," as Trollope later told the story.[56]

any novel-reading capacity" (chap. xliii), and it was the ordinary novel reader, with his interest in the twists and turns of a plot, that Trollope addressed. In this respect the novel has little to be said for it.

But Trollope thought of the book also as "A Tale of the Famine Year in Ireland" (chap. xliv), and very early (chap. vii) recalls the essays he published in the *Examiner* at the time. A substantial part of the work, then, is a firsthand account of what Trollope himself had seen—the starving mothers and children, the soup kitchens, the makeshift public works undertaken so that the relief would be payment for labor, not charity. (His description of crews sent out, without tools or adequate direction, to cut away the hills and level the roads—thus leaving the roads in many cases impassible morasses—sound not unlike more recent experiences with similar relief efforts in the Great Depression.) "The great object was gained; the men were fed, and were not fed by charity. What did it matter, that the springs of every conveyance in the county Cork were shattered by the process, and that the works resulted in myriads of wheelbarrows [hastily assembled in too great numbers for the projects]" (chap. xviii). Herbert, who worked hard at organizing the local relief committee, felt bound by the prevailing doctrines of "political economy" (Benthamite radicalism), yet "there were but few days in which he did not empty his pocket of loose silver. . . . [Money should be] expended with forethought and discrimination. . . . But the system was impracticable, for it required frames of iron and hearts of adamant. It was impossible not to waste money in almsgiving" (chap. xvi). The novel is a tribute to its author's affection for Ireland, undertaken at the moment of his permanent return to England.

The *Saturday Review*, though it found Trollope "well worth reading on the Irish famine," was very lukewarm to the book. "Mr. Trollope has reached the stage in which he may justly claim the character of an excellent literary workman . . . but . . . he has also arrived at the point when he makes a novel just as he might make a pair of shoes, with a certain workmanlike satisfaction in turning out a good article, but with little of the freshness and zest which marked his earlier productions."*[57]

---

*Trollope's earliest surviving comparison of a novelist to a shoemaker was made in a letter of April 13, a month before this review appeared.[58]

Chapter VIII

1860

The remarkable success of the *Cornhill Magazine* did much to change the aspect of British publishing in the latter part of the century. The sale of 109,274 copies of its first number gave to *Framley Parsonage* by far the greatest circulation ever achieved by a Trollope novel. George Smith's roster of contributors contains nearly every name of note in Victorian literature: besides Thackeray and Trollope, there were George Eliot, Elizabeth Gaskell, Harriet Beecher Stowe, John Ruskin, Wilkie Collins, Matthew Arnold, W. S. Gilbert, Charles Lever, Tennyson, Elizabeth Barrett Browning. Dickens was not among these, for he was conducting a journal of his own and was not, moreover, on cordial terms with Thackeray; he was induced, however, to write an obituary notice of Thackeray early in 1864. Smith simply determined to obtain the writers he wanted by paying prices far beyond what they had ever received elsewhere; Trollope, who had edged upward to £600 for *Castle Richmond,* published in three volumes, now quickly moved beyond the £1,000 mark and reached £3,000 from Smith for *The Small House at Allington* in 1862 and £2,800 for *The Claverings,* which was somewhat shorter.[1] Smith also insisted on the right to publish the *Cornhill* serials in book form himself, and thus required his authors to give up their former publishers for these works at least. The Chapmans were good-natured about Trollope's temporary defection, but Blackwood was more than a little grieved when George Eliot succumbed to the wiles of a man he regarded as "the enemy" and something of a buccaneer.[2] Had *Romola* been of the length Smith first wished, he would have paid her £10,000; in the end, because it was shorter, he gave £7,000. In 1868 Smith gave Browning £400 for the book rights to *The Ring and the Book,* the largest sum Browning had ever received for any of his works. Though the figure was amended to £1,250 through the extension of the contract to five years, one begins to wonder why anyone should want to write poetry.[3] The pattern of novel publishing was changing: the bargain offered by the shilling magazine, with segments of a novel—or even of more than one novel—and a great deal of other material as well, began to call in question the worth of publishing the novel by itself in shilling parts, and the huge circulation of the magazine made the old three-volume form at thirty-one shillings sixpence a questionable investment for the circulating libraries like Mudie's, who had been the chief purchasers of such editions. When Smith, Elder published *Framley Parsonage* in book form, they charged only twenty shillings for the three volumes; the complete novel in the *Cornhill* had cost sixteen shillings. And then, the success of the *Cornhill* spawned a great many imitators, so that novelists had a broader market for their wares.

For more than four years, scarcely a number of the *Cornhill* appeared without its pages of Trollope. When *Framley Parsonage* concluded, only three months elapsed before the eight-part *Struggles of Brown, Jones, and Robinson* began (August, 1861, through March, 1862). Then after a lapse of five months the twenty-part *Small House at Allington* ran from September, 1862, through April, 1864. In addition, three essays of his appeared in the same four years. (Tom Trollope also wrote for three numbers in the first year, and his second wife Frances Eleanor began to contribute in the fourth year.)

Smith celebrated his success with the institution of monthly "Cornhill dinners" at his home in Gloucester Square, Paddington. At the first of these, Trollope tells us, "I first met many men who afterwards became my most intimate associates. It can rarely happen that one such occasion can be the first starting-point of so many friendships! It was at that table, and on that day, that I first saw Thackeray, Charles Taylor (Sir)—than whom in latter life I have loved no man better,—Robert Bell, G. H. Lewes, [W. H.] Russell of the *Times,* and John Everett Millais."[4] G. A. Sala was there, Monckton Milnes, and M. J. Higgins,[5] whose pseudonym, "Jacob Omnium" ("Jack of all Trades") may have suggested to Trollope the name for his most splendid nobleman, the Duke of Omnium ("Duke of All Things"). (Then, from the well-known bastard Latin phrase "Omnium Gatherum," he coined the name "Gatherum Castle" for the Duke's seat in West Barsetshire.) Sala remarked:

> Anthony Trollope was very much to the fore, contradicting everybody, subsequently saying kind things to everybody, and occasionally going to sleep on sofas, chairs, or leaning against sideboards, and even somnolent while standing erect on the hearthrug. I never knew a man who could take so many spells of "forty winks" at unexpected moments, and then turn up quite wakeful, alert, and pugnacious, as the author of "Barchester Towers," who had nothing of the bear but his skin, but whose ursine envelope was assuredly of the most grisly texture.[6]

Nevertheless, that first celebration provided its embarrassments. When Smith took Trollope up to introduce him to Thackeray just before dinner, Thackeray curtly said "How do?" and turned on his heel. Trollope was so furious that he came to Smith next morning to say that had it not been for the courtesy owed to his host, he would have walked out of the house; he would never speak to Thackeray again. It was later explained that Thackeray, in poor health, at the moment of the introduction had been seized with a sudden spasm of intense pain; and so all was forgiven.

Another episode was perhaps even more embarrassing because it befell unexpectedly after a lapse of four months. On May 26, the *New York Times* published a column of gossip from its London correspondent, full of *personalia,* and among other things telling a story of an occurrence at this first *Cornhill* dinner, the point of which was to hold Smith up to ridicule as "a very good man of business, but totally unread."[7] With questionable taste, the *Saturday Review* in London quoted liberally from the column by way of showing the inferiority of American standards of decency, where such gossip could be published by one of "the most respectable American papers," and be read.[8]

The whole affair was silly and hardly worth notice, except for the fact that the *New York Times* column was known to have been written by Edmund Yates, who was still angry at having had his name stricken from the rolls of the Garrick Club two years earlier, after more than ten years of membership, as a penalty for having published some gossip on Thackeray which the latter said could only have been based on a conversation at the club, the confidentiality of which had thus been breached. Yates was a clerk in the secretary's office of the Post Office, sixteen years younger than Trollope, and the embarrassment arose from Trollope's consciousness that it was he who had told Yates some of the occurrences at the dinner. When he confessed to Smith, Smith responded very angrily and Trollope replied meekly, "I know I have been wrong, and you may say anything you like to me."[9] In the same column in the *New York Times* Yates told his American readers that, "with the exception of Dickens and Thackeray, perhaps Anthony Trollope is making more money than any English novelist" and that Trollope's friends were urging him to leave the Post Office and devote all his time to writing, but Trollope was reluctant to risk giving up his secure salary of over £800 a year.

かた

John Everett Millais was fourteen years younger than Trollope, charming, handsome, and a very successful artist. When Smith began thinking of illustrations for *Framley Parsonage,* he apparently had not yet engaged Millais to do the work, for though he asked Trollope to suggest a subject for an illustration for the third installment (chaps. vii–ix) he did not mention the artist. Trollope's suggestion—the aged Lord Boanerges trying to explain to Miss Dunstable the scientific principle of surface tension by means of soap bubbles—had comic possibilities, but was utterly insignificant to the story. Trollope (who had never dealt with an illustrator before) was prepared to require him—whoever he might be—to read *Doctor Thorne* to see what Miss Dunstable looked like.[10] Then came the intimation from Smith that Millais might consent to do the work. "Should I live to see my story illustrated by Millais no body would be able to hold me," Trollope replied.[11] (In *The Warden* Trollope had adorned Tom Towers's luxurious apartment with "a singularly long figure of a female devotee, by Millais," viewed as representative of the Pre-Raphaelite school [chap. xiv].) Millais' first illustration accompanied the fourth installment, in the April number, and was far more appropriate: the romantic hero Lord Lufton and the heroine Lucy Robarts parting at the gate to her brother's house after Lufton had met her by chance and escorted her home. Clearly Millais had read carefully Trollope's description of the scene. For the next illustration (in the sixth installment) Millais also made the choice—Lucy lying in despair on her bed after having assured Lord Lufton, out of regard for his mother's wishes, that she could never love him. Trollope innocently suggested the title, from his text: "Was it not a lie?" Then he saw the proof of the plate and was distressed beyond measure: "The picture is simply ludicrous, & will be thought by most people to have been made so intentionally. It is such a burlesque on such a situation as might do for Punch, only that the execution is too bad to have passed muster for that publication." If Millais cannot pay more attention to his work than this, perhaps it would be better to give up altogether the idea of illustrating the book.[12] Trollope was too quick in making his judgment: most of the picture consists of a large heap of flounces and crinolines, with Lucy's head on the pillow at one end and her foot stretched out to the floor at the other, and it is undoubtedly the most memorable of the illustrations. It has more of comedy than pathos, but a young lady cannot always change into something subdued before giving way to grief, and even Trollope admitted two months later, "I saw the *very pattern of that dress* some time after the picture came out."[13] The epigraph of the picture, "Was it not a lie?" became thematic in the latter part of the novel, and Lucy and her husband recur to it with some emphasis in the very last pages, perhaps because Millais' illustration had so impressed itself on Trollope's mind.

From that time on, he expressed nothing but delight with Millais' illustrations. "As a good artist, it was open to him simply to make a pretty picture, or to study the work of the author from whose writing he was bound to take his subject. . . . In every figure that he drew it was his object to promote the views of the author." Millais became his favorite illustrator, and by Trollope's calculation drew altogether eighty-seven illustrations for his tales.[14]

Framley Parsonage was the first Trollope novel to come out in segments and the first to be illustrated. Of the thirty-seven novels he published thereafter (not counting *Castle Richmond,* which was overlapped by *Framley Parsonage*), sixteen were illustrated and all but three were published serially in parts or in a journal.

ভ়

The *Cornhill* in its early years had a general policy of anonymity for its prose works (Tennyson and Matthew Arnold could sign their poems from the outset), a policy that was only gradually modified. And therefore the authorship of *Framley Parsonage* was subject to some speculation among the uninformed. Smith was obliged on one occasion to disabuse the fond father of a young lady in the West Country who had claimed to all her friends and relatives that she was the authoress. Needless to say, the claim became a subject of amusement in the Trollope family: when in September an elaborate traveling case mysteriously arrived at Waltham House, apparently a gift, Rose suggested, "It's the lady who said she wrote your book intending to make you some amends."[15]

The novel is more closely integrated in its characters and plot with the other Barchester novels than *Doctor Thorne* had been, and also with the later parliamentary series through the Duke of Omnium, the Marchioness of Hartletop, and their crowd. Mrs. Proudie is once more at her best. Trollope seems to have been especially fond of his creation of Miss Dunstable, no-nonsense heiress whose patent-medicine fortune had attracted young men of social position but short means in *Doctor Thorne.* Toward the end of that earlier novel he tells us that some ill-natured gossips "contrived to spread the report that Dr. Thorne, jealous of [his niece's] money, was going to marry [Miss Dunstable]." Was this merely a random remark that he later remembered and made use of, or was he already planning the event with which *Framley Parsonage* concluded?

Tom Trollope's wife Theodosia thought *Framley Parsonage* Anthony's best novel and Tom was inclined to agree, though he had not yet been able to pry *Castle Richmond* away from his mother.[16] The book shows remarkable variety, from the tragic figure of the Reverend Josiah Crawley of Hogglestock (a development from Mr. Quiverful of Puddingdale, without the overtone of farce implicit in those names) to the hilarious scene of Mrs. Proudie's righteously interrupting a pompous lecture by an ambitious politician and to the high comedy of the drawing-room encounter between the disreputable Whig Duke of Omnium and the rigidly moral Tory Lady Lufton. The innocent but socially ambitious vicar of Framley comes close to disaster through guaranteeing a loan of unspecified amount taken by a member of an ancient Barsetshire family, Nathaniel Sowerby.

Many years earlier, perhaps while Anthony and Tom were in lodgings together in London, Tom had rescued a friend who had fallen victim to the same swindle, and, having signed two blank notes, was later confronted with them in the possession of a man he had never seen, with the figures filled in to very large amounts. [17] Sowerby himself, a generous good fellow who has lived a carefree life of debt, faces ruin as the creditors close in, but both he and the vicar are rescued, though Sowerby only to the extent he deserved. (The moving description of the bailiffs' invasion of the vicarage to catalogue the contents for auction, with the family in misery in the study [chap. xliv], may carry some remembrance of what occurred in Trollope's own family home at Harrow, though the passive, affectionate sympathy of the vicar's wife was very unlike the energetic measures taken by Mrs. Trollope to thwart the invaders.) The young Lord Lufton falls in love with the vicar's sister, a heroine in every way, but the marriage is sternly opposed by his mother, the patroness of Framley; her honest change of heart at the end is foreshadowed early in the novel when she goes from her home to the vicarage to apologize to the vicar's wife for giving her an undeserved rebuke. Like *Barchester Towers* with its occasional epic tone, this novel plays on the mock-heroic with the classic battles of the gods and the giants in Parliament (chap. v), and there are, as in the former novel, occasional Addisonian essays on social life such as the humorous contrast between the dinner party and the "conversazione" (sherry party or cocktail party in our twentieth century) (chap. xvii). "I wish Mr. Trollope would go on writing Framley Parsonage for ever," wrote Mrs. Gaskell to George Smith. "I don't see any reason why it should come to an end, and every one I know is always dreading the *last* number." [18]

The popularity of Trollope's tale led to solicitations to write for other magazines that sprang up in imitation of the *Cornhill*. As *Framley Parsonage* drew to an end, Mrs. S. C. Hall asked him to join the staff of contributors to her new *St. James's Magazine,* but he was obliged to decline. [19] When pressed, he did send his essay on "The National Gallery," which appeared in the September, 1861, number. Then the proprietor of *Temple Bar,* which began eleven months after the *Cornhill,* in August, 1861, asked an old friend of Trollope's family to approach him about taking over the nominal editorship from Sala, at £1,000 a year for three or five years, including a novel. "All the real work of Editorship will be performed as heretofore by Mr. Edmund Yates, who would act with you as Subeditor." Trollope replied "that I would put my name to nothing as to which I did not do what my name imported that I would do, and that I was too busy to undertake the work." When the story reached the newspapers, the amount of the offer had been doubled in the report, and a fellow Post Office surveyor in some amusement told Trollope he would be

glad to lend *his* name to the proprietors for £100, since surveyors' salaries
did not seem to be on the rise.[20]

ॐ

Trollope's new postal district was essentially Essex, Suffolk, Norfolk,
Cambridge, and Huntingdonshire, with the eastern edge of Bedfordshire
and Hertfordshire on a line that included Biggleswade, Hitchin, Hatfield,
and Barnet. The first novel he began after his transfer, *Orley Farm,* was set
in his new district, and so too were many subsequent ones, including a
large portion of *The Way We Live Now.* Place-names like Clavering and
Ongar, in *The Claverings,* though not there used in their actual geographical sense, are drawn from the district, and so too is Belton of *The Belton
Estate.*[21]

Trollope's routine duties are reflected in the memoranda preserved in
the minute-books of the Post Office. A junior clerk in the Colchester post
office was suspended for a week for carelessness, on Trollope's report, and
warned to mend his ways. The postmaster at Yarmouth was reimbursed
for fitting up a temporary office. A new pillar-box was erected at Thetford
and the messenger's wages were raised two shillings a week for making
collections from it. On the other hand, two letter boxes requested by
postal patrons in Saffron Walden were disapproved by him and not erected. Rural postmen from Bury St. Edmunds whose walks were sixteen
miles daily had their wages increased from twelve to fourteen shillings a
week. An ancillary letter carrier at Bury was promoted to letter carrier and
stamper. Trollope proposed a new arrangement for the post town serving
Narborough and Pentney. The postmaster of Newmarket was required to
resign, but the new appointee, despite Trollope's recommendation, was
not granted an increased stipend. Rural deliveries in the neighborhood of
Enfield were rearranged on his plan, as were those for Ongar and the areas
round Romford and Brentwood. Several postmasters' salaries were increased, though in one instance a clerk's position was left vacant and the
postmaster was required to assume the duties.[22]

His replies to complaints and suggestions have augmented the stocks
of autograph collectors. He explained to the M.P. from Hertfordshire who
had forwarded a memorial from some constituents that a later hour for the
mail cart through Much Hadham to Bishop's Stortford would delay the
posts in the latter place and could not be granted. Lady Stradbroke had to
be told that the postmaster at Wangford, for whom she interceded, had
held office so long that he had regarded it as a right and absolutely
neglected his duties despite warnings, so that a new one had been appointed. Sir Bartle Frere's brother seemed to have no ground for complaint about a letter's taking two days from Diss to Kenninghall: it had

been posted too late in the afternoon. The rector of Skeyton was told that it would be too expensive to send a messenger to collect from a pillar-box he wanted erected in his parish. Trollope would call upon the vicar of Runham to ascertain the circumstances of his complaint. Captain Henry Byng, R.N. (of the family of the admiral executed *pour encourager les autres*) had written on behalf of Cook the mail cart contractor; but Cook had been going slower and slower, and so his contract had been canceled. If he should submit a new tender competitive with others, it would be accepted and the experience would be sure to speed him up.[23] One of Trollope's earliest moves in his new district brought him one of his earliest complaints. Seeing that there were more letters per day for East Bergholt than for Lawford, Trollope had reversed the circuit for delivery out of Manningtree so that it went to East Bergholt first and Lawford last. This was by no means satisfactory to the rector of Lawford, Charles Merivale, older brother of the John Merivale with whom Trollope had explored the abandoned mansion that inspired *The Macdermots*. The two had not met since Charles Merivale left Harrow in 1824, though Trollope on two occasions had reviewed parts of Merivale's *History of the Romans under the Empire* for the *Dublin University Magazine*. The present grievance served to renew the acquaintance. A few years later (1866), at Trollope's suggestion, Merivale joined him as a member of the committee of the Royal Literary Fund. But on postal matters Merivale continued to grumble: "The P. O. is constantly blundering, notwithstanding . . . the numerous complaints I make myself to Trollope about it," he wrote to his mother.[24] Merivale may have sympathized with the vicar of Bullhampton, who "carried on a perpetual feud with the Post-office authorities" because his village "unfortunately was at the end of the postman's walk, and as the man came all the way from Lavington, letters were seldom received much before eleven o'clock." It was the vicar's "great postal doctrine that letters ought to be rained from heaven on to everybody's breakfast-table exactly as the hot water is brought in for tea," and "being an energetic man, [he] carried on a long and angry correspondence with the authorities aforesaid" (chap. xxii).

や

Sir Rowland Hill was absent on prolonged sick leave when the *Times* on March 29–30, 1860, published a long article on the shortcomings of the Post Office, especially in the metropolitan area, and urged a parliamentary inquiry. "Want of room, want of improved system, and want of a properly paid and efficient staff, are fast giving rise to such disorganization as almost calls for the interference of the Legislature." The accusations were that the Post Office regarded itself as a source of revenue, not as a service, and that the lower staff—the people who actually handled the letters—were underpaid and overworked. Tilley, as assistant secretary, instantly requested comments from the responsible officers, and at the suggestion of William Bokenham, controller of the Circulation Department, recommended to Lord Elgin, the postmaster general, appointment of a committee from the Post Office to examine the charges; Bokenham and Thomas Boucher of the Circulation Department, Frank Ives Scudamore, the receiver and accountant general, R. Parkhurst of the Secretary's Department, and Trollope were named on April 2. Group after group of Post Office workers filed petitions to be heard by the committee, and the unrest grew to a point where Tilley needed reassurance from Boucher that it would not reach the proportions of a strike.[25]

But Sir Rowland Hill in his seclusion saw matters slipping out of his control. First of all (obviously after consultation with him) his brother Frederic, an assistant secretary nominally on a par with Tilley but several years his junior in appointment, instructed the committee "not to take any steps which they have any reason to believe would not be approved by both the Assistant Secretaries, without first reporting the case for instructions." Instantly the committee resigned. Tilley furiously asserted his seniority to F. Hill and urged that the resignations not be accepted. Three days later (April 24) Sir Rowland suspended the committee. Fears of the workers' discontent then became urgent, and on April 30 Sir Rowland instructed the committee to get back to work, under certain restrictions. The committee insisted that it would not do so without assurance that its inquiry might be unfettered, and Frederic Hill responded that unless they took up their task they would be regarded as disobeying their chief's orders. Trollope's signature of course appears on each statement issued by the committee in this interchange.

The committee of inquiry was then reconstituted to include two representatives of the Treasury, which after all would have to approve any measures that involved salaries; Boucher stepped down but Trollope remained. Bokenham in a printed flyer assured the employees that the committee would begin its investigation without delay and warned that they must abstain from "any proceedings tending to agitation, or inconsistent with the rules of the Department, in respect of the form in which their representations should be brought before" their superiors. Deliberations of the committee began on May 16, and in seventeen sessions over the next seven weeks the committee examined 116 witnesses, 92 of them delegates of the postal employees' groups who had signed memorials to the committee. One of the many complaints was the system of spying on suspected pilferers and entrapment through marked currency. Trollope moved from the committee table to the witness's chair to describe the system of "restrictive sorting" whereby all the contents of a single letter box went through the hands of only four people in the post office, so that responsibility could be fixed without espionage. On July 21 the committee completed its twenty-seven-page report, with recommendations for significant improvements in salary scale for the lower employees, and accompanied it with a printed transcript of evidence and memorials that ran to 242 folio pages. Sir Rowland urged the postmaster general of the new government, Lord Stanley of Alderley, to let all but the least complex of the committee's proposals wait for adoption until his return from his leave of absence.

Sir Rowland in fact regarded the committee and its operations as a "cabal" against him. From his Hampstead home on January 16, 1861, he sent a long and severe stricture on the work of the committee, with some bitter personal remarks on Tilley, whom he blamed for the entire inquiry and accused of thereby letting the discipline of the service collapse.[26] The committee was reconvened to reply to Hill on February 28; Tilley defended himself, and Lord Stanley of Alderley affirmed that it was not Tilley but the postmaster general who had the responsibility for naming and commissioning the body (a bit of fiction, of course; the postmaster general acted on Tilley's advice).

Meanwhile, on January 4 Trollope gave a public lecture at the General Post Office on "The Civil Service as a Profession" and the lecture was fully reported in the newspapers next day. It was an open challenge to Hill on one issue:

> If any plan could enable a job-loving [favoritizing] senior to withstand the spirit of the age and put unfairly forward his special friends, it was the system of promotion by merit as at present sanctioned.*. . . . I trust we shall live to see it overthrown, or rather to overthrow it—(cheers). . . . The question should not have been decided for us without an expression of the opinion of the profession in general. (Cheers.) Such an expression might easily have been elicited; but that had not been done, and an enormous change had been made affecting all our worldly interests with an importance that could not be exaggerated. And that change had been made without any attention to the wishes of the profession and so made in accordance with the Utopian theories of a very few men.

Now one of Sir Rowland's proudest accomplishments was (in the words of his nephew's article on him in the *Dictionary of National Biography*) that "by establishing promotion by merit he had breathed fresh life into every branch of the service." And so Hill informed Trollope that the postmaster general had expressed disapproval of the lecture (the disapproval of course put into his mouth by Hill).[27]

---

*Merit, that is, as distinguished from seniority.

Then Trollope published the lecture in the February number of the *Cornhill.* Hill first told Tilley that, though its publication in a time of latent insubordination in the secretary's office might be incendiary, he did not blame Tilley for not rebuking Trollope, "considering his position with reference to Trollope." He then asked Lord Stanley of Alderley to censure Trollope officially, but Stanley confessed that Trollope had shown him the article in proofs a fortnight earlier, and so he was in no position to speak. More than a year later Hill wrote in his diary:

> Matthew [Hill] has had a correspondence with Trollope. T. takes the opportunity of speaking highly of me, and of defending his own conduct. Don't believe in T's sincerity—no man both clever and honest could be a party to the elaborate misrepresentations in the two Reports of the committee on the Circulation office, and as T. is undoubtedly clever, it follows in my opinion that he is dishonest.— E[dward] Page to whom I mentioned the circumstance assures me, also in confidence, that T. has recently spoken of me in his presence, in a manner quite inconsistent with his present professions.[28]

The issue of promotion by merit was resolved, even before Sir Rowland retired, in accordance with Trollope's views. Tilley agreed with him at least insofar as assenting to the proposition that the superior officers could have little opportunity of assessing in detail the respective merits of a large number of the employees in the lower ranks. Tilley and Trollope on April 26, 1860, had testified together before a parliamentary select committee on Civil Service appointments (an appearance that had been deferred three days because of the urgency surrounding the constitution of the Post Office's committee of inquiry). Their testimony was largely concerned with Trollope's old bugaboo of the inappropriateness of the Civil Service Commission's examinations to the posts that the examinees were to fill.* But the other matter was very much in everyone's mind. The promotion on April 10 of two clerks to higher ranks over the heads of three (in one case) and six (in the other) men senior to them led to a memorial to the postmaster general in protest, signed by a large number of clerks in three departments; the memorial was one of those placed before the committee of inquiry. The postmaster general requested that heads of departments be canvassed for their opinions, and Trollope on June 13 replied briefly: "Excepting always Staff appointments, . . . I think that all promotion should go by seniority, *and as a matter of right,* a certificate of general competence being only required." Tilley's advice to

---

*Sir Stafford Northcote and Monckton Milnes were members of the committee, which expressed special pleasure with Trollope's testimony.

the postmaster general led to the formulation of a policy that directly contravened Hill's convictions: at the lower levels, promotion would be by seniority, provided the competence of a man for the new level was assured; for the higher positions, promotion by merit was to be maintained. "'Promotion by merit' looks well on paper," Tilley wrote, ". . . but I believe that, if it be adhered to, you will in a few years, have an amount of dissatisfaction and indifference in your Public Offices that will be very difficult to contend with. Even in the higher grades of the service it is sometimes nearly impossible to decide who is positively the best man."[29]

The question arose once more three years later; heads of departments were again canvassed to see if they retained their former opinions, and Trollope once again (May 24, 1863) affirmed his conviction, this time at greater length: "I feel very sure that the system of promotion by merit, as it is called, cannot in truth be carried out, and that it is injurious to the service. . . . The system demands that promotion shall be given to the best man, let the merits of those who are to be superseded be what they may,—and let the years of service and well-grounded expectations of the senior candidates be also what they may." No matter how long a man has worked, giving his best services; no matter that he may have married on the assured conviction of his promotion; no matter that he is perfectly fit for a higher place, he may lose it all if someone better come along at the last minute. "No amount of excellence is safe, because a greater amount of excellence must always be possible."

> To know whether a man be absolutely fit or unfit for certain duties is within the capacity of an observant and intelligent officer;—but it is frequently altogether beyond the capacity of any officer however intelligent and observant to say who is most fit. Zeal recommends itself to one man, intelligence to a second, alacrity to a third, punctuality to fourth, and superficial pretense to a fifth. There can be no standard by which the excellence of men can be judged as is the weight of gold.

And what of the good men who are cruelly passed over under this system? "The man who is competent and has exerted himself and is yet passed over, cannot but be broken-hearted; and from a broken-hearted man no good work can be obtained."[30]

ॐ

Waltham House is described by one of Trollope's long-standing friends and frequent guests, Sir Frederick Pollock, as "an old-fashioned red-brick

house of about William the Third's time, with a good staircase and some
large rooms in it, and standing in equally old-fashioned grounds." Besides
the main part of the house there were two wings, one for the stables in
which he kept his hunters, the other serving as an office for the Post Office
clerks who worked under him.[31] Trollope described Rose's responsibilities there to an American friend: "She has a house, and children &
cows & horses and dogs & pigs—and all the stern necessities of an English
home." The rural delights were later recalled by a friend who was a guest
there more than a decade later. "At Waltham House, . . . among his
cows, and roses, and strawberries, [Trollope] delighted to welcome at his
quiet dinner-table some half-dozen of intimate friends. Those who were
occasional guests there remember how, in the warm summer evenings,
the party would adjourn after dinner to the lawn, where wines and fruit
were laid out under the fine old cedar-tree, and many a good story was
told while the tobacco-smoke went curling up into the soft twilight."[32]

One of the delights of Irish life for Trollope had been riding to the
hounds, and this he kept up regularly during the season in England. The
experience of "Pollock, the heavyweight sporting literary gentleman" in
Can You Forgive Her, was too often his own. Pollock chose the gate rather
than the difficult jumps, and though the ground was easy riding, his poor
horse labored and grunted sorely, so that Pollock began desperately to
hope that the fox would quickly be caught while he could still be in at the
finish. But "the pace soon became too much for the good author. His
horse at last refused a little hedge, and there was not another trot to be got
out of him. That night Pollock turned up . . . about nine o'clock, very
hungry,—and it was known that his animal was alive;—but the poor
horse ate not a grain of oats that night, nor on the next morning."[33] "We
had a wretched day of it today," Trollope told a friend in March, 1861,
"ploughing about thro the mud & rain—all day in the woods—our great
success was the digging out of one fox. The run was 10 minutes—The
digging out 50."[34] Nevertheless he enjoyed the sport.

Waltham House quickly became the center of the sort of hospitality
Trollope loved to dispense and to receive. Dinner guests were always
welcome to spend the night if there was no urgent need for them to return
to London. The Boston publisher James T. Fields (who was then bringing
out Hawthorne's *Marble Faun* in America while Smith was publishing it
in London) was the occasion of a Waltham House dinner party on May 19,
1860, at which Tom Trollope and Smith were guests, and Fields communicated a letter of February 11 from Hawthorne:

> It is odd enough that my own individual taste is for quite another
> class of works than those which I myself am able to write. If I were to
> meet with such books as mine by another writer, I don't believe I

should be able to get through them. Have you ever read the novels of
Anthony Trollope? They precisely suit my taste,—solid and substantial, written on the strength of beef and through the inspiration
of ale, and just as real as if some giant had hewn a great lump of earth
and put it under a glass case, with all its inhabitants going about
their daily business, and not suspecting that they were being made a
show of. And these books are just as English as a beef-steak. Have
they ever been tried in America? It needs an English residence to
make them thoroughly comprehensible; but still I should think that
human nature would give them success anywhere.[35]

Hawthorne's enthusiasm is that of a new convert; only a year and a half
earlier he had not read a line of Trollope's. He was in England at the
moment but could not return to London at Fields's urging to meet Trollope, and sailed for New York almost at once.[36]

At just this time Edward FitzGerald told a friend that he was awaiting a box of books from Mudie's Library that would, he hoped, include
some novels of Trollope. "I am glad to go into Society so easily as one does
in a good Novel. Trollope's are very good, I think: not perfect, but better
than a narrower Compass of perfection like Miss Austen's."[37]

Trollope's career as a London club man, which gave him such great
pleasure for the rest of his life, began when he asked Monckton Milnes to
put him forward for membership in the Cosmopolitan; he was elected in
mid-April the next year (1861). The Boston historian John Lothrop
Motley describes it as a "club which meets late in the evenings twice a
week, Sundays and Wednesdays, in a large room which is the studio of the
painter Phillips, in Charles Street, leading from Berkeley Square. The
object seems to be to collect noted people and smoke very bad cigars."[38] It
became the prototype for the Universe Club in *Phineas Redux*. When
Trollope had to spend the night in town he lodged in Garlant's (or
Garland's) Hotel, Suffolk Street—a cul-de-sac off Pall Mall East and close
to the stage door of the Haymarket Theatre. In *The Last Chronicle of Barset*
he describes it as "a certain quiet clerical hotel at the top of Suffolk Street,
much patronized by bishops and deans of the better sort," and Eleanor
Arabin stays there; so too does the dean of Brotherton in *Is He Popenjoy?*[39]

George Smith's ambitious and fertile mind devised a triple proposal:
that Trollope supply a short serial when *Framley Parsonage* was completed,
that he do another long serial, and that he go out to India and write a two-
volume book on that country, the last for £3,000, including three papers
on India for the *Cornhill*. For a moment this last caught Trollope's fancy.
"But [I] will not break my heart if the plan falls to the ground. Per se
going to India is a bore,—but it would suit me professionally." The
Indian project was abandoned, but Smith bought *Brown, Jones, and Robin-*

son for serialization in eight issues of the magazine at £75 per part, and Trollope set about completing that work.[40] India remained the one major part of the British Empire that Trollope did not visit and write about.

One of the warmest friends he made at the first *Cornhill* dinner was G. H. Lewes, with whom he was closely associated in literary projects for the next decade. In the spring Lewes and George Eliot went to Italy, and on their way home late in June picked up Lewes's son Charles, who had just finished his schooling at Hofwyl, near Bern. Lewes inquired of Trollope respecting a position for the lad in the Post Office, and Trollope within a week had secured for him from the postmaster general a nomination to a vacancy in the secretary's office, where Trollope had made his own start. The nomination was only a first step, since there were always more nominees than vacancies and the choice was made by competitive examination in handwriting, dictation in English (i.e., spelling), arithmetic through the "rule of three" (simple proportion), and composition. With a fatherly interest and some excitement at the notion that the young man would be following his own footsteps, Trollope warned him to cram for the examination. "The danger to young men educated on the continent is in spelling & in ordinary English idioms. My belief is that if you took the 12 most popular authors in England they would all be beaten. For myself I should not dream of passing. I sd. break down in figures & spelling too, not to talk of handwriting."[41] When the results were announced a month later, Charles Lewes was at the top of the list, and Trollope now helped with the technical advice that would give him seniority over the other young men appointed at the same time: he must be the first of the successful candidates to report to the secretary's office. A year and a half later, Trollope was lunching with the Leweses and learned that Charles was still in his original position in the missing letter branch. His parents had not been aware that this was unusual, but Trollope knew that something was wrong, made inquiry, and was told that the boy was well behaved and well disposed, but utterly failed in making himself useful; "He is careless & very slow; and will not exert himself," was the report.[42] This news was shocking to Lewes, but the couple's affection for the boy and Trollope's advice surmounted the problem; Charles won his first promotion the next year, secured normal advancements thereafter, and remained with the Post Office until 1886. Lewes in late 1860 returned Trollope's favor by securing information for him about Swiss schools in which he had some thought of placing Henry and Frederic (who, however, both remained at Bradfield College, near Reading, which they had entered early in the year).[43]

❧

Anthony's planned journey to Florence, with some travels in Holland en route, had to be deferred from the spring to the end of September because of the Post Office committees, and the "Dutch excrescence" (as Tom called it) was cut off for the time being. He reached Florence about October 1, 1860, went to Rome with Tom on the twelfth, but could not proceed to Naples because of the hostilities between the Garibaldian and the Neapolitan armies; they returned to Florence by the twenty-seventh.[44] Old Mrs. Trollope was by now very feeble indeed and could scarcely hold a pen in her hand. Anthony seems this year to have made more acquaintance with the British literary colony in Florence than formerly. The Brownings were in Rome, but returned to Florence before he left, and he called on them promptly, on October 11. Elizabeth had only recently recommended his books to her brother George; now she wrote (after a second visit from him), "Robert and I both consider him firstrate as a novelist—*Framley Parsonage* is perfect it seems to me— . . . I like both brothers very much. Anthony has an extraordinary beard to be grown in England, but is very English in spite of it, & simple, naif direct, frank—everything one likes in a man—anti-Napoleonist of course, & ignorant of political facts more than of course, & notwithstanding that, caring for *me*—which is strange, I admit."[45]

He came to know their friend Isa Blagden and actually, on his return to London, persuaded Smith to publish her novel *Agnes Tremorne,* which he had carried home with him.[46] He and Tom called on the eighty-five-year-old Walter Savage Landor, and Landor was moved to read his novels, "admiring them for their unaffected beauty of purpose and truth to nature." (Whether Landor actually said this is open to doubt; the judgment was published after his death by Kate Field, who knew that Anthony would see the remark.)[47] But the friend who most endeared herself to him was this lovely twenty-two-year-old Irish-American girl Kate Field, who was staying in Florence with her mother and had become a close friend of Tom and Theodosia. "[Trollope] is a very delightful companion. I see a great deal of him. He has promised to send me a copy of the 'Arabian Nights' (which I have never read) in which he intends to write 'Kate Field, from the Author,' and to write me a four-page letter on condition that I answer it." He kept his promise the instant he returned to London.[48] Kate indeed had thoroughly charmed all the English circle in Florence, including the Brownings and Landor, and only a few months earlier had read *The Three Clerks* and *The Bertrams.* Already she was a warm advocate of women's liberation, and it was probably her lively discourses on the subject that led Trollope to create the character of Mrs. General Talboys (as well as similar female American advocates in his later novels).

Trollope concluded *Framley Parsonage* with a chapter of marriages, in which he adopts a rather conventional cynical pose. If "the happiness of marriage is [not] like the Dead Sea fruit—an apple which, when eaten, turns to bitter ashes in the mouth," it certainly is the end of the romantic delights of life; "the bread and pudding of married life are then in store for [a man];—or perhaps only the bread and cheese." "As for feast of reason and for flow of soul, is it not a question whether any such flows and feasts are necessary between a man and his wife? How many men can truly assert that they ever enjoy connubial flows of soul, or that connubial feasts of reason are in their nature enjoyable?" G. H. Lewes protested against this view, and Trollope responded: "As to myself personally, I have daily to wonder at the continued run of domestic & worldly happiness which has been granted me;—to wonder at it as well as to be thankful for it. I do so, fearing that my day, also, of misery must come;—for we are told by so many teachers of all doctrines that pain of some sort is mans lot. But no pain or misery has as yet come to me since the day I married; & if any man should speak well of the married state, I should do so."[49] Lewes, who apparently had not previously met Rose, dined and spent a night at Waltham a few days later. "He has a charming house and grounds, and I like him very much, so wholesome and straightforward a man. Mrs. Trollope did not make any decided impression on me, one way or the other."[50]

↜

For Mr. Podsnap, in Dickens's *Our Mutual Friend,* "the question about everything was, would it bring a blush into the cheek of the young person?"[51] It was a question publishers often had to ask themselves, and there was a good deal of uncertainty about the answer. On July 29, 1860, Trollope told George Smith that he had within the last ten days completed a story set in Palestine, called "The Banks of the Jordan" (or, alternatively, "A Ride across Palestine"). Smith asked to see it, and within a week offered to publish it, but only on condition that certain passages be much modified for reasons of delicacy. The story was of an English youth who attached himself to the narrator in Jerusalem for a sightseeing tour of the Holy Land, since both were alone and there would be some economy as well as security in traveling together. The youth had assured the narrator that he could endure hardship; "as for sleeping accommodation, he did not care if he kept his clothes on for a week together." The lad withdrew to a distance and did not join in the stripped-down bathing in the Dead Sea or in the Jordan, and when, early in the journey, the awkward Turkish saddle chafed the insides of the youth's thighs unmercifully, and the narrator offered to massage the skin with brandy, the youth silently declined. An English-style saddle was luckily procured and the journey continued. But as the pair reached the port of Jaffa to embark for Alexandria, they were overtaken by a seventy-year-old English baronet who revealed that the youth was in fact his runaway *niece.* "The affair of the saddle," replied Trollope to Smith's demands, "and that other affair of the leg—(I think I said leg—) could be arranged; . . . but you city* publishers are so uncommonly delicate, whereas anything passes at the West End."[52] The story did not appear in the *Cornhill*.

Early in November, however, when Trollope was just returned to London from Italy, Smith found himself several pages short for the December number, and asked Trollope to do a story on the instant. Trollope promised; "Mrs. General Talboys" was completed in four days, Smith sent it to the printer without looking at it, and then, when he and Thackeray read it, promptly returned it; to Thackeray fell the duty of explaining. This story was of the wife of an English general, sojourning in Rome with only a twelve-year-old daughter, friendly with a group of artists and an enthusiastic spokesman for the freedom of women from conventional restraints, including that of marriage. One of the artists had quarreled with his wife and "comforted himself in his desolation"; Mrs. Talboys had seen the fruits of his "comfort in another love" and declared them "the children of innocence." Her language was so vigorous and enthusiastic that the same artist persuaded himself that she was inviting his familiarity, and proposed to elope with her to Naples. To everyone's surprise she was indignant at the "premeditated insult" of "the base-hearted churl [who] failed to understand the meaning of true honest sympathy, . . . the feelings of a true-hearted woman." But Trollope's representation of her language with respect to the illegitimate children had been too strongly sympathetic for his editor and publisher. Thackeray indeed was acquiring some skill in expressing *Cornhill*'s prudery; he wrote to Elizabeth Barrett Browning on April 2, 1861, to decline her "Lord Walter's Wife": "Our Magazine is written not only for men and women but for boys, girls, infants, sucklings almost; and one of the best wives, mothers, women in the world writes some verses which I feel certain would be objected to by many of our readers." Thereupon she good-naturedly sent him another poem in its place.[53] Trollope's reply to Thackeray was friendly, but "I will not allow that I am indecent, and profess that squeamishness—in so far as it is squeamishness and not delicacy—should be disregarded by a writer." He then gave quite enough instances of illegitimacy and impropriety in modern novelists to make his point, including Beatrix in *Henry Esmond* and an incident in *The Virginians;* "I am another, am I?" replied Thackeray. Trollope did, however, acknowledge that "pure morals must be supplied, and the owner of the responsible name must be the Judge of the purity."[54] The December *Cornhill* remained some pages short of its normal length.

---

*The Cornhill is a street in the City; the Marble Arch, which Trollope humorously said he should use as title for the magazine he would establish to publish the story, was in the West End.

But the end was not yet. Responding to a request from the proprietor of a weekly paper, the *London Review,* he sold eight stories of a second series of *Tales of All Countries* to that journal; the first two published were "The Banks of the Jordan" and "Mrs. General Talboys." The *London Review,* still in its first year, had hoped for great things from Trollope's name, but the outcry against these stories was prompt and loud. The "mildest" of the protesting letters affirmed: "I shall immediately destroy the supplements containing the two tales that have as yet come out and if they are continued I shall be compelled to give up the paper. . . . You must make your election whether you will adapt your paper to the taste of men of intelligence & high moral feeling or to that of persons of morbid imagination & *a low tone of morals."* The letter by which one of the proprietors conveyed that condemnation was inscribed by Trollope, "a wonderful letter," as indeed it was.[55] The remaining tales of this group were passed on to *Public Opinion,* where they appeared apparently without incident. (Without incident as to morality, that is. Before they could be turned over to the new publisher, the proprietor of the *London Review* was obliged to have them all recopied, at a cost to Trollope of about a guinea and a half.[56] Trollope rather thought the price was a bargain, and modern editors faced with the problem of making out his handwriting will understand why.)

Trollope was indeed not "squeamish," though there is little that would bring a blush into the young person's cheeks, partly because one must read very attentively to get the thrust of his sportiveness. The birth of Madeline Stanhope Neroni's daughter too soon after her marriage, in *Barchester Towers,* has been mentioned. Then there is the remark in *Doctor Thorne* that "of course Lady Arabella could not suckle the young heir herself. Ladies Arabella never can. . . . Nature gives them bosoms for show, but not for use" (chap. ii). And there is the back-of-the-hand remark on American prudery when in *The West Indies* he speaks of "screw boats—propellers as the Americans call them with their wonted genteel propriety."[57] These remarks are not prurient, but precisely in the same tone as "In her heart of hearts Mrs. Grantly hated Mrs. Proudie—that is, with that sort of hatred one Christian lady allows herself to feel towards another."[58] The Widow Greenow in *Can You Forgive Her?* condemns those women who "look as though matrimony itself were improper, and as if they believed the little babies were found about in the hedges and ditches. . . . You remember [the old song] 'The poker and tongs to each other belongs.' So they do, and that should be the way with men and women" (chap. lxiv). When she tells Farmer Cheesacre that a young woman's heart "is breaking beneath her stays," Trollope comments, "This almost improper allusion had quite an effect on Mr. Cheesacre's sensitive bosom" (chap. lxxviii).

Times changed. Seventeen years later Trollope was asked again to supply a story which might give a new weekly paper the same good start the editors of the *London Review* had hoped for in 1861. The editor of *Light,* Robert Buchanan (the man who, skulking behind a pseudonym, had written the savage attack on Rossetti's immorality in "The Fleshly School of Poetry") wrote, "I don't presume to dictate, but we strongly desire a tale with great sexual interest."[59] Trollope sold him "The Lady of Launay," which was perfectly unexceptionable, except, perhaps, that the hero and heroine traveled from Avranches in Normandy to Somersetshire without a chaperone, before their marriage—a journey passed over in silence. And in 1879 Trollope recorded in his life of Thackeray some of Thackeray's extempore verses which had stuck in the mind of an old friend:

> In the romantic little town of Highbury
> My father kept a circulatin' library; . . .
> Mamma was an inhabitant of Drogheda,
> Very good she was to darn and to embroider."

"There may, perhaps, have been a mistake in a line, but the poem has been handed down with fair correctness," remarked Trollope innocently. There was indeed a mistake in a line; as the poem came to Trollope, the final line above read: "Where my dear Pa fust met and enjoyed her."[60] Trollope was quietly turning the tables on Thackeray's ghost—or had the censors once more spoiled his fun?

Chapter IX

1861-62

With *Castle Richmond* completed on March 25, 1860, and *Framley Parsonage* on June 30, Trollope plunged into the writing of *Orley Farm* on July 4. He had already arranged for its publication in twenty monthly parts by Chapman and Hall, starting May 1, 1861, for a price of £2,500. Chapman consulted Smith, Elder, and they spoke confidently of its probable success as a serial.[1] Millais was engaged to do two illustrations for each part, and these, said Trollope, "are the best I have seen in any novel in any language." He urged that Millais go down to Harrow to see the farm house there, "Julian Hill," to use as an illustration for the first number; Millais did so.[2] Chapman soon decided that he would prefer to begin issuing the parts in March instead of May; since this might be held to conflict with the last two numbers of *Framley Parsonage* in the *Cornhill,* Smith's consent was sought and gladly given. And so publication began when the thirteenth number was not quite finished; the novel was not completed until June 22.

Down at the General Post Office in St. Martin's-le-Grand a series of public lectures was set up in the early months of 1861 to provide money for fitting out a new reading room for the Post Office Library and Literary Association, and inevitably Trollope was asked both to lecture and to recruit lecturers. He turned to his new friends from the *Cornhill;* Thackeray declined, but Lewes lectured on "Life from the Simple Cell to Man" on February 15 and Robert Bell spoke on "Shakspeare and His Times" on May 24. The first two lectures were by members of the Post Office staff who already had established literary reputations, Trollope himself "On the Civil Service as a Profession" (January 4) and Edmund Yates "On Good Authors at a Discount" (January 18). Other lecturers were Tom Trollope, Thomas Hughes, Thomas Hood, and Frank Ives Scudamore, the Post Office administrator who had the task of actually arranging the lectures.[3] As has been noted, Trollope's lecture was an open challenge to the program of "promotion by merit" advocated by Sir Rowland Hill, and much offended Hill, especially when it was given wide attention in the newspapers and was published in the *Cornhill Magazine.*[4] It is possible that Trollope's essay on "The National Gallery" was also written for this series, and scheduled for June 7, but it was not delivered.[5]

An invitation to dine with Lewes and George Eliot on July 4, and then take tea with the Carlyles in Cheyne Row, was one Trollope could not resist.[6] He had been all his life somewhat ambivalent toward Carlyle's writing; his style, Trollope later remarked, was (like that of Dickens, also parodied in *The Warden*) "created by himself in defiance of rules," yet "with this language, such as it is, the writer has satisfied the great mass of the readers of his country." Yet, alas! both these writers "have done infinite harm by creating a school of imitators."[7] Indeed, the publisher's reader for *The New Zealander,* as we have seen, accused Trollope himself of being such a "feeble" imitator. Lewes fancied that both the Carlyles liked Anthony,[8] but in fact his boisterous self-confidence seems to have been little to the taste of the master. Trollope of course told of his method of writing, and Carlyle replied that a man should neither read nor write on a train, but "sit still and label his thoughts." In March, 1864, Trollope again called on Carlyle. "Oh, heavens;—what a mixture of wisdom & folly flows from him!"[9] There was some subsequent exchange of civilities between them (since Trollope was later able to supply a friend with Carlyle's autograph[10] and apparently once asked Carlyle to give Jane his love). The last letter Carlyle wrote to Jane before her death—a letter from Scotland that never reached her—asked her to "write to 'trollope' . . . that I can't dine anywhere, and must not."[11] "Fat Trollope" was Carlyle's way of referring to him—"Fat Trollope (if you know Trollope and his fat commonplaces)," he wrote to Emerson on June 14, 1865.[12] And when Trollope reviewed Ruskin's *Sesame and Lilies* unfavorably in the new, liberal *Fortnightly Review* (which Carlyle loathed), Carlyle lashed out with a letter to Jane: "Trollope, in reviewing it with considerable insolence stupidity and vulgarity, produces little specimens far beyond any Trollope sphere of speculation. A distylish little pug, that Trollope; irredeemably imbedded in commonplace, and grown fat upon it, and prosperous to an unwholesome degree. Don't *you* return his love; nasty gritty creature, with no eye for 'the Beautiful, the' etc.,—and awfully 'interesting to himself' he be." William Dean Howells quotes Carlyle as saying "that Trollope could never lack for characters, so long as there were thirty millions of people in Great Britain, mostly bores."[13] As for Trollope's judgment of Carlyle at almost the same moment, it was that Carlyle's hard blows are harmless, for one has "the feeling that they are all struck in the dark, & may probably, after all, not be deserved."[14]

Back in May of 1847, Frances Trollope took Tom to the annual anniversary dinner of the Royal Literary Fund in London.[15] Fourteen years later her younger son was a steward at the anniversary dinner, and responded to the toast to "The Literature of England." (A "steward" was one who contributed a fixed sum in excess of the ordinary cost of a ticket for the dinner—usually three guineas instead of one—and who in addition was expected to bestir himself in the sale of tickets and in inducing monetary gifts from purchasers.) The Royal Literary Fund, started in the late eighteenth century and chartered in May, 1818, exists to offer temporary financial relief to "persons of genius and learning, or their families, who shall be in want" and who apply to it for assistance. The relief was in the form of a single gift, not a continuing pension, though an application might be renewed if further need occurred. Most of the recipients are now unknown, but among those assisted during the two decades Trollope was associated with the fund were Henry Mayhew, G. A. Sala, Thomas Hood, Julian Hawthorne, Henry Kingsley, and the widows of Mark Lemon and Shirley Brooks, successive editors of *Punch*. The anniversary dinner was the principal source of income for the fund, and on this occasion in 1861 Trollope's contribution of £13 10s. 0d. made him a life member of the corporation. He was enlisted as speaker and steward by Robert Bell, and at dinner on that occasion sat with Bell, Thackeray, E. S. Dallas, Frederick Pollock, and the publisher Frederic Chapman. For the rest of his life he was actively engaged in the affairs of the fund, which became one of his best-loved enterprises.[16]

"I now felt that I had gained my object. . . . I had created for myself a position among literary men, and had secured to myself an income on which I might live in ease and comfort—which ease and comfort have been made to include many luxuries. . . . Though the money has been sweet, the respect, the friendships, and the mode of life . . . have been much sweeter."[17]

ॐ

Trollope's brief visit to New York at the end of his West Indies mission whetted his appetite for more, especially since his mother's reputation had been so firmly fixed on the foundation of her *Domestic Manners of the Americans,* and the abandoned notion of a trip to India and a book thereon led him on March 20, 1861, to sign an agreement with Chapman and Hall for a book on North America, with an initial payment of £2,000.[18] Then came the need to request a leave of absence from his Post Office duties.

"There is, so far as I am aware, no precedent for such an application as the enclosed from Mr. Trollope, and I need not add that an absence of seven months on the part of a Surveyor is in many respects objectionable," wrote Sir Rowland Hill on April 9 in laying the request before the postmaster general, thereby setting in motion one of the most humiliating episodes in his conflict with Trollope. Hill proposed that, in consideration of Trollope's valuable service in Egypt and the West Indies, the leave might be granted "with the distinct understanding that the indulgence be considered a full compensation for the special services on which he rests his claim." Lord Stanley of Alderley, instead of merely initialing

Hill's memorandum, raised the question whether Trollope might help bring to a conclusion some of the current negotiations over postal arrangements between England and the United States, and whether indeed he might not gain valuable information for coming to an understanding with both North and South should the two finally be separated. "The employment of Mr. Trollope in the duties described above would be objectionable," replied Hill on April 12, and Stanley then initialed the original memorandum. [19]

It would appear that he had intended to approve the leave, but not the conditions Hill had stated; Hill took the initials as approving the entire memorandum and imposed those conditions. Trollope protested. On April 23 Stanley wrote to Hill:

> I consider that the valuable services rendered by Mr. Trollope to the Department, justified me in granting the leave requested, though somewhat out of the ordinary course. I never thought that Mr. Trollope made any claim for compensation, nor did I intend that the Leave now granted should be considered as such. Mr. Trollope's services discharged with Zeal Diligence & Ability will always give him that claim to consideration, which the exhibition of such Qualities must entitle any officer to expect from the PMG, and the leave now granted can in no respect be considered as diminishing such claims on the part of Mr. Trollope.

And so Trollope got his leave for seven months.

One must be aware of the normal relation between secretary and postmaster general to sense the force of the rebuff to Hill: the postmaster general conventionally did not reverse his secretary, and perhaps nowhere else in the minute-books has so firm a tone been taken, and at such length, against a secretary. It may be, though the evidence does not exist, that Tilley had intervened with Stanley behind Hill's back; Trollope himself indicates that before making the application at all in official form, he had laid his plan before the postmaster general, who, indeed, was a member of the Cosmopolitan Club to which Trollope was elected at just about this time. In any case Hill remembered the wound. "*Trollope* is suspected of neglecting his official duties to attend to his literary labours," he wrote in his journal on September 6, 1862 (after some earlier complaints that Trollope was reported to have disparaged the penny post in some remarks he made in America). "Engagement in connection with the Cornhill Magazine and another periodical whose name I do not recollect—numerous novels—Trip to the United States . . . and work thereon—In confirmation see in Athenaeum of this day letter from Trollope in which he speaks of earning 'his bread by writing'—as though literature were his 'profession' &c." (Trollope had written to the *Athenaeum* on the harm done to English authors by the American disregard of their copyrights.) It should be added that conflict with Lord Stanley of Alderley was one of the principal causes of Hill's retirement in 1864.[20]

Precisely at this point the open hostilities of the War of Secession began, and while Trollope was making his arrangements he read in the papers the account of the Confederate victory at Bull Run on July 21. As he wrote to Kate Field, whom he had asked for advice on accommodations in the States, and who was still in Florence but soon to return to America, the defeat of the Federal armies made compromise impossible and presaged a long bloodshed.[21]

ॐ

The Cunarder *Arabia* left Liverpool on August 24 with Rose and Anthony aboard; after touching at Halifax on September 3, it delivered them to Boston at seven o'clock on the morning of the fifth. He was well provided with letters of introduction to Americans, and on the very day of his arrival went out to Quincy to call on William Barlow Lee, whose lovely lawn he admired. The next day he dined with the Unitarian minister Dr. Samuel Kirkland Lothrop, who knew his friend W. W. F. Synge; Senator Charles Sumner and Charles Homans were of the company. He was back in Quincy the day after this, to dine with Charles Francis Adams, son of John Quincy Adams and a successor to his father in the United States House of Representatives. Meanwhile the publisher James T. Fields was gathering some of the great literary figures for a dinner with Trollope on his return from a visit to Newport with Rose.[22]

Newport was a disappointment. Although the summer had not yet gone, their huge hotel, the Ocean House, with accommodation for six hundred guests, had in fact only about twenty-five. Since smoking was forbidden in the only attractive common room, the men slipped away to the bar to "liquor up" or to the "comfortless reading room among a deluge of American newspapers" to smoke, leaving their dozen or so wives forlorn, "on various sofas at terrible distances,—all strangers" in a room designed to accommodate two hundred. The children dined with their parents, even at the age of three or four! The hotel itself was out of sight of the ocean and half a mile from the sandy bathing spot, where men and women bathed together and therefore had to wear decorous costumes. "My idea of sea-bathing for my own gratification is not compatible with a full suit of clothing. I own that my tastes are vulgar and perhaps indecent, but I love to jump into the deep clear sea from off a rock, and I love to be hampered by no impediment as I do so." A day of horseback riding the length of the island was a waste of time: the scenery was nothing remarkable and the horses were poor; "that which my wife rode was altogether ignorant of the art of walking." They did see Mary Knower, an American girl whom they had entertained at Waltham Cross after Anthony met her and her mother on shipboard on his way home from New York in 1859.[23]

The dinner at Fields's house on Charles Street, Boston, took place on September 16; Emerson and Hawthorne came in from Concord, James Russell Lowell from Cambridge, and Oliver Wendell Holmes from his house a few doors down the street. Lowell thought the guest of honor "a big, red-faced, rather underbred Englishman of the bald-with-spectacles type. A good roaring positive fellow who deafened me . . . till I thought of Dante's Cerberus." He sat on Trollope's right, then came Emerson, then Holmes; Holmes teased Trollope with paradoxes to which Trollope replied vigorously and loudly, while Lowell and Emerson crouched down out of the line of fire and had some very good talk of their own. It was clearly one of those occasions that are pleasant at the time, but rather tedious in the description, especially since there was so much debate on the relative merits of the customs and food of the two countries. Hawthorne sat opposite, and when appealed to on the comparative excellence of English and American peaches, remarked, "I asked an Englishman once who was praising their peaches to describe to me exactly what he meant by a peach, and he described something very like a cucumber." No doubt Trollope had this remark in the back of his mind when he wrote of a similar debate in Dubuque, where he ate the best apple he ever encountered, but would not concede to his American hosts that English peaches had no flavor. "My idea had been that good peaches were to be got in England only. I am beginning to doubt whether my belief on the matter has not been the product of insular ignorance, and idolatrous self-worship. It may be that a peach should be a combination of an apple and a turnip." "I rather liked Trollope," said Lowell ultimately, and, according to Fields, "Trollope fell in love with [Hawthorne] at first sight and . . . swears [he is] the handsomest Yankee that ever walked this planet."[24] Two years later Trollope read Hawthorne's travel sketches of England, *Our Old Home,* as he was writing *Can You Forgive Her?* and denied that his Lady Monk, though a woman of about fifty, was "verging to that state of body which our excellent American friend and critic Mr. Hawthorne has described as beefy and has declared to be the general condition of English ladies of Lady Monk's age.[25] Lady Monk was not beefy" (chap. xxxiii). Hawthorne did not live to read this tribute.

The day after this literary dinner party Anthony and Rose left for Portland, Maine, whence they traveled through the White Mountains and on into Lower Canada. Canada was then administratively in a period of transition: Upper and Lower Canada (i.e., Ontario and Quebec) had been united, and a new capital city was being built at Ottawa (which Anthony and Rose visited), but the Maritime Provinces of Nova Scotia, New Brunswick, and Prince Edward Island had not yet been united with them, nor had the territories west of Ontario. Their tour took them to Quebec, where they dined with the governor, Sir Edmund Walker Head, then to Sherbrooke, Montreal, Ottawa, Toronto, and Niagara Falls. From Buffalo they went westward across Canada and then through Detroit, Grand Haven, Milwaukee, and La Crosse to St. Paul, encountering encampments of recruits for the war. At the Mississippi Hotel in St. Paul Trollope "saw an immense lot of luggage in the hall, which I was told belonged to a young lord who was going to be skinned by the wild Indians between that place and the Rocky Mountains"; the young lord turned out to be Viscount Milton, grandson of the Earl Fitzwilliam who was a friend of Rose's father at Rotherham. Milton and his companion W. B. Cheadle were gathering materials for their book on *The North-West Passage by Land,* and were in fact not skinned; five years later it fell to Trollope to propose Milton's health at the dinner of the Royal Literary Fund. And twenty years later the Earl of Knocknacoppul's daughter (in *Marion Fay*) was unable to put off her marriage because the Irish baronet, her fiancé, "says that if she delays any longer he'll go on a shooting expedition to the Rocky Mountains, and then perhaps he might never come back."[26]

A broken paddle wheel on the steamer downriver to Dubuque gave Trollope a chance to step ashore and visit some of the woodcutters' cabins; he was hospitably received by the families and went away much impressed with their cheerfulness, their affectionate relationship with their children, their hospitality, and the books and newspapers in evidence, including "Harper's everlasting magazine."[27] The journey then took them eastward through Chicago, Cleveland, Buffalo, Utica, and West Point to New York City. Naturally Trollope stopped at the great post office in Chicago to talk to the postmaster, and they took a day to visit Trenton Falls, near Utica, which Anthony's father had visited with Tom, and his mother later visited with his two sisters.[28] West Point was included both for its beauty and because a knowledge of the military academy would be needed for the book he was writing, and in New York City he inspected as many of the "institootions" as he could—"schools, hospitals, lunatic asylums, institutes for deaf and dumb, water works, historical societies, telegraph offices, and large commercial establishments . . . in a thorough and conscientious manner." And they also made the acquaintance of the historian George Bancroft.[29]

The streetcars in New York (horse drawn, of course) were Anthony's special bane: he never quite learned how his fare was to be paid, he always dropped his change on the straw-covered floor, and he never could see through the foggy windows the street names that would tell him where to dismount. The payment of fares was complicated by the fact that if two or three women entered the car at the same time with him, they would hand him their coins and expect him to make the transaction on their behalf.

There was another act of chivalry they demanded on a crowded car. "[A woman] looks square at you in the face, and you rise to give her your seat. . . . She takes the place from which you have moved without a word or a bow. She twists herself round, banging your shins with her wires [hooped skirts], while her chin is still raised, and her face is still flattened, and she directs her friend's attention to another seated man, as though that place were also vacant, and necessarily at her disposal." Two decades later, Matthew Arnold in Boston managed things better. According to newspaper reports, as he sat on a crowded car he asked a lady swinging from a strap in front of him how far it was to the Hotel Vendome, and when she told him, remarked, "Good; I'll get off there and then you can have this seat."[30]

The Trollopes had hoped to find Kate Field in New York, but in vain. Through James Fields they got her address—in Boston, as it turned out—and Trollope urged her to come up to their hotel there (the Tremont House) on the evening of their return, November 12. Ten days later she accompanied them to hear Edward Everett deliver his lecture on "The Causes and Conduct of the Civil War" at Roxbury; Anthony found himself "honoured by being placed on the platform among the bald-headed ones and the superlatively wise." He thought Everett a splendid orator— or rather a splendid actor—but observed that he was careful to say only what his audience wanted to hear, though it was not what he himself had advocated only a few short years before. "The lecture gave me a poor idea of Mr. Everett as a politician." It contrasted with another lecture he had heard on the very night of his arrival (perhaps also with Kate): Everett "was neither bold nor honest, as Emerson had been." Emerson's lecture on "American Nationality" drew some three thousand people to the Tremont Temple on November 12; it lacked all emotional appeals to the flag, all mysticism and platonism, and was straightforward, sound, and sensible. It provided Trollope with one remark he thought "in itself worth an hour's attention": "Your American eagle is very well. Protect it here and abroad. But beware of the American peacock." Four years later he quoted the remark to Carlyle, who repeated it with pleasure to Emerson.[31]

Boston was a city of lectures; on the twenty-seventh he and Kate heard a rabid abolitionist discourse from Wendell Phillips, who appeared unwell and had constantly to be urged by his audience to speak louder. He was especially offensive to Trollope by his constant disparagement of the British: "It was a well-known fact," he asserted, "that Lord Palmerston was hostile to [Americans]. Nothing but hidden enmity,—enmity hidden or not hidden,—could be expected from England." The language was so irresponsible that "after that I heard no more political lectures in Boston."[32] But he did accompany Kate Field to hear the spiritualist poetess Elizabeth Doten—amusing to hear, dull to read. He cautioned

Kate that she was running after false gods in running from one such lecture to another, "seeking the excitement of ultra ideas and theoretical progress, while you begrudge the work of your brain, and the harder work of your fingers and backbone. Those lectures are but an intellectual idleness, an apology for sitting without a book to read or a skirt to hem or a shirt to fell. . . . You want to go ahead of other folks,—you know you do; but you wish to do it lazily."[33]

Boston's "institutions" also came under his scrutiny, including the seven-year-old Boston Public Library with its free circulation of books to all of the city's 200,000 inhabitants. "Of course I asked whether a great many of the books were not lost, stolen, and destroyed; and of course I was told that there were no losses, no thefts, and no destruction." It did not diminish Trollope's admiration for the library to be told that his own "productions were in constant demand."[34]

ᔐ

Rose sailed for home on Wednesday, November 27, and the second half of Trollope's investigation of America began. There were a few more visits to make in New England—to Emerson and Hawthorne at Concord, to Longfellow in Cambridge, to the factories at Lowell. He dined as Emerson's guest at the Saturday Club on the last day of the month, and once more was in the literary company he loved. Then he went to New York, to Philadelphia (where he saw one of the Biddles and William Bradford Reed), to Baltimore (where he met John Pendleton Kennedy and visited the army camps and barracks), and to Washington, where he stayed for a month in a private lodging house conducted by a colored man named Wormley at 305 I Street N.W., not far from the Capitol, a place obtained for him by William Barlow Lee and one he was very pleased with.[35]

Washington itself, however, did not please him in this wartime winter weather, where all was a sea of mud churned up by thousands of troops and where the town was still far from completion, where maps showed streets but the eyes could see only fields. He was eager to get into the secession states, but the farthest he could go was to George Washington's house at Mount Vernon. For a large part of his month he was plagued with a carbuncle on his forehead, which at first confined him to his house, and which had to undergo a surgeon's knife from time to time. Nevertheless he worked as hard as he could at gathering materials for his book; "I have seen most of the bigwigs here except the President," he told Kate Field early in January, and he interviewed the secretary of the treasury on the government's scheme for financing the war.[36] To James

Fields he reported, "I am dining out & *teaing* out, & doing a deal of talk, but somehow the place is dull to me. I don't care for such convivialities if the people are merely strangers." Richard Henry Dana, the lawyer-author who had written *Two Years Before the Mast* and whose book *To Cuba and Back* was published almost simultaneously with Trollope's *The West Indies*, had failed in an attempt to invite the Trollopes in Cambridge, but succeeded with Anthony in Washington, where his initial verdict after entertaining him at breakfast was that Trollope was "intolerable, no manners, but means well, & would do a good deal to serve you, but says the most offensive things—not a gentleman." Dana did, however, earn Trollope's gratitude by reading in manuscript chapters of *North America* and using his legal expertise to help Trollope avoid errors based on his misunderstandings of American laws and customs.[37]

The hostility of the orators and the newspapers toward England was intensified by the navy's interception of the British mail vessel *Trent* on November 8 and removing from it two Confederate envoys to London, who were then taken to Boston. There was no conceivable legal ground for such seizure, but the bold, decisive step by Captain Charles Wilkes was so popularly applauded as to make it difficult for the federal government to concede the release of the men at the request of the British Government. In Washington there was less anti-British sentiment than there had been in New England, but the situation was still uncomfortable. British subjects were warned by their embassy to be ready to depart at a moment's notice. "A man-of-war did come to the Potomac, ready to take away Lord Lyons [the English Minister to Washington] and his suite. In Washington, we heard that on the next day war was to have been declared,—unless Mr. Lincoln and Mr. Seward yielded." "I dined with Mr. Seward on the day of the decision [December 27], meeting Mr. Sumner at his house, and was told as I left the dining-room what the decision had been" (the decision, that is, to return the envoys to the British).[38] And so Trollope could continue with his tour of America. He actually met Captain Wilkes, and recalled the encounter without pleasure. "Abuse of England is, no doubt, a prevalent topic of conversation in the Northern States," he remarked in his lecture on the American Union; "but such conversation has never been pursued in my hearing, after it was known that I was an Englishman. Never,—with but one exception. The sole transgressor was that Commodore Wilkes who gained such immortal glory by his valour in the *Trent* affair!"[39]

He went westward as far as St. Louis and Rolla, now in the borderland between loyalty and rebellion, visiting Union camps, talking to officers and men and to civilians. Of course he went to Cincinnati, where he was shown the building erected for his mother's "bazaar." "I was assured by the present owner [that it] was at the time of its erection considered to be the great building of the town. It has been sadly eclipsed now, and by no means rears its head proudly among the great blocks around it. It had become a 'Physico-medical Institute' when I was there, and was under the dominion of a quack doctor on one side, and of a college of rights-of-women female medical professors on the other. 'I believe, sir, no man or woman ever yet made a dollar in that building,' [remarked the owner]." Mrs. Trollope's name was still remembered in the states; indeed Rose was obliged to protest to someone who saw the name tag on her luggage that she was *not* that Mrs. Trollope, and a newspaper correspondent at the army headquarters in Rolla asked Anthony, "Air you a son of the Mrs. Trollope? . . . Then, sir, you are an accession to Rolla."[40]

Although Trollope was astonished by the way in which life went on much as usual, apart from the visible works of the military, he was much moved also by one circumstance in the border states of Maryland, Kentucky, Missouri, all slave states that had not seceded but whose populations were divided in their sympathies. There in Baltimore, for example, "beneath [the Federal] artillery, were gentlemen hotly professing themselves to be secessionists, men whose sons and brothers were in the southern army, and women—alas!—whose brothers would be in one army, and their sons in another. That was the part of it which was most heartrending in this border-land. . . . Fathers were divided from sons, and mothers from daughters. Terrible tales were told of threats uttered by one member of a family against another. Old ties of friendship were broken up. Society had so divided itself, that one side could hold no terms of courtesy with the other."[41] Therein lay the plot of a short story he wrote after his return to England, "The Two Generals" (included in his volume *Lotta Schmidt and Other Stories*).

In St. Louis he met Dr. William Greenleaf Eliot, a friend of Kate Field's and founder of Washington University there. (T. S. Eliot was his grandson.) He was grieving at that time for the death of a child, but had some conversation with Trollope about Kate. " 'Let her marry a husband,' said he. 'It is the best career for a woman.' I agreed with him—and therefore bid you in his name as well as my own to go & marry a husband." Three months later (May, 1862) readers of *Orley Farm* saw that Lady Staveley held the same view respecting her daughter Madeline: "When some one had once very strongly praised Florence Nightingale in Lady Staveley's presence, she had stoutly declared her opinion that it was a young woman's duty to get married. For myself, I am inclined to agree with her." She by no means desired "that her daughter should take to the Florence Nightingale line of life, . . . should withdraw herself from the

world, and give up to sick women what was meant for mankind."* Mr.
Peacocke, the central figure in *Dr. Wortle's School* (1880), had spent five
years as "vice-president of a classical college at St. Louis, in the State of
Missouri," and then returned to England "with a beautiful American
wife, and the necessity of earning an income by his erudition."[43] Kate
never followed her friends' advice to take a husband.

From St. Louis Trollope returned by much the same route he had
taken westward; there were a few days in Baltimore, in Washington, in
Philadelphia, and then more than a week in his favorite Boston to renew
his friendships there. And there he had the new and exciting experience of
seeing "the world of Boston moving itself on sleighs. There was not a
wheel to be seen in the town. The omnibuses and public carriages had
been dismounted from their axles and put themselves upon snow runners,
and the private world had taken out its winter carriages [sleighs], and
wrapped itself up in buffalo robes." He tried his hand at driving a lady in
such a conveyance, on March 8, behind a pair of horses that promptly ran
away, but fortunately did not overturn him, and he got her home without
disaster. In this adventure he found the subject for another short story in
the *Lotta Schmidt* collection, "Miss Ophelia Gledd," a very Henry Jamesian narrative of the conflict of two cultures, Bostonian and English. On
March 12 he sailed from New York, and reached Liverpool on the twenty-
fifth.[44]

The book he had contracted to write was forwarded to Rose in
manuscript as he wrote it; about two-thirds of it were completed by the
time he got to Cincinnati on his way eastward in mid-February.[45] It
passed rapidly through the press after he reached England, and was published in two large volumes about May 19, 1862, at the rather high price
of thirty-four shillings. The £1,250 for which he had sold it to Chapman
had covered his expenses of travel and left him £625 profit.[46]

His own verdict on the book is still valid: "It was not well done. It is
tedious and confused, and will hardly, I think, be of future value to those
who wish to make themselves acquainted with the United States. . . . I
can recommend no one to read it now in order that he may be either
instructed or amused,—as I can do that on the West Indies."[47] It desper-

---

*After his visit to South Africa Trollope somewhat modified his view, not of
marriage but of "the Florence Nightingale line of life." He could not speak kindly enough
of the hospitals at the Diamond Fields—"hospitals, which have caused infinite labour and
are now successful;—especially one which is nearly self-supporting and is managed ex-
quisitely by one of those ladies who go out into the world to do good wherever good may
be done. I felt as I spoke to her that I was speaking to one of the sweet ones of the earth. To
bind up a man's wounds, or to search for diamonds among the dirt! There is a wide
difference there certainly."[42]

ately needed revision to prune out the repetitions; a narrative moves from event to event and so is amenable to Trollope's method of composition without extensive revision, but not a treatise like this. Moreover, it tried to be too many things at once—a travelogue, a sociological study of American culture, and an account of the undoubtedly important events then occurring in the states, which the British only incompletely understood. A comment he makes on his discussion of the *Trent* affair is in many ways characteristic of large parts of his book, and also rather characteristically Trollopian: "I do not pretend to understand [the legal authorities] or even to have read a single word of any international law. I have refused to read any such, knowing that it would only confuse and mislead me. But I have my common sense to guide me."[48] Yet to Americans indeed the book does still have an interest, and it is also full of evidence of Trollope's industry in seeking out information at every point. Where he had professional knowledge—in the management of postal affairs—his grasp of the situation in America is most illuminating. And so too is his firsthand observation of the details of American life in the uncertain first twelve months of the secession.

ঞ

Trollope's sale of some of his short stories to *Harper's New Monthly Magazine* appeared to Harpers to give them some claim to his other works also, and by the spring of 1862 they had published as books in New York *The Three Clerks, The Bertrams, Castle Richmond, Doctor Thorne, Framley Parsonage* (with Millais' illustrations), *The West Indies,* and *Brown, Jones, and Robinson. Orley Farm,* also with Millais' illustrations, was running in *Harper's* while Trollope was in America. American copyright law offered no protection to foreign authors, and was indeed framed essentially as part of the protectionist policy in favor of American manufacturers rather than as guaranteeing the rights of authors; until very close to the present day an American citizen whose work was manufactured abroad had no copyright in that work in the United States. And so Harper had paid to Trollope's publishers in England only what fees Harper deemed appropriate.[49] The British publishers were powerless, since once a book was out there was nothing to sell; prior to publication they could negotiate a price to provide the American publisher with advance copies of the text or with plates of the illustrations, but that was all. Moreover, an American publisher himself had no protection against one of his brethren with respect to the publication of a foreign book. Trollope asked the advice of James T. Fields, as a member of the trade, and learned that the only hope—a very slight one—of being paid by the Americans for his work was to engage the goodwill of an American publisher on his behalf.

A call upon Fletcher Harper in New York brought no promise of change; Harper expressed himself very happy with the current state of affairs. Trollope asked whether, if he should contract with another American publisher, Harper would print a competitive issue, and Harper replied that, though he would be sorry to lose Trollope as an author, he would not under these circumstances produce a rival edition. But there was nothing in writing to this effect, and Harper later denied that he had made such a promise. His view was, in fact, that his firm had made a considerable investment in bringing Trollope's name before the American public and would in all prudence have to profit from that investment by continuing to add to their list of Trollope's works.

Trollope, however, did contract with the Philadelphia publisher J. B. Lippincott to supply early sheets of the London edition of *North America;* Lippincott could then hope to bring the work out before Harper could get a market copy of the London edition, and he promised to pay Trollope a royalty of $12\frac{1}{2}$ percent on all copies sold after the first two thousand (which would be free of royalty). He "thereby [saves] himself from any payment to me if the sale be small, at the cost of a large payment if the sale be large," Trollope told Fields. Lippincott actually called on Harper in New York (where he was negotiating the agreement with Trollope) and came away with the conviction that Harper would market the book in any case, and try to undersell him; Trollope did not on this occasion speak with Harper. The agreement seems to have been a rather foolish one on Lippincott's part and a pointless one on Trollope's; "I do not much mind" what happens, he told Fields,[50] and indeed almost implies that his principal concern is to strike a blow for international copyright in general, not to protect his own income.

If the scheme was to succeed, the details had to be handled with great care. The advance copy would have to be sent to Philadelphia well before London publication, and Lippincott would have to use reasonable speed in getting his edition on the market. But things were not so attended to. Both Trollope and Chapman were eager to get the book out, and therefore it was on sale in London on May 19, only seven weeks after Trollope landed. Moreover, Lippincott was dilatory; his handsome two-volume edition was ready by June 22, but "the current half year being then near its close, (a time when we are always compelled to withhold our new publications and await semiannual settlements) we were not able to distribute the book to our correspondents as promptly as would otherwise have been done." Harper's copy of the London edition was forwarded by his agent with promptness, his printery was under the same roof as his offices in Franklin Square, New York, and (wrote Lippincott) "they made the greatest efforts to forestall us in the market, stopping their other operations as I understand in order to bring out your book at the earliest possible moment."[51] Within three days of the arrival of his copy in New York, Harper had his book on the market, in one volume, clothbound, priced at sixty cents; Lippincott had to do the best he could to recover his losses, and Trollope got nothing. "They undoubtedly have been very smart," Trollope remarked of Harpers. He used the occasion to fire a salvo in the London press against the unjust American copyright laws, a matter in which he tried to rally his New England friends to his side, but his indignation produced no remedies;[52] indeed, as we have seen, his letter merely offended Sir Rowland Hill. Harper continued to publish Trollope's books—thirty-one titles by the end of Trollope's life, for most of which he paid almost nothing.[53]

૨⁂

Orley Farm was still appearing in parts when Trollope returned to England, and the book publication in two volumes occurred about December 3, 1861, and September 25, 1862. The bound volumes were priced at eleven shillings each (one shilling more than the component parts), and the sale, at least of the first volume by itself, was disappointing. But "who the deuce buys the first volume of a book?" Trollope asked Chapman from America. "I fear we made a mistake about the shilling."[54]

When Trollope committed himself to the publication of *Orley Farm* in twenty monthly parts, he was following the example of Thackeray, Dickens, and a good many other contemporary novelists against whom the accusation of "mechanical" writing is not commonly made as it has been made against Trollope after his boast in *An Autobiography*. And yet a novel in parts, regardless of the author, is a novel in a most rigorous straitjacket, with which considerations of internal structure and aesthetics have nothing to do. Each of the twenty parts would have to contain precisely thirty-two pages, for no other reason than that the printers conventionally folded a sheet of paper into sixteen pages, and it was uneconomical to bind a "part" in any other than a multiple of sixteen pages. And so every monthly number was within about 200 words the same length as every other monthly part.

Trollope speaks of its plot as "probably the best I have ever made," but this assertion must be taken in the context of another remark, that "a good plot . . . is the most insignificant part of a tale,"[55] and also of Trollope's common use of the term "plot" to describe the dominant characteristic of the story of mystery, like Wilkie Collins's *The Woman in White* (1860) or Mary Elizabeth Braddon's *Lady Audley's Secret* (1862). He was tempted, indeed, to call his book *The Great Orley Farm Case,* but that was too awkward a title; and though the genre of the suspense story was in his mind, he deliberately resolved the mystery of the doubtful will with

Lady Mason's confession precisely halfway through the book. Lady Mason was the second wife of an elderly London merchant who was eager that his by then nearly forty-year-old son (by his first wife) should become a landed gentleman and who therefore bequeathed to him both a large estate in Yorkshire and a more modest estate, Orley Farm, about twenty-five miles from London. When he became the father of another son, the mother was eager that the farm be left to the infant, and when two years later Sir Joseph Mason died, a codicil to his will was found to that effect. It was this codicil that was questioned, and that Lady Mason had in fact forged. The novel becomes, then, a very sensitive study of the effect of a secret guilty act on the characters of the essentially decent perpetrator and of those who are linked to her by family, affection, or even hatred as they learn or gradually suspect the truth. The suspense consists in seeing how she will survive a court trial for perjury, with the irony of an actual acquittal when nearly all the world except her son has become convinced of her guilt. The son Lucius is especially well done, though by no means an engaging young man; he is conscientious, self-righteous, eager to be his widowed mother's protector, and hurt by her apparent lack of openness with him, but firm in the conviction of her innocence until her confession removes all doubt; then he insists on turning over his wrongful inheritance to the legal (and thoroughly obnoxious) heir, his older half-brother, and, though he perceives his life as ruined, he remains his mother's protector in exile as long as she will let him.

The lawyers and the law courts dominate the book, and may well draw at least somewhat on Trollope's recollection of his barrister father. Not only did Lady Mason's barrister friend Thomas Furnival at one time live in Keppel Street, Bloomsbury, where Trollope was born, but his chambers were in the Old Square, Lincoln's Inn, where Anthony as a schoolboy had to live in his father's rooms during the vacation time while his mother was in America. It is indeed not impossible that some of his courtroom scenes were based on memories of having watched his father in his professional duties. The *Saturday Review,* commenting on *The Three Clerks* in 1857, asked: "Why do not novelists consult some legal friend before they write about law? Is it impossible to find a barrister who has a hobby for criminal law, and also a hobby for criticising novels, and who would bring his skill in both lines to bear upon the correction of a layman's mistakes?" Trollope acknowledged this criticism in his next novel, *Doctor Thorne* (1858), and jestingly expressed his willingness to pay his share of the cost of such a learned gentleman. "When we've got that barrister in hand, then if I go wrong after that, let the blame be on my own shoulders—or on his."[56] To whom Trollope turned for assistance in legal matters we do not know, but at least one modern lawyer who had a hobby for criminal law and a hobby for criticizing novels has commented that *Orley Farm* is "remarkably free from legal mistakes, except for occasional slips in small matters purely technical. . . . Trollope, by this time, has apparently met and talked to some real lawyers."[57] It is likely that club life in London was beginning to broaden his experience. In the novel, Mr. Chaffanbrass is once more called upon to confuse the witnesses, and at his suggestion the drawing up of the brief for the defense is put into the hands of a Jewish solicitor named Solomon Aram, a man whose office was above an eating establishment in central London and whom the county aristocracy regard as likely to contaminate them by association, but who is in fact clever, considerate, and entirely estimable.

The novel is largely a picture of life among the country gentry, and as such is most agreeable. The lively hunting scene, with its nearly fatal fall that leads a young couple to a happy marriage, is one of Trollope's best. His commercial travelers are caricatures of a sort that scarcely demands his talent, and Millais represents them with a drawing in a vein unusual to him and reminiscent of some of "Phiz's" illustrations of Dickens. One quite minor figure, the successful barrister's neglected wife, Mrs. Furnival, wins our sympathy rather because of than in spite of her dullness. Elizabeth Barrett Browning, who had thought *Framley Parsonage* "superb," "perfect," told Isa Blagden in the spring of 1861 that despite Trollope's occasionally atrocious style (of which she gave some examples) she greatly admired the excellent, straightforward movement of the early numbers of *Orley Farm,* so unlike the more recent work of Thackeray, who "goes round and round till I'm dizzy, for one, and don't know where I am." She did not live to read beyond the fourth number.[58]

There is a passage about halfway through the second volume in which Trollope speculates on what may be the most enviable time of life with a man.

> I am inclined to think that it is at that period when his children have all been born but have not yet began to go astray or to vex him with disappointment; when his own pecuniary prospects are settled, and he knows pretty well what his tether will allow him; when the appetite is still good and the digestive organs at their full power; when he has ceased to care as to the length of his girdle, and before the doctor warns him against solid breakfasts and port wine after dinner; when his affectations are over and his infirmities have not yet come upon him; while he can still walk his ten miles, and feel some little pride in being able to do so; while he has still nerve to ride his horse to hounds, and can look with some scorn on the ignorance of younger men who have hardly yet learned that noble art. As regards men, this, I think, is the happiest time of life.[59]

He was a few days short of forty-six when he wrote this.

Chapter X

1862–64

Ten days after his arrival at home Trollope was elected to membership in the Garrick Club (April 5, 1862), proposed by Robert Bell and seconded by Thackeray.[1] It was the favorite of the half-dozen clubs to which he belonged, for the congenial conversation and especially for the afternoon rubbers of whist which he enjoyed (but felt somewhat inclined to apologize for when he wrote *An Autobiography*). Not many months after his election the club moved from its original home in an old "family hotel" in King Street to a new building designed by the architect Frederick Marrable in New King Street, near Leicester Square; the name of the street was then changed to Garrick Street. The members (either at the time of Trollope's election or very soon afterwards) included artists (Millais, Leighton, Rossetti, Frith, Woolner), theatrical people (Planché, German Reed, Squire Bancroft), musicians (M. W. Balfe, Sir Arthur Sullivan), publishers (Fred Chapman, Alexander Macmillan, J. M. Langford), and a very large proportion of the principal literary figures including Harrison Ainsworth, Shirley Brooks, Wilkie Collins, E. S. Dallas, Mark Lemon, Charles Lever, Robert Lytton, Theodore Martin, David Masson, George Meredith, John Morley, and Charles Reade. Dickens was in and out— elected 1837, resigned 1838; rejoined very quickly but resigned in 1844; accepted a pressing invitation to return in 1854, but resigned finally in 1865 when his friend and subeditor W. H. Wills was blackballed for membership. Two others of the group Trollope met at the first *Cornhill* dinner and esteemed affectionately thereafter were members, W. H. Russell and Sir Charles Taylor. And since possible sources of the names of Trollope's fictional characters are of some interest, there were among the members a Palliser, a Mildmay, a Maule, and a Round (as well as Marrable, the architect). When Thackeray died at the end of 1863 Trollope replaced him as one of the committee, and soon thereafter joined Sir Charles Taylor as a trustee of the club. Tom Trollope was elected in 1864 and young Harry Merivale Trollope in 1867.[2]

A few months before he sailed for America Trollope was asked by George Smith to write another novel for the *Cornhill*, about the same length as *Framley Parsonage* (it turned out to run to twenty numbers, however, not sixteen); the agreement was signed on July 6, 1861, and *The Small House at Allington* was written between May 20, 1862, and February

11, 1863.[3] It began its publication in the September number of 1862, and for the first eleven months overlapped with George Eliot's *Romola,* which had been running since July. Anthony had dinner with Lewes and George Eliot in late May to welcome Tom Trollope, just arrived from Florence for a few weeks' visit, and when a month later he received his new *Cornhill* Anthony wrote to her most enthusiastically: *Romola* was her greatest work. "The descriptions of Florence,—little bits of Florence down to a door nail, and great facts of Florence up to the very fury of life among those full living nobles,—are wonderful in their energy and their accuracy. . . . I wonder at the toil you must have endured in getting up your work,—wonder and envy. But I shall never envy your success."[4] The success that Trollope might have envied was Smith's offer of £10,000 for *Romola* only seven months after he had offered Trollope £3,500 for *Small House.** (For reasons that are not clear in the correspondence, the payment for *Small House* was actually only £3,000).[5] In fact, Trollope was not a man disposed to envy. He had a strong sense of his own worth, but also a practical awareness of market forces that made distinctions between one writer and another in the cash value of a novel. Tom Trollope took to himself the credit for having made her so thoroughly acquainted with Florence when she and Lewes had visited that city.[6]

One more request for a novel came early in April from a distinguished Scottish Presbyterian clergyman, a friend of Trollope's and a fellow member of the Garrick Club, the Queen's chaplain Norman Macleod. The Scottish publishers Alexander Strahan and William Isbister, having moved to London, projected a journal that would appeal to the religious mind, though not a theological journal, and induced Macleod to become its editor; the first number of the monthly *Good Words* appeared at the same time as the first number of the *Cornhill.*[7] Strahan later was founder and publisher of the *Contemporary Review* (1866), with its Church of England connections, and though he worked with titular editors it was he who made most of the decisions. Therefore it may be assumed that Macleod's letter to Trollope was written on Strahan's initiative—Strahan, to whom Macleod referred in the letter as "my publisher . . . as sensible a fellow as I know—truthful, honorable, generous—and with enterprise fit to cement again the American Union." The circulation of *Good Words* was 70,000, and Macleod promised that Strahan would pay handsomely if

---

*Thackeray indeed *did* envy her that bargain. About this time he chatted gloomily with Lord Stanley (later Earl of Derby) at the Cosmopolitan Club about how "the public had got tired of him. . . . His last book had not paid its expenses. . . . Miss Evans got £7,000 for one of her novels, [whereas] *Esmond,* which he thought his best, had brought him only £1,500, for a year's hard work." He "praised Trollope highly: could not read the sensation writers of the day, Wilkie Collins, etc."

Trollope would contribute a novel. "I think that you could let out the *best* side of your soul in Good Words—better far than even in Cornhill." Trollope was perhaps too little warned by the tone of that sentence. Strahan's first notion was for a short serial at £600; later in the year he amended the offer to £1,000 for a longer tale, to appear in the magazine from July to December, 1863. Trollope accepted the latter proposal, then bargained to sell the book rights to Chapman for £500 for a first edition of 1,500 copies.[8]

Meanwhile Strahan offered £100 for a short Christmas tale for the January, 1863, number of *Good Words*. "Dr. Macleod thought 'Out of Work' would make a seasonable story, but of course you will do what you consider best for the Magazine."[9] Acting on the suggestion, Trollope sent "The Widow's Mite" on December 8, a story of a young woman who wore her ordinary clothes at her wedding in order to contribute the price of her wedding gown and veil to feed Lancashire mill workers unemployed because the supply of cotton had been cut off by the American Civil War. The marriage between an English girl and an American man in this tale was a motif which, with its counterpart of an American girl and an Englishman, Trollope used frequently after his American tour.

ea

Of course Trollope had to fall back into his routine of traveling about his district on Post Office business, but it must be confessed that the district was a very pleasant one. If, for example, he was on the move for the first ten days of September, his temporary base was the popular North Sea resort of Cromer, and his daily business took him from there to such resorts as Sheringham, Trimingham, and Aldeburgh. A ten-day leave of absence in the middle of the month let him make the journey to Holland he had planned two years earlier; John Tilley seems to have been with him.[10] The seven-page anonymous article on "My Tour in Holland" in the November *Cornhill* is devoted largely to the art collections he saw there; he also describes the cheerfulness of the Amsterdam fair, the roar of voices in the Amsterdam stock exchange, a tourist show-village (Broek) that made him angry because he was badgered by guides and touts with their hands out, and the university and wonderful collection of stuffed birds at Leyden. He found the Dutchmen not fat, as in the conventional image, but compact and tidy—a fact that came home to him when he had to hire a bathing costume at Scheveningen and discovered that "no moderate-sized Englishman could have clothed himself in the garment provided for my use." He ventured to affront the decencies by going into the water notwithstanding, but (once again) "for myself I do not love

[bathing] machines, and prefer bathing *au naturel*." For the article he was
paid £15.[11]

In the autumn the bricklayers took over Waltham House to make
some enlargements.[12] When the weather became colder the seaside was
less attractive, but the hunting season opened, and "I have become a slave
to hunting,—as men who do hunt must do at this time of the year." He
was out every Wednesday and Saturday in December, and his house was
full of guests, "all more or less in the boots & breeches line."[13] And he
also composed a lecture on "The Present Condition of the Northern States
of the American Union," which he delivered in the provinces late in
December and in London on January 13, 1863. He asked George Smith to
print two dozen copies for him and sent one to James T. Fields in Boston
for publication in the *Atlantic*. "The small country audience received it
well—what a larger London audience may do, I cannot say."[14] But Fields
did not publish it. In truth, it is a rather poor piece, superficial, plati-
tudinous. Future prosperity lies with the Northern states; in these days
Russia is going ahead faster than Spain, for in the North God has given
his best gifts to the inhabitants, not to the soil, "and the man has been
more productive than the soil." "Good living for the masses, for God's
wide people,—that is the object; it is that to which civilization tends; it
is that which civilization means." His gift of prophecy remains, naturally,
what it was in *North America:* North and South will separate; the secessionists will succeed in that sense, and "I regard it as impossible that
senators from Georgia and Massachusetts should ever again sit in the same
Assembly."[15] He brought the lecture out again on January 26, 1864, in
response to a request for a discourse before the Athenaeum at Bury St.
Edmunds, in his postal district.[16]

ð

The moment *The Small House at Allington* was finished Trollope sent its
concluding chapters to Smith, from two motives: fear lest it should
through some mishap burn up, and the expectation of being paid for it at
once. (The fate of the early draft of Carlyle's *French Revolution* makes the
former motive not altogether irrational.) February saw him confined to his
bed for a fortnight with a liver ailment, and in March one of the most
important additions was made to the household: Rose's sister's daughter,
Florence Nightingale Bland, both of whose parents died about this time,
came to live at Waltham.[17] She was then only about eight years old, but
as she grew up she became her uncle's amanuensis, as well as his traveling
companion on his last journey to Ireland in 1882. The greater part of his
literary manuscripts in his last four or five years of life are in her hand,
which is far more legible than his own by this time.

Three weeks after completing *The Small House,* Trollope began his novel for *Good Words.* He had worked so comfortably with Millais in the illustration of *Framley Parsonage* and *The Small House*—calling the artist's attention to scenes that might make good illustrations but still allowing him a free hand—that he planned to use him again for the new novel, and indeed Millais was already doing Biblical illustrations for *Good Words.*[18] Unfortunately lightning was about to strike.

When Macleod formed his plans for *Good Words,* he determined to include not only religious articles, but the best products of the pens of writers of all schools of theology and all departments of literature, provided only that the writings be not essentially out of harmony with the Christian faith, and he was able through ties of personal friendship to command the work of men like Charles Kingsley, the liberal Anglican theologian A. P. Stanley, and Anthony Trollope. One line he did draw: "No one whom I could not receive, so far as character is concerned, into my family" was permitted to write for his magazine. He reached his decision, he assured a correspondent, not lightly but prayerfully— "*prayerful,* not as a mere phrase, but as expressing a real fact."[19] The implication no doubt was that the Lord was in full agreement with his policy—or at least had registered no objection.

The Christmas number (dated January, 1863, but published December 23 preceding) not only contained "The Widow's Mite" but announced the serial by Trollope with illustrations by Millais.[20] When the first installments of the manuscript reached Strahan, he sent them to the printer without troubling Macleod with Trollope's difficult handwriting. Meanwhile, however, in April the Evangelical Anglican journal, the *Record* (which Matthew Arnold described as "the Evangelical hyaena" for its implacable enmity to liberalism)[21] attacked *Good Words* at great length on the grounds of heterodoxy, and reprinted its diatribe as a pamphlet, *"Good Words:" The Theology of Its Editor and of Some of Its Contributors,* in the writing of which it employed the Scottish Presbyterian minister of a chapel in Chelsea. The thrust of the attack was that "many thousands of our youth of both sexes will get to know Messrs. Kingsley, Stanley, [Llewelyn] Davies, Trollope, and others of the like sort, *for the first time,* in the pages of *Good Words,* attracted there by the names of the Evangelical men whose writings adorn its pages."[22] (Macleod remarked with some cogency that it was probably the other way round—that the readers were attracted to the Evangelical theologians by the distinguished names of the other contributors.) The attack seems to have been motivated very personally against Macleod, and Trollope's name was mentioned only as representative of the class of novelists, not because any fault was found with his contribution. His was, quite simply, the best-known name among all the writers for *Good Words.*

Macleod's indignation at the attack was great, and of course righteous. "I have no doubt *Good Words* will be injured," he wrote to Strahan, "but it will perish before I truckle to any party." Nevertheless, "Let us be very careful not to admit through oversight one sentence which ought to pain a Christian, however weak he may be."[23] Not truckling, then, but being very careful, especially with the work of a novelist whose name had been singled out as representative of a class unfit to enter a decent home, Macleod, reading *Rachel Ray* for the first time in galleys, discovered that, though there was no slightest suggestion of immorality, nevertheless meetings of the Dorcas Society were shown to be dull and dancing until four in the morning was shown to be pleasant; moreover, a clergyman of Evangelical tendencies, Prong, was ridiculed (he was, in fact, a minor, provincial replica of Barchester's Obadiah Slope). Why could not the novelist have made the Dorcas Society pleasant and dancing abominable? He wrote a long letter to Trollope, therefore, on June 11, explaining why he could not publish the novel. It was not a bad letter—indeed its tone was conciliatory—but Macleod could not quite avoid shifting the blame to his contributor: he really had hoped Trollope "could with [his] whole heart produce another novel which instead of showing up what was weak, false, disgusting in professing Christians might also bring out, as has never yet been done, [what] Christianity as a living power derived from faith in a living Saviour" can effect in the world, though naturally he had thought it unnecessary to specify such a hope in advance. "I thought you would . . . bring out more fully the positive, good side of the Christian life than you had hitherto done," whereas Trollope was of opinion that his previous novels had made perfectly clear to Macleod what the new one would be like. Macleod prefaced his letter with an amiable "*nota bene*": "This letter will keep cold till you are at peace with all the world, with a pipe well filled, and drawing well. Read it then, or a bit each day for a month."[24]

Even before Macleod's letter came Strahan had told Trollope of the decision, and Trollope paused long enough in his writing the concluding pages of the story to resettle the commercial affairs: from June 10 to 14 there was no composition. He also promptly warned Millais that the magazine had thrown him over: "They write me word that I am too wicked."[25] Inasmuch as he had contracted to sell the serial rights to *Good Words* for £1,000 and the book rights for an edition of 1,500 copies to Chapman and Hall for £500, he immediately ascertained that Chapman would double his sum for double the number of copies, then wrote sternly to Strahan demanding payment of the £500 he stood to lose, with the threat that if the money were not instantly forthcoming Strahan would be taken to court for the full £1,000; there was also the implication that by practically branding Trollope as a writer unfit to appear in the decent company of *Good Words,* the proprietor might be held to have libeled him. Strahan paid the £500 and subsequently made a virtue of having done so; in fact, he had some claim to virtue, for he assured Trollope from the start that he was quite prepared to do what Trollope thought right in the matter of remuneration.[26]

Trollope was not really wrong to say, when he told the story in *An Autobiography,* that the editor's letter was full of "wailing and repentance." The novel "certainly is not very wicked." The dancing was "described, no doubt, with that approval of the amusement which I have always entertained." "It is more true of novels than perhaps of anything else, that one man's food is another man's poison." He wrote to Macleod's brother Donald after Macleod's death in 1872: "I need not say that Dr. Macleod's rejection of the story never for a moment interfered with our friendship. It certainly raised my opinion of the man."[27] They did indeed remain friends—a testimony no doubt to Macleod's personal charm and to Trollope's seldom holding a grudge for long. With Strahan Trollope continued to have business relations, and Strahan felt comfortable enough in them to ask Trollope to propose him for membership in the Garrick Club.[28]

Moreover, despite the fiasco with *Rachel Ray, Good Words* continued to provide a market for Trollope's writings: another Christmas story for 1863 (that about the two brothers from Kentucky who were generals in the opposing armies in the Civil War), a few more short stories in subsequent years, and (when Donald Macleod succeeded to the editorship) two novels and a novelette: *The Golden Lion of Granpere* (1872), *Kept in the Dark* (1882), and *The Two Heroines of Plumplington* (1882), a final brief venture into Barsetshire. Trollope's exuberance still needed restraint, however. In *Kept in the Dark,* his manuscript word "damnable" is printed "pernicious" or "wicked," "damning" becomes "condemning," "blessed change" becomes "blissful change," "d—— my relatives" becomes "never mind my relatives," "By G——!" becomes "Good Heavens!" "I'm d——d if" becomes "I'll be whipped if," "an infernal shame" is merely "a great shame," "She is more of a devil than you are" becomes "She has more mischief even than you have," and any number of expletives are simply deleted.[29] Only a few months after this, Trollope wrote to another Scottish editor (Blackwood) who was publishing a novel serially: "As I go on [I] will endeavour to put out all the profanities."[30] But the profanities came naturally, and were especially offensive in Scotland. Trollope "was the only man I had heard swear in decent society for uncounted years. The swearing, which was repeated, was the most disagreeable of all [his traits]: the actual asseverating, by the Holiest Name, of some trumpery statement." Such was the recollection of one who met him at the home of John Blackwood, at St. Andrews.[31]

Late in 1879 the Reverend R. S. Oldham concocted with Trollope a scheme for persuading some of the more eminent writers of the day to do a series of short novels on social subjects for publication by the Society for Promoting Christian Knowledge—novels "dealing with prevailing evils," as Edmund McClure, the society's editorial secretary, understood it. Trollope promised to use his good offices with such writers as William Black and R. D. Blackmore, and offered to write a story himself illustrative of "commerical honesty" for only £250 for the entire copyright, half his current rate. Doubtless recalling *Rachel Ray,* he also offered to allow the society to reject the work after the manuscript had been received, "because it is incumbent on the Society to put forth nothing but that of which it approves. It is altogether contrary to my usual habit. Indeed I have not accorded such a privilege to any purchaser for more than 20 years."[32] Despite McClure's initial enthusiasm, the scheme seems to have come to nothing.

❧

We have seen that Trollope's postal arrangements brought him a renewed acquaintance with his very old Harrow friend, the Reverend Charles Merivale; on March 11, 1861, he was guest at Merivale's home as he was making his rounds and "looking after his letters" (as Merivale said).[33] It was doubtless at Trollope's suggestion that Merivale was chosen to propose the toast to "The Writers of Fiction" at the annual dinner of the Royal Literary Fund on May 13, 1863. Then, the day before the dinner, Trollope learned that it would be his task to respond to the toast. And so on that evening Merivale called upon "one eminent in writings of fiction, eminent as a novelist, one from the keenness of whose analysis of human nature we have all smarted, statesmen, bishops, lawyers, and country parsons, members of parliament, and newspaper editors, but again by whose genial humanity we have all been comforted and reassured. I beg to give you the name of my excellent friend Mr. Trollope." In response, Trollope said,

> [I must profess] my belief that that branch of the profession of literature is distinct, and is established, and is good, and is useful, and is ornamental. . . . The days are not far gone,—many of us here, who have grey hairs and bald heads remember them,—in which a novel was looked upon as a bad production—as an evil thing. Our daughters were not allowed to read them, and we were not sure that they were good for our sons. Now, I maintain that we who are fathers, look upon novels as good things. They instruct our

daughters and they instruct our sons. . . . Instead of using words of humility as I sit down, I will use words of pride, and say here, that now, at this present day, the Novel Writers of the country are the great instructors of the country. They help the church and they are better than the law. They teach ladies to be women, and they teach men to be gentlemen.

When the Quaker's daughter Marion Fay, finding herself in love with Lord Hampstead in the novel Trollope wrote sixteen years later, reflects on the social positions of herself and the young lord, she remarks, in language reminiscent of Trollope's speech, "[God] has made me better [than a lady]. He has made me a woman."[34]

A month later the general committee of the fund (of which Trollope was not yet a member) was rocked by scandal. Thomas Macknight, author of popular biographies of Burke, Bolingbroke, and contemporary political figures such as Disraeli (as early as 1854) on June 10 was awarded his second literary fund grant of £50 (the first came in July, 1839). Exactly a week later his wife brought suit for divorce, and her testimony, faithfully reported in the Times,[35] presented a sordid account of misery and quarrels that ended with his living for three years as titular husband of an actress named Sarah Thorne. Stern letters were addressed by the committee to Macknight's recommenders, among them his publishers Chapman and Hall, who responded in shocked horror that they were severing their connection with Macknight. (Five years earlier another Chapman and Hall author left his wife and took up with an actress, but the publishers then showed no eagerness to sever their connection with Charles Dickens.)

Tom's wife Theodosia had become an invalid; Tom brought her and their daughter Beatrice ("Bice") from Florence early in July for a change of climate, then returned to Florence alone to look after his mother. Later in that month Anthony and Rose took their sons and their niece Edith Tilley on a four-month tour of Switzerland: from Thun to the Oberland with a guide and horses, to Grindelwald, over the Grimsel to the Rhone Valley, then over the Gemmi and north via Baden to the Rhine and Cologne. At St. Goar they met Robert Bell and his wife. Anthony augmented his cellar with a shipment of wine from Germany.[36]

Only a month after his return he again went to the Continent, this time escorting Theo and Bice back to Florence; young Harry, now seventeen, accompanied them. Mrs. Trollope's memory had failed her several years before, but she still enjoyed her afternoon walk on her older son's arm in the garden of the Villino Trollope on the Piazza dell'Independenza, and brightened at the thought of Anthony. Her granddaughter's lovely voice caroling forth some Tuscan song made her exclaim softly, "Dear creature! Dear creature!" About two weeks after Anthony returned home she died peacefully on October 6; her last words were "Poor Cecilia." She was buried in the Protestant cemetery in Florence, the cemetery in which Elizabeth Barrett Browning lay and where, a year later, Walter Savage Landor would be buried; her stone bears a Latin inscription by Tom.[37] Anthony forwarded a concise summary of her life to the editor of the *Athenaeum;* it was turned into a graceful anonymous paragraph on her career by Dr. John Doran in the issue of October 10 (p. 469).

About two weeks before he finished writing *The Small House,* and five weeks before he began to write *Rachel Ray,* Trollope on January 26, 1863, signed an agreement with Chapman for a new novel to be issued in twenty parts of thirty-two pages each, like *Orley Farm,* beginning January 1, 1864. For the right to publish 10,000 copies (in any form) Chapman would pay £3,000. With his experience with Harper fresh in his mind, Trollope stipulated that any money resulting from the disposal of sheets of the work to foreign publishers was to go entirely to himself. The novel was to become *Can You Forgive Her?* which he began to write on August 16, between his return from Switzerland and his journey to Florence. The book was completed on April 28, 1864, four months after the publication of the first part.[38]

Trollope had written about ten chapters of the new book when, on the very eve of his departure for Italy, Chapman suggested in conversation that they launch a new weekly magazine with Trollope as editor, and that the new novel be made the staple from the start. Robert Bell was also to be involved in the project, presumably as Trollope's assistant editor. "As to the name I think the 'New Weekly'—would be best," wrote Trollope. "The new weekly conducted by Anthony Trollope." There would be about twenty-eight pages of miscellaneous matter per week, and an installment of the novel eight pages long—Chapman had sample pages sent out to Italy for Trollope's inspection. Trollope ruled out printing in double columns, thought that the novel portion could be collected in colored covers once a month, and speculated how the same setting of type could be used for both parts and volume issues.[39]

It was, in fact, a rather strange proposal for Chapman to have made. The apparent model was Dickens's very successful weekly, *Household Words,* begun in 1850 and published by Bradbury and Evans. After a decade Dickens quarreled with Bradbury and Evans, withdrew from *Household Words,* and began a new weekly on the same pattern, *All the Year Round,* published by the proprietors (of which Dickens was principal). Bradbury and Evans carried on the pattern with a rival *Once a Week,* to which Tom Trollope was a contributor. But the exclusive rights to distribute *All the Year Round* outside of London were held by Chapman and Hall, who with their new proposal to Trollope would be competing with themselves (though of course they had no managerial control over *All the Year Round*). In any case, the scheme was broached too hastily to be launched by the first of the year, as Chapman proposed, and nothing more is heard of it.[40]

Books were passing frequently this year between Trollope and George Lewes and George Eliot. The first was *Romola,* in volume form, which she sent him in July. "Were you now departing from us, . . . you might go satisfied that you have written that which would live after you," he wrote in acknowledgment. "It will be given to but very few latter day novels to have any such life. The very gifts which are most sure to secure present success are for the most part antagonistic to permanent vitality." In October he sent her his newly published *Rachel Ray.* "You know that my novels are not sensational. In Rachel Ray I have attempted to confine myself absolutely to the commonest details of commonplace life among the most ordinary people, allowing myself no incident that would be even remarkable in every day life. I have shorn my fiction of all romance." She replied gracefully when she had read the book:

> Rachel has a formidable rival in The Small House, which seems peculiarly felicitous in its conception & good for all souls to read. But I am much struck in Rachel with the skill with which you have organized thoroughly natural everyday incidents into a strictly related well proportioned whole, natty & complete as a nut on its stem. Such construction is among those subtleties of art which can hardly be appreciated except by those who have striven after the same result with conscious failure. . . . But there is something else I care yet more about, which has impressed me very happily in all these writings of yours that I know—it is that people are breathing good bracing air in reading them—it is that they, the books are filled with belief in goodness without the slightest tinge of maudlin. They are like pleasant public gardens, where people go for amusement, & whether they think of it or not, get health as well. . . . Such things are rather the result of what an author is than of what he intends.

Then in December Lewes sent Trollope the newly revised edition of his *Life and Works of Goethe.* "Alas, me," lamented Trollope, "—for 11 years I learned Latin & Greek—& know it now . . . {very} superficially. Of German of course I know nothing. Shall I hereafter have an action against my pastors & masters?"[41]

❧

A significant aspect of *Doctor Thorne* had been the question of the marriage between two people of very different social level; Frank Gresham, nephew of the Earl de Courcy and heir of a landed family in Barsetshire whose wealth had been squandered, was barred from marrying the woman he loved, Mary Thorne, orphaned niece of a country doctor, until it was learned that she was heiress of one of the largest industrial fortunes in the country. *The Small House at Allington* is devoted almost entirely to variations on the theme of marriage for money and marriage for social position. The wealthy old bachelor squire of Allington, Christopher Dale, provided a home for his widowed sister-in-law Mary Dale and her two daughters, Bell and Lily, but was little inclined to provide the girls with a dowry. Lily falls in love with a handsome young London west-end club man and civil servant, Adolphus Crosbie, who proposes marriage to her but then has second thoughts, both because she is only a country girl and because he has insufficient income for the kind of life he likes to lead. He jilts her in favor of Lady Alexandrina de Courcy, the by no means young daughter of the Earl who is eager for marriage and who can provide him with both money and social position. (The motif of Lady Alexandrina's pursuit of Crosbie is repeated in the pursuit of Lily's forlorn suitor Johnny Eames by Amelia Roper, daughter of his lodging-house keeper.) Squire Dale wishes that his other niece, Bell, should marry his nephew and heir to the Allington estates, Bernard Dale, but she does not love him and marries a plain country doctor, James Crofts. The mental gyrations of these people as they weigh the advantages and disadvantages of their various matings are carried on at perhaps too great a length. Trollope, however, was fond of the novel, and found that his readers were especially moved by Lily Dale's grief and her commitment to the life of an old maid.*[42] One episode from *Doctor Thorne* so pleased the author that he deliberately repeated it in *The Small House,* with an explicit reference to the earlier book. In the former, Frank Gresham horsewhipped Gustavus Moffat outside his Pall Mall club for having jilted Augusta Gresham (chap. xxi). In the latter, Johnny Eames, desperately in love with Lily Dale and beside himself with rage at Crosbie's treatment of her, encounters the latter on the platform of Paddington Station, assails him, and blackens his eye; they fall into the railway bookstall of W. H. Smith, among the shilling yellow-back novels (Trollope's own would soon be on those shelves) (chap. xxxiv).

---

*At some time during his few years of personal acquaintance with Thackeray, Trollope was praising *Henry Esmond*—"not only his best work, but so much the best, that there was none second to it. 'That was what I intended,' [Thackeray] said, 'but I have failed. Nobody reads it. After all, what does it matter? . . . After all, Esmond was a prig'." The phrase so stuck in Trollope's mind that when he wrote about the novel in his life of Thackeray in 1879 he used that word as the key to the hero's character, and three years earlier in *An Autobiography* he described his darling Lily Dale as "a female prig."[43]

Significant segments of the novel are set in London, and not surprisingly Trollope is sensitive to the tone of the various parts of town. Crosbie lives on Mount Street, near Berkeley Square in Mayfair, and loathes the middle-class region of St. John's Wood where his sister-in-law to be lives with her lawyer husband. The distinction between the heart of Belgravia and its Pimlico edge is made very clear. New housing along the Bayswater Road is acceptable, for it gives a glimpse of Hyde Park; Portman Square, in the part of town where Trollope lived most of his London years, might be better. Undergraduates who have to live near the British Museum will recognize, not altogether with delight, Mrs. Roper's boardinghouse on Burton Crescent (now Cartwright Gardens), where Johnny Eames and his friend Cradell lived, northeast of Russell Square.

"Thackeray," says Trollope, "often refers in his writings, if not to the incidents at any rate to the remembrances of his own life."[44] London club life is now far more important than it was in earlier novels, just as it had become for its author. Sir Raffle Buffle, first commissioner of the Income Tax Office, where Eames worked, is remarkably like, in his behavior, to Colonel Maberly of the Post Office, under whom Trollope worked. "He used to arrive about eleven o'clock, and announce his arrival by tearing at the bell for his breakfast," Edmund Yates recalled of Maberly. "This bell brought the head messenger, whose services he arrogated to himself, who, being a venerable-looking and eminently respectable personage, probably well-to-do in the world, was disgusted at having to kneel at the Colonel's feet, and receive the Colonel's dirty boots into his arms with the short adjuration, 'Now, Francis, my straps.'" Sir Raffle's private secretary gave up that post "because he could not endure the tones of Sir Raffle's voice," and warned his successor, "I hope you like being rung for, like a servant, every minute, for he's always ringing the bell. And he'll roar at you till you're deaf. . . . And, sometimes, when he has sent [his messenger] out about his private business, he'll ask you to bring him his shoes." Trollope himself affirmed that "Sir Raffle was intended to represent a type, not a man; but the man for the picture was soon chosen, and I was often assured that the portrait was very like. I have never seen the gentleman with whom I am supposed to have taken the liberty."[45] It may be supposed that Trollope here was being somewhat disingenuous; Maberly, it might be added, lived long enough to have read *An Autobiography*. Of Bell and Lily Dale Trollope remarked that they were both "very fair, so that the soft tint of colour which relieved the whiteness of their complexion was rather acknowledged than distinctly seen. It was there, telling its own tale of health, as its absence would have told a tale of present or coming sickness" (chap. vi). The memory of his sisters' fate was still very present to him.

Though the book was among the half-dozen collected as "The

Chronicles of Barsetshire" in 1878, its connection with the town and diocese of Barchester is very tenuous. Crosbie, waiting between trains there, most improbably goes to service in the cathedral, and in so doing steps back into the past: he is struck by the fragile figure of the old precentor, converses with him, and is taken by him to see Hiram's Hospital, of which Harding is sure Crosbie must have read in the newspapers. On the other hand, Plantagenet Palliser makes his first appearance in the novel, and by the end of it we have also met Lady Glencora MacCluskie and have heard of Burgo Fitzgerald. The old Duke of Omnium, lords Brock and de Terrier, were introduced in *Framley Parsonage*. And so we have the connecting links between Barchester and the parliamentary novels, of which the first, *Can You Forgive Her?* was already appearing before *The Small House* ended its run in the *Cornhill*.[46]

※

Trollope's description of *Rachel Ray* as being confined to "the commonest details of commonplace life among the most ordinary people" is a fair statement: it is set in a fictitious small town in Devonshire called "Baslehurst," near Totnes, where the muddy beer from the brewery of Bungall and Tappitt fights a losing battle with Devonshire cider. Bungall's nephew and heir, Luke Rowan, arrives on the scene, falls in love with the younger daughter of the widowed Mrs. Ray, and ultimately persuades a reluctant Tappitt to retire from the brewery in Rowan's favor. (Tappitt had his worst fears about retirement confirmed: "The days of [his] domestic dominion were over, as is generally the case with a man who retires from work and allows himself to be placed, as a piece of venerable furniture, in the chimney corner. . . . No man should abdicate; . . . happiness in this life . . . is hardly compatible with that diminished respect which ever attends the relinquishing of labour. Otium cum dignitate is a dream" [chap. xxx].) Mrs. Ray's older daughter Dorothea, also a widow, is a severely evangelical religionist who believes the newcomer is surely a wolf in sheep's clothing (a figure Trollope uses almost *ad nauseam*) and for a time disrupts the family by her opposition to Luke's courtship of Rachel, but in the end he proves his worth and marries his beloved. The older sister Dorothea herself almost yields to the marriage proposal of the Reverend Samuel Prong, a sanctimonious product of the Church Missionary Society's training college at Islington (chaps. v, xiv). But though she is willing to put herself in his hands in most respects, she cannot bear to be told that "Voting for Members of Parliament is a thing which ladies naturally are not called upon to understand," nor is she to be persuaded that if she does not surrender her modest widow's income to him upon marriage, she will be sinfully disobedient to her spouse, her lord and master (chap. xxiv). Prong is obnoxious in his pious language and his manner, but not absolutely vile or immoral.

In fact, the uproar over the proposed publication of the novel in *Good Words* was entirely unwarranted. Trollope designed a tale in which true virtue was entirely compatible with the pleasantness of life. The condemnation is against Dorothea, who "would have been quite willing to see her sister married, but the lover should have been dingy, black-coated, lugubrious, having about him some true essence of the tears of the valley of tribulation" (chap. xxix). Trollope was even careful that Luke Rowan should say the Lord's Prayer nightly at bedtime, and that grace should be said before dinner (chaps. xiii, xx). It was indeed a moral tale for a good Christian magazine.

Mrs. Ray is the most entertaining character in the novel, an affectionate woman whose instincts are all on the right side but whose intellect is not able to stand up to the arguments of her older daughter or her clergyman, or, indeed, her neighbors. Trollope lets his humor play sweetly with her. When Dorothea flings out of the cottage where she had been living with her mother and Rachel, vowing never to return so long as Rachel is so wicked as to walk out, and even to dance, with young Rowan, Mrs. Ray "stood at the door of her house with her handkerchief to her eyes." Then she said to Rachel, "It will make a great difference in the housekeeping," and "went to work at her little accounts" (chap. ix). She is convinced that Rowan's intentions are honorable after "he took his tea here quite like a steady young man. He drank three large cups" (chap. xii). Since Trollope began to write *Rachel Ray* only three weeks after completing *The Small House,* it is not surprising that he repeated the motif of a heroine pining into illness when her glamorous lover apparently deserts her; fortunately in this cheerful novel Rachel is not after all abandoned by the young man.

Young John Addington Symonds, who as an undergraduate at Oxford had read *Framley Parsonage* in the *Cornhill* at the library of the Union, was overwhelmed with delight by *Rachel Ray,* "the Idyll of love which I now look upon with most pleasure. . . . It is an excellent novel." "The whole story is a piece of Life, & I sympathize more than I ought to with the fresh strong unconscious youth of these two commonplace people. I would give everything I possess, my education, my passionate enjoyment of poetry & music & all Arts, & every scrap of money or interest or expectation I possess, for that hour at the Churchyard stile, for the difficulties surmounted, the strong nerves, the true love, the simple life, the real work of those visions in Mr. Trollope's brain."[47]

Chapter XI

1864

On the day before Christmas in 1863, Thackeray died suddenly at his home in Palace Green, Kensington. "I felt [his death] as a very heavy blow," Trollope wrote to George Smith the next day. "I have not the heart to wish anyone a merry Christmas."[1] Trollope was among the 1,500 or more people who attended the funeral at Kensal Green Cemetery on December 30. Thackeray had read proofs of three installments of *Dennis Duval* for the *Cornhill,* and there was only one more chapter in reserve, but the novel had not actually begun its run. (Acting on the advice of Dickens and Trollope, Smith printed all that had been written, from March through June, 1864.)

The friendship between the two men had been quite extraordinary. They had had common friends, such as Follett Synge, who had met Thackeray in America before he encountered Trollope in San José, Costa Rica, but they had no personal relationship until Trollope wrote to Thackeray from Ireland, asking to be among the contributors to the new *Cornhill Magazine.* Thackeray's reply was most flattering, but they did not see each other in the course of Trollope's quick trip to London soon thereafter, where he settled the *Cornhill* business entirely with Smith. After the unfortunate first meeting at the *Cornhill* dinner of January, 1860, however, they became very warm friends. Thackeray was the sort of man who did not keep his business acquaintances at a distance: there was a personal warmth in all his correspondence. When Trollope replied to his rejection of "Mrs. General Talboys," Thackeray was ill but asked one of his daughters to read the letter; as he reported to Trollope, when she had done so she told her father, "He is an old dear and you should write him an affectionate letter."[2] An amiable note to decline a request to lecture at the Post Office had the postscript, "Have you a mind to dine here on Monday at 7:30?" A note to Synge of uncertain date asks: "Hadn't you better dine here on Sunday? Bring the ladies & Trollope too. 7 o'clock."[3] That invitations passed the other way is evident from a letter Trollope sent to Millais early in June, 1863: "Do . . . settle a day with the Thackerays and [Charles] Collinses . . . for the consumption of . . . our cream and strawberries."[4]

In his later biography of Thackeray Trollope remarks on Thackeray's diffidence with respect to his own powers, in contrast with Dickens's self-confidence: "'They don't read it,' he said to me of *Esmond*. . . . No little wound of the kind ever came to him but he disclosed it at once" (p. 16). And certainly such modesty can be engaging. "I think Trollope is much more popular with the Cornhill Magazine readers than I am: and doubt whether I am not going down hill considerably in public favor. It doesn't concern me very much," Thackeray wrote to an American friend in May of 1861.[5] In view of the promptness with which Smith requested a full-length novel of Trollope when Trollope quite unexpectedly approached Thackeray only two months before the first issue of the *Cornhill* was printed, Thackeray cannot fully be credited when he tells Charles Lever that he deliberately "sang small, wishing to keep my strongest for a later day, and give Trollope the honors of *Violono primo*": the question Trollope asked in *An Autobiography* cannot be answered so. "How had it come to pass that . . . the Editor and the proprietors were, at the end of October, without anything fixed as to what must be regarded as the chief dish in the banquet to be provided?"[6]

Trollope and Thackeray were both members of the Cosmopolitan Club and the Garrick Club. Thackeray resigned the editorship of the *Cornhill* in May, 1862, finding himself temperamentally and physically unequal to the task; he "was far too tender-hearted to be happy as editor. He could not say 'No' without himself suffering a pang as keen as was inflicted by that 'No' on the rejected contributor himself," said Smith.[7] But the close association between the two novelists continued. On May 11 of that year Trollope and Thackeray dined at the Star and Garter in Richmond; Thackeray had come without his wallet and Trollope advanced his portion of the dinner bill, £5 17s. 6d. "He sent me a cheque for the amount in rhyme, giving the proper financial document on the second half of a sheet of notepaper."[8] At almost precisely the same moment, Synge, about to depart for the kingdom of Hawaii on a Foreign Office mission, wrote to both friends most distressing letters revealing his immediate and desperate need of a large sum of money, about £2,000. As luck would have it, Trollope and Thackeray chanced to meet at the Horse Guards as they were passing between St. James's Park and Whitehall, and discussed the matter as they stood between the two motionless mounted sentries. "'Do you mean to say that I am to find two thousand pounds?' [Thackeray] said, angrily, with some expletives. I explained that I had not even suggested the doing of anything—only that we might discuss the matter. Then there came over his face a peculiar smile, and a wink in his eye, and he whispered his suggestion, as though half ashamed of his meanness. 'I'll go half,' he said, 'if anybody will do the rest.'" "I have just met a Trojan of the name of Trollope in the street, . . . and the upshot is that we will do what you want between us," Thackeray wrote. "My dear old Synge, come and talk to me on Friday before twelve." And so Thackeray lent £1,000 and Trollope £900 (Trollope apparently never knew of the difference), at 5 percent interest; by the time Thackeray died Synge had repaid each of them £500.[9]

It fell to Trollope to tell Synge of Thackeray's death. "I saw him for the last time about ten days before, . . . and sat with him for half an hour talking about himself. I never knew him pleasanter or more at ease as to his bodily ailments. How I seem to have loved that dear head of his now that he is gone." Thackeray "was a man to be loved even more than he was liked," Trollope told a correspondent. "He was tender-hearted in the extreme, and had much of the softness and sometimes also . . . of the weakness of a woman." He is quoted by Thackeray's daughter as having said (rather uncharacteristically), "If I thought I should never see old Thackeray again, I should be a very unhappy man."[10]

The first issue of the *Cornhill* to go to print after Thackeray's death (February, 1864) contained memorial sketches by Dickens and Trollope, both of whom declined payment. At the same time the *Cornhill*'s rival and contemporary *Macmillan's Magazine* carried memorials of Thackeray by Henry Kingsley and the editor, David Masson.[11] Kingsley's and Masson's essays are tedious and self-gratifying in their display of literary craftsmanship. Dickens's short piece is remarkably perceptive in its reminiscences of Thackeray the man, and keeps its eye well on the object. Trollope, also writing warmly about a subject he loved, lets his rhetoric, and especially his figures of speech, run away with him. The *Spectator* gave three columns to a discussion of these tributes, seeking to define the qualities that a biography of Thackeray would need. "The graphic, manly, and perfectly simple expression of grief and personal love for our great satirist from the pen of Mr. Dickens—is exactly what it aims to be," but "who would believe that the writer of [the following] wonderful sentence was the acomplished author of 'The Warden' and 'Barchester Towers'?—'He carried his heart-strings,' says Mr. Trollope, 'in a crystal case, and when they were wrung, or when they were soothed, all their writhings were seen by friend and foe.'" "Mr. Trollope's few words, coming as they do from a mind conspicuous for manly sense, fine intelligence, and easy simplicity of style,—furnish a very remarkable illustration of the danger that the responsibility of writing Thackeray's biography may embarrass rather than stimulate the intellect of a true friend."[12] (Trollope's language was not quite so silly as the reviewer made it appear: he actually wrote "all their workings," not "all their writhings.")

Far across the Atlantic, Emerson, gathering notes for a lecture on "Greatness," noticed that "The 'Spectator' says of the three obituary notices of Thackeray by Dickens, Trollope, and Kingsley, that only Dickens's is equal to the subject: the others strain to write up, & fail. . . . The experience is familiar, day by day, that of two persons, one of character & one of intellect, Character will rule & intellect must bow."

The essay was published late in Emerson's life, without this reference; the observation on Trollope and Dickens remained hidden for more than a century in Emerson's notebook. [13]

In March, Trollope went to the sale of Thackeray's books and furnishings and came away with a dish as memento of his friend. [14]

æ.

About a month before Thackeray died (November 13, 1863) Trollope signed an agreement with Smith to supply a novel for the *Cornhill* that would run for sixteen numbers. When he came to write it, nine months later, he gave it the title of *The Claverings;* it was the narrative of the family of Sir Hugh Clavering, eleventh baronet, who lived at Clavering Park, near Clavering, in the diocese of Barchester. A neighbor of Thackeray's Pendennis was Sir Francis Clavering, ninth baronet, who in the 1830s lived at Clavering Park, near Clavering, in the West Country, on the River Brawl; the line went back to Sir Poyntz Clavering, whose effigy in the costume of the time of James I might be seen in the Clavering Church. [15] There is no reminiscence of the earlier book in Trollope's novel, and indeed there is a town of Clavering, with a nearby Clavering Park, in Essex, in Trollope's postal district. Yet the use of the name as a family name, and the moving it to the West of England, is no accident: Trollope was unobtrusively paying his respects to his late friend.

In fact, from the date of the publication of *Barchester Towers* Trollope had been referred to by reviewers as a Thackerayan novelist (a lesser Thackeray, to be sure, but then Thackeray had been before the public eye longer, with *Vanity Fair, Pendennis, Henry Esmond,* and *The Newcomes*). About the time *Vanity Fair* began to appear in monthly parts (January, 1847), Trollope's *Macdermots* was published, and he had already begun his second Irish novel. But there can be little question that thereafter he learned a great deal from Thackeray's "novel without a hero": "Heroes and heroines, as so called, are not commonly met with in our daily walks of life," he remarks in *The Three Clerks* (chap. xlvii); "If [the novelist] attempt to paint from nature, how little that is heroic should he describe!" he tells us in *The Claverings* (chap. xxviii). [16] The "realism" Trollope admired in Thackeray was equally characteristic of his own work from the start, as were the lucidity and ease of style. [17] He was only briefly tempted by Thackeray's love of parody (Dr. Pessimist Anticant and Mr. Popular Sentiment in *The Warden,* "Crinoline and Macassar" in *The Three Clerks*), but he never gave up the trick he pretended to reprobate in Thackeray, indulging "too frequently in little confidences with individual readers, in which pretended allusions to himself are frequent. . . . The book is robbed of its integrity by a certain good-humoured geniality of language, which causes the reader to be almost too much at home with his author."[18] This aspect of both novelists was most severely criticized by Henry James and William Dean Howells.[19]

A contemporary novelist remarked on the delight Thackeray seemed to take in the names he invented in *Vanity Fair*.[20] Label names go back a long way in English fiction and drama, and they were used by other novelists in the nineteenth century, but by few with such wit as Thackeray—and Trollope not only shared his delight, he often shared his names. "Ah, my friend, from whom I have borrowed this scion of the nobility!" Trollope remarks in a footnote to the name Cinquebars* in *Can You Forgive Her?* (chap. xvi) about three months after Thackeray's death. "Had he been left with us he would have forgiven my little theft, and now that he has gone I will not change the name." We first see the name of Lady Glencora's dissolute but handsome admirer Burgo Fitzgerald in March of 1864—a curious name, but one familiar to the reader of *Vanity Fair* (chap. xxvii), where Mrs. Major O'Dowd was the daughter of Fitzjurld Ber'sford de Burgo Malony. The name of Gatherum Castle, seat of the Dukes of Omnium, is constructed on the same principle as Thackeray's "Snobbium Gatherum" in *The Book of Snobs,* and the names of Trollope's Lord Grassangrains, Mr. Chaffanbrass, the groom Hayonotes, and the hostler Wutsanbeans are formed after *Vanity Fair*'s Lord Portansherry. Both novelists give to their scenes, especially in London, "a local habitation and a name" recognizable even to the modern visitor.

There is little point in arguing whether Trollope is a lesser Thackeray, or whether indeed the greater reputation of Thackeray in his day was merely the consequence of his being earlier in the field, and, perhaps, more attractive personally. Both were naturally witty, but Trollope's was the instant recognition of an inherently ridiculous remark or situation, whereas Thackeray's gives the sense of being contrived, of inventing the situation (and the language) in order to show off the wit. Trollope himself says of novelists, "Different readers are affected in a different way. That which is one man's meat is another man's poison. . . . It is a matter of taste and not of intellect, as one man likes caviare after his dinner, while another prefers apple-pie."[21]

ॐ

On March 1, 1864, the news reached Trollope that Rowland Hill had resigned his secretaryship at the Post Office; at the same time a copy of Hill's revised pamphlet on *Results of Postal Reform* came to him from the author. He wrote courteously the next day:

> I cannot but have felt for the last year or two since I was called upon to make one of a committee of inquiry during your illness, that you

---

*A five-barred gate that only a skilled horseman dares to jump.

have regarded me as being in some sort unfriendly to your plans of postal reform. I am not going to trouble you with any discussion on that matter, but I cannot let your resignation from office pass without assuring you of my thorough admiration for the great work of your life. . . . There are national services, for which a man can receive no adequate reward, either in rank or money, and it has been your lot to render such a service to the world at large. I hope that you may live long to enjoy the recognition of your own success.

The courtesy not unnaturally gave pleasure: "Among the numerous letters of congratulation are . . . some even from men whom I have had too much reason to believe unfriendly," Hill wrote in his journal. "There is an excellent letter, among others, from Trollope." But Trollope's personal judgment of Hill as an administrative officer remained what it had always been, and when after both men were dead his expression of that opinion was made public in *An Autobiography,* Hill's son, zealous like all members of the family for Sir Rowland's glory, published this letter with a view to showing that Trollope either misrepresented his opinion of Hill in his autobiography or was an insincere and fulsome flatterer. Edmund Yates, though a friend of the younger Hill, quite properly thought the two sentiments expressed were compatible: admiration of the institution of the penny post did not necessarily negate an opinion that Hill was not a good administrator. No reader of Hill's private journals can think other than that, for all Hill's great service to the world, rewarded ultimately with burial in Westminster Abbey, Trollope's judgment of him was right. He was vain and suspicious almost to paranoia, and such a man might indeed "have put the great department with which he was concerned altogether out of gear . . . had he not been at last controlled."[22]

Frederic Hill continued in his assistant secretaryship for some years after Sir Rowland's resignation; he sometimes attempted by devious means to thwart the new secretary's administration and he conveyed to his brother the news of events at the Post Office. Trollope is said to have told a story about him that was passed on in the memoirs of another Post Office man. By way of cementing a peace after recent quarrels, Frederic Hill invited Trollope to dinner at his Hampstead home. When Trollope arrived, he found that he and his host were the only men in a company of twenty or thirty ladies—who, moreover, had already dined. Host and guest went down to dinner, where the only viands were part of a cold leg of mutton at one end of the table and a salad at the other; no potatoes, no other vegetables, not a drop even of water to drink. Hill told Trollope to sit opposite the mutton, and he himself sat by the salad, which he devoured entire while Trollope made the most of the mutton. They then went upstairs to the drawing room, where the ladies were seated in a large circle with a chair in the middle for the principal guest. "The ladies will now proceed to interrogate you upon various matters," said Frederic Hill—and they did. What the matters were, the story does not tell.[23]

The annual report of the postmaster general (still Lord Stanley of Alderley) for 1864 announced Hill's retirement because of failing health, then went on: "I have appointed Mr. Tilley, who was the senior assistant secretary, to succeed Sir Rowland Hill, and the place vacated by him has been filled up by the promotion of Mr. Scudamore, who, amongst other able men whose claims I fully considered, seemed to me to possess the highest qualifications for the office." Tilley's appointment was hardly a surprise; for several years as assistant secretary he had carried the greater part of Hill's burden and he was the senior man in the office. For the first time in Trollope's experience, moreover, a secretary had been appointed who had risen through the ranks. But the appointment of Frank Ives Scudamore was a surprise: he was from quite another branch of the Post Office, the receiver and accountant general's office, though he had been seconded to the secretary's office on special assignment. Trollope was sadly disappointed at not securing the assistant secretaryship for himself, and his firmest principles respecting the service were offended by the appointment over him of someone six years his junior.[24] That Scudamore was an excellent administrator was beside the point. Scudamore's principal achievement in the Post Office was the taking over of private telegraph companies and making that service part of the Post Office monopoly.

Much to the point, however, was Trollope's sense that Tilley had been responsible for the selection. The postmaster general—who came and went with the changes of party in power—could exercise authority if he wished, but almost invariably accepted the advice of his permanent secretary, the highest continuing officer in the Post Office. Indeed, it was Tilley who wrote the annual report, the language of which has just been quoted. Tilley was one of Trollope's oldest friends; his first wife had been Trollope's sister and his second wife was also connected with the Trollopes. The strain between the men was not long in showing itself.

Nearly a decade earlier, on April 17, 1855, the English surveyors had sent a memorial to the postmaster general protesting that their salaries had been set at a scale £100 per annum lower than those of the heads of departments in London, though their work was fully as responsible. Tilley, acting for Hill, recommended that their protest be rejected. Again in May, 1859, the English surveyors requested equality in salary with the heads of departments, and again Tilley advised against honoring their request. Trollope was not party to these petitions, since he was still in Ireland.[25] But he was present at a meeting of the nine English surveyors at Bedford on April 6–8, 1864, and signed the memorial they there framed. By this time they could protest not only the difference in the established scale, but also the fact that it had recently "been found expedient to

encrease by special allowances the Salaries of all these officers" (i.e., heads
of departments and assistant secretaries) in so general a manner that it
appeared a matter of policy, but the surveyors had enjoyed none of these
increases. With the authorization of Lord Stanley, Tilley responded to the
surveyors as a group that there had been no such general policy—that
every increase beyond the scale had been for special services, and that a
general revision of salaries was not to be undertaken. He seems to have felt
no embarrassment in the fact that he himself had benefited from such
special increments.[26]

Trollope expected the surveyors to be convened as a body to consider
this reply, and when no meeting was called he addressed, on July 8, a very
long letter to the secretary protesting both the decision itself and the
apparently calculated rudeness with which the argument of the surveyors
was brushed aside. There are many signs of haste in the letter; though
nominally addressed to the secretary as "you," it refers to "Mr. Tilley" in
the third person. "I do not think he will for a moment assert,—otherwise
than with the general latitude of loose official phraseology, that he, as
assistant Secretary, performed any special services. He did his work that
was not special in a way that by the consent of all of us deserved the
reward it has received; and, no doubt, before that supplemental allowance
was awarded to him, he was paid insufficiently for the ordinary work of his
office." "Special services were alleged,—but I am not aware, nor as far as I
know is any Gentleman in the department aware, that special services had
been rendered,—except by Mr. Scudamore, the late Receiver and Accountant General, whose great services on the part of the Crown have been
altogether exceptional." When special circumstances are alleged as a reason for widespread, but still selective, increases, the extra payments "are
in every way objectionable. They lead to endless heartburns and jealousies. They are given,—and must be ever given when given,—in a
spirit of partisanship. And they are unjust alike to the department and to
the public." Trollope was right, and Tilley, who was under no illusions
about how the criterion of "merit" was used in the public service, must
have known he was right, had he not been understandably offended by
other parts of the letter. "I have served under the Secretaryship [as had
Tilley, of course] of Sir F. Freeling, Colonel Maberly, and Sir Rowland
Hill," Trollope went on, "and I feel assured that no application from the
whole corps of Surveyors would have been answered in so studiously
offensive a manner [Tilley underscored these last four words when he read
the letter] by either of those Gentlemen. . . . I also think that I am
justified in asking his Lordship to recommend the newly appointed Secretary to be more considerate of the feelings of those Officers among whom
he passed his official life, till he received his promotion."[27]

"I send to your Lordship for perusal before submitting it to you officially this most intemperate letter from Mr. Trollope," wrote Tilley to Stanley, and then to Trollope:

> His Lordship is at a loss to understand why you should come forward alone to question a circular letter which was addressed to yourself as only one of a body. He can only conclude that none of your colleagues felt aggrieved or if they did that no one else could be found to put his signature to a document such as [Tilley first wrote "so improperly worded as"] that which you have forwarded. Be that as it may, Lord Stanley . . . desires me to express his regret at its tone and at the temper which you have displayed and to say that you have adduced no reasons which appear to him to call for a reconsideration of his decision.

Such was the weak reply that Tilley drafted; Lord Stanley gave it his approval.[28]

Now Trollope attempted to take his case to the postmaster general directly, with a letter of July 18 from a holiday at Windermere. He was, after all, on terms of personal friendship with Lord Stanley, at whose house he was an occasional dinner guest; they had laughed together over Sir Rowland Hill's indignation at the Post Office lecture on the Civil Service.[29] Tilley's reply to the surveyors' petition, he wrote, had studiously ignored the merits of their argument. "It was exactly the way in which Oliver was treated when he came forward on behalf of the Charity boys to ask for more;—and I own that I thought Mr. Tilley was very like Bumble in the style of the answer he gave us." There was of course no such thing as addressing the postmaster general directly; the letter went to Tilley, as Trollope knew it would, and Tilley replied that the postmaster general had nothing to add to his earlier communication. And there the matter was dropped.

It is painful to see two old and dear friends in a conflict of this sort. If Trollope may seem to have been unnecessarily aggressive and personal, it must also be observed that he was right in his argument. He wrote to an associate that, while reluctant to take such a course without listening to the advice of his friends, "My feeling is that a man should fight to the last if he feels himself to be right."[30] And there can have been nothing more frustrating than to know that there was no appeal: that Tilley was at every point putting his own words into the mouth of the postmaster general, and that unless Tilley were disposed to admit that he had been in error, there was no chance that Trollope's cause could gain a hearing. It might be added that Tilley's stance got its just response—letters from individual surveyors making claims on their own behalfs for supplementary increases in salary for "special services." Trollope made no such application.[31]

A few months later (February 10, 1865), Tilley proposed that Trollope be sent on an official mission of nine months to Gibraltar and Malta, Egypt, Bombay and possibly Calcutta, Ceylon, Shanghai, and Japan. It was clearly something he thought Trollope would enjoy and Trollope's first disposition was to accept; after nearly a fortnight's consideration, however, he declined. But all was well again between him and Tilley, and Tilley's letters resumed their affectionate form of address—"My dear Tony."[32]

Meanwhile Sir Rowland Hill in his retirement was writing in his journal: "I must own that I am not very sorry to learn that the conspirators against me are now quarrelling as to the division of the spoil. There has, I learn, been a fearful passage of arms between Trollope and Tilley— Trollope, of course, being the aggressor."[33]

꒰ꙮ

One of the most distinguished of the London clubs is the Athenaeum, of which the common bond of the members is literary, artistic, or intellectual interest (as other clubs have their common bonds in Liberalism, Conservatism, university connection, the military and naval services); it is elegantly housed in a building on Waterloo Place, near what would soon be the office of Smith, Elder. Membership might be obtained in the ordinary way through nomination and seconding by members and vote by the membership, but in order to ensure a high level of distinction there was also provision that as many as nine persons a year should be elected by the committee for "distinguished eminence in science, literature, or the arts, or for public services." Among members so elected were Ruskin, Thackeray, John Forster, T. H. Huxley, Charles Merivale, Sir Rowland Hill, Wilkie Collins, Robert Browning, Benjamin Disraeli, and J. E. Millais. Dickens, Macready, Monckton Milnes, and A. P. Stanley had been elected under a comparable provision at a time of great expansion of the membership in 1838. The death of Thackeray no doubt served to call the committee's attention to Trollope; at any rate, he was elected by the committee in 1864. He was often at the club, though he felt greater affection for the Garrick, and was best known as a frequenter of the card room, where he might be seen engaged at whist with W. E. Forster and Abraham Hayward.[34] (Forster was Matthew Arnold's brother-in-law, and Arnold was also a member of the club.)

A modification of the club rules that must have made the card room more pleasant for Trollope is sometimes credited to Thackeray. Prior to 1862 "people could no more smoke in the Athenaeum than they could smoke in church," but in that year one small room at the top of the building was converted into a smoking room, and then, little by little, the privilege was extended to the underground billiard room, then to the morning room on the ground floor.[35]

At the annual general meeting of the Royal Literary Fund on March 9, Trollope was elected to fill a vacancy on the general committee of twenty-four who actively superintended the operation of the fund (of course with the help of a paid secretary who during all Trollope's years with the fund was Octavian Blewitt). The committee met monthly, and sometimes even more frequently, during nine months of the year, and its principal business, the distribution of grants, required its members to study some six or eight applications for each meeting. Membership on the general committee was on the whole very distinguished and devoted: Lord Stanhope, Lord John Manners, J. A. Froude, Dean Stanley, and Bishop Wilberforce were among those who sat with Trollope, and in 1866 he successfully proposed for the committee his old friend Charles Merivale. Trollope himself served on the committee for the rest of his life. His chief efforts were directed to increasing the size of the grants (it was during his membership on the committee that the ordinary maximum rose from £50 to £100, and the rare grant by the end of his life got as high as £200) and to securing the assent of his colleagues to the notion that each year's gifts to the fund be spent entirely on relief, not left to accumulate. He seldom missed a meeting unless he was out of the country.

At the anniversary dinner for 1864, with the Prince of Wales in the chair, he responded to the toast proposed by Earl Russell, "Prosperity to English Literature, and the Health of Mr. Anthony Trollope." His remarks were largely devoted to the memory of Thackeray, whom the Prince had already mentioned and who had been linked by Russell to Cervantes.

> He is one whom we all loved with an especial love [said Trollope], because no man's hand was ever open more often than his, and no man's hand was ever opened wider. . . . I do not think that we yet know how great that man was—I do not think that we have felt how deep was his pathos, how soft he was in his tenderness, how true he was in his delineations of character, how gracious he was in his conduct [cheers]. . . . If any man has trod upon the heel of Cervantes it is Thackeray. There is in his writings a touch of that love of the sublime, joined to that appreciation of the ridiculous, which, if we think of it, makes up the characters of all those friends whom we love the fondest, and whom we trust the most firmly.[36]

Trollope's four-year association with Thackeray was the turning point of his literary life: from this time on, writing was the principal source of his income, and Anthony Trollope was a person of recognized significance in literary society.

Chapter XII

1864–65

In addition to his Post Office work and his novel writing, Trollope was coming more and more to be in demand as a lecturer. After speaking on January 26, 1864, at the Athenaeum, Bury St. Edmunds, about the state of the American Civil War,[1] he suspended work on *Can You Forgive Her?* for a fortnight in February to write and deliver a lecture on Thursday the eighteenth on "Politics as a Daily Study for the Common People" at the Leeds Mechanics' Institution and Literary Society.[2] (The date had to be negotiated with a view to leaving his Saturday free for hunting near his home.) On February 25 he lectured again on the American Civil War at the Literary and Mechanics' Institution in Halstead, Essex (in his Post Office district) at the invitation of the vicar of Halstead, Charles Burney.[3] And he spoke to the Shakespeare Foundation Schools in London on May 11.[4] The "lecture at Bury went off magnificently," he told Lewes. "I went there in a carriage with a marquis, who talked to me all the way about the state of his stomach—which was very grand; and the room was quite full, and the people applauded with thorough good nature, only they did so in the wrong places;—and two or three Lady Janes told me afterwards that it was quite nice;—so that I was, as you see, quite in a little paradise of terrestrial Gods and Goddesses." The morning after the lecture he got off at six to a hunt meeting thirty miles away.[5]

Young Harry Trollope had stayed in Italy to study with tutors; he now returned with his uncle Tom, and his father asked Lord Houghton to help procure for the lad a nomination to the Foreign Office from Lord Russell. Nothing came of the proposal, and the eighteen-year-old young man went to Paris in early October, escorted by his father.[6]

The Trollopes' holiday this year was divided between a comfortable house, "Greenbank," at Grasmere in the latter half of July and a visit to Freshwater, on the Isle of Wight, in early October. Trollope complained to George Smith that the former sojourn was by no means a holiday—he worked harder than he had ever worked before (on *Miss Mackenzie*) because of the time he had lost sitting for the portrait Smith had commissioned from Samuel Laurence. But when the finished portrait arrived as a gift from Smith, he found it "wonderfully vigorous. . . . When I look at the portrait I find myself to be a wonderfully solid old fellow. The picture is certainly a very good picture & my wife declares it to be very like,—& not

a bit more solid than the original."[7] On the ferry crossing to the Isle of
Wight on October 8 another of his portraitists was a fellow passenger, the
photographer Julia Cameron. William Allingham sat next to Anthony
outside the coach to Freshwater, Allingham on his way to stay with the
Tennysons. "[Trollope] asked a great many practical questions about the
houses and lands which we drove past—did not seem interested about
Tennyson. Told me he had been in every *parish* in Ireland. He [and Rose]
put up at Lambert's Hotel." Tennyson turned the tables many years later
(after Anthony's death), when Allingham told him he was reading some of
Trollope's novels "and felt my estimate of his powers to be higher than it
used to be." "But they're so dull," said Tennyson; "—so prosaic: never a
touch of poetry."[8] Within ten days of his return, Trollope wrote the
chapter of *The Claverings* that described Lady Ongar's visit to Freshwater.

Julia Margaret Cameron had bought the house nearest to Tennyson's
in 1860, was given her first camera in December, 1863, and within a few
months had achieved professional success as a portrait photographer. She
scarcely needed an introduction to Trollope, for Thackeray had been an
old friend and Henry Taylor, author of *Philip van Artevelde,* was one of her
favorite guests and models. She lost no time in securing Anthony; during
his five-day holiday he posed for at least two portraits, one very familiar,
hatless, and one relatively unknown, with a hat and with the same
wrinkles in his jacket (illus. 6).[9]

る

The choice of Hablot Knight Browne ("Phiz") to supply the forty illustrations for *Can You Forgive Her?* was Chapman's, and signified no break
between Millais and Trollope. Millais' explanation, indeed, is undoubtedly true: Chapman and Hall had paid Trollope so much for his novel
(£3,000) that they wished to save on the illustrations.[10] Millais' fee of £25
for each drawing would have come to £1,000 for the entire book; Chapman procured Browne's services for substantially less. Browne had been
the illustrator for ten of Dickens's novels, beginning with *The Pickwick
Papers* in 1836 when he was only twenty-one; Chapman and Hall were the
publishers. He had also supplied the twelve illustrations for the three-
volume edition of Mrs. Trollope's *Charles Chesterfield* in 1841.

Trollope had worked well with Millais, and Millais had been very
attentive to the careful descriptions Trollope's texts provided for the
figures. He did not know Browne. "I specially want to see your artist
before he goes to work. When can I meet him? He should have read the
work first," Trollope wrote to Chapman in October, 1863. "If I meet
your artist on Friday, pray arrange that he shall have read the numbers
first." By Christmas the illustrations for the second (February) number

were done, and Trollope had chosen the subjects for those of the third
number. In another month he had marked the subjects for numbers four
and five. At the end of March he indicated the subjects for numbers seven
and eight. But long before that he had determined that Browne must go.
When Millais dined at Waltham Cross on January 10, Trollope proposed
that Millais take over the work, and was so eager as to wish to pay him out
of his own pocket. But Millais declined.[11]

Browne's drawings were etched on metal, whereas Millais' had been
cut on wood. Browne's figures were therefore much smaller, there was
greater detail, and his plates often were more crowded. He was essentially
a caricaturist, moreover, and his illustrations were far less suited to Trollope's usual matter than they had been to Dickens's. Indeed, Trollope
early complained that he had to adapt his choice of subjects to Browne's
limitations. "I hope he will take a little trouble about his horses. The
farm yard is the best. You see as regards all of them I am drawn to choose
some subject that is almost burlesque," he told Chapman on January 30,
as he returned drawings for parts four and six.[12] In Browne's defense it
might be said that a good deal of the early part of *Can You Forgive Her?* is
suited to caricature, with the figures of the Widow Greenow and her
suitors, and since Browne had before him only the parts on which he was
working, he could not foresee the tone that would be appropriate for the
whole book (in fact, only about half the book was written before publication began). As Trollope said, the "farmyard" was very good indeed:
Farmer Cheesacre proudly displaying heap after heap of manure and straw
(muck) "raised like the streets of a little city," as evidence of his prosperity, while among the barnyard animals a huge hog stands reduplica-
tively behind the farmer. The widow he hopes to persuade into matrimony shows an eager interest, but the niece she likes to think of as
Cheesacre's "intended" stands a little back with a large, presumably
perfumed, handkerchief held to her nose and mouth (plate no. 8, chap.
xiv). Other illustrations, like the widow's sentimentally looking at her
late husband's picture while her next husband's whiskers brush her widow's cap (plate no. 20, chap. xl) well reflect Trollope's humor, and the
plates with Burgo Fitzgerald (nos. 15 and 17) are full of character. On the
whole, and especially in view of the handicap under which he worked
(though he had worked under the same handicap with Dickens, illustrating stories of which he could read only a part at a time), Browne did not
do badly. But he was certainly unlike the Millais with whom Trollope's
works were by now associated. Curiously, none of Browne's illustrations
was signed.

When George Smith apparently proposed Browne as illustrator for
The Claverings in the *Cornhill* Trollope wrote bitterly: "I think you would
possibly find no worse illustrator than H. Browne, and I think he is

almost as bad in one kind as another. He will take no pains to ascertain the thing to be illustrated. I cannot think that his work can add any value at all to any book." At the time (August, 1864) Browne's work was still appearing in the monthly parts of *Can You Forgive Her?* but Trollope went on to tell Smith that he had employed a lady for the last ten numbers of that novel, at £5 5*s.* 0*d.* a drawing. This was a Miss E. Taylor of St. Leonard's, in Sussex, of whom nothing further seems to be known; her drawings were cut on wood and bore some resemblance to Millais'. "She has as yet done two drawings on wood. They are both excellent, and the cutter says that they will come out very well. . . . Why not employ her [for *The Claverings*]?"[13] But she too was a disappointment; he seemed to be unable to arrange meetings with her to talk over the work, and in desperation told her to choose her own subjects. Though he professed to like some of her wood blocks,[14] her drawings were in fact sad failures. Meanwhile poor Browne found himself discarded also by Dickens, whose *Our Mutual Friend* began to appear from Chapman and Hall on April 30 with illustrations by Marcus Stone. "Confound all authors and publishers, say I. There is no pleasing one or t'other," he wrote.[15]

❧

Trollope had so much enjoyed his Swiss tour in July and August of 1863 that he could not resist placing some early chapters of his new novel in Basel. "I have just returned from Switzerland," he told his readers at the beginning of part 2 of *Can You Forgive Her?,* written between August 24 and September 2, and the description of the mighty Rhine as seen from the balcony of the hotel there (which modern tourists will recognize as The Three Kings) is a part of the novel few readers forget.[16] Equally impressive is his description of the Fells in the Lake District (chap. xxxi), where Squire Vavasor lived near Penrith, once the home of John and Cecilia Tilley, the town to which Anthony had brought his bride in 1844 to meet his family. The description was written in mid-November, 1863, and actually appeared while Trollope and Rose were tramping about near Grasmere in the summer of 1864. "I have sat me down and slept among those mountain tracks," he told his readers, recalling earlier years, "— have slept because nature refused to allow longer wakefulness. But my heart has been as light as my purse, and there has been something in the air of the hills that made me buoyant and happy in the midst of my weariness."

An important motif of *The Small House* had been, as Trollope re-marked in *An Autobiography,* the jilting of his heroine by a snob. Perhaps it was this motif that called up to his mind his early, unpublished, unperformed, and (to his public) unknown play, *The Noble Jilt.* In any case, *Can You Forgive Her?* was conceived as a transformation of this play set in late eighteenth-century Bruges into a novel set in the England of his own day. The serious part of the play dealt with the wavering of the heroine between two suitors, a worthy, wealthy, and dull gentleman on the one hand and a swashbuckling, high-spirited revolutionary politician of no principles on the other; the latter is aided by a sister who is the heroine's best friend. This plot is mirrored by the comedy of a rich widow sought by a sober, wealthy (and alas "podgy") citizen and by a good-looking, impoverished, bragging military man. Trollope said he did not dare to call his novel "The Noble Jilt" "lest criticism might throw a doubt on the nobility"; unfortunately the title he did adopt suggested a memorable witticism to a twenty-two-year-old critic just beginning his literary career: "Can we forgive Miss Vavasor?" asked Henry James. "Of course we can, and forget her, too, for that matter."[17] Trollope kept alive the idea of the jilt, however. The old squire startled his granddaughter when he applied the term to her: "Poor Alice! she was a jilt; and perhaps it may have been well that the old man should tell her so" (chap. xxxii). As the novel drew to a close, Alice remarked to her fiancé, "I shall never cease to reproach myself. . . . I have been—a jilt." He replied, "The noblest jilt that ever yet halted between two minds!" (chap. lxxiv). Trollope informed his readers that the story of his heroine's waverings had been present to his mind for many years (chap. xxxvii), though he did not explain here how that was true. That a dull play should have become a serious and interesting novel perhaps shows how right Trollope was to think that "plot" as such was not of the greatest importance in his novels.

But though the story of the "jilt" who must be forgiven is the starting point of the novel, the greatest interest, both for Trollope and his modern reader, was unforeseeable throughout most of the first half of the novel. It lies in yet another parallel plot that is not introduced at all until part 5—the story of Lady Glencora's wavering between the handsome rake Burgo Fitzgerald and her worthy, but dull, husband Plantagenet Palliser. (There is a factitious link among the heroines of the three plots: Mrs. Greenow is Alice Vavasor's aunt and Lady Glencora is Alice's cousin.) Alice had been engaged to the man she "jilted"; young Glencora, by virtue of the strong pressure from her family, was actually married to the man she was tempted to abandon. Once again Trollope learned he was on dangerous moral ground; the suspense resided in wondering whether Lady Glencora would yield to temptation, and unfortunately, since the tale appeared in monthly parts, the readers could not quickly look ahead for reassurance. "There came to me a letter from a distinguished dignitary of our Church, a man whom all men honoured, treating me with severity for what I was doing. It had been one of the innocent joys of his life, said the clergyman, to have my novels read to him by his daughters. But now I was writing a book which caused him to bid them close it! Must I also turn away to vicious sensation such as this? Did I think that a wife contemplating adultery was a character fit for my pages? I asked him in return, whether from his pulpit . . . he did not denounce adultery to his audience; and if so, why it should not be open to me to preach the same doctrine to mine."[18] Lady Glencora, of course, did not yield.

It has been remarked that she and her unworthy suitor were already named, and her marriage to Palliser told, in the preceding novel, *The Small House at Allington*. But since *The Small House* and *Can You Forgive Her?* were both published serially and since the latter began its appearance before the former ended, Trollope must have relied on his readers to keep current with both novels at once: the Fitzgerald-Glencora romance was first mentioned in *Small House* in March, 1864, and then slipped over to the fifth part of *Can You Forgive Her?* in May of that year. Burgo's introduction in the latter novel is most memorable. Trollope indulged himself in an elaborate description of a hunting scene (in which, as we have noted, he placed himself in the guise of Pollock, "the heavy-weight sporting literary gentleman"). As the fox made a last desperate escape after a long hard run, the few surviving riders rushed in pursuit.

> There was a huge ditch and boundary bank there which Sir William [the master of the hounds] had known and avoided [by using a nearby gate. But] Maxwell and Burgo Fitzgerald, followed by Vavasor, went straight ahead. . . . Maxwell, whose pluck had returned to him at last, took it well. His horse was comparatively fresh and made nothing of it. Then came poor Burgo! Oh, Burgo, hadst thou not have been a very child, thou shouldst have known that now, at this time of the day,—after all that thy gallant horse had done for thee,—it was impossible to thee or him. But when did Burgo Fitzgerald know anything? He rode at the bank as though it had been the first fence of the day, striking his poor beast with his spurs, as though muscle, strength, and new power could be imparted by their rowels. The animal rose at the bank, and in some way got upon it, scrambling as he struck it with his chest, and then fell headlong into the ditch at the other side, a confused mass of head, limbs, and body. His career was at an end, and he had broken his heart! Poor noble beast, noble in vain! To his very last gasp he had done his best, and had deserved that he should have been in better hands. His master's ignorance had killed him. There are men who never know how little a horse can do,—or how much! (Chap. xvii)

The thoughtless, utterly selfish man here shown will a few chapters later generously buy a meal in an Oxford Street public house on the night before Christmas Eve for a homeless sixteen-year-old streetwalker. As they part she presses his hand to her lips. "'I wish I might once see you again,' she says, 'because you are so good and so beautiful.'. . . Poor Burgo! All who had seen him since life had begun with him had loved him and striven to cherish him. And with it all, to what a state had he come!" (chap. xxix). When the girl encountered him once again late in the novel, she remarked, with little ambiguity, "Shouldn't I like to be good to such a one as him!" (chap. lxvi).

Can You Forgive Her? expands greatly on the attention given to parliamentary elections and parliamentary politics in *Doctor Thorne,* and it expands also on the simple proposition there that "No other great European nation has anything like [a seat in Parliament] to offer to the ambition of its citizens; for in no other great country of Europe, not even in those which are free, has the popular constitution obtained, as with us, true sovereignty and power of rule" (chap. xvii). In the new novel, the general proposition is given a very direct and personal application to Trollope himself:

> There is on the left-hand side of our great national hall . . . a pair of gilded lamps, with a door between them, near to which [a] great policeman . . . guards the pass. Between those lamps is the entrance to the House of Commons, and none but Members may go that way! It is the only gate before which I have ever stood filled with envy,— sorrowing to think that my steps might never pass under it. There are many portals forbidden to me, as there are many forbidden to all men; and forbidden fruit, they say, is sweet; but my lips have watered after no other fruit but that which grows so high, within the sweep of that great policeman's truncheon. . . . Not to have passed by the narrow entrance between those lamps,—is to die and not to have done that which it most becomes an Englishman to have achieved. (Chap. xlv)

"I do not see why a man should not live honestly and be a Member of Parliament as well," remarked Plantagenet Palliser (chap. lxxiv).

There is a markedly different relation between reader and novel when the entire book is in the reader's hands at once and when it comes to him only in installments, so different that it would be well if the modern reader could know, as one usually cannot, what the original part divisions of a nineteenth-century novel were. In *Vanity Fair,* for example, a chapter on the civilian panic in Brussels at the roar of the cannon of Waterloo ends with the abrupt sentences: "Then at last the English troops rushed from the post from which no enemy had been able to dislodge them, and the Guards turned and fled. No more firing was heard at Brussels—the pursuit rolled miles away. The darkness came down on the field, and city: and Amelia was praying for George, who was lying on his face, dead, with a bullet through his heart" (chap. xxxii). The modern reader must then go through two and a half chapters that deal with other matters before he hears anything further about Amelia, but this can be done rather quickly; the original reader would have had to wait a full month before he could get those three following chapters in his hand. Thackeray's abrupt ending to his part 9 was unusually theatrical; Trollope does not commonly play such a trick. The story of Lady Glencora's temptation at the hands of Burgo Fitzgerald at his aunt's large party, and of her rescue from temptation by Plantagenet Palliser (chaps. xlix–l) is told in the same installment. But the preparations for the party had been described the month before, and along with them were two chapters of the George and Alice Vavasor plot and one of the Widow Greenow's story. Trollope allowed his novel to begin its publication when it was barely more than half written, but he was too methodical to permit himself any further delays, and there was no scrambling, as with Dickens, to keep ahead of the printer's desperate cry for copy: he completed the twentieth and final part just as the fifth part was printed off. (He had the additional motive for finishing quickly that he was paid for each part as it reached the publisher's hands; the more rapidly he worked, the sooner he got the whole of his £3,000.) There is, none the less, a jogging, donkey-cart kind of pace imposed by the method of publication in parts that the readers of *Barchester Towers* and *Doctor Thorne* had not felt.

ॐ

Much of the story of *Can You Forgive Her?* is set in Trollope's Post Office district—Yarmouth, Norwich, Cambridgeshire—and the place-names occur frequently in his diaries. Nevertheless, those diaries show that about 1864 his traveling diminished drastically. One may assume that his supervision of his district could more and more be delegated to his assistants. But it is also notable that the year 1864 saw perhaps his most prodigious output of fiction—half of *Can You Forgive Her?* and all of *Miss Mackenzie* and *The Claverings,* for a total of more than half a million words. Publication of course lagged behind composition, but the effect of this effort showed in his accounts for 1865, when his income from writing leaped to £5,866 15*s.* 7*d.* (as against £2,271 12*s.* 6*d.* in 1864); in 1866, thanks to the sale of many of his earlier copyrights to W. H. Smith for publication as "yellow backs," it rose to £6,291 10*s.* 0*d.*[19]

   As he looked back on this period in *An Autobiography* he admitted that he "crowded [his] wares into the market too quickly, because the reading world could not want such a quantity of matter from the hands of one author in so short a space of time." But he denied that the rapidity of production caused inferior work; in fact, "I believe that the work which has been done quickest has been done the best." And his argument is persuasive; indeed once the characters are invented they take a life of their own and follow the courses of their own natures. (In the few instances in which his preliminary sketches of his plots have survived, we can see how this has occurred.) The vividness of his characters would only fade if there were undue delay in writing down their stories. The principal danger of speed, of intense periods of composition, was to style—to lucidity, even to grammatical regularity. And there he confessed that he was not immune to criticism, though he had early developed the habit of clear writing, as a skilled musician has the habit of producing well-articulated music, the telegraph operator the habit of transmitting and receiving messages, the compositor of setting up type.[20] One other respect in which his haste left its mark is his occasional forgetfulness of locale. In *Can You Forgive Her?* for example, Lady Monk's house (from which Burgo hopes to elope with Lady Glencora) is explicitly placed in Gloucester Square (north of Hyde Park), yet often it is referred to as being in Grosvenor Square (east of Hyde Park), not only by simple lapse of the pen but by the actual geography of the streets along which Burgo walks.

The agreement Trollope made with Chapman and Hall on February 23, 1864, called for a novel in two volumes of the same length as *Rachel Ray,* for which he was to receive £1,200 for the first three thousand copies.[21] But it was not merely in length that *Miss Mackenzie* resembled *Rachel Ray.* The ordinary lower-middle-class society of Rachel's "Baslehurst" is not unlike that of Miss Mackenzie's "Littlebath." And as Baslehurst had its Evangelical clergyman Mr. Prong, so Littlebath has the Reverend Mr. Stumfold and his wife and his curate Jeremiah Maguire. Stumfold "was always fighting the devil by opposing those pursuits which are the life and mainstay of such places as Littlebath. His chief enemies were card-playing and dancing as regarded the weaker sex, and hunting and horse-racing—to which, indeed, might be added everything under the name of sport—as regarded the stronger" (chap. ii). If the Sabbatarianism of this group did not achieve Mrs. Proudie's objective of banning Sunday trains, it did succeed in forbidding the postmen to deposit mail on Sundays in the houses of the faithful (chap. xiv).

Margaret Mackenzie was the youngest in her family of three, and was brought up in the part of London in which Trollope was born. (The chambers of her lawyer Mr. Slow may well have been modeled on Thomas Anthony's chambers, though the address is not quite the same [chap. xvii].) For eighteen years she had nursed, first an invalid father, then an invalid brother who was a minor civil servant; when she was thirty-four the death of the latter released her and provided her with a reasonable financial competence. Until then she had known nothing of society and was thought of as hopelessly plain (if she was thought of at all). She moved to Littlebath in the hope of finding friends, and fell into the hands of Mrs. Stumfold, the stern ruler of the Stumfoldians. Her anti-Stumfoldian neighbor, Miss Todd, would have offered friendship, but there was no dividing one's allegiance in that community, and the neighbor ironically remarked, "I always see that when a lady goes evangelical, she soon finds a husband to take care of her; that is, if she has got any money" (chap. xiii). It was not long, therefore, before the curate Maguire got wind of her fortune and was courting Miss Mackenzie. But so too were the son of her remaining brother's partner in the oilcloth business in London, an agreeable but vulgar young man who meant well but could not keep himself honest, and a widowed cousin of hers, aged about fifty and heir to a baronetcy but to no money. Gradually she gained confidence both in the strength of her mind and the acceptability of her appearance: as she looked in the mirror she saw that her eyes were bright and her smile was dimpled; her hands told her that her hair was soft and silken and her cheek youthful; as she drew her scarf tighter across her bosom she felt its firmness (chap. ix). Her first thought was to marry Maguire so that her money would be put to good use in furthering his religion, but gradually she learns that she must live for herself, not sacrifice herself, and the discovery is fortunate, for Maguire turns out to be a thorough scoundrel. Her growing self-confidence makes her willing also to resist the various selfish criticisms of her relatives and to wait until she is sure which suitor she wants. Trollope once thought of calling the novel *The Modern Griselda,* and toward the end he refers to Margaret as "Griselda" so often, in his discourses with the reader, that he once absent-mindedly lets a cousin address her by that name instead of "Margaret" (chap. xxix). (Griselda, of course, was the name of Archdeacon Grantly's daughter, but she, as Lady Dumbello and the Marchioness of Hartletop, was anything but a "modern Griselda" in character.)

Trollope was a firm believer in the notion that a "gentleman" could always be distinguished by his manners and social grace, and amuses himself with the gaucheries of the tradesmen and their wives in the novel. Margaret's sister-in-law engages a butler for the evening and a caterer to serve a fancy dinner, but is sure that one bottle of champagne will suffice and is humiliated when the butler fills the glasses even of those guests he had been told to pass by, so that the principal guests get none. In every respect the dinner is a disaster. At tea on another occasion, the young partner in the oilcloth business wears bright yellow gloves, has his hair molded in waves with perfumed grease, and offers his arms simultaneously to *two* ladies instead of one (chaps. viii, ix). The general embarrassment is perhaps more painful than comic, especially as Trollope himself was often accused of social gaucherie. As always, his own gentlemanly education can be recognized in the literary allusiveness of his language—a phrase from Shakespeare or from Milton, a quotation from Horace, the "Shadrach Fire Assurance Office" and the "Abednego Life" (chaps. xviii, xix). Once he actually introduces a character with the sole purpose of quietly using the language of Edward FitzGerald's famous parody of Wordsworthian blank verse, "A Mr. Wilkinson, a clergyman" (chap. x).[22] He remembered with such pleasure his epigram in the speech at the Royal Literary Fund's dinner in 1863 that he repeated it in his characterization of one of Margaret's friends: "Had she not been so much the lady, she would have been more the woman" (chap. ix).

Unquestionably the complications are drawn out far too long before Margaret in fact marries the bald-headed widower, and Trollope also introduces an irrelevant chapter (xxvii) toward the end of the novel with the purpose of ridiculing charity bazaars; as he had told Mrs. Henry Wood only a few months earlier, "I hate these bazaars as methods of charity, believing the tendency of them to be altogether bad."[23] (Mrs. Wood had asked him to sign a sheaf of bookmarks so that she might sell them at a bazaar.) The bazaar in *Miss Mackenzie* was held in South Kensington for the benefit of orphan children of Negro soldiers killed in the American Civil War, and brought out an array of Trollopian characters who have no other function in this novel—the Duchess of St. Bungay, Lady Glencora Palliser, the Marchioness of Hartletop. If *Miss Mackenzie* is not one of Trollope's better novels, it nevertheless treats with a lively mind a social milieu one does not usually associate with him. The book was published about February 18, 1865.

多

"You are a jilt,—that is all," says young Harry Clavering to the lovely Julia Brabazon at the beginning of the *The Claverings,* when she tells him, in the garden, that she is throwing him over in favor of the wizened old (thirty-six) alcoholic Earl of Ongar, who has an income rumored to be about £60,000 a year. Once again the word *jilt* is the keynote of a novel. For when Julia marries, Harry falls in love with a plain but sweet girl, younger daughter of a provincial civil engineer to whom he has become apprenticed and whose wife has already married off her older daghters to previous apprentices; Harry and the girl soon become engaged. And then Lady Ongar returns to London, widowed and rich after less than a year of married life on the Continent, and Harry's old love grows warm again. Will he now jilt Florence Burton for the woman who formerly jilted him? In his uncertainty he agrees to marry the widow, who confesses she still loves him, but after a long struggle he in his turn jilts Julia. Julia accepts, with dignity and intelligence that win our sympathy, the fact that she must for the rest of her life pay the price for having sold herself for Lord Ongar's fortune.

The social level of the characters is once more in the upper range. Julia is the daughter of a lord "whose peerage had descended to him in a direct line from the time of the Plantagenets," Harry is first cousin to an eleventh baronet, whose title, as it turns out, he will inherit. The snobbery shows itself in Harry's first impression of Florence's cotton-gloved brother as "the man who dusts his boots with his handkerchief" (the vignette at the initial letter of the tenth installment in the *Cornhill* shows him doing it), but the warmth of the family life of these Burtons at their home in Onslow Crescent, only a few steps from the house in Onslow Square where Thackeray lived when Trollope first met him, wins Harry completely, and Florence's mother later expresses a view that is not out of keeping with the tone of the novel: "I wish there was no such thing as a gentleman;—so I do. Perhaps there would be more honest men then" (chap. xxxii). There is nothing but admiration in this novel for the few middle-class characters.

Comedy is at the expense of the empty-headed members of the sometimes Wildean upper class. Archie Clavering (younger brother of the current baronet) and his friend Captain Boodle (a man with a Thackerayan name and the same fondness for the adverb *doosed*—"devilish"—that Major Pendennis has) plot to win Lady Ongar and her fortune for Archie, and enlist the aid of a Franco-Polish countess, Sophie Gordeloup, who is Julia's frequent companion. As Boodle is convinced she is a Russian spy, she is clearly bribable, and she quickly relieves Archie of any concern for delicacy by taking his money and asking for more (chap. xxiv). If she is venal she is also very shrewd and blunt, and so utterly confounds Boodle in a superb scene (chap. xxx) that he is convinced she has supernatural insight—is "a medium—or a media, or whatever it ought to be called" (chap. xxxix). And therefore he is terrified when in a rage she foretells that Sir Hugh and Archie, who are off on a fishing expedition in Norwegian waters, will in fact be "locked up . . . [in] what you call Davy's locker." With the somewhat contrived assistance of Trollope, however, she ensnares Boodle and carries him off to Paris as her purser.

The "witch's" prophecy comes true, Sir Hugh and Archie are drowned, and the title passes to Harry's father. In a final scene meant to balance the opening chapter, Harry once more parts from Julia in the garden of Clavering Park and devotes the rest of his life to his marriage with Florence and to the preservation of game on the estate he will inherit. The novel is linked to the Barsetshire novels by a slender thread: Clavering Church is in the diocese of Barchester and Bishop Proudie, when he takes over the diocese, puts an end to the fox hunting of Harry's father the rector. It is one of Trollope's very best, especially for the ultimately generous character of Julia.

Trollope's contract with Smith, Elder for *The Claverings*, dated November 13, 1863, called for the novel to be published in sixteen numbers of the *Cornhill* beginning any time between January and October, 1865.[24] The manuscript was finished on the last day of December, 1864, but about three weeks before that Smith asked if publication could be postponed to begin in January, 1866, and Trollope agreed; Smith in turn agreed to pay Trollope in full when the manuscript was delivered to him early in 1865.[25] In fact, the novel began its run in February, 1866. Arrangements for the illustrations were made at the last minute: Smith knew of a twenty-six-year-old artist, Mary Ellen Edwards, of whom he thought highly, and as late as December 21, 1865, Trollope wrote to him to suggest the subjects for both the vignette at the opening of the novel and the full-page illustration for the first installment; he designated also what should be the legend under the picture, for which he ordinarily preferred a quotation from his text.[26] It may be supposed that the remaining fifteen illustrations and vignettes were similarly chosen by him. "M. E. E." had a long career as an illustrator, and her drawings for *The Claverings* were at least satisfactory, sometimes more than that. The work was published in two volumes, with the full-page illustrations but not the vignettes, about April 20, 1867.[27]

Chapter XIII

1865–66

When Trollope expressed the fear that he had been induced, by his service to two publishers, to crowd his wares into the market too quickly, he was speaking of his novels as published by Chapman and Hall and by Smith, Elder—*Rachel Ray, Can You Forgive Her?* and *Miss Mackenzie* by the former, for example, and *The Small House at Allington* and *The Claverings* by the latter. But it was not only novel writing that was involved; it was the temptation to follow a new career of journalism, and the seduction was offered by two new periodicals from these two publishing houses.

On October 29, 1864, the professor of poetry at Oxford, Matthew Arnold, lectured on "The Function of Criticism at the Present Time"; the lecture was published simultaneously in Walter Bagehot's new *National Review*. In a memorable passage, Arnold asked, "What is at present the bane of criticism in this country?" and answered his question:

> It is that practical considerations cling to it and stifle it. It subserves interests not its own. Our organs of criticism are organs of men and parties having practical ends to serve, and with them those practical ends are the first thing and the play of mind the second; so much play of mind as is compatible with the prosecution of those practical ends is all that is wanted. An organ like the *Revue des Deux Mondes,* having for its main function to understand and utter the best that is known and thought in the world, existing, it may be said, as just an organ for a free play of the mind, we have not. But we have the *Edinburgh Review,* existing as an organ of the old Whigs, and for as much play of the mind as may suit its being that; we have the *Quarterly Review,* existing as an organ of the Tories, and for as much play of mind as may suit its being that; we have the *British Quarterly Review,* existing as an organ of the political Dissenters, and for as much play of mind as may suit its being that; we have the *Times,* existing as an organ of the common, satisfied, well-to-do Englishman, and for as much play of mind as may suit its being that. And so on through all the various fractions, political and religious, of our society; every fraction has, as such, its organ of criticism, but the notion of combining all fractions in the common pleasure of a free disinterested play of mind meets with no favour. Directly this play of

mind wants to have more scope, and to forget the pressure of practical considerations a little, it is checked, it is made to feel the chain. . . . It must needs be that men should act in sects and parties, that each of these sects and parties should have its organ, and should make this organ subserve the interests of its action; but it would be well, too, that there should be a criticism, not the minister of these interests, not their enemy, but absolutely and entirely independent of them. No other criticism will ever attain any real authority or make any real way towards its end,—the creating a current of true and fresh ideas. [1]

Arnold's remarks served to give focus to the conversations of a group of men who were meeting in the autumn of 1864 to discuss the founding of a new periodical. Precisely who made up the group is, curiously enough, uncertain; Trollope was a leader, and with him were Frederic Chapman, Henry Danby Seymour, and James Cotter Morison. [2] Involved in the planning was a young novelist named George Meredith, who became a reader of manuscripts for Chapman and Hall in 1860. He had already publicly declared *Barchester Towers* "decidedly the cleverest novel of the season [1857], and one of the most masculine delineations of modern life in a special class of society that we have seen for many a day." [3] In 1859 Meredith published *The Ordeal of Richard Feverel.* By that time he had some personal acquaintance with Trollope, for he wrote to Tom Taylor that when Anthony returned from the West Indies and finished the book he was writing on his experiences there, he might be glad to contribute to *Once a Week*, the journal Bradbury and Evans were setting up to compete with Dickens's *All the Year Round.* He became a fellow member of the Garrick Club in 1864, and thereafter was for a good many years associated with Trollope in the world of publishing and journalism. In November, 1864, he wrote to Chapman that Danby Seymour "thinks the Magazine will have a fair chance, and hopes that I shall have the *de facto* running of it." [4]

But Arnold's lecture changed that. The group resolved to form a small stock company to publish not a magazine but a "journal similar to the *Revue des Deux Mondes,* treating of subjects which [should] interest cultivated and thoughtful readers, and published at intervals which are neither too distant for influence on passing questions, nor too brief for deliberation. . . . We shall ask each writer to express his own views and sentiments with all the force of sincerity. He will never be required to express the views of an Editor or of a Party." [5] Like the *Revue,* it would be published twice a month. All articles would be signed (in contrast with the practice of most reviews then published, and even of the *Cornhill* at first). There was general agreement, Trollope said, that "we would be neither conservative nor liberal, neither religious nor free-thinking, neither popular nor exclusive;—but we would let any man who had a thing to say, and knew how to say it, speak freely." Then, quite inconsistently (as he was driven to admit when he thought back on the matter), Trollope insisted "that nothing should appear denying or questioning the divinity of Christ." In accordance with their plans, the journal was called the *Fortnightly Review,* an unfortunate choice, since when less than two years after its beginning the journal became a monthly, copyright laws prevented any change in name without an entire reorganization. (For the same reason, the *Nineteenth Century* continued under that name until well into the twentieth century.) Trollope claimed entire responsibility for the choice of the title, and admitted that he felt it an embarrassment, a bad joke, every time he picked up the journal after it became a monthly. The enterprise was capitalized at either £8,000 or £9,000; Trollope's investment, which as he recalled it was what others also had put in, was £1,250, so that there were presumably seven proprietors.[6]

The management was under the direction of a board, of which Trollope was chairman. The business office was the Piccadilly address of Chapman and Hall, who were publishers (but not at first proprietors) of the journal, and the printer from the first was Cotter Morison's brother-in-law James Sprent Virtue, a well-established printer and publisher with offices in the City Road; he attended the fortnightly meetings of the board and became a friend and admirer of Trollope's. It was while the organization was under discussion that Trollope wrote his description of a "committee" in *The Claverings:* "It is necessary to get a lot of men together, for the show of the thing,—otherwise the world will not believe. That is the meaning of committees. But the real work must always be done by one or two men" (chap. xxxii).

Chapman and Trollope were both eager that Lewes should undertake the editorship; he accepted early in December, then changed his mind in mid-December. But on December 30, 1864, he dined with Seymour, Chapman, Trollope, and Laurence Oliphant, and tentatively once more undertook the editorship. Matters were not firmly settled, however, until Trollope lunched at Lewes's on March 21, 1865, and took him along to a meeting of the board.[7] Four days later the first advertisements appeared.

In one matter Trollope was overruled: he was mildly opposed to the inclusion of fiction, but the board of management determined that fiction should be a part of each issue. And so on January 30, 1865, he began *The Belton Estate,* which started its serial appearance in the first number on May 15; he did not finish writing it until September 4. He did at least make clear to Lewes that he preferred that the novel be not always placed first in an issue, "as it indicates an idea that it is our staple;—which indicates the further idea that the rest is padding."[8] The *Fortnightly* also gave Anthony the opportunity to discuss in articles of some length matters of considerable interest to him—"Public Schools" (October 1, 1865), "The Civil Service" (October 15, 1865), Sabbatarianism (January 15, 1866)—and to write a substantial number of book reviews.

The journal was in fact the most intellectual of the reviews and magazines of its day, and came closest to Arnold's ideal. Arnold himself was a faithful reader from the outset, printed nine essays in it (from 1877 to 1887), and often alluded to it. (Frederic Harrison's "Culture: a Dialogue," in the *Fortnightly* for November, 1867, was the principal stimulus for *Culture and Anarchy*.) Meredith was a frequent contributor to the journal, and after his friend John Morley took over the editorship, he became even more heavily involved in "the running of it."

The *Fortnightly* was not at the beginning a financial success. By August 22, 1866, the board determined to suspend the mid-month issue, and from November 1 the journal appeared monthly. Trollope in his *Autobiography* explained that "a fortnightly issue was not popular with the trade through whose hands the work must reach the public; and, as our periodical had not become sufficiently popular itself to bear down such opposition, we succumbed."[9] Since each number cost two shillings (twice the price of a number of the *Cornhill*), and that price was continued when the journal became a monthly, the monthly cost to purchasers was cut in half, and the reduction may well have helped increase the sales.

The *Fortnightly* spawned an imitator a year later in the *Contemporary Review,* published by Alexander Strahan in the interest of the Church of England and first edited by the dean of Canterbury, Henry Alford. Nearly a century later, in January, 1955, the *Fortnightly* was incorporated into its rival, which continues to this day. (The *Cornhill* ceased publication in 1975.)

ঌ

On the last day of 1864 Trollope wrote to George Smith, "How about the Evening? The fortnightly is still hanging dubious. I will see you before long and we will tell our respective stories." Smith's projected evening newspaper, the *Pall Mall Gazette,* was indeed closer to publication than the *Fortnightly;* by the middle of January Trollope was busy writing articles for it.[10] The first issue appeared on February 7, 1865, and in it were an anonymous note by Trollope on Napoleon III's *History of Julius Caesar* (just then published) and his signed "Letter on the American Question."[11]

The aim of the *Pall Mall* was much the same as the aim of the *Fortnightly:* it was to put "the full measure of thought and culture" into journalism (to use the language of its first editor, Frederick Greenwood).

Every number contained a digest of the day's news culled from the morning newspapers, along with two or three articles on political and social questions of a sort then commonly treated in such weeklies as the *Spectator* and the *Saturday Review*.[12] It embarked on what has become known as "investigative journalism" with such a venture as sending an anonymous reporter to spend a winter night in the "casual" ward of a poorhouse to see for himself what the conditions were like; a few years later a new editor caused a major scandal with a study of prostitution in London, called "The Maiden Tribute of Modern Babylon." There was significant overlap between the writers for the *Pall Mall* and for the *Fortnightly:* even before he accepted the editorship of the latter, Lewes agreed to become an adviser for the former, and Trollope was a member of its "staff" (not a salaried position, but someone who could be called upon to perform assignments or who could volunteer to write upon subjects that interested him). Matthew Arnold was a contributor from late in the first year, and when Greenwood resigned the editorship in 1880 John Morley was his successor. The overlap with Smith's *Cornhill* was naturally even greater, including Greenwood himself. Arnold's *Friendship's Garland* letters were first published in the *Pall Mall*, and so too were Trollope's *Hunting Sketches* (which began in the third number of the new paper), his *Travelling Sketches* (August 3 to September 6, 1865), and his *Clergymen of the Church of England* (November 20, 1865, to January 25, 1866). He contributed more than seventy pieces of varying length to the paper in its first three and a half years, and was paid £331 17s. 0d. in 1865 and 1866.[13] There was once a contretemps between Trollope and Smith when Smith's payment for an article seemed beneath Trollope's dignity and Trollope returned the check, but Smith's explanation mollified him. "I am so fond of the P.M.G.—and so greatly admire your energy and skill and I may say genius in the matter—that I really dislike doing or saying anything which may terminate my connexion with it," Trollope wrote to him.[14]

In his *Autobiography* Trollope speaks in the highest terms of his fellow contributors, and remarks, "I have met at a Pall Mall dinner a crowd of guests who would have filled the House of Commons more respectably than I have seen it filled even on important occasions." He recalls also an assignment given him by Smith to attend the entire season of the May meetings of the Evangelicals in Exeter Hall. After attending the first meeting on May 5—six sermons in four hours on promoting Christianity among the Jews—he wrote in agony to Smith declining to attend any more at any price. "Suicide would intervene after the third or fourth, or I should give myself up to the police as the murderer of" one of the reverend gentlemen. His son Harry went along, in the hope that he might attend some future meetings in his father's stead, but he "found so ready a resource in somnolence, that to him a May meeting would simply mean sleep for the future." The sermons were tedious and odious, yet one would hardly dare to ridicule them publicly. [15] He did write one paper on the subject, "The Zulu in London" (May 10, 1865), expressing his fictitious visitor's astonishment at the speaker's reliance on the astronomy of the Book of Joshua over Copernicus and Galileo and his disgust at the disrespect for the female intellect implied in the speaker's plea that the minds of the ladies "not be vexed with . . . reasonings."*[16]

Clergymen of the Church of England provoked from the dean of Canterbury, Henry Alford, "the most ill-natured review that was ever written upon any work of mine." What stung most was Alford's snobbish remark that Trollope did not understand Greek—but as he wrote *An Autobiography* he forgot the context: Alford actually found fault with a slovenly style that could say "sympathy *for*" when the Greek root clearly requires "sympathy *with*" ("sym-" meaning "with"; but our modern dictionaries are not so insistently pedantic as Alford). Alford was especially severe with Trollope for his making superficial statements about church organization, statements that were simply not true. [17] Perhaps Alford was picking up the gauntlet Trollope threw down with his definition of a dean as "a Church dignitary who . . . has little to do and a good deal to get."

Trollope's articles were generally on subjects close to his heart—patronage or "jobbery" in Civil Service appointments, the justice of the Northern cause in the American Civil War, the merits of the English public schools, fox hunting, literal acceptance of Scripture by the Evangelicals as authority for scientific truth. "Manners makyth men," as he quoted the motto of Winchester College; "and for us in England the manners of the best among us have been made for us at our public schools." A letter on Lincoln's assassination, which he signed, drew an anonymous criticism from the *Saturday Review* on "Mistaken Estimates of Self," ridiculing Trollope for thinking that the public had any interest in what *he* thought of a matter so far removed from his competence:

> "The whole letter is an extraordinary illustration of the way in which a charming novelist may flounder about in platitudes and almost penny-a-lining commonplaces when he turns political philosopher. And it is an excellent illustration of that mistaken estimate of self which induces a man of reputation to suppose that under all possible circumstances he ought to make the public acquainted with his

*J. W. Colenso, sent as missionary bishop to Natal, translated the Bible into the Zulu tongue with the assistance of a native, and the detailed scrutiny of the text led him to question the literal accuracy of Scripture in *The Pentateuch and the Book of Joshua Critically Examined* (1862, with later additions). The book aroused a storm of controversy, and the *Times* (February 16, 1863) remarked, "Instead of Dr. Colenso converting the Zulu, the Zulu converted Dr. Colenso." It is this Zulu Trollope used as his spokesman.

sentiments. There is a wide difference between the political temper
and the knack of writing graceful love-letters and understanding the
feelings of agreeable young ladies and gentlemanly government
clerks.[18]

The *Pall Mall* sprang to his defense with nice irony. But after Trollope's
death Greenwood almost echoed the *Saturday*'s opinion. Trollope was a
man "with the aspect of a wild boar, and with not infrequent resemblance
to the manners of the same." He was "extraordinarily ambitious to figure
as a politician, but a politician he was not born to be: he was born to write
Barchester Towers."[19] The more one reads of Trollope's political writing,
the more true this judgment sounds.

  After a few years, Trollope gave up his work for the *Pall Mall*,
having by that time undertaken the editorship of a journal of his own.
Meanwhile, however, he had successfully proposed Smith and Greenwood
for membership in the Garrick Club.[20]

᷒

In 1863 an overweight London undertaker in his sixties, William Banting, published a thirty-two-page pamphlet that made his name a household word not only in England but in France and Germany as well. He
had suffered great physical discomfort from his girth (he could no longer
lace his boots); his ankles would not support him when he descended the
stairs; exercise only made him the hungrier; and then he discovered the
effect of a diet that increased his consumption of protein foods and drastically reduced sugar and starch, lost weight significantly, and published
his discovery as *A Letter on Corpulence, Addressed to the Public*. In mid-
December, 1864, George Eliot told her Warwickshire friend Charles
Bray, "I have seen people much changed by the Banting system. Mr. A.
Trollope is thinner by means of it, and is otherwise the better for the self-
denial." Almost seventeen years later Trollope's President Neverbend,
who devised mandatory euthanasia at sixty-eight for the inhabitants of the
South Pacific colony of Britannula, gloried in the thought "that my
memory would [be] embalmed with those who had done great things for
their fellow-citizens. Columbus, and Galileo, and Harvey, and Wilberforce, and Cobden, and the great Banting who has preserved us all so
completely from the horrors of obesity, would not [be] named with hon-
ours more resplendent than that paid to the name of Neverbend."[21] We
do not know how long Trollope imposed restraints on his diet; one other
indulgence he showed no signs of curtailing at this moment. Since his
visit to the West Indies he had been an importer of cigars, for himself and
his friends, and in the spring of 1865 he announced to George Smith that

he had just then received a consignment of 12,000 cigars; Smith must let him know how many he wanted.[22]

Early in 1865 Anne Thackeray, still suffering from the pain of the parting from her father as well as the recent death of her grandmother, went to Waltham Cross for a stay with the Trollopes. The Merivales were there too. "It was a sweet old prim chill house wrapped in snow." She was astonished to hear Trollope called by the servant every morning at four to take up his writing task for the day. The Trollopes maintained their affectionate relationship with Anne, who recalls another occasion when Mrs. Millais organized a pleasant July walking party at Knole Park, Sevenoaks, Kent, that included Millais, the Trollopes, and one or two others. They came upon an artist at work in a little wood; Millais stopped to inspect the work, remarked, "Why, you have not got your lights right. Look, *this* is what you want," and taking the brush out of the painter's hand made a line or two on the picture, then nodded to him and walked away. Trollope, noticing the man's bewilderment, said he should be told who had made those brush strokes, and ran back to explain. Then it became necessary for Annie to run back and point out that this second person had been Anthony Trollope. And finally yet another returned to state that the last messenger was Thackeray's daughter.[23] It is to be hoped that the man kept his painting, if only for its associations.

On April 13, Tom's wife Theodosia, who had long been ailing but had not been actually an invalid, died unexpectedly in Florence. Two days later Anthony made a quick trip out, and by April 30 was back at Waltham House, accompanied by Tom's daughter Bice. It was at the railway station at Culoz, in the valley of the Rhone, on this return journey that Trollope learned of the assassination of Lincoln, which led to his letter of lamentation in the *Pall Mall Gazette* (May 5, p. 4), expressing the fear that the delicate balance of judgment needed to restore and preserve peace could not be attained without the president. Characteristically, Rose and Anthony took their ten-year-old niece warmly into their home; since she loved music, they engaged Frances Eleanor Ternan, older sister of Dickens's mistress the actress Ellen Ternan, as her music teacher. Frances Eleanor had been a music student in Florence some years earlier, and had come to know Tom; a warm friendship had sprung up between her and Theodosia, and she became very fond of Bice. (It was through Tom's introduction that she came to know Anthony and Rose back in London.) Tom planned to follow Anthony and Bice to England as soon as he disposed of his house on the Piazza dell'Independenza in Florence, but the sale involved him in a lawsuit there that kept him engaged until August.[24]

Meanwhile Anthony spent a month in Glasgow and Belfast, from about mid-May. "Enjoying myself!" he wrote from the former place in reply to a note from Lewes; "revising a post office with 300 men, the work and wages of all of whom are to be fixed on one's own responsibility! Come and try it, & then go back to the delicious ease & perfect freedom of your Editor's chair." One of his tasks was to speed up the service to and from London. It was not easy; Tilley wrote to him, "Any acceleration—even five minutes—in the arrival of the limited Mail at Glasgow is entirely out of the question." Trollope evidently had some success, however, since he pointedly made Phineas Finn in London read a letter from Lady Laura Kennedy on the very evening of the day it was written in Glasgow.[25]

ॐ

Young William Dean Howells, though still in his twenties, was just now completing four years as American consul at Venice, and had written a book on that city. (His consulship had been the reward for his writing a campaign biography of President Lincoln, just as Hawthorne's consulship in Liverpool had been the reward for his writing a campaign biography of President Franklin Pierce.) Howells stopped in London on his way home, and, armed with a letter of introduction, wrote to Trollope in the hope that Trollope might help him find a publisher for the Venetian book. He was invited to spend a night at Waltham Cross on July 16 or 17, but (according to his daughter, to whom he must have told the story) Trollope scarcely spoke to him, and offered him no help or advice on the subject of publishers; Howells was too shy to press the matter and came away disappointed. (Nevertheless, the first edition of *Venetian Life* did come out in England, published by Trübner.) Howells later unconsciously gave what may be a clue to his unsatisfactory visit: in his Venetian years, he tells us, "I was not yet sufficiently instructed to appreciate Trollope, and I did not read him at all."[26] There is doubtless a certain imprudence in approaching a distinguished author about whose work one is entirely ignorant.

In his later years, Howells expressed contradictory opinions of Trollope's writing. There was a savage anonymous review of his *Thackeray* in the *Atlantic Monthly* in August, 1879 ("Mr. Trollope was simply unfit for the work to which he was appointed"), and a Henry Jamesian condemnation of both Trollope and Thackeray in *Criticism and Fiction* (1891) for spoiling their artistic illusion by interposing themselves casually and familiarly to discuss their narratives with their readers. And yet only a few years later he remarked that had Trollope had a more delicate sense of humor (he "jokes heavily or not at all"), "I should . . . make bold to declare [him] the greatest of English novelists; as it is, I must put before him Jane Austen, whose books, late in life, have been a youthful rapture with me. Even without much humor Trollope's books have been a vast pleasure to me through their simple truthfulness. . . . It is their serious fidelity which gives them a value unique in literature, and which if it were carefully analyzed would afford a principle of the same quality in an author who was undoubtedly one of the finest of artists as well as the most Philistine of men."[27]

Another weekend visitor to Waltham House was Norman Macleod, who was in London in mid-August. By that time Tom Trollope had joined the family there, as he saw his *History of the Commonwealth of Florence* through the press. Anthony had been an intermediary between Macleod and Mark Drury's granddaughter Anna Drury in her attempt to place one of her novels in *Good Words*. Later in the year, Trollope was chosen to propose Macleod's health at the festival of the Scottish Hospital in London, a task he performed "eloquently," according to a correspondent in the *Times*.[28] Two weeks earlier than this festival Macleod had addressed the Presbytery of Glasgow on "The Lord's Day," an address against rigorous and (as he held) unscriptural restraints on the Christian's use of the Sabbath, a speech which, when published as a pamphlet, led to Trollope's supporting summary of Macleod's position in a *Fortnightly* article on "The Fourth Commandment." Mrs. Proudie would have been horrified and indignant. Once again the *Saturday Review* criticized him for venturing into areas in which his opinion was of no importance. "Let the shoemaker stick to his last," they proclaimed in a page and a half on "An Amateur Theologian." "With the opinions expressed in those pages we have scarcely any fault to find," but "are not his novels, especially considering the speed with which they succeed each other, enough to fill his time? . . . Favoured by practice and original endowment, he can write novels as easily as a hen lays eggs." This time Trollope himself returned to the attack in the *Pall Mall*: "The *Saturday Review* has no special fault to find with my remarks,—always excepting the great vice of a novelist choosing to make remarks. . . . I am forced to declare that, shoemaker as I am, I will employ my time in any way that seems fit to me,—the wrath of the *Saturday Review* notwithstanding."[29]

&

On August 28, 1865, the Foreign Office issued, over the signature of Earl Russell, a passport for "Mr. Anthony Trollope (British Subject) accompanied by his wife, son and Miss Ternan, travelling on the Continent."[30] The son was Fred, and the party was augmented by Tom and Bice. Rose gives us a summary of their journey, which began on September 16: Aix-la-Chapelle (Aachen), Coblentz (where Harry met them), Cassel, Dresden and the Saxon Switzerland, Prague, Ratisbon (Regensburg), and on to Salzburg. Tom and Bice (and presumably Fanny Ternan) left the group at

Dresden. At Salzburg they met E. F. S. Pigott. The tour continued to Königssee, to Hallein (where they went down a salt mine), to Bad Gastein, Werfen ("with the many beds"), Abtenau ("with no beds"), Hallstatt, Ischl, Gmunden and the Traun Falls, then on to Linz, where there was a sad parting for Rose. Pigott, Anthony, and Fred went on to Vienna, and from there Fred left for Australia, where he planned to settle. It was agreed that he would return home when he was twenty-one (1868), and he did so, but the emigration was in fact permanent, and his descendants— the only survivors of Anthony's branch of the family—still live there. Anthony had asked George Smith, and no doubt others, for letters of introduction for Fred before they left England. Anthony returned to Linz, picked up Harry and Rose, and went home via Passau (where a horse nearly broke Rose's leg), Nuremberg, Frankfurt, and Brussels.[31] The journey was pleasant and, so far as Trollope's writing was concerned, significant; he had frequently reflected his travels in his fiction, especially in his *Tales of All Countries,* but the medieval picturesqueness of Prague and Nuremberg soon produced a pair of novels quite unlike his other work, *Nina Balatka* and *Linda Tressel*; the former, indeed, was begun on November 3, only four days after he reached home.[32]

&

About a fortnight after their return, word came that Mrs. Gaskell had died. Her *Wives and Daughters* was running in the *Cornhill,* and she was two installments in advance of the printer, but her final chapters could only be guessed at. "I do not know how often I was to have met her at your house, and yet never did so," Trollope wrote to George Smith. "I regret it greatly now. . . . It will have shocked you greatly,—and your wife. . . . Had she finished her story for you?"[33]

At this time he was entering into negotiations with Fred Chapman and Smith for the publication of a cheap edition of all his works—or as many of them as he could arrange. The proposal originated with W. H. Smith, proprietor of railway bookstalls all over Britain; after some months of negotiations, during which Trollope rather hoped that George Smith would be willing to buy the copyrights and publish the cheap edition, an agreement was reached with W. H. Smith and Chapman. Chapman and Hall were to publish for W. H. Smith a "Select Library of Fiction," bound in illustrated pasteboard covers; the imprint was theirs but Smith owned the copyrights, the stereotyped plates, illustrations, and wrapper blocks. For the use of his copyrights Trollope received the lump sum of £2,000.[34] The first of his novels to appear was *Doctor Thorne,* number 85 in the series, published about May, 1866; it was followed a month or two later by *The Macdermots of Ballycloran,* number 86. Within two years there were eleven of his novels on the list, and when in July, 1881, W. H. Smith sold his entire interest in the series of more than four hundred titles to Ward, Lock and Company, there were twenty-seven of Trollope's novels and short story collections. Ward, Lock added three more, and a four-volume edition of *Australia and New Zealand*. The Trollope novels published by Bentley, Longman, Blackwood, Chatto and Windus, and Smith, Elder, twenty-one titles in all, were never included. But at last a reader could buy in one volume even *La Vendée,* that had long since gone out of print.[35]

The three series of sketches Trollope wrote for the *Pall Mall Gazette* were published in three small volumes soon after their appearance in the newspaper, the eight *Hunting Sketches* about May 10, 1865, the eight *Travelling Sketches* about February 10, 1866, and the ten sketches of *Clergymen of the Church of England* about March 29. The first and third are disappointing—too generalized, without the kind of shrewd, individual perceptions one has come to expect from the author. We do far better to read about Archdeacon Grantly and the Reverend Josiah Crawley than to read the sketches of "The Archdeacon" or "The Curate," and when Trollope looks down in general terms on "The College Fellow who has taken Orders," one has to remind himself that Trollope's grandfather Milton was such a man. The hunting scenes in the novels are far better done than these hunting sketches; "The Hunting Parson" is a tedious discussion of the rights and wrongs of clerical hunting that is pale beside the robust figure of the dean of Brotherton in *Is He Popenjoy?* But Rose's manuscript notes of their Continental travels show that both she and Anthony had a sharp eye for the idiosyncrasies of their fellow travelers, and these idiosyncrasies (which are noticed also in many of the *Tales of All Countries*) enliven the *Travelling Sketches*. Anthony was doubtless writing for Rose when he observed: "Men there are bold enough to stay from church on Sundays, to dine at their clubs without leave, to light cigars in their own parlours, and to insist upon brandy-and-water before they go to bed; but where is the man who can tell his wife and daughters that it is quite unnecessary that they should go up the Rhine?"[36]

૨▲

The Belton Estate is one of the most subtle of Trollope's novels. Its theme is the disastrous consequence of the utter dependence of the women in society upon the men. It is a somewhat surprising thesis for the same pen that later ridiculed Olivia Q. Fleabody and the Baroness Banmann, but the two positions are not necessarily inconsistent. The heroine, Clara Amedroz, is left penniless when her brother commits suicide after running up large gambling debts, and the family estate, entailed upon male heirs, goes to a distant cousin when her father dies. Every penny she can have for the rest of her life depends upon the generosity of men, for which they are likely to expect the repayment of a marriage in which she will always be reminded that she brought nothing to the union. The motif is repeated in many other situations. Mrs. Askerton, a charming, kind, intelligent woman, has married a man who took her to India and brutalized himself with drink until her life was unbearable; her only release is to accept the offer of a generous and upright military man and to elope with him. The two are married as soon as the husband drinks himself to death within a few years, but both second husband and wife—especially the latter— pay a lifetime penalty of social ostracism and isolation. With some irony the woman speaks to Clara of "that decent feeling of feminine inferiority which ought to belong to all women" (chap. xxxi).

Clara herself is intelligent, affectionate, proud, and able to assert herself, but also sensitive to the pain of her position. When she goes, out of kindness, to stay with a widowed aunt who is evangelical in her Sabbath observances, the aunt's nephew and heir is also visiting there; he announces that he is obliged to go away on Saturday, and Clara states her case in a remarkable passage that is thematic for the book:

> "I [too] don't like Sundays at Perivale at all, and . . . I should do just as you do if I had the power. But women—women, that is, of my age—are such slaves! We are forced to give an obedience for which we can see no cause, and for which we can understand no necessity. I couldn't tell my aunt that I meant to go away on Saturday."
>
> "You have no business which makes imperative calls upon your time."
>
> "That means that I can't plead pretended excuses. But the true reason is that we are dependent."
>
> . . ."Dependence is a disagreeable word," he said; "and one never quite knows what it means."
>
> "If you were a woman you'd know. It means that I must stay at Perivale on Sundays, while you can go up to London or down to Yorkshire. That's what it means."
>
> "What you do mean, I think, is this;—that you owe a duty to your aunt, the performance of which is not altogether agreeable.". . .
>
> "It isn't that. . . . My aunt has been kind to me, and therefore I am bound to her for this service. But she is kind to you also, and yet you are not bound. That's why I complain. You sail always under false pretences, and yet you think you do your duty. You have to see your lawyer,—which means going to your club; or to attend to your tenants,—which means hunting and shooting. . . . But I can't; we

ain't allowed to have clubs, or shooting, or to have our own way in anything, putting forward little pretences about lawyers." (Chap. vii)

Clara becomes engaged to the nephew, Captain Aylmer, who is gentlemanly and means well, but conventional and unthinking. He knows that his mother is difficult to please, dictatorial, overbearing, yet it is a matter of course to him that Clara must yield to every whim of his mother. Now (says Trollope) "There is nothing so irritating to an engaged young lady as counsel from her intended husband's mamma" (chap. xvi). Clara's visit to the Yorkshire home of Aylmer's family is a superb episode in which Clara's iron will stands up perfectly to Lady Aylmer's bullying.

Clara breaks off the engagement to the captain and in due course marries the distant cousin who has inherited her father's estate. This cousin, Will Belton, is a Norfolk farmer like Farmer Cheesacre in *Can You Forgive Her?* with some of the latter's impetuosity and bumptiousness, but Belton is not a clown; he is sensitive to the needs and feelings of others and the match will doubtless be a good one. Nevertheless, the social dilemma of "the miseries of female dependence" (chap. xxix) is not resolved by the success of one firm-minded young lady.

This is a novel with no villains; Trollope is remarkable in the care with which he makes certain that we see the ordinariness of the thinking even of persons like Aylmer and his mother, whose chief faults are lack of intelligence and a ready acceptance of commonplace and convention. Trollope's own evaluation of the novel—and he confessed that by the time he wrote *An Autobiography* he could scarcely remember it—is a sad underestimate: "It has no special merits, and will add nothing to my reputation as a novelist." More accurate is his description of it at the time to Tilley: "I have told the publishers to send you a copy of a good book, called Belton Estate, which will improve your mind, and the minds of your children if you and they will attend to it."[37] It is in fact one of his best. Shortly before it drew to a close, Jane Carlyle wrote to a friend, "I hope you read that tale going on in the 'Fortnightly'—'The Belton Estate' (by Anthony Trollope). It is charming, like all he writes;—I quite weary for the next number, for the sake of this one thing; the rest is wonderfully stupid." And Browning too praised it to his Florentine friend Isa Blagden.[38]

The novel is a good deal shorter than the ones Trollope had been writing for the *Cornhill* (if we exclude *Brown, Jones, and Robinson*) and indeed is only half the length of *Can You Forgive Her?* It is about the equal of *Rachel Ray* and *Miss Mackenzie*. It ended its run in the *Fortnightly* on January 1, 1866, and was published in three volumes a day or two before that—the three volumes somewhat to his displeasure, since he had intended it to be in two, like its equals.[39] Its successor in the *Fortnightly* was Meredith's *Vittoria;* only a few months earlier Meredith wrote that he was beset with proofs for *Rhoda Fleming,* "and with Trollope and Lewes at me to get up steam for *Vittoria* I have been hardly capable of a word to my ghostly adviser."[40]

➸

Nina Balatka was a token of Trollope's enthusiasm for that Central Europe with which he had made his first acquaintance in the autumn of 1865. He began the writing as soon as he reached home, and completed it by the end of the year. Not since *Doctor Thorne* (1858) and *The Bertrams* (1859) had he embarked on a novel without a prior agreement as to its publication, and even in those two cases agreements were made before the novels were completed.

Perhaps the most striking landmarks in Prague are the Old Synagogue, one of the oldest in Europe, with foundations dating from the sixth century and a superstructure from the thirteenth, and the Jewish cemetery with inscriptions as old as the beginning of the seventh century. These are the center of the once strictly segregated Jewish sector, all around which is, of course, the Roman Catholic capital of Bohemia. The Catholic piety is symbolized by the shrine of the martyred St. John of Nepomuk on the ancient Charles Bridge over the Moldau, in which the saint was drowned by the King's order in 1393. High above in the huge, many-windowed eighteenth-century castle, still lived the feeble-minded ex-Emperor Ferdinand of Austria, supplanted in 1848 by Kaiser Franz Josef.

Prague gave Trollope his first view of an East European ghetto and for all his sturdy, matter-of-fact Victorian anti-Semitism, the actual sight of apartheid moved him. *Nina Balatka* springs from the tourist's impression of the irreconcilable differences between the Jews and the Christians: Nina, a Catholic, and her Jewish lover Anton Trendellsohn horrify their relatives in both communities by engaging themselves to be married. At times the description of Prague seems almost like a guidebook. But Trollope, who knows English life intimately and from the inside, is entirely outside the lives of the people of Prague, and there is, as Blackwood remarked when he first read it, "the sort of air of hardness about the story that one feels in reading a translation."[41] There is a touch of melodrama also as Nina threatens to slip suicidally from St. John's shrine on the bridge into the black rushing waters, but is rescued by the firm arms of her Jewish friend Rebecca. The story ends happily with the marriage of Nina and Anton and their escape from Prague to a freer life in the West.

It is not easy to accept at face value Trollope's explanation of his wish to publish *Nina Balatka* anonymously. "It seemed to me that a name once earned carried with it too much favour. . . . I felt that aspirants coming up below me might do work as good as mine, and probably much better work, and yet fail to have it appreciated. In order to test this, I determined to be such an aspirant myself, and to begin a course of novels anonymously, in order that I might see whether I could succeed in obtaining a second identity,—whether as I had made one mark by such literary ability as I possessed, I might succeed in doing so again." The venture, so conceived, is a bit quixotic: the reviewer in the *Spectator* guessed that Trollope was the author, yet was puzzled at the anonymity, for "Mr. Trollope's name is worth a great deal in mere money value to the sale of any book."[42] Short though the novel is (about half the length of *The Belton Estate*), one has difficulty in believing that Trollope would have offered it to the *Cornhill* for anonymous publication at £300 if he had thought he could get a much higher price with his name. On the other hand, the *Saturday Review*'s remark that he dropped novels as easily as a hen drops eggs may have been a timely caution, repeating in vivid language what his publishers had been hinting at for some time, that he was saturating the market. Certainly the world has known prolific writers to establish several identities through pseudonyms, for exactly this reason.

Whatever the motive, however, Trollope offered *Nina Balatka* to George Smith on March 9, 1866, for anonymous publication either in the *Cornhill* or as a book for £300, or for publication in both forms for £500. It took Smith less than two weeks to decline. And then, perhaps urged by Lewes and George Eliot, he approached Blackwood's London representative, Joseph Langford, who forwarded the manuscript to Edinburgh; *Blackwood's Magazine* still persisted in the old-fashioned custom of publishing its fiction as well as its articles without author's name. John Blackwood wrote a long critique of the manuscript—something Trollope had never theretofore received at the hands of his publishers—and indicated some uncertainty: it was skillfully told, but would probably not be profitable in magazine or in volumes unless he could obtain it for a very small sum. The amount agreed upon was £250 for the magazine publication, £200 for the remainder of the copyright. Alas, Blackwood's estimate was right: in its first six months in volume form, the anonymous book sold fewer than 500 copies.[43]

Blackwood nevertheless expressed his gratification at Trollope's confidence in him, "a personal stranger," and was pleased "by his desire to have a tale of his in the old Magazine." They presumably met when Blackwood was in London in May, and thereafter became good friends as well as business associates; four more of Trollope's novels appeared in "Maga" and Blackwood also published his *Commentaries of Caesar* and (posthumously) *An Autobiography* and *An Old Man's Love.*

Trollope had sold several short stories to the publisher Strahan for use in *Good Words* since the amicable settlement of their difference over

the publication of *Rachel Ray*. Now Strahan begged from him a contribution to the *Argosy,* a new magazine, popular in aim, of which Strahan was
proprietor, and Trollope agreed to supply four short stories at £60 each.
Only three of these were published, and the second of them, "Lotta
Schmidt," was also a product of Trollope's tour of Central Europe. It is set
in Vienna, the city of wine and roses, waltzes and rococo, Schubert and
Johann Strauss. The tale is a little love story, set in a beer garden and a
dance hall, and the older suitor wins Lotta over the more elegant younger
man because of the way he pours out his soul in playing the zither in the
beer garden where (like Strauss) he conducted the orchestra.

Chapter XIV

1866

Trollope was eminently a social person, and his membership in the Cosmopolitan, the Garrick, and the Athenaeum Club brought him the friendship of a good many men of political and literary importance. Very often these same men were his associates on the staffs of the *Cornhill* and the *Fortnightly;* especially with reference to the latter he was energetic in cultivating possible contributors.

It had been Tennyson's friend Monckton Milnes, then a member of Parliament and not long thereafter created Baron Houghton, who (at Trollope's request) put him forward for membership in the Cosmopolitan, to which he was elected in April, 1861. Trollope was invited to lunch with Houghton, Rose called on Lady Houghton, and in due course they were both invited to spend a week at Houghton's Yorkshire seat of Fryston in mid-January, 1866. Also at the house party was Lady Rose Fane, daughter of the Earl of Westmorland, who wrote to her mother, "I wish I had never seen Mr. Trollope; I think he is detestable—vulgar, noisy & domineering—a mixture of Dickens vulgarity and Mr. Burtons selfsufficiency—as unlike his books as possible." Rose was "a quaint sort of woman, & wd. be well enough only she has perfectly white hair which [she wears without a cap]—in the most fashionable way with (last night) a little rose stuck in it wh: looks most absurd."[1] A year and a half later a guest at another house party, "Barry Cornwall's" widow Anne Procter, told Houghton that she met the Trollopes at Bulwer-Lytton's home, Knebworth (Hertfordshire), and "found Trollope very pleasant." (Bulwer-Lytton, not yet personally acquainted with Trollope, had written a letter to him in December, 1865, praising *Miss Mackenzie* in particular and Trollope's novels in general. Trollope replied in kind, indicating that his own work had been much indebted to *Pelham*. The invitation to Knebworth was clearly a fruit of this correspondence.) A decade later Augustus Hare found Rose "a beautiful old lady with snow-white hair turned back" when he met the Trollopes at a party at Lord Houghton's which had "every one there, from Princess Louise to Mrs. Anthony Trollope."[2]

Trollope invited Lord Houghton to the dinner of the *Fortnightly* staff on April 11, and at one or another of their encounters the conversation must have turned to book and manuscript collecting, for Trollope presented Houghton with what William Longman assured him was the very last copy of the first edition of *The Warden,* the book which provided him with his first regular income from writing. Not long thereafter he consulted Houghton about the commercial value of a collection of alleged letters by a Southern gentleman written during the course of the Civil War.[3] Trollope was often willing to oblige his bibliophilic friends: he gave Frederic Locker-Lampson (who knew Trollope at the Cosmopolitan, the Athenaeum, and the Royal Literary Fund, "where he was amusingly combative," and with whom he exchanged dinners) the "bulky manuscript" of *The Small House,* bound in dark morocco and with "the aspect of our Family Bible."[4] Lord Houghton was also a strong supporter of the Royal Literary Fund, of which he served as a treasurer for twenty years prior to his resignation early in 1877; from 1869 Trollope became one of Houghton's fellow treasurers, a post he held until his death.

It was Houghton who brought Trollope into contact with Tennyson, whose periodic visits to town were the occasion of dinners nearly every night, often with Trollope, Milnes (Houghton), Tom Taylor, Spedding, Thomas Hughes, or Lord Stanley among the guests.[5] And Browning was Trollope's guest at a *Fortnightly Review* dinner at St. James's Hotel, Piccadilly, on March 14, 1866. "Your coming will not be taken, nor is our wish for you to come intended, as in any way binding you to anything more on our behalf than the light of your face on our little dinner. Not but that we are *most anxious* for your stouter assistance if at any time you can give it to us," he wrote, and Browning replied in acceptance, "You are all too kind and generous—and I have nothing but the gratitude for that to give in return." It would appear that Trollope was hinting that Browning might write for the review, but Browning seems to have understood that he was being asked to invest money. He regarded the *Fortnightly* as "very good and respectable, but hardly successful, I should fear, as a speculation. The 'Pall Mall,' which was in a very sorry condition, is now in high vogue,—so do things alter."[6]

The "Lord Stanley" mentioned as among the guests at dinners for Tennyson was the Lord Stanley of Alderley who as Whig postmaster general had been Trollope's superior from March, 1860, to June, 1866. Lady Stanley was an energetic political hostess of the sixties, at whose assemblies Trollope was occasionally seen. He dined at her house on February 10, 1866; "later in the evening her ladyship gave an assembly which was numerously and fashionably attended," and Anthony no doubt stayed on. Lady Stanley's daughter was married to Earl Russell's son, Viscount Amberley, and she too entertained him. "We had a little dinner of Huxley, Anthony Trollope, Lady Russell, and Mr. Knatchbull Hugesson whom Amberley brought home from the H[ouse] of C[ommons]. Dinner was very pleasant, Ly. R. enjoyed it very much and was pleased to make acquaintance with Trollope and Huxley. A[mberley] and

I thought T's voice too loud, he rather drowned Huxley's pleasant quiet voice which was certainly better worth hearing," Lady Amberley recorded in her diary. Trollope may have stayed on into the evening, when Lord Russell dropped in with George Lewes, "whom I made acquaintance with for the first time and liked; though he was desperately ugly, small, dirty looking, long hair and bad complexion," Lady Amberley wrote. The day after one such party Trollope sent to the *Pall Mall Gazette* for publication a vigorous reply to the *Saturday Review*'s attack on Lord Russell.[7] From about this time, Trollope's novels begin to carry his readers into the political and social circles with which he was now becoming acquainted.

੨▲

On February 9, Trollope took the chair at a dinner in honor of William Bokenham, who was retiring as controller of the Circulation Department of the Post Office, where he had been employed since Trollope was five years old. Over a hundred of Bokenham's friends attended the dinner, which "included every delicacy of the season, and reflected the greatest credit upon . . . the proprietor" of the London Coffee-house, Ludgate-hill. Trollope, having proposed the mandatory toasts to the Queen and the royal family, gave an "admirable" testimonial to Bokenham and presented him on behalf of his associates with a "magnificent tea and coffee service in pure silver."[8]

The Circulation Department was the branch that handled the distribution of letters within the metropolitan area. In 1856 London had been divided into postal districts for the sorting and delivery of mail; despite the ridicule of the *Times* in 1860 that letters marked "N.W." and "S.W." (North West and South West London) were sent to North Wales and South Wales, Tilley could affirm that during the day a letter would be delivered within an hour if it was addressed to the same postal district in which it was deposited.[9] (There were then about a dozen collections and deliveries in a day.) The Post Office committee of 1860–61, of which Trollope had been a member, did not take up in any detail the organization of the London postal system, but it did recommend that more high administrative staff was needed in the Circulation Department. By the time Bokenham retired it was clear that the task of supervision was too great for the single controller, and Tilley in late March, 1866, informed the postmaster general that he was eager to make eight of the ten metropolitan postal districts (excluding West Central and East Central, the area around the General Post Office, which would continue as they were) each into a separate "post town" under its own postmaster, and all under a newly created surveyor, on analogy with post towns in the rest of England. In order to examine the feasibility of the scheme, he asked for authority to appoint some competent person to draw up a report. The competent person was Trollope.[10]

The report itself was submitted with a speed that clearly shows the move was a foregone conclusion: on May 9 Tilley was able to say that Trollope had furnished "abundant evidence of the advantages to be gained by the change." By June 15 the scheme was in effect and Trollope had been assigned the temporary surveyorship, as well as direct responsibility (functioning as "postmaster") for the Western and the North Eastern districts of London. His headquarters were fitted out in the Vere Street post office, just off Oxford Street and near Cavendish Square.

The transition was by no means easy. One of the most difficult problems was the reassignment of all the staff in such a way that the altered needs of the new arrangement would not jeopardize their seniority; in the end, most of the old staff retained their old titles, though inappropriate to the new structure. Trollope worked with his customary energy. Question after question was resolved in written reports, and at the same time he attended to such details as the inspection of the physical aspects of the district post offices. (In one of them he found the water closets and urinals objectionably near to the windows of the kitchens in the basement and requested £40 to provide the necessary alterations.) One gets the impression that he went about his business with an irresistible force: if he contravened an order from above, or neglected the sensibilities of his colleagues, he brushed the offense aside with a "So sorry!" and continued on his way.[11]

On June 20 Tilley offered him the permanent surveyorship of the Metropolitan District, at a salary which would in the first year be the same as his current salary of £700, but which would rise in four years to £800; the normal maximum for surveyors was still £700. Trollope instantly declined with thanks, it may be supposed somewhat to Tilley's surprise. By August 8 he returned to his district, accompanied by an expression of appreciation from the postmaster general "for the Services which he has rendered to the Department in carrying to a successful issue a difficult arrangement which involved no little labour and contrivance" (the words were of course Tilley's).[12]

≈●

Nina Balatka had been completed less than a month and was still unpublished, *The Claverings* was just now starting in the *Cornhill*, when Trollope about January 30, 1866, proposed to George Smith the publication of another novel he was beginning to write, one in the Barsetshire series that might be published in twenty monthly parts like *Orley Farm*. The market, however, was changing rapidly, and Smith was afraid that the monthly installment priced at a shilling might be obsolete before the new work was ready. "A new sixpenny periodical would leave us very little hope of success with a shilling serial." And so, though he was prepared to offer £3,000, he wished to reserve the right of determining later whether to publish in twenty parts (at a shilling each) or thirty parts (at sixpence each). Trollope pointed out that he should know in advance how he must divide his work: a book designed for twenty parts cannot be automatically divided into thirty. Still, if necessary he *could* plan precisely equal chapters of which six would constitute a twentieth of the whole, four would constitute a thirtieth; "there will be some trouble in this, but having a mechanical mind I think I can do it. If you wish it I will do so." Smith at first committed himself to the thirty-number length, but after he began to calculate the price when the sixpenny parts were bound in two volumes (including a shilling for binding each volume), he discovered that thirty-two parts brought him to a neater figure (eighteen shillings) than thirty parts (seventeen shillings). And so thirty-two parts were settled on (but the bound volumes actually were priced at twenty shillings). By this time Trollope had already made a start on his manuscript, and so some rearranging was necessary. Whether the numbers would appear weekly or monthly was left open, but Smith leaned to the former, and so it was arranged. Trollope wrote *The Last Chronicle of Barset* between January 21 and September 15, and the parts appeared weekly from December 1, 1866, to July 6, 1867. When John Blackwood expressed some surprise at this weekly mode of publication, Trollope replied:

> The period of its coming out was Smiths idea & not my own, & frightened me when I first heard of it. How far it answers I do not know. It is his own speculation, & he is a man of such pride of constancy that I should not dare to propose to him any change. He will never complain to me, being in that respect made of the same stuff as yourself. As regards the workmanship of the story I believe it to be as good as anything I have done. A weekly novel should perhaps have at least an attempt at murder in every number. I never get beyond giving my people an attack of fever or a broken leg.

The entire book was set in type before the first number appeared.[13]

Reviewers of the early numbers pointed out, with courteous approval, the innovation of weekly parts. Whether the plan was financially successful cannot now be determined, though there is some suggestion that it may not have been so. Parts issues brought their publishers profit not only through sales to the public, but also through the pages of advertising bound with each number, and in the later numbers of *Last Chronicle* the advertising pages had almost withered away to Smith, Elder's own announcements. Moreover, when Trollope wrote *An Autobiogra-*

phy early in 1876, he complained that he had not received a penny beyond the initial £3,000, by way of his share of the profits on the sale of additional copies, and so it may be supposed that there was no such sale.[14] Soon after the two-volume edition was published, Trollope asked Smith if he would like to bring out all the Barsetshire novels in a series,[15] but Smith did not do so, and though he and Trollope remained on good terms and Trollope continued to write for the *Pall Mall Gazette, The Last Chronicle* was the last novel of Trollope's to be published by Smith, Elder.

The Trollopes continued to exchange dinners with Millais and his wife, with whom they dined on March 16. Naturally Anthony hoped he could persuade Millais to illustrate this new book, and though Millais had for the most part given up book illustration he had remarked, in conversation, that he might sometime lend a hand to Trollope in such a venture. Therefore Trollope in mid-August pressed him, reminding him how familiar he was with the Barsetshire people. The necessity of producing an illustration each week proved more than Millais could face, and he declined. By September 11 Smith secured George H. Thomas, who had illustrated Wilkie Collins's *Armadale* for the *Cornhill;* Trollope hoped he would make his people look like those Millais had drawn, and was only moderately pleased with the result. "Crawley before the magistrates is very good. So is the bishop. Grace is not good. She has fat cheeks, & is not Grace Crawley. . . . Mrs. Proudie is not quite my Mrs. Proudie."[16]

One of the most famous anecdotes in *An Autobiography* is Trollope's explanation of how he "killed my old friend Mrs. Proudie."

> It was thus that it came about. I was sitting one morning at work upon the novel at the end of the long drawing-room of the Athenaeum Club,—as was then my wont when I had slept the previous night in London. As I was there, two clergymen, each with a magazine in his hand, seated themselves, one on one side of the fire and one on the other, close to me. They soon began to abuse what they were reading, and each was reading some part of some novel of mine. The gravamen of their complaint lay in the fact that I re-introduced the same characters so often: "Here," said one, "is that archdeacon whom we have had in every novel he has written." "And here," said the other, "is the old duke whom he has talked about till everybody is tired of him. If I could not invent new characters, I would not write novels at all." Then one of them fell foul of Mrs. Proudie. It was impossible for me not to hear their words, and almost impossible to hear them and be quiet. I got up, and standing between them, I acknowledged myself to be the culprit. "As to Mrs. Proudie," I said, "I will go home and kill her before the week is over." And so I did. The two gentlemen were utterly confounded, and one of them begged me to forget his frivolous observations.[17]

Perhaps it didn't happen quite that way. According to his writing calendar for *Last Chronicle,* Trollope wrote the chapter in which Mrs. Proudie died about the middle of August, 1866, but indeed her death had been prepared many chapters earlier in that terrible scene in which the bishop tells his wife, "I do not know how I shall ever speak again. You have disgraced me" (chap. xlvii). In any case, since no part of the novel was published before December of that year, the conversation at the club could not have referred to *Last Chronicle.* Grantly, Mrs. Proudie, and the bishop had last appeared significantly in *Framley Parsonage* in April, 1861; they were barely mentioned in a late chapter of *Small House* in April, 1864. Trollope's clerical clubmen must have been nursing their grievance for quite some time before they expressed themselves in his presence, or the magazines in their hands must have been rather old, if his account is even partially credible.

ॐ

The *Last Chronicle of Barset* was Trollope's longest novel to date, and indeed only one longer was yet to come, *The Way We Live Now.* "Taking it as a whole, I regard this as the best novel I have written," he said in early 1876,[18] when a dozen or so novels were still unwritten. It has three plots, essentially separate though slightly linked to one another: the story of Josiah Crawley, perpetual curate of Hogglestock, who is surrounded by the Barsetshire people we know from *Framley Parsonage;* the narrative concerning Lily Dale, John Eames, and Adolphus Crosbie carried on from *The Small House at Allington,* and the account of a new group that in many ways looks forward to the associates of Lopez in *The Prime Minister* and of Melmotte in *The Way We Live Now.* These last are Dobbs Broughton, Mrs. Van Siever (widow of a wealthy Dutch merchant), and Augustus Musselboro (the prototype of Lopez and Melmotte), who "wears a lot of chains, and has elaborate whiskers, and an elaborate waistcoat, which is worse; and . . . doesn't wash his hands as often as he ought to do" (chap. xxiv). These three were partners in a financial enterprise operating out of a small courtyard in the City near the Bank of England and the Stock Exchange, though Mrs. Van Siever was a somewhat silent partner. What the enterprise actually was is obscure: perhaps the brokerage of questionable stocks, and certainly moneylending. It was sufficiently prosperous for a time to enable Broughton to provide his wife (who had the Thackerayan maiden name of Maria Clutterbuck)[19] with a fine house in Palace Gardens, just to the west of the park and only a few steps from Thackeray's last home in Palace Green. Theirs was a wealthy-looking parvenu society living in the new, elegant Victorian mansions which one can still see in Porchester Terrace off the Bayswater Road and north of the park. Mrs.

Dobbs Broughton "loved her husband in a sensible, humdrum way, feeling him to be a bore, knowing him to be vulgar, aware that he often took a good deal more wine than was good for him, and that he was almost as uneducated as a hog. Yet she loved him, and showed her love by taking care that he should have things for dinner that he liked to eat" (chap. xxvi). But speculations in the City became more and more desperate, Broughton drank more and more wine, and in his drunkenness ultimately shot himself in the head in the courtyard near his office. His widow, faced with absolute poverty, married Musselboro. Her friend Madalina Demolines, whose mother was the widow of a physician knighted for some service to royalty, is reaching the age at which the chances of matrimony may be slipping away, and she engages in a serious flirtation with Johnny Eames that ends in a farcical scene in which Johnny has to enlist the aid of a policeman to escape from her house. Why a woman's strenuous efforts to marry a man should be subject for farce, when Johnny's persistence in trying to marry Lily Dale moves our sentiments, is perhaps more clear to Trollope than to the modern reader.

But Lily will not marry Johnny. The memory of her former ill-advised desertion of him in favor of Adolphus Crosbie haunts her, and his claim to fidelity is undermined when she gets wind of his flirtation with Madalina. She was, Trollope remarked, a favorite character with his public, though he himself had reservations. "She made her way into the hearts of many readers, both young and old; so that, from that time to this, I have been continually honoured with letters, the purport of which has always been to beg me to marry Lily Dale to Johnny Eames. Had I done so, however, Lily would never have so endeared herself to these people. . . . It was because she could not get over her troubles that they loved her."[20]

The principal plot of *Last Chronicle,* however, is the story of Josiah Crawley's tribulations when he is accused of the theft of a check for £20, and here Trollope tried his hand at the sort of story he seldom attempted, the mystery tale like Mary Elizabeth Braddon's *Lady Audley's Secret* and Wilkie Collins's *Woman in White.* Though murder and terror were not involved, there was an accusation of theft that came close to ruining a man's life. Lord Lufton had written a check for £20 (payable to bearer, so that it could circulate like currency until presented to the bank for payment), then Lufton's agent lost the pocketbook containing it—he thought at Crawley's house, but Crawley denied having seen it. Some time later, however, Crawley cashed the check to pay his butcher's bill, and when the question was raised by the agent Crawley said he thought he had received the check from Dean Arabin. But Arabin and his wife by now had left for the Continent—the dean indeed for Jerusalem—and when asked by letter, the dean denied having given Crawley the check.

Crawley was committed to trial for the wrongful conversion, was generally viewed by the public as a thief, and began to doubt his own sanity.
This is as much as the reader knows through most of the novel.

If the unraveling of the mystery lacks the gothic trappings of the
"tale of terror," there was the disappearance of a carriage driver from the
local inn, the Dragon of Wantly, who was generally believed to have
sneaked off to New Zealand, and there was a red-nosed scoundrel who
wore his hat indoors and out and who lurked and spied out of dark corners
and through windows. Crawley's cousin and lawyer, Toogood, ultimately
discovers that the missing pocketbook had fallen out of the agent's pocket
in the carriage hired from the inn, the driver had sold the check at a
discount to the red-nosed scoundrel and left town, and the red-nosed
scoundrel had used the check at face value to pay some rent long overdue
to Mrs. Arabin. On the eve of his departure, Dean Arabin, knowing
Crawley's desperate straits, put ten five-pound banknotes into an envelope
for Crawley, and Mrs. Arabin, wishing to augment the sum, slipped the
check into the envelope. The proud Crawley reluctantly put the banknotes
and the check aside, but gradually drew on the cash and then, dunned by
the butcher, sent a lad to the bank to cash the check also and paid off the
butcher. Mrs. Arabin is summoned home in time to testify that she gave
the check to Crawley, the true thief is exposed, the scoundrel leaves town,
and Crawley is given the more profitable living of St. Ewold's in place of
the underpaid curacy of Hogglestock. As Trollope acknowledged, too
much is made to depend on Crawley's forgetfulness, and he acknowledged
also "that I have never been capable of constructing with complete success
the intricacies of a plot that required to be unravelled."[21]

Archdeacon Grantly maintains well the character he established in
the earlier books—generous and self-willed at the same time. He felt, in
the matter of the appointment to St. Ewold's, that "it was his special duty
to do the best he could for Mr. Thorne [the squire of the parish], but it
was specially his duty to do so without consulting Mr. Thorne about it"
(chap. lxxxii). At his first appearance in the book, he and his wife carry on
a discussion as they dress for dinner, she in her bedroom, he in his
adjoining dressing room, but he is so outraged that "all unaccoutred as he
was, he stood in the doorway between the two rooms, and thence fulmi-
nated at his wife" (chap. ii)—the echo of Cassius's heroic speech in
Shakespeare's *Julius Caesar* serves to call attention to the undignified
appearance of the archdeacon in his underwear. But he behaves well in the
end, and when Crawley, whose daughter is to marry Grantly's son Henry,
expresses the wish that he and the archdeacon stood on more equal
grounds as regards money, the archdeacon replies, "We stand on the only
perfect level on which such men can meet each other. We are both
gentlemen" (chap. lxxxiii). (Trollope was earlier at some pains to show

that despite his poverty, Crawley was a gentleman, and was recognized as one by parishioners whose coats were no worse than his own [chap. xx].)

Mrs. Proudie, who has now resided above ten years in Barchester (chap. lxvii), is at the center of two parallel scenes in the bishop's study that mark the transition from the comedy we have associated with her to the tragedy of her—alas!—unlamented death. She bullies her husband and Crawley until the curate turns on her with the remark that astounds us all: "Peace, woman. . . . You should not interfere in these matters. . . . The distaff were more fitting for you" (chap. xviii). Under similar circumstances during the bishop's interview with a cleric of greater prestige, Dr. Tempest, Tempest insists that either she or he must withdraw from the room; she refuses, he departs, and the bishop is left with the sense that he has been disgraced (chap. xlvii). "It cannot be said that she was a bad woman, though she had in her time done an indescribable amount of evil. She had endeavoured to do good, failing partly by ignorance and partly from the effects of an unbridled, ambitious temper" (chap. lxvi). The depth of the bishop's sense of disgrace utterly incapacitates him for the work of the diocese. "I wish I could forget myself," he tells her. "You have ruined me. I wish I were dead." He threatens to leave her, publicly. "At the bottom of her heart she knew that she had been a bad wife. And yet she had meant to be a pattern wife!" She withdraws to her bedroom and almost on the instant dies of a heart attack. Mr. Harding must also be disposed of in the ripeness of his years, and his closing scenes are described by Trollope with superlative emotion (chap. lxxxi).

Trollope's friends would recognize their author's familiar tastes. The Post Office surveyor could not forget Mrs. Proudie's attempt to halt the Sunday mails in Barsetshire (chap. lxxiv) and the civil servant could not forget the doctrine of competitive examinations for promotion, with "Devil take the hindmost." (Since "hindmost candidates were often the best gentlemen, . . . the Devil got the pick of the flock" [chap. xv].) He saw to it that his favorite Latin authors, Caesar and Cicero, were on Crawley's bookshelf (chap. iv). When Henry Grantly and Johnny Eames, then unknown to each other, traveled in the same compartment of a train from Paddington to Guestwick, Grantly carried the *Times,* Eames the *Daily News;* one had the *Saturday Review* and one the *Spectator,* but both had that "enterprising periodical" the *Pall Mall Gazette* (chap. xxvii). Trollope had named one of the best-known characters in *The Warden* from the passage (127:5) in the Book of Psalms, "Happy is the man that hath his quiver full of [children]"; now Mr. Toogood comforts himself over his dozen children "with the text about the quiver you know" (chap. xxxii; also chap. xl). The author of *Clergymen of the Church of England* can repeat his conviction that "a dean can go where he likes. He has no cure of souls to stand in the way of his pleasures" (chap. xxxii); the archdeacon "had never been a hunting man, though in his early days many a clergyman had been in the habit of hunting without losing his clerical character by doing so" (chap. xxxiii), and there is even a deliberate sketch of a new kind of clerical character, the ecclesiastical lawyer (chap. xxxiv). The painter Conway Dalrymple says that "the worst of success" is "that when won by merit it leads to further success, for the gaining of which no merit is necessary" (chap. li)—precisely the reasoning which Trollope advanced for publishing *Nina Balatka* anonymously. There was a foreshadowing of Lizzie Eustace's romantic dream of being carried off by a Byronic lover when Toogood's daughter Lucy lamented that no Corsair or Giaour ever came to Tavistock Square to carry off a girl. "Were not those the days to live in! But all that is over now, you know, and young people take houses in Woburn Place, instead of being locked up, or drowned, or married to a hideous monster behind a veil. I suppose it's better as it is, for some reasons" (chap. xl). The pathos of Crawley's stubborn pride, his learning, his instructing his daughter in the classical languages, coupled with his humiliating poverty, his consciousness that he cannot provide even minimal comforts for his family, is reminiscent, perhaps, of Thomas Anthony Trollope in the wretched farmhouse at Harrow Weald.

Not long after *Last Chronicle* was published, Trollope tells us, the manager of the new Gaiety Theatre, John Hollingshead, asked him to do a piece for his stage, and Trollope did so in the spring of 1869, using the Crawley plot for a comedy he called *Did He Steal It?*[22] In the play Crawley retains his school but is not a clergyman. Mr. Goshawk is a magistrate and managing director of the school, and he and his wife combine the functions of the Proudies and the Grantlys—Mrs. Goshawk's son, a captain, is in love with Grace Crawley and her daughter has married wealth. Like Mrs. Proudie, Mrs. Goshawk dominates her husband and is sternly rebuked by Mr. Crawley's "Peace, woman!" The matter of the check is resolved when Mrs. Lofty, a "benevolent old lady belonging to Silverbridge," storms into the Dragon of Wantly, having returned posthaste from Rome, thunders at Mrs. Goshawk, "Madame, you've put your foot in it," and reveals that she had given the check along with the banknotes to Crawley. Much of the dialogue is patched together from the novel, though one remark of the henpecked Goshawk is new: "A man can't sew a woman's mouth up; he can't send her to bed,—he can't very well beat her. I couldn't at least. He can go to his club, and that's about all he can do. Women don't like clubs. Mrs. G. doesn't like the club. I tell her clubs come from nagging,—and it's true."

All flavor of tragedy has disappeared, and we are left with a rather thin farce. The play was rejected by the theater manager on grounds

Trollope could not recall only a few years later, but a handful of copies were printed up for the author in 1869 by James Virtue.

ॐ

Holiday plans for 1866 were preempted by Tom's engagement and remarriage. Anthony and Rose spent a short time in September at Glengariff on Bantry Bay in Southern Ireland, in abominable weather, then on October 1 Anthony went out to Florence. "I knew you would," had been his response when Tom announced that he was about to marry Frances Eleanor Ternan. Dickens wrote a warm congratulatory letter, claiming credit for having been the "unconscious instrument" of Tom's happiness when he gave Frances Eleanor and her mother a letter of introduction to old Mrs. Trollope in Florence eight years earlier.[23] Anthony, Tom and Frances traveled together to Paris, where they were joined by Rose, Harry, and Frances's mother, and where the wedding took place on October 29. Somehow, Anthony cut his leg with a knife on the train—a misfortune Rose recalled nine years later but which seems to have had no serious consequences. By the beginning of November the family was back in Waltham Cross.

Alfred Austin, who had been a member of the group that founded the *Fortnightly* and who later became Poet Laureate, spent the winter of 1864–65 in Florence, met and much liked Tom Trollope, and indeed moved in with him at the house in Piazza dell'Independenza when Theodosia died. He came to know and like Anthony also, and makes an interesting comparison between the two: "Unlike his brother Anthony, who, though likewise a delightful companion, and brimming over with active intelligence, was in no accurate sense of the word intellectual, and as unhelpful and impatient an arguer as I ever met, Thomas Adolphus Trollope rejoiced in threshing out afresh the old metaphysical and theological problems, handling them with a rare dialectical skill. . . . Many years later, his brother Anthony said to me, . . . when staying [at my house], 'You know how attached I am to you. But there is one thing for which I cannot forgive you. You have made my brother Tom a Conservative.'" Austin said that Frances Eleanor, "though thoroughly feminine in every respect, had an almost masculine mind in the sphere of serious intellectual deliberations." As for politics, Austin pointed out that after Anthony revisited Ireland at the end of his life, he himself became a Unionist and denounced Gladstone and all his works.[24]

ॐ

Early in November, 1866, George Lewes resigned the editorship of the *Fortnightly* for reasons of health, leaving the December number ready for the press. The resignation came as no surprise, but was subject of special regret for Trollope. "I hate the breaking of pleasant relations; and am distrustful as to new relations. I have felt however . . . that your time was too valuable to be frittered away in reading Mss. and in writing civil,—or even uncivil—notes," Trollope wrote to him.[25] The principal candidate for the vacant post was a young writer for the *Saturday Review,* John Morley, a friend of Cotter Morison's. Morley later recalled but one thing about Trollope's interview with him for the editorship. "'Now do you,' he asked, glaring as if in fury through his spectacles, and roaring like a bull of Bashan, 'do you believe in the divinity of our blessed Lord and Saviour Jesus Christ?' He had not a perfect sense of the shades and delicacies of things, nor had he exactly the spirit of urbanity." On November 9, the decision as to a successor had not been made; should the committee of management appoint Morley, or should Trollope, as chairman of the board, undertake the editorship on a temporary basis without salary, relying largely on the work of Lewes's subeditor John Dennis, whom the committee much liked? Trollope had filled in for Lewes the preceding June and July while Lewes was traveling abroad. Only three weeks later, Morley (then twenty-eight) was in place and was asking Trollope's permission to pay his friend Swinburne twenty guineas for a poem, "Child's Song in Winter"; Trollope consented, and the poem appeared in the January number. The transition, however, was not easy; Morley did not like working with Dennis and wished to be rid of him at once. Dennis sought Trollope's aid, but "what can I do?" "I do not specially dislike Morley, but I do not care for his style of work, & cannot interest myself in the thing," he wrote in the middle of May following.[26] A later judgment is more balanced: Morley "has done the work with admirable patience, zeal, and capacity. Of course he has got around him a set of contributors whose modes of thought are what we may call much advanced: he being 'much advanced' himself, could not work with other aids. The periodical has a peculiar tone of its own; but it holds its own with ability, and though there are many who perhaps hate it, there are none who despise it." Meanwhile, the proprietors, having exhausted their capital, sold the journal to Chapman and Hall "for a trifle"; in due course it became "a good property."[27] But at best its circulation was of a quite different order of magnitude from that of the *Cornhill,* even after the latter's drop from its original hundred thousand.

It is not clear precisely when the ownership of the review was transferred to Chapman and Hall; Trollope's correspondence shows that the original proprietors were still involved in decisions at least through May, 1867. Trollope's own interest in the next few years fell off from the *Fortnightly* because of his preoccupation with *St. Pauls Magazine,* but he was clearly not without influence, since Tom's novel *Leonora Casaloni* was serialized from March to December, 1868, and Frances Eleanor's *Anne Furness* from July, 1870, to August, 1871. By that time Anthony was once more an important *Fortnightly* author: *The Eustace Diamonds* began its serialization in July, 1871, and *Lady Anna* in April, 1873.

His farewell to the *Fortnightly* for the moment is a brief review (perhaps actually accepted by Lewes, though published in Morley's second number) of a moral ballad by the nearly seventy-year-old Mrs. Mary Sewell, *The Rose of Cheriton,* aimed at persuading Parliament to put down drunkenness among the working classes "by shutting up beer-shops," as Trollope said. (Mrs. Sewell's daughter Anna has gained an immortality not granted her mother, by writing *Black Beauty*.) Unfortunately, the ballad (in his judgment) is so unthinking, so given to the presumption that one side is entirely wrong, that it "will be thrown aside with a feeling . . . that it is preachy-preachy for preaching sake." As for the results of the prohibition she advocates, it would "create the illicit sale of articles which would become more deleterious and more seducing by the very fact of their illegality," and Trollope points to the failure of the attempts in some American states to "prevent brewers from brewing and distillers from distilling." "Let her push her argument . . . to the end, and she must, I think, find that she comes to a quarrel with her Creator, because there is beer in the barley and wine in the grape." Were brewing and distilling forbidden, her ballad declares, there would be

> "Plenty of food upon the children's plate,
> The wife at home,—men would not emigrate;
> And strikes would end."

No emigration—"Would she have had no America and no Australia?" asks Trollope, with a son now in the latter. "And as to the question of strikes, . . . on so large, so vital, so all-absorbing a question as that, she should have paused before she ventured to condemn the whole theory as being positively bad,—out of all question bad,—bad as drunkenness itself is bad!" (It was not Trollope, after all, who wrote *Hard Times*.) "But for pious little books, no thought, no caution, no delay, no sifting of opinions, is deemed necessary. The good intention is all in all. The good intention of Mrs. Sewell no one will dispute."[28] Not every Victorian author, nor every Victorian journal, would have ventured to express such opinions as these.

Chapter XV

1866–67

The decade of the sixties was remarkable for the very great number of new periodicals that had their beginning then. *Macmillan's Magazine* antici-pated the flood by a few months (November, 1859); we have already encountered in this narrative the *Cornhill Magazine* (January 1, 1860), *Temple Bar* (December, 1860), the *Fortnightly Review* (May 15, 1865), and two of the magazines started by the Scottish publisher Alexander Strahan, whose *Good Words* began on the same day as the *Cornhill* while Strahan was still publishing in Edinburgh, and whose *Contemporary Review* started on January 1, 1866, nearly four years after his migration to London. In December, 1865, Strahan also inaugurated a sixpenny magazine aimed at a less sophisticated audience, the *Argosy*. This last got off to a slow start, and on April 3, 1866, Strahan asked Trollope for "a short sketch of say ten or twelve pages, and I will gladly pay you on your own terms." The journal "must do well yet for it is very good and very cheap," and he intends soon to ask Trollope for a full-length novel; for the present can Trollope supply the short story by April 16 or 17? "Father Giles of Ballymoy," an amusing anecdote of a traveler in a rural Irish hotel that has an autobiographical note, appeared in the May number and brought Trollope £60. He was promptly paid, and agreed to write three more stories at the same price; these were "Lotta Schmidt" (July), "The Misfor-tunes of Fred Pickering" (September) and, presumably, "The Last Aus-trian Who Left Venice," which, however, arrived after Strahan had sold the magazine and was therefore published in *Good Words*.[1]

These and three other stories from *Good Words,* with two stories published elsewhere, were collected in a volume called *Lotta Schmidt and Other Stories,* of which Strahan sent Trollope the "first budget of proofs" on March 7, 1867. Strahan was a notoriously ambitious publisher who be-haved most generously in payments to first-rate authors (he became Tennyson's publisher in 1868 by guaranteeing him payments of £4,000 annually for the right to publish all his poems for four years, and to publish his new poems at 5 percent commission), but he was perennially short of funds and so he wrote to Trollope, "Finding [your book] would make 2 Vols of fair novel size, I thought it as well to make 2 of it. This will enable me to spend a good deal more in advertising it and making it more widely known. And if I make a little more profit to myself I am sure you will not object." Trollope did object; "I have always endeavored to give good measure to the public." Strahan had originally agreed to publish the tales in one volume, at ten shillings sixpence; now he plans two at, presumably, twenty shillings, the pages showing "such a poor rill of type meandering thro' a desert of margin, as to make me ashamed of the idea of putting my name to the book." Still, not wishing to make Strahan pay too dearly for his folly, Trollope offered to share the expense of setting the type anew. The book was published in one volume, about August 24.[2]

Trollope had first planned to call the book *Tales of All Countries, Third Series*, but Strahan wanted a slightly more saleable title. The stories, one of which had been first published as early as 1861, draw upon Trollope's knowledge of the Caribbean ("The Journey to Panama"), the border states in the American Civil War ("The Two Generals"), the west of Ireland ("Father Giles"), the northern coast of Cornwall near Tintagel ("Malachi's Cove"), the factory region of western England ("The Widow's Mite"), Venice at the end of the Austrian occupation, Boston society ("Miss Ophelia Gledd"), and the Viennese beer halls ("Lotta Schmidt"). The ninth, "The Adventures [or "Misfortunes"] of Fred Pickering," tells of a young man trying to support a wife and infant child by making his way through journalism and literature in London—the sort of person Trollope had often encountered through the Royal Literary Fund. Alas, Fred failed: when he sent a careful analysis of *Samson Agonistes* to one editor, it was returned with the remark that the journal "never admitted reviews of old books," and Fred had to go back to Manchester as clerk in a law firm. Like Trollope's other collections of short stories, these are essentially anecdotes, some very entertaining, others not.

We have seen that there had already been two attempts to involve Trollope in the editorship of a new magazine, that by the publisher of *Temple Bar* in 1861 and the tentative scheme by Fred Chapman in 1863 for "*The New Weekly,* conducted by Anthony Trollope," in which project Robert Bell would be associated.[3] When fiction was to be the staple of a magazine, it behooved the proprietor to secure the name of a novelist whose books appealed to the public he aimed at, whether the novelist had a talent for editorial work or not, and so the offer respecting *Temple Bar* had explicitly called the post an "ostensible" editorship, the "real work" to be performed (in this case) by Edmund Yates. By the same token, if the journal was to appeal to a readership with a religious cast, it behooved the proprietor to secure the name of a well-known religious figure; thus Strahan secured Norman Macleod as nominal editor of *Good Words* and the dean of Canterbury, Henry Alford, to edit the *Contemporary Review*. We have seen how much of the success of the *Cornhill* was due, not to the skill and business acumen of Thackeray, but to the initiative and financial venturesomeness of the publisher George Smith. Although Trollope would not "undertake a mock Editorship," by 1866 his work with the *Fortnightly* was giving him a good deal of experience with all aspects of bringing out a periodical.

The printer of the *Fortnightly* was James Virtue, who attended all the meetings of the board of proprietors and who may himself have been one of them, as was his brother-in-law Cotter Morison. He was a well-established, prosperous publisher, born, indeed, in the lodgings in Ivy Lane, near St. Paul's Cathedral, above the shop in which his father conducted a book selling business. When the Virtue firm acquired the *Art Journal*, they set up a printing establishment in the City Road to cope with the specialized needs of that magazine, and thereafter conducted the printing and publishing business in tandem; printing was done on a large scale for other publishers as well.[4]

Virtue, then, had been closely associated with Trollope in the publication of a periodical for more than a year and a half when conversations began between them about the establishment of a new magazine. Which of them began the conversations is not clear; almost certainly it was Virtue, who would have to set up and finance the venture. Trollope's account is entirely credible, except for his own ignorance of the extent of Virtue's publishing business: Virtue

> asked me to edit a new magazine for him, and . . . offered me a salary of £1,000 a year for the work, over and above what might be due to me for my own contributions. I had known something of magazines, and did not believe that they were generally very lucrative. They were, I thought, useful to some publishers as bringing grist to the mill; but as Mr. Virtue's business was chiefly that of a printer, in which he was very successful, this consideration could hardly have had much weight with him. I very strongly advised him to abandon the project, pointing out to him that a large expenditure would be necessary to carry on the magazine in accordance with my views,—that I could not be concerned in it on any other understanding, and that the chances of an adequate return to him for his money were very small. He came down to Waltham, listened to my arguments with great patience, and then told me that if I would not do the work he would find some other editor. Upon this I consented to undertake the duty.[5]

It was presumably after that visit to Waltham Cross that Virtue wrote to Trollope on November 15, 1866, a letter that showed the planning well along. Both men would have known of the *Argosy's* difficulty, and there had been some thought of taking it over from Strahan, but they were reluctant to continue a magazine that had already established its character (not too successfully) and even, necessarily, had a back-log of accepted contributions, and so, a few weeks later, the *Argosy* became the property of Mrs. Henry Wood, author of the prototypical Victorian melodramatic *East Lynne,* who conducted the journal pros-perously for many years. "What say you," wrote Virtue,

> to a new Magazine to be started say—Jany 1 [i.e., 1868], to be edited by you and so announced.
> Editors salary to be £*1000* per annum, this to include all Editorial Expenditure.
> All arrangements with contributors to be made by you entirely, upon such terms as we may agree upon together, but the manage-ment of the literary portion and Illustrations must be entirely in your hands.
> Your own writings would of course be paid for, same as if you wrote for any other Magazine.
> I should propose to get up a Magazine similar in appearance to the Argosy, but upon better paper and with more pages,—but if you feel inclined to entertain the idea we can discuss the details, if we can first agree upon main principles, such as Editor's salary and the like.
> I am sure there is room for a good Magazine, under your manage-ment, it will be hard if we cannot hold our own against such as "Belgravia" and "Temple Bar."[6]

Trollope's reply was prompt, and a further letter from Virtue next day was perfectly amenable to the suggestions and conditions Trollope had apparently laid down.

> About the novel to commence with—I have nothing whatever in contemplation for this, my experience lies so little in that way that I fear I should have to look to you entirely for the Literature—Is there no possibility of arranging even for a short one of your own. But perhaps when you have thought over the matter more fully—you would lay out roughly your plan for the whole Magazine and then we might determine which portion should be illustrated & such like. . . . I calculate that a sale of 25,000 would pay,—but I cer-tainly expect a far higher circulation.

Without waiting another instant Trollope began writing *Phineas Finn* on November 17.[7]

By December 13 Virtue was committed firmly to the project; there remained the questions of a name for the magazine and the date of its beginning. Trollope preferred October 1 for the latter, since if his salary would not commence before the first number he could hardly afford to work longer on the project without compensation. For the former, he rejected out of hand *Trollope's Monthly;* possibly, he thought, the *Monthly Westminster* or the *Monthly Liberal.* (He later conceived that the *Whitehall Magazine* might do.)

> I would propose to have every month a political article,—one month on foreign politics and one month on home politics. I would have but very little reviewing;—*or none.* None, unless on some very rare occasion. I would begin with a novel myself, & would propose to carry it thro 20 numbers. . . . Would you think well to have a second novel, of course written on cheaper terms? Even so it will cost more than ordinary matter, but not much more—perhaps 25/ a page instead of 20/. It makes the work of getting the number out much easier, and saves sometimes the necessity of using indifferent matter. I think that during the Session I would endeavour to explain in a few pages what Parliament is doing.[8]

He fixed the price of his own novel at £3,200. Memoranda of agreement were signed by January 24, 1867, and the title of *St. Pauls,* from the part of London where Virtue's publishing house stood (on the analogy of the *Cornhill* from the location of Smith, Elder's house) was fixed sometime after the middle of April.[9]

By that time Trollope had already written to ask his friend Robert Bell to be his subeditor (whose salary was to be paid out of the annual £1,000 Trollope received as editor), but Bell was obliged to decline on grounds of health. Fortuitously, Trollope's friend Sir Charles Taylor in mid-January consulted him about Mme. Blaze de Bury's wish to sell a still unwritten novel; Trollope offered to interest himself in it when it was complete so that he could read it entire, and, as it happened, he purchased it as the second novel for the opening numbers of *St. Pauls.* (She was a British woman married to a Frenchman, whom Tom Trollope had known in Paris in 1840 as "one of my most charming friends of those days.")[10] As these plans were taking shape, the publisher George Routledge was also planning a new magazine, the *Broadway,* and asked Trollope to write for it, but "I fear I shall be too busy all thro' the autumn and to the end of the year to do anything."[11] He did not explain at what he should be busy.

૨૪

"Dear old Robert Bell died this morning," Trollope wrote to George Smith on April 12, 1867, and enclosed an obituary notice for the next day's *Pall Mall Gazette.* "He was a very manly fellow. I loved him well." Within a month he had drawn up a petition to be presented to the prime minister, Lord Derby, by the president of the Royal Literary Fund, Lord Stanhope, asking for a government pension for Bell's widow, and had solicited signatures from the publisher John Murray, from Wilkie Collins, and from Dickens (among others, no doubt). When he learned that Bell's library was to be sold at auction, he arranged to buy the lot—nearly four thousand volumes—at a valuation substantially higher than the auction would have brought: "We all know the difference in value between buying and selling of books." He enlisted Chapman's help in moving them to Waltham Cross. [12]

It was Bell who had first introduced Trollope to the Royal Literary Fund, and when at the anniversary dinner of May 15 he responded to the toast to "Imaginative Literature," he paid tribute to Bell's invaluable work on behalf of the fund. Once again there was a last-minute aspect to the speech: on the very day of the dinner he was writing to the secretary of the fund to say that he could not be counted on. But that evening he was there to hear the president (Stanhope) speak of an "invention, attended with most successful results, of which, as far as I know, the original merit belongs to M. de Balzac; the plan being that the characters of one work of fiction are not confined to that work, but reappear in subsequent adventures in other works." (Thackeray, of course, preceded Trollope in this practice in England.) Sir Francis Hastings Doyle, newly elected successor to Matthew Arnold as professor of poetry at Oxford, proposed the literary toast at great length, and repeated the president's theme: "We are all of us familiar with the gallery of portraits which Mr. Trollope has given to the world: we all of us scramble every week for the new number of the last novel now in progress [*The Last Chronicle of Barset*], and we hope to finish that and see many others from the same fertile pen, delighting us for many years to come (cheers)." And so Trollope responded: "I should be very happy, after what has been said by the President of the Society, to drink long life to M. de Balzac [who died in 1850]. I am told that he was the man who invented that style of fiction in which I have attempted to work. I assure any young men around me who may be desirous of following the same steps that they cannot possibly find any style easier. The carrying on of a character from one book to another is very pleasant to the author; but I am not sure that all readers will participate in that pleasure." [13] Perhaps this public acclaim did something to assuage the wrath caused a year earlier by the two clerical critics he may have overheard at the Athenaeum.

Trollope's letter to Dickens soliciting support for Mrs. Bell's pension brought a prompt and friendly response:

> My dear Trollope,
>   The instant I got your letter at my office, I of course went over to the [Royal Literary Fund office at] Adelphi Terrace and signed the Memorial. I had heard with much satisfaction that poor Mrs.

Bell had found a friend in you, for I knew she could have no
stauncher or truer friend.

Faithfully Yours Always

Anthony Trollope Esquire   Charles Dickens

There is a good deal of uncertainty about the relations between Dickens
and Trollope. Two years later Trollope told an autograph seeker, "It is not
often that I chance to hear from [Dickens], but such things do occur now
& then"; still, he could not at that moment lay his hand on any letter of
Dickens's, [14] and in fact the one on Robert Bell's widow is the single piece
of correspondence between the two to have survived. Dickens met Trollope's mother very soon after the publication of *The Domestic Manners of the
Americans,* and presented himself at her door (and Tom's) in Florence in
1844. Thereafter he was in frequent friendly correspondence with Tom,
whom he invited (along with Tom's wife Theodosia) to write for *All the
Year Round.* [15] Tom's second wife, Frances Eleanor Ternan, also contributed to *All the Year Round.* But there were reasons which may have made
Anthony prefer to keep his distance from the most popular novelist of his
day. Dickens had quarreled with Thackeray, he had withdrawn in a rage
from the Garrick Club, and he had actively campaigned against the Royal
Literary Fund. Trollope had parodied Dickens (quite skillfully) as "Mr.
Popular Sentiment" in *The Warden,* and he had expressed himself firmly
against the picture of the Civil Service as the "Circumlocution Office" in
Little Dorrit, but writers must expect disagreement with their ideas now
and then, and public differences of opinion on such matters need not in
themselves be causes of hostility. That vicious scandalmonger Edmund
Yates told the story (after both Dickens and Trollope were dead) that John
Forster, then a guest at Gad's Hill Place, greeted Dickens at lunch with
the remark that he was reading Yates's first novel, *Broken to Harness*
(1864); "It is really very good, my dear Dickens—quite as good as Mr.
Anthony Trollope." "That is not very high praise," said Dickens. [16] The
story of course may not have been true; Yates was quite capable of publishing a falsehood. Nevertheless, had Dickens and Trollope been close,
the evidence would have survived.

Indeed, it is entirely possible that the common effort on behalf of
Mrs. Bell marked a turning point. There is about Dickens's letter a
certain air of formality, but Dickens is allying himself warmly with a
project close to Trollope's heart. The following autumn Trollope accepted
an invitation to be one of the stewards (i.e., financial backers) of a dinner
to be given on November 2 on the occasion of Dickens's journey to
America. "You . . . know that I am not specially in that set, but having
been asked I did not like to refuse," he told a friend. Tom Trollope was

also a steward, along with a whole roster of literary friends of Trollope's. At the dinner Anthony responded to the toast to "literature." Taking the occasion of a "banquet . . . to grace a great chieftain in literature," he undertook to confute the well-known prophet of woe who had just then published "Shooting Niagara—and After," and who had cautioned them, "Fiction, O my friend! you will have to think how perilous and close a cousinship it has with lying." In reply Trollope named characters or cited scenes from "the five great artists of modern fiction," the authors of *The Newcomes, Jane Eyre, Adam Bede, Eugene Aram,* and *Oliver Twist,* and asked: Are these characters and scenes lies? "We who write fiction have taught purity of life, nobility of action, and self-denial, and have taught those lessons with allurements both to the old and the young which no other teacher of the present day can reach, and which no prophet can teach." He was received with general and prolonged cheering.[17]

Trollope's insistence on the moralistic didactic function of novels—an idea which is a constant in his public utterances on the subject—takes on the air of a cliché of the period when one hears the words with which Sir Francis Grant, president of the Royal Academy, had introduced Trollope at the anniversary banquet previous to the public opening of the exhibition on May 4, 1867: "In regard to works of fiction, we artists, and, indeed, mankind in general, most warmly appreciate those works which, combining sound morality and wholesome instruction with poetic imagination, are alike strong in graphic truth and perfect fidelity to nature. In these important qualities few authors have equalled, and none have surpassed, Mr. Anthony Trollope. (Hear, hear.)" Trollope responded to the toast to "The Interests of Literature" "in felicitous terms," and the company then separated; he was the last speaker in a long evening that began with the Prince of Wales.[18]

಄

With *Phineas Finn* still more than a month from completion, Trollope looked ahead to the writing of yet another novel set in the Central European cities he had visited two years earlier, and inquired of Blackwood's London agent Joseph Langford whether "Maga" might be receptive to another such anonymous work. John Blackwood replied on April 3: "I am pleased to hear of Trollope's disposition for further relations. When you see him give him my compliments, and say I am quite inclined. 'Author of "Nina Balatka"' may become a very convenient *nom de plume,* especially for such a very prolific writer as our friend." Acting on this encouragement, Trollope began *Linda Tressel* on June 2, less than three weeks after finishing *Phineas,* sent the manuscript to Blackwood on July 10, and promptly accepted his offer for £450 for the full copyright. Blackwood was aware that *Nina Balatka* had aroused curiosity about its authorship—

that it was "telling although not selling"—and now discovered that fewer than five hundred copies had been sold, "which is a great shame & a heavy loss but I trust that the well earned reputation [that] could not help Nina herself will help Linda." The personal friendship between author and publisher is indicated by Trollope's invitation to Blackwood (and his wife, if she were with him) to dine and spend the night of July 1 at Waltham Cross, Blackwood being then in London. [19]

When the publisher read the first part of *Linda Tressel,* however, he felt obliged to write on September 13 that he was "very sorry to say that I fear you have made a blunder and so have I," and gave a lengthy and pointed critique. Trollope instantly replied that Blackwood must feel "quite at liberty to give up the story" and must "feel quite sure that your returning it to me will moult no feather between you & me." Blackwood did not return it, and by mid-December felt more comfortable; it had now run for three months in the magazine and "as far as I can judge the public seem to be liking [it]." It was, unfortunately, a financial failure like its predecessor. [20]

&

Nuremberg, prior to the devastation of World War II, was one of the most romantic towns of Germany, with its river flowing between pictur-esque houses and dividing around the large Schütt Island. Trollope was struck, on his visit there, by the fact that though the fourteenth-century Church of Our Lady was Catholic, other large gothic churches of the same era, such as those of St. Sebald and St. Lawrence, were Protestant, albeit Bavaria as a whole was Catholic. Into that setting he placed the story of Linda Tressel, an orphaned young lady of twenty who was being brought up on the island by a strictly Calvinistic aunt in a house which Linda will inherit. Linda loves a lad her own age, but the aunt insists that she marry Peter Steinmarc, an elderly, shuffling, beer-drinking, pipe-smoking lodger who in fact would like to become the owner of their house. When-ever Linda rebels, her aunt in all sincerity throws herself upon her knees and prays that grace may be shown to her sinful niece. The Calvinism of the aunt, indeed, sets her off socially from the Lutherans as well as the Roman Catholics of the town. But the story is almost without episode and without character, except for "that wicked old saint," the aunt (chap. xii). In the end Linda flees to the home of relatives in Cologne and there dies, not from any named illness but from the loss of a will to live. It was one more "tale of all countries"—indeed the story is almost the same as that of "La Mère Bauche"—with the ornamental trimmings of a foreign set-ting, but the Calvinism (in contrast to Trollope's handling of some British Puritanical figures in other novels) is a mere caricature. John Blackwood had been right: the book was a blunder.

In mid-July John Lothrop Motley met Trollope at a dinner party at Stirling Maxwell's. "I liked Trollope very much; he was excessively friendly, and wants me to come down to him where he lives in the country—I forget where: perhaps I shall," Motley told his wife.[21]

The Trollope holiday in the summer of 1867 was divided between ten days at Clovelly with Rose in early June and a Continental tour with her from July 17 to August 21. Anthony went ahead for a few days at the Paris Exhibition; she joined him there and they journeyed eastward through Reims, Nancy, Metz, and down to Remiremont in the Vosges. From there they crossed Switzerland to Chur (Coire), where Harry joined them; they spent some time in the Engadine—Savognin, over the Albula to St. Moritz and Silvaplana, back over the Julier. They crossed the St. Bernard Pass to Locarno and Lake Orta, then over the Simplon in the dark, down the Rhone Valley to Geneva and home. On September 1 Trollope began to write *The Golden Lion of Granpere*, a novel set in Lorraine, in eastern France, which he had just then visited.[22]

☙

Trollope must have given Tilley some explanation for declining the offered surveyorship of the newly established London postal district, but if so the explanation has not been recorded. One might speculate that he already had his resignation from the service in mind; even if it were only a faint idea he would be abandoning the option if he took on a new and very important responsibility. (Edmund Yates commented that toward the end of his Post Office career, Trollope's involvements in literature had become more strenuous, his interests in the service less overwhelming.)[23] Or perhaps he simply felt comfortable in his way of life at Waltham Cross, which he would have to give up if he moved to a new district. His own Eastern District had been expanded somewhat by the addition of the area around Peterborough in a rearrangement of surveyors' districts he had helped to define earlier in 1866. Under this arrangement his seventy-seven post towns were the largest number in any district, though the average weekly circulation in it of 747,336 letters was sixth of the ten.[24] In *An Autobiography* he tells us that his thought of resigning was motivated largely by the hurt when Scudamore was appointed assistant secretary. "I did not wish . . . that any younger officer should again pass over my head. I believed that I had been a valuable public servant, and I will own to a feeling existing at that time that I had not altogether been well treated."[25]

The agreement to edit *St. Pauls* sealed the resolution, and also, by giving him a secure income of £750 a year for at least two years (the thousand pounds promised by Virtue would have to be reduced by the £250 he paid to his assistant editor), made the resignation financially feasible. For in resigning he gave up all claim to a pension, for which he would have had to work another eight years (to age sixty) and which would then in any case have amounted to a mere £500 a year or less. Indeed he had already laid aside enough of his literary earnings to produce an income more than equal to the pension he abandoned. On October 4, 1867, Tilley forwarded Trollope's resignation to the postmaster general, the Duke of Montrose, with a long letter outlining the terms in which the Duke might wish to express his appreciation of Trollope's long years of service to the department. The Duke took his cue and assented to Tilley's language; six days later Tilley could forward Trollope's response: "You will be glad to see that Mr. Trollope is pleased with his letter." Indeed he was: he copied it verbatim into *An Autobiography,* with only the very slightest suggestion of irony that shows his awareness of the personal relationship between the actual author of the letter and himself. Tilley had secured the Duke's endorsement of the proposition that "in spite of the many calls upon his time Mr. Trollope has never permitted his other avocations to interfere with his Post Office work which has always been faithfully and indeed energetically performed."[26]

The resignation took effect on October 31, and almost his last official act was to resist attempts to reduce salaries and cut back services in his district. "The early morning delivery should be maintained at these suburban towns. If it were taken off, the second delivery would be later than at present, & men would get no letters or papers before they went to business. I feel sure that great complaint would arise. I also [believe] that less than the proposed salaries would not be found to be sufficient remuneration for the work required."[27] The surveyorship was taken over by Charles Rea, who had deputized for him during his journey to the United States and more than once subsequently during his leaves of absence and duties elsewhere.

A decade after Trollope's death Yates, who was notorious for his literary quarrels, wrote in his weekly gossip sheet, the *World:*

> A man with worse or more offensive manners than Trollope I have rarely met. He was coarse, boorish, rough, noisy, overbearing, insolent; he adopted the Johnsonian tactics of trying to outroar his adversary in argument; he sputtered and shouted, and glared through his spectacles, and waved his arms about, a sight for gods and men. . . . By the officials who were subordinate to him . . . he was pretty generally hated for the particularly objectionable manner in which he treated them. . . . I have heard of several instances, [however,] and I know of one, to prove that he had a kind heart.[28]

The records of the Post Office reveal the quarrelsomeness and the occasional bullying; they also reveal a man who on principle worked hard for the well-being of all civil servants, not merely himself, and whose intelligent energy in the interest of the Post Office is not easily matched.

A farewell dinner was given for Trollope by his colleagues on the evening of Thursday, October 31, at the Albion Tavern. One wonders what irony put Scudamore in the chair and made Yates vice-chairman. Tilley was of course present. "The toast of the evening was very cleverly proposed by Mr. Scudamore, and that of the visitors, very facetiously by Mr. Edmund Yates, and a very successful evening was spent," reported the *Times*.[29] It was a much quieter occasion than the grand public dinner given for Dickens two days later on his departure for America.

For the first time in nearly thirty-three years Trollope was not a civil servant. When Tilley in 1878 became discouraged with his own work in the Post Office and asked Trollope's advice on whether he should retire (since his pension would be as large as his salary), Trollope replied:

> A man who works for his bread is so much nobler than he who takes his bread for nothing. . . . You say of me:—that I would not choose to write novels unless I were paid. Most certainly I would;—much rather than not write them at all. The two points to be looked at are, your happiness,—(provided that the happiness of others dependent on you is indifferent in the matter,—) and your duty. What future employment do you propose for yourself? In some respects you have limited yourself more closely than many men. You cannot stand in a club window; you cannot play cards; you cannot farm. Books must be your resource. I hardly know whether you can be happy four hours at a spell with a book. I do know that such happiness comes only from practice, and that the habit will not be acquired late in life. As to duty I am convinced that you ought to go if you believe it to be better for the service that you should do so;—or to remain for the same reason. . . . If it be that weariness tends to make your work unserviceable, I think you should go. If there be no such conviction, I think that for your own sake you should remain another term. Your happiness is so much to me that I cannot but write about it much in earnest.

Tilley remained in the service another two years, then retired upon the death of his third wife.[30]

᪥

Trollope's conviction that *Saint Pauls* should have a strong political flavor—"every month a political article," and "during the Session I would endeavour to explain in a few pages what Parliament is doing"—clearly determined the subject of the novel he wrote for it; there are times when

Phineas Finn reads more like a treatise on nineteenth-century parliamentary government than a work of fiction. Trollope spent much time in the gallery of the House of Commons to observe the etiquette and the flavor of debate.[31] The principal concerns of both parties in the latter years of the sixties were reform (making the qualifications for the franchise much broader and redistributing the constituencies to reduce the absolute control of wealthy patrons over certain seats in Parliament) and the Irish problem (disestablishment of the Anglican Church of Ireland, and protection of agricultural tenants against arbitrary dispossession by their landlords); these questions are discussed at some length in the novel.

For the hero is a Roman Catholic Irishman from Killaloe, on the River Shannon, not far from Trollope's first Irish residence in Banagher;* he represented an Irish constituency which he owed to the blessing of an Irish Earl, and was a Liberal by party allegiance. When the Earl became angry with him he was given the English constituency of Loughton by the Earl of Brentford—so conspicuously a pocket borough as to be embarrassing to a Liberal member, a constituency marked for abolition under redistribution. One aspect of election reform before the House was the substitution of secret ballot for open voting in elections; Finn, like Trollope, was hostile to the ballot (a man should have the courage to declare his opinion openly), and he hoped to make his first speech in the House in opposition to the change, but lost his nerve. The hardest lesson for him to learn was the necessity to support his party every step of the way, whether he agreed with them or not: "I shall go [into Parliament] as a sound Liberal,—not to support a party, but to do the best I can for the country," he declared at the outset (to the disgust of his political mentor) (chap. ii), and his promising career terminated five years later when, having seen something of the miseries of his native land, he voted in favor of Irish tenant rights at a moment when the prime minister was unwilling to support such a move.

The ladies in the novel are far more interesting than the gentlemen (except perhaps for Phineas), and Trollope concerns himself once more with the problem he had made the focus of *The Belton Estate*—the position of women in society. To Lady Laura Standish, the energetic and intelligent daughter of the Earl of Brentford who delighted in politics, "It is a great curse to have been born a woman," since woman's lot is one of

---

*In *An Autobiography* (p. 318), Trollope says he was led to make his hero an Irishman "by the circumstance that I created the scheme of the book during a visit to Ireland." It is true that, as we have seen, he and Rose had a short holiday in Southern Ireland (not the western country from which Finn came) about two months before he began to write the novel, but the Hibernian origins of Finn certainly owe much more to the current importance of Irish problems in British politics.

dependence. Lady Laura marries a Scottish Calvinist of great wealth and a cabinet member in the hope that she can gain influence that way, but learns that she has subjected herself entirely to his dictates, dictates the more intransigent because "the laws of God" require his dominance; it is "the performance of his duty to his Maker" (chaps. xxxii, lxviii). Her friend Violet Effingham is horrified to hear her story. "This makes me feel that I never will be married." "And yet what can a woman become if she remain single? The curse is to be a woman at all." "I have always felt so proud of the privileges of my sex," said Violet. "I have never found them" said [Lady Laura]; "never. I have tried to make the best of its weaknesses, and this is what I have come to!" And so Violet declares that she will "knock under to Mr. Mill,* and go in for women's rights, and look forward to stand for some female borough" (chap. li). But even Violet found that she could not "be independent in her life, as a man is independent, if she chose to live after that fashion," and dwindled into a wife (chap. lxxii).

Another recurrent subject in Trollope's novels about this time is the British attitude toward Jews, to which he had recently been directed in large part by his visit to Prague and the writing of *Nina Balatka*. The thoroughly charming and generous Austrian widow Madame Max Goesler, whose wealth and manners gave to her little house in Park Lane an envied position in London society, was sought in marriage by the old Duke of Omnium, and she reflected that she had a perfect right to accept him: "There was no slur on her name; no stain on her character. What though her father had been a small attorney, and her first husband a Jew banker!" But Lady Glencora Palliser, who indeed had liked Madame Max but whose position was threatened by the contemplated marriage, saw the matter quite differently: "That such a man as the Duke should be such a fool!—The widow of a Jew banker! He, the Duke of Omnium,—and thus to cut away from himself, for the rest of his life, all honour, all peace of mind, all the grace of a noble end to a career which, if not very noble in itself, had received the praise of nobility! And to do this for a thin, black-browed, yellow-visaged woman with ringlets and devil's eyes, and a beard on her upper lip,—a Jewess,—a creature of whose habits of life and manners of thought they were all absolutely ignorant; who drank, possibly; who might have been a forger, for what any one knew; an adventuress who had found her way into society by her art and perseverance,—and who did not even pretend to have a relation in the world" (chap. lxii). The tragedy of Ferdinand Lopez in *The Prime Minister* is here foreshadowed.

---

*On May 20, 1867, John Stuart Mill moved to substitute the word *person* for *man* in defining the electorate under the new Reform Bill; two years later he published *The Subjection of Women*, setting forth doctrines he had long advocated.

As always Trollope loved to refer to events of his own life. On June 15, 1867, he had been obliged to defend himself to a correspondent who accused him of technical errors in the description of Crawley's "theft" of the check in *Last Chronicle;*[32] by that time he had perhaps already written this passage in *Phineas Finn:*

> The poor fictionist very frequently finds himself to have been wrong in his description of things in general, and is told so roughly by the critics, and tenderly by the friends of his bosom. He is moved to tell of things of which he omits to learn the nature before he tells of them,—as should be done by a strictly honest fictionist. He catches salmon in October; or shoots his partridges in March. His dahlias bloom in June, and his birds sing in the autumn. He opens the opera-houses before Easter, and makes Parliament sit on a Wednesday evening. And then those terrible meshes of the Law! How is a fictionist, in these excited days, to create the needed biting interest without legal difficulties; and how again is he to steer his little bark clear of so many rocks,—when the rocks and the shoals have been purposely arranged to make the taking of a pilot on board a necessity?" (Chapt. xxix)

Thereafter, however, Trollope was more careful to take advice on legal matters in his fiction. The manuscript of *He Knew He Was Right* shows that he consulted a lawyer on the circumstances under which a father might claim custody of a child when the parents were separated. He inquired of the vicar of Harrow where the title deeds and maps of glebe lands were deposited, information he wished to use in *The Vicar of Bullhampton.* His friend Charles Merewether wrote an opinion as to the legal status of Lizzie Eustace's diamonds—were they heirlooms or "paraphernalia"? And since the plot of *Lady Anna* revolved around a nobleman's marriage to two women, one perhaps merely pretended but the authenticity of the second depending on whether the first was real, he outlined the situation and had a legal friend write comments in the margin.[33]

Phineas, about to become a barrister, plans to take chambers in the Old Square, Lincoln's Inn, where Thomas Anthony Trollope had had his chambers (chap. vii). He whiles away his time at a dull house party working his way gallantly through a couple of volumes of Sir Archibald Alison's *History of Europe during the French Revolution,* and "read away till he nodded"—the book out of which Trollope had made *La Vendée* (chap. xxxii). Mary Flood Jones's servant in County Clare is named Barney (chap. lxix), after the Irish groom whose duty it was to wake Trollope every morning so that he might be at his writing desk by 5:30.[34] The money-lender who begs that Phineas "be punctual" in his repayments (chap. xxi) has appeared in earlier novels, out of Trollope's memories of his early impoverished days as a Post Office clerk. Phineas's friend Laurence Fitzgibbon felt that the bill-collector "should be treated as you treat organ-grinders. They are a nuisance and must be endured" (chap. xxii).

The novel ends with Phineas marrying his boyhood sweetheart, and their living in Ireland on a government appointment that appears to have been a sinecure. Though the story comes to a proper close, there is some suggestion that we may be permitted to watch Phineas resume his political career in another novel. But that will be several years off.

From the first, readers found the account of political events so real that they could not resist identifying the politicians of the novel with the men they knew. On March 31, 1869, the *Daily Telegraph* devoted its first leading article to fiction and journalism which take as their subject the private lives of public men. Trollope, always an interesting writer (the *Telegraph* remarked), makes the special subject of *Phineas Finn*

> an exhibition of several living portraits very thinly disguised. Thus we have Lord Derby as Lord de Terrier, Mr. Disraeli as Mr. Daubeny, Lord Russell as Mr. Mildmay, Mr. Gladstone as Mr. Gresham, and under the name of Turnbull we have Mr. Bright. In the fancy picture representing the President of the Board of Trade Mr. Trollope has 'stuck in' some little traits. The Mr. Bright of the novel is made arrogant and offensive in private society, incapable of comprehending a joke, and even probably harsh and overbearing in his own home. Is it gentlemanlike to paint portraits thus? We do not ask whether the sketch is a good likeness.

Trollope replied instantly in a letter published the next day:

> In the character of Mr. Turnbull to which allusion is made, I depicted Mr. Bright neither in his private or public character; and I cannot imagine how any likeness justifying such a charge against me can be found. The character that I have drawn has no resemblance to the chairman of the Board of Trade in person, in manners, in character, in mode of life, or even in the mode of expressing political opinion. It was my object so to draw the character that no likeness should be found in our own political circles for the character so drawn. I have been unlucky,—as the charge brought by you against me shows; but I protest that the ill-luck has not been the result of fault on my part.[35]

Since Trollope's assistant editor for *St. Pauls,* Edward Dicey, was a leader writer for the *Daily Telegraph,* Trollope may have known who wrote the article.

Only about eight months before he began to write *Phineas Finn* Trollope reviewed R. H. Hutton's *Studies in Parliament*—personal sketches of seventeen public men—for the *Fortnightly Review;* it was no doubt a book that helped prepare him for writing the novel. And his first point in the review is one he might have turned against his critic: Hutton and Trollope published over their own names, whereas political journalism—including, of course, the *Telegraph*'s attack—was anonymous. In the review Trollope seconds Hutton's sketch of Bright as a man of closed mind, unable to listen to any opinion not his own; he "always makes his opponents feel that he condemns, if he does not scorn them for their belief," said Hutton.[36] If such a man is important in the political life of the country, then Trollope is entirely right to make Turnbull such a man. A novel set in Parliament must represent points of view, and even political tactics, actually current in parliamentary debate, and it must attach its fictional names to those points of view. But this is quite different from invading the domestic and social lives of actual politicians, or asserting that fictional characteristics belong to identifiable people, and this Trollope did not do. When he wrote *Phineas Finn,* the Conservatives were in power; in the novel the Liberals are in power. The "ill-luck" he refers to was in part that the Liberal administration of Gladstone came in while the novel was running its serial course, and in that government Bright became president of the Board of Trade. (Turnbull, by the way, did not hold any office in *Phineas Finn;* the president of the Board of Trade, until he resigned over the same issue that led Phineas to resign his official position, was Joshua Monk, a man of very different character and altogether admirable.) Trollope in the winter of 1866–67 could perceive the dominant issues before the House, but he had no gift of prophecy: he could not foresee the course of events between his writing of the novel and its publication as a completed book in early March, 1869.

Nevertheless, the question whether *any* of his politicians were either portraits or characters continues to tease his readers. Trollope himself said that he had taken "certain well-known political characters, such as Disraeli and Gladstone . . . as models for such fictitious personages as Daubeny and Gresham," and if indeed Daubeny's opportunism reflects Trollope's opinion of Disraeli's charlatanism (he refers to both as "Cagliostros," after the well-known swindler immortalized by Carlyle) it is still more accurate to say that in Daubeny Trollope has drawn a Machiavellian politician—of which species there are always examples—than that the figure of Daubeny "is" (fairly or unfairly) Disraeli. "There has been no distant idea in my own mind of any living person. [My political characters] are pure creations."[37]

Chapter XVI

1867–68

Phineas Finn was the third Trollope novel in eight years to launch a new journal. This time the journal was Trollope's own.

It is not easy to get accurate information on the publishing of Victorian periodicals—information on their rates of pay to contributors, their circulation, even (sometimes) on who actually owned them, since the named publisher was not always the actual proprietor. One source of income is almost always inaccessible to us—the income from advertising. Moreover, some of the payments originally charged to the magazine would be recouped by the publisher elsewhere—for example through subsequent book publication when the publisher had bought the copyright entire. The cost of *Phineas Finn,* prorated for its twenty installments, was £160 per issue—the bookstall price of 3,200 copies of a shilling magazine; the remaining matter in *Saint Pauls* would come to about £100 per issue at the rate Trollope and Virtue planned to pay contributors, the price of another 2,000 copies. Editorial salaries amounted to the price of 1,866 copies of each issue. Illustrations would add to the cost. And of course since the journal was discounted to distributors, the sale would have to be considerably more than 7,000 copies merely to pay the contributors and editors. The cost of manufacture and delivery would have to come on top of all these. But Virtue actually published in book form the two novels with which *Saint Pauls* began, as well as the series on *British Sports and Pastimes* and Charles Lever's (anonymous) three-part fiction, *Paul Goslett's Confessions.* Of these four, three could be republished within the first year; *Phineas Finn,* because of the length of its run as a serial, had to wait until the second year. Thus some cost could be recovered outside the sale of the magazine. No doubt this was what Trollope meant when he remarked that he thought magazines not generally very lucrative, but that they were "useful to some publishers as bringing grist to the mill."[1] (Bibliographers have sometimes expressed surprise that Trollope himself had so many different publishers for his novels, but the explanation almost invariably is that he sold the novels to publishers of magazines who then had the right to republish in volume form. From 1860 onward, when *Framley Parsonage* was published in the *Cornhill,* fourteen of his novels which first appeared in journals were republished as books by the firms associated with those journals.)[2]

Moreover the competition among magazines was great and increasing, and circulations were dropping. Everyone remembered *Cornhill*'s more than 100,000 copies of the early numbers, but by 1868 its circulation was about 26,000; *Temple Bar,* which started in December of 1860 with a circulation of 30,000, had dropped to 11,000 around 1866 and leveled off at 13,000 by 1870. The *Fortnightly* was at 1,400 when its original proprietors sold out, and reached only 2,500 by 1872.[3] The *Broadway* began in mid-August, 1867, and varied the usual pattern by selling at sixpence instead of a shilling; it reached an instantaneous sale of about 90,000, but quickly dropped off. (One could meet the competition both by pricing and by offering more pages for the money; *Saint Pauls,* like *Cornhill,* had 128 pages per issue, whereas *Temple Bar* had 144.) Edmund Yates resigned the editorship of *Temple Bar* to launch *Tinsley's Magazine* at the end of July, 1867; after two months the proprietors of the new journal determined to put out the monthly issues on the fifteenth rather than at the end of the month, in order to avoid the simultaneous competition with the other monthlies. A large sale like that of the *Broadway* initially was of course publicized, but it is hard to believe that Virtue knew the market very well when he expected "a far higher circulation" than 25,000 for *Saint Pauls.*[4]

The rate of pay Trollope proposed—about twenty shillings a page for nonfiction, twenty-five shillings a page for a novel other than his own (and Mme. Blaze de Bury was held strictly to twenty shillings for her *All for Greed*)—appears to be about average, though it did not compete with the *Cornhill,* which at this time was paying Matthew Arnold about twenty-eight shillings a page for his essays. (He liked the *Cornhill,* he said in 1863, because it "both pays best and has much the largest circle of readers.")[5] The price Trollope charged *Saint Pauls* for his own novels was very much higher than most popular magazines were paying, though it was entirely in keeping with what he was currently receiving from other publishers; as has been remarked, Virtue must have expected to recoup much of that cost from book publication rather than from the sale of the magazine. *Saint Pauls* was just beginning its second half-year when Trollope wrote to Blackwood on the economics of book publishing:

Touching the mode of publication & sale of novels, I have a strong conception that publishers must make a change in their mode of business, and must eschew the half guinea volume system;—and I am led to this opinion by observing that the public have unconsciously learned to expect that the best novels of the day are to be obtained by them in a different form. They think,—without thinking—that they will get the best novels in the magazines, and that novels which have been published in magazines, should appear not in 3 vols.—but in one or two.

And for novels which appear with illustrations at 20/- (in 2 vol)— there is a sale among private people, whereas for those published in 3 vol at 31.6d. there is none [since the only sale is to the lending libraries, at a huge discount]. It must however be remembered that the 2 volume novel at 20/ is a much longer work than the 3 vol at 31-6d. All the details respecting this I should much like to discuss with you. I find no difficulty whatever in selling a novel for £3,000: (—Let this be private)—But I cannot tell how the publisher gets back his money.[6]

The last sentence is revealing, since Trollope controlled the purse strings for the authors in his magazine.

The new monthlies were all very much alike—one or two novels serially, and miscellaneous articles on matters of current interest. They were distinguished from one another by the audience at which they aimed, the intellectual tone they adopted. The *Cornhill* was serious and of high quality; *Temple Bar* set out to rival it, but quickly (1862) fell into a more popular mode with the sensational fiction of writers like Mary Elizabeth Braddon (who in due course became editor and principal novelist of *Belgravia,* which began in November, 1866). Mrs. Henry Wood was of course principal novelist for her *Argosy,* but she sometimes had a second novel running in another magazine.[7] Trollope clearly aimed at an audience like that of the *Cornhill,* though he sought to give *Saint Pauls* a character of its own through his attention to political matters both at home and abroad.[8]

One decision, whether made by Trollope or by Virtue or jointly, is surprising and nowhere accounted for in the surviving correspondence: contributions other than novels were published anonymously, or at most with the author's initials (and these last were signed chiefly to the poems).[9] Despite the *Fortnightly*'s innovation in insisting on signed articles, a policy which Trollope had praised, the *Cornhill* continued for the most part its practice of anonymity (though writers like Matthew Arnold and Trollope signed their names). The practice of other rival journals varied: *Belgravia* advertised the names of most of its contributors, as did the *Broadway,* whereas *Temple Bar* did not. One might suppose that those which obtained the best-known writers would use signatures for publicity, but that seems not invariably to have been the case. The argument Trollope had used in reviewing Hutton's *Studies in Parliament* that the signature guaranteed the responsibility of the writer seems not to have prevailed with himself.[10] Even the novelists were often identified, in *Saint Pauls* and other magazines, not by name but as "the author of———,"so that their names to this day sometimes are not known. Very soon after the editorship passed out of Trollope's hands, *Saint Pauls* began to identify most of its contributors.[11] The fact is, however, that Trollope, after writing "On Anonymous Literature," had had second thoughts: literary honesty is the aim, but the signed article is not always honest and the unsigned one may be very good indeed. [12]

੩ล

With the date for the first number of *Saint Pauls* drawing closer, it is hardly surprising that Trollope's correspondence shows increasing involvement in his editorial duties (and of course a great deal of the correspondence has not survived). Naturally he turned first to his friends and acquaintances; fortunately he had a wide range of them. When Robert Bell could not undertake the subeditorship, he chose Edward Dicey, a fellow member of the Garrick Club and an experienced journalist who had been foreign correspondent for the *Daily Telegraph* from 1862 and a leader writer for that paper. When Trollope was dropped from the editorship of his magazine early in 1870, Dicey became for three months editor of the *Daily News*, and then for eleven years editor of the Sunday *Observer*. As early as February, 1867, Trollope forwarded to his brother Tom what would appear to have been a formal request by Virtue for contributions from both Tom and his wife; in any case, both did become contributors. [13] In mid-July he approached Austen Henry Layard for the political articles he wished to include in each number; Layard declined to do those on domestic politics but did agree to write on foreign affairs. [14] Layard had been undersecretary for foreign affairs in the Whig ministries of Palmerston and Russell and would become chief commissioner of works in Gladstone's government of December, 1868; a year later he became British minister at Madrid. Presumably reluctant, for political reasons, to sign his articles, he received assurance from Trollope, "I will bear in mind what you say about not mentioning your name. Not but what these things get out." In August Trollope begged Millais (who had already agreed to illustrate *Phineas Finn*) to plan the cover for the new magazine; since the cover illustration is not signed, we do not know his response. [15]

The first number (for October) duly made its appearance at the end of September. After an "Introduction by the Editor," first place went to an article on the Reform Act of 1867 by George J. Goschen, who had been in Russell's cabinet and was to sit in Gladstone's cabinet of December, 1868, as president of the Poor Law Board. Then came the first chapters of Mme. Blaze de Bury's novel *All for Greed*, an article by Dicey on "The Ethics of Trade Unions," an article on horse racing by Francis Lawley, one "On Sovereignty" (the symbolic function of the monarchy) by Trollope himself, on "Taste" by Henry Nelson O'Neil, and the opening chapters of *Phineas Finn*. Lawley was a friend of Dicey's on the *Daily Telegraph*, where he was a writer on sports, and in the early 1850s had been Gladstone's private secretary and had sat in Parliament for Beverley as an advanced

Liberal. O'Neil was a close friend of Trollope's and Millais', who in 1870 was to dedicate his *Satirical Dialogues* to Trollope, the thinly disguised "Author" in the first dialogue. Trollope wrote O'Neil's obituary in the *Times* in 1880,[16] and described there the crowds which had clustered around his paintings of "Eastward Ho" and "Home Again" at the Academy's exhibitions of 1857 and 1858. It was an opening number of which Trollope and Virtue might well be proud. Trollope celebrated its appearance with five days in the hunting field.[17]

Though there is no record of the sale, the press's reception was on the whole kind. The publisher was able to quote favorable comments from twenty-eight of the London, Dublin, and provincial newspapers in a full-column advertisement in the *Athenaeum* in the middle of October. The *Bookseller* predicted that it would be "one of the most successful of modern literary ventures," one that distinguished itself from *London Society, Temple Bar, Belgravia,* and *Tinsley's* by the solidity of the articles in addition to the interest of the novels. The *Spectator*'s long review, however, is more reserved: "It is a readable magazine, a cultivated magazine, a magazine without anything that jars upon the taste, or offends the judgment; but the first number is tame, has exceedingly little vivacity, and no intensity of purpose. There is a colourlessness about it." If we now look at the qualifications of the writers and feel inclined to commend Trollope, the *Spectator* is of opinion that "Mr. Trollope is trusting, we suspect, too much to men of made reputation, who have lost the spring and the zeal of their first spirit of belief and enterprise."[18] The reviewer was almost certainly R. H. Hutton; the same stylistic sensitivity which had recognized Trollope's authorship of *Nina Balatka* was able also to identify his authorship of the article "On Sovereignty" here.

There was no poetry in the first number, but Trollope in his "Introduction" announced, "If a poet will send us his poetry, it shall certainly be used." The invitation was promptly accepted by Cecilia Meetkerke, wife of a cousin of Trollope's father, whose attempts had been submitted to Trollope for criticism and improvement at least since 1863.[19] William Allingham, approached no doubt on the strength of the acquaintance made on the journey to the Isle of Wight a few years earlier, contributed poems to the December number and that for April; Tom Hood, founder of *Fun* and *Tom Hood's Comic Annual,* sent one for January; Thomas Miller, "the basket maker," one for February, and Edwin Arnold (later author of *The Light of Asia*) one for March. But the most faithful poet was a young man in his twenties, a civil servant at the Board of Trade, whose "Une Marquise" appeared in March, 1868. This was Austin Dobson. Trollope worked hard to help Dobson improve his work, and the young man "gratefully inscribed to Anthony Trollope" his first volume, *Vignettes*

1. Anthony Trollope, about 1860

3. Anthony Trollope, October 15–18, 1861

2. Thomas Adolphus Trollope in Florence, autumn 1857 (?)

4. Anthony Trollope, November, 1861, or March, 1862

5. Rose Trollope

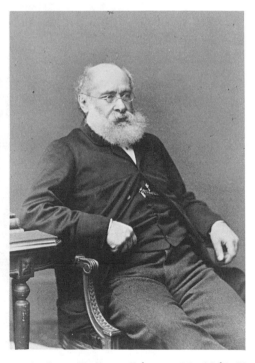

6. Anthony Trollope, October 9–13, 1864   7. Anthony Trollope, February 15, 1867 (?)

8. Kate Field, May, 1868 (?)

9. Anthony Trollope, May 4, 1871 (?)

10. Cover for the weekly parts of *The Last Chronicle of Barset* (1866–67)

George MacDonald   J. A. Froude   Wilkie Collins   Anthony Trollope
W. M. Thackeray Lord Macaulay Bulwer Lytton Thos. Carlyle Charles Dickens
GROUP OF CONTEMPORARY WRITERS

11. Group of Contemporary [Prose] Writers

12. "Posy and Her Grandpa" (Posy Arabin and Mr. Harding)

POSY AND HER GRANDPAPA.

13. "A Memorable Whist Party at the Athenaeum"

Anthony Trollope.   Right Hon. W. E. Forster.
    Abraham Hayward.   Sir George Jessel.
A MEMORABLE WHIST PARTY AT THE ATHENÆUM.

14. Anthony Trollope

15. Cover for the monthly parts of *The Way We Live Now* (1874–75)

16. "Siege of the Deck Cabin," June, 1878

in Rhyme (1873), which included poems Trollope had published in *Saint Pauls.*[20] One might observe that Trollope had pretty much the same rate of payment for verse as for prose, twenty shillings a page: the typical poem was worth two, three, or five pounds.

Volunteers came forward, many of them with novels, but precisely there Trollope could not afford to welcome a newcomer. At least two writers of articles in the first year, James Hutton and James Leakey, later applied to the Royal Literary Fund (of which, of course, Trollope was an officer) for financial assistance. Hutton was granted £60, but Leakey's appeal was denied on the ground that he had written too little. And there was one other who never quite contributed: the Irishman Richard Shew affirmed in his application, "As an instance of the complete physical depression I am in, I may mention that last year I communicated with Mr. Trollope, with respect to some articles on Art for St. Paul's Magazine, & after I had mapped out the outlines, the effort so exhausted me I could not almost read a book for many days through the action of the nervous system" (May 14, 1870). His claim was disallowed, as having insufficient literary merit.[21]

ॐ

The pace of Trollope's novel writing was spectacular, in view of all his other activities. *The Golden Lion of Granpere* was held up for a fortnight in early September, 1867, by Trollope's work on *Saint Pauls,* but he completed it on October 22. He much preferred to have his publication contract in hand before he began a novel, but this one was a labor of love, and, as it befell, the manuscript lay in his desk nearly five years before it was published. His next undertaking was far more ambitious—a novel as long as *Last Chronicle,* to be published like that work in weekly numbers; he began to write *Mrs. Trevelyan* the day he proposed it to Virtue, and Virtue accepted the proposal two days later, on November 15. The price was £3,200.[22] Since the agreement had nothing to do with *Saint Pauls,* it would appear that there was some notion of Virtue's becoming Trollope's regular publisher. The writing was finished on June 12, 1868, and at some time before publication the title was changed to the more striking *He Knew He Was Right.* It made its appearance in thirty-two six-penny weekly parts from October 17, 1868, to May 22, 1869, and in eight monthly two-shilling numbers from November to May, with illustrations by Marcus Stone.[23] Before he left for America, Trollope also contracted to do a serial for *Once a Week,* to be delivered by the beginning of May, 1869; he began writing *The Vicar of Bullhampton* in Washington on June 15, three days after putting "Finis" to *He Knew He Was Right.*

On their summer holiday in 1867 Anthony and Rose had taken the beautiful road built through the Vosges by Napoleon III from Remiremont in Lorraine eastward through Munster to Colmar in Alsace. A few miles to the west of Munster he placed the tiny village of Granpere, with its hotel, the Golden Lion, as the setting for his short novel. The region interested him because its inhabitants were partly Roman Catholic, partly Protestant, but the two groups got on amiably and mixed marriages were common; in fact religion is of no great importance in the debates over the marriage which is at the center of his story. The son of the proprietor of the Golden Lion and the niece of the proprietor's second wife fall in love, the father regards their doing so as an impertinence and the son leaves home to become manager of a hotel in Colmar owned by a distant cousin, a widow. Meanwhile a marriage is arranged between the niece and a cloth merchant from Basel. After many misunderstandings the son and the niece are reunited and the cloth merchant departs, having been taken on a family picnic in the mountains to soothe his feelings. The story moves even more slowly than *Linda Tressel* and is even more repetitive—a scene or conversation is presented, then we see or hear it again as one of the characters goes back over it in his mind. The attempts at local color are modest, and one is even tempted to speak slightingly of Anthony's own zest for sightseeing when he remarks that in Colmar—a fascinating old town with varied architecture and wonderful paintings—"there is not much to interest you" beyond the statue of General Rapp in the Champ de Mars. It is a tepid story, but perhaps better suited to the readers of *Good Words* (where it found a home) than *Rachel Ray* would have been. Between the writing and the publication of the story the Franco-German war had transferred the entire region from France to Germany, and some patching up was needed, but the narrative takes place while the region was still French; indeed the hero at one point reports that the pro-German element in Colmar had been thoroughly discomfited.

Trollope made several attempts to publish the manuscript. In the summer of 1869 Frederic Chapman had an inquiry about a Trollope novel for publication in *Appleton's Magazine* in New York; Trollope offered to sell the copyright of the *Golden Lion* for £700, or the magazine rights for £500; "I do not think you can make more than £200 out of a one volume novel." When nothing came of this negotiation, he offered the book in February, 1871, to Blackwood as third of the series of short novels in a foreign setting (and now with permission to use his name); Blackwood sadly declined—*Nina Balatka* had sold 480 copies out of 1,250 printed in volume form for a loss of £8 15s.; *Linda Tressel* 275 copies out of 750 printed for a loss of £16. By this time Strahan had taken over publication of *Saint Pauls,* and purchased the entire novel for £550, primarily for use in *Good Words* (January–August, 1872) but also as a volume to be brought out by his associate William Tinsley. It was Trollope's last contribution to *Good Words* while his friend the editor Norman Macleod was still alive. Strahan engaged Francis Arthur Fraser to illustrate it in the magazine, and to illustrate *Ralph the Heir* for *Saint Pauls*. When *The Golden Lion* was set in type, Trollope was in Australia, and his friend Sir Frederick Pollock read the proofs—"but there was really nothing for me to do" because the manuscript was so clear.[24]

At the beginning of 1868 the Reverend Edward Bradley, a prolific author and illustrator better known by his pseudonym "Cuthbert Bede," found himself a dinner guest at a country house (presumably near Stilton in Huntingdonshire) where Trollope was staying for a few days during the hunting season; Trollope had brought his horses with him, and was on his way to visit his cousin Sir John Trollope, at Casewick, near Stamford in Lincolnshire. Bradley was amazed by Trollope's energy—up at five in the morning to write, then hunting, dining, playing whist and smoking until the small hours. He received a bundle of proofs for *Saint Pauls* in the morning mail, and when Bradley returned after a night spent elsewhere he begged Bradley's assistance in greatly curtailing an article on the Irish Church—a difficult and delicate work which Bradley undertook. "While I was [so] engrossed, . . . he looked over other proofs and wrote several letters. I was much struck with the rapidity he showed in getting through this business, and also in keeping up a running conversation with those present, at the same time that he was reading proofs and writing letters." The business of the day concluded, he had a hearty breakfast, spent the whole day hunting, and had dinner and whist at another house some miles distant from the one in which he was staying. Bradley perceptively makes the point (which the present biography hopes to keep before the reader) that though the greater part of the day was apparently given to recreation, in the pursuit thereof Trollope was also gathering materials for his writings.

Trollope professed to be entirely happy in his career as a writer, but was bothered and harassed by the editorial work on *Saint Pauls,* and by nothing quite so much as the to him heartbreaking work of returning a manuscript, "declined with thanks," to some hopeful young writer. Bradley confessed that he had often seen his own manuscripts come back, but that he was persistent in sending them off at once to some other editor, and then if necessary to a third, "and so on." But he was surprised to learn that Trollope too had known complete failure, especially with his writings for the stage. At a somewhat later date, Bradley was able to amuse him with a photograph of Trollope he had purchased in Birmingham, which the shopkeeper had displayed as a portrait of Martin

Farquhar Tupper, a notoriously dull but extraordinarily popular moralizing poet.[25]

                                    🐦

On June 18, 1867, a postal convention between England and the United States was signed in London to replace the convention of 1848. The chief British negotiator was Sir Rowland Hill's brother Frederic, as supervisor of the mail packet service. Frederic Hill was an ardent advocate of the doctrines of "political economy," a free trader of the Manchester school. And so he willingly acceded to the American views which left each country free to fix its own rates for international mail (below a specified maximum rate agreed upon) and to ship its mails by whatever vessels it found least expensive. How Tilley was lulled into accepting the agreement is not clear. For in so agreeing, Hill knowingly went counter to Tilley's doctrine of the primacy of speed and efficiency, which he conceived would be best achieved by long-term contracts with a single packet company operating over the most direct route—in this case Cunard between New York and Queenstown—on a schedule fixed by the Post Office and with strict provision for penalties in case of tardiness. But Cunard declined to bid on a contract that gave them the mails in one direction only, and the United States was keeping its end open, partly at least with a view to using mail contracts in future to subsidize American ships. And so only six months after the convention was signed, the British Post Office gave the required twelve months notice that it would terminate the agreement on December 31, 1868, and wished to reopen negotiations.[26]

"It will be necessary to send a strong man" wrote Tilley to the Duke of Montrose on December 12, 1867, "and I think of proposing to you to ask Mr. Trollope to undertake the revision as we shall get the benefit not only of his ability but of his personal popularity with the Americans. I know of no one else who would do the work so well."[27] Trollope accepted the commission formally on February 29 (informally of course he had accepted it some weeks before that), and by way of giving dignity to the mission was presented at the Prince of Wales's levée on March 17. He received his instructions on April 9 with full assurance that whatever he agreed to within their framework would be accepted, and sailed from Liverpool on April 11. The pay was five guineas per diem plus passage and actual expenses. It was a chance to earn extra money, to visit a country he liked, and to see old friends; no doubt the business with *Saint Pauls* could be put sufficiently in order and in any case he would not be gone long. But that sailing was the beginning of a miserable quarter of a year.

In the first place, when Trollope reached Washington on the twenty-fourth, the impeachment trial of President Johnson was occupying the attention of Congress and the uncertainty of the verdict made the tenure in office of the American postmaster general, Alexander W. Randall, also uncertain; he declined to deal with Trollope until the trial was over. And so Trollope went off to Boston from May 6 to 15. Johnson was acquitted on Saturday, May 16, and Randall and his senior clerk, Joseph H. Blackfan, superintendent of foreign mails (for whom Trollope formed a high regard as "the man who really understands the question") gave over the whole of the following Monday to Trollope, but only so that they could make clear to him that they would not bind themselves to a regular schedule of ships or a manner of payment in harmony with the British. " 'Do you do as you like, and let us do as we like.' That is their argument; and that, they say—no doubt with truth—, was our argument also when the last convention was a making." (Randall even quoted at length a letter from Frederic Hill written during the previous negotiation, in support of his position.) Randall, moreover, was perfectly content to do without a postal agreement between the two countries, if it came to that. Trollope suspected that the German steamship lines (which called at Southampton, but not Queenstown) had him in their pocket, but it is clear that American shipping interests were also involved.

In view of the impasse, Tilley on June 8 urged the British Treasury—which had to approve the negotiations—to let Trollope simply make the best deal he could. "It is not desirable to detain Mr. Trollope in America longer than is absolutely necessary." There was no reply; meanwhile Trollope was getting restless, for he could not leave Washington, and a city which in April and May is delightful grows unbearable in late June. "Take pity on Trollope and let us have an answer," Tilley urged the Treasury on June 17, and again on June 27: "Might I ask you . . . to come to a decision as to the American postal convention. . . . Trollope went out to please me at some inconvenience to himself and he is most anxious to get back."[28] Trollope, sadly, was writing his epitaph:

> Washington has slain this man,
> By politics and heat together.
> Sumner alone he might have stood
> But not the Summer weather.

"This place is so awful to me, that I doubt whether I can stand it much longer. To make matters worse a democratic Senator who is stone deaf and who lives in the same house with me, has proposed to dine with me every day! I refused three times but he did not hear me, and ordered that our dinners should be served together. I had not the courage to fight it any further, and can see no alternative but to run away." A decade later he still remembered that "in June the musquito of Washington is as a roaring lion."[29] He could allow himself only brief excursions, to Richmond and

Baltimore in May and to New York in June; even the last was cut short by a cable from London. He wrote desperately to Scudamore for another thousand dollars. At last the telegram went out to him on July 1: "Make Treaty on the best terms you can."

The terms were indeed bad ones. Trollope forwarded two newspaper clippings to support his view that "the motive power in all this is the influence of certain members of Congress who know and care nothing for the transit of mails, but who do know and care a great deal about certain Companies." One of these was a leading article from the *Washington Morning Chronicle* of July 2: "That [former] treaty secured important advantages in the reduction of the rates of postage, but the wiseacre who controls the British Postal Department in the interest of a subsidized line of steamers" has canceled it and proposes that all mails both ways be carried on British ships. "This is a very pretty little plan, and Mr. Anthony Trollope has come over here . . . for the purpose of negotiating an arrangement whereby it may be carried into practical effect." He was obliged to get authorization for further retreat from the British position. Then Randall went off to the Democratic national convention in New York, leaving Trollope to endure the heat of Washington a few days longer.

"I cannot but feel that they have had the whip hand of us altogether," he wrote. The treaty he concluded on July 11 settled almost nothing except an agreed rate of postage per letter of twelve cents or sixpence and a provision that each country might keep whatever fines it collected for insufficient prepaid postage instead of having to account to the other country. Trollope rushed to New York on the twelfth, spent a night in Boston, and sailed from New York on the fifteenth. Even the cool spray of Niagara Falls was denied him.[30] He reached home on the twenty-sixth, to conclude a mission of 111 days, for which he received £582 15s. and a message of thanks from the Duke of Montrose, who regarded the mission as a failure but was "satisfied that no exertions on [Trollope's] part were spared to attain the end in view."[31]

There was a lapse of several years before he could use his experience with American legislators in his novel *The American Senator* (not the deaf one he knew), or add his American lecturer, Olivia Q. Fleabody (*Is He Popenjoy?*) to the list of those he fancied surrounding Kate Field in America—"Janet L. Tozer, Annie B. Slocum, Martha M. Mumpus, Violet Q. Fitzpopam etc."[32]

He also had carried with him to America, at his own request, a commission from the Foreign Office to make an effort to secure an international copyright agreement between the United States and Great Britain.[33] Trollope had long been a warm advocate of reciprocal copyright protection for British and American authors; on October 4, 1866, a paper of his "On the best Means of Extending and Securing an International Law of Copyright" was read (not by himself in person) at the Congress of the National Association for the Promotion of Social Science at Manchester. His advocacy was not uniformly approved by the publishing industry, even in his own country; one of the trade journals, noting that a new German law removing copyright protection from works of authors long dead had produced editions of classical German texts for as little as threepence, sixpence, or a shilling, "commend[ed] these facts to the attention of Mr. Anthony Trollope, who thinks that copyright tends to make books cheaper."[34] There is obviously no record of this aspect of his American mission in the Post Office archives. It bore no fruit, but it did lead to his membership in the Copyright Commission of 1876 (likewise a fruitless enterprise).

As the Cunarder *Scotia* carried Trollope into the New York harbor on April 22, another Cunarder, the *Russia,* had already cast off from the dock and was waiting in the bay; aboard her was Charles Dickens. "What was my amazement," Dickens wrote to James T. Fields from shipboard, "to see [Anthony] with these eyes come aboard in the mail tender just before we started! He had come out in the Scotia just in time to dash off again in said tender to shake hands with me, knowing me to be aboard here. It was most heartily done." At that very moment Kate Field was crossing the harbor on the ferry from Manhattan to Jersey City to catch the train for Washington, and waved a symbolic farewell to Dickens. Two years later Trollope recalled that he found Dickens "with one of his feet bound up, and he told me, with that pleasant smile that was so common to him, that he had lectured himself off his legs; otherwise he was quite well. When I heard afterwards of his labours in the States and of the condition in which those labours had been continued, it seemed to be marvellous that any constitution could have stood it."[35]

Trollope this year stayed at his former lodgings in Washington with Wormley, on I Street. On his first day there, he met Kate as they both visited the Capitol. "Same as ever," she recorded in her diary, and he called on her that evening. They met again at the Capitol on April 27, and on the twenty-eighth, the day of his departure for New York, they visited the Capitol together.[36] On his two-week excursion to Boston at the beginning of May he was with Fields and his wife; Mrs. Fields described it in a letter to Kate as a very pleasant visit. "Good whole-souled Mr. Trollope. A few such men redeemed Nineveh. He always seems the soul of honesty." But he expressed "in no mild or measured terms his disgust for Washington and Impeachment."[37] There are far fewer records of this visit than of the one six years earlier; there was, in fact, very little time for the friendly literary encounters of the previous occasion. The *Boston Evening Transcript* described his appearance a month later:

> He is a strange looking person. His head is shaped like a minnie ball, with the point rounded down a little, like the half of a lemon cut transversely in two. It is small, almost sharp at the top, and bald, increasing in size until it reaches his neck. His complexion and general bearing are much like Dickens's. His body is large and well preserved. He dresses like a gentleman and not like a fop, but he squeezes his small, well-shaped hand into a very small pair of colored kids. He 'wears a cane,' as all Englishmen do.

"I never wear gloves," Trollope told Kate when she sent him this description. "What fools people are." He was back in Washington just in time to hear the verdict of acquittal for Johnson in the Capitol.[38] Several letters to the *Pall Mall Gazette* and articles in *Saint Pauls* are the fruit of his observations of American politics.

Kate sent Trollope from New York a short story she had published earlier in the year, and the beginning of a manuscript of another she was writing. He was kind and helpful in his replies; she could write well, he said, but had reflected too little on the art of narration. The first function of a story is "to charm and not to teach." "Teach, and preach, and convince if you can;—but first learn the art of doing so without seeming to do it." "If you are writing an essay, you have to convey of course your own ideas and convictions, to another mind. You will of course desire to do so in fiction also, and may ultimately do so (when your audience is made) more successfully than by essay writing. . . . When you have learned the knack of story telling, go on to greater objects." A friend of hers, Charles Wyllys Elliott, who lived at the Bible Hotel in the Bowery, sent Trollope a sheaf of manuscript novels, and even proposed that Trollope publish one of them in England as his own. (Trollope, unfamiliar with some of New York's odder street names, read the address as "No. 44 Bible Bower." "I cannot believe that there is as yet in New York any so near approach to the Elysian Fields."[39]

When they met in New York early in June Trollope asked Kate to do something for *Saint Pauls,* and she was eager to try, but by the time she had something to offer his connection with the magazine had ceased. "I would willingly see myself in some little way helping you in a profession which I regard as being the finest in the world," he told her. He took her, on this visit, to the studio of a photographer who (though tipsy) made portraits of both of them. "I should like one of you standing up, facing full front, with your hat," he told her. As he left for England, he sent her his kindest love, "with a kiss that shall be semi-paternal—one third brotherly, and as regards the small remainder, as loving as you please." "I wish I thought I might see your clever laughing eyes again before the days of spectacles;—but I suppose not."[40]

Chapter XVII

1868–69

It had been "a most disagreeable trip to America," "a most odious summer," he wrote upon his return, and two months later he was still writing to Kate Field that he would never see her again unless she came to England. "I am becoming an infirm old man, too fat to travel so far."[1] He was still, however, to circumnavigate the world twice and make a journey to South Africa.

He plunged instantly into work on *Saint Pauls.* Virtue thought it would be well to have a special Christmas story number some time in the latter part of November, and Trollope solicited a narrative in verse from Robert Lytton (Bulwer-Lytton's son and heir), whom he had met at Knebworth, as well as prose stories from George MacDonald and Charles Lever. MacDonald complied, Lytton and Lever did not; by the time Lever's refusal came at the end of August, Anthony was perceiving that an extra Christmas number would be impractical and persuaded Virtue to give it up. He found waiting for him three articles on Italy—contemporary and historical—from his brother Tom, which he published over the next year. A novel by Tom's wife Fanny, *The Sacristan's Household,* had already begun its serialization in July, with illustrations by Marcus Stone. (Stone, toward the end of the year, began to do illustrations for the weekly numbers of *He Knew He Was Right,* also published by Virtue.) Tom Trollope was paid at the going rate of a pound a page; Virtue determined the compensation for Fanny's novel to avoid embarrassment for Anthony. One fiction writer, whose short story, "For a Year," he had previously accepted to appear in the June number, was Annie Thomas Cudlip, one of Chapman and Hall's novelists; their reader, George Meredith, had reported on a book of hers, "She has studied Trollope with advantage and throws in her hunting-bits very cleverly. It is written for the market and will suit the market."[2] The magazine's contents were improving, and showed the energy with which Trollope sought out contributors—Leslie Stephen, Peter Bayne (whose article on Palmerston Trollope drew upon in his own little biography of Palmerston a decade later), Adam Gielgud (a Polish scholar, for Eastern European affairs), Edward Pigott (the examiner—or censor—of plays, for an article on Yachting). He turned down an article on Darwin, because "I am myself so ignorant on it, that I should fear to be in the position of editing a paper on the subject." G. H. Lewes did an essay on "The Dangers and Delights of Tobacco" for November, and Juliet Pollock, wife of Frederick Pollock, did several pieces, including a review of George Eliot's *Spanish Gipsy*. A year and a half earlier, when Rose and Anthony spent the night at the Pollocks' house in Montagu Square, Anthony came to breakfast (after his usual early stint of writing) with the remark, "I have just been making my twenty-seventh proposal of marriage" (this one in *Phineas Finn*).[3]

His first busy day in London gave him just time to catch the Royal Academy's summer exhibition (its centenary year), and tired as he was he spent some time among the pictures.[4] In the latter part of August and early September he and Rose went to Scotland, first to stay with John Blackwood in his home, Strathtyrum, overlooking the golf course at St. Andrews. Anthony tried his hand at golf, but violated the etiquette of the game by talking loudly and constantly. Once, after a particularly bad stroke, he collapsed in a mock faint and fell upon a spare golf ball in his pocket; then the uproar was greater than ever. A large party of Scottish dignitaries was invited to meet him at dinner on August 19, including the publisher Chambers, Principal Tulloch of the University, and the Reverend A. K. H. Boyd. Boyd had refreshed his memory of the wonderfully delicate, beautiful and powerful passages of *Last Chronicle,* but was shocked to find that the man had none of the delicacy of the book. "He was singularly unkempt, and his clothes were very wrinkled and ill-made." The expected melodious accents did not come; instead there was repeated profanity, offensive to clerical ears. He did not endear himself to the company when he pronounced Scott's novels so dull that they could never find a publisher in the contemporary world. Since Boyd knew Trollope had praised Scott in print, he was puzzled to know which was Trollope's real view. Did he merely wish to give his fellow guests a slap in the face?[5]

❧

By what may seem to be a peculiarity of the election laws, Trollope for most of his life was ineligible to vote for a member of Parliament: many civil servants, like lunatics, lords, and of course women, were without the franchise.[6] His political preferences, however, were not secret; his closest friends were Liberals. There was of course political business in some of Trollope's earlier novels, including the campaigning in *Doctor Thorne,* but the earliest detailed examination of an election was that of George Vavasor in *Can You Forgive Her?* (1864), the first novel of what we have come to call the "parliamentary" series, where the frustration and ruinous expense of winning a by-election, only to lose the seat almost immediately through a dissolution of Parliament, drove Vavasor out of his mind.

Vavasor is the villain of the novel, but Trollope makes us sympathize with the force of his desperation.

Again and again in his novels he had expressed the view that the highest honor to which an Englishman might aspire was the privilege of passing through the members' entrance to the House of Commons. From the moment of his retirement from the Post Office, therefore, Trollope looked about him for an opportunity to sit in the House. As early as the end of November, 1867, he wrote to a correspondent: "I [can] give no decided answer to your question, but [I have] no present intention of standing for one of the boroughs in question."[7] He was urged by Andrew Johnson, one of the leading Liberals of the county, to stand for South Essex, the prevailingly Liberal district near which he resided; then Johnson changed his mind, stood himself, and what looked like a sure seat for Trollope disappeared. Where the suggestion came from that he stand for the Yorkshire borough of Beverley is not clear—presumably from Liberal party offices.[8] But candidacy in Beverley was quite a different matter and the service required of a Liberal candidate there was not to win, which was impossible, but to let the Conservatives show their hand and disqualify themselves (under newly revised statutes) by corruption. The population of Beverley was about 12,000, of whom somewhat more than 2,000 were registered electors. The number was barely sufficient to escape the provisions of the new distribution of seats in 1867, and the borough continued to send two members to Parliament. The Conservative candidates in 1868 were Sir Henry Edwards, one of the directors of a local factory who had represented the borough since August, 1857, and Captain Edmund H. Kennard, a new man and an outsider looking for a safe seat. Trollope's colleague on the Liberal side was the Hon. Marmaduke Constable Maxwell, son of the Earl Herries, who lived near Beverley.[9]

Trollope's agents distributed his printed election address, dated October 28, 1868; he appeared in person before the voters on October 30 and again on November 9, 11, 12, 13, and 16.[10] "Parliamentary canvassing is not a pleasant occupation. Perhaps nothing more disagreeable, more squalid, more revolting to the senses, more opposed to personal dignity, can be conceived. The same words have to be repeated over and over again in the cottages, hovels, and lodgings of poor men and women who only understand that the time has come round in which they are to be flattered instead of being the flatterers."[11] At some time during the campaign he also sat on the platform at a crowded meeting in St. James's Hall, Regent Street, London, in support of the candidacy of John Stuart Mill for reelection for Westminster (the seat that Melmotte later won in *The Way We Live Now*), and the clear, ringing accents of his short and forcible speech were said to have contrasted most strikingly with the candidate's voice, which could scarcely be heard by those nearest to him.[12] If the newspaper reports from Beverley make his speeches sound tepid, they were at least intelligent and to the point. One of the issues to which he addressed himself was the long overdue provision of elementary education for all the people (a promise the Liberals fulfilled with Forster's Elementary Education Act of 1870); another was the disestablishment of the Anglican Church of Ireland, which came in 1869. He had to skirt the issue of the secret ballot, which the Liberals advocated as a guard against corruption and which Trollope himself disliked as unmanly.* The election of 1868 was in fact the last general election conducted by open voting. For the most part he seemed to rest on the self-evident proposition that the populace of an industrial town had far more to expect from the Liberals than from the Conservatives. He ignored the immediate cash benefits the Conservatives were paying to the voters. Trollope was of course present on the day of the election, November 17. Up until about eleven o'clock he and Maxwell were still leading, but at the close of the polls it was announced that Edwards received 1,132 votes, Kennard 986, Maxwell 895, and Trollope 740. Maxwell's margin over Trollope may be attributable to his being a local man. (Since each elector had two votes, more than 39 percent of the electors voted for Trollope.) Speaking from the hustings when the poll was announced, he said: "It may be that I shall appear before you again, and if I do I shall hope that you will think I have done nothing to forfeit your friendship." His formal farewell address dated from Waltham Cross the next day expressed the same hope. According to the Liberal *Beverley Recorder* Trollope and Maxwell were greeted by the crowd with an ovation that seemed to belie the announcement of their defeat then being made.

But Beverley had sent its last members to Parliament. The local Liberal committee immediately filed a petition charging corruption and asking that the election be set aside. The case was heard before Sir Samuel Martin, a Baron of Exchequer, on March 9–11, 1869; 109 witnesses testified (Trollope was not among them), and at the conclusion Martin announced that he would report to the speaker of the House "that, in his opinion, this election was void at common law; that a very large number of electors of this borough were bribed and did sell their votes under the influence of bribery" (Martin estimated the number at more than 800), and—most important of all—that he felt obliged to make a special report on the matter to the attorney general.[13] Trollope instantly set Dicey to work on an article on "The Election Petitions" for the April number of *Saint Pauls*. A commission of three lawyers was set up by the government, which in thirty-eight days of hearings from August 24 to November 17

---

*As early as February, 1833, his mother had remarked in a letter, "I do not love . . . election by ballot."

examined over 700 witnesses. Trollope appeared before them in Beverley
on September 3. Much of the testimony was devoted to the municipal
election at Beverley only fifteen days before the parliamentary election,
and it was established that by general consent a bribe accepted in the
former was held to include payment for a vote in the latter. The committee reported on January 29, 1870, that corrupt practices had prevailed at
Beverley at both parliamentary elections in 1857 and at those in 1859,
1860, 1865, and 1868; it appended a list of over 600 persons (including
both Edwards and Kennard) guilty of corruption at one or more of these
elections. (Edwards's margin of victory over Trollope was less than 400.)
Trollope and his colleague were not under suspicion. The government
prepared, and Parliament passed, a bill depriving Beverley of its parliamentary representation (henceforward its voters would help elect the
member for the East Riding of Yorkshire), and permanently disfranchising all those listed by the commission as bribers or bribed.[14]

The cost to Trollope was about £400 plus a share in the actual
expense of holding the election, including beer for the officers at the polls;
the entire amount was about £440.[15] There is no evidence that any of the
expenses of the proceedings subsequent to the election fell on him, since
he was not one of the petitioners. He had done good service for his party;
if he did not help them to secure two Liberal voices behind the Treasury
bench, he at least helped them get rid of two Conservative voices on the
other side. More interesting to him than the practical aspect was his
conviction that he had struck a successful blow against the degradation of
electoral corruption. And whatever illusions he may have allowed himself
during the campaign, he must have known (indeed on his own testimony
he had been told in advance) that this was the service he had been sent to
perform.[16] Nevertheless, what he really wanted was a seat in Parliament.
"I shall have another fly at it somewhere some day, unless I feel myself to
be growing too old," he told a friend.[17] But by the next general election
(1874) he was fifty-nine. His novels continued to express his sense that
such a seat is the highest position to which an Englishman may aspire.
Dickens, who had declined to stand for Birmingham in the election of
1868, did not agree: "The House of Commons . . . is a dismal
sight. . . . Its irrationality and dishonesty are quite shocking. . . . Anthony's ambition [at Beverley] is inscrutable to me. Still, it is the ambition of many men; and the honester the man who entertains it, the better
for the rest of us, I suppose."[18]

"What an idea does [Cicero] give as to the labour of a candidate in
Rome!" Trollope wrote in 1880. "I can imagine it to be worse even than
the canvassing of an English borough, which to a man of spirit and honour
is the most degrading of all existing employments not held to be absolutely disgraceful."[19] But this much contact with public life had been

profitable to Trollope, not only in the strong political sense it gave his novels, but in his vivid perception of the political careers of Cicero and Palmerston, whose lives he published in 1880 and 1882. Lord Bryce, a Liberal cabinet minister of a somewhat younger generation who knew Trollope personally, took a somewhat different view of the matter; he regretted that Trollope was not elected, since "with his quick eye for the superficial aspects of any society, [he] might have described the House of Commons admirably had he sat in it himself," whereas "the pictures of political life which are so frequent in his later tales have not much flavour of reality. They are sketches obviously taken from the outside." In Bryce's opinion, Trollope "was a direct and forcible speaker, who would have made his way had he entered Parliament."[20]

ૠ

Shorter articles for *Saint Pauls,* frequently topical, could be provided with relatively little advance planning, but for the novels it was best to arrange well beforehand, especially if good work by good novelists was to be obtained. And so as the end of the year 1868 approached, Trollope laid various proposals before Virtue. *Phineas Finn* would end with the May number of 1869, and Fanny Trollope's *The Sacristan's Household* in June. A novel in sixteen parts by Mrs. Oliphant, *The Three Brothers,* was engaged for the place left vacant by *Phineas,*[21] and he hoped for a six-part tale by Hamilton Aïdé to succeed Fanny's novel. It would be cheap; "the last 7 months of 1869 will thus be much cheaper to you than the previous 20 months" (when his own expensive novel was running). He had already published a two-part fiction by Aïdé at the price of £25 for thirty-eight pages. There was room, then, for a high-priced novel beginning in January, 1870: he would supply one to run eighteen months for £2,520, or, "if you would prefer that I should apply to George Eliot, I will do so. I think she would charge you double what I should. . . . Do not for a moment suppose that there will be any feeling of rivalry between her & me. I should like to do exactly what you think best."[22] Aïdé's novel did not materialize, and Trollope himself filled up part of the gap with a series of "An Editor's Tales," half a dozen short stories in eight installments.

On reflection, Virtue determined to accept Trollope's novel (*Ralph the Heir*), to begin its run on January 1, 1870.[23] But something else was in the wind, as Trollope learned from his conversation with Virtue— Virtue was looking for another publisher to take on *Saint Pauls.* Fred Chapman had apparently remarked earlier that he would be glad to have it. Chapman and Hall had been publishing *Colburn's New Monthly Magazine,* but Harrison Ainsworth, who was both proprietor and editor, moved it to the firm of Bentley on July 1, 1868, leaving Chapman with no periodical of this type. By January 1, Ainsworth and his magazine were back with Chapman, however,[24] and so when Virtue pursued the matter three months later, Chapman was no longer interested. When Virtue accepted Trollope's terms for *Ralph the Heir,* then, on April 13, he asked that he might be "free to use the tale in any other Magazine, in case we shall, in the mean time, make any new arrangements for St Pauls Magazine—you are aware that nothing is yet absolutely decided, although many things are discussed." He guaranteed the monthly payment of £140, to begin in January 1870.[25]

The hazards of magazine publication were experienced by Trollope well before the subsequent misfortunes of *Saint Pauls.* His Garrick Club acquaintance E. S. Dallas took on the editorship of *Once a Week* for the publishers Bradbury and Evans in January, 1868, at a salary of £800 that included all editorial expenditures,[26] and he immediately asked Trollope for a novel (January 5). An agreement was reached for a tale the length of *The Claverings,* at a price of £2,800, to be ready for publication beginning the first week of May, 1869. "Mind I expect a stunner," wrote Dallas. Trollope wrote *The Vicar of Bullhampton* between January 15 and November 1, 1868. As the time for publication approached, Dallas, apparently in conversation, asked permission to defer the serial for three months, and Trollope rather hotly objected that since he had agreed not to publish another novel during the first six months of its run, he was being disadvantaged financially by the proposal. He soon reconsidered, but Dallas could not resist remarking in a letter of January 21, 1869, that Trollope had overcharged the publishers for his wares: "You know best how many publishers there are in London who would accede to such terms."[27]

Almost immediately there was an even graver problem. Bradbury and Evans had purchased the right to publish an English translation of Victor Hugo's *L'Homme Qui Rit* in *Once a Week,* beginning in January, but Hugo had delayed French publication from week to week until it was apparent that the translation could not begin its run until April at the earliest, and with Trollope's novel beginning in July the two together would take up all the pages of the magazine. Would Trollope therefore object if Bradbury and Evans published *The Vicar* in the *Gentleman's Magazine,* a veteran journal more than a century old which they had recently purchased and refurbished? It "is raised in character—is extremely well done—& will do you no discredit," urged Dallas on March 22. Trollope refused indignantly, with the righteous wrath of a man who had kept his part of the agreement, had even made a concession, and was now being thrust aside for a writer who had *not* kept his agreement, who was a Frenchman, whose recent novels were "pretentious and untrue to nature," who was merely a "sententious French Radical."[28]

There was more to the publishers' conduct than met the eye, and one is led to wonder how much Dallas foresaw when he wrote. For in response to Trollope's refusal, they transferred the Hugo novel to the *Gentleman's Magazine,* commencing with the May number, and advertised "a new story by Anthony Trollope, of great interest, and specially designed for 'Once a Week,' [to be] commenced at the end of June."[29] By the end of June, however, they were completing the sale of *Once a Week* to another publisher who would cut the price from ninepence to twopence, Dallas had lost his editorship, and *The Vicar* was advertised for monthly publication in shilling parts, with illustrations, to commence shortly.*[30] As a book, it appeared in a single volume, with thirty illustrations by Henry Woods, early in April, 1870.[31] And Trollope abated his price for the novel by £300.[32] Meanwhile he published in *Saint Pauls* (July, 1869) a sixteen-page scornful review of *L'Homme Qui Rit* by his friend Juliet Pollock. The gifted French author, she said, has "touched nothing which he did not disfigure," but the tedium of Hugo's satire (and it is tedious) is more than matched by the tedium of her review.[33]

≈

Trollope described the years 1867 and 1868 as "the busiest in my life,"[34] years in which he wrote almost ceaselessly—*Phineas Finn, Linda Tressel, The Golden Lion, He Knew He Was Right, The Vicar of Bullhampton,* and articles for *Saint Pauls* and the *Pall Mall Gazette*—and at the same closed out his work with the Post Office, edited his magazine, traveled on the mission to America, and stood for Parliament.

In *Phineas Finn* he had almost accidentally, it would seem, created a character in Robert Kennedy who was obsessively determined to control his wife and was jealous of her friendships with other men, to the utter destruction of the marriage. For his next long novel—indeed one-third longer than *Phineas*—he made a husband's obsession for control the center

---

*Trollope gave this account of Dallas's editorial failure in a letter to Lord Houghton on May 19, 1870, in reply to Houghton's claim that Dallas had offered Disraeli £10,000 for *Lothair:*

> Two years ago Dallas was editing the paper called Once a Week:—and, as it happened, I sold a novel, through him, to the proprietors of that paper just at that time, for publication in the paper. My price was not exorbitant:—i e it was exactly at the rate I was being paid for the article from other sources. I found that he was running a muck among novelists, offering to buy this and that, buying indeed this & that, and in the mean while the paper had to be disposed of as worthless. It was sold I believe for all but nothing. My bargain had been made bona fide with the proprietors, and my novel was written for them. But I was obliged to assent to another mode of publication, and to abate my price. Therefore I regard an offer made by Dallas as no genuine offer,—even though his offer were for Lothair.

of his story. Kennedy had affirmed that "the laws of God" required his dominance (chap. lxviii); Louis Trevelyan of *He Knew He Was Right* stood upon the language of the marriage ceremony, "that obedience which she had sworn at the altar to give him" (chap. lxxxiv). And therefore, just as in *Phineas,* there is a good deal of discussion of the place of women in society. "It is a very poor thing to be a woman," said Trevelyan's wife Emily to her sister. "You can't be otherwise than a woman. And you must marry. . . . A woman must be decent; . . . she can't die, and she mustn't be in want, and she oughtn't to be a burden" (chap. v). The sister, indeed, had already told herself that "The lot of a woman . . . was wretched, unfortunate, almost degrading. For a woman such as herself there was no path open to her energy, other than that of getting a husband" (chap. iv).

Trevelyan's obsession, however, was not merely a reflection of a universal condition of society; it was much more complex and individual. In 1877 Trollope's friend George Meredith would remark on the healing power of the comic spirit: "Each one of an affectionate couple may be willing, as we say, to die for the other, yet unwilling to utter the agreeable word at the right moment; but if the wits were sufficiently quick for them to perceive that they are in a comic situation, as affectionate couples must be when they quarrel, they would not wait for the moon or the almanac . . . that they should join hands and lips."[35] Trevelyan and Emily did love each other, but "each desired that the other should acknowledge a fault, and neither of them would make that acknowledgment" (chap. xi). When Colonel Osborne, a friend of Emily's father, called on her, Louis became jealous (although indeed the man was older than her father, and may even have been her godfather—her father found it very difficult to recollect godparents accurately). He wished her to cut off the acquaintance, though a sense that he was being silly left him incapable of taking a firm stand. Emily, outraged at the implied distrust of her virtue, insisted that he be precise in his instructions to her and in the terms of his accusation. And Osborne, sensing what was going on and fancying himself something of a Lothario, persisted in calling on her and writing to her. Trevelyan sent his wife and infant son to stay with friends in Devonshire, hired a detective to watch her, and then realized that he had publicly made a fool of himself. He knew that the contact with the detective disgraced and degraded him, and lost all self-respect. "He would sooner have shot himself than have walked into his club, or even have allowed himself to be seen by daylight in Pall Mall, or Piccadilly. He had taken in his misery to drinking little drops of brandy in the morning, although he knew well that there was no shorter road to the devil" (chap. lix). And yet with the detective's aid he kidnapped the child and fled to

Italy, where he lived in solitude at a farmhouse in the hills near Siena. Tragedy, not comedy, is the mood, and Trollope echoes the language first of the jealous Othello, then of the mad King Lear.[36] In the end, Emily, out of love and pity, goes far beyond the concessions she had formerly refused to make, admits her error in terms so ambiguous as to suggest to Louis that she may even have been attached to Osborne, and persuades her husband, insane, emaciated, so weak he can hardly walk, to return to England, where she sadly nurses him until he dies. It is a moving tale, a tragedy that was quite unnecessary as regards the parents, and the worse because of the unhappiness of the innocent child. "Oh God, to what misery had a little folly brought two human beings who had had every blessing that the world could give within their reach" (chap. xcii). "The pity of it!" as Louis had said to himself, recalling Othello in Othello's own city of Venice, whither Trollope had no doubt deliberately taken him to stress the parallel (chap. xlv).

Because the story is so moving, one can too easily overlook the fact that it takes up only about a third of the book. It is "a recognised fact in society that young ladies are in want of husbands," says Trollope (chap. xxxv), perhaps recalling the opening sentence of *Pride and Prejudice.** There are four other couples in the novel whose romances must be narrated: "It is the nature of a complex story to be entangled with many weddings towards its close" (chap. lxxxviii), and the last ninety pages produce the four weddings, as a lovely girl from Providence, Rhode Island, marries the heir to an English peerage, Emily's sister Nora marries a radical journalist with whom she had fallen in love at first sight, a quiet provincial girl blossoms under the admiration of a provincial banker, and a silly clergyman from the cathedral chapter at Exeter marries a silly girl who has pursued him. The journalist, indeed, bears some resemblance to Trollope; he had been schooled at Harrow, and when he takes a leave of absence from his newspaper he must provide a substitute to write articles on the Irish Church and on the state of society in modern Rome (the subjects of articles in *Saint Pauls* from the pens of Anthony and Tom) (chap. xix).

One of the most entertaining of the characters is an elderly spinster, Miss Jemima Stanbury of Exeter. Trollope had lived in Exeter for a time when he was reorganizing rural posts in England, but he had known the city even earlier, for his mother's sister Mrs. Mary Clyde lived there, and

*"It is a truth universally acknowledged, that a single man in possession of a good fortune must be in want of a wife." Nora Rowley refused to elope with her young man (chap. xc) because "of all things in the world I don't want to be a Lydia"—i.e., presumably, a Lydia Bennet of *Pride and Prejudice.*

so did a distant cousin, Fanny Bent, who was something of a model for Miss Stanbury. Miss Jemima had a heart of gold, but she was fond of having her own way, she would not allow her niece to read modern novels, she distrusted pillar-boxes for letters, "regarded penny postage as one of the strongest evidences of the coming ruin," and "in the matter of politics she had long since come to think that every good thing was over" (chaps. vii–viii). She was the generous aunt of one of the brides and one of the grooms in the story, and for a time had been patroness of the silly clergyman.

Trollope makes good use of his travels—in the Alps, in Italy (there is an especially fine description of the hill country near Siena), in North America (with his occasionally satiric characterization of the American people), in the West Indian colonies (where he had learned something about the colonial governors like Emily Trevelyan's father). Lest we doubt the reality of some of his earlier characters, we find passing mention (along with Disraeli, Robert Lowe, and Lord Derby) of Lady Glencora, Lord Cantrip, the young Irish undersecretary for the colonies (Phineas Finn), Bishop Proudie, and (somewhat less in passing) lawyer Bideawhile. There is fine humor in the book—the gossipy tea and whist party at Exeter (chap. xv), the description of the two sisterly rivals for the hand of the foolish clergyman (like "two pigs at the same trough, each striving to take the delicacies of the banquet from the other, and yet enjoying always the warmth of the same dunghill in amicable contiguity" (chap. xliv), and a misanthropic young woman's description of the blessing her mother invokes upon their humble meal, with "a grace hovering in the air different to that which she says: . . . 'Pray, God, don't quite starve us, and let everybody else have indigestion'" (chap. xcvii).

Trollope did indeed get into trouble with Kate Field over his creation of the American poetess Wallachia Petrie, the "Republican Browning," who dominated every conversation with her affirmations of woman's independence, of the effeteness of British civilization, and of the regrettable falling off from principle of her dear friend who got married. "I never said you were like W. Petrie. I said that that young woman did not entertain a single opinion on public matters which you could repudiate,—and that she was only absurd in her mode of expressing them," he replied to Kate's protest.[37] One wonders a bit why he chose the name of Trevelyan for the man who "knew he was right." He had become a friend of Sir Charles Trevelyan since the days when he created Sir Gregory Hardlines in *The Three Clerks,* and indeed Sir Charles was currently a contributor to *Saint Pauls.* Perhaps he was keeping the peace when he made one of the American girls remark, "Mr. Trevelyan! What a pretty name. It sounds like a novel" (chap. xxxvii).

Altogether this is one of Trollope's most varied novels, and Marcus

Stone's illustrations harmonize well with the text to give it an even fuller meaning.

෨

The Vicar of Bullhampton, which Trollope tentatively entitled *I Count Her Wrong* when he planned it,[38] is preceded by a preface in which he justifies having portrayed sympathetically "a girl whom I will call,—for want of a truer word that shall not in its truth be offensive,—a castaway." Carry Brattle, the youngest daughter of the miller of Bullhampton, was "such a morsel of fruit as men do choose" (chap. v), and was seduced by a young lieutenant in the army; when the miller discovered the fact, he beat the young man "to death's door," "left him all but lifeless," but was so justified in the popular mind that the law dared not touch him. Carry disappeared, presumably banished from the paternal roof, and miserably followed that nameless occupation. She returned to the neighborhood of Bullhampton in the company of a pair of scoundrels, one of whom was later convicted of bashing in the skull of a local farmer in a burglary attempt, and she was there discovered by her younger brother Sam and by the vicar of Bullhampton, Frank Fenwick, who found respectable lodgings for her, braved the scandal spread by a hostile Marquis of Trowbridge decrying his visits to the rooms of such a woman, and sought without success to persuade her relatives or parents to take her in. Carry refused to be sent to a shelter for fallen women, was understandably bored by the isolation of the lodging that had been found for her, and made her way across country on foot to the old mill, where she was welcomed by her mother and sister and ultimately accepted also by her father; there she spent the rest of her days, comfortable in the love of her family and their forgiveness, but always conscious of the disgrace which marked her off from the rest of the village world. One is struck with the way in which the early part of the story runs parallel to the opening of *Doctor Thorne,* with its seduction of a laboring man's sister and the brutal punishment meted out to the seducer by the girl's brother; one is struck also by the way in which the girl in the earlier story is married to a worthy man and reabsorbed into society (in America, to be sure) without a great fuss. In fact, for all the bravado of Trollope's preface to *The Vicar,* he is very uncomfortable with Carry's story and sadly ignorant of the sociology of prostitution.

But Carry's story is actually almost lost in the novel, obscured by the characteristically Trollopian romance between a beautiful twenty-one-year-old orphan friend of the vicar's wife (tall, graceful, "her back . . . as lovely a form of womanhood as man's eye ever measured and appreciated") (chap. i) and, on the one hand, the squire of Bullhampton, on the other the girl's impoverished cousin, a captain in the army home on leave from

India. She and the captain fall deeply in love, but through a misunderstanding she supposes he intends to marry another and she agrees to marry the squire (who is, like Trollope, a Harrovian). She has not learned the lesson another young woman in the story later formulates, that "one ought to be very fond of a young man before one falls in love with him" (chap. lviii). But the misunderstandings are resolved, the captain inherits a baronetcy and a comfortable fortune, the heroine marries him, and the poor squire, brokenhearted and humiliated, leaves Bullhampton and the company of his friends.

There is also the story of the hostile Marquis, the principal landowner of Bullhampton, who to spite the vicar gives to the minister of a Primitive Methodist congregation a plot of land just at the vicar's gate, on which to build a hideous chapel whose bell shall be louder than that of the church, and through the open doors of which the sermons of Mr. Puddleham shall echo into the vicar's house. Luckily neither the Marquis nor Mr. Puddleham had looked up the title to the property: it turned out to be glebe land—land attached to the Church of England benefice for the use of the incumbent—and the chapel had to be dismantled and moved to a more remote spot.

Trollope's village setting and the lives of the humbler folk are a change from his recent novels of metropolitan life and the aristocracy; the miller and his family are especially well done. Bullhampton is a fictitious village on Salisbury Plain, its location very precisely fixed on the first page of the novel (but unfortunately not very logically; if "Bullhampton" is on the railway line from Salisbury to Yeovil, it cannot be closer to Marlborough than to Salisbury).* It is generally the part of the country we have learned to know as "Barsetshire," and indeed the inn at Salisbury is given the same name ("Dragon of Wantley") as the inn in Barchester.

Not long after he completed *The Vicar* Trollope wrote to an acquaintance, "With me, it often comes as a matter . . . of regret, that I can express what I wish to express only by the mouths of people who are created—not that they may express themselves, but that they may amuse."[39] So many of Trollope's women have rebelled at the idea of marriage that it is interesting to see here that his heroine "longed to be a wife"; "Marriage is the most proper and the happiest thing for the young woman" (chaps. xxxvii, lxvii). Speaking apparently in his own voice, he adds: "Nature prompts the desire, the world acknowledges its ubiquity, circumstances show that it is reasonable, the whole theory of creation requires it." And not only of women: "Let men be taught to recognise the

---

*There is similar apparent precision in the way in which Trollope repeatedly gives both date and day of the week for letters and events, and yet is utterly inconsistent in terms of the calendar for any actual years.

same truth as regards themselves, and we shall cease to hear of the necessity of a new career for women." This is indeed the Trollope who lectured publicly on higher education for women at about this time.[40]

About a month after he finished *The Vicar* Trollope was reminded that he had not yet paid his annual subscription to the Early English Text Society; he paid up for both 1868 and 1869.[41] With his usual irony, he had recently said of one of the characters in *The Vicar,* "His whole time was spent among his books, and he was at this moment engaged in revising and editing a very long and altogether unreadable old English chronicle in rhyme, for publication by one of those learned societies which are rife in London" (chap. xliii).

&

When *The Vicar* was completed on November 1, 1868, Trollope had to give his attention immediately to the Beverley election; then—except for a few articles he wrote for *Saint Pauls*—he could rest his pen for a bit. But two days after Christmas he began a short novel, first called *The House of Humblethwaite,* that he finished in a month and then sought a publisher for. "My story is a common love story—but one that ends sadly," he told Alexander Macmillan when the publisher responded with interest to an inquiry whether he would like it for *Macmillan's Magazine.* Macmillan agreed to purchase the entire copyright for £750, publication in the magazine to begin in January, 1870. "It is complete," Trollope assured him. "You can have the manuscript when you please."[42] The only hitch in the arrangements came when Macmillan sold the book publication rights to Hurst and Blackett and Trollope early in October, 1870, learned that they planned to issue it in two volumes. "As one pound of tea won't make two by any variance in packing the article,—so neither will a one-volume tale make two volumes."[43] It was a replay of Trollope's quarrel with Strahan over the publication of *Lotta Schmidt* three and a half years earlier. Although Blackett responded to Macmillan that nearly half the book was already in type, and that in any case the book was precisely the same length as the last novel they had published in two volumes, an accommodation was made and Trollope had his way.* Though he might win the skirmishes, however, he could not win the war: by 1879 his own firm of Chapman and Hall were bringing out in two volumes each his *Cousin Henry* and *An Eye for an Eye,* each of which was almost exactly the same length as *Sir Harry Hotspur of Humblethwaite.*

The novel itself is curiously uncertain in tone. Its title suggests

*Macmillan had the book printed up by his own printer, Richard Clay; we don't know what financial adjustment was made.

comedy—the nickname of a fiery fourteenth-century nobleman made famous by Shakespeare, and here supplied with an alliteratively named estate. In the novel the title character is a nineteenth-century North of England baronet of ancient family whose pride in the class to which he belongs—the gentry, not the nobility—governs his sense of duty and his way of life: he must "so live as to do his part in maintaining that order of gentlehood in England, by which England had become—so thought Sir Harry—the proudest and the greatest and the justest of nations" (chap. i). When he was forty-five he married an earl's daughter of twenty-five who "even yet" (nearly thirty-five years later) "had not forgotten the deference which was due to his age," and though her title showed her noble rank ("Lady Elizabeth Hotspur," not "Lady Hotspur") she "was known,—where she was known,—simply as Sir Harry's wife."

Humblethwaite was in Cumberland, not far from Penrith; there are fine descriptions of the English lakes, the streams and mountains north of Keswick (chap. iii) and those near Penrith and Ullswater (chap. viii). Sir Harry also had an estate in County Durham. But naturally he had a town house in Mayfair, on Bruton Street off Berkeley Square (where the Proudies, Lady Lufton of Framley, and the Longestaffes of *The Way We Live Now* had their town houses also). Here he honored his daughter with a magnificent ball at which

> there were some very distinguished people indeed,—persons whom it would hardly be improper to call illustrious. There were two royal duchesses, one of whom was English, and no less than three princes. The Russian and French ambassadors were both there. There was the editor of the most influential newspaper of the day,—for a few minutes only; and the Prime Minister passed through the room in the course of the evening. Dukes and duchesses below the royal degree were common; and as for earls and countesses, and their daughters, they formed the ruck of the crowd. The Poet-laureate didn't come indeed, but was expected; and three Chinese mandarins of the first quality entered the room at eleven, and did not leave till one. Poor Lady Elizabeth suffered a great deal with those mandarins. From all this it will be seen that the ball was quite a success. (Chap. vi)

We seem to be in a world of social comedy. The mandarins foreshadow the Emperor of China later to be honored by Melmotte's ball in *The Way We Live Now.*

But the story is not a comedy, it is melodramatically tragic. Sir Harry's only son dies at the outset, and though the baronetcy passes on by the laws of primogeniture to the nearest male heir, a cousin George Hotspur, Sir Harry has perfect freedom to bequeath all the property as he wishes. Since George turns out to be (despite his birth) no gentleman—he lies, cheats his creditors, lives off the income of an amiable actress whose husband has deserted her, and swindles young innocents at the card table—Sir Harry determines to leave the estate entire to his daughter, with the understanding that her future husband (whoever he may be) will take the surname of Hotspur. Even George's misdeeds are awkwardly narrated; we get ominous hints of the card-sharping, but the facts are not disclosed until the end of the story, though there has been no technical reason to mystify the reader. Unfortunately, young Emily falls in love with George, engages herself to him, and when Sir Harry forbids the marriage, vows never to marry another. The parents take Emily to Italy to distract her mind from its grief, but as they move northward to Switzerland for the summer, they see among the notices in the *Times* at Lugano that George has married his actress, whose husband has fortuitously died in San Francisco. Emily begs them to stay longer in Lugano, and there, four months later, they bury her in the small Protestant cemetery, brokenhearted in the knowledge that the man she loved had courted her only for her money. Sir Harry, childless, now wills his estate to his wife's nephew, the current Earl, and property which had seemed to the reader unlimited in its magnitude when it supported the magnificent ball in London is now described as so much smaller than the Earl's that the bequest "to him would be little more than additional labour."

The novel was begun only a few months after Trollope's visit to his distant relative Sir John Trollope, the seventh baronet, whose estate at Casewick had been in the family since 1621. The first three baronets of the line had all been sheriffs of County Lincoln. The family traced among its ancestors that notable warrior in the Wars of the Roses, Sir Andrew Trollope, who at the battle of Wakefield in 1460 (mentioned in *Henry VI, Part III*) captured the Yorkist Richard Plantagenet, third Duke of York, later beheaded. An Elizabeth Plantagenet, illegitimate daughter of Edward IV, later married into the family. And as early as 1390 an earlier John Trollope had acquired the manor of Morden, in County Durham. It is hard to avoid the conclusion that Trollope conceived the novel, with its titular allusion to those medieval wars, as a result of his visit to Casewick. And yet he would not have known quite how to treat the subject so as not to be too conspicuously critical or satirical of his host, whom in any case he probably was not inclined to criticize.

The reader who thinks only of the pathos of the story will agree with one modern critic who calls it "the story of the destructive power of truth and single-mindedness, the tragedy of the pure in heart."[44] But another modern critic remarks that Trollope "apparently did not see the incongruity of a master of the comedy of manners wrestling with a plot bad enough to be rejected by a librettist of Italian opera."[45] Trollope's contemporary, the poet Charles Kent, who had arranged the banquet for

Dickens on the eve of his journey to America, reviewed the book for the *Sun,* and called it "not only a brilliant example of Anthony Trollope's powers as a novelist, but . . . in a very striking manner a radiant specimen of English imaginative literature." In acknowledging the copy of the review Kent sent him, Trollope wrote: "I only hope [your praise] may have been deserved. I am always most doubtful about my work;—and in some moods am altogether beyond doubt." Trollope was by no means always doubtful about his work, but in this case he knew he had cause. "Humblethwaite is too gloomy and wretched," he told a friend.[46]

Chapter XVIII

1869–70

Keeping the promise he had made in 1865, Fred Trollope returned home in December, 1868, "had a season's hunting in the old country," then departed permanently for Australia from Plymouth in late April of 1869; he was now twenty-one years old. His original departure had been "a great pang to his mother and me," Trollope wrote, but Fred had "resolved on a colonial career when he found that boys who did not grow so fast as he did got above him at school." His purpose remained fixed, and thereafter if his parents were to see him they must journey to Australia.[1]

A few months later Trollope thought he had found a useful occupation at home for his older son Henry—he purchased for him a one-third partnership in Chapman and Hall at the price of £10,000.* "I have had an immense deal of trouble in arranging it," he told Lewes on August 13. "It is a fine business which has been awfully ill used by want of sufficient work and sufficient capital." J. M. Langford, the director of Blackwood's London office, was helpful in making the arrangements, and to Blackwood Trollope reported in October, "Harry is hard at work and comes home freighted with Mss. What he does with them I don't know; but I feel glad that I am not an author publishing with Chapman & Hall as I fancy he goes to sleep over them with a pipe in his mouth." Nevertheless he was proud: "I should tell you that Chapman & Hall are in truth Chapman & Trollope, and that the Trollope is my son," he told a friend a year and a half later. But the work did not suit Henry; he withdrew himself and the money about September, 1873, and devoted himself to traveling and independent writing.[3]

❧

Trollope was confined to his bed for a great part of March, but recovered in time to attend the elaborate and elegant banquet with which the citizens of Liverpool honored Charles Dickens at St. George's Hall on April 10 to mark the close of his series of farewell readings from his works. Dickens was uneasy about the occasion—the hall was much too large, the acoustics poor, the program too long, and then G. A. Sala was

---

*Henry had just then (June 7, 1869) been called to the bar from Lincoln's Inn.[2]

to respond to the toast to "The Newspaper Press," and "he is certain to be drunk." He had no uneasiness respecting Trollope, who would respond (with Hepworth Dixon) to the toast to "Modern Literature." Seated together at the chief table, but at some distance from their fathers, were "Mr. A. Trollope, jun." (presumably Henry) and Mr. C. Dickens, jun. The report of the event in the *Liverpool Daily Courier* was remarkably frank: "Mr. Anthony Trollope has not an agreeable voice, but his short speech was marked by manliness, good sense, and a touch of quiet humour." "If we [novelists] can . . . amuse you," he said, "without making the purity of woman less pure, without making the manliness of man less manly—then, I say, we do a great and good work." As it befell, it was not Sala (who made "a modest, sensible, but most effective speech") who was drunk, but his introducer, Lord Houghton. Houghton had been called upon early in the evening to respond to the toast to the Parliament of Great Britain, and now late in the evening was obliged to toast the newspapermen. His speech "became curiously hazy towards its close, and consequently was received with good-natured impatience. . . . How much more potent a fluid is champagne than nepenthe." Houghton's friends could not have been surprised. Three years earlier a guest at the Cosmopolitan Club described "Anthony Trollope, cracking jokes before the fire" and Lord Houghton arriving, "maudlin with drink."[4]

As plans were being made in January for this year's anniversary dinner of the Royal Literary Fund on May 5, it was felt that the common bond between the great nations on both sides of the Atlantic should be honored with a toast, and Trollope suggested that the new United States minister, Reverdy Johnson, be invited to reply. He "is able to talk on any subject or on none without stint."*[5] Johnson fulfilled the prophecy: when the shorthand notes of his remarks were transcribed for printing in the annual report, they were so long and so rambling that Johnson's friends had to be called on confidentially to suggest drastic excisions. Trollope himself responded to the toast to "Literature," proposed by his schoolfellow at Winchester, Lord Justice Sir George Giffard. His was an agreeable speech that did not notably repeat what he had said at Liverpool a month earlier; he spoke on the rewards and the disappointments of the rapidly growing profession of writing, a talk based at least partly on his experience as editor of *Saint Pauls*.

---

*Trollope was never unaware of the distinction between a private and a public expression of opinion: in his last letter to the *Pall Mall Gazette* from Washington in late June, 1868, he wrote: "I will not finish this . . . without expressing the great gratification I feel at the selection of Mr. Reverdy Johnson as Minister to England. He is about the best man that this country has to give to such a service; and she has no better to give to any other service."[6]

The men and women who now earn their bread by writing what others shall read, or at least by what others shall purchase, may be counted by thousands. Doubtless this profession is of all the most precarious, and yet it is of all the most alluring. It may be begun without capital, without patronage, and without favour. It may be carried on under any circumstances of residence, amidst the whirl of fashion, or in the silence of the most secluded retreat. A table and a chair, a little paper, a pen and ink, and the young aspirant hopes that he may be able to touch the pulses of the world. . . . We, who are so intimately acquainted with the affairs of this Corporation, are bound to know how great are its difficulties, and how heart-breaking, how sad are its reverses. . . . [But] the rewards of this profession are so sweet. . . . They are the esteem of men whose estimation is honour; reputation amongst those who have already been reputed great; and a name widely spread amongst our countrymen. Added to this is that feeling, which is so common to us all, that it is much more pleasant to teach, or even to amuse, than it is to be taught or to be amused.

The talk was interrupted from time to time with cheers or laughter, and Trollope sat down to the sound of great cheering.[7] Sala was present at the dinner, and next day wrote to a friend: "Reverdy Johnson (that interminable old magpie and stump orator) . . . said he was glad to find himself among the literary men of England. He was among Trollope. . . . I don't quarrel with the L. F. for serving up the eternal Trollope. The fund is a good charity." Four years later Sala himself was obliged to apply to the fund for a grant because of a painful and disabling illness. At the meeting of the general committee, Trollope seconded the motion by which Sala was given £100.[8]

ॐ

The publishing business was highly speculative, whereas two occupations upon which it depended—papermaking and printing—were a good deal more predictable as to their profits. It is not surprising, then, that a publisher like Strahan should be heavily in debt to his paper suppliers, Spalding and Hodge, and to his printer James Virtue. As early as July 12, 1866, Strahan had borrowed £15,000 from the one and £10,000 from the other. Part of the agreement was that Virtue should print and bind all periodicals and books published by Strahan (including, therefore, the *Contemporary Review*), and the copyrights in the various periodicals served to secure the loan.[9] The publication of a magazine required not only editorial talent, but also careful supervision of the business side as well, and Virtue was apparently finding that *Saint Pauls* was taking more time than he could afford. When the sale to Chapman and Hall came to nothing, and Strahan's debts grew greater and greater, Virtue transferred *Saint Pauls* to Strahan in mid-May, 1869, and along with it a substantial portion of his list of books, including *Phineas Finn* (just then published in book form) and *He Knew He Was Right,* which Strahan promptly brought out in two volumes, with its sixty-four illustrations; the part issues were completed by the end of May. The transaction was not a "sale," it was essentially a transfer for managerial purposes and Virtue retained his financial control over the journal, but having turned the management over to Strahan he would in future decline to intervene. It was apparently Virtue's hope that Strahan's expertise with periodicals would make *Saint Pauls* profitable. Trollope was undoubtedly kept well informed of Virtue's intentions, since they saw each other frequently, but surviving correspondence tells us little.

Trollope was not entirely comfortable with Strahan, whom he regarded as rather irresponsible in making payments and even in handling manuscripts sent to him. (It was not long after this that Matthew Arnold had trouble collecting payment for an article in the *Contemporary.*)[10] The transition was not perfectly easy: Trollope as usual authorized a payment for Austin Dobson, but the new publisher's clerks had no address for such a person and Dobson had to wait. Another manuscript sent to Strahan's office never reached Trollope, presumably because the Strahan people supposed it was intended for *Good Words.* "There has been a change of office though none really of management or ownership," he explained to Dobson.[11] He naturally gave up his editorial office at Virtue's printing house and borrowed space at Chapman and Hall's on Piccadilly rather than work out of Strahan's office. His term as editor was ensured through September, 1869, and in fact continued (apparently without formal extension) beyond that time. After the transfer to Strahan, Trollope ceased to keep his record of payments to contributors, but he may have continued to exercise control over them until he gave up the editorship with the July number of 1870. He wrote to Austin Dobson on May 21, 1870: "In my endeavour to establish the Saint Pauls on what I considered to be a good literary footing, I insisted on myself naming the remuneration to be paid. It has not been very great, but it has been fairly good. The object now is to make the magazine pay. What may be the result of that resolve to contributors in the way of remuneration will never be known to me after June. I fear it may not be altogether satisfactory."[12]

The contract for the publication of *Ralph the Heir* was unchanged by the transfer: Trollope wrote the novel from April 4 to August 7, so that it was ready in plenty of time for serialization in *Saint Pauls,* beginning in January, 1870. And the greater part of his surviving correspondence from 1869 and the first half of 1870 is concerned with his editorial labors.

He and Rose did manage a holiday of several weeks in May at Bolton Abbey and elsewhere in Yorkshire, and a longer one in France late in the summer. Anthony took Rose to Paris on August 13, but returned at once in order to testify before the Beverley Bribery Commission on September 3. Immediately thereafter he met her at Caen for what must have been a most pleasant tour of Normandy and Brittany—Granville, Avranches, St. Malo, Dinan, Brest, Nantes, Angers, and their old favorite, Chartres.[13]

The half-dozen "Editor's Tales" by which Trollope bridged the gap in his supply of fiction for *Saint Pauls* are for the most part whimsical embroideries of his own experiences with would-be contributors. There is the lively young woman who wins his heart despite her lack of talent, and to whom he gives the name of his grandmother Mary Gresley; there is the small group of young men with one slightly older woman who resolve to found the perfect magazine, the *Panjandrum,* much as the *Fortnightly* had been founded, but with substantially less success, since they dissolved in squabbles before the first number could be assembled. One especially whimsical story must have been designed to catch the eye of a couple to whom Trollope was himself very much devoted. "Josephine de Montmorenci" was the pen name, in the story of that name, of an English writer of fiction, rather too fond of metaphysics, who was reluctant to deal with an editor except through an intermediary. Her name was actually Maryanne, though she was called "Polly" by her relatives, one of whom, named Charles, worked at the Post Office and smoked incessantly. Now "George Eliot" was a pseudonym designed to disguise a woman named Marian, nicknamed "Polly," who had a metaphysical bent. Her common-law husband George Henry Lewes was constantly buying cigars from Trollope, and indeed had written an article on tobacco smoking for *Saint Pauls.* Moreover, his son Charles worked in the Post Office. Obviously it was not a story about Lewes and George Eliot, but the coincidences must have been intentional.

"The Spotted Dog," however, is not whimsical but deeply tragic: a brilliant, well-educated young man who had been a scholar of a Cambridge college becomes a desperate drunkard, marries an alcoholic wife and struggles both to get himself out of his miserable way of life and to support four children. An opportunity comes his way to do the index of a learned treatise on classical meters by a rural clergyman; he takes the manuscript home, but his wife in a drunken rage tears it up and burns it. The translator gives his children money to go out and buy themselves breakfast, then cuts his throat. "And that was the end of Julius Mackenzie, the scholar." The scraps and ashes of the manuscript are locked in a box and taken home by the rector as if they were a funerary urn, but he never unlocks the box or attempts to reconstruct his book.

Three of the stories had appeared in *Saint Pauls* when Strahan offered

Trollope £150 for the right to republish them in a book which appeared about July 1, 1870.[14]

ea

Strahan and Company remained in financial difficulties, and on January 25, 1870, Strahan used the occasion of sending Trollope's check for *Ralph the Heir*—a payment that gave him "much pleasure"—to "take the opportunity of letting you know that we have been thinking . . . that perhaps 'Saint Pauls' might be allowed to follow the example of 'Blackwood' and 'edit itself,' that is put up with such editing as publishers can give." At the same time Virtue wrote to express his personal regret that the magazine and Trollope should part company. "Our relationship together has been so genial & pleasant that I much regret that any change should have become necessary." He apologizes for not intervening, as he might do, for "although I am largely interested in Strahan's business—I have always declined and intend to decline—any active share in its management."[15] The date first set for Trollope's termination was the June number, but he continued his tenure for an extra month, and there was no diminution of his editorial activities during those final months.* One curious decision Strahan had already made was to publish *Ralph the Heir* both as a monthly supplement bound with *Saint Pauls* (which was of course correspondingly reduced in size) and in monthly sixpenny parts, in the hope of attracting two sets of buyers.

Strahan's decision as to the editorship was entirely reasonable in terms of the practice with other magazines of the day, and indeed at the same time he also dropped Dean Alford as editor of the *Contemporary Review*. Trollope had already learned by experience that Thackeray was a figurehead as editor of the *Cornhill* and Macleod as editor of *Good Words,* and when he wished to place a novel in *Blackwood's* or *Macmillan's* he wrote to their publishers John Blackwood or Alexander Macmillan. Blackwood's friend A. K. H. Boyd put the matter very well:

> I am quite sure that a publisher makes the best Editor. He is much less likely than a man of letters to fill a periodical with unreadable papers which echo his own crotchets. He is much more accurate. He is absolutely without jealousy. He knows nothing but the success of his magazine or review. . . . John Blackwood . . . had an absolute genius in discerning what would hit the popular liking. . . . Success is the touchstone here. It may be a Philistine test. But, thus tried,

---

*His name as editor appeared for the last time with the advertisements for the July number.

John Blackwood's thirty years of management of the magazine were years of triumph. Shrewdness and geniality were his outstanding characteristics.[16]

It is certainly an easy oversimplification to blame the ultimate fate of *Saint Pauls* on Trollope. Not long after his death, R. H. Hutton, a generally sympathetic critic and long-time editor of the *Spectator*, remarked: "His editing of *St. Paul's Magazine* was conventional. He did not really know how to use contributors, how to make the most of them."[17] But we have already seen Hutton's review of the first number of the magazine; did he in fact have any knowledge of Trollope's editorial practices, beyond this outsider's impression? John Morley, also a successful editor, asserted that "no periodical was ever less intelligently edited, or made less mark, though the pains that Trollope took were infinite. He even read through every manuscript that any simpleton chose to pester him with—a waste of time absolute and unredeemed."[18] Morley's comment was a bit too superficial: the success of a periodical depended a great deal more on the publisher than the editor, and in that heyday of magazines a great many, even with experienced editors, had shorter lives than *Saint Pauls.* Edmund Yates found when he undertook the editorship of the new *Tinsley's Magazine,* which started two months before *St. Pauls,* that "triumphant success, such as had attended the establishment of *Cornhill* and *Temple Bar,* was no longer to be commanded by the proprietors of shilling magazines," even though "this new enterprise was started with all liberality and energy, with a number of excellent contributors."[19] By the beginning of February, 1869, Yates was obliged to give up his editorship after a tenure more than a year shorter than Trollope's was to be.[20] Dallas was editor of *Once a Week* for a mere nineteen months, and he too was an experienced journalist. Circulation itself is not the only key to success. The *Fortnightly,* in terms of endurance and quality, was one of the best of the new periodicals; its circulation was a mere 2,500 by 1872. Its rival, the *Contemporary,* was reaching 10,000 about that time. Trollope's figure for the peak circulation of *Saint Pauls* was "nearly 10,000."[21] What was needed, however, was a publisher with plenty of capital and a willingness to put more into the journal than he would receive, if it should be necessary to do so. But Strahan had no capital.

Trollope more than once expressed his sense of grief at the necessity of declining work submitted for his journal; a letter to Austin Dobson at the moment of his retirement shows the corresponding pleasure of an editor: "I cannot refrain from saying how much gratification I have had during the last two years and a half in meeting with two or three contributors whom I have not known before,—(in your case have not even yet known in the flesh) and as to whom I have felt that they would grace our literature hereafter."

With respect to Dobson in particular, he said: "No contributor who has worked with me has given me more pleasure than yourself."[22]

After Trollope's editorship ended, *Ralph the Heir* of course continued, but only two more articles of Anthony's appeared (in August and November, 1870).[23] Both Tom and Fanny Trollope, however, continued to be frequent contributors, and so were some others of Trollope's team. Strahan attempted to change the apparent character of the magazine by advertising it as "light and choice," as distinguished from the *Contemporary* ("theological, literary, and social"), and he secured Nathaniel Hawthorne's posthumous last novel, *Septimius,* for serialization from January through June, 1872. But the number of pages dropped off. Illustrations were discontinued with the January number of 1872. In March of that year Strahan's creditors forced him to give up his association with the firm of Strahan and Company, Ludgate Hill, and he was obliged to leave behind him such lucrative journals as *Good Words;* he found shelter with the new firm of Henry S. King, who took over some of his books and such journals as the *Contemporary* and *Saint Pauls,* with Strahan presumably still giving whatever editing there was. Records of the King firm show that the circulation held at about 8,000 at the beginning of 1873.[24] The magazine expired with the issue of March, 1874, leaving one serial novel only in its early chapters. Probably the fairest and best-informed account of the venture is after all that in Trollope's *Autobiography:*

> It did fail, for it never paid its way. . . . The enterprise had been set on foot on a system too expensive to be made lucrative by anything short of a very large circulation. Literary merit will hardly set a magazine afloat, though when afloat it will sustain it. Time is wanted, —or the hubbub, and flurry, and excitement created by ubiquitous sesquipedalian advertisement. Merit and time together may be effective, but then they must be backed by oeconomy and patience.[25]

Though the range of his subjects in some measure had reflected his own intellectual bias, it had been on the whole responsive to the current interests of the intelligent, Liberal readers. His contributors had been for the most part distinguished in their fields, many of them also writers for the *Cornhill* and the *Fortnightly.*

As for Virtue, he continued on friendly terms with Trollope, and whenever Trollope had a piece of printing that needed doing—as with the text of a lecture, the catalogue of his library, or the account of his journey to Iceland—it was Virtue to whom he turned.

ঽ৯

Trollope's love of hunting led him often to introduce a hunting scene into his novels; now he hit upon the idea of portraying some characters he knew well, but who are not commonly thought of in that context—the man who makes the riding breeches and the man who makes the riding boots. Thomas Neefit, the prosperous breeches maker of Conduit Street with a pleasant rural cottage at Hendon, north of London (newly accessible by the underground railway), has a practical wife and a pretty, quick-witted daughter Polly for whom he entertains social ambitions. Mrs. Neefit was less ambitious: let her husband only "content himself with going to town four times a week [instead of six], and take a six weeks' holiday in the autumn. That was the recognised mode of life with gentlemen who had made their fortune in trade. . . . But above all things he ought to give up measuring his own customers with his own hands" (chap. v). One of Neefit's best customers was Ralph Newton, heir under an entail to the estate of his uncle Squire Gregory Newton of Newton Priory, in Hampshire on the border of Berkshire; Ralph was the perfect gentleman in his habits, but with an income altogether inadequate to his tastes, and his uncle hated him because he stood in the way of transmitting the estate to the uncle's much-loved but illegitimate son, another Ralph Newton. Therefore Ralph the Heir fell increasingly into debt to his tradesmen, and Neefit saw his opportunity: he invited Ralph to dinner at Hendon, with the understanding that he court Polly; should the two become engaged, Neefit would give Ralph outright £20,000.

There was, however, the bootmaker Moggs, of Booby and Moggs, Old Bond Street, whose son Ontario (christened in honor of a Canadian godparent) had known and admired Polly for many years. "He was a tall, thin, young man, with long straggling hair, a fierce eye, very thick lips, and a flat nose,—a nose which seemed to be all nostril;—and then, below his mouth was a tuft of beard, which he called an imperial. It was the glory of Ontario Moggs to be a politician;—it was his ambition to be a poet;—it was his nature to be a lover;—it was his disgrace to be a bootmaker." He was a regular attendant at meetings of his debating club at the Cheshire Cheese, where "he was great upon Strikes" and "had horrible ideas about co-operative associations, the rights of labour, and the welfare of the masses" (chap. viii). He even held that "ladies should understand politics as well as men; and . . . that they ought to vote" (chap. xxvi). Readers of Matthew Arnold's *Culture and Anarchy* will recognize the names of Moggs's heroes, Odger and Beales of the Reform League, and the allusion to the Hyde Park riots of 1866—"Down with them golden railings" (chap. xvi). To Neefit's distress, Moggs showed up at the cottage at Hendon on the very evening that Ralph Newton was to dine and propose to Polly, and Mrs. Neefit asked him to stay for dinner. The scene at the cottage is one of many of Trollope's superb bits of comedy in the book. There was no proposal of marriage that evening.

Ralph the Heir is a thoroughly decent, well-meaning young man.

He does indeed propose marriage to Polly in due course as he had promised, not once but twice, even though he wonders if he could ever make a
lady of her, "would be able to teach her to call Mr. Neefit her papa" rather
than her father (chap. xix). But, to adapt an old saying, "a man is only as
strong as his weakest moment" (chap. xxvii). There is a retired barrister,
Sir Thomas Underwood, who is Ralph's guardian, and to one of whose
daughters Ralph had once declared his love. Then came an orphaned niece
of great beauty to live with Sir Thomas and his daughters—her father was
"some old general who used to wear a cocked hat and keep the niggers
down out in one of the colonies"—and when Polly will not have him
Ralph, seeing how lovely the niece is, reflects regarding his declaration to
the daughter, "Does any one suppose that a man was bound to marry the
first girl he kisses,—or if not the first, then why the second, or the
third?" (chap. xlii, xxxviii). In the end he marries a newcomer to the scene
whose prudent mother has three unmarried daughters in their twenties
and who lays her trap well.

The complexities of the plot need not be described, but Trollope has
some events of his own life well in view. Sir Thomas, who once sat in
Parliament and was for a few months solicitor general, is persuaded to run
again, this time for the perfectly corrupt borough of Percycross; Trollope
had learned a good deal about election bribery at Beverley, and though the
Percycross election differs in some details from that at Beverley, its results
also are overthrown on a petition and the borough is permanently disfranchised after a hearing. In one respect, Sir Thomas alas comes close to
home to many academics: from the age of twenty-four he had "devoted
himself to the writing of a life of Lord Verulam, and had been at it ever
since. But as yet he had not written a word. . . . And yet Sir Thomas was
always talking to himself about Sir Francis Bacon, and was always writing
his life" (chap. xl). As old age overtook him, there came "the conviction
that everything is vanity, that the life past has been vain from folly, and
that the life to come must be vain from impotence" (chap. li).[26]

The Hampshire countryside Trollope describes with such affection
when he speaks of Newton Priory is near Heckfield, where his grandfather
Milton had been vicar; indeed the early part of the hunt on which Squire
Newton fell and was killed took place "within a field of Heckfield church"
(chaps. xi, xxxi). A decade later Trollope himself moved to a country
house that was only about twenty-five miles from Heckfield.

The women of the story show more variety than those in a good
many of Trollope's novels, but they are well aware of their dependence
upon men for the marriage they must look forward to. "A woman can
only be still and endure," Clarissa Underwood lamented to herself (chap.
xli). And when Sir Thomas stands for Parliament, his niece says, "I shall
feel so proud when uncle is in Parliament again. A woman's pride is
always vicarious;—but still it is pride" (chap. xxii).

Trollope near the end of the book makes an apology for choosing an amiable weakling as his central character. Every novelist has the desire to teach, so that his readers will not only love characters like Jeanie Deans and Henry Esmond, but hate the Becky Sharps and Barry Lyndons. Ralph Newton was not vicious; in real life he would not have been held to have disgraced himself. Nevertheless, "the faults of a Ralph Newton, and not the vices of a Varney or a Barry Lyndon are the evils against which men should in these days be taught to guard themselves;—which women also should be made to hate. Such is the writer's apology for his very indifferent hero, Ralph the Heir" (chap. lvi). These words were written very near to the time when Trollope was formulating his lecture "On English Prose Fiction," a lecture in which he declares his admiration for Jane Austen: "Miss Austen was surely a great novelist. . . . What she did, she did perfectly. Her work, as far as it goes, is faultless. She wrote of the times in which she lived, of the class of people with which she associated, and in the language which was usual to her as an educated lady. . . . In the comedy of folly I know no novelist who has beaten her. The letters of Mr. Collins, a clergyman in 'Pride and Prejudice,' would move laughter in a low-church archbishop. Throughout all her works . . . a sweet lesson of homely household womanly virtue is ever being taught."[27] In many a passage of *Ralph the Heir* Trollope too excels in "the comedy of folly": the irony of tone and speech makes his craftsmanship in this book almost unsurpassed among his works.

Its publishing history is curious. Eighteen of the nineteen monthly parts published by Strahan had illustrations by F. A. Fraser, some of them superb. The three-volume first edition published on April 6, 1871, by Hurst and Blackett (who at this time were apparently eager to contract for first-edition rights in order to supply the lending libraries), had none of these. Strahan's first one-volume edition, published in the summer of 1871, had eleven, and a year later, with Strahan in financial difficulty, Routledge brought out the same edition with all eighteen plates.[28]

&

About the tenth of October, 1869, Blackwood learned that Trollope planned to lecture in Edinburgh and promptly invited him to stay at his home. "I shall be very happy to be your guest," Trollope replied. "Some learned pundit,—at least he was a doctor,—kindly offered to give me the 'hospitality of the city,' which, as it means a half-formed introduction to the pickled snakes and a visit to the public library & the like I viewed with horror and did not accept. I lecture about novels, and shall expect Mrs. Blackwood to go and hear me. . . . You [however] must know more about novels than I can tell you." The Edinburgh lecture "On English Prose Fiction as a Rational Amusement" was given on January 28, following the delivery of the same discourse at Hull on the twenty-fourth and Glasgow on the twenty-seventh. In Glasgow he stayed with George Burns, the shipping magnate whose son eight years later arranged a pleasant excursion to Iceland with Trollope and others, and he also had an evening with his friend R. S. Oldham. After Edinburgh the lecture was delivered at Birmingham on January 31. His fees for two of the lectures were £15, for the other two £10.[29]

Blackwood showed him two new little books—synopses of the *Iliad* and the *Odyssey* with which the Rev. W. Lucas Collins was inaugurating a new series of "Ancient Classics for English Readers." "You would have been delighted as I was to hear how enthusiastic he was about your Iliad & the whole scheme," Blackwood wrote to Collins. "As he is about the most shrewd & practical man of letters going it was very cheering to hear him." His practicality led him to write an admiring review of the two books for *Saint Pauls** (March, 1870) and his enthusiasm led him to volunteer to do Caesar's *Commentaries* for the series, a project upon which he began work instantly, while he was still staying with Blackwood. One of his very earliest published writings, his review of Charles Merivale's *History of the Romans,* had required a careful study of Caesar, and now after nearly twenty years he could fulfill the wish then formulated to write at greater length upon "probably the greatest man who ever lived."[30] Only two years earlier he had made Ralph the Heir quote in Latin Caesar's famous victory proclamation "veni, vidi, vici" (chap. xlii), which he uses several times in his new little work. Merivale's book supplied much of the background and Trollope also made some use of Napoleon III's book on Caesar, about which he had written in the *Pall Mall Gazette* five years earlier.[31] As he worked on the book, he told Blackwood, "I have enjoyed it amazingly. . . . It has been a change to the spinning of novels, and has enabled me to surround myself with books & almost to think myself a scholar." It has "taken me back to the old books which I read when I was young," he told Dobson.[32]

The task was finished with remarkable speed from January 29 to April 16; he altogether set aside for the moment *The Eustace Diamonds,* on which he had been working since December 4. He sent the first half, when it was completed, to Blackwood with some trepidation, but Blackwood was much pleased, and so too was Collins, whose editorial suggestions Trollope welcomed. "I do not know that for a short period I ever worked harder. . . . I was most anxious, in this soaring out of my own particular line, not to disgrace myself. . . . Perhaps I was anxious for something more. If so, I was disappointed." When the work was done,

---

*The volumes are "very pleasant reading;—almost as good as a novel we might say."

Collins invited Anthony and Rose to visit him at his vicarage of Kilsby, near Rugby, and they spent two nights there at the end of May. "We like them very much," Collins told Blackwood; "—him especially, he was so very pleasant to talk to, and at the same time so perfectly unassuming. What I like best in Mrs. T. is her honest and hearty appreciation of her husband."[33] "I do like a woman that can thoroughly enjoy her husband's success," said Madame Max Goesler in *Phineas Redux* a few months later. "When she is talking of [him] she is completely happy" (chap. xxxvii).

When, however, he sent a copy of the little work to Merivale in June, 1870, Merivale simply thanked him for his "comic Caesar." "I do not suppose he intended to run a dagger into me. Of any suffering from such wounds, I think, while living,* I never shewed a sign; but still I have suffered occasionally. . . . Nevertheless, having read the book again within the last month or two, I make bold to say that it is a good book."[34] It is not easy to believe than an old friend like Merivale would have made a remark that could hardly be taken as amusing; quite possibly he merely thanked Trollope in a handwriting no more illegible than Trollope's own for his "Com^ies Caesar."

The little book is a private rebellion against the conventional, un- imaginative literalness of the Latin lessons he had received at Harrow and Winchester, but it is also a clear proof that he had learned there a great deal more of that language than he pretended. When he describes Caesar's bridge across the Rhine, he asks, "Is there a schoolboy in England, or one who has been a schoolboy, at any Caesar-reading school, who does not remember those memorable words, 'Tigna bina sesquipedalia,' with which Caesar begins his graphic account of the building of the bridge?" (chap. v). A full century after Trollope, schoolboys and schoolgirls in America were still building models of that bridge and were converting into miles the *milia passuum* Caesar so often logged on his marches. But Trollope's thrust is not merely to narrate, briefly, what happened, but imaginatively to make the events intelligible in terms of our own era—or that of Queen Victoria. The conquests in Gaul, Britain, and Germany which Caesar narrates in his *Commentaries* are precisely like the growth of Victoria's empire in India, of the Spanish empire in America, and of the United States in Trollope's day. "The humane reader of history execrates, as he reads, the cruel, all-absorbing, ravenous wolf. But the philosophical reader perceives that in this way, and in no other, is civilisation carried into distant lands" (chap. ii). On the other hand, the barbarous German tribes "are communists as to the soil, and stay no longer than a year on the same land. These customs they follow lest they should learn to prefer

---

*Trollope arranged to have *An Autobiography* published posthumously; hence this rather strange-sounding expression.

agriculture to war; lest they should grow fond of broad possessions, so that the rich should oppress the poor; lest they should by too much comfort become afraid of cold and heat; lest the love of money should grow among them, and one man should seek to be higher than another. From all which it seems that the Germans were not without advanced ideas in political economy" (chap. vii).

Trollope makes intelligible the broad outlines of a story that in the original is too often mired in detail. And his sense of irony occasionally leads him to smile at the humorlessness of Caesar's narrative, as when Caesar tells us without blushing that his troops were victorious because their immediate commander inspired them with faith in Caesar's greatness (chap. ix). Trollope praises Caesar's conciseness of language (which he demonstrates with a certain amount of verbosity on his own part) (chap. ix). Caesar's cruelty is repeatedly stressed; his greatness consists not in humaneness but in determination and efficiency. And though we depend for our judgment only on what Caesar himself tells us, "The reader always feels inclined to believe the Commentary, even when he may most dislike Caesar" (chap. viii). If classical texts are ever to have readers other than students of philology, they must be presented as Trollope here presented his Caesar. "The intention is to create that feeling of lightness which is produced by the handling of serious matters with light words, & which is almost needed in such a work."[35] Trollope's lightness was acknowledged in an anonymous review by Mrs. Oliphant: he "has told the story of the great Julius with much ease and spirit; almost too clearly, brightly, and well for a subject which we associate with mighty tomes and heavy periods. . . . The skill of the practised narrator conveys an unusual charm to the history." "I cannot read [Mr. Trollope's 'Caesar'] without laughing—it is so like Johnny Eames," she told Blackwood as she worked on her review.[36]

When he had corrected the final proofs, Trollope told Blackwood, "It is a dear little book to me,—and there is one other thing to be said about the little dear. I think the 1st of June is your birthday. At any rate we'll make it so for this year, and you will accept it as a little present."[37] The first of June, day of the book's publication, was not Blackwood's birthday and Trollope knew it was not, but his was a delicate compliment that gave Blackwood much pleasure.

৯৯

The subject of Anglo-American copyright naturally continued to engage attention, and on February 16 some sixteen authors and publishers met in John Murray's dining room on Albemarle Street to discuss the subject.

The publisher George Bentley jotted in his diary some characterizations of the participants; what they said was confidential and not recorded. "Dickens seemed in good health, & spoke with his accustomed warmth, as also did Anthony Trollope; Sir Charles Trevelyan was paradoxical & unreasonable. . . . Dickens every one knows; his Vandyke shaped head, his face charged with electricity, full of power, his deep blue eye, his energetic manner. Froude quiet & unobtrusive, with a sensible, 'middle-class' face. Trollope large-headed, bushy eyebrowed—heavy bearded, full faced, quick, fiery-eyed, but generous & warm." The meeting had to be resumed a month later to complete its business, and again on March 16 Bentley recorded that "Lord Stanhope took the chair. . . . Trollope told me that his brother Adolphus would be likely to leave Italy, his wife being desirous of coming to England. . . . Dickens looks better & is as genial as ever. One of his best characteristics, is his sound business habits, & good common sense."[38] Tom's move to England, however, did not take place in Anthony's lifetime.

Bentley's concern for Dickens's health was widely shared; his optimism, unfortunately, was not justified. It was a bad season for the literary world. On May 23 Mark Lemon, longtime editor of *Punch* and a good friend of Dickens's, died, and only seventeen days later Dickens was fatally stricken at his desk at Gad's Hill Place at the age of fifty-eight. Fanny Trollope's younger sister Ellen was with him when he died.

As Trollope took up his pen to write a memorial of Dickens for *Saint Pauls,* he was inevitably reminded that he and Dickens had both written on Thackeray's death for the *Cornhill* six and a half years earlier. The article—signed with Trollope's name and published in the last number of the magazine he edited—is very graceful, written, one feels, with his eye on the object. He speaks especially of Dickens's immense popularity,[*] and his unique ability to make his whole range of characters prototypical. "The man with whom something is ever about to turn up, is well-known to us, and is always considered by us to be going under an alias when he is not called Micawber." Dickens had been entirely devoted to literature, to the exclusion of all else.

> Men in so-called public life were to him . . . so placed as to be by their calling almost beyond the pale of sincerity. To his feeling all departmental work was the bungled, muddled routine of a Circumlocution Office. Statecraft was odious to him. . . . I never heard any man call Dickens a radical; but if any man ever was so, he was a radical at heart,—believing entirely in the people, writing for them,

---

[*]When Trollope wrote of the magnitude of Dickens's sales, he was not uninformed; he was intimately associated with Dickens's publishers.

speaking for them, and always desirous to take their part as against some undescribed and indiscernible tyrant, who to his mind loomed large as an official rather than as an aristocratic despot. He hardly thought that our parliamentary rulers could be trusted to accomplish ought that was good for us. Good would come gradually,—but it would come by the strength of the people, and in opposition to the blundering of our rulers.[39]

One more point presented itself to Trollope with some force: " 'Edwin Drood,' like 'Denis Duval,' and 'Wives and Daughters,' [the novel on which Mrs. Gaskell was engaged when she died,] will be left unfinished."

As he prepared his lecture "On English Prose Fiction" for future occasions, Trollope slipped into his printed text a leaf of manuscript which should bring up to date what he had been saying about the great English novelists no longer alive, and which summed up his ultimate public verdict:

> When I first prepared this lecture one was still living who certainly bore the second rank among us in our catalogue of British novelists, if he did not contest the first with Walter Scott. I speak, of course, of Charles Dickens,—who, alas has died since I gave this lecture last year at Glasgow and at Edinburgh. I would he were still living because I loved the man,—because he was a friend to literature, & because he was a beneficent man doing good to all around him,— active, wise, and humane. I know not well how to speak of him with sufficient praise on this occasion. One does not willingly make comparisons between one's dear friends;—and yet, in going through the task now before me, I am bound to do so.
>
> In the first place I may tell you with absolute truth that no novelist has ever enjoyed the popularity among English readers that has fallen to the lot of Charles Dickens. The sale of his books here and in America is a thing of itself,—and is so great as almost to induce a belief that Pickwicks and Oliver Twists are consumed in families like legs of mutton. Against a verdict from the public so palpable and plainly expressed as this no critic should lightly demur. He who has charmed millions,—and has done so, as Dickens did, without ever teaching an evil lesson,—may be held to be above criticism, and to have achieved that end to which the critic should direct the artist.
>
> Having said this, in which I am sure that you will agree with me, I will add,—feeling by no means equally sure of your assent,—that to me the characters of Dickens have not the likeness to human nature which I find in Thackeray or in Fielding. As Scott was too prone to grace his heroes and heroines with more than human dig-

nity, so has Dickens clothed his in raiment more than humanly grotesque. The heroism of Rowena is perfect but cold; and the virtues of Smike are transcendental, though very quaint. But we have never perhaps known a Rowena or a Smike as we have an Amelia Booth and a Major Pendennis.[40]

※

Busy as he was with his writing, Trollope was also on the move a good deal in 1870, though we know relatively little about his errands. He and Rose went again to Bolton Bridge in May—"the prettiest spot in England." A year later he used it as the setting for *Lady Anna*. He divided the last fortnight of June between an excursion to Ireland and a visit to his friend Sir Charles Taylor at Beauport, near Battle in Sussex. Before the year was out he had written a new, short novel in an Irish setting (*An Eye for an Eye*, written from September 13 to October 10). The outbreak of the Franco-Prussian War in mid-July prevented the annual tour of the Continent; he and Rose went to the English Lakes in August, and there he completed *The Eustace Diamonds* on August 25.[41] And on October 23 he started work on *Phineas Redux*. *The Eustace Diamonds* was contracted with Chapman for the *Fortnightly Review* to begin in July, 1871, and he was beginning to build up a backlog of manuscripts.

At Taylor's request he devoted a good deal of energy toward the end of the year to helping Lord Brougham oversee the publication of his older brother's memoirs—the well-known *Edinburgh Review*er, statesman, and lord chancellor, a universal genius of whom it was told in Edinburgh that if only he had known a little of the law, he would have known something of everything. This undertaking required a visit from Trollope to Brougham Hall, near Penrith, in September, and the book was ultimately published, but the second Lord Brougham seems to have taken very little of Trollope's advice.[42]

Chapter XIX

1871

At least as early as April 15, 1870, Anthony and Rose were planning their journey to visit Fred in Australia in the spring of 1872. As the date drew closer, the pressure became greater, especially as they were giving up their house at Waltham Cross with a view to moving into London on their return. The pace of Anthony's writing did not let up for a minute, however, and when he set sail he left behind him the manuscripts of two long novels and two short ones. A problem arose about *The Eustace Diamonds*, which was to begin publication in the *Fortnightly* on July 1, 1871; Fanny Trollope's *Anne Furness* had been running there since July, 1870, and late in March Morley wrote to Henry Trollope to suggest that perhaps his aunt could cut it short to avoid overlapping with her brother-in-law's work—or else Anthony might consent to a postponement of the beginning of his novel. Anthony indignantly held his ground, and Fanny's. "It seems to me that the redundancy of Fanny Trollope's work is entirely owing to [Morley's] own carelessness in not seeing that a proper proportion was inserted in each number of the Review."[1] Anthony won his point, and in July and August the two Trollopes appeared together. Strahan on April 14, 1871, purchased one of Anthony's short novels, *The Golden Lion of Granpere*, for publication in *Good Words*, to begin in January, 1872. Publication of his other two manuscript novels, *An Eye for an Eye* and *Phineas Redux* (completed April 1, 1871), had not yet been arranged.[2]

One very festive occasion was a small luncheon party given by Lewes and George Eliot at "The Priory" on April 23, where Trollope was to meet Ivan Turgenev; after the luncheon there was a larger assembly that included the Burne-Joneses, Mrs. Arthur Hugh Clough, and Pauline Viardot, the operatic mezzo-soprano who "sang divinely and entranced every one, some of them to positive tears." She and Turgenev had been together at Baden, and took refuge in England from the Franco-Prussian War. Among her songs that afternoon was the wonderful aria "Que farò senza Euridice" from Gluck's *Orfeo*. Next morning Turgenev was to have met Trollope at the Athenaeum Club, but they missed each other; Trollope procured for him guest privileges at the club, however. A young man who knew them both about this time described Turgenev as "a big man rather like Anthony Trollope."[3]

At the end of April, 1871, Charles Lever, in failing health and making his last visit to England from his consular post in Trieste, "had luncheon with George Eliot and dined with Trollope—a feast for Lucullus in food, and capital talking." Trollope a few years later told Lever's daughter, "[Your father and I] dined together [the evening before I started on my first journey to Australia] and I little thought that I should never see him again."[4] At the end of the decade he told Lever's biographer that Lever "was an intimate friend of mine whom I dearly loved. . . . Of all the clever men I have known, his wit was the readiest. . . . His was a kind friendly nature, prone to cakes and ale, and resolved to make the best of life when, as you no doubt know, things were often very sad with him."[5] Lever was, at least when he wrote to a close friend, a bit less enthusiastic about Trollope. "I don't think [him] *pleasant,* though he has a certain hard common-sense about him and coarse shrewdness that prevents him being dull or tiresome. His books are not of a high order, but still I am always surprised that he could write them. He is a good fellow, I believe, *au fond,* and has few jealousies and no rancours; and for a writer, is not that saying much?"[6]

ह≥

His lecture on prose fiction was still very much in Trollope's mind as he wrote *The Eustace Diamonds,* and he devoted a good part of one chapter (xxxv) to making clear that the novel which is a picture of life cannot have heroes and heroines who are perfect; indeed, despite the popular notion, they may be very imperfect. Just as the lovers of painting have come to expect the perfection of a Venus,

> so also has the reading world taught itself to like best the characters of all but divine men and women. Let the man who paints with pen and ink give the gaslight, and the fleshpots, the passions and pains, the prurient prudence and the rouge-pots and pounce-boxes of the world as it is, and he will be told that no one can care a straw for his creations. With whom are we to sympathise? says the reader, who not unnaturally imagines that a hero should be heroic. Oh, thou, my reader, whose sympathies are in truth the great and only aim of my work, when you have called the dearest of your friends round you to your hospitable table, how many heroes are there sitting at the board?

But the term *novel* has many meanings: Lady Linlithgow, a cantankerous old woman but one of taste, had Miss Edgeworth's novels downstairs, *Pride and Prejudice* in the bedroom, and did not subscribe to Mudie's Library "because when I asked for 'Adam Bede,' they always sent me the

'Bandit Chief'" (chap. xxxiv). Her very unintellectual companion Miss Macnulty was "a great devourer of novels" of another sort, and could talk for three weeks "about the sorrows of the poorest heroine that ever saw her lover murdered before her eyes, and then come to life again with ten thousand pounds a year" (chap. xxii).

Lizzie Eustace, whose diamonds give the novel its title, is one of Trollope's subtlest portraits, altogether a fascinating character. Trollope is quite misleading when he calls her, early in the novel, an "opulent and aristocratic Becky Sharp" (chap. iii). Becky had a firm purpose and was ruthless in its pursuit; Lizzie was a paradoxical weathercock. She was clever, but ignorant, especially as to practical matters. She "was quick as a lizard in turning hither and thither, but knew almost nothing" (chaps. ii, x). Her most charming quality is her devotion to poetry—Shelley, Byron, and the new Arthurian idylls of Tennyson—with her conviction that "poetry was life and life was poetry." She could sit on the rocks overlooking the sea near her Scottish castle and dream of the Corsair she was sure would sweep her away (chaps. lxv, xxvi). She craved "poetry, together with houses, champagne, jewels, and admiration" (chap. lxviii). She "liked lies, thinking them to be more beautiful than truth" (chap. lxxix). "True love, true friendship, true benevolence, true tenderness, were beautiful to her,—qualities on which she could descant almost with eloquence, and therefore she was always shamming love and friendship and benevolence and tenderness. . . . She knew that she herself was ever shamming, and she satisfied herself with shams" (chap. xiv). She simulated anger, but "was almost incapable of real anger" (chap. ii). She had a wonderful gift with language, and along with her drawing-room accomplishments was a superb horsewoman. "She's a very great woman," said her brother-in-law,—"and if the sex could have its rights, would make an excellent lawyer" (chap. lxxii).

She is surrounded by some extraordinarily seedy characters who are frequently dull, but occasionally provide comedy—as when Mrs. Carbuncle ("that horrid American woman that nobody knows anything about") energetically procures from her acquaintances wedding presents for her niece (chaps. xlvi, lxv). The man Lizzie ultimately marries is a converted Central European Jew (a reminiscence of Trollope's visit to Prague a few years earlier) who had become an exceedingly eloquent evangelical Church of England clergyman. Trollope treats him with an uncomfortably heavy hand—"a nasty, greasy, lying, squinting Jew preacher; an impostor, . . . a creature to loathe," though possessed of "a certain manliness" (chap. lxxiii). He anticipates Lopez in *The Prime Minister*, but Lopez is handled with far greater delicacy and sympathy.

As a whole, the novel is slow-moving and repetitive; the plot—the double theft of the diamond necklace—is clumsy. And yet the character of Lizzie is a masterpiece.

Though it is commonly regarded as one of the "parliamentary" novels, it has very little of politics in it. We see Plantagenet Palliser struggling with the problem of converting the coinage from the duo-decimal to the decimal system (a problem most Continental nations had already resolved, and one which was very much to the fore in England when the novel was written, as Matthew Arnold makes clear to us in "The Function of Criticism"). Palliser is determined to build upon the farthing (a "fourthing," or quarter of a penny); but there are forty-eight farthings (twelve pence) in a shilling, and the decimal system demands fifty, so that there should be a hundred farthings in a two-shilling piece. (The govern-ment that finally adopted the decimal coinage in 1971 was far bolder, abandoned both the farthing and the shilling and decreed that the former two-shilling piece should contain but ten pence instead of twenty-four.) Then comes the question of a name for the new "farthing," if it is no longer a "fourth" of anything. Well, "the 'Fortnightly Review' comes out but once a month, and I'm told that it does very well," as it brings its readers novels like *The Eustace Diamonds* (chap. lv).

The book seems especially rich in allusion to contemporary events and the London scene. Lizzie supplies her guests in Scotland with hampers of food from Fortnum and Mason of Piccadilly (chap. xxiii). One takes the new Underground to Swiss Cottage (chap. xviii). Mrs. Carbuncle's com-plexion was so lovely people said as a matter of course that she "had been made beautiful forever" (that is, had been treated in the beauty establish-ment of Mme. Rachel in New Bond Street) (chap. xxxvi). Scotland is the place to travel; "Switzerland and the Tyrol, and even Italy, are all redolent of Mr. [Thomas] Cook" (chap. xxxii). Old Lady Linlithgow is called "the duchess, after a certain popular picture in a certain popular book" (*Alice in Wonderland*) (chap. xxxiii). Lizzie and her friends go to the Haymarket Theatre to see "a new piece, 'The Noble Jilt,' from the hand of a very eminent author," but do not much care for it (chap. lii). (It was Trollope's unproduced play.) Lizzie reads Tennyson's *Holy Grail,* which was pub-lished almost at the moment Trollope wrote the chapter (xix). Trollope makes clear the social distinctions between the two parts of the West End, the more elegant section south of Oxford Street, extending from Mayfair through Belgravia and Pimlico, and the less elegant part "somewhere north of Oxford Street" where the Trollopes would buy a house on their return from Australia (chap. xiii).* Trollope's handling of the hunting

---

*For all his precision, however, Trollope cannot make up his mind whether Lady Linlithgow lives on Bruton Street or Brook Street.

scene in this book is perhaps more satisfying to those who do not know the sport, since he adopts the device of having Lord George Carruthers explain it all to Lizzie as they take part in it. In his recent novels, Trollope has taken to giving from time to time both date and day of the week for letters or events. In *The Vicar of Bullhampton* these were quite inconsistent with one another; here, all but one will fit into a pattern of 1865, 1866, and 1867 successively.

The book closes with the promise of a sequel (*Phineas Redux*), on which indeed Trollope set to work within two months of finishing *The Eustace Diamonds*. Not long after the book appeared, Disraeli met Trollope at Lord Stanhope's dinner table and remarked: "I have long known, Mr. Trollope, your churchmen and churchwomen; may I congratulate you on the same happy lightness of touch in the portrait of your new adventuress?" The compliment was the greater because Disraeli was not a frequent reader of novels; "When I want to read a novel, I write one."[7]

An Eye for an Eye is a novel about the same length as *Nina Balatka* and *Linda Tressel,* with its setting at the spectacular Cliffs of Moher in County Clare on the west coast of Ireland—an area familiar to Rose and Anthony from Anthony's Post Office work the year after they were married. The Protestant heir to the earldom of Scroope, which has its seat at Scroope Manor, about eleven miles from Dorchester in southwest England, falls in love with the Roman Catholic daughter of a presumed widow who lives in a cottage near the top of the cliff; he is serving in the army and stationed at Ennis. Like many of Trollope's heroes of this period, he is generous, well-meaning, and weak; the girl has already become pregnant when he inherits the earldom and decides that he cannot properly make her a Countess. He good-naturedly returns to the cottage to announce his decision; the girl's mother, beside herself, pushes him to his death over the six-hundred-foot sheer precipice, and spends the rest of her life in an asylum repeating the scriptural phrase "An eye for an eye." The story analyzes the motives of the young man so repetitively as to lose the reader's attention. Trollope allows himself only a very little local color: when the young heir went back to the cottage after an absence of several weeks,

> he was sick indeed, of everything Irish, and thought that the whole island was a mistake. . . . How ugly the country was to his eyes as he now saw it. Here and there stood a mud cabin, and the small, half-cultivated fields, or rather patches of land, in which the thin oat crops now beginning to be green were surrounded by low loose ramshackle walls, which were little more than heaps of stone, so carelessly had they been built and so negligently preserved. A few

cocks and hens with here and there a miserable, starved pig seemed to be the stock of the country. Not a tree, not a shrub, not a flower was there to be seen. The road was narrow, rough, and unused. The burial ground which he passed was the liveliest sign of humanity about the place. Then the country became still wilder, and there was no road. The oats also ceased, and the walls. But he could hear the melancholy moan of the waves, which he had once thought to be musical and had often sworn that he loved. Now the place with all its attributes was hideous to him, distasteful, and abominable. (Chap. xvi)

෨

Phineas Redux—"Phineas Brought Back"—is first of all, of course, the planned sequel to *Phineas Finn.* That promising young Irish politician had surrendered his post as undersecretary for the colonies and given up his seat in Parliament over a difference with his Liberal party chiefs on Irish tenant rights, which he wished to see protected; he had retired to a minor Civil Service post in Ireland and married his boyhood sweetheart. As the new novel begins, their brief marriage has already ended with her death and the Liberals have been displaced in power by the Conservatives under Prime Minister Daubeny. Finn's friends remember his charm and promise, and induce him to return to England and stand for Parliament in a general election in the hope of strengthening their position in the House; he assents and becomes a candidate for the fictitious coal-mining and manufacturing borough of Tankerville, in the county of Durham, an utterly corrupt constituency that bears great resemblance to its neighboring borough of Beverley. Finn is defeated by a very narrow margin, but the election is overthrown on the grounds of bribery, Finn is seated and the Conservative candidate is subjected to criminal penalties. (This was no doubt the result Trollope in his rosier dreams had hoped for at Beverley.) And so Finn thinks to resume the path to glory he had given up in the earlier novel.

Phineas Redux is more firmly embedded in contemporary British politics than any other of Trollope's novels, and is interesting for its discussions of political theory that supplement what he had been writing for the evening *Pall Mall Gazette* and *Saint Pauls Magazine.* (He makes a backhanded allusion to the former paper when he lets the scandalmongering editor of the *People's Banner,* Quintus Slide, speak of "the hextent of the duties, privileges, and hinfluences of the daily press;—the daily morning press, that is; for I look on those little evening scraps as just so much paper and ink wasted" [chap. xxii].) Phineas, in the Tankerville campaign, had spoken in favor of disestablishment of the Church of England, sound Liberal doctrine though Finn's party had not made it part of their platform in this campaign. Then Daubeny, aware of the success of Disraeli's Conservatives in carrying urban household suffrage in 1867 after repeated failure by the Liberals to bring in an acceptable reform bill, determined once more to "dish the Whigs" by introducing legislation to disestablish the Church: the Liberals then would be forced either to support a Prime Minister they wished to unseat, or to oppose legislation they were on principle in favor of. They chose the latter course, Daubeny's government had to yield to the Liberal government of Mr. Gresham, and Finn's prospects were hopeful. In all the discussion of the issue in the novel, Trollope kept before his readers the Disraeli-Gladstone conflict as well as the success of the Conservative Sir Robert Peel in 1846 with the repeal of the Corn Laws, a decidedly Liberal measure which the Liberals had been unable to carry through.

Unfortunately Finn's friendship for Lady Laura Kennedy rose up to haunt him. Lady Laura had left her husband in the earlier novel, finding his doctrine of matrimonial dominance and of rigid Calvinist religious observance intolerable; Kennedy assumed, incorrectly, that Lady Laura had left him out of love for Finn, and when Finn at Lady Laura's request visited her in Dresden, where she was living in exile with her father, Kennedy wrote an angry letter for publication in the *People's Banner* libeling Finn. Hoping to forestall publication, Finn called on Kennedy in his London hotel, where the unbalanced husband fired a pistol at Finn's head (but missed his mark altogether). Kennedy was clearly insane, and was recognized as insane by his family, but the scandal was published by Slide in the *Banner* in the interest of "purity of morals," and, by the way, of selling a great many copies of the paper (chap. xxii). The scandal, together with Finn's having supported Church disestablishment in his Tankerville campaign and with the hostility of one of the rising powers in the Liberal party, Mr. Bonteen, kept Finn from any lucrative appointment in the government and left him thoroughly discouraged.

But a sequel had been promised to another, more recent, work, and *Phineas Redux* is in fact two novels rather weakly patched together. Lizzie Eustace "was a most interesting young woman," said Lady Glencora (now Duchess of Omnium), "and I sincerely hope we have not got to the end of her yet" (*Eustace Diamonds,* chap. xlvi). Lizzie, like Lady Laura, left her thoroughly disagreeable husband Joseph Emilius and was championed by Mr. and Mrs. Bonteen. One night, after an open quarrel between Finn and Bonteen at their club, the Universe, Bonteen had his head battered in on the dark street; two people, Finn and Emilius, had been known to hate him, but the evidence seemed to point to Finn as the murderer; he was remanded for trial and imprisoned in Newgate. The second half of the novel is devoted to the melodrama of the trial, in which a last-minute bit of evidence shakes the case against him and he is acquitted. Emilius is found guilty of bigamy, having left behind a wife in Cracow before he married Lady Eustace, but, though his principal alibi is disproved by the efforts of Madame Max Goesler, the evidence that he was the murderer was never strong enough to bring him to trial for that crime. Unfortunately the "interesting young woman" of the Duchess of Omnium's recollection scarcely appears in this novel, and there is here nothing memorable about her beyond Trollope's valedictory: "She would still continue to play her game as before, would still scheme, would still lie; and might still, at last, land herself in that Elysium of life of which she had been always dreaming. Poor Lizzie Eustace! Was it nature or education which had made it impossible to her to tell the truth, when a lie came to her hand? Lizzie, the liar! Poor Lizzie!" (chap. lxxii). There remains the question of the relation between literature and life. One of the principal fools in the story, Thomas Platter Spooner, "remembered," as he thought of a young lady's rejection of him, "that he had read . . . that lovers in novels generally do persevere, and that they are almost always successful at last," and so he tried again to persuade the young lady, but in vain (chap. xix). On the other hand, the Duchess tells another prospective young husband who hopes that "the romance and poetry do not all vanish" with marriage that "romance and poetry are for the most part lies, . . . and are very apt to bring people into difficulty" (chap. lxxvi). For this second young suitor, a rather mindless fellow only slightly superior intellectually to his utterly selfish, idle father (both of them excellent comic characters) Trollope has chosen the surname of "Maule," whether deliberately or not; Anthony's mother, with Tom and Cecilia, had spent a few weeks in lodgings at Dover in early September, 1838, before establishing themselves in York Street, and there they had seen much of the Reverend Mr. Maule, rector of St. Mary's, Dover, who was married to one of Mrs. Trollope's Bristol cousins.[8]

Anthony had introduced himself into *Can You Forgive Her?* as the hunting gentleman, Bouncer, who did a day's work at his writing desk before dawn; "old Bouncer, the man who writes," was also present at the Universe Club on Charles Street when Bonteen and Finn quarreled, and he testified at the trial (chap. lxi). The Universe was in fact the Cosmopolitan, of the same address, a club at which Trollope spent many very pleasant evenings. And Emilius, when he lost his church because of the separation from Lizzie, took the lodgings Trollope himself lived in as a young man in London, on Northumberland Street, where the lodging-house keeper in the novel had the symbolic name of "Mrs. Meager" (chap. lvi). She was able to testify that Emilius took the house key away with him when he journeyed to Prague, where he might have had a duplicate made, though he said he had left it in a drawer; "we always knows what's in the drawers."*

Phineas in the earlier novel had rescued Kennedy from the attack of a thug, and thereafter he carried with him a "life preserver," a short stick with a heavily loaded end, as protection against night attacks, against "ruffians in the street" (chap. lx). It was his carrying this weapon that led to the suspicion that he had murdered Bonteen, but in fact he had only been following the prudent advice of the worldly-wise newspapers of real-life London. This was by no means the advice Trollope would follow; in an early number of *Saint Pauls* he had written an article on "The Uncontrolled Ruffianism of London, as Measured by the Rule of Thumb," and his "rule of thumb" was personal experience, against the fearful published statistics: he himself had never known anyone who was attacked, nor even anyone who knew anyone who was attacked. As for pickpockets, the closest he had come was his wife's claim that a handkerchief was taken from her as she got out of a cab; but "we who knew the habits of the lady always thought that that handkerchief had been left upon the cab-seat." And so, despite the horrors told about Professor Fagin's establishment in *Oliver Twist,* he would continue to carry a pocket watch and money and "go mooning along the pavements as we have done every day for the last thirty years," without a knobstick, certainly without a revolver, but "accompanied by a somewhat soft and ancient umbrella, which we love well"—an umbrella "with a large knob," as he described it to a friend at whose house he left it a few years later.[9]

Even the reader who finds the melodrama a bit overdone will be kept alert and happy by the unexpected wit so often encountered, the worldly wisdom that explodes sentimentality, and the illumination of the Victorian political and judicial system. The book seems especially rich in literary allusion, as phrases from the Bible and the *Aeneid,* from Terence and Horace, Shakespeare, Milton, even Elizabeth Barrett Browning, are so often at the tip of the author's pen.

&

Before starting [for Australia] there came upon us the terrible necessity of coming to some resolution about our house at Waltham. It had been first hired, and then bought, primarily because it suited my Post Office avocations. To this reason had been added other attractions,—in the shape of hunting, gardening, and suburban hospitalities. Altogether the house had been a success, and the scene of

---

*"We victuallers ken well aneugh what goes on in our ain houses," said Meg Dods, the innkeeper in Scott's *St. Ronan's Well.* "And what for no? — . . . I e'en listened through the keyhole of the door" (chap. xiv).

much happiness. But there arose questions as to expense. Would not a house in London be cheaper? There could be no doubt that my income would decrease, and was decreasing. I had thrown the Post Office, as it were, away, and the writing of novels could not go on for ever. Some of my friends already told me that at fifty-five I ought to give up the fabrication of love-stories. The hunting, I thought, must soon go, and I would not therefore allow that to keep me in the country. And then, why should I live at Waltham Cross now, seeing that I had fixed on that place in reference to the Post Office? It was therefore determined that we would flit, and as we were to be away for eighteen months, we determined also to sell our furniture. So there was packing up, with many tears, and consultations as to what should be saved out of the things we loved.

As must take place on such an occasion, there was some heart-felt grief. But the thing was done, and orders were given for the letting or sale of the house. I may as well say here that it never was let, and that it remained unoccupied for two years before it was sold. I lost by the transaction about £800. As I continually hear that other men make money by buying and selling houses, I presume I am not well adapted for transactions of that sort. I have never made money by selling anything except a manuscript. In matters of horseflesh I am so inefficient that I have generally given away horses that I have not wanted. [10]

Needless to say, making the arrangements for departure was accompanied by "great bustle and perturbation," as Trollope wrote to James T. Fields, but worse was at hand: he and Rose had booked passage from Liverpool on May 6, but "Alas for us, the wretched ambition which wrecked the Queen of the Thames on its homeward journey* has caused our vessel to be postponed 18 days, & we do not sail till the 24th,— which is an incredible nuisance to us, being as we are homeless wanderers. We are in all the misery of living about among friends and pot-houses,— going through that very worst phase of life which consists in a continuous and ever failing attempt to be jolly, with nothing to do. . . . My only doubt as to finding a heaven for myself at last, arises from the fear that the disembodied and beatified spirits will not want novels." On May 24 they finally got off aboard the *Great Britain,* and the next day he began to write *Lady Anna.* [11]

---

*The *Queen of the Thames* ran aground and was wrecked near the Cape of Good Hope on March 18, on a return voyage from Melbourne. Since she had made a record-breaking run out, the *Times* (April 28, p. 9e) conjectured that she had run too close to shore in the attempt to save a few miles and make an even speedier return. For whatever reason, since the weather was clear and calm, her navigator was patently incompetent.

The motif of the novel was one he was to use again a few years later in *Is He Popenjoy?* Was the heroine "Lady Anna Lovel" or was she more properly "Miss Anna Murray"? Earl Lovel had married Josephine Murray in due form at Applethwaite parish church in Cumberland, but within six months he thrust her out, pregnant and penniless, with the announcement that he had a prior wife in Italy still living at the time of the marriage. The English wife, and the daughter born to her, were given shelter and money by a Benthamite Radical tailor and his son in Keswick. The villainous Earl was of a type Trollope was beginning to like—Lord George de Bruce Carruthers and Sir Griffin Tewett in *The Eustace Diamonds,* the Marquis of Brotherton in *Is He Popenjoy?*—the vicious aristocrat common also in contemporary sensation novels like *The Woman in White.* After the wicked Earl's death, litigation established the mother's right to the title of Countess Lovel and the daughter's to the courtesy title due to an Earl's daughter, Lady Anna Lovel. Even more important, the litigation established their right as widow and legitimate daughter to inherit the almost limitless fortune of the Earl. Here, as elsewhere, Trollope shows his delight in forensic argument.* The heir to the title, a distant cousin, was left with no inheritance beyond a small entailed property, and so the Lovel family was eager to arrange a marriage between him and Lady Anna. She, however, had fallen in love with the tailor's son (also a tailor) and insisted on keeping her pledge to marry him. When her mother, proud of her now established rank, was horrified at the girl's plan to marry an ordinary tradesman, she kept them apart and treated Lady Anna with such bitterness that the girl fell desperately ill; fortunately she did not die of a broken heart as Emily Hotspur had done. With operatic melodrama the Countess attempts to kill the young tailor; her pistol shot wounds him seriously but he recovers.

For reasons never apparent, unless to make the date correspond more nearly to the time of the Trollope/Tilley move to Penrith, in the same region, the novel is set back in time to the early part of the century: Lady Anna was born in 181— and married in the thirties, while William IV was still on the throne; it appears, in fact, that Trollope had the calendar for 1835–36 before him. Stagecoach and coastal steamer were still the means of travel. Thomas Thwaite, the tailor father, knew Southey and Wordsworth (died 1843 and 1850) in Keswick and Rydal, and indeed a whole chapter is devoted to an interview between Daniel Thwaite and "the Keswick poet" in which Trollope once more discusses the relation between poetry and life. "I have written much of love," the poet says,

---

*As with *The Eustace Diamonds,* he sought the advice of a barrister friend on the legal technicalities; among his working papers is a sheet of questions in his handwriting, with answers by the unidentified consultant. [12]

"and have ever meant to write the truth. . . . But the love of which we poets sing is not the love of the outer world. It is more ecstatic, but far less serviceable. It is the picture of that which exists, but grand with imaginary attributes, as are the portraits of ladies painted by artists who have thought rather of their art than of their models. We tell of a constancy in love which is hardly compatible with the usages of this as yet imperfect world" (chap. xxvi). On the other hand, the lawyer who argues on "some romantic idea of abstract right" rather than from partisan interest acts "in direct opposition to all the usages of forensic advocacy as established in England," and "ought to have been a poet" (chap. xxxiii).

Trollope summarized his aim in a letter to a friend and fellow novelist, Lady Wood (a widow who began to write fiction at the age of sixty-four to bolster her income):

> Of course the girl has to marry the tailor. It is very dreadful, but there was no other way. The story was originated in my mind by an idea I had as to the doubt which would, (or might) exist in a girls mind as to whether she ought to be true to her troth, or true to her lineage, when, from early circumstances the one had been given in a manner detrimental to the other—and I determined that in such case she ought to be true all through. To make the discrepancy as great as possible I made the girl an Earls daughter, and the betrothed a tailor. All the horrors had to be invented to bring about a condition in which an Earls daughter could become engaged to a tailor without glaring fault on her side.[13]

Daniel Thwaite's egalitarian Radicalism is eloquent and well reasoned, though he fully intends to abide by the laws and customs which will give him absolute control of his wife's fortune. "For a man with sound views of domestic power and marital rights always choose a Radical!" Trollope comments, ironically (chap. xlv). A great part of the book is devoted to the debate on equality and to the definition of a gentleman, in which a delicate balance is held between the points of view. "Sir William Patterson was a gentleman as well as a lawyer,—one who had not simply risen to legal rank by diligence and intellect, but a gentleman born and bred, who had been at a public school, and had lived all his days with people of the right sort" (chap. xviii), and it is Sir William who persuades Daniel Thwaite to less rigid and hostile ways, and wins his friendship. In very many respects Thwaite is a reincarnation of Ontario Moggs of *Ralph the Heir,* and perhaps also of George Eliot's Felix Holt, the Radical.

Trollope's own life again finds its echoes in the novel. Lady Anna's mother moves from Wyndham Street (where Anthony lived as a young clerk in the Post Office) to Keppel Street, where he was born, and the banns for Lady Anna's marriage were published in Bloomsbury Church, where Anthony was baptized. (In the event, however, the wedding took place in Cumberland.) A very pleasant excursion is taken to Wharfedale and Bolton Abbey, where Anthony and Rose had recently spent their summer holidays. "There isn't a better inn in England than the Devonshire Arms;—and I don't think a pleasanter spot" (chap. xiv). The young Earl Lovel's two cousins went to Harrow (chap. v).

As so frequently of late, especially in his less complex novels, Trollope becomes very repetitious, indeed as a matter of art. His characters review in their minds events we already have seen, in a kind of stream of consciousness that serves to explain their course of action. In the end, Thwaite and Lady Anna marry and emigrate to the egalitarian world of Australia, on whose shore Trollope would land on July 27, eight days after penning the concluding lines that tell of their decision. Once more he promises a sequel, no doubt intending to use the life he would see there as material for this new novel; but the sequel was not written.

Chapter XX

1871–72

Australia in 1871 was a geographical rather than a political entity; it was made up of six separate colonies (Victoria, New South Wales, South Australia, Queensland, Tasmania, and Western Australia), each with its own legislature (chosen by various methods) and its own governor sent out from London. Their populations ranged from three-quarters of a million to 25,000, and there were also 600 souls in the vast Northern Territory which existed almost exclusively as the base for the overland telegraph line that was then linked to London. In nothing, perhaps, was the separateness of these colonies so marked as in the existence of customs barriers between them; the London government had decreed that if the colonial legislatures set up any trade barriers at all, these must be applied uniformly against other Australian colonies and against other nations.

Practically speaking, the colonization of Australia had occurred entirely within the fifty-six years of Trollope's lifetime; he would have said within his memory: "Distance is a term of comparison. A hundred years back is very little. There are many among us who remember well the greater part of the period themselves, and know the other part by the memory of their parents. The history of the French Revolution is to us as the history of our own times."[1] The white population was almost entirely European-born. First there had been the penal colonies to which convicts like Abel Magwitch in *Great Expectations* (1860–61) were sent; then as voluntary emigration increased the exportation of convicts was discontinued. But remnants of the convict population remained, some still in prisons, others in honorable positions in the community, though liable to be referred to as "lags." Until their sentences expired there were some restrictions on their movements, and when Trollope wanted to travel from Western Australia to South Australia he was obliged to obtain a magistrate's certificate that he "[was] not and never [had] been a prisoner of the Crown in Western Australia." (He was less offended by the indignity than by having had to pay a shilling for the certificate.)[2]

Australia and New Zealand were important places of refuge from the overpopulation of the crowded home islands, and there was in fact considerable movement back and forth. The chancellor of the Exchequer in London when Trollope made his voyage, Robert Lowe, practiced law in New South Wales from 1843 to 1850 and was a member of the Legislative

Council there; the Irish rebel Sir Charles Gavan Duffy, after some years as member of the Imperial Parliament in Westminster, emigrated and was for many years a member of the Parliament of Victoria; he was premier of Victoria when Trollope was there. Matthew Arnold's oldest brother Thomas spent the years 1847–56 in New Zealand and Tasmania. Alfred Tennyson d'Orsay Dickens went out in 1865 and his brother Edward Bulwer Lytton Dickens followed three years later. (India was a much less favorable alternative: Walter Landor Dickens was commissioned in the East India Company's army and died in India.) For many an Englishman, Irishman, Scotsman, and Welshman Australia would be a future home, and Trollope's journey there was not to be merely a holiday visit to his son: he determined to gather as much data about the colonies as he could, travel as strenuously as he could to see conditions for himself, and write a book which should be not a mere travelogue but a compendium of sociological information. The concluding paragraph of his book sums up his aim:

> For men who can and will work with their hands, for women who can cook and be generally useful about a household, for girls who are ready to learn to cook and to be generally useful, these colonies are a paradise. They will find the whole condition of life changed for them. The slight estimation in which labour is held here [in England] will be changed for a general respect. The humbleness, the hat-touching, the servility which is still incidental to such work as theirs in this old country, and which is hardly compatible with exalted manhood, has found no footing there. I regard such manhood among the masses of the people as the highest sign of prosperity which a country can give.[3]

The book on India which George Smith had wanted him to write a decade earlier was never undertaken; this in a sense took its place, and is a prodigious achievement. When he left England he had signed an agreement with Chapman and Hall for the publication of the book (for which they would give £1,250), and with the *Daily Telegraph* for the publication of a series of letters he would send home currently.[4]

He carried with him introductions and (though the letters seem not to have survived) he had written in advance to people who might be helpful, so that his mission was well known and he was followed with interest by the newspapers, which enable us to trace his travels.[5] It appears that after their arrival at Melbourne (Victoria) he and Rose embarked for Sydney (New South Wales); there Rose traveled westward to Fred's sheep-raising station at Mortray while Anthony continued by ship to Brisbane in Queensland. It was more than two and a half months before he rejoined her at the station.

My wife had brought a cook with her from England who was invaluable,—or would have been had she not found a husband for herself when she had been about a month in the bush. But in spite of her love, and her engagement to a man who was considerably above her in position, she was true to us while she remained at M[ortray], and did her best to make us all comfortable. She was a good-looking, strong woman, of excellent temper, who could do anything she put her hand to, from hair-dressing and confectionery up to making butter and brewing beer. I saw her six months afterwards,—'quite the lady,' but ready for any kind of work that might come in her way. When I think of her, I feel that no woman of that kind ought, as regards herself, to stay in England if she can take herself or get herself taken to the colonies. I mention our cook because her assistance certainly tended very greatly to our increased comfort.[6]

There was the usual newspaper confusion between Rose and her late mother-in-law: "While the author is upon his excursion," said the Sydney *Empire*, "the authoress his wife, is quietly mingling with bush society, the guest of her son, and his friends and neighbours."[7]

Wherever he went, Trollope enjoyed hospitality as though he were an official guest; he was given temporary membership in the chief clubs, or was entertained in the homes of government officers. Dinners were given in his honor. He observed the colonial legislatures in action. Within two months of his arrival, George William Rusden, clerk of the Legislative Council of Victoria, dedicated to him a pamphlet on the history of Melbourne; the two became good friends.[8] Whenever he expressed a curiosity about anything, his hosts arranged for him to see it— sometimes, indeed, with a persistence that was a trifle bothersome. He was eager to descend into a gold mine, but quickly discovered that one visit showed him all he wanted to see; yet whenever he got near a mine he was pressed to descend.

I went down a mine at Wallaroo, finding it always to be a duty to go down a shaft on visiting any mining locality,—and I came up again. But I cannot say that I saw anything when I was down there. . . . I went through it like a man, without complaint,—and was simply very much fatigued. As I rose to the air I swore I would never go down another mine, and hitherto I have kept my vow. . . . [At] one gold-field I found a young man whom I had known at home, who had been at school with my sons, and had frequented my house. . . . [He and his mate] had found no gold as yet, and did not seem to expect to find it. . . . He had been softly nurtured, well educated, and was a handsome fellow to boot; and there he was eating a nauseous lump of beef out of a greasy frying-pan with his pocket knife, just in front of the contiguous blankets stretched on the ground, which constituted the beds of himself and his companion.[9]

It gave Trollope great pleasure to note that a mining company named the Disraeli Company apparently paid no dividends. In due course a new shaft at Ballarat was named "Sir Anthony Trollope" in honor of his visit; whether this shaft paid off is not disclosed.[10]

Everywhere he went he encountered people he had known, or whose families he had known, at home. At Rockhampton, the grandnephew of Henry Hart Milman, late dean of St. Paul's, was engaged in boiling down tallow at a meat-processing establishment.[11] An innkeeper in a village in the midst of a forest had been butler in the house of a friend at home. A legislator in Tasmania was a former convict whose family he had known in Ireland.[12] A Winchester schoolfellow, who had once served in the Prussian army (as it had once been proposed that Anthony serve in the Austrian cavalry), was resident magistrate at Albany, Western Australia.[13] The commissioner of police at Adelaide had been his schoolfellow at Harrow, and the owner of a large cattle station in South Australia had also been an (older) Harrow contemporary.[14] In New Zealand, one of the founders of the Canterbury settlement was John Robert Godley, "whom I remember as a boy at school [Harrow] thoroughly respected by all his schoolfellows," and at Picton, a little farther to the north, he "found the son of an English friend, who himself had been among the earliest of the New Zealand settlers, superintending the creation of a railway from thence to Blenheim." The town of Drury, near Auckland, was "so called from my old friend and [Harrow] schoolfellow, Captain Drury, Lord Byron's godson, who surveyed the coasts in these parts, and selected the site of the capital."[15] When Fred Trollope first went out to Australia he carried a letter of introduction from Millais and his wife to Effie's brothers George and John Gray, though as they did not respond when he wrote to them he never met either until 1884. In 1881 Fred met a man named Russell in the Lands Office who had been Anthony's fag at Harrow. "He said that you once had a great fight and at last beat your man," Fred wrote to his father.[16]

After his travels in Queensland and a few towns in northern New South Wales, Anthony spent some three weeks (about October 20 to November 12) at Mortray, his son's station near Grenfell. At Grenfell he stopped to pick up Fred's fiancée, Susannah Farrand, daughter of a police magistrate at Forbes, whom he found very much prettier than her photograph—"a good humoured pleasant little girl; who, I think will make Fred a Good wife." They lost their way in the forest as they drove to Mortray, but managed to find it, and found Fred hard at work washing his sheep. The house was better than Anthony had expected. At Mortray he could observe Australia's most important commercial enterprise, sheep grazing, at first hand. The work was very strenuous, and required great physical stamina. The "squatter" (proprietor of the large sheep station, who owned the stock and fenced the paddock, but did not own the land) "should be social,—for he must entertain often and be entertained by other squatters; but he must be indifferent to society, for he will live away from towns and be often alone with his family. . . . The joy that mostly endears his life to him is the joy that he need not dress for dinner." By evening the men were thoroughly fatigued, and so "the recreations of the evening consisted chiefly of tobacco in the verandah."

> I did endeavour to institute a whist table, but I found that my friends, who were wonderfully good in regard to the age and points of a sheep, and who could tell to the fraction of a penny what the wool of each was worth by the pound, never could be got to remember the highest card of the suit. I should not have minded that had they not so manifestly despised me for regarding such knowledge as important. They were right, no doubt, as the points of a sheep are of more importance than the pips of a card, and the human mind will hardly admit of the two together. Whist is a jealous mistress;—and so is a sheep-station.[17]

His son did, however, stage a kangaroo hunt for him, and "I confess that in the absence of fox-hunting I enjoyed it very much."[18] Six months later he participated in another variety of the Australian version of his favorite sport—following the Melbourne staghounds. The season opened with "a great hunt breakfast—or luncheon," then the two hundred or so participants wandered up and down on their steeds, uncertain when the chase would begin or what they would be pursuing—perhaps a dingo, thought Trollope. He never found out. When the chase began his horse nobly cleared some high barriers, but then he rode straight through what appeared to be an opening. Neither the horse nor the near-sighted rider saw a wire stretched across it; "the two of us were rolled over in ignominious dismay." The horse recovered and ran off, while Anthony was left to wander lost in a forest of gum trees. Fortunately he was rescued by other huntsmen and even his horse was recovered to carry him the twelve miles to his stopping-place for the night. The newspapers called attention to his misfortune, but one of them was at least kind enough to add that a memorable number of accidents had occurred on that day.[19]

Rose now joined him in his travels, the first month of which was spent in and near Sydney. He visited schools, gave expert testimony before a select committee on the Civil Service, and was a guest at a picnic of cabinet ministers which was followed by a boat excursion down the Hawkesbury River, "among river scenery as lovely as any which I ever beheld." One of the reaches of the river was subsequently named after him.[20] They then went on to Melbourne, where he gave a public lecture on "Modern Fiction as a Rational Amusement," which got much advance publicity in the newspapers but proved disappointing to the audience: many could not hear it, and those who could found the subject altogether unfamiliar.[21] It was now close to the heart of the summer; temperatures reached 106 degrees, and though in general Melbourne's water supply was excellent, on this occasion neither at the house in town nor at a friend's house in the country could a bathtub be filled.[22] He amazed himself "at the diligence with which [he] walked through institutions of every kind"—lunatic asylums, other hospitals, jails—and since Melbourne is built on two hills and the valley between them, "these afford rising ground sufficient to cause considerable delay to the obese and middle-aged pedestrian when the hot winds are blowing."[23] His detailed account of Melbourne and Ballarat (down to the observation that there were "84 miles of streets, 164 miles of foot pavement,—there ought to be 168, if every mile of street were fairly dealt by") makes clear the alert attention with which he wrote his descriptions: it is a book that combined the statistical with lively observation. "I am afraid that domestic details may not be very interesting to general readers, but they may serve to afford to some intending emigrant an idea of the fate which he would meet."[24]

At Ballarat, "the gold-field city," there were again many "institutions" to visit. He and Rose were guests of the mayor one evening at a performance at the Theatre Royal, then, after taking her back to the hotel, he and the mayor, escorted by a police sergeant, "took a tour of Ballarat East at a later hour, and had an opportunity of witnessing a picture of life amongst the Chinese and the free and easy Europeans"; "the wickedness of the town" was as much a subject of his inquiry as its schools, hospitals, libraries, hotels, and public gardens.[25]

Whether Rose accompanied him to any other of the Australian colonies is not clear; probably she remained at Mortray. In Hobart, at the beginning of the new year, he made the acquaintance of the premier of Tasmania, James Milne Wilson, "and I thought that I had not met a sounder politician in Australia."[26] There the Church of England cathedral was being replaced, but "funds are needed" and he gave his lecture on "Modern Fiction as a Recreation for Young People" for the benefit of the building fund.[27] It was characteristic of Trollope to wish to repay favors. When in Western Australia tribal inmates of a prison put on a "corroboree," or dance, for him he purchased five shillings worth of tobacco for distribution among the performers, and "was assured that the evening would be remembered as a very great occasion in the prison."[28]

He had reached Western Australia by steamer from Melbourne to Albany, then journeyed to Perth, the colony's capital, in company with a young Scotsman, in a specially hired conveyance which was on the road for four days, but allowed them to stop and sleep at night.

This we did, taking our own provisions with us, and camping out in the bush under blankets. The camping out was, I think, rather pride on our part, to show the Australians that we . . . could sleep on the ground, *sub dio,* and do without washing, and eat nastiness out of a box, as well as they could. There were police barracks in which we might have got accommodation. At any rate, going and coming we had our way. We lit fires for ourselves, and boiled our tea in billies; and then regaled ourselves with bad brandy and water out of pannikins, cooked bacon and potatoes in a frying-pan, and pretended to think that it was very jolly. My Scotch friend was a young man, and was, perhaps, in earnest. For myself, I must acknowledge that when I got up about five o'clock on a dark wet morning, very damp, with the clothes and boots on which I was destined to wear for the day, with the necessity before me of packing up my wet blankets, and endeavoured, for some minutes in vain, to wake the snoring driver, who had been couched but a few feet from me, I did not feel any ardent desire to throw off for ever the soft luxuries of an effeminate civilisation, in order that I might permanently enjoy the freedom of the bush. But I did it, and it is well to be able to do it.[29]

In Perth he was the guest of the police magistrate Edward Wilson Landor, a young cousin of Walter Savage Landor, who had emigrated with a broken heart when he was deemed by her father unsuitable to marry Landor's daughter Julia.[30] E. W. Landor placed his study at Trollope's disposal, where he could do his writing. More than half a century later two people who remembered Trollope's visit recalled that he accompanied the Landor family to an evening party at which the hosts's daughter made her debut. He showed up in everyday clothes with a blue shirt that shocked the host and other guests in their evening costumes. (It seems quite likely that, with so much of his traveling being done on horseback or under other difficult circumstances, he had no evening clothes with him.) But worse was to come: seated in a place of honor next to the debutante, he had the misfortune to upset a cup of coffee on her new white frock. When he returned to England, he sent Mrs. Landor a specially bound, inscribed copy of *The Claverings.*[31]

He next did a month's tour of South Australia, then went overland through Victoria to Mortray, which he reached about the middle of June. While he and Rose were visiting Sydney and Melbourne the preceding December Fred had married Susie (December 14). They expected their neighbor Alfred Dickens for dinner on June 17. Toward the end of the month Anthony, Rose, and Fred went to Sydney, then sailed round to Melbourne. Before he left Sydney, Anthony applied to the premier of New South Wales to have Fred made a magistrate in the Forbes district, and the appointment was duly made. At Melbourne Anthony and Rose were guests at the governor's annual ball (July 24, at Government House), and were reported by the newspapers to have danced the first set. On July 29, the parents sailed for New Zealand. "Bad farewell to my dearest Boy—very sad—Ah me!"[32]

ঽ৯

Trollope began writing his book on Australia on October 23, 1871, immediately after his first arrival at Mortray; thereafter, there were periods in which he wrote with his accustomed regularity and, as might be expected, occasional long lapses.[33] From mid-January to March 24, 1872, there were only five days of writing, when he was on shipboard from Melbourne to Albany, Western Australia (March 2–6). From mid-April to May 25 he was traveling strenuously in South Australia and western Victoria and wrote on only three days while he was relaxing at the house of a friend at Colac. On board ship to New Zealand (July 30–August 3) he wrote two introductory chapters on Victoria, which called up a whole list of questions for Rusden to answer.[34] There were sixteen days of writing out of his two months in New Zealand; then he worked nearly every day on shipboard from New Zealand to San Francisco (about October 4 to November 4) and from New York to England (about November 27 to December 6). There was a little tidying up to do in London, so that he was writing on Christmas day, and he missed his contractual deadline of December 31, 1872, by about a fortnight.[35] His eleven letters to the *Daily Telegraph,* signed "An Antipodean," were written at the same time as the corresponding sections of the book, and indeed all but three were published after he had begun his homeward voyage.[36]

New Zealand was, in itself, a more exciting adventure than Australia had been; its settlement was more recent and impinged more on his adult consciousness. As recently as 1844, Macaulay, seeking a parallel for the Reign of Terror in the French Revolution, remarked that the space of "a few months had sufficed to degrade France below the level of New Zealand." The Maoris had been far more successful in their combats with the settlers than the aborigines of Australia had been, and in addition the Maoris were cannibals. Though the war against them ended as recently as 1865, there were still raids, and one notable Maori hero named Te Kooti was still evading capture when Trollope was there.

> I found myself struck, for a moment, with the peculiarity of being in New Zealand. . . . New Zealand had come up in my own days, and there still remained to me something of the feeling of awful distance with which in early years I had regarded the young settlements at the Antipodes,—for New Zealand is, of all inhabited lands, the most

absolutely Antipodean to Greenwich. I remembered the first appearance in public of the grim jokes attributed to Sidney Smith, as to the cold curate, and the hope expressed that Bishop Selwyn might disagree with the cannibal who should eat him. The colony still retained for me something of the mysterious vagueness with which it was enveloped in early days,—so that when landing at The Bluff I thought that I had done something in the way of travelling. Melbourne had been no more than New York, hardly more than Glasgow, certainly not so much as Vienna. But if I could find myself in a Maori pah [native fort],—then indeed the flavour of the dust of Pall Mall would for the time depart from me altogether. . . . But when I had got as far as Invercargill [his first stopping point], the capital of Southland, I felt exactly as I might have felt on getting out of a railway in some small English town, and by the time I had reached the inn, and gone through the customary battle as to bedrooms, a tub of cold water, and supper, all the feeling of mystery was gone. I began to inquire the price of tea and sugar, and the amount of wages which men were earning;—but had no longer any appreciation of my Antipodean remoteness from the friends of my youth.

As for the Maoris, he heard the story of Rauparaha, who "had been a great cannibal, and had been a horrible scourge to the Maoris of the Middle Island, of whom he had devoured many. But he had a great reputation for wisdom, and managed, after all his troubles, to die in his bed at a fine old age." And then Trollope "had the pleasure of meeting his son at the Governor's table [at Wellington], and of playing battledore and shuttlecock with him in the Governor's hall. For this Rauparaha also is a great man among Maoris, and is very friendly with the white man. It is said of him,—the present man,—that he has killed men, but never eaten them."[37]

The season was winter in the antipodes, and Trollope was roundly scolded, again and again, for coming to see and report on the country "at a time in which her roads were all mud, and her mountains all snow," for visiting "the coldest part of New Zealand in the depth of the winter." Most transportation in New Zealand was by sea, as it had been in Australia, but Rose and Anthony wanted to see the country; they were obliged to send most of their luggage by steamer, "as it was impossible to carry overland more than one or two leather bags, and . . . it was long before we regained our boxes. . . . After a long and painful separation we and our luggage did come together again; but there was much of intermediate suffering. A hero, but nothing short of a hero, might perhaps sit down comfortably to dinner with the full-dressed aristocracy of a newly-visited city in a blue shirt and an old grey shooting jacket."[38]

His account of New Zealand is in general written with the same object as that of Australia—to tell the readers at home what they might expect if they emigrated. The New Zealanders themselves regarded their country as "the cream of the British empire," and in that judgment they included a superiority to England itself. Trollope was willing enough to suspend judgment as to the future, but at the time of his visit he found life there less comfortable, less prosperous, than in Australia. There was, however, "one point as to which the New Zealand colonist imitates his brethren and ancestors at home,—and far surpasses his Australian rival. He is very fond of getting drunk." On one occasion, in the northern province of Auckland in Maori country, the natives

> came and sat alongside of me [at the inn],—so near that the contiguity sometimes almost amounted to an embrace. The children were noisy, jovial, and familiar. As far as one could judge, they all seemed to be very happy. There was a European schoolmaster there, devoted to the Maori children,—who spoke to me much of their present and future condition. He had great faith in their secular learning, but had fears as to their religious condition. He was most anxious that I should see them in school before I departed on the next morning, and I promised that I would do so. Though I was much hurried, I could not refuse such a request to a man so urgent in so good a cause. But in the morning, when I was preparing to be as good as my word, I was told that the schoolmaster had got very drunk after I had gone to bed, had smashed the landlord's windows, and had been carried away to his house by two policemen,—greatly, I hope, to the sorrow of those Maori scholars. After this little affair, it was not thought expedient that I should trouble him at an early hour on the following morning.[39]

The excursion into Maori country, under primitive and arduous conditions, was undertaken so that he might both see some of the loveliest scenery in the world (including Lake Taupo) and learn more of the Maoris at first hand. The scenery was indeed magnificent—he could even imagine its future development into holiday resort country—and he did, without a moment of terror, spend time in a Maori "pah," even in a small Maori hut by himself for a night, with "a little door just big enough for ingress,—hardly big enough for egress,—and a heap of fern-leaves, and a looking glass, and a bottle which looked like perfumery,—and the feeling as of many insects." His final verdict on the Maoris was that

> they are certainly more highly gifted than other savage nations I have seen. They are as superior in intelligence and courage to the Australian Aboriginal as they are in outward appearance. They are more

pliable and nearer akin in their manners to civilised mankind than are the American Indians. They are more manly, more courteous, and also more sagacious than the African negro. One can understand the hope and the ambition of the first great old missionaries who had dealings with them. But contact with Europeans does not improve them. At the touch of the higher race they are poisoned and melt away. There is scope for poetry in their past history. There is room for philanthropy as to their present condition. But in regard to their future,—there is hardly a place for hope.[40]

When he and Rose had first arrived at Wellington on August 27 he found a note from Dr. John Logan Campbell, one of the leading merchants in Auckland; Campbell had known Tom Trollope during a long sojourn in Florence in the mid-sixties and had heard of Anthony's plan to visit New Zealand. He therefore offered them the hospitality of his large home in central Auckland; they arrived on September 13, and Rose remained his guest during Anthony's fortnight in the lake country (September 16–30). As Edward Landor had done in Western Australia, Campbell supplied him with a small writing room where he could work without interruption. Trollope made much of his methodical practices, so that Campbell remembered them to the end of his life, but apparently spoke little of what he was writing, for Campbell supposed it to be a novel.[41]

On October 3 they sailed from Auckland on the American steamer *Nebraska.* A few days earlier (September 27) Fred's first child, Frank Anthony, was born; obviously the grandparents were not at hand. They had been assured that they could go through to San Francisco on one ship; instead they were obliged to transfer at Honolulu to the *Idaho;* they spent some twenty-four hours there (October 21–22). "Nothing could be better than the *Nebraska,*—nothing worse than the *Idaho.*"[42] They were in San Francisco on November 6, then crossed North America by train with a few short stops on the way, including a call upon Brigham Young at Salt Lake City.

> I . . . [sent] to him my card, apologising for doing so without an introduction, and excusing myself by saying that I did not like to pass through the territory without seeing a man of whom I had heard so much. He received me in his doorway, not asking me to enter, and inquired whether I were not a miner. When I told him that I was not a miner, he asked me whether I earned my bread. I told him I did. "I guess you're a miner," said he. I again assured him that I was not. "Then how do you earn your bread?" I told him that I did so by writing books. "I'm sure you're a miner," said he. Then he turned upon his heel, went back into the house, and closed the door.

I was properly punished, as I had been vain enough to conceive that he would have heard my name.

On November 25 they reached New York, spent two nights at the Brevoort House, then sailed for England, where they arrived ten days later.[43]

ॐ

In his absence, Trollope's name was kept alive in England by the serialization of *The Eustace Diamonds* in the *Fortnightly:* it began a month after he sailed and was still running when he got home. *The Golden Lion of Granpere* appeared in *Good Words* while he was abroad. He also left behind in a strong box the manuscripts of *Phineas Redux* and the much shorter *An Eye for an Eye.* "If . . . The Great Britain . . . had gone to the bottom, I had so provided that there would be new novels ready to come out under my name for some years to come."[44] When, therefore, he received in Wellington a letter from Arthur Locker, editor of the weekly newsmagazine the *Graphic,* requesting a novel to inaugurate a new policy of running serial fiction, Trollope was prepared and promptly offered him *Phineas Redux.* The publisher's letter of acceptance was waiting for him when he reached London and the serial began its publication in mid-July, 1873. On one point, as Trollope recalled, he stood firm:

> The editor of that paper greatly disliked the title, assuring me that the public would take Redux for the gentleman's surname,—and was dissatisfied with me when I replied that I had no objection to them doing so. The introduction of a Latin word, or of a word from any other language, into the title of an English novel is undoubtedly in bad taste; but after turning the matter much over in my mind, I could find no other suitable name.

Trollope's asking price of £2,500 was divided equally between the *Graphic* and the publishers of the book, Chapman and Hall.[45]

Another of his novels, however, suffered a fate during his absence that distressed him a great deal. *Ralph the Heir* was drawing to a close in *Saint Pauls* when he sailed for Australia, and indeed had already made its appearance in book form. The novelist Charles Reade, a fellow member of the Garrick Club and a friend whose work Trollope professed to admire, was also a dramatist ever on the lookout for plots. In Trollope's novel he thought he had found one, based on it the play he called *Shilly-Shally,*[46] and offered it to John Hollingshead of the Gaiety Theatre. "I gladly accepted it," said Hollingshead. "This brought [Reade and myself] more together, and I learnt to know and appreciate one of the most earnest,

singular, and genuine men who ever struck root as an author and journalist."[47] Reade clearly meant well: though the laws of copyright gave
him the free right to dramatize the plot of a published novel without
permission and without acknowledgment, he would, he said, have sought
Trollope's prior consent—but Trollope was on the opposite side of the
world, Reade was in a hurry and so was Hollingshead. The play began its
month's run on Easter Monday, April 1, with an excellent cast headed by
the most popular comic actor of the day, John L. Toole. Reade did seek
the advice of Henry Trollope with respect to whether he "should describe
the Comedy as my work according to the custom of adaptors, or give the
original inventor his just due upon the bill. The latter seems the fairest to
me, and is to the advantage of the novelist by throwing the doors of the
theatre open to him on some future occasion." He invited Harry to dine
and attend the first night's performance with him.[48] The play was advertised as by "Anthony Trollope and Charles Reade," it was reviewed as "a
new comedy in three acts by Anthony Trollope and Charles Reade," and
when an enthusiastic audience on the first night called loudly for the
author, "the stage manager of the Gaiety came forward to announce that,
being at the Antipodes, Mr. A. Trollope could not acknowledge the
compliment." The play ran nightly (except Sundays) until May 1 (a
benefit night for Toole), then ended its run with a matinee on Saturday,
May 4, when it was paired with Arthur Sullivan's operetta *Cox and Box.*
That evening it gave way to the opening of Dion Boucicault's *Colleen
Bawn.* It had appeared twenty-eight times.[49]

All this was history by the time Trollope learned anything about it.
Reade's letter to him, though dated March 7, did not reach him at
Melbourne until after the middle of May. It was a rather foolish letter,
making a virtue of giving Trollope his "just honor" despite the laxity of
the copyright law, and promising to send him a prompt copy, "since you
ought to make a good deal of money by it if produced in Australia under
your own eye." Trollope instantly sent under cover to George Smith,
publisher of the *Pall Mall Gazette,* a letter denying any responsibility for
the work. "If the play has appeared with my name to it, or if it be
advertised to appear with my name, will you kindly insert the enclosed,"
he wrote to Smith. "I cannot understand how any author can act in such a
way. It is monstrous that I should be made to appear as a writer of plays
without my own permission,—or that I should be coerced into a literary
partnership with any man." The public letter (of which he sent a copy to
Reade) was mild and generous in its reference to "my friend, Mr. Charles
Reade." "I would as lief enter into such a partnership with Mr. Charles
Reade as with any man I know, because I recognize his genius and admire
his work; but I think that no such partnership should be proclaimed to the
world without the consent of both parties. I feel bound to make it known

that I have given no such consent."[50] A second letter from Reade reached him on May 31, with a copy of the play. "I admire your genius and value your friendship, and am anxious that there should be no quarrel between us," Trollope replied. "But I think you have done towards me what should not be done, and I should be pusillanimous were I not to express my opinion"—and therefore he was writing to the *Daily Telegraph* to disclaim any connection with the play.[51]

For the English newspapers had also reached Melbourne, and in the *Daily Telegraph* was a review published the morning after the first performance, charging the play with coarseness, indelicacy, with containing "many things . . . that must make a modest woman blush." To be sure, the reviewer said that none of these questionable passages had been written by Trollope; all were Reade's, and he had disgraced his brother author. Reade's angry letter of reply in the *Telegraph* also reached Australia, pointing out publicly that the reviewer was a jealous playwright—in fact, though he named no names, Clement Scott, whose play had been supplanted at the Gaiety by *Shilly-Shally*. Trollope's letter to the editor appeared two months after it was written: "My name has been used without my sanction, and my plot adopted without my knowledge. Mr. Reade has told me by letter that he is legally entitled to do as he has done. It may be so. . . . [But] I think that one author should not require the law to protect him from such usage at the hands of another."[52]

Unfortunately, Reade, whose nature was more prickly even than Trollope's, would not let the matter drop; he replied in the newspaper the day he read Trollope's letter, affirming that he had "decided to give Mr. Trollope half the receipts of 'Shilly-Shally,' and, by the same rule, half the credit. . . . [He] objects to his name being connected with the play, though two-thirds of the lines are from his pen. I submit; and henceforth his only connection shall be with the receipts." A common friend, the artist Henry Nelson O'Neil, tried to bring about a reconciliation; Trollope restated his case in a letter which does not survive, and Reade, to whom O'Neil showed it, claimed that Trollope had distorted Reade's meaning. But "having given him one good cause of offence, . . . I paid half the English profits to his credit. He might have declined them without affronting me: but he did affront me: and it seems to me that in his letter he clings to the affront, and says he will not be brought to believe I intended to pay him any money when I brought out the play." No other evidence survives that Reade ever offered, or paid, half the profits, nor would such an offer justify his presumption in Trollope's eyes.[53] Blackwood's London agent, J. M. Langford, summed up the matter thus at the end of December: "[Trollope] is involved in a quarrel with Charles Reade about dramatising *Ralph the Heir*—that is C. R. quarrels but Trollope will not. I am sorry for I have always stood up for

Reade but in this case he was wrong from the beginning and has at last written a very bad letter headed 'Mr. Trollope,' getting himself more into the mud at every step he has taken."[54]

Reade had announced in the *Telegraph* that he had instructed his solicitor to bring suit against some of his reviewers for slander in view of their charges of indecency. By the time the suit was heard in the Court of Common Pleas on February 10, 1873, Trollope was home and could see the whole matter stirred up again. Reade of course affirmed that there was no indecency, but (as Trollope must have read in the *Times*) that "he had softened down many passages in Mr. Trollope's novel," thereby suggesting that Trollope's novel verged on indecency. The lord chief justice, Sir Alexander Cockburn, properly observed that this had nothing to do with the question. The jury awarded Reade damages of £200 against the proprietors of the offending newspaper, the *Morning Advertiser*.[55] But Reade's behavior throughout justifies the comment Trollope made in *An Autobiography:*

> There is no writer of the present day who has so much puzzled me by his eccentricities, impracticalities, and capabilities as Charles Reade. I look upon him as endowed almost with genius, but as one who has not been gifted by nature with ordinary powers of reasoning. . . . He means to be honest. He means to be especially honest,—more honest than other people. . . . And yet of all the writers of my day he has seemed to me to understand literary honesty the least. . . . [In the matter of *Shilly-Shally*] I could not . . . make him understand that he had done wrong, and could only escape from the absurdity of a personal quarrel with a man I esteemed by suggesting to him that nothing more should be said about it by either of us.

They were thereafter inevitably thrown together constantly, and Reade told his future biographer that "for a considerable period they glared at each other in silence, and . . . they were actually wont to participate in a game of whist at the Garrick without deigning to speak to each other."[56]

After trying for a year and a half to persuade Hollingshead to bring the unfortunate play back to the stage, Reade determined to print the play, and asked Trollope's permission. Again there was potential for misunderstanding, for Trollope was out of town and did not receive the letter for some seven weeks. His reply shows his awareness of the delicate relationship. "I am sure you will not think that I omitted to answer it after receiving it. Print Shilly-Shally with or without any notice as you may please."[57] Peace was apparently declared. In the spring of 1878 Trollope secured Reade as one of the "stewards" (financial backers) for the annual dinner of the Royal Literary Fund, and at much the same time dunned him "to give a pound or two for Thackerays bust at the

Garrick."[58] This, of course, was some years after *An Autobiography* was written. But even in *An Autobiography* there is a reference to "My friend Charles Reade" (p. 211).

The litigation brought an apologetic letter from another of Trollope's friends, the producer John Hollingshead, but Trollope assured him that he never felt any bitterness against him in the matter. Not long afterward, Hollingshead asked Trollope's support in extending copyright protection to include adaptation of a novel for the stage. In his memoirs Hollingshead said Reade had told him that he had asked and had obtained Trollope's permission for the use of the novel, but this statement, made over twenty years after the event, is probably a convenient failure of memory. As for the alleged indecency, the jury could not find any in the language of the script, but Reade himself pointed out in another context that the actors in a farce can by their tones and gestures be very suggestive. Certainly Trollope was innocent. At best, the play was described as "sad stuff" by Reade's friend Percy Fitzgerald, who was embarrassed at having to review it in the *Observer*.[59]

Chapter XXI

1872–73

Rose and Anthony found temporary living quarters for the autumn of 1872 at No. 3 Holles Street (a short street that runs from Cavendish Square to Oxford Street) and despite the inconvenience of being without most of his possessions Anthony plunged with great vigor into his customary routine. He dutifully attended a meeting of the Royal Literary Fund committee on December 11, then threw himself strenuously into the pleasures of the hunt: on the twenty-first he "had 2 h. 45 min. after the same fox, . . . the biggest bellyful of hunting I ever had in my life, almost without a cheque; first 30 minutes very fast and a kill. I never had such a day before. Buff [his horse] carried me through it all as well as ever. But was *very tired*. He and a second horse I had out were both too tired to be got home. . . . I have four in all."[1] At first he returned to the familiar fields of Essex, then moved his horses to Leighton Buzzard in Bedfordshire, where Baron Meyer de Rothschild kept his pack and where there was stag hunting as well as fox hunting. But he preferred his former grounds, and the next winter moved his hunters back to Essex, though that meant a longer early-morning cab ride across London to get to the proper railway station, three days a week during the season.[2] He was once more able to buy supplies of cigars from friends who imported them—though they were become so expensive that "for the future I give myself to pipes. If I can not smoke a small cigar under eight pence, I will not smoke them at all." It is unlikely that he intended to keep his resolution. He wrote to Lewes and George Eliot from Australia late in February, 1872: "You in your comfort smoke cigars. . . . I am reduced to the vilest tobacco out of the vilest pipe, and drink the vilest brandy and water." When he wrote that letter he had just received the first volume of Forster's *Life of Dickens*.

> [It] is distasteful to me,—as I was sure it would be. Dickens was no hero; he was a powerful, clever, humorous, and, in many respects, wise man;—very ignorant, and thick-skinned, who had taught himself to be his own God, and to believe himself to be a sufficient God for all who came near him;—not a hero at all. Forster tells of him things which should disgrace him,—as the picture he drew of his own father, & the hard words he intended to have published of his

own mother; but Forster himself is too coarse-grained (though also a very powerful man) to know what is and what is not disgraceful; what is or is not heroic.

Trollope knew Forster, of course, because of their common connection with Chapman and Hall. Anthony lunched with the Leweses and Edith Simcox on December 13, and talked so energetically that George Eliot could not get to know her new admirer.[3]

One very troublesome matter was awaiting Anthony and Rose: their son Henry had fallen in love with "a woman of the town" (as Lewes recorded it in his diary) and wanted to marry her. The parents responded affectionately but firmly, and Harry proved amenable: he went off to Australia on a prolonged visit only a fortnight or so after their return. The following September, immediately after he came back, he withdrew himself and his money from Chapman and Hall. He was away for about nine months.[4] Rumor had it that the woman was a French actress.

And of course Trollope had to see *Australia and New Zealand* through the press, an "agony of endeavouring to get [it] out before the end of [January]." He corrected the last sheet of index on January 31, and copies were on their way to Rusden and other Australian friends by February 5. "The making out of an index . . . is of all efforts in letters the meanest, the most enervating, and at the same time the most difficult." (It is so, though his index is a very thin one indeed.) The life in Australia and New Zealand, he told a friend, is "a very much better life than we have here. There a man who will work has enough of all that he wants. The horror of this country is that let men work as they will there is not and cannot be enough for them all. A man who is not properly fed cannot be a man fit either for God's work or for man's work." "I know that in many matters I must be inaccurate," he told Rusden. "The necessities of the work . . . demanded that it should be written quickly. I can not accuse myself of having spared myself labour in writing it; but I found myself driven to attempt details which should have received more work in verifying them, than the time allowed me to give to them." He liked the book less than the one on the West Indies, which was far the livelier, and feared that the new volumes were "dull and long."[5] They are, certainly, somewhat prolix and repetitive, but on the whole represent a magnificent intellectual achievement.

෪

As urgent as the completion of his book was the finding of a new house; by February 1, 1873, he had contracted to purchase No. 39 Montagu Square, near the north end of the west side of the square and about half a mile west of the temporary quarters in Holles Street. It was close to the York Street house which he had shared with his mother, and to the church in which his sister had been married to John Tilley. He arranged with Chapman for prompt payment of money due him for *The Eustace Diamonds* so that he could put down his deposit. Then there was the necessity of buying furniture, papering and painting, and somewhat remodeling the house, especially with reference to the provision of a room in which he could write. His good friend Sir Frederick Pollock, who was a member of the Cosmopolitan and the Athenaeum clubs and sat with Trollope on the general committee of the Royal Literary Fund, lived on the opposite side of the square at No. 59. It is "not a gorgeous neighbourhood, but one which will suit my declining years and modest resources," he said—somewhat too disparagingly, for it is a very pleasant neighborhood. "Our first work in settling here was to place upon new shelves the books which I had collected round myself at Waltham. And this work, which was in itself great, entailed also the labour of a new catalogue. . . . Only those who have done it know how great is the labour of moving and arranging a few thousand volumes. At the present moment I own about 5,000 volumes, and they are dearer to me even than the horses which are going, or than the wine in the cellar, which is very apt to go, and upon which I also pride myself," he wrote some three years later.[6] James Virtue, whose firm was printing the Australian book, printed up a few copies of the library catalogue for him. And whatever Trollope may have thought of John Forster, he presented him with an inscribed copy of this catalogue.[7] Indeed, in *An Autobiography* Trollope speaks of Forster as "an intimate and valued friend," and recalls "that room in Lincoln's Inn Fields in which . . . Dickens had given that reading of which there is an illustration with portraits in the second volume of his life," published in 1872–74.[8] The move was made about Easter (April 13). By this time the hunting was over—"nothing to do beyond the writing of a novel or two till November next. In some coming perfect world there will be hunting 12 months in the year."[9]

There were in fact two novels on the fire. On March 28 he signed an agreement with Chapman for a novel the length of *Orley Farm,* to be published in twenty shilling parts of thirty-two pages each; the first half was to be delivered by the end of October. This was the novel that became *The Way We Live Now,* and, substantially larger than *Orley Farm,* was his longest novel. But less than a fortnight after he began work on this, he received a letter from Arthur Locker offering £450 for a long Christmas story for the *Graphic,* and so he devoted the month of June (having completed fifteen chapters of the longer novel) to writing *Harry Heathcote of Gangoil* (ultimately published as a book after its magazine appearance, and by far the shortest of his novels). As he had done with *Phineas Redux,* which was still running in the *Graphic* when the Christmas novel appeared, Locker found fault with the title of the new story, but once more Trollope was firm. "There are matters in which a man must go by his own judgment."[10] Trollope was soon to get his own back: the *Graphic*'s illustrator for *Phineas Redux,* Frank Holl, unable to draw horses, introduced a picture of a champagne picnic into the middle of a chapter about a fox chase (as Trollope told Shirley Brooks in a shout across the room at the Garrick Club).[11]

It was inevitable that Trollope should have written a novel about Australia; indeed an Australian publisher had much puzzled him out there by telling him that he had already bought from Chapman the right to republish Trollope's novel about that country. (It turned out that the man had actually purchased *Australia and New Zealand.*)[12] *Harry Heathcote* is a straightforward story of a sheep farmer, a "squatter," who was threatened by the hostility of some lawless neighbors who tried to burn him out by setting grass fires in the dry season. The natural hostility between squatter (who used public land) and "free selector" (who was able at will to choose and purchase land within the area used by the squatter) was removed when a free selector helped Harry put out the fires and indeed became engaged to Harry's sister. Harry was in fact, at least as regarded his situation in life, Fred Trollope; Trollope used almost the same language to describe Harry's reason for emigrating as he was to use some three years later about Fred: "Boys less than himself in stature got above him at school."[13] In keeping with his repeated experience out there, Trollope made the sergeant at the local police post an Oxford graduate, son of a clergyman, who had sought a livelihood in the antipodes. Trollope made much of the paradox that in the Southern Hemisphere the heat at Christmas is almost unbearable, and he introduced the required seasonal sentiment with his close: " 'That's what I call a Happy Christmas,' said Harry, as the party finally parted for the night."[14]

Meanwhile Chapman bought for £1,200 the copyright of *Lady Anna,* which began serial publication in the *Fortnightly* two months after *The Eustace Diamonds* ended.[15]

❧

April 5 brought a mild shock to the Trollope home. A short time earlier, Anthony was invited to James Virtue's house at Walton-on-Thames and there he met Leslie Ward, with whom he took a pleasant walk to St. George's Hill. "While Trollope admired the scenery," Ward recorded, "I noted the beauties of Nature in another way, committed those mental observations to my mental note-book, and came home to what fun I could get out of them." For Ward was "Spy," the celebrated caricaturist for

Vanity Fair, and his drawing appeared in color in the first number for April. "I . . . portrayed Trollope's strange thumb, which he held erect whilst smoking, with his cigar between his first and second fingers, his pockets standing out on either side of his trousers, his coat buttoned once and then parting over a small but comfortable corporation." There were also a fierce and slightly idiotic face, and hair brushed upward on both sides of a bald head, like feathery wings. Trollope told Virtue in no uncertain terms that his treachery had been intolerable, and Virtue (who had hoped Ward's caricature would be more flattering) wrote stiffly to Ward; but the storm blew over. Meanwhile Edmund Yates was delighted and offered Ward the post of regular caricaturist to his projected new weekly, the *World* (an offer Ward declined, on reflection).[16] The "Spy" drawing was Trollope's second appearance in caricature within a year: on the preceding June 1, while he was still in Australia, a revivified *Once a Week* published Frederick Waddy's well-known sketch of him sitting on a stack of his clerical novels and holding in his hand a puppet clergyman, of which he was pulling the string.[17] As for Yates's new venture into "society journalism," which began in July, 1874, he planned a series of illustrated articles on "Celebrities at Home" for which he invited Trollope to pose, but Trollope declined: "I allow that your articles are cleverly done, and without the least offence," he wrote, "also that you have many very distinguished people in your gallery. But I would rather not." His refusal, Yates observed, could not have been based on an objection to the *World,* a notorious gossip sheet, since twice Trollope proposed to supply a novel for that journal, proposals that Yates in his turn declined. In the manuscript of *An Autobiography* Trollope referred to Yates as "a literary gutterscraper,—one who picked up odds and ends of scandal from chance sources, and turning them with a spice of malice into false records, made his money of them among such newspapers as would pay him." The passage was canceled before publication, and so although Yates had seen *An Autobiography* before he wrote his own *Recollections,* his complacency about Trollope's judgment of him had not been upset.[18]

Hospitality was certainly easier at Montagu Square than it had been at Waltham Cross, where it was almost obligatory to offer dinner guests overnight accommodation, and the Trollopes' social life was quickly resumed in their new home. Robert Browning dined with them on June 11. Kate Field was in London from early June until the last of July, and on June 10 she was their guest at a dinner where she met Wilkie Collins. "She is adored by everybody, and I am all ready to follow the general example," Collins wrote in response to Trollope's invitation. She dined in Montagu Square at least twice thereafter, early in July and again a few days before her departure. Trollope called on her frequently of a morning.[19]

"Two of the wildest of your countrymen, Joaquin Miller & Mark

Twain, dine with me at my club next week," Trollope wrote to her early in July. "Pity you have not yet established the rights of your sex or you could come and meet them, and be *as jolly as men.*" Thirty-four years later, almost to the day, Mark Twain dined once again as a guest at the Garrick Club, and

> could dreamingly see about me the forms and faces of the small company of that long forgotten occasion. Anthony Trollope was the host, and the dinner was in honor of Joaquin Miller, who was on the top wave of his English notoriety at that time. . . . Tom Hughes addressed remarks to [me] occasionally; it was not in his nature to forget or neglect any stranger. Trollope was voluble and animated. . . . Joaquin Miller . . . was affecting the picturesque and untamed costume of the wild Sierras at the time, to the charmed astonishment of conventional London, and was helping out the effects with the breezy and independent and aggressive manners of that faraway and romantic region. He and Trollope talked all the time and both at the same time, Trollope pouring forth a smooth and limpid and sparkling stream of faultless English, and Joaquin discharging into it his muddy and tumultuous mountain torrent. . . .
> It was long ago, long ago! and not even an echo of that turbulence was left in this room.

Miller himself claimed to have hunted with Trollope and others (obviously not in July) and on a challenge to have ridden bareback and "left them all behind and nearly every one unhorsed."[20] As for Mark Twain, he must have recognized a fellowship in humor with Trollope, for he quietly copied a line from *Phineas Finn* in Pudd'nhead Wilson's calendar:

> [Aspasia Fitzgibbon] was greatly devoted to her brother Laurence, so devoted that there was nothing she would not do for him, short of lending him money (*P.F.,* chap. v).
>   The holy passion of Friendship is of so sweet and steady and loyal and enduring a nature that it will last through a whole lifetime, if not asked to lend money (*P.W.,* chap. viii).

২঵

Trollope preserved a great deal more evidence of his writing method for *The Way We Live Now* than for any other of his novels. There was of course the usual record of progress—the number of pages written per day, set opposite a day-to-day calendar. He calculated two pages of manuscript (at the average rate of 260 words a page) to each page of print, and the first three "parts" (thirty-two printed pages, five chapters, to each part) occupied him for the entire month of May. All of June was devoted to writing *Harry Heathcote*. Parts 4–6 were written from July 3 to 30, even during a ten-day grouse-shooting holiday in Inverness beginning July 13.[21] He wrote steadily and rapidly from August 11 to September 19, with the regularity he always boasted but almost never achieved—one sixty-four-page (manuscript) "part" every five days. Most of this stint was done while he and Rose were on a six-week holiday in Killarney, but on his last ten days there he laid down his pen. They returned to London on September 30, and he devoted the first ten days of October to rereading his manuscript: ten of the fourteen parts now completed had been promised to the publisher by October 31. The last six parts came at a slightly more leisurely pace, and for one week in December, when he was halfway through his last part, he was prevented from writing at all by a bad foot. The final stretch was December 17–22. On that last date he proudly noted that though he had allowed thirty-two weeks for the writing, he had actually completed the novel in twenty-nine weeks if the time consumed by *Harry Heathcote* were deducted.[22] But it may have been the "bad foot" that caused the issuance of the first part to be postponed from the end of December to the end of January.[23]

Before he began the composition, he jotted down memoranda on the characters he planned. The chief character was to be Lady Carbury, who at first thought was housed on Bryanston Square, a few steps west of Montagu Square; then, by a quick change of mind, she was moved to Welbeck Street, closer to Trollope's temporary home on Holles Street—Welbeck Street, the street on which nearly a decade later Trollope would die. Her son and daughter, Sir Felix and Henrietta, are sketched, and so is her cousin by marriage, Roger Carbury. Life at his Suffolk home, Carbury Hall, and Roger's relations with the neighbors were to be developed at length. His friend Paul Montague's role also was mapped out: "Gets into some scrapes which must be devised," and the nature of the device was then indicated by the marginal note, "Mrs. Hurtle. Winifred." Paul was to be housed on Suffolk Street in London—the little street at the head of which was Trollope's favorite hotel, the one in which he would be staying when he fell fatally ill. The other country gentry are sketched, and the London editors, molders of literary opinion. The bishop of Elmham was to be modeled on Trollope's headmaster at Harrow, "old Longley," whose name in the novel was arrived at by reversing the letters (Yelgnol), then contracting them to Yeld. And Father John Barham was modeled on a priest Trollope had known at Waltham.

This was indeed to have been what Trollope then called it, his "Carbury novel." Other characters were added, rather tentatively. There was to be an heiress, Marianna Treegrene (the name presumably to suggest "Greenbaum"), the daughter of Emanuel S. Treegrene, the great American swindler. But before he wrote more, he determined that she should be Marie Melmotte and he Augustus Melmotte, the French swindler. Then came Madame Melmotte, "fat Jewess." The Beargarden Club, the Grendalls, and Ruby Ruggles with her father and her suitor John Crumb are listed, and that is about all. Marginally he indicated that the presumed period of the action was 1873 and that it should begin on February 25 of that year. In fact, it begins on February 25, but not 1873; of two letters described in the opening chapter one is dated "Thursday," and another written at the same sitting is dated "25th February, 187—," whereas February 25, 1873, was a Tuesday. Most of the dates later in the story can be matched with 1872.[24]

Another leaf of notes shows the commercial emphasis increasing, with a new "American swindler" introduced in the person of Hamilton K. Fisker, and the name of the "South Central Pacific and Mexican Railway," as well as some events planned for the fifth number of the book. Most of these were kept; a few details were discarded. Then comes a list of fifty-five episodes planned as the subjects of the chapters in parts 10–20. As these chapters were written, Trollope inserted the number opposite the episode, increasingly altering their projected order or discarding proposed episodes altogether until, after the eightieth chapter was written, the list was no longer useful. Among the discarded plans were the death of Sir Felix, apparently in consequence of the attack by John Crumb (reminiscent of the fate of Dr. Thorne's brother), and five chapters (93–95, 97–98) dealing with the trial and imprisonment of Melmotte. In fact, up to the very moment of concluding the chapter on Melmotte's disgrace in Parliament, Trollope left open the possibility of composing one of his favorite courtroom scenes: first he wrote "on the following morning the maid-servant found him asleep," then crossed out "asleep," wrote "dead," and added the sentence that now concludes chapter lxxxiii.* The title of the novel was settled very late: a final list of chapter titles is still headed "Carbury Novel." To one side is written "The Life We Live Now," and then "Way We Live Now," hardly more than a month before planned publication.[25] The final decision was apparently made on November 17, and it was advertised by name on December 6, when it was still due to begin publication on January 1; by December 27 it was advertised to begin on January 31.[26] The title is unique among Trollope's works: it was meant to be provocative, to suggest satire on the unscrupulous commercialism of contemporary English life, and it provoked responses from the reviewers accordingly.

---

*"Drunk as he had been, — more drunk as he probably became during the night, — still he was able to deliver himself from the indignities and penalties to which the law might have subjected him by a dose of prussic acid."

Trollope himself discovered and engaged the illustrator of the book, Lionel Grimston Fawkes, an officer in the Royal Artillery. The young man (twenty-four years old) was apparently suggested to Trollope by his uncle, a Mr. Pain, and Trollope invited Chapman to meet him at breakfast in Montagu Square on July 23, 1873. Less than two months later he reported to Chapman that he had received one drawing from Fawkes and found it on the whole satisfactory. "It is time something should be decided."[27] Fawkes was engaged. The choice was not a success. Trollope wrote to Mary Holmes immediately after the fourth number appeared: "What you say of illustrations is all true,—not strong enough in expression of disgust. But what can a writer do? I desire, of course, to put my books into as many hands as possible, and I take the best mode of doing so."[28]

❧

The Way We Live Now is Trollope's longest and most complex novel. As the *Times* reviewer pointed out when the book was published, it makes its point not by satiric exaggeration but by letting the characters behave in perfectly ordinary human fashion, and none of them is altogether bad; some, like Lady Carbury, perceive their faults and try to reform them. The reader is guided by Trollope's ironic comments, but much of the moral analysis is made by characters themselves, and then the reader must apply his own values in judging what the characters have said.

The principal spokesman in the novel against the way we live in the latter part of the nineteenth century is of course Roger Carbury, whose ideal is the country gentleman, residing on an estate that bears the family name and has been handed down from generation to generation. "The very parish in which Carbury Hall stood,—or Carbury Manor House, as it was more properly called,—was Carbury parish. And there was Carbury Chase" (chap. vi). The squire's energies are directed to the productivity of the estate agriculturally, and he regards his possession of it as a trust; we have seen the same idea put forward in *The Belton Estate* and in the concept of "Ralph Newton of Newton" in *Ralph the Heir*. "Dear Roger was old-fashioned, and knew nothing of people as they are now. He lived in a world which, though slow, had been good in its way; but which, whether bad or good, had now passed away," his cousin Lady Carbury reflected (chap. xxx). "People live now in a way that I don't comprehend," he himself remarked (chap. xlvi). At quite another social level Mrs. Pipkin, the Islington landlady, thought about "the new dispensation" that had come during the past fifteen years, so that her niece Ruby went unchaperoned to the theater, presumably with a young man, and got home after midnight; she could send and receive letters from the gentleman without inspection. Mrs. Pipkin merely knew that "the world was being changed very fast" (chaps. xliii, xlviii). The theater in question was an actual music hall in Shepherdess Walk, just off the City Road in the East End: the Eagle Tavern and Grecian Theatre was a notorious haunt of prostitutes, which Trollope delicately described as "half music-hall, half theatre, which pleasantly combined the allurements of the gin-palace, the theatre, and the ball-room, trenching hard on those of other places" (chap. xliii).[29]

The great corrupter, of course, was money, and the representative of money on a grand scale was the unscrupulous swindler Augustus Melmotte, who two years earlier had moved, under pressure, from Paris to London (after earlier exploits that had nearly landed him in prison in Hamburg), and had taken a magnificent house on the south side of Grosvenor Square in the heart of Mayfair. Though everyone was convinced that he was dishonest and though he was personally unattractive, he could gather round him, socially and in business, the most elevated of people, all of whom hoped that they themselves would gain wealth while he was fraudulently draining the fortunes of others through his manipulations. The hand of his daughter Marie was the great prize; Lord Nidderdale, a fairly decent young man and heir to the Marquis of Auld Reekie, entered the competition and "offered to take the girl and make her Marchioness in the process of time for half a million down"; "he had an idea that a few years ago a man could not have done such a thing—that he would be held to show a poor spirit should he attempt it; but that now it did not much matter what a man did,—if only he were successful" (chaps. iv, liii). Georgiana Longestaffe, daughter of a Suffolk squire who had married into the aristocracy and had ambitions beyond his financial resources, becomes engaged to Brehgert, a wealthy Jewish business man, to her parents' distress; but Georgiana is able to plead that the times have changed: "People don't think about that as they used to, papa. He has a very fine income" (chap. lxxviii). "You couldn't have loved him, Georgiana." "Loved him! Who thinks about love nowadays? I don't know any one who loves any one else" (chap. xcv). And to the aristocratic young gamblers in the Beargarden Club "there had filtered, through the outer world, a feeling that people were not now bound to be so punctilious in the paying of money as they were a few years since" (chap. lxxiv). The Beargardeners gambled and drank gin the night through, and there is even a hint of opium.

The literary and religious worlds shared the general corruption. The novel opens with Lady Carbury writing to the editors of three influential journals attempting to bargain for a favorable review for her forthcoming potboiling book. The amiable bishop of Elmham tolerates Melmotte because he has given £200 to the Curates' Aid Society. "Such a gift shows him to be a useful member of society,—and I am always for encouraging useful men. . . . The country is changing." "It is going to the dogs, I think;—about as fast as it can go," responded Roger. "They who . . . set the example go to his feasts, and of course he is seen at theirs in return. And yet these leaders of the fashion know,—at any rate they believe,— that he is what he is because he has been a swindler greater than other swindlers. What follows as a natural consequence? Men reconcile themselves to swindling. Though they themselves mean to be honest, dishonesty of itself is no longer odious to them. Then there comes the jealousy that others should be growing rich with the approval of all the world,— and the natural aptitude to do what all the world approves. It seems to me that the existence of a Melmotte is not compatible with a wholesome state of things in general." On the contrary, replied the bishop, "men on the whole do live better lives than they did a hundred years ago. There is a wider spirit of justice abroad, more of mercy from one to another, a more lively charity, and if less of religious enthusiasm, less also of superstition" (chap. lv). His broad tolerance is mirrored in the indifference of Georgiana Longestaffe, whose sole interest in religion is the social respectability it carries, and who demands of her mother, "What possible difference can it make about a man's religion?" (chap. xcv). She, her mother, and her sister, when in church, "knelt on their hassocks in the most becoming fashion, and sat during the sermon without the slightest sign either of weariness or of attention," as Trollope remarked with fine irony (chap. xxi).

British social prejudice is constantly before one in the novel—feelings about Jews especially, but also about Americans and even, in passing, about Methodists: "Young what's-his-name married the tallow-chandler's daughter, . . . but [the proposed marriage to Brehgert] was worse than that," said Lady Pomona Longestaffe. "Her father was a methodist" (chap. lxxix). From the moment he first heard of the American woman, Mrs. Hurtle, "Roger had regarded her as a wicked, intriguing, bad woman. It may, perhaps, be confessed that he was prejudiced against all Americans; . . . he pictured to himself all American women as being loud, masculine, and atheistical" (chap. lxxxvii). But it is the nineteenth-century English feeling about Jews that Trollope presents most thoroughly, as he handles characters like Cohenlupe, Goldscheiner, Brehgert, and Madame Melmotte. As to whether Melmotte himself was Jewish there is ambiguity; perhaps, indeed, he was Irish, but the general view was that there was a strong Jewish strain in his blood. Brehgert attempts to explain the matter to Georgiana: "Fifty years ago, whatever claim a Jew might have to be as well considered as a Christian, he certainly was not so considered. Society was closed against him, except under special circumstances, and so were all the privileges of high position. But that has been altered. Your father does not admit the change; but I think he is blind to it, because he does not wish to see" (chap. lxxix). A great many characters in the book did not wish to see. Yet Brehgert is thoroughly honorable, kind, even generous, as when he silently returns to Melmotte evidence of Melmotte's forgeries. As for Trollope's own opinion of the matter, "One of the greatest judges in the land is a Jew" (chap. lxxviii)—Sir George Jessel, made master of the rolls on August 30, 1873, only about two months before Trollope wrote this chapter; Jessel was a friend associated with Trollope in the activities of the Royal Literary Fund,[30] and a whist partner at the Athenaeum Club.

Mrs. Hurtle wins the respect of Roger, of the reader, of Trollope himself: "I think . . . that Mrs. Hurtle, with all her faults, was a good-natured woman" (chap. xcvii). As she reflects on how she had given herself to Paul Montague, then been discarded, she becomes aware of the different standards by which men and women were measured: she and Paul "had played a game against each other; and he, with all the inferiority of his intellect to weigh him down, had won,—because he was a man. She had much time for thinking, and she thought much about these things. He could change his love as often as he pleased, and be as good a lover at the end as ever;—whereas she was ruined by his defection" (chap. xcvii).

Events in the novel often parallel recent or current events in England. Newspapers for some months, beginning in March, 1873 (two months before Trollope started to write), were filled with reports of a swindle amounting to over £100,000 against the Bank of England, perpetrated by a group of American forgers. The figure of Melmotte had its origins in the speculator and forger John Sadleir, a member of Parliament who, when he failed in 1856, committed suicide with prussic acid; Trollope had mentioned him in his unpublished book, *The New Zealander,* of that year. And there was the "Railway King," the "Railway Napoleon," George Hudson (1800–1871), whom Carlyle in *Latter-Day Pamphlets* cited as a symptom of the moral degeneracy of his countrymen, who worshipped such a creature out of greed.[31] Railway investments, especially in American enterprises, were very popular: the *Times,* for example, carried an advertisement for the 7 percent gold bonds of a railway with the geographically improbable name of the "Atlantic, Mississippi, and Ohio Railroad."[32] (Not all these schemes were fraudulent: Matthew Arnold had reason to be content with his investment in American railways.) While Trollope was writing his earliest chapters England was looking forward to the official visit of the Shah of Persia (June 18 to July 5, 1873), and his description of Melmotte's dinner for the Emperor of China was written only two months after the Shah's departure.[33]

There is a temptation, perhaps unwarranted, to find also some literary model for the novel and its characters. On November 13, 1873, Trollope addressed the Liverpool Institute—a lecture that combined his discourse in defense of novel reading with reflections, suitable to the occasion, upon popular education. He spoke especially of Lord Frederick

Verisopht as typical of Dickens's powerful descriptions of "a set of foolish, idle, vicious young men"—a comment that suggests a link between *Nicholas Nickleby* (1838–39) and the Beargardeners and reminds us that Ralph Nickleby, the promoter of a fraudulent stock in the United Metropolitan Improved Hot Muffin and Crumpet Baking and Punctual Delivery Company, ended by hanging himself. A parallel has also frequently been drawn between Melmotte and the swindler Merdle in *Little Dorrit* (1855–57), who was also a member of Parliament and who committed suicide. (The *Liverpool Daily Post,* reporting Trollope's lecture, remarked: "The incessant toil which the production of so many works entails is making itself apparent, for he looks a much older man than when he last made a public appearance in Liverpool—on the occasion of the Dickens banquet. . . . Mr. Trollope is no orator; he has a somewhat thick utterance, and last night had a husky voice, but he succeeded in interesting the audience for very nearly an hour.") In recognition of his discourse, the directors elected him a life member of the institute.[34]

The Way We Live Now is saturated with familiar places. The Suffolk region where Roger Carbury lived, and its coastal resort of Lowestoft, were in Trollope's district as Post Officer surveyor from 1859 to 1867 and he knew them thoroughly. (The King's Head tavern in Bungay, where John Crumb and Ruby Ruggles had their wedding breakfast, still survives.) His new home was in the Marylebone region of London; when Melmotte's fraud and suicide became known, his parliamentary constituency of Westminster never forgave him, but "Marylebone, which is always merciful, took him up quite with affection" and even "spoke of a monument," no doubt like the one to Hudson which provoked Carlyle's pamphlet (chap. lxxxviii). Clubland, south of Piccadilly, and Mayfair, which separated it from Marylebone, he of course knew well. There are a few echoes of his travels in America—Mrs. Hurtle speaks of hearing the seals howling at San Francisco, and the proposed South Central Pacific and Mexican Railway would run from Salt Lake City ("thus branching off from the San Francisco and Chicago Line") through Mexico City to Vera Cruz (chaps. xlii, ix). The myth of the "glorious west, . . . those golden shores which the Pacific washes" (chap. xcviii) may have been fostered by the luncheon with Mark Twain and Joaquin Miller. Lady Carbury's publisher gives her the same advice Hurst and Blackett's foreman had given to the young Trollope: "Whatever you do, . . . don't be historical. Your historical novel, Lady Carbury, isn't worth a———" (chap. lxxxix).[35] The enemies of lawyer Squercum said he must be a Jew, because he never came to his office on a Saturday, but "they who knew the inner life of the little man declared that he kept a horse and hunted down in Essex on Saturday"—where Trollope continued to hunt even after he gave up his house at Waltham Cross in Essex (chap. lviii). There was the question for the Herald's officer to decide with reference to the seating at Melmotte's dinner for the Emperor of China: "Which ought to come first: a director of the bank or a fellow who writes books?" But it turned out to be unimportant: though two poets had received tickets, and "a novelist was selected," "as royalty wanted another ticket at the last moment, [this] gentleman was only asked to come in after dinner" (chaps. xliv, xxxv). When a telegram from London intercepted Marie Melmotte's elopement at Liverpool, Trollope wrote: "It may well be doubted whether upon the whole the telegraph has not added more to the annoyances than to the comforts of life. . . . Poor Marie, when she heard her fate, would certainly have gladly hanged Mr. Scudamore"—Frank Ives Scudamore, Trollope's colleague who was responsible for the Post Office telegraph service and who had presided over the farewell dinner given to Trollope on his retirement (chap. l).

His opinion of Disraeli is brought forward in this, as in more than one of his other novels. "Melmotte was not the first vulgar man whom the Conservatives had taken by the hand, and patted on the back, and told that he was a god," reflected Beauchamp Beauclerk, one of the party leaders, as he watched Melmotte's campaign, which he was energetically supporting (chap. liv). When Brehgert became engaged to Georgiana, he suggested that she might call him "Ezekiel" instead of "Mr. Brehgert"; she hesitated, and he volunteered that his late wife had called him "Ezzy"—Trollope's ridicule of Disraeli's nickname of "Dizzy." Georgiana "did not think it possible that she should ever call him Ezzy" (chap. lx). Trollope explained the origin of Father Barham, the priest befriended by Roger Carbury, who was modeled on George F. L. Bampfield. "When at Waltham, I became acquainted with the R. C. priest there, & opened my house to him in full friendship. He was a thoroughly conscientious man, an Oxford man, what we call a pervert and you a convert, and a perfect gentleman,—so poor that he had not bread to eat. I & my wife were as good to him as we knew how to be;—but he would never desist for a moment from casting ridicule and opprobrium on my religion, though I would not on any account have hinted a slur upon his. I was obliged to drop him. He made himself absolutely unbearable," he wrote to Mary Holmes, a Roman Catholic correspondent who had once annoyed Thackeray by attempting to convert him.[36] Trollope took his revenge by subjecting his priest to a scornful humiliation at the hands of Melmotte (chap. lvi). When Ruby and John Crumb were married, Crumb's friend Joe Mixet made a speech in which he quoted Scripture: "'Appy is the man as 'as his quiver full of 'em" (chap. xciv), recalling the passage to which a principal character of *Barchester Towers* owed his name.

Only a fortnight before the last number of the novel was published—indeed two months after it had appeared in volume form—a first leading article in the *Times* castigated the corruption of the age in two angry columns that seem to echo *The Way We Live Now* (though Trollope and his book are not mentioned). "It is a simple matter of fact that these last twelve months have been marked by a succession of disgraceful scandals. . . . There is increasing audacity, increasing greed, increasing fraud, increasing impunity; and these are stimulated and fed by increasing indulgence and ostentation. . . . Gentlemen of family and station are competing for the honour of helping Canadian, American, French, and German adventurers to fleece English society, and English society has allowed its greediness for exorbitant gains to hurry it blindfold into the trap." Trollope's friend, Lord Justice Wilbourne William James, is quoted as having said, "In this state of things these gentlemen apply to a body of English gentlemen of position and say to them, 'Pretend to be shareholders, pretend to be promoters, pretend to have made a contract with us, and invite the world to join you as shareholders. . . . We will find you the shares, we will indemnify you against all the expenses, we will have the contract made by ourselves cut and dried ready for signature, and we will give you a part of the purchase-money which we are to receive in money or shares, and, besides that, you will have your profits as Directors of this Company.' And that body of English gentlemen consented and condescended to become the retainers on these terms of some unknown adventurers from the other side of the Atlantic." "Unhappily," the article goes on, "the same recklessness, with the inevitable consequence of dishonesty, is showing itself in a hundred forms all about us. We believe there never was so much card-playing for high stakes as there is now, . . . in classes [of society] where a night's bad luck may easily be a life's ruin, and where the impulse is, not that the gamblers have money, but that they want it, and cannot get it by other means. Yet there are those who will play with them, to reap a harvest out of misery and ruin."[37] The writer, commonly supposed to be John Delane, editor of the *Times,* seems to have looked at contemporary English life through the glass of Trollope's novel. It is scarcely surprising that about two weeks later Lady Barker's (anonymous) review of the novel in the same newspaper should praise its "too faithful . . . portraiture of the manners and customs of the English at the latter part of this 19th century." "This is one of Mr. Trollope's very best stories," she says,[38] and readers more than a century later tend to agree with her.

Chapter XXII

1873–75

In Shirley Brooks's opinion, Trollope "roar[ed] more than ever since Australia." The foreign correspondent for the *Times,* William Howard Russell, and Trollope were his dinner guests early in 1873 and between them made so much noise that Brooks good-naturedly threatened them with the police. "Then Anthony said we were conventional tyrants, and Russell said in a weeping voice that Ireland was accustomed to be trampled on."[1] Perhaps the volume of the roaring can be attributed in part to the condition Anthony sadly reported to Lady Pollock in October:

> I have been troubled and in some sort unhappy. I fear I have lost the hearing of one ear for always. For such troubles a man ought to be prepared as he grows old; and this is comparatively so small a trouble, that I ought not to feel it a grievance. But for a time it frets me, and confuses me. I fancy that I am always going to be run over, and everybody seems to talk to me on the wrong side. I am told that a bone has grown up inside the orifice. Oh dear! One does not understand it all. Why should any bones grow, except useful, working, bones? Why should anything go wrong in our bodies? Why should we not be all beautiful? Why should there be decay?—why death?—and, oh why, damnation? The last we get out of by not believing it, but when a man has a bone in his ear, so that everything makes a rumbling noise and nothing is heard distinctly, he does believe it. But why;—why is it there? I suppose I have done something or left undone something, which if left undone or if done, would have saved me from the bone. But for the moment I cannot get it out of my head. I wish I could![2]

Brooks's predecessor as editor of *Punch,* Mark Lemon, died on May 23, 1870, and a month later Brooks addressed Trollope very earnestly in support of an application for relief from the Royal Literary Fund on behalf of the widow. Trollope lent his support at the meeting of the general committee, and Mrs. Lemon was given £100. Less than two years later, *Punch* could announce that the Gladstone administration had granted her an annual pension of £100.[3] And then in February, 1874, Brooks himself died, leaving an impoverished widow, and Trollope once again was called upon to support an application to the literary fund. She too received £100 from the fund, three months after her husband's death. In this case the widow's emotional distress was such as to make it exceedingly painful for her to call in person at the fund's office for her check, and Trollope intervened to have the ordinary procedure waived.[4] He did more: he acted as treasurer and "beggar-in-chief" to a small committee of Brooks's friends who raised a subscription of more than £1,000 by private donations for her relief; he said he wrote "some hundreds" of letters about the business early in May, and some fifteen of his notes or receipts have survived. At the same time he set in motion a petition to Disraeli's government to secure a Civil List pension for her, and she was granted an annual £100 in June, 1876.[5]

Trollope was no stranger in the pages of *Punch*. A cartoon in 1871 showed a tall, handsome, shallow young man in the firm embrace of a skinny elderly woman he had married for money. He petulantly tells her he doesn't so much mind her petting him in private, but he wishes she would not do so in front of his friends. "And why not, my Phoebus?" she replies, being "up in Mr. Anthony Trollope." "Should not a Woman *Glory* in her Love?" "O, Bother!—" says the husband. A few years later the Reverend Duodecimus Lazarus Quiverful is shown pushing a three-wheeled carriage full of sleeping children, and about the same time a cartoon satire on bad table manners is called "The Way We Live Now."[6] Trollope's granddaughter was told that when Anthony returned from Australia, there was a cartoon of "Mr. Punch" welcoming him home.[7]

Only a month before Brooks's death, he had joined Trollope, Millais, and thirteen others at the home of the Queen's surgeon, Sir Henry Thompson, to sign the statement that brought into existence the Cremation Society, of which Thompson became president. Trollope himself died two years before cremation became legal in England.[8]

≈

Two months after the first number of *The Way We Live Now* appeared, Trollope signed an agreement with Chapman and Hall for a new novel (not named in the contract), and on the next day (April 8, 1874) he began to write *The Prime Minister*. Later in the year Effie Millais expressed her discontent with having to read novels in installments, and he replied: "I quite agree with you about reading novels in numbers, but am glad that all are not of your way of thinking,—as I should never earn any money."[9] The issuing of novels in parts, which had been so successful in the case of Dickens (and was still being used in posthumous cheap editions of Dickens's novels), was beginning to fall into disuse with the proliferation of magazines and Trollope's publishers tried in vain to rescue that form. The pattern of twenty monthly parts at a shilling each was altered after

Orley Farm and *Can You Forgive Her?* to weekly sixpenny parts for *Last Chronicle*. *He Knew He Was Right* was published concurrently in weekly and monthly parts. *The Vicar of Bullhampton,* when the magazine to which it had been sold failed, came out in monthly parts. *Ralph the Heir* was published as a supplement to the monthly *St. Pauls Magazine* but was concurrently available in separate parts. *The Way We Live Now* went back to monthly shilling parts, and now *The Prime Minister* was planned for eight double-sized monthly parts at five shillings each. It was Trollope's last venture in parts publication (as distinguished from serial publication in a magazine). His contract promised him £2,500 for the copyright; since the stipulated length was four-fifths that of *The Way We Live Now,* the rate of payment was slightly higher for the new novel.

In *The Prime Minister* the Duchess of Omnium contrasts her own talents with those of her husband: "He never wants to say anything unless he has got something to say. I could do a Mansion House dinner to a marvel" (chap. lvi). Not long before Trollope wrote this passage in early August, 1874, he had been one among some three hundred guests the lord mayor and lady mayoress had entertained in the Mansion House on July 21, to honor the principal representatives of literature and art in England, France, and Belgium. Mrs. Oliphant found it an "amusing" occasion; she sat next to Matthew Arnold and liked him better in person than in his books. She saw Trollope and Charles Reade but very few other representatives of literature; the newspapers, however, reported that Browning, Swinburne, Ainsworth, Wilkie Collins, G. A. Henty, Rhoda Broughton, Sala, and Yates were there, as well as "Billy" Russell of the *Times.* The ladies of the Queen were striking in their finery. The dinner was served "with the accustomed splendour" in the Egyptian Hall, but alas! the food was poor, in Mrs. Oliphant's view, and the speeches as reported in the *Times* were certainly exceedingly dull;[10] the speakers had not "got something to say."

Anthony and Rose spent a fortnight in Paris (April 17–30), where they picked up Tom's daughter Bice and brought her home, and then from mid-July to mid-September they took her on a tour of the Black Forest and Switzerland that almost repeated the tour they had so much enjoyed in 1857.[11] On the Continent they met the New England author Richard Henry Dana and his wife and had many good talks together. Trollope later told Dana's son that his father "was one of the most entertaining *raconteurs* he had ever met and spoke of his wit and wide information, all which made conversation where he was present so entertaining."[12] Harry Trollope, who was now living on the Continent, joined their party for the Black Forest portion of their tour and came to visit them in London for a week or two soon after their return. Then he went back to Germany. The manuscript of *The Prime Minister* traveled with them, of course, and increased in size almost daily as Trollope lingered amid the lovely scenery of the Hoellenthal and Hoechenschwand and enjoyed the fantastic view from Felsenegg, a health resort above Lake Thun.

But their tour did not close without incident. They took their homeward tickets from Basel through Strasbourg, Luxembourg, Brussels, and Ostend to London. The advertisements had said the price was 124 francs (about £6 4s.) per person; they were charged 130 francs. The advertisements had said luggage up to 56 pounds per passenger was free; they were charged for every pound. They had been told they were on a through carriage to Ostend, and it was so labeled, but they were obliged to change at Brussels. The only opportunity to purchase any refreshment between Basel at 3:00 P.M. and Brussels at 7:00 A.M. was a fifteen-minute halt at Strasbourg. But they were singled out for a special misfortune—the conductor tearing a coupon out of one of their ticket books at Strasbourg managed to drop the whole book down the window frame. Officials gathered round; all were infinitely polite and sympathetic, but the book was irretrievable and of course the gentleman had to pay for a new ticket.

Nearly twenty years earlier Trollope had satirically remarked in *The New Zealander:*

> The threat of [writing a letter to the *Times*] is now the common and immediate resource of impotent anger. An unreasonable lady makes some monstrous request to a railway official, and a refusal immediately brings down an assurance of a letter to the Times. An unfortunate custom house officer is unable to do all that some hot-tempered traveller requires in his haste, and the promise of a letter to the Times is the immediate result. That men should threaten in their anger is not surprising nor disgraceful. The Times newspaper affords us in this the discreeter way that we now have of uttering an oath in our anger. Of the two practices the Times newspaper is the better, if the matter be there allowed to drop. With the majority it does so drop. By the mean spirited, the malignant, and often by the vain, the matter is carried further, and the letter is written. Of such a judicious Editor culls the most fitting, and public opinion is so created.[13]

Precisely a week after his return, Trollope dated his letter to the *Times* from the Garrick Club, recounting his experiences and "warning travellers against the direct route between London and Basle, *via* Strasburg, Luxemburg, and Brussels." The *Saturday Review* lost no time in making sport of one of their favorite victims, and wrote that in handling his travel arrangements Trollope had shown "more than that average amount of ignorance and weakness" for which the managers of railway lines can be expected to make provision. This accusation drew from him an instantaneous second letter to the *Times.* Two months later a third letter reported that he still had not got his money. Early in December he received restitution of his overcharges, along with a request that he now tell the readers of the *Times* that the money had been paid; he did so, with the observation that twelve weeks had been a long time to wait, and that he might at least have expected an apology he never received.[14] Meanwhile he was explaining to the readers of *The Prime Minister* that the traveling world "divided itself into Cookites and Hookites,—those who escaped trouble under the auspices of Mr. [Thomas] Cook, and those who boldly combated the extortions of foreign innkeepers and the anti-Anglican tendencies of foreign railway officials 'on their own hooks'" (chap. lxvii).

∂

In many respects *The Prime Minister* is a reworking of the social problems Trollope had dealt with in *The Way We Live Now*. The moral corruption of commercial society, and especially the speculative commerce of the investors in the City, is again central, and more than once we have echoes of the comparative language of the former novel, the "now" and the "formerly." "The world was changing around him every day," thought old Abel Wharton, barrister and member of the landed gentry. "Peers' sons were looking only for money. And, more than that, peers' daughters were bestowing themselves on Jews and shopkeepers" (chap. ix). "The world as it was now didn't care whether its sons-in-law were Christian or Jewish;— whether they had the fair skin and bold eyes and uncertain words of an English gentleman, or the swarthy colour and false grimace and glib tongue of some inferior Latin race" (chap. xiv). The present age was "surrendering itself to quick perdition" (chap. xvi). Not surprisingly, characters are carried over from the one novel to the other—Sir Damask and Lady Monogram (chap. ix), Mr. Broune of the *Breakfast Table* and his wife Lady Carbury, and poor old Booker of the *Literary Chronicle* (chap. xi). (There had been only a most tenuous link between the people in *The Way We Live Now* and the earlier novels: Lord Nidderdale was a cousin of Lady Glencora, Duchess of Omnium.) The central figure of this commercial aspect of the novel is Ferdinand Lopez, a handsome man of thirty-three with a bachelor flat in Westminster, who dresses meticulously, rides well on a splendid horse, was educated at a good English private school and a German university, then returned to work in a London stockbroker's office. But though a good worker he was restless under the direction of others and turned to speculation of his own, including the purchase of shiploads of guano from South America and of kauri gum from New Zealand (a cheaper substitute for amber), stock in a newly invented concoction from the bark of central African trees, called "Bios," and in a mining venture in Guatemala. These investments were not unlike the South Central Pacific and Mexican Railway; they absorbed money but were very likely to pay back nothing, and Lopez obtained the funds for his investments by borrowing or cajoling wherever he could (chaps. i, xliii, lii, liii). Like Melmotte he was, in English eyes, a "nasty foreigner," and probably of Jewish descent (chap. xiii), but whereas Melmotte was an unpleasant bully without a shred of commercial morality, Lopez wins our sympathy and the love of Wharton's daughter Emily: he is charming, intelligent, well educated. Ambitious of acceptance into the society of his intellectual equals, he seems forever barred by his lack of property and by the English sense that he is not one of them; even the generous hero of the novel, Arthur Fletcher, while denying Wharton's description of him as "a nasty Jew-looking man," feels obliged to say that though "he's a hand-some man, with a fine voice," he is "dark, and not just like an Englishman" (chap. xv). "When a man has connections, a father and mother, or uncles and aunts, people that everybody knows about, then there is some guarantee of security," but as for Lopez, "No one knows anything about him, or where to inquire even" (chap. v). Lopez makes some headway into society through his marriage to Emily and through attracting the attention of Glencora, Duchess of Omnium, who promises to help him win a seat in the House of Commons for the Omnium family constituency of Silverbridge, but none of his schemes for gaining a fortune pay off, and he faces a life not very different from that of his associate, "Sexty" Parker, a very ordinary person, "not quite a gentleman" (chap. xliii), with a dull wife whose accent is decidedly lower-class. Emily's father is too careful with his money to commit much of it to his son-in-law's speculations; new election laws (including the secret ballot) make family patronage of constituencies unethical and ineffectual, and Lopez loses money to no purpose in his bid for the seat. As matters get worse he becomes less scrupulous—and less pleasant. He bullies Emily; he drives Parker to financial ruin and alcoholism. And yet, "to give him his due, he did not know that he was a villain" (chap. liv). Unlike Melmotte, he puts his own money into the fraudulent speculations—and loses it. Perhaps his overbearing insistence that Emily unquestioningly obey his commands is the aspect of his behavior we are least likely to condone, and yet his language to her is in fact not very unlike that of the Duke of Omnium when the Duchess attempts to assert her own ideas (chaps. xxxii, xlii).

Having met Lizzie Eustace, Lopez conceived the notion of recovering his fortune by eloping with her, "but Lizzie Eustace had £4000 a year and a balance at her banker's. 'Mr. Lopez,' she said, . . . 'I think you must be a fool'" (chap. lv). And so early one morning he dressed carefully, kissed his wife affectionately, took the underground to Euston Station, and bought a first-class ticket to a very busy junction point six or seven miles distant. He paced the platform there, and as "the morning express down from Euston to Inverness was seen coming round the curve at a thousand miles an hour," he turned toward a ramp that led down to the tracks, and "with quick, but still with gentle and apparently unhurried steps, he walked down before the flying engine—and in a moment had been knocked into bloody atoms" (chap. lx). These were the final words of part 6; readers would have to ruminate on the event for another month before they learned the sequel. For the third time (Dobbs Broughton, Melmotte, and Lopez) a shady speculator in a Trollope novel took his own life.

A husband's dominance over his wife is a recurrent theme. "Of course I know it would be wrong that I should have an opinion," said the Duchess to the Duke. "As 'man' you are of course to have your own way. . . . Really you are becoming so autocratic that I shall have to go in for women's rights." "In all things there must at last be one voice that shall be the ruling voice," said the Duke. "And that is to be yours,—of course," she replied (chap. xxxii). The question even became a parliamentary one: "Mrs. Gresham got her husband to make that hazy speech about women's rights, so that nobody should know which way he meant to go" (chap. li). Mrs. Finn was sure that equality for women was coming, though she thought legislation on the matter would defeat its own ends (chap. xi).

The candidacy for Silverbridge provided the link with the familiar figures from the "parliamentary" novels. Plantagenet Palliser, Duke of Omnium, becomes prime minister in a coalition government that holds things together for three years until his own hereditary party, the Liberals, can organize themselves again, and there is a good deal of political discussion that reflects Trollope's own views as an "advanced conservative Liberal."[15] Though the coalition ultimately fails on an issue of electoral reform (anticipating the Reform Act of 1884), the "great political questions of the Commonwealth" were "Labour and Capital, . . . Unions, Strikes, and Lock-outs." On the other hand, Sir Orlando Drought, first lord of the Admiralty and the chief Conservative in the coalition, seeks glory by "the building four bigger ships of war than had ever been built before,—with larger guns, and more men, and thicker iron plates, and, above all, with greater expenditure of money"—a doctrine that has a familiar modern ring; his battle cry for the coalition was to be "the Salvation of the Empire" (chap. xxxii).

Naturally there is a good deal of Trollope's personal experience in the novel. A letter posted in a pillar-box in London between three and four o'clock in the morning was delivered to Wharton Hall in Herefordshire late that same evening (chaps. xxii–xxiii). Dick Roby proudly serves Trollope's favorite claret, '57 Léoville (chap. x). Remembering how he himself had helped in the disfranchising of his opponents at Beverley on the grounds of bribery, he saw to it that the candidates at Silverbridge carefully avoided all suspicion of bribery; "A brewer standing [for election], and devil a glass of beer!" complained one veteran elector (chap. xxxiv). [16] The style of the novel is urbane, sophisticated, abounding in the literary allusions and classical quotations that showed it to be the work of an educated man; Trollope, like Lopez during his courtship, "talked . . . of books,—and especially of poetry. Shakespeare and Molière, Dante, and Goethe had been . . . dear to him" (chap. xliv).

Unfortunately, his pen slipped on one classical allusion. Soon after the book's publication, Browning met Lord Acton on the street, and Acton was setting right "a strange blunder of . . . Trollope's," who had said that "the Spartan boy did not even make a grimace when the wolf bit him beneath his frock" (chap. lxxiii). Poor Anthony! it was a fox, not a wolf—and indeed he had got it right only a few years earlier in *The Claverings,* (chap. xxxii). One of his most enthusiastic admirers, Edward FitzGerald, found *The Prime Minister* "the only dull novel I have read of Trollope's."[17] There is in the book more weighty discussion of serious matters than is usual with him, but he does not abandon his lightness of touch. When Lopez becomes desperate for money, the extent of his economy is to take away his wife's subscription to Mudie's Lending Library and to instruct her that she shouldn't wear things that wanted washing (chap. xlvii). Only a savage, "or perhaps an Irishman," can banish care (chap. xxv). "Who, that ever with difficulty scraped his dinner guests together, was able afterwards to obliterate the signs of the struggle?" (chap. xxx). The description of Sir Alured Wharton, the Herefordshire baronet of ancient lineage, is a masterpiece of "character" writing: "All his happiness was to be drawn from the past. There was nothing of joy or glory to which he could look forward either on behalf of his country or his family" (chap. xiii). Though a good many reviewers agreed with FitzGerald, Trollope was right in his staunch affection for this novel.[18]

A month after completing *The Prime Minister,* and this time with no contract for publication, on October 12 Trollope began another long novel, *Is He Popenjoy?*

❧

The news from Fred at Mortray was not good: there had been prolonged drought, and the station was proving too small to be manageable at a profit. And so his father determined on another journey to Australia. "My boy in Australia is all in the right way. If he dont succeed in the long run I can no longer believe in honesty, industry, and conduct. But I believe I can give him a helping hand by going out. I can see what money I can advance to him out of my small means, and settle certain things with him," Trollope wrote to John Blackwood. [19] By the end of September, 1874, he told his plans to an American friend, Harriet Knower: he would go to Australia in the spring of 1875, and would return via San Francisco and New York. "That will be my 5th visit to the States, and on each occasion I have felt sure that I should never make the journey again." He complained that he did not like his London house nearly so well as the one at Waltham Cross. "But I suppose I shall live here now till I die. I do not know anything that should make us change." [20] There would, however, be something—the love of the countryside—that was after all to make him change after seven years at Montagu Square.

Trollope's meeting with Rhoda Broughton at the Mansion House dinner may have been their first encounter. While in America in 1868 Trollope had purchased her novel *Not Wisely but Too Well* on the recommendation of a lady friend and wrote to the authoress to praise it and also, as much her senior, to offer criticisms: "You fall into the common faults of the young, making that which is prosaic in life too prosaic, and that which is poetic, too poetic. . . . [But I] came to the conclusion that there had come up another sister among us, of whose name we should be proud." Though in fact he does not mention *Saint Pauls,* it is possible that he was intending to invite a contribution from her, but he never received one. In any case, she wrote from North Wales in October of 1874 to tell him that she was coming to London and would like to meet George Eliot. "George Eliot is not now in town. She is somewhat difficult to know. I will tell you more about her when I have the pleasure of seeing [you]," he replied as he invited her to lunch with himself and Rose on November 3. Some fifteen months later he praised her, among the modern novelists, in *An Autobiography:* "She has the gift of making [her personages] speak as men and women do speak." But "in [her] determination not to be mawkish and missish, she has made her ladies do and say things which ladies would not do and say. They throw themselves at men's heads, and when they are not accepted only think how they may throw themselves again." [21] This from the writer who had just completed the portrait of Arabella Trefoil in *The American Senator!*

The beginning of the new year brought some misfortunes to himself. First came "a very nasty liver attack," so that by January 6 he was "so weak I can only just crawl. But I am attaining to a slow but manly desire for mutton chops and sherry, and am just beginning to think once again of the glories of tobacco." He had indeed been seriously alarmed. But six days later he reported that he was "better and am hunting again, and do not mean to die this bout." Perhaps the hunting came too soon: on the sixteenth "I got into a muddy ditch, & my horse had to blunder over me, through the mud. He trod 3 times on my head. When I saw the iron of his foot coming down on my head, I heard a man on the bank say—'He's dead.' I am strapped up with plasters as to my forehead, but otherwise quite uninjured. You may imagine that in the scrimmage I had a queer moment."[22]

As for the tobacco, Trollope was wavering. On February 12 he told an inquirer: "I have long been an habitual smoker consuming about four cigars a day. I left it off a short time ago as an experiment for a fortnight, and found no effects, good or ill,—except the saving of the money." He was still smoking on the Australian journey, but by the end of 1875 he told one of his Australian friends who was visiting London, "A terrible misfortune has happened. I have 'swore off' smoking. But you shall have your pipe (the old tobacco) or cigars among the books. It will be quite a delight." Still, he had not quite "swore off." Five months later he wrote to a friend, "You will, after what you have written to me about tobacco, be glad to hear that I have gotten down from 6 cigars a day to *one a week,*—which is about equal to the horse's allowance of straw a day. But I, up to this, am not brought to apparent death." In the year of his death he summed up his experience with tobacco for another inquirer: "I have been a smoker nearly all my life. Five years ago I found it certainly was hurting me, causing my hand to shake, and producing somnolency. I gave it up for two years. A doctor told me I had smoked too much (three large cigars daily) and that smaller cigars would not be injurious. Two years since I took it up again, and now smoke 3 small cigars (very small) and so far as I can tell without ill effect. I am 67."[23]

There were a good many matters to attend to before he could get away. Rose was not to go with him, but would "roam about" (to use her words) on the Continent, probably with Harry and Florence Bland—to Hamburg, Danzig, Dresden. The problem of letting the house in Montagu Square had not been resolved when he left: they had offered it to John Blackwood, but he was not coming to town then, and so Trollope feared he would have to "bar up the library" and let it to strangers.[24] How Rose resolved the matter we do not know. An application for assistance from the Royal Literary Fund by Jane Mill needed his attention, for his fellow members of the committee wanted a judgment on her literary merit; he took time from his packing to report that he had "read sufficient of [her] work to enable me to express an opinion that the literary merit, though not high, should be acknowledged—I think that if the case be properly substantiated a small grant should be made. The lady is evidently industrious." On the strength of this recommendation she was given £30 at the next meeting of the committee.[25] Two days before he left town he finished reading proofs for *The Prime Minister.*[26] And he had to secure permissions from various of Tom Trollope's publishers for the collection into two volumes of Tom's recent magazine tales. One of these publishers was George Bentley, who granted the permission and at the same time asked Anthony for a novel for *Temple Bar;* Anthony agreed to supply one for publication in sixteen numbers, beginning in April or May, 1876, "if we could agree about the price." That agreement required negotiation: "I could not take the sum you offer," Trollope told Bentley, but he accepted £600 in monthly installments and £1,200 from Chapman for the rest of the copyright.[27] Apparently he first intended to use *Is He Popenjoy?* for the purpose, but ultimately let Bentley have *The American Senator,* begun in Australia on June 4.

&

Is He Popenjoy? was completed at sea between Ceylon and Melbourne on May 3, 1875. The only echo of the journey is Jack De Baron's threat to go to the island of Perim, at the south end of the Red Sea, in order to escape marriage—a threat he could not carry out (chaps. lix, lxiii). Trollope's ship had touched at Perim on the way to Australia, "a miserable little island" with a tiny garrison and a single officer.[28]

Doubtless the name of the novel needs explanation. "Lord Popenjoy" is the courtesy title of the oldest son and heir of the Marquis of Brotherton (whose family name is Germain); it derives from the (fictitious) name of the property in the black country of the midlands, from the coal of which the Germains derive their wealth. The question "Is He Popenjoy?" is first raised when the wicked Marquis returns from many years in Como, Italy, accompanied by an Italian wife and an infant son; neither marriage nor birth had been previously announced to his family in England, and there was naturally some doubt whether the boy was really Lord Popenjoy or a child born out of wedlock. When both the youngster and the wicked Marquis die, the speculation shifts to whether the coming child of the new Marquis (younger brother of the wicked one, and a principal character of the book) will be a boy (and hence Lord Popenjoy) or a girl. It is indeed Popenjoy (one chapter from the end of the book) and there is much rejoicing.[29]

The novel starts in a manner not unlike *Barchester Towers:* a fictitious cathedral city of Brotherton in the county of Brothershire in the midlands (bearing much resemblance to Staffordshire) has its bishop, its dean (father of the heroine) with whom the bishop generally disagrees, and a rigorous puritanical bishop's chaplain named Groshut who is even more hostile to the dean. He was (like Lizzie Eustace's second husband, Joseph Emilius) a converted Jew, and like his prototype Obadiah Slope of *Barchester Towers* he bullies his bishop too much and is ultimately sent away. The dean expresses doubt "whether any good is ever done by converting a Jew," and when reminded that St. Paul was a converted Jew is driven to fall back on the argument that in those days there was no other possibility (chap. xliv).

But the novel really focuses on the marriage between the dean's daughter, Mary Lovelace, and Lord George Germain, younger brother of the wicked marquis. It was not a love match; Lord George had loved another woman but she had refused him because neither he nor she had any money. The dean was a wealthy widower whose substantial fortune was inherited from his tradesmen parents, and his daughter was attractive, so that Lord George next sought her hand and was accepted. She was eager to be a good wife and to love her husband, but the task was not easy: he liked dull life in the country, had no interest in lakes and mountains (no travel to Switzerland and Italy) and none in the gaiety of London. His first act after the marriage was to set a reading list for her; for a start she was to spend an hour after breakfast each day with Gibbon (chap. iii). They were to live with his widowed mother and three unmarried sisters, who devoted their days to making petticoats for the poor and visiting the sick of the neighborhood, and who looked down on the dean as the product of a marriage between a livery stable keeper and the daughter of a rich candlemaker. There were no novels at all in their home "except those of Miss Edgeworth, which were sickening to [Mary]" (chap. xlv). The dean enjoyed life and intended that his daughter should do so also, and so he insisted that the couple spend their winters in a house he helped them take, overlooking St. James's Park near Storey's Gate and only a few steps from the Houses of Parliament and Westminster Abbey. (Not least of the dean's offences in the eyes of Brotherton society was his love of hunting; Trollope handled the problem very much as he had done in his hunting sketch of "The Hunting Parson" ten years earlier, and he gives us a spirited description of a hunt early in the novel.)

Mary took real pleasure in the social life of London, in dances and lively converstaion; "I often think that my young ladies have been popular, not because they have been true to nature, but because they have been lively," Trollope wrote to a friend three months before he began the novel.[30] Lord George was constantly disapproving: he forbade her to waltz, for example, as unbecoming the sister-in-law of a Marquis. She meets a young officer whose conversation she enjoys and who indeed falls in love with her, but who never tells her so and never for a moment crosses the bounds of propriety. Lord George presumes that the husband's will must prevail, and forbids her to see the young officer. "I trust that you do not wish to contest the authority which I have over you" (chap. xxxix). He intends to be "masterful and marital" (chap. xxxii) and even drags her away from a large party at which the dancing seems to him too frivolous (chap. xxxviii). She must be above suspicion, like Caesar's wife. "That the power of a husband was paramount he was well aware"; nevertheless "he did not exactly see his way to the exercise of it." For Mary is far from submissive, being fully conscious of her own innocence and indeed her loyalty to him.

Meanwhile, the woman who had turned him down because he was without money married a man much older than herself who had that qualification and no other, and became a member of the same social group in London. She frankly sought to resume the former amatory relationship with Lord George, and he, although too honest to engage in an affair with another man's wife, was too simple-minded to know how to avoid it. He knew they were "bound by honour, by religion, and equally by prudence" to avoid each other (chap. xx), but whenever she summoned him to her house in Berkeley Square he went to her. Intending to show Mary another letter, he inadvertently directs her to a most passionate epistle from the lady, and though he does not actually see her read it he realizes what he has done. Yet never once does she mention it to him, or show any distrust of him. He is slow to realize the devotion to him that her silence shows, and slow also to understand what his sister Lady Sarah explains to him: "She cannot feel as you do in all things any more than you feel as she does. . . . Each must give way to the other if there is to be any happiness" (chap. xlix). "What a fool a man must be not to see that he is preparing misery for himself by laying embargoes on the recreations of his nearest companion" (chap. xxxix). But if the husband ought not to tell his wife not to waltz, neither should the wife tell the husband not to smoke.

The comic background to this theme is "The Rights of Women Institute. Established for the Relief of the Disabilities of Females" (generally referred to merely as the "Female Disabilities"), in the Marylebone Road. This was headed by Lady Selina Protest, "a very little woman with spectacles, of a most severe aspect." At the only meeting Lady George Germain attended, there were two distinguished speakers from abroad, Miss Doctor Olivia Q. Fleabody from Vermont and the Bavarian Baroness Banmann, "a very stout woman, about fifty, with a double chin, a considerable moustache, a low broad forehead, and bright, round, black eyes, very far apart," who waddled rather than walked (chap. xvii). The harmony of this occasion unfortunately did not continue; as the months passed the Baroness found herself thrust aside by the admirers of Doctor Olivia, whom she sputteringly referred to as "that *female,*" with little regard to consistency with the principles which had brought them together (chap. lx). The burlesque of the "Disabilities" is the reverse of the coin which carried "Caesar's wife" on the obverse.

Once again, as in *Last Chronicle,* we find a dean using the little hotel in Suffolk Street as his London base (chap. xxvi). The Post Office telegraph has reformed the English style by teaching us "the pith and strength of laconic diction" (chap. xx). When Trollope calls the huntsman of the Brotherton Hunt "George Scruby," he is remembering the countryside near Rose's home of Rotherham, where one of the local hunts regularly assembled at Scrooby Inn.[31] And the device of making the wicked Marquis *twice* marry his wife (in case the first marriage should turn out to have been illegal) is of no consequence to this story, but the same device was to become quite central to the plot of the later *Mr. Scarborough's Family*. *Is He Popenjoy?* has the same theme as *He Knew He Was Right*, but without the melodrama and the insanity: its characters are varied, but are normal people in normal situations, and in its ironic observation of human pomposity it is one of Trollope's best.[32]

The novel remained unpublished for two and a half years; then the younger Charles Dickens brought it out in *All the Year Round* from mid-October, 1877, to mid-July, 1878. Once again Trollope proved too improper for an editor's taste; he failed to draw the line between innocent flirtation and outright adultery with sufficient rigor. And so Dickens would not let him refer to "that commandment which [Lord George] weekly prayed that he might be permitted to keep" (chap. xix). Trollope might say that it was "so hard to be a Joseph," but he might not go on: "The Potiphar's wife of the moment has probably had some encouragement,—and after that Joseph can hardly flee unless he be very stout indeed" (chap. xxxii). A married woman was not permitted to speculate with whom her husband "consoles himself," nor to say, "I hope someone is good-natured to him, poor old soul" (chap. xxxv). All calculations as to the expected arrival date of the infant must be banned, nor might the farmer point out that *his* baby would arrive much sooner after his marriage than Lord George's (chap. lxiii). And of course Mary was not permitted to announce that she would nurse her own baby (chap. lxiii).[33]

ᶑ

The publisher Nicholas Trübner, having learned of Trollope's planned journey to Australia, apparently proposed that he write a series of letters from abroad for weekly publication in provincial newspapers, and Trollope welcomed the proposal. "I should endeavour to deal chiefly with the social condition of the people among whom I found myself," he said. The agreement provided payment of £15 for each of twenty letters, and an additional £5 each if the number of newspapers subscribing should reach eighteen (as it did not). And so he set off on his journey equipped with a supply of addressed envelopes and a "manifold writer" (apparently a device employing carbon paper, which by the end of the journey became quite useless). The prudent Trübner wanted a second copy of each letter sent by some conveyance other than that which carried the first copy. "I find working with that multiplying apparatus is a bore, not but that it is easy enough while you are doing it, but that it is so long & troublesome to arrange, and then it dirties your fingers in a disgusting manner," he wrote to Rose. His experience with the Post Office enabled him to fix with some precision the dates his letters would arrive in London;[34] the fine art of keeping track of the schedules of mail ships is one which has disappeared only since the middle years of the present century, not altogether to our advantage.

The letters, which deal with Italy, the Red Sea and Aden, Ceylon (four letters), Australia (ten letters), Fiji and colonization in the South Seas (two), New Zealand, and California, are lively accounts, obviously much briefer than his *Australia and New Zealand,* less scholarly, and based principally on observation and conversation. It is especially interesting to read him on the subject of colonization at a time when the British Empire seemed to be expanding without limits:

> Men who are at the same time politicians and philanthropists—or who, in other words, concern themselves with the welfare of their own country and of the world at large—find an almost invincible difficulty in the colonization of new lands. That the teeming populations of old civilised countries should find new fields for their labours in the fertile lands about the world—lands which, when found by them, are populated only in the sparsest manner—seems to be not only expedient but absolutely necessary for carrying on God's purposes with the earth. It is impossible to regret that North America and Australia and South Africa have been opened to British enterprise and British life; and yet we have to acknowledge to ourselves that in occupying these lands we commit a terrible injustice. Though we have struggled against the injustice, it always comes. We have endeavoured to console ourselves by thinking that the peoples would at any rate have become Christians before they had utterly perished. I will not here go into that very vexed question of the possible Christianising of the savage races. But experience seems at any rate to show that the extermination always comes before the Christianity has been realised. The land becomes ours with its fatness—and the people disappear. They cannot endure contact with us—even when, as in New Zealand, we make the most determined struggle to be just. They cannot endure contact with us—even when, as in New Zealand, they are endowed with gifts of intellect and courage much higher than those generally found among savage tribes. It is terrible to think of this extermination. The Maoris are going. The blacks of Tasmania have perished to the last man. The

aborigines of Australia are perishing in part, and partly being driven into the barren interior of their own country.[35]

Something at least of his distaste for the colonial mission was the result of the experience of Commodore James Goodenough, who in conversation had rebuked Trollope for disparaging the native islanders' "aptitudes for lessons of a high order" and told him "that his experience taught him to think that they were fit recipients for any good tidings which might be brought to them." Within a few weeks, Goodenough had sailed for the Santa Cruz Islands, north and east of Australia, and there, in the course of what appeared to be a friendly bartering session with the natives, he was shot with an arrow and the wound proved fatal. Trollope had just arrived at Sydney on his return from Mortray when Goodenough died; "we buried him with his two shipmates upon the hill, on the north shore, over Sydney harbour, in one of the loveliest spots ever formed by nature. . . . We had all of us to remember that in this futile attempt to make friends with the few natives of a little island, England had lost one of her best seamen—a man tender as he was brave, a man of science, full of the highest aspirations, fit for any great work—such a one as no nation can afford to lose lightly."[36]

Trollope left England on March 1, crossed France into Italy (where his train was snowed in at Bologna), met Tom at Rome and traveled with him to Naples, which he found not particularly interesting, nor the bay equal in charm to several others he had seen. A visit to Pompeii, recently excavated, fascinated him, and Tom took him also to the picture gallery, then on March 8 at Brindisi he boarded the ship *Nigani* for Alexandria. The Suez Canal, still only dreamed of when he undertook his postal mission to Egypt in 1858 (and Trollope had then been skeptical of the dream), now carried the larger vessels plying between London and India, but not the smaller ones that called at Brindisi; the rail between Alexandria and Suez was now complete, however, and he did not need the services of a camel. At Suez he caught the *Peshawar,* which had come from London and Southampton, and was carried round India to Point de Galle at the southern tip of Ceylon.[37] This, he tells us, "is that Tarshish whence, once in three years, came the ships of Solomon, 'bringing gold and silver, ivory, apes, and peacocks.'"[38]

In Ceylon a young man tried to sell him an interest in a coffee forest; "If you have a few thousands, you can't do better." (Five years later a blight wiped out the coffee industry, and Ceylon turned to production of tea and other exports.) He traveled about the island, and spent a week at the favorite mountain resort of the English at Nuwara Eliya, "with my very old friend the present viceroy," his Harrow schoolfellow William Gregory of Coole Park, Galway. "He is a very good fellow, but his house was dull and there was nothing to do or be done. I do not think he enjoys his life there very much himself. A Governor has a great deal of luxury but very little comfort. He can admit no equals, and lives in a sort of petty bastard vice royalty which would kill me."[39]

In Australia he was known for his book on the colony, of course, and when he stepped off the *Golconda* in Melbourne on May 3 he at first fancied that almost everyone looked at him with offended indignation. Soon, however, he found himself a celebrity among friends; immediately on his arrival at Sydney an acquaintance from the earlier visit, the premier of New South Wales, John Robertson, invited him to be one of an official party to see off the New Guinea Scientific Expedition the next day, May 18. Six days later he was of the governor's party that reviewed the military forces of the colony on the Queen's birthday.[40] He then spent more than two months at this son's station. "[Here] I have no sherry and bitters, though plenty of smoking. I dont always get my boots cleaned, and other personal attendance I have none. I write for four hours a day, then ride after sheep or chop wood or roam about in the endless forest up to my knees in mud. I eat a good deal of mutton, smoke a great deal of tobacco, and drink a moderate amount of brandy and water. At night I read, and before work in the morning I play with my grandchildren,—of whom I have two and a third coming. Fred, my son here, is always on horseback and seems to me to have more troubles on his back than any human being I ever came across. I shall be miserable when I leave him because I do not know how I can look forward to seeing him again without again making this long journey. I do not dislike the journey, or the sea, or the hardship. But I was 60 the other day, and at that age a man has no right to look forward to making many more voyages round the world."[41] It was decided that Mortray should be sold, and Anthony helped with making the arrangements, but after he left, some of the bankers and business men he had talked to behaved as scoundrels in their dealings with Fred. The station was sold at a loss of £4,600, which the father scraped together from the proceeds of his novels. Fred looked about without success for a place as manager and part owner of a larger station, then purchased some undeveloped land which his bad health never allowed him to work, and by the end of 1876 had obtained an inspectorship of conditional purchases in the Lands Department, a post he held until only a few months before his death. At Mortray Anthony began to write *The American Senator*.[42]

On his return to Sydney he was honored at an elaborate picnic up the Nepean and the Warragamba by boat, arranged by many public figures. The chief justice, Sir James Martin, toasted him as a man who "has won our personal esteem as well as our admiration, and . . . we have as much affection for his character as we have respect for his attainments." Trollope responded, "I feel that I am in the midst of old and dear friends, whose

sympathy and kindness it will be quite impossible for me ever to forget."
A week later, on August 28, he sailed from Australia aboard the *City of
Melbourne,* called at Auckland and Honolulu, and landed at San Francisco.[43] A visit to Yosemite was arduous and tedious, but the rail journey
across the continent was made very pleasant by the friendliness of his
fellow travelers. The train stopped thrice daily for twenty minutes for
meals. "If [the traveler] wishes the solace of wine or spirits he should take
them with him. He will find himself provided with an excellent bed and
with ample accommodation for washing his hands and face. The need of a
bath at the end of the journey is certainly much felt."[44]

There is little record of his brief stay in New York and New England. He saw Oliver Wendell Holmes in Boston and no doubt other
friends as well. Despite stormy seas he enjoyed his fellow travelers on the
Bothnia from New York to Liverpool. One of them, Henry James, found
him "the dullest Briton of them all," with "a gross and repulsive face and
manner," who nevertheless appeared to be a good fellow when you talked
to him. Trollope had the ship's carpenter fit him out with a writing desk
in his cabin, and "he drove his pen as steadily on the tumbling ocean as in
Montagu Square." (Later, when James met Trollope at dinner in London,
he found him "a very good, genial, ordinary fellow—much better than he
seemed on the steamer.")[45] He had finished *The American Senator* as he
crossed the Pacific, and was now at work on *An Autobiography.* The ship
reached Liverpool on October 30.

A group of Boston and Cambridge friends of Trollope's were organizing a fund-raising fair for the Massachusetts Infant Asylum, and part of
the effort was the publication of half-a-dozen leaflets as a lighthearted
serial called *Sheets for the Cradle* in the second week of December, 1875, at
a subscription price of one dollar. James Russell Lowell was a contributor,
and the editor was Susan Hale, sister of Edward Everett Hale (whose more
serious periodical, *Old and New,* had carried *The Way We Live Now* until it
collapsed in May, 1875). Such a mock journal needed a "novel," and
probably while in Boston Trollope agreed to supply one—a "novel" in
three "volumes," each consisting of three chapters about two hundred
words long, entitled "Never, Never—Never, Never." The author of
some of the longest novels in English was cheerfully parodying, in one of
the shortest, his own *Small House at Allington*—and a witty and delightful
parody it is, unfortunately almost unknown. He was determined to confute Bret Harte, who was reported to have said he had no sense of humor.
The notion of a short parody had occurred to him at least two years earlier,
when he asked three artist friends to illustrate a novellette in three volumes, each volume on a sheet of note paper, which he intended as "a
present to a very pretty girl whom I have known for some years."[46] But of
this earlier parody we know nothing more.

Chapter XXIII

1875–76

The publisher Bentley demurred at Trollope's title for *The American Senator,* since he had stipulated "a tale of modern English life," and when Trollope stood firm ("I am sure that nobody can give a name to a novel but the author"), Bentley in the advertisements added in parentheses, "The Scene of which Story is laid in England." As the novel progressed in the magazine, Bentley told the author that he liked the work.[1] In the matter of the title, Trollope seems to have had a very late repentance, for he began his last chapter by saying that his book "might perhaps have been better entitled 'The Chronicle of a Winter at Dillsborough.'" Dillsborough is a fictitious small market town in the county of "Rufford," northwest of London (chap. i). The novel is essentially the story of two women in search of husbands, Mary Masters and Arabella Trefoil. Mary was a sweet-natured person about twenty-one years old, daughter of the town's more important attorney by his first wife, whose father had been a clergyman. Mary's social position was ambiguous—an attorney is not of the gentry, but a clergyman is by definition a gentleman; and then the attorney's second wife was merely the daughter of an ironmonger. Mary was sought in marriage by Larry Twentyman, a prosperous yeoman farmer of the vicinity, but Mary, much as she liked him, did not love him, and, not being inclined to be bullied by her family, refused the proposal. She had been brought up to believe that "young women should be quiet and wait till they're sought after" (chap. xxvi), and so for much of the book it appeared that she would be the Lily Dale to Larry's Johnny Eames, but ultimately the squire of the village, a bachelor of forty who had inherited nearby Bragton Park, and whom she had known and loved since she was a child, plucked up his courage and asked her to marry him. The question of whether husband or wife should rule was settled more pragmatically than it had been in *Popenjoy:* "I mean it to be understood that [as your true husband] I take you into partnership on equal terms, but that I am to be allowed to manage the business just as I please. . . . Only as you are practical and I am vague, I don't doubt that everything will fall into your hands before five years are over, and that I shall have to be told whether I can afford to buy a new book, and when I am to ask all the gentry to dinner" (chap. lxxi).

The Trefoils (apparently not related to the old dean of Barchester,

whose death is recorded in *Barchester Towers*) were of the highest nobility;
the head of the family was Duke of Mayfair, with the fine country estate of
Mistletoe in Lincolnshire. The Duke's younger brother, Lord Augustus,
himself with no financial resources, had married a banker's daughter,
squandered her money, and then lived apart from her and their child,
Arabella. It was the aim of the Trefoil women's lives to secure a suitable
husband for Arabella; they spent most of the year as guests of various
people who could not easily turn them away, and the pursuit of the male
was "the work to be done" (chap. xvii). More than one engagement
Arabella thought secure collapsed, and when nearly thirty she was still
single. She had met a British Foreign Service officer on a visit to Washington with her mother, was affianced to him, but did not really care for
him, and while visiting at his house near Dillsborough began to wonder if
she could not "pull off" an engagement with a more attractive bachelor,
Lord Rufford (chap. xx). "She had long known that it was her duty to
marry, and especially her duty to marry well" (chap. xii). She had very
large, beautifully blue eyes, perfect eyebrows, and a brilliant complexion
which, if owing a great deal to art, concealed the art skillfully. Tall and
big, hers was a somewhat Germanic beauty (chaps. xii, xxviii), and she
was intelligent as well. But as the American Senator observed when he
learned that her fiancé had died, "From what I see and hear, I fancy that
here in England a young lady without a dowry cannot easily replace a
lover. I suppose, too, Miss Trefoil is not quite in her first youth" (chap.
lxviii). Hers is a situation rather unjustly held by many to be comic, but
she gains the reader's respect despite her scheming and her energetic
pursuit of the male quarry (so opposite to Mary Masters), and we are well
content when at the end she inherits £5,000, marries another Foreign
Service officer named Mounser Green, and accompanies him on a diplomatic mission to Patagonia. If it is customary to speak of Lizzie Eustace as
Trollope's Becky Sharp, it would not be amiss to find the same resemblance in Arabella. And only at the end do we perceive the irony of
Trollope's comment when early in the story Mounser Green remarked,
"I'm a poor man, but I wouldn't take her with £5,000 a year, settled on
myself." "Poor Mounser Green!" added Trollope (chap. xxviii).

One of the hunts near Rose Trollope's home of Rotherham was the
Rufford Hunt[2] (Rufford Abbey was a mansion close to Ollerton, in Sherwood Forest), and there is a good deal of hunting in the novel. Again and
again the hunt is treated as a metaphor for Arabella's pursuit of Lord
Rufford, and even that devoted sportsman justified her in his mind: "As
for hunting him,—that was a matter of course. He was as much born and
bred to be hunted as a fox" (chap. lxvii). Trollope is speaking for himself
when he makes Reginald Morton, the squire of Bragton, ridicule "a letter
[I have had] this morning from a benevolent philosopher [who] wants me

to join a society for the suppression of British sports as being barbarous and antipathetic to the intellectual pursuits of an educated man" (chap. lxxiii). (A few months later in *An Autobiography* he used much the same language to summarize E. A. Freeman's position in his *Fortnightly* article against hunting.)[3] And when one of the sportsmen is in fact killed by a kick in the head after he has been thrown from his horse (chap. xxii), we are aware of Trollope's recollection of his own recent narrow escape on the hunting field. In the eyes of the senator, a hunt consists of "a hundred harum-scarum tomboys [riding] at their pleasure over every man's land, destroying crops and trampling down fences, going, if their vermin leads them there, with reckless violence into the sweet domestic garden of your country residences; and . . . no one can either stop them or punish them!" (chap. lxxviii).

The figure of Elias Gotobed, Republican senator for the great western state of Mickewa, has nothing to do with the plot; he has come to England from Washington at his own expense from a sense of duty to inquire into "the most material institutions of the country" (chap. li). And it is his presence that leads Trollope subsequently to speak of himself as a "satirist" in writing this novel, whose part it is "to be heavy on the classes he satirises,—not to deal out impartial justice to the world; but to pick out the evil things."[4] The device is a familiar one in satire; the American Senator in England is Goldsmith's Chinese "Citizen of the World" or Swift's Gulliver among the Lilliputians. Perhaps it is the satirist's slight distancing from reality that leads Trollope to choose far more label names for his characters than he has lately been accustomed to use: Mr. Wobytrade, the undertaker; Platitude and Monsoon of the Foreign Office, Ribbs, the butcher, Lord Lambswool (chaps. lxiv, lxv, lxxvii), Lady Ushant. Mounser Green's aunt defended his Christian name as not "a kind of chaff" but a family surname, "as good a Christian name as Willoughby or Howard" (chap. lxxv), and Senator Gotobed's name is in fact also an authentic English surname, no more a kind of "chaff" than, say, the surname "Trollope." The contemporaneity of the story is emphasized by Trollope's placing its events explicitly in the winter and spring of 1874–75.

The senator of course is himself object of the conventional British amusement at American idiosyncrasies. He understands the word *hunt* as an American would (i.e., as "shoot," in "hunting" wild animals), uses "fix" as "to prepare" (a dinner), is fond of "I guess," and addresses an opponent in an argument as "Mister" (without a surname: "You think he's a scoundrel, Mister"). When he calls at the Foreign Office Mounser Green apologizes for not having a spittoon, " 'but the whole fire-place is at your service.' The senator could hardly have heard this; it made no difference in his practice" (chap. xxviii). The senator's earnest inquiries into

English life range through the lack of central heating, the inequities of the franchise (prior to the Reform Act of 1884, obviously) and of clerical patronage, "feudalism," or the privilege of rank in "this aristocratic country," and the economics of landlordism. No doubt recalling Mark Twain and Bret Harte, Trollope lets a friend assure the senator "that the serious American is not popular [in England], whereas the joker is much run after" (chap. li). His point of view is properly characterized by one of his hosts as "utilitarian" (chap. lxviii)—i.e., Benthamite or Millite rationalist; this is not Trollope's own doctrine. The senator of course expresses his opinions everywhere in conversation, in two long letters to a congressman from his home state, and by way of culmination in a lecture on "The Irrationality of Englishmen" at St. James's Hall that requires two of Trollope's closing chapters and that is curtailed when the police become alarmed by threats of a riot. "The British heart might be all right; but the British head was,—ah,—hopelessly wooden! It would be his duty to say so in his lecture" (chap. lxix).

Some of Trollope's favorite subjects recur here: competitive examinations for the Civil Service (chap. xxviii), "Caesar still clinging to his Commentaries as he struggled in the waves" (chap. xliv), the quality of clarets (about which of course the senator reveals his utter ignorance) (chap. xlii). There is the local postmaster who was almost persuaded to turn over to her mother a letter of Mary Masters, but who remembered at the last moment the duties he had learned from "one of those trusty guardians of our correspondence who inspect and survey our provincial post offices" (chap. xxxiv). Trollope was gathering his thoughts for the writing of *An Autobiography,* and his description of farmer Goarly's disreputable house is in fact very close to the description he would soon be writing of his father's farmhouse at Harrow Weald.[5]

The book was written in anticipation of Trollope's fifth visit to the United States; it was completed two days before he landed at San Francisco. When, therefore, he was back in London he had the manuscripts of two finished novels with him and could choose which he wanted to use in *Temple Bar.* "I wish to consult you about our novel," he told Bentley as he invited him for a late breakfast on November 11, 1875. The choice they made was *The American Senator.* Then Trollope himself apparently had second thoughts; he was eager to do a sequel to *The Prime Minister* that might be more successful than a novel on a new subject. But *The Prime Minister* would not complete publication in parts before June, 1876, and Bentley wanted to begin the serialization of his novel before that date. And so on January 17, 1876, Trollope wrote to him, "It is now too late to change the subject of the novel for the Temple Bar. 'The American Senator' must therefore stand."

Chapman and Hall were to bring out the three-volume edition about a month before the tale would end in the magazine, and it occurred to Bentley that it would be more convenient if Chapman's printers (Virtue & Co.) struggled with Trollope's manuscript than if his own printers had to do so. But Chapman was apparently reluctant to pay for the typesetting a year and a half before he could sell a copy of the book (published June 2, 1877), and so Bentley's printers had to make the best of the scrawl. Initially also Bentley had thought of buying from Chapman the right to issue the one-volume "popular edition," no doubt using the same typesetting as *Temple Bar,* but that too fell through, and Chapman turned over the one-volume edition to his neighbor on Piccadilly, Chatto and Windus, who published it at the beginning of November, 1877.[6]

હ

Anthony's sixtieth birthday, April 24, 1875, fell while he was on shipboard between Ceylon and Melbourne, and seems to have brought upon him gradually the sense that he was becoming an old man. "As to that leisure evening of life, I must say that I do not want it," he wrote to a friend in June, 1876. "I can conceive of no contentment of which toil is not to be the immediate parent. As the time for passing away comes near me I have no fear as to the future—I am ready to go. I dread nothing but physical inability and that mental lethargy which is apt to accompany it."[7] With the awareness that he must give up smoking and hunting came also the impulse to look back upon his career. And so as he crossed the Atlantic on his voyage home from Australia and North America he wrote the first two chapters of his memoirs.[8] While on shipboard he had to rely, of course, entirely on his memory for the account of his early years; when he reached home, he had access to his carefully preserved correspondence with publishers and his contracts with them, as well as to whatever other correspondence he had kept. Presumably at his suggestion, Rose jotted down for his use brief notes of her recollection of their year-by-year activities from the time of their marriage.

Trollope had once dined with John Stuart Mill at Blackheath, and he wrote a letter to Mill's stepdaughter at the very time she was publishing Mill's posthumous *Autobiography* (though as that letter has not survived we do not know what he said); it seems likely, therefore, that he read Mill's book soon after it appeared in 1873.[9] Mill begins with the modest disclaimer that his own career in itself can be of no interest to the public, but he believes that the history of his education and the development of his opinions may provide for his contemporaries and posterity a valuable record of the age's intellectual movement. Trollope begins with the same disclaimer: he has written "the autobiography of so insignificant a person as myself" in order that through revealing "what I, and perhaps others round me, have done in literature; my failures and successes such as they have been, and their causes," he may show what "opening . . . a literary career offers to men and women for the earning of their bread" (chap. i). There is, therefore, a good deal of discussion of payments from publishers, ending with a table of "the sums I have received" for "the books I have written" (chap. xx). Art, he continues to insist, is as much the trade of the artist as shoemaking is the trade of the cobbler. [10] It is a commonplace of modern scholarship that this commercial frankness postponed all chance of a posthumous reputation for him for some half a century, but evidence is seldom adduced to support this improbable view. If the image of the gentleman author, who wrote to occupy his leisure and with no thought for profit, at all endured into the nineteenth century, the spectacular industry and financial success of a Dickens must have destroyed that image some years before Trollope set down his confession.

Trollope had also recently encountered another bit of autobiography, that in which Dickens wrote of the anguish of his four months of humiliating work in Warren's Blacking warehouse at the age of twelve, a fragment Forster published in the first volume of his *Life of Charles Dickens,* which Trollope read in Australia at the beginning of 1872. Consciously or unconsciously Trollope echoed this passage as he described his unhappy schooldays at Harrow, when he was about the same age, and the miseries of both lads were closely linked to loss of social status caused by the father's desperate and unexpected poverty. The wretched schooldays have become as much a part of the Trollope myth as the Blacking Warehouse is of the Dickens myth. [11]

The *Autobiography* is only partially a chronological account. As he had promised, he discusses contemporary novelists; he devotes some pages to the theory of fiction, and echoes what he said in the lectures that he was so frequently asked to give on that subject.* He talks about reviews of fiction and ridicules the author who tries to win favor by flattering the critic, as Lady Carbury had done in his recently published *The Way We Live Now.* He very carefully sets up the image of his unhappy youth at the beginning, so that in the midst of his prosperity he can reflect on the contrast between the lad who had "crawled up to school with dirty boots and trousers through the muddy lanes" and the sweetness of "the respect, the friendships, and the mode of life which has been achieved" (chap. ix).

---

*He gave one such lecture, "On the Art of Reading," before the students at the Quebec Institute on Lower Seymour Street on March 2, while he was at work on *An Autobiography.* As in that book (chap. xii), he lays great stress on morality among the great novelists of his day: he did not think that Scott, Thackeray, or Dickens ever wrote anything impure. He used essentially the same lecture when he distributed prizes at the City and Spitalfields School of Art in November. [12]

A year after he wrote his memoir, he defended Cicero for saying that the orator may "garnish his good story with little white lies,—'mendaciunculis.' The advice does not indeed refer to facts, or to evidence, or to arguments. It goes no further than to suggest that amount of exaggeration which is used by every teller of a good story in order that the story may be good. Such 'mendaciuncula' are in the mouth of every diner-out in London and we may pity the dinner parties at which they are not used. . . . Either invent a story, or if you have an old one add on something so as to make it really funny. Is there a parson, a bishop, an archbishop, who if he have any sense of humour about him does not do the same?"[13] One must be prepared as one reads *An Autobiography* to suspect some "little tiny exaggerations." Trollope put it more simply in *The Way We Live Now:* "Who tells the whole truth in giving the story of his life?" (chap. xlvii).

Often he adopts the tone of a letter—a letter written in 1876—as when he remarks that his boyhood friend John Merivale "is going to dine with me one day this week" (chap. iii), or laments, "Alas! at this very moment I have [a Christmas story] to write, which I have promised to supply within three weeks of this time" (chap. xx). His actual correspondence of this period often discusses matters he takes up in the book, as for example the letters he wrote to Mary Holmes about *The Way We Live Now* and *Daniel Deronda*.[14] (There exists a presentation copy of *Deronda* inscribed to Trollope "with the affectionate admiration and regard of George Eliot.")[15] Indeed the memoir is not an authoritative factual account of what happened, but a retrospect from the point of view of the months in which he wrote it (with a few corrections in footnotes written about three years later); it is as firmly emplaced in his sixty-first year as the novels he wrote immediately before it and after it, and it occasionally echoes the autobiographical comments he made in those novels.

No doubt he did not deliberately misrepresent the facts, but his memory was sometimes remarkably false to them, as when he spoke of the Ireland to which he was transferred early in his Post Office career as "a country in which there was not a single individual whom I had ever spoken to or ever seen" (chap. iv), though his Harrow schoolfellow William Gregory lived near his headquarters and was frequently his host. When he professed that he "never lived in any cathedral city,—except London, never knew anything of any Close" (chap. v), he quite forgot his schooling at Winchester, where indeed St. Cross Hospital gave him some sense of the life he portrayed in Hiram's Hospital. The statement that "we always spent six weeks at least out of England" while living at Waltham Cross (chap. xv) is far from literally true. If we are to believe that the plot for *Doctor Thorne*, which was suggested to him by his brother Tom, "was the only occasion in which I have had recourse to other source than my own brains for the thread of a story" (chap. vi), what becomes of the theories of certain modern scholars that his plots drew heavily on the Elizabethan and Jacobean dramas he was so fond of, and in which he delighted to "search their plots and examine their characters"? (chap. xx).* And one of the landmark dates in the book—the year in which he began to write *The Warden*—is mistaken: it was in July of 1853, not 1852 (chap. v). (As he thought the matter over, he was puzzled that "on looking at the title-page, I find it was not published till 1855.") His son Henry, in preparing the *Autobiography* for publication, set the date right.

Trollope completed the book before his birthday in April, 1876; "Since I saw you I have written a memoir of my own life," he told his Australian friend G. W. Rusden. "Now I feel as though every thing were finished and I was ready to go. No man enjoys life more that I do, but no man dreads more than I do the time when life may not be enjoyable."[17] He put it in his safe, and placed with it a letter to Henry, to be opened only after his death. The letter contained instructions for the book's publication, if in Henry's judgment it ought to be published, and though it permitted him to omit anything he thought ought to be omitted, it forbade additions. Henry, with the concurrence of Tom Trollope, submitted the book to Blackwood for publication rather than (as Anthony had suggested) to Chapman, since by that time the firm of Chapman and Hall had passed to other proprietors and Fred Chapman was no longer owner, but manager on their behalf.[18] Consistent to the end, he instructed Henry to drive a satisfactory bargain for the book, and Blackwood gave him £1,000 for the first 4,000 copies, plus two-thirds of the profits on all other copies sold. It was published about October 15, 1883. Sir Rowland Hill's daughter, who probably meant no compliment in view of the picture Trollope drew of her father, calls the book "one of the greatest, and certainly not the least amusing, of his many works of fiction."[19] Whatever her intention, her remark is true, and not in the least disparaging. It was with full awareness that Henry's would be the first eye to see the manuscript that Trollope wrote: "My son Henry . . . has . . . taken

---

*By the time of his death he had written marginalia and critiques in each of his copies of 257 plays and duly recorded the dates of his reading them. But if one is to look for a relationship between the novels and the early English plays one should probably avoid seeking direct borrowing of plots and characters. He drew upon them unconsciously; drew upon them for various comic devices, and perhaps modeled upon them his fondness for plot lines only loosely linked to one another, as in *Can You Forgive Her?* Certainly he was not deliberately seeking his plots in those plays before the time he wrote *An Autobiography* (1876), though a later novel like *The Fixed Period* (1881) has legitimately been paired with the comparable plot of *The Old Law*, by Massinger and others (read by Trollope in July, 1876), and *Mr. Scarborough's Family* (written 1881) may have drawn on Jonson's *Volpone* (re-read by Trollope in August, 1882) for the deviousness with which the old man played upon the greed of his presumed heirs.[16]

himself to literature as a profession. Whether he will work at it so hard as his father, and write as many books, may be doubted."[20]

ช่ว

Young George Leveson Gower, nephew of Earl Granville, knew Trollope as an annual visitor to the rectory of William Lucas Collins at Lowick, where George was a private pupil. Anthony customarily brought along a string of seven horses for hunting, and he and the lad rode out together with the Woodland Pytchley. But not after 1876, when Trollope recorded in *An Autobiography,* "My resolution has been taken. I am giving away my old horses, and anybody is welcome to my saddles and horse-furniture" (chap. xix). "The abnegations forced upon us by life should be accepted gracefully. I have not therefore waited to drain the cup to the last drop," he explained to a friend. "Alas yes, Essex hunting is over for me," he wrote to Anna Steele on March 25, 1876.[21]

Another recreation was threatened: while out in Australia he learned that a former member of the Horse Guards whom he specially disliked had stirred up dissension at the Garrick Club and had driven away Trollope's dear friend Sir Charles Taylor. "If I find when I return that I cannot get a decent rubber there, I shall be driven among the ponderosities of the Athenaeum where I can neither smoke nor have a glass of sherry and bitters."[22] Taylor, Trollope wrote in *An Autobiography* (chap. viii), "was our king at the Garrick Club. . . . He gave the best dinners of my time, and was,—happily I may say is,—the best giver of dinners." The parenthetical remark had to be amended within a few months, and Trollope wrote to Rusden in Australia, "He was thoroughly manly, and among the friends of my later life there was no one whom I more thoroughly loved— what the Garrick will do, which he managed as though it were his own house, we do not yet know."[23] Fortunately for Trollope's whist, the obnoxious horseguardsman also died.

A new lord mayor of London on May 6, 1876, gave a grand banquet at the Mansion House to nearly three hundred representatives of literature in its various branches. Trollope was there, of course, and may have sat at the same table with Mr. and Mrs. Matthew Arnold, Robert Browning, and Harrison Ainsworth.[24] The speeches were apparently extemporary, and as reported in the *Times* were exceedingly dull. Sala spoke on behalf of the drama, and Edmund Yates said a few words on behalf of the "Journalists, Novelists, and Art Critics." Another guest was the younger Charles Dickens, and quite possibly the conversation on this occasion led to his buying *Is He Popenjoy?* for *All the Year Round,* a weekly for which Anthony was not invited to write while it was conducted by the senior Charles Dickens.

The appearance of Kate Field on the London and provincial stage in

1876[25] was no doubt what prompted Trollope's remarkably affectionate tribute to her in *An Autobiography*. In his manuscript Trollope referred to her, not by name, but as "an American woman"; the book when published referred to her merely as "a woman," and an Englishwoman of whom Anthony was not fond publicly claimed, in *Women of the Day*, to be the person alluded to.[26] Kate's lodgings were on New Cavendish Street, Portland Place, not far from Montagu Square, and Anthony doubtless saw her frequently. She had Christmas dinner with Anthony and Rose that year.

The death of Earl Stanhope late in 1875 had a twofold impact on Trollope. Stanhope had been president of the Royal Literary Fund for a dozen years; the general committee invited Lord Derby to assume that position. And only two months before his death Stanhope had been appointed to the chairmanship of the new Copyright Commission; the vacancy in the chairmanship led to the replacement of four others of the fifteen-member commission, and one of the four new members was Trollope. The commission held forty-eight hearings, beginning May 8, 1876, and ending May 8, 1877; Trollope was present at all but one of the meetings. (Only his friend Dr. William Smith equaled that record; even the new chairman, Lord John Manners, missed three hearings.)

The hearings of the royal commission established very clearly the chaotic state of the laws both within the empire and internationally. Trollope had felt the sting of American practices from the time Harper undercut his agreement with Lippincott for publication of *North America*, but even in the colonies protection of English authors was uncertain. He had also been angered by Reade's adaptation of *Ralph the Heir*, and one of the witnesses before the commission was John Hollingshead, the producer of *Shilly-Shally*, who had helped form an Author's Protection Society; he testified on what he conceived to be the proper relation of copyright to the adaptation of a novel for presentation on the stage.[27] The commission produced its report on May 24, 1878. "With the great body of it I agree. . . . But in regard to this question of international copyright with the United States, I think that we were incorrect in the expression of an opinion that fair justice,—or justice approaching to fair,—is now done by American publishers to English authors by payments made by them for early sheets," Trollope remarked in an addendum to *An Autobiography*.[28] New legislation was naturally slow to follow the commission's report, and Trollope did not live to see it.

જ

In mid-October, 1876, Anthony, Rose, and Florence Bland returned from a two-month holiday in what were becoming favorite mountain resorts of theirs, Höllenthal in the Black Forest and Felsenegg in Switzerland; though ill at both places Anthony worked steadily at the manuscript of the novel variously entitled *The Ex-Prime Minister, Lord Silverbridge,* and (finally) *The Duke's Children.* Their return journey took them through Brittany and Bruges. A few days after they reached Montagu Square he completed the book on October 29.[29]

Nine months after he ceased to be prime minister the Duke of Omnium, with his Duchess and their three children, Lord Silverbridge, Lord Gerald Palliser (aged 20), and Lady Mary Palliser (aged 19), spent a year on the Continent; a fortnight after their return to England, and on the second page of the novel, the Duchess was dead, presumably of influenza. The novel is an account of the Duke's difficulties in facing the problem of looking after his children, and especially in reconciling himself to the spouses the eldest and the youngest of them seemed determined to choose. Lady Mary had fallen in love with Frank Tregear, the impecunious son of a Cornish gentleman; the Duke wished for a suitably noble son-in-law. Lady Mary, echoing Archdeacon Grantly's remark to the Reverend Josiah Crawley when Henry Grantly and Grace Crawley were to be married,[30] "asserted that as the gentleman was a gentleman there need be no question as to rank, and that in regard to money there need be no difficulty if one of them had sufficient" (chap. xxiv). Again and again throughout the novel the Duke reflects on the parallel between Lady Glencora's passion for Burgo Fitzgerald and his daughter's love for Tregear, and persuades himself that it is his duty to prevent their marriage. Lord Silverbridge proposed marriage to Lady Mabel Grex, daughter of the selfish spendthrift Earl Grex, but she, partly to avoid seeming to jump at the offer of a very wealthy husband, declined his proposal, and before he had a chance to renew it, he met and fell in love with Isabel Boncassen, daughter of a wealthy American scholar who had brought his wife and daughter to London so that he might study in the library of the British Museum. Boncassen was himself son of a dock worker, and although his daughter had no trace of the usual American nasal speech, his wife's language was quite uncultivated. Again, the Duke was distressed at the impropriety of the marriage, but Silverbridge was convinced that the world was changing: "Some years ago it might have been improper that an American girl should be elevated to the rank of an English Duchess; but now all that was altered" (chap. lxi). (Quite possibly Trollope was alluding to the marriage on April 15, 1874, of Lord Randolph Churchill, younger son of the Duke of Marlborough, to Jennie Jerome, daughter of a wealthy New York speculator. Lord Randolph was at about the same time elected to Parliament for the family constituency of Woodstock, just as Silverbridge was elected for the Omnium family borough in Barsetshire.)

The Duke ultimately gave his consent to both marriages, after a good deal of rather repetitive meditation by all parties.

But the real heroine of the book is Lady Mabel Grex, who had loved her cousin Frank Tregear but had given him up because neither of them had sufficient money to live on, and who had unselfishly turned down Silverbridge; "A girl unless she marries becomes nothing, as I have become nothing now," she reflects at the close of the book (chap. lxxvii).

The novel gathers together not only most of the characters from the previous "parliamentary" novels, but also people from others of Trollope's books. Gotobed, the American Senator, is now the American minister in London (chap. lxx),* and Captain Glomax's Ufford and Rufford United Hunt is mentioned (chap. lxii). The Beargarden Club is somewhat less disreputable than it was in *The Way We Live Now,* but a good many of our old acquaintances are still members. Naturally there is a good deal of discussion about American women, not at all unlike the similar views expressed in *An Autobiography.* Trollope satirized the sentimentality of much American literature by introducing Ezekiel Sevenkings, "the great American poet from the far West." "Do you not regret our mountains and our prairies," he asked Isabel Boncassen in London; "our great waters and our green savannahs?" "I think more perhaps of Fifth Avenue," she replied (chap. lxx).

There is very little of political discussion in the novel. Lord Silverbridge distresses his father by standing as a Conservative for the family constituency, instead of as a Liberal like the Duke; "We've got to protect our position as well as we can against the Radicals and Communists," he told his father (chap. vii). The Conservative government that succeeded Omnium's coalition had its prime minister in the House of Lords, Lord Drummond; the leader of the House of Commons was Sir Timothy Beeswax, chancellor of the Exchequer. Beeswax was far more of a parliamentary manager than a statesman, one who "had so mastered his tricks of conjuring that no one could get to the bottom of them." "No one was more warmly attached to parliamentary government than Sir Timothy Beeswax," because it gave him access to power; "but I do not think that he ever cared much for legislation" (chap. xxi). This, of course, is the kind of language that Trollope customarily used about Disraeli, and the situation was not unlike that when the older Lord Derby was prime minister and Disraeli, as chancellor of the Exchequer, was the most powerful man in the House of Commons. In February, 1868, Derby resigned and Dis-

---

*Only a few weeks before he began the novel, Trollope heard that R. H. Dana had been nominated by President Grant to that post, and wrote to express his gratification. But the nomination was not approved by the Senate, and Dana did not come.[31]

raeli became prime minister, but by the end of the year the Liberals were in power and Gladstone was prime minister. Disraeli's sponsoring of the Reform Act of 1867 had been the same sort of move to retain power without regard for party principle that Trollope attributed to Beeswax. Beeswax and Drummond fell out, Beeswax broke up the cabinet by resigning, and the Liberals came back into power with the Duke of Omnium as lord president of the council.

Trollope had planned the novel in twenty parts, like *The Way We Live Now,* but when the time came it seemed best to publish it in a magazine. The younger Dickens paid him £400 to bring it out in *All the Year Round,* as he had done with *Is He Popenjoy?* but apparently he wanted to give up no more space than the roughly nine months he had devoted to the former novel, and so Trollope cut his manuscript by 20 percent, meticulously pruning from beginning to end but never cutting so big a segment as a whole chapter: the original number of eighty chapters remained. Chapman paid him £1,000 for the book copyright, £200 less than he had paid for *Popenjoy.* As Trollope remarked in a later footnote to *An Autobiography,* "Since the date at which this was written I have encountered a diminution in price."[32]

Trollope tells us (correctly) that the £2,800 he received from George Smith for the serial and volume publication of *The Claverings* in 1866 was "the highest rate of pay that was ever accorded to me"—the largest amount, that is, in proportion to length. Trollope was more aware than many modern scholars that pay bore some relation to the number of pages. The largest amount he received for a single novel was £3,525 for *Can You Forgive Her?* in 1864; the novel was half again as long as *The Claverings.* His receipts remained at approximately £2,500–£3,000 for a full-length novel through *The Prime Minister* in 1876, then fell off markedly.[33]

❧

Trollope's consistent admirer Edward FitzGerald was as strong in his feelings about Disraeli as Anthony, and was accustomed to use much the same language Trollope used; from a holiday in Lowestoft, he wrote to a friend early in 1877: "[At a circulating library] I got [a novel] of Trollope's, 'Phineas Redux,' and have been glad to be back with him—a clever, and right-hearted, Man of the World. It is a Political Novel: much better than D'Israeli's, I think: whose writings are to me what his Politics are—showy and shallow. It really is a Disgrace for England's Aristocracy to be dragged about by this Jewish Adventurer."[34]

Patriotism for most Englishmen, said Trollope, is "a feeling that they would like to lick the Russians, or to get the better of the Americans in a matter of fisheries or frontiers."[35] The burning political issue of 1876 was the "Eastern Question"—the conflict between Turkey and Russia and the attempt of the Balkan peoples to tear themselves free of the Turkish empire. Gladstone especially was moved to campaign against the policy of Disraeli's government to speak softly to Turkey, even in the face of reported vicious massacres by the Turks in the Bulgarian communities. "Here we are all talking of war,—or rather of peace. The truth is that Gladstone has raised among the people such a flame of indignation against the Turks, that it would be impossible for any English Minister to go to war in their defence," Trollope wrote to Rusden on October 27.[36] On December 8, an all-day conference on the Eastern Question was held in St. James's Hall, "which was crowded in every part," said the *Times* reporter. (This, of course, was the hall in which Senator Gotobed had delivered his discourse on "The Irrationality of Englishmen.") Trollope sat on the platform, and was called on to speak. Times had changed, he said, since England fought in the Crimea to support Turkey against Russia—and the Turks and the Russians were changed. We must, regretfully, decide that our old friends will not reform their morals. "The Turk does not see the difference between good and evil as we see it. . . . He is the worst citizen in the world, because arms are his glory, and he has no glory except in arms. Industry, commerce, agriculture, science, literature are all ignoble to him. (Hear, hear.) To hold men in dominion by his sword and by his gun is to him the only ambition worthy of a nation or of a man. Therefore, England must now declare that if the Turk is to live in Europe, it must be under other laws than his own, and he must adopt other customs than those which outrage the feelings of civilized humanity. (Cheers.)" Thomas Hardy was in the audience, and saw something the *Times* did not record. "Trollope outran the five or seven minutes allowed for each speech, and the Duke [of Westminster], who was chairman, after various soundings of the bell, and other hints that he must stop, tugged at Trollope's coat-tails in desperation. Trollope turned round, exclaimed parenthetically, 'Please leave my coat alone,' and went on speaking."[37]

It was perhaps on this occasion that one hearer described Trollope as "all gobble and glare."[38] Nevertheless Lord Bryce thought Trollope's appearance on the platform in discussion of an issue then of the highest importance in parliamentary politics was evidence of his "continued interest in public affairs." One must bear in mind, along with this, a comment Bryce made in another context about the "views which [Trollope] was prompt to declare and maintain. There was not much novelty in them—you were disappointed not to find so clever a writer more original—but they were worth listening to for their solid common-sense, and you enjoyed the ardour with which he threw himself into a discussion."[39]

Chapter XXIV

1877–78

As the new year of 1877 began, Trollope was occupied with his more routine, noncreative obligations. The Copyright Commission was meeting two afternoons a week; the Royal Literary Fund had its business. Trollope procured its new president, the Earl of Derby, as chairman for the anniversary dinner on May 9; he was engaged in the search for someone to replace the resigning Lord Houghton as one of the treasurers, and there were the usual examinations into the qualifications of applicants for relief. When Helen Angelina Crickmaur, "a dear old lady" (six years younger than Trollope himself) who had been a schoolmistress but who was now almost starving at writing children's stories for small periodicals, was judged by the committee to have insufficient literary merit, Frederick Locker, a member of the committee, gave Trollope a sovereign to pass on to her.[1] Trollope's financial scruples extended to conveying the formal thanks of the committee to Lord Derby in a longhand letter, rather than pay the cost of engrossing, and he looked carefully into the capital resources of the fund in order to support his position that larger grants might be given and that each year's income might be spent in full. (The letter of thanks to the chairman of the annual dinner seems routinely to have indicated how much money the dinner had raised, so that the distinguished chairman might judge his popularity and effectiveness.)[2]

As for the Copyright Commission, the *Times* reported in February that it was still engaged upon the cheerful occupation of taking evidence, and had not yet even begun to talk about framing the report. The evidence taken already had reached the proportion of a moderately full library, and more than £1,000 had been paid to the shorthand writers who recorded it.[3] A year earlier, Lord John Manners remarked to John Blackwood that several members of the commission were given to making speeches instead of asking questions—and "Trollope too is rather in the speech-making line." But after testifying for nearly two hours, Blackwood was relieved to report to his wife that both Lord John and Trollope told him, "You did capitally."[4] At the time Trollope embarked for South Africa, the commissioners were reported to be endeavoring to find a basis for their report by formulating a series of resolutions: there were then about seventy of them, and it was expected that their number would reach a hundred.[5]

Henry James was back in London at the beginning of the year under the wing of Lord Houghton, who provided him with a guest membership to the Cosmopolitan, "a sort of talking club, extremely select." On his first visit, "amid a little knot of Parliamentary swells," he "conversed chiefly with . . . Trollope." On another occasion, Trollope introduced James to an American woman, a Miss Van Rensellaer, whose "American 'chattiness' exhilarated [James] more than any anglaise I have talked with these six months, and though she was vulgar, made me think worse of these latter, who certainly are dull, and in conversation quite uninspired." Two years later he was bemoaning "the bother of being an American! Trollope, Thackeray, Dickens . . . were free to draw all sorts of unflattering English pictures, by the thousand," whereas he himself, in a newspaper review of *Daisy Miller and Other Stories,* was taken severely to task for misrepresenting English ladies.[6]

❧

Trollope began to write *John Caldigate* (earlier known as *John Caldigate's Wife* and *Mrs. John Caldigate*) on February 3, 1877; by the time he sailed for South Africa on June 29 he had completed thirteen parts, of which he left the manuscript with Chapman. He wrote the final three parts aboard the steamer, finished them on July 21 and sent them also to Chapman when he landed at Cape Town next day. He had first approached Bentley as publisher, but when Bentley declined he turned to Blackwood, who paid him £600 for the use of the novel in *Blackwood's Magazine.* There it was published anonymously (as was the custom with that journal) from April, 1878, to June, 1879.* Chapman and Hall purchased the book copyright for £1,200 and brought out the three-volume edition (with Trollope's name) about May 30, 1879.[8]

One might easily imagine that from the time Trollope encountered his sons' schoolfellow prospecting for gold in Currajong, New South Wales,[9] he had it in his mind to use that experience as the subject of a story; in any case, John Caldigate, a Harrovian and a graduate of Cambridge, cut off by his father for extravagance, set out for Australia with his college friend Dick Shand in search of riches. On shipboard he became attracted to an intelligent adventuress, about twenty-four years old, who called herself "Mrs. Smith" and whose husband was reputed to have

---

*Trollope mistakenly assumed that the publication of *Nina Balatka* and *Linda Tressel* in *Blackwood's* without author's name was merely a part of his scheme for testing his success independently of his reputation. And therefore he wrote to Blackwood, "I suppose you would publish [*John Caldigate*] with the name which was withheld as to L. T. and N. B."[7]

drunk himself to death within a year of their marriage. As the voyage drew to an end she admitted that she was in love with Caldigate and he engaged himself to her, but she professed reluctance to marry him until he had had more time for reflection and they separated when the ship reached Melbourne. Caldigate and Shand made their way to the New South Wales gold fields—to "Nobble" and "Ahalala" (which have been identified with Grenfell and Currajong). [10] Shand became a hopeless drunkard and eventually went off to tend sheep in Queensland, but Caldigate found gold, then sold his holdings to his partner Crinkett, and returned home rich.

Trollope is perhaps not quite fair to his reader in his handling of a crucial aspect of the Australian adventure; he certainly does not adhere to the doctrine he had proclaimed in *Barchester Towers* (chap. xv): "The author and the reader should move along together in full confidence with each other." He tells us that Caldigate had no correspondence with Mrs. Smith for more than a month after they parted at Melbourne, then he learned by chance that she was dancing professionally in the theater at Sydney under the name of Mademoiselle Cettini and went to see her there. From this point the story is told only as presented in his letters home, and "it need hardly be said that there was no mention . . . of Mrs. Smith" (chap. xiii). Caldigate, after returning to Cambridgeshire, married the daughter of his father's banker, Hester Bolton, whose lovely eyes he had cherished in memory all the time he was gone, though he had scarcely talked to her on the occasion of their single previous meeting. The remainder of the novel is set in Cambridge, Suffolk, and Essex—Trollope's district when he was Post Office surveyor and the heart of the Puritan country of the seventeenth century. Hester's mother indeed was a very strict, puritanical woman and even their country home was called "Puritan Grange."

The book now quickly takes on the shape of the novel of mystery and intrigue. Crinkett and Mrs. Smith have joined forces and write to demand money of Caldigate on the ground that the mine he had sold them had suddenly failed, and when he declines to send it they show up in England and charge him with bigamy: he had, they claim, been married in Australia to Mrs. Smith. For the first time we learn that she had indeed joined him at Ahalala, had lived with him there, and was sometimes referred to as "Mrs. Caldigate." John denied the marriage, but the evidence at his trial for bigamy was such as to gain his conviction and a two-year sentence in prison.

Then Dick Shand came home; he wore yellow trousers purchased in San Francisco, a very large checked waistcoat and a short coat of the same material, and he was prepared to swear that there had been no marriage. But it was his word against theirs, and many people echoed the views of

Caldigate's cousin, the wife of the Reverend Augustus Smirkie, rector of Plum-cum-Pippins: "Did you ever see such trousers? I would not believe him upon oath" (chaps. xlix, lvi, li). A part of the evidence against Caldigate had been an envelope addressed in his handwriting to "Mrs. John Caldigate" at Nobble, and postmarked in the Sydney post office on May 10, 1873. Caldigate admitted having written the name, but denied that he had posted the envelope, and indeed it did not have the customary backstamp it should have received on its arrival at Nobble. A conscientious Post Office official, Bagwax, whose specialty was postmarks, suspected forgery but could not prove it; even after the trial he continued to study photographs of the envelope with the typical praiseworthy zeal of the Trollopian civil servant (not at all like the Dickensian employee of the Circumlocution Office). Suddenly he was struck by an aspect of the adhesive stamp itself. English postage stamps of the nineteenth century bear in their corners mysterious letters of the alphabet in various combinations; the postage stamp on the incriminating envelope carried a *P* in each lower corner, and Bagwax learned that stamps with *P*'s in the lower corners were not printed before 1874—therefore the letter could not have passed through the mails in 1873 and the date stamp had been falsified in the Sydney post office at a later date! Caldigate was released by a special pardon from the home secretary. In a footnote Trollope apologized to his "friends at the Sydney post-office" for this account: "I know how well the duties are done in that office" (chaps. lii, lxiv).*

Caldigate was cleared of bigamy, but the question remained in the minds of Hester's family and neighbors: was the characteristic lawlessness of a colonial mining village sufficient justification for his manifest immorality in living with Mrs. Smith? Hester consoled herself that this early infatuation was like a child's attack of measles, "which have been bad and are past and gone. Euphemia Smith has been her husband's measles. Men generally have the measles" (chap. li). (*Blackwood's* editor allowed Trollope this observation.) And so the novel ends happily. The criminal complications and complexity of the plot, the long suspense of the trial, and the conspiracy against Caldigate are not the usual substance of a Trollope novel; indeed they are the sort of thing he meant to repudiate

---

*It is curious that Trollope himself should have misunderstood the meaning of those letters—or did he merely assume that his readers would not perceive the error? The so-called check letters indicated the position of each stamp on the engraved sheet of 240 stamps. The top row of stamps would be lettered *A-A*, *A-B*, *A-C*, etc., to *A-L*, the second row *B-A*, *B-B*, *B-C*, etc., to *B-L*, for twenty horizontal rows and twelve vertical columns, i.e., to *T-J*, *T-K*, *T-L*.[11] What Bagwax might have learned was that in 1874 the number of vertical columns of stamps on a sheet was increased at least to sixteen (letter *P*). I cannot find that this was true. Moreover, stamps of this period from New South Wales do not show the corner letters in question.

when he said he thought "plot" was not a merit in novels. The book does not stand up very well among his more characteristic works. Tom Trollope, who was in London when he read the first four installments in *Blackwood's,* asked Anthony who was the author. "He was much surprised when I told him," said Anthony. [12]

ॐ

The writing of *John Caldigate* was interrupted for about three weeks from February 22, 1877, when Trollope wrote simply "Cicero" on his calendar. [13] This was the substantial two-part article for the *Fortnightly Review,* "Cicero as a Politician" (April, 1877) and "Cicero as a Man of Letters" (September, 1877). Trollope himself traced his love of Cicero's oratory back to his years in the upper forms at Harrow. [14] His review (May, 1851) of Charles Merivale's book on the subversion of the Roman republic by Pompey and Caesar necessarily also dealt with Cicero's vain search for some way of preserving the traditional form of government, a search that ultimately cost him his life. It was at the time of this review, Trollope tells us, that he first projected his biography, [15] and Merivale figures large in *The Life of Cicero.* Some of his reflection about method is expressed in a review of Merivale's subsequent volumes five years later, where Trollope insists that works of classical history must be written in good English style, not Latinate. [16] He himself freely quotes Latin on the assumption that many of his readers will understand it, and that the original has overtones no translation can catch,* but quoting Latin is different from writing in a hybrid, Latin/English jargon. The ideal of a readable style is one to which he adhered in his writings on the classics perhaps even more rigorously than in his novels. George Meredith wrote to John Morley that Trollope's first Cicero article "shows him to have a feeling for his hero. It reads curiously as though he were addressing a class of good young men. This is the effect of the style, or absence of style. One likes him for working in that mine." [17] Clearly Trollope was encouraged by the success of the articles to move on to his full-length biography of his hero.

There is a strong personal element in his *Life of Cicero,* even to his supposition that he might leave the manuscript unpublished (as he had done with *An Autobiography* less than a year before), "so that it may be left for those who come after me to burn or publish as they may think proper"

---

*"In translating a word here and there as I have done, I feel at every expression my incapacity. There is no such thing as a good translation. If you wish to drink the water with its life and vigour in it, you must go to the fountain and drink it there" (2:11–12). In his translations Trollope was extraordinarily careful to avoid mechanical fidelity and to be sure both idiom and circumstances would be clear to a modern English reader.

(1:1). It was of the utmost importance to Trollope that Cicero and his contemporaries should be recognizable human beings, behaving essentially as we might do, though with visible differences that may be pointed out. More than once his hero, seeking election, had to face "bribery, . . . intimidation, and a resort to those dirty arts of canvassing with which we English have been so familiar."[18] Nevertheless, Cicero was opposed to the secret ballot, as Trollope had been. "It is, alas, useless now to discuss the matter here in England. . . . It is, however, strange to see how familiar men were under the Roman Empire with matters which are perplexing us to-day" (2:379). At one point, when he was eager to get on with his writing, Cicero complains that he can get nothing done because he is overwhelmed by celebrity-seeking visitors. "No English poet was ever so interviewed by American admirers!" says Trollope (1:351). The faith in auguries and portents among the Romans (whose leaders played upon such superstition for political ends) reminds him of a recent assertion by the Scottish Sabbatarians, reported in the newspapers, "when the bridge over the Tay was blown away, that the Lord had interposed to prevent travelling on Sunday!" (2:24). Trollope relies very heavily on Cicero's statements about himself in the correspondence which has fortunately survived in such abundance, though he faults modern scholars for not reading these letters in their context: "If truth is to be expected from them, [they] have to be read with all the subtle distinctions necessary for understanding the frame of mind in which they were written" (2:166). Mommsen, whose history gives Trollope much of the factual background of events, is praised for his "research and knowledge," but "I cannot accept his deductions as to character" (1:314).*

Cicero was in fact "a modern gentleman" (2:300). He was broadminded toward those "allurements" which Nature herself has produced, and to which "not only youth, but even middle age, occasionally yields itself" (2:37). He was "an Epicurean,—as we all are" (2:337). "What a man he would have been for London life! How he would have enjoyed his club, picking up the news of the day from all lips, while he seemed to give it to all ears. How popular he would have been at the Carlton. . . . And then what letters he would write! With the penny post . . . at his command, and pen instead of wax and sticks, or perhaps with an instrument-writer" such as the one Trollope used to send back the copies of his newspaper letters from his recent Australian tour, "he would have answered all questions and solved all difficulties" (1:37–38). About a letter of moral precepts which Cicero wrote to his brother Quintus, Trollope comments, "Let the reader . . . ask himself what precepts of Christianity

---

*Trollope had to use W. P. Dickson's translation of Mommsen, "as I do not read German" (1:79).

have ever surpassed it." "I find a note scribbled by myself some years ago in a volume in which I had read this epistle, 'Probably the most beautiful letter ever written'" (1:337, 340). Indeed, Cicero's book on moral duties, *De Officiis,* is "one of the most perfect treatises on morals which the world possesses" (2:383).

"It is because he was so little like a Roman that he is of all the Romans the most attractive" (1:20). "I may say with truth that my book has sprung from love of the man" (1:2). "It has seemed to me that he has loved men so well, has been so anxious for virtue, has been so capable of honesty when dishonesty was common among all around him, has been so jealous in the cause of good government, has been so hopeful when there has been but little ground for hope, as to have deserved a reputation for" (in the words of his eighteenth-century biographer Conyers Middleton) "'sanctity of heart and morals'" (1:143). And he was (like Trollope himself, perhaps) an "almost inexhaustible contributor to the world's literature" (2:370).

He who had recently written *An Autobiography* remarks of Cicero's letters, "It is best to take a man's own account of his own doings and their causes, unless there be ground for doubting the statement made" (1:62). On the other hand, "the need of biographical memoirs as to a man of letters is by no means in proportion to the excellence of the work that he has achieved. . . . The man of letters is, in truth, ever writing his own biography" (1:32). Meantime, accidentally and in passing, Trollope gives us (from Cicero) the origin of the title of one of his own greatest novels: "Sed quid agas? Sic vivitur!"—"What would you have me do? It is thus we live now" (2:133).

Because he was writing altogether without the irony that so often prevails in the novels, his own beliefs are expressed in the *Life of Cicero* with a remarkable directness and honesty. To take only two of the more significant:

> *On property.* Property, speaking of it generally, cannot be destroyed. . . . But it is within human power to destroy possession and re-distribute the goods which industry, avarice, or perhaps injustice have congregated. They who own property are in these days so much stronger than those who have none that an idea of any such re-distribution does not create much alarm among the possessors. The spirit of communism does not prevail among people who have learned that it is in truth easier to earn than to steal. But with the Romans political economy had naturally not advanced so far as with us. (1:234–35)

> *On the efficacy of prayer.* Then [Cicero] reminds the people of all that the gods have done for them, and addresses them in language which makes one feel that they did believe in their gods. It is one instance,

one out of many which history and experience afford us, in which an honest and a good man has endeavoured to use for salutary purposes a faith in which he has not himself participated. Does the bishop of to-day when he calls upon his clergy to pray for fine weather believe that the Almighty will change the ordained seasons, and cause his causes to be inoperative because farmers are anxious for their hay or for their wheat? But he feels that when men are in trouble it is well that they should hold communion with the powers of Heaven. So much also Cicero believed, and therefore spoke as he did. (1:281)

It was in preparation for the *Fortnightly* articles that he "completed [reading] all Cicero's works from beginning to end" by December, 1876. The vigor with which he devoted himself to his study of Roman writers, and of Cicero especially, in these years is truly remarkable. There survives a set of 178 volumes of Latin authors, published in Paris between 1826 and 1839, with parallel texts in Latin and French, in most of which he has recorded the dates of his reading, and in nearly half of which he has noted down comments and observations. The densest annotations are in the thirty-six volumes of Cicero, and many of his comments are echoed in his *Life of Cicero*. Some, at least, of these books accompanied him on his Australian journey of 1875, for in one of them, a group of Cicero's orations, he noted, "This is the volume that was found out of doors at Forbes in N.S.W." His memoranda are dated from March, 1876, to December 24, 1879, and his readings include Livy, Suetonius, Tacitus, Quintilian, Ovid, and Horace, several of them from beginning to end more than once.[19] After three and a half years he told his son Henry (May 26, 1880), "I have done [writing] my Cicero,—but have not read it, which now remains for me to do."[20] He did more than read Cicero's works in preparation for his book; he read, with an alert and critical mind, the scholarship about Cicero, and one has a sense that though he may some-times have lacked learning (and that but seldom) his good sense made him more reliable than the pedants. The slowness with which he composed the book undoubtedly contributed to a certain repetitiveness in it, and per-haps reveals the merit of his usual speed of composition, but the book is a very important piece of work. (And a long one—longer than *Barchester Towers,* longer than any novel he wrote after the *Cicero.*)[21]

The manuscript was not, after all, left to the mercies of "those who come after me." "The correction of the Cicero will be a great trouble, as every word of it must be verified,—quotations I mean, & such like," he told his son. "It will be very tedious." On June 29, 1880, Chapman and Hall agreed to pay him a straight royalty on all copies sold, and a few days later he sold the American rights to Harper.[22] The book was published in London about December 1. Reviews were on the whole ample and friendly, but not uniformly so. The narration was judged to be skillful and characteristically lucid, and the book full of common sense. "Mr. Trollope's scholarship is quite equal to his task." Trollope deals with Cicero "as if he were in the habit of meeting him at the Garrick." And W. Lucas Collins, for whose series of "Ancient Classics for English Readers" Trollope had done the *Commentaries of Caesar* ten years earlier, and who himself had done Cicero for that series, remarked, "We have here perhaps the first Life of Cicero which will take its place on the drawing-room table."[23] It is futile to lament, no doubt, that this genuine masterpiece is now almost forgotten.

One day in the spring, Trollope paid a visit to a building in St. Martin's-le-Grand that had not existed while he was employed in the Civil Service—the large Telegraph Office recently built opposite the General Post Office. Here somewhat more than eight hundred young women were employed in dispatching, relaying, or receiving messages in a service which had become a Post Office monopoly only eight years earlier. Trollope's account of these "Young Women at the London Telegraph Office," published in *Good Words* for June, 1877, is a warm expression of pleasure in the beneficence of the service to which he had been devoted, as regarded the humane employment of young women. And the humanity was rewarded by efficient performance. True, on the rare occasion when serious discipline was demanded, the secretary to the Post Office himself was called upon to rule—"an officer of majestic power outside the Telegraph Office, who may be supposed to be a sort of Jupiter up in the clouds," Trollope's brother-in-law John Tilley. Trollope also wrote a short story on "The Telegraph Girl."[24]

ॐ

When Austin Dobson sent Trollope a copy of his *Portraits in Porcelain* in mid-May, 1877, Trollope could not resist doing what he had always done with Dobson's poems when he published them in *St. Pauls:* noting the passages he thought Dobson might improve by a little more "elbow grease." This time, however, he did not have the editor's privilege of indicating them precisely to Dobson, and so made only the general remark that he had noticed such passages (an observation that must rather have frustrated the author, who could not defend himself, even to himself, against such vague criticism). "Vers de Societe are for me unalluring unless I can sympathize with the feeling, and find a pathos even in those which are nearest to the burlesque. It is because that touch is never wanting to you that I always thought and still think that you will surely be known sooner or later as a master in your art."[25]

The letter closes with an invitation to Dobson and his wife to dine in Montagu Square a fortnight hence. As one reads Trollope's surviving correspondence one is struck with the frequency with which he offers hospitality. At Waltham Cross an invitation to dinner usually entailed the offer of a night's accommodation; in Montagu Square such an offer was unnecessary. In either case a staff of servants was of course a blessing, but this abundant sociability speaks exceedingly well for Rose. We really know little about Rose, except that whenever her husband refers to her, he does so in terms of the highest affection. About this time, moreover, there are rather unexpected and revealing references to her literary judgment in Trollope's letters home from South Africa. Their son Henry was trying to establish a literary career for himself: he had been ghostwriting for Bianconi's daughter a biography of the proprietor of "Bianconi's cars," Ireland's principal pre-rail means of public transportation; he had undertaken *Corneille and Racine* for Blackwood's series of "Foreign Classics for English Readers," and he was submitting articles for publication (or refusal) by the leading periodicals. Trollope was warmly interested, and he wrote to Henry from Port Elizabeth on August 9, "I am sure your mother could help you a good deal [with the Bianconi book] if you will let her." Two months later, writing from the Transvaal, he urged Henry to place his name on the title page "if the book be good. . . . And I should take mamma's advice as to the goodness for she is never mistaken about a book being good or bad." And a few weeks later he was reassured to hear from Rose that the book "is very good reading." Rose may be inferred to have played a greater role as domestic critic of Anthony's writing than she is usually credited with.[26]

At least by May 19 Trollope had decided to journey to South Africa as soon as possible to look at the affairs of the colonies there.[27] The immediate stimulus was probably the controversial annexation of the Transvaal by Sir Theophilus Shepstone, acting on behalf of the British crown but without explicit authorization from Disraeli's government; this move occurred on April 12, 1877, and Trollope confessed that he "had never heard much and . . . had been interested not at all" in this remote district "till six months before I started on my journey." Yet "when I left home my main object perhaps was to visit it."[28] Affairs in South Africa were indeed a warm political issue, and were the subject of discussion at a meeting of the Royal Colonial Institute on June 7, when Donald Currie, founder of the Castle Steamship Company which for five years had linked England with Cape Town, spoke on the future of South, Central, and Eastern Africa. Trollope was called on by the president of the institute and briefly explained why he was about to set out for the Cape.[29] There can be no doubt that his principal reason was to look into the condition of the blacks; he had been horrified at the virtual extinction of the native populations of Australia, New Zealand, and North America, and hoped to find something more creditable to England in South Africa. The day after the Colonial Institute meeting, he booked his passage on one of Currie's steamships—booked it through Currie himself in fact; there is some advantage in knowing the president of the company personally.[30]

Preparations for his journey occupied him for the month of June (though he did a normal amount of work on *John Caldigate*); he called on the colonial secretary, Lord Carnarvon,* asked Sir Henry Barkly, who had just completed a tour as governor of the Cape Colony, for letters of introduction, and procured others from still other acquaintances with South African connections. Barkly's letter to the prime minister at Cape Town was somewhat skeptical: "Of course he will write a dissertation on South Africa, which may or may not be more impartial than the productions of other literary men, but as it is better that he should have the opportunity of getting correct information if he chooses, I shall recommend him to your good offices." He carried with him a bound notebook, the gift of his son Henry, to use as a travel diary.[31] His departure on the SS *Caldera* from Dartmouth on June 29 was announced well in advance in the *Times*.[32] The date prevented his fulfilling an engagement to distribute the prizes at the school of Tom Trollope's sister-in-law, Ellen Ternan Robinson, and her husband at Margate, but Frances Ternan Trollope came over from Florence to fill in, and stayed in Montagu Square for a few nights to bid him farewell.[33]

❧

Trollope spent less than two weeks in Cape Town and its vicinity, met all the members of the Cape Parliament, dined as guest of Lady Frere at Government House (Sir Bartle Frere could not act as host, since he had received word of his sister's death), and of course visited the post office: "Wherever I go I visit the post-office, feeling certain that I may be able to give a little good advice. . . . But I never knew an instance yet in which any improvement recommended by me was carried out."[34] Quickly he moved on by ship to Port Elizabeth, then journeyed by Cape cart—a two-wheeled vehicle with large wheels "admirably adapted for the somewhat rough roads of the country"—to King Williamstown, capital of the short-lived colony of British Kafraria, which after a separate existence of only four years had been annexed to the Cape Colony in 1864. Here he was called upon by a delegation of Kaffirs whose spokesman, a chief named Siwani, was very bitter about British rule, and especially about being obliged to wear trousers instead of going naked. But, Trollope observed, "the Kafir who has assiduously worn breeches for a year does feel, not a moral but a social shame, at going without them." After half an hour of oratory the chief let it be known that he required money for

---

*After his return, Trollope was an occasional guest at Highclere Castle, Lord Carnarvon's seat in Hampshire.

tobacco and grinned broadly when Trollope gave him half a crown. "The Kafir boy or girl at school and the Kafir man at work are pleasing objects; but the old Kafir chief in quest of tobacco,—or brandy,—is not delightful."[35]

Trollope was well aware that white colonization had entailed taking land, whether the black inhabitants wished it or not, and indeed he looked forward to a political enfranchisement of the blacks, dependent upon an educational qualification: "In coming ages a Kafir may make as good a Prime Minister as Lord Beaconsfield"—a very ambiguous statement in view of Trollope's opinion of Disraeli—"but he cannot do so now,—nor in this age,—nor for many ages to come. It will be sufficient for us if we make up our minds that at least for the next hundred years we shall not choose to be ruled by him." But he insists more than once that ultimately "South Africa is a country of black men,—and not of white men." And these are tribes that, unlike the Maoris of New Zealand and the aborigines of Australia, are "menaced by no danger of extermination." "As I am glad to see all political inequalities lessened among men of European descent, so should I be glad to think that the same process should take place among all men." He admires the Kaffirs, and has "no doubt that the condition of the race has been infinitely improved by the coming of the white man."[36]

At Pietermaritzburg, the capital of Natal, which he reached by vessel to Durban and thence by rail, he promptly went to hear Bishop Colenso preach. Colenso, missionary bishop to the Zulus in Natal since 1853, had been appointed a mathematics teacher at Harrow by Longley, shortly after Trollope left the school, but after his elevation to the episcopacy had stirred up much controversy by publishing a book pointing out the mathematical inconsistencies scattered through the books of the Pentateuch, and declaring that clearly these books could not have been divinely inspired.[37] When he was deprived of his see for heresy by Bishop Gray of Cape Town in December of that year, he went off to London to appeal to the judicial committee of the Privy Council, which set aside Bishop Gray's decision, and among the subscribers to a fund to help defray his legal expenses was Anthony Trollope. On that occasion, "I remember being asked to dinner by a gushing friend. 'We have secured Colenso,' said my gushing friend, as though she was asking me to meet a royal duke or a Japanese ambassador. But I had never met the Bishop till I arrived in his own see, where it was allowed to me to come in contact with that clear intellect, the gift of which has always been allowed to him."[38] One of Trollope's *Clerical Sketches* had been "The Clergyman Who Subscribes for Colenso" (January 25, 1866) and when he reluctantly accepted an assignment from the *Pall Mall Gazette* to attend a missionary meeting at Exeter Hall, he wrote as "The Zulu in London" (May 10, 1865). On

September 6 the Mayor of Pietermaritzburg gave a dinner for Trollope at which Colenso was a guest. "I do not know that I ever heard so many good speeches before on a so-called festive occasion. . . . Everybody had something to say, and nobody was ashamed to say it." The Colenso group was "almost afraid lest [Trollope] should fall completely into the hands of the officials and be hoodwinked," yet they were confident he would "prove too keen an observer for them to deceive him." "Father is a great admirer of Trollope," wrote Colenso's son. "The *Barchester Towers* series give him immense enjoyment."[39]

❧

Thus far the journey had been easy enough, but from Pietermaritzburg to Pretoria in the Transvaal, Kimberley in the Diamond Fields, Bloemfontein in the Orange Free State, and back to Cape Town—over 1,500 miles under the worst conditions—the journey was "awful to me." He began to see why he had been told again and again that he was much too old for the venture; his bulk of more than sixteen stone (224 pounds) and his wretched eyesight were no help.[40] A salesman of farm equipment joined Trollope as a traveling companion; they purchased a Cape cart and four horses and hired a black driver at £5 a month plus his keep and the cost of his return home. In the first week of travel from the border of the Transvaal they "pulled off [their] clothes but once"; what called themselves hotels were uninviting and short of beds. It was still September when they reached Pretoria (the season corresponded to March in the Northern Hemisphere).[41] There Trollope stayed at Government House, where he was well entertained, but Sir Theophilus Shepstone was away and Trollope was obliged to leave without seeing "the one person whom I was most anxious to see in South Africa."[42] The twenty-one-year-old Henry Rider Haggard, returning from a mission late one night, went to the room in Government House which he had formerly occupied, "began to search for matches, and was surprised to hear a gruff voice, proceeding from my bed, asking who the deuce I was. I gave my name and asked who the deuce the speaker might be. 'Anthony Trollope,' replied the gruff voice, 'Anthony Trollope.' Mr. Trollope was a man who concealed a kind heart under a somewhat rough manner, such as does not add to the comfort of colonial travelling."[43] Thus was repeated the experience which many years earlier in Ireland had led to the story of "Father Giles of Ballymoy."

On the journey from Pretoria to the Diamond Fields, begun on October 1, one of the horses, the sprightliest of the four, fell ill; he did not respond to dosages of chlorodyne and alum, nor indeed even to whiskey, but lay down and died at Anthony's feet. They were able to replace him at Potchefstroom and went on laboriously to Kimberley.[44] Two more of the horses exhausted themselves and had to be replaced with a hired pair, and another had to be bled from the ear to be relieved of the agony of colic. At Kimberley they sold their team, cart, and harness at auction, the auctioneer proclaiming to the assembled bidders "that the horses had all been bred at 'Orley Farm' for [Anthony's] own express use."[45]

The first diamond was found in South Africa in 1867, only ten years before Trollope reached Kimberley. Indeed the diamond-digging industry did not begin until 1872. Trollope found the immense hole there, nine acres in area, 230 feet deep, open to the sky and divided into tiny separate working claims, most interesting; he descended to the floor of the pit (in 140-degree temperature) to observe the process.[46] Kimberley itself was interesting because so many of the natives were employed and earning money; "I know no other spot on which the work of civilizing a Savage is being carried on with so signal a success. . . . Here . . . a healthy nation remains and assures us by its prolific tendency that when protected from self-destruction by our fostering care it will spread and increase beneath our hands."[47] For the rest, flies, dust, and heat made Kimberley "as little [alluring] as any town that I have ever visited."

> There are places to which men are attracted by the desire of gain which seem to be so repulsive that no gain can compensate the miseries incidental to such an habitation. I have seen more than one such place and have wondered that under any inducement men should submit themselves, their wives and children to such an existence. I remember well my impressions on reaching Charles Dickens' Eden at the junction of the Ohio and Mississippi rivers and my surprise that any human being should have pitched his tent in a place so unwholesome and so hideous. I have found Englishmen collected on the Musquito Coast, a wretched crew; and having been called on by untoward Fate and a cruel Government to remain a week at Suez have been driven to consider whether life would have been possible there for a month."[48]

He was still thinking of these wretched places when a few months later, in *Ayala's Angel*, he makes Frank Houston reflect that in proposing to an heiress he was doing his duty,—"just as another man does who goes forth from his pleasant home to earn his bread and win his fortune in some dry, comfortless climate" (chap. xiv). At the Diamond Fields he encountered a Major Lanyon, "whom I found administering the entangled affairs of [the area]. . . . When last I had seen him, and it seems but a short time ago, he was a pretty little boy with a pretty little frock in Belfast." Among other friends from the home country he also met Napier Broome at Pietermaritzburg, who had reviewed (anonymously) *He Knew He Was Right, The Eustace Diamonds,* and *Australia and New Zealand* for the *Times.*[49]

All the time he was traveling, "day by day . . . I have written my book. The things which I have seen have been described within a few hours of my seeing them. The words that I have heard have been made available for what they were worth,—as far as it was within my power to do so,—before they were forgotten. A book so written must often be inaccurate; but it may possibly have something in it of freshness to atone for its inaccuracies."[50] He also wrote and sent home periodically to his agent Nicholas Trübner fifteen letters on South Africa for publication in various provincial British newspapers, and these began to be published also in the *Cape Times* on November 10, nearly a month before he left for home.[51] In London the *Times* kept its readers informed of his movements; he was aboard the SS *Nubian,* which landed in London on January 3, 1878.[52] As he crossed the Bay of Biscay he wrote the final chapter of *South Africa* and delivered it to Virtue (whose services as printer he had especially requested) the day after his arrival.[53] The book was published by Chapman and Hall about February 9. He was called on to speak at a meeting of the Royal Geographical Society devoted to the geography and economy of "the new British Dependency," the Transvaal, on January 14, addressed the Working Men's Club and Institute Union about South Africa on March 30, [54] and published an article on "Kafir Land" in the *Fortnightly Review* of February 1. (Most of the information in the article was contained in his book, but it was especially timely because of the outbreak of one of the Kaffir wars against the British.) The rapid sequence of events and the publicity were evidence of the great public interest in that part of the world. Though he did not visit the Zulus on their own land, "his dreaded Majesty King Cetywayo . . . at this moment, January, 1878, is I fear our enemy," and it took little foresight for him to say, "I am very far from recommending an extension of British interference; but if I know anything of British manners and British ways, there will be British interference in Zulu-land before long."[55] By the end of 1878 the British had confronted Cetywayo with an ultimatum and on January 22, 1879, the British troops suffered a disastrous defeat and massacre at Isandhlwana.

    South Africa was warmly praised by the reviewers for its lively style, the energy shown by the author in examining everything for himself, and the timeliness of the book. The *Saturday Review* remarked that "there is scarcely a dull page"; Trollope, despite warnings, "went, and did endure much discomfort, and found his journey very laborious. But he survived the trial, collected his materials, irradiated them with his facile style, and has now published the result in as good and complete a notice . . . as any home-staying Englishman could wish to have." The reviewer then summarized at great length and with complete agreement what Trollope had said. The *Times* reviewer also observed that "the world ought to be very much obliged to Mr. Trollope," and devoted more than two columns to an approving summary.[56]

Chapter XXV

1878

Back in London Trollope energetically plunged into his former activities. John Blackwood and his wife had a "cheery dinner" at the Trollopes' on February 24; "Anthony has come back in great force," and Lord John Manners had told Blackwood that "he is like to drive them all mad at the weary Copyright Commission going over all the ground that has been discussed in his absence."[1] Before he left, the commission's hearing of testimony had been completed, but much work on the report had been done in his absence, and by the time of Blackwood's remark Trollope had attended two meetings of the commission (the first only six days after his landing from South Africa). Their work was drawing to a close: the commission completed its report on May 11. The main thrust of their deliberations was that English and foreign authors should be treated alike with respect to copyright, regardless of whether foreign governments granted reciprocal protection to English authors. (They could publicly announce that they wished to set a good example, but no doubt they were also influenced by the repeated testimony as to the extent to which American authors suffered from the flooding of the American market with unprotected British works.) They recommended that the right of dramatizing a novel or other work should be reserved to the author, and should be coextensive with the copyright, on the ground that under the current unrestricted use the author might be injured not only pecuniarily but in reputation "if an erroneous impression is given of the book." One sees in this language Trollope's old indignation over the reviewers' accusations of impropriety in *Shilly-Shally*, though nothing in the report attributes the point to him. Like several other members of the commission Trollope added a note of his own to the report. Copyright registration was to be made compulsory, and the commission wished to enforce it by permitting a continuing sale of any unauthorized copies printed before registration; Trollope demurred at the potential magnitude of the penalty and sensibly urged the simple payment of a fine.[2]

On the same day he attended the Copyright Commission's meeting on January 9, Trollope took the chair at the meeting of the general committee of the Royal Literary Fund. There a grant of assistance·was made to a colleague of Matthew Arnold's, one of Her Majesty's inspectors of schools, John Reynell Morell.[3] But the principal business was to lay plans for the coming anniversary dinner; at Trollope's suggestion W. E. Forster was asked to take the chair on the occasion, and Forster agreed (perhaps over the whist table at the Athenaeum).[4] Trollope bestirred himself with especial energy to enlist "stewards": Matthew Arnold (who would of course be present when his brother-in-law presided), Charles Reade, Sir Henry Thompson (founder of the Cremation Society), Millais, Dicey, Sir Henry James, Trollope himself, and nearly a dozen others. Alexander Kinglake, author of *Eothen* and, currently, of a multivolume history of the Crimean War, first sent a frosty reply, then thought better of it: "My indifference about the 'Literary Fund' gave way . . . in a moment when I perceived that you felt a personal interest in the matter; & well indeed might this be, for I am always mindful of the unnumbered hours of pleasure that I owe to your delightful books. And, apart from the pleasure, it is so good for one, I imagine, to see the play of healthful English life as you with your genius present it!"[5]

Trollope's constant scrutiny of the applications for the fund's assistance gave him some sense of personal acquaintance with the applicants, and occasionally he dipped into his own pocket or touched the generosity of his friends to supplement a grant. One frequent and successful applicant was Charlotte Anne Smith of Guildford, afterwards Mrs. Hodgkins, whose marriage did not improve her circumstances. "As for the mother [presumably mother-in-law], and all the rest of the horrors, that is human nature," Trollope commented to Blewitt (November 20, 1876). "I am very glad to hear that you have decided to return to your husband. I send a small trifle for your present wants," he wrote to her on March 23, 1878. Both times the fund granted her £25. Later in 1878, at the moment he received an application from Mrs. George Linnaeus (Isabella Varley) Banks, authoress of several books of poetry and about sixteen novels, Trollope chanced to be in Manchester to deliver a lecture and there heard the mayor at a public dinner declare his admiration for the most popular of her books, *The Manchester Man*. Trollope took the opportunity of telling the mayor privately "how far [her] rewards in literary life had fallen short of [her] deserts," and the mayor gave Trollope some money for her. "Had you heard the language in which he spoke of your book that would at any rate have given you unmixed pleasure," Trollope kindly wrote to her. At that time the committee gave her £40; before Trollope's death she had received £355 from the fund.[6]

Then arose a last-minute emergency. At the end of April Forster broke his leg in a carriage accident in the South of France; he sent a letter of regret and a contribution of £25. Trollope was not present at the special meeting of the general committee that instructed Froude to ask Arthur Stanley, dean of Westminster, to serve in Forster's stead. Stanley was willing, but both he and Froude thought Matthew Arnold would be the better choice. Arnold, however, declined, his brother Edward having just then died, and Stanley took the chair.[7]

Kinglake's letter is only one of many expressions of pleasure in Trollope's novels by his literary contemporaries, many of which never reached his eye. Twenty-seven-year-old Robert Louis Stevenson wrote to his parents:

> Do you know who is my favourite author just now? How are the mighty fallen! Anthony Trollope. I batten on him; he is so nearly wearying you, and yet he never does; or rather, he never does, until he gets near the end, when he begins to wean you from him, so that you're as pleased to be done with him as you thought you would be sorry. I wonder if it's old age? . . . I have just finished the *Way of the World* [*sic*]; there is only one person in it—no, there are three—who are nice: the wild American woman, and two of the dissipated young men, Dolly and Lord Nidderdale. All the heroes and heroines are just ghastly. But what a triumph is Lady Carbury! That is real, sound, strong, genuine work: the man who could do that, if he had had courage, might have written a fine book; he has preferred to write many readable ones.

And Edward FitzGerald, now nearly seventy, was following *Is He Popenjoy?* in its weekly installments in *All the Year Round:* "I wish it, or its like, would continue as long as I live."[8]

Anthony's future biographer, T. H. S. Escott, who in a few years would succeed Morley as editor of the *Fortnightly Review,* resolved to do a good turn for two friends by bringing together in a cordial atmosphere Trollope and Edmund Yates, and so on February 18 he entertained them at dinner with five others (including Froude) at the Thatched House Club. (Trollope had formerly been a member when it was called the Civil Services Club, but he had long since dropped out.) "How did you manage to bring them two together?" whispered one of the guests, an Irishman, to their host; they had been strangers to one another for a decade. "Perhaps modern English literature might be searched in vain for men at once so eminent, so touchy, so ready to take offence with each other, and with all the world besides, as [Yates, Dickens, Thackeray, and Trollope]," remarked Escott. But "the dinner turned out very pleasantly," said Yates, who especially enjoyed Trollope's recollections of their years under Rowland Hill in the Post Office.[9]

৯⅃

On April 25, 1878, while on a holiday near Bolton Abbey, in Yorkshire (where he had gone to "get out of the East Wind" of London, which he

feared might be fatal to him, [10] Trollope sat down to begin a new novel—
the first he had begun in more than a year. As he wrote *Ayala's Angel** he
was clearly in high spirits, and undertook to follow the courtships of no
fewer than five young ladies, who did indeed pose a problem for him
before the book was done: "With the affairs of so many lovers and their
loves, it is almost impossible to make the chronicle run at equal periods
throughout" (chap. xlviii). The problem was fully as great for the City
financier Sir Thomas Tringle, who, as father of two of these young ladies
and guardian of two others, was sometimes tried beyond endurance,
especially since his son Tom was pining for love of one of them. "He was
becoming sick of the young ladies. . . . 'They are a pack of idiots together,' he said, 'and Tom is the worst of the lot.' With this he rushed off
to London, and consoled himself with his millions" (chap. xlii).

For women, marriage was the one necessary in life: "It seemed,
[Ayala] said to herself, that people thought that a girl was bound to marry
any man who could provide a house for her, and bread to eat, and clothes
to wear" (chap. xxvii). "Unless I marry I can be nobody," said Imogene
Docimer to Frank Houston. "I can have no existence that I can call my
own. I have no other way of pushing myself into the world's notice. You
are a man. . . . You can live and eat and drink and go where you wish
without being dependent on any one" (chap. xxviii). But it was equally
incumbent upon the men to look out after their financial interests, and
poor Sir Thomas's distress comes largely from having to deal with the
dowry expectations of one suitor after another. His younger daughter's
admirer made the mistake of eloping with her to Ostend, where, as it
happened, they could find no Anglican clergyman before Sir Thomas, in
pursuit, could intervene and bring her home. The husband of the older
daughter condescends to point out to his future brother-in-law where the
mistake lay: "It makes one feel that you can't make a demand for money as
though you set about it in the other way. When I made up my mind to
marry I stated what I thought I had a right to demand, and I got it. He
knew very well that I shouldn't take a shilling less. It does make a
difference [in your case] when he knows very well that you've got to marry
the girl with or without the money" (chap. lxii). The young woman's
feeling of desperation over procuring a husband reminds one of the sad
situation of Arabella Trefoil in *The American Senator;* as it happens the
country house in which Ayala is entertained is in the county of Rufford,

---

*No doubt the title should be explained. Ayala Dormer, nineteen at the time her
artist father died and very beautiful, had a romantic dream that she would be carried off in
marriage by an "Angel of Light." When the red-haired, homely Colonel Jonathan Stubbs
courted her, she admired, even loved him, but nearly lost him because she was so slow to
realize that he was indeed her "Angel of Light."

and we meet some of the characters from the earlier book, including the now fat Lord Rufford, father of a brood, at the hunting meets there. It was nearly seven years since Major Caneback's fatal fall (chap. xxiii).

Trollope indulges his fancy in coining significant personal names: Septimus Traffick, M.P., who supplied this financial wisdom to his future brother-in-law, is the second son of Lord Boardotrade; two of the minor characters are Lord John Battledore and Tom Shuttlecock; Sir Thomas Tringle's financial house is Travers and Treason. The surnames of the principal characters are Dormer, Dosett, and Docimer, as if Trollope were playing with the sounds, and Imogene Docimer's brother's given name is Mudbury. Nevertheless, the London in which most of the story is set is very meticulously and realistically characterized, with all the proper distinctions socially between Brook Street, Queen's Gate, Onslow Gardens, and Notting Hill. (In Onslow Gardens, where Ayala's father lived, Thackeray's daughters bought a home after their father's death, and Egbert Dormer, like Thackeray, was buried at Kensal Green.) Lovesick Tom Tringle, despondent, intoxicated, and soaking wet in the rain, "walked, as fast as he could, round Leicester Square" at midnight. "He did not make his way round the square without being addressed, but he simply shook off from him those who spoke to him" (chap. xliv). A century later, a young man walking round Leicester Square at midnight would find a similar amiability amongst the denizens of the square. The calendar for the novel is that of 1878–79, and the properly Conservative Sir Thomas Tringle, advising Tom on stopping points on a journey round the world, included Kabul: "By that time I dare say we shall have possession of Cabul. With such a government as we have now, thank God! the Russians will have been turned pretty nearly out of Asia by this time next year." (The allusion is to Disraeli's Afghan War [chap. lxi].)

The social comedy is of a high order, especially in the vanity of Tringle's older daughter Augusta, who at twenty-five marries the forty-five-year-old Traffick. He "will probably be in the government some day," she told Ayala. "Won't he be very old before he gets there?" Ayala asked. "This was a terrible question. Young ladies of five-and-twenty, when they marry gentlemen of four-and-fifty, make up their minds for well-understood and well-recognised old age. They see that they had best declare their purpose, and they do declare it. . . . But at forty-five there is supposed to be so much of youth left that the difference of age may possibly be tided over and not made to appear abnormal. Augusta Tringle had determined to tide it over in this way. The forty-five had been gradually reduced to 'less than forty'—though all the Peerages were there to give the lie to the assertion. She talked of her lover as Septimus, and was quite prepared to sit with him beside a stream if only half-an-hour for the amusement could be found" (chap. v).[11] Augusta's younger sister

Gertrude and Ayala's older sister Lucy were married in a joint ceremony at a fine country house; Gertrude reflects that if the ceremony had actually taken place at Ostend, "I don't suppose anybody would have given me anything. Now there'll be a regular wedding, and, of course, there will be the presents." The joint display of the wedding gifts was indeed "satisfactory," but Augusta remarked privately to Ayala, "No doubt I had twice as much as the two put together. . . . But then of course Lord Boardotrade's rank would make people give" (chap. lxii). At the outset of the story Lady Tringle had chosen to take the orphaned Ayala into her home as more attractive than Lucy, but Ayala "turned out on her hands something altogether different from the girl she had intended to cherish and patronise" (chap. viii), and was passed on to another aunt in exchange for Lucy.

Once again Trollope has his sport with Victorian prudery. Lucy Dormer's suitor Isadore Hamel was a sculptor whose slight income came from portraits. " 'Heads,' suggested Sir Thomas. 'Busts they are generally called,' [said Hamel]. 'Well, busts. I call them heads. They are heads. A bust, I take it, is—well, never mind.' Sir Thomas found a difficulty in defining his idea of a bust" (chap. xxxiii).

The author we have come to know is everywhere visible. "I regard ['64 Léoville] as the most divine of nectars" (chap. v). Trollope the experienced traveler allowed Gertrude to predict that her brother Tom would recover his spirits in New York: "There's no place in the world, they say, where the girls put themselves forward so much, and make things so pleasant for the young men" (chap. lxi). He amused himself with the British self-satisfaction: the Marchesa Baldoni "was thoroughly well dressed, and looked like a Marchesa;—or perhaps, even, like a Marchioness" (chap. xv). On the other hand, English social customs are defended: "Conventions are apt to go very quickly, one after another, when the first has been thrown aside. The man who ceases to dress for dinner soon finds it to be a trouble to wash his hands" (chap. xvii). It is on the whole a very lively and youthful book.

The writing of *Ayala's Angel* was suspended from May 1 to June 17, but Trollope took the manuscript with him on his holidays to Wemyss Bay, near Glasgow, and then to Iceland, in late June and early July, and to Felsinegg, Switzerland, and Höllenthal in the Black Forest from late July to late September; it was completed at the latter resort on September 24. When he began the novel, he still had on hand the manuscript of *The Duke's Children,* written nearly two years earlier; he sold publication rights for that book only in June, 1878, and indeed had to take time from the writing of *Ayala's Angel* to revise and curtail the earlier novel. Contracts for publication of *Ayala's Angel,* therefore, were not signed until November, 1880, after *The Duke's Children* had been published. These were with

Chapman and Hall for the three-volume edition and with the National Press Agency for newspaper distribution in Great Britain; the former was published about May 14, 1881, but serialization in the newspapers has not been traced. [12]

By now the diminution in the payments he received for his novels, which he mentioned in *An Autobiography,* was becoming very marked. One reason may have been his commitment to Chapman and Hall as publishers, since they were falling on hard times. For *Is He Popenjoy?* they paid £1,200 in January, 1877, and for *The Duke's Children* (slightly longer) £1,000 in June, 1878; each had been published serially in *All the Year Round* at £400. (These novels were about the same length as *The Claverings,* for which he was paid £2,800 in 1866–67.) *Ayala's Angel* (slightly shorter) in late 1880 brought him only £750, with a contract for speculative serial publication in newspapers at £200. The best he could do with *Mr. Scarborough's Family* (the same length as *Popenjoy*) in 1882 was £600 for the three-volume edition from Chatto and Windus, and the same amount from them for the projected *Landleaguers. All the Year Round* paid £400 for serialization of the former. All this at a time when, as he was explaining just then to the readers of "Why Frau Frohmann Raised Her Prices," money was "not much more than half what it used to be" (chap. v). Perhaps even more galling was the dignified letter he felt himself bound in honor to write to Chapman's accountant on August 13, 1880: the firm had lost £120 by *The Duke's Children.* "I cannot allow that. It is the first account I have ever seen of one of my own books. . . . I will repay to the Company the amount lost, viz. £120, if you think that fair." [13] The publishers did think it profitable to issue an inexpensive one-volume edition in the same year.

෨

If Trollope devoted the greater part of his energy to building up a supply of novels for future publication, there were also frequent requests from editors that he contribute shorter fiction to their journals. One of these has already been mentioned: Robert Buchanan was undertaking to launch a new weekly, *Light,* and asked Trollope to write a story in six parts, 24,000 words, for £110. Trollope promised him that most, indeed probably the whole, of the story would be in his hands by March 18, 1878, and "The Lady of Launay" was published in the first six numbers of the new journal, beginning on April 6. It was not sufficient to ensure prosperity for the venture; *Light* survived for precisely seven months. [14] The tale is far from the best of Trollope's shorter stories, but begins, curiously, with a situation parallel to one he used a month later at the beginning of *Ayala's Angel:* a wealthy but very rigid woman adopts the lovelier of two orphaned sisters, then believes herself obliged to send her away because her son falls in love with the young woman and the marriage in the mother's opinion would be unsuitable.

Donald Macleod, who became editor of *Good Words* on the death in 1872 of his brother Norman, continued to draw on Trollope. The publisher of the journal was now William Isbister, who had come down from Scotland with Alexander Strahan in 1853, and who ultimately succeeded to the proprietorship of Strahan's firm in the complicated arrangements that followed Strahan's bankruptcy.[15] On October 24, 1876, the younger Macleod asked Trollope for a "storiette" ("a short title which might divide into two parts") for early 1877: "I hope you will undertake this—if for nothing else—for the sake of 'Auld lang syne.'" For old time's sake, then, Trollope agreed to supply by January 31 a thirty-page (double-columned) story at a reduced rate of £175; Macleod actually divided "Why Frau Frohmann Raised Her Prices" into four parts, beginning in February, 1877.[16] The "short stories" of Trollope's last years are controlled as to length by the demands of the editors and are not all "short"; "Frau Frohmann" is about half the length of some of his separately published novels like *The Fixed Period* and *Cousin Henry.* They turn on a single event, and (as with his earlier short stories) sometimes impel him to draw on his observations of life abroad. Frau Frohmann was the widowed proprietress of a holiday resort inn near Innsbruck, which she managed with impeccable regard for the quality of the food and services, in the interest of a clientele much of which returned year after year. Her conservatism, indeed Toryism, made her unwilling to raise her prices over the years, and equally unwilling to pay more for the supplies she purchased from local purveyors. The story is almost couched as a lesson in "political economy," but is lighthearted in tone and ends with general rejoicing when she takes the steps necessary to preserve her financial stability and the quality of her services.

At one point she fears that she may have to give up her active management of the inn and retire to a nearby village. "But, when she came to think of it in her solitude, she did not wish to go. . . . What did retirement mean? Would it not be to her simply a beginning of dying? A man, or a woman, should retire when no longer able to do the work of the world" (chap. vii). These words had scarcely been written, and had not yet been published, when Tilley asked Trollope's advice about retiring from the Post Office and received the reply that almost repeated these words.[17]

Christmas stories were much in demand, and "Catherine Carmichael; or, Three Years Running," written for the *Masonic Magazine,* was indeed a strange Christmas tale, some 10,000 words written in eleven days early in October, 1878, for the sum of £100.[18] "Christmas at Thompson Hall" (the *Graphic,* 1876) had been the cheerful account of an

English wife who, journeying with her husband from Pau to a Christmas gathering of her family near London, in the dark halls of a Paris hotel had blundered into the wrong room and placed on the bare chest of a sleeping man a mustard cataplasm she had made in the deserted dining room for the relief of her husband's sore throat. Since her name was embroidered on the handkerchief on which she had spread the mustard, the whole hotel knew of her guilt when the victim awakened in the agony of a fiery chest; then fate made him their companion every inch of the journey to Thompson Hall, where he was introduced as the fiancé of her only sister. But "Catherine Carmichael" was set in the crude mining and sheep-raising country of New Zealand on three successive Christmases. On the first, Catherine, left an orphan by the deaths of both parents within a year, was married to a crude, parsimonious sheep farmer who needed a domestic servant. As they departed from the ceremony, which was only a brief episode on a four-day journey from her home to his, she reflected: "She was the man's wife, and she hated him. She had never known before what it was to hate a human being." On the second Christmas she sat on the verandah of their house as neighbors deposited beside her the drowned body of the hated husband. On the third Christmas she is made happy by the arrival of her husband's young cousin, whom she had secretly loved, though between them during their previous acquaintance there had been no sign of love.

ે

On the last day of May, 1878, Trollope was one of a large number of guests at a dinner given by George Joachim Goschen and his wife to present George Eliot and Lewes to the Crown Prince of Prussia (later Emperor Frederick III of Germany) and his wife, Queen Victoria's oldest daughter. Among the other guests were Dean Stanley, Froude, Kinglake, and John Morley. Though gratified by the royal recognition of his wife, whom the Prince and Princess urged to call upon them when next in Berlin, and pleased by a casual remark which showed that the Princess was aware of George Eliot's mammoth translation of Strauss's *Life of Jesus,* Lewes confessed that he was "knocked up" by the time he got home at midnight. [19] Exactly six months later (November 30) Lewes died, and Trollope was called upon to commemorate him in the journal of which, at Trollope's insistence, Lewes had been the first editor, the *Fortnightly Review* (January, 1879).

Trollope was frankly incapable of dealing with Lewes's achievements in science and philosophy—"To me personally Lewes was a great philosopher only because I was told so"—and so for more than a fifth of his essay he drew upon the pen of Frederic Harrison. His account of the founding of the *Fortnightly* is naturally much like the one he gives in *An Autobiography*. He also tells the story of an article Lewes wrote on Dickens two years after the novelist's death, in which he offended John Forster by saying that "Dickens by the strength of his imagination so subordinated his readers that they do not perceive . . . that want of reality which pervades his characters." Forster attacked the article in his biography of Dickens, and in his turn hurt Lewes's feelings. "John Forster is dead also. They were two loving honest friendly men, both of them peculiarly devoted to genius wherever they could find it." As for Lewes, "the humourist was to me a joy for ever. Sure no one man told a story as he did. . . . There was never a man so pleasant as he with whom to sit and talk vague literary gossip over a cup of coffee and a cigar." No mention is made of George Eliot. Only a month after Lewes's death, Trollope dated his own last will.[20]

More than a decade earlier Trollope had been introduced by Norman Macleod to the Cunard Steamship Company's chairman, John Burns, and spent social evenings with him whenever he was in Glasgow.[21] The steamship company was about to put into service a new steam yacht, the *Mastiff,* but before it entered upon its duties the yacht conveyed on a fortnight's excursion to Iceland (June 22 to July 8) a party of sixteen friends, with Burns of course as host, and Trollope as the senior guest. Rose was not of the party. The yacht sailed from Wemyss Bay, in western Scotland, where Burns had his home in Castle Wemyss; they stopped at St. Kilda, then visited Thorshavn, capital of the Faeroe Islands (a Danish possession) from 10:30 P.M. to 1:30 A.M. on the night of June 25–26. The midnight sun was of course shining. Trollope met the postmaster, who spoke English, and was eager to question him about the extent of his supervision from Copenhagen, but refrained. How many English postmasters could speak Danish, Trollope wondered. They were in Iceland from early morning on June 28 until July 5, with a most pleasant visit to Reykjavik (where they met all the most important people) and an arduous excursion on horseback to the geysers; Trollope, now at even more than sixteen stone, had difficulties, but not so great as those of his horse, who in desperation repeatedly turned around and tried to go back to his stable. The return voyage was by another route. The strenuousness of the overland expedition and no doubt lack of sleep left him "shattered moderately," "so knocked about" that for a fortnight he could hardly attend to business.[22]

Trollope quickly wrote an account of Iceland for the *Fortnightly Review* (August, 1878), generally informative like most of his travel writings, and another account, very personal and anecdotal, which was printed by James Virtue and elaborately bound as a souvenir folio at the request of Burns. *How the 'Mastiffs' Went to Iceland* was generously illustrated with drawings by one of the party, Mrs. Hugh Blackburn, and three photographs; Trollope's massive figure is at the center of most of the drawings. He speaks from the experience of many a holiday in Germany and Switzerland when he describes the harvesting of eiderdown, "of which are made those stuffy, fluffy, soft, slippery coverings which always fall off a German bed when an Englishman tries to sleep in it" (p. 25). The book was apparently in much demand, for Trollope quickly ran out his allotment of copies. [23]

Immediately after his return he distributed the prizes at the school conducted by Ellen Ternan Robinson's husband at Margate, the date having been moved back to accommodate his voyage. He repeated in his speech the erroneous assertion that in the dozen years of his schooling he never got a prize. [24] Then he and Rose went off to Felsenegg and the Black Forest until late September.

ક

Trollope wasted little time after he came home from the Continent before beginning his next novel: *Cousin Henry* was written between October 26 and December 6, 1878. In mid-November he was in Manchester to lecture on South Africa, and there met Alexander Ireland, publisher of the *Manchester Examiner and Times* and the *Manchester Weekly Times;* learning that Trollope was working on a new novel, Ireland arranged to publish it in the latter and in the *North British Weekly Mail,* and paid £200 for the two. He seems also to have chosen the novel's title from among three Trollope proposed to him (the other two were *Getting at a Secret,* which Rose said sounded like claptrap, and *Uncle Indefer's Will*). Chapman brought it out in two volumes about September 27, 1879, and paid £300 for the book rights. [25]

Cousin Henry was in structure very like the long short stories Trollope was at this time writing for the periodicals. It consisted of a single incident, from which it never diverted its attention. An elderly unmarried Welsh gentleman named Indefer Jones (now between seventy and eighty years old) owned the large estate of Llanfeare, near Carmarthen, which had been in his family for generations; it had been entailed upon him, but the entail had not been renewed when he came into possession. Like Frau Frohmann, he was a thorough conservative to whom "the idea of raising a rent was abominable" (chap. ii). When his sister died and her husband remarried, he invited his orphaned niece Isabel Brodrick to live at Llanfeare with him; she made herself much beloved to her uncle, the tenants, and the servants. But there was also his brother's son, Henry, who bore the family name of Jones, and the old man was obsessed with the idea that the estate should always go to a Jones. Through the making of a succession of wills he wavered between his nephew and his niece; when she flatly refused to take the name of Jones by marrying Cousin Henry, he made what was to be a final will in Henry's favor, and left a modest sum of money to Isabel (without, however, making provision for drawing upon the estate for the money).[26] At the last minute, sensing the approach of death, he secretly recopied that will, exchanging the names of Henry and Isabel, had two tenants witness his signature, and in a few days died. No one knew what had become of this deathbed will, but Cousin Henry, straightening out his uncle's room, carried the volume of Jeremy Taylor's sermons from his uncle's bedside back to their place on the bookshelves and as he did so discovered the missing document tucked in its pages. He could bring himself neither to reveal it nor to destroy it.

The spineless Henry spent the succeeding months, nominally in possession of his inheritance, in an agony of uncertainty. There is a degree of sympathy for him, the "poor, cringing, cowardly wretch" (chap. xvii), whose very lack of character made him despised by all around him— indeed so despised that they could not refrain from telling him they despised him. The Carmarthen newspaper forced his hand by running a series of articles that, if untrue, were clearly libelous. Advised by his uncle's lawyer, he brought criminal libel charges against the newspaper, then sat day after day in terror at the thought of undergoing cross-examination at the hands of one of Great Britain's cruelest barristers, John Cheekey. Daily he resolved to burn the will and swallow the ashes; twice daily he repeated the Lord's Prayer without the petitions on temptation and evil (chap. xx), but he could not take a step that would be irretriev-able. Isabel, having been assured at her uncle's deathbed that "It is all right. It is done" (chap. iv), was convinced that the will in her favor was in the house; still, she was "a woman, with a woman's propensity to follow her feelings rather than either facts or reason" (chap. xvi). The family lawyer, however, as the affair approached the decisive moment, reconstructed the old man's last hours with a deductive accuracy that anticipated Sherlock Holmes, and on the day before the trial he was able to call on Cousin Henry, walk directly to the book of sermons, and pick out the incriminating volume. Poor Cousin Henry: "To be commonly wicked was nothing to him,—nothing to break through all those ordi-nary rules of life which parents teach their children and pastors their flocks, but as to which the world is so careless. . . . But to burn a will! . . . To do that for which he might be confined to Dartmoor all his life, with his hair cut, and dirty prison clothes, and hard food, and work to do! . . . He was not the man to do it,—neither brave enough nor bad enough." Moreover, "though he was a knave, he was not cunning" (chaps. xx, xxiv). And so he went back to his clerk's desk in London, with "the security of lowliness into which to fall back" (chap. xxii).

Chapter XXVI

1879

For a span of nearly nine years Trollope had talked to audiences in Britain and Australia on the reading of novels and had indeed devoted a substantial portion of *An Autobiography* in 1876 to the subject. Even earlier he proposed to do an article for the *Cornhill* defending the moral usefulness of novels against an attack by Archbishop Thomson of York, but dropped the idea.[1] The concurrent appearance of new editions of Thackeray and Dickens led him to cast his remarks in the form of a review of those editions and to offer them to the editor of the *Quarterly,* his friend Dr. William Smith, in October, 1878. He had no "purport of reviewing their works, but making their names simply a groundwork for my remarks."*[2] Smith did not take the article, but James Knowles published it in his very successful new monthly, the *Nineteenth Century* (January, 1879). A substantial part of the article is lifted nearly verbatim from what Trollope had already written in *An Autobiography;* much of the rest is revised from parts of his lecture "On English Prose Fiction as a Rational Amusement," delivered in Edinburgh on January 28, 1870.[3]

Almost at the same moment chance threw in his way an opportunity for even fuller discussion of the craft of fiction. John Morley was editing for Macmillan a new series of relatively short biographies of "English Men of Letters," and Trollope was to do a life of Thackeray. Trollope's devotion to Thackeray's memory was no secret; earlier in 1878 he had dunned fellow members of the Garrick Club for contributions to commission a bust of Thackeray by Joseph Boehm for the club rooms—an enterprise that was fresh in his mind when he wrote the book for Morley.[4] We know little about the negotiations between Morley and Trollope, but there were obstacles. Thackeray had wanted no biography, and certainly the new project could not be carried out without the help of his survivors. Trollope was very close to the older daughter, Annie, and had been on good terms as well with the younger one, Minnie, before her death in 1875; both

---

*This writing an essay under pretext of writing a review was an honorable custom with the *Quarterly* and the *Edinburgh:* when Carlyle in 1859 published his "Signs of the Times" in the latter journal, he prefixed to the essay two fictitious book titles and one tract by his friend Edward Irving that was there for comic purposes, not because it was mentioned in the essay.

Annie and Minnie's widowed husband Leslie Stephen (who had by now succeeded to the editorship of the *Cornhill*) gave their friendly assent to the project.[5]

These little biographies treated authors as far back as Chaucer, but even in the case of writers recently dead like Landor and Dickens there were already sizable biographies which Morley's writers could condense; they could also, of course, draw upon their own sources of information, and the focus was generally on the works rather than the lives. Trollope, however, had no such biographical resource. He did look into works like W. C. Macready's recently published diaries.[6] He sent several sheets of questions to Annie, and these she answered as best she could; he also procured from her the names of friends from whom he might seek information.[7] Morley expressed the hope "that you will give us as much as ever you can in the personal vein, by way of background to the critical and descriptive,"[8] and the evidence that Trollope followed at least some of Annie's suggestions is visible in the comments he quotes from Thackeray's friends, some named and others anonymous.* Apart from these quotations, we have none of the correspondence he must have had with Thackeray's friends, but FitzGerald remarked in late February that Trollope had written "for some particulars of Thackeray between 1830–40. . . . I could tell him very little, having burned nearly all the letters that [WMT] wrote me during that time. . . . I am glad Trollope has the job if to be done at all: he is a Gentleman as well as an Author—was a loyal friend of Thackeray's, and so, I hope, will take him out of any Cockney Worshipper's hands." A few weeks later FitzGerald said that "two or three particulars which Annie T. had given him, I was able to prove wrong."[10] In fact, however, Trollope had less than nine weeks to write the work—a book nearly as long as *Cousin Henry*. Morley fixed the length and set the fee at £200.

Since Trollope moved in much the same literary circles as Thackeray, and was only four years younger, his remarks throw light on both his own work and Thackeray's,[11] and his judgments, while not necessarily at one with our own, speak to the ideas current at the time. Indeed, his final chapter, on "Thackeray's Style and Manner of Work," is a comprehensive discussion of his own ideas of "realism": "It is the object of the author

---

*For example, "As I write this I have before me a letter from Thackeray to a friend describing his own success when *Vanity Fair* was coming out" (pp. 118–19), and "I have had sent to me for my inspection an album of drawings and letters, which, in the course of twenty years, from 1829 to 1849, were despatched from Thackeray to his old friend Edward Fitzgerald" (p. 30). It was only two years earlier that FitzGerald complained that Annie Thackeray had lost "all the Drawings—which were all I had, save two—of her Father's." Trollope sent proof sheets of the biographical chapter to four of Thackeray's friends, including FitzGerald, William Howard Russell, and George Smith, and incorporated their corrections.[9]

who affects it so to communicate with his reader that all his words shall seem to be natural to the occasion. . . . And yet in very truth the realistic must not be true,—but just so far removed from truth as to suit the erroneous idea of truth which the reader may be supposed to entertain" (pp. 184–85). He insists upon the moral purpose of the novel, and draws upon his own experience: "Having been for many years a most prolific writer of novels myself, . . . I regard him who can put himself into close communication with young people year after year without making some attempt to do them good, as a very sorry fellow indeed" (p. 202; also p. 107). And yet the novel's "only excuse is to be found in the amusement it affords," for it will never instruct "unless it hides its instruction and amuses" (p. 191).

It is rather curious, in view of Trollope's own practice, to read that Thackeray's "most besetting sin in style,—the little earmark by which he is most conspicuous,—is a certain affected familiarity. He indulges too [often] in little confidences with individual readers, in which pretended allusions to himself are frequent" (p. 201).[12] Even in this biography, Trollope speaks often of himself: "I remember once, when I was young, receiving advice as to the manner in which I had better spend my evenings; I was told that I ought to go home, drink tea, and read good books. It was excellent advice, but I found that the reading of good books in solitude was not an occupation congenial to me" (p. 41). Trollope also gives warrant to those of us who link novels to the lives of their authors when he remarks, after quoting Thackeray's description of Barnes Newcome, "Thackeray had lately seen some Barnes Newcome when he wrote that" (p. 117). The current events of Trollope's life appear in the biography. Would he have thought of speaking of the "personal flavour" of Kinglake's *Invasion of the Crimea* (p. 200) if he had not recently had the pleasant correspondence with Kinglake which has been quoted in the preceding chapter? or of praising the peculiarly American humor of "The Heathen Chinee" (p. 192) if he had not almost at the moment of writing entertained Bret Harte at dinner at the Garrick Club?[13] In one respect his ridicule was soon overtaken by events: he expresses the view that "literature can herself, for herself, produce a rank as effective as any that a Queen's minister can bestow. Surely it would be a repainting of the lily, an adding a flavour to the rose, a gilding of refined gold to create tomorrow a Lord Viscount Tennyson, a Baron Carlyle, or a Right Honourable Sir Robert Browning. And as for pay and pension, the less the better of it for any profession, unless so far as it may be payment made for work done" (pp. 37–38). Five years later Tennyson was made a baron by Gladstone; on June 2, 1897, Lord Salisbury's government bestowed on Rose Trollope a Civil List pension. At the end of the book Trollope reverts to the monument Smith, Elder had created in the form of the deluxe edition of Thackeray's works they were currently publishing at £33 12*s*.

"It is understood that a very large proportion of the edition has been already bought or ordered. Cost, it will be said, is a bad test of excellence. It will not prove the merit of a book any more than it will of a horse. But it is proof of the popularity of a book" (p. 206). Cardinal Manning, a schoolfellow of Trollope's at Harrow, in acknowledging a presentation copy of the biography, wrote: "When the memories of your readers run back over your many works they will bear to you the witness you bear to Thackeray. And that is one of signal honour."[14] The book is required reading for Trollope's devoted admirers, an appendix to *An Autobiography*.

When the book appeared about May 31, it disappointed some readers. FitzGerald wrote to Lord Houghton (whose poem on Thackeray's death Trollope quotes with high praise) that Trollope had "made but an insufficient account of WMT, though all in gentlemanly good Taste, which one must be thankful for."[15] Reviews were mixed, from the *Literary World's* view that it was the most readable of the "English Men of Letters" volumes yet to have appeared to the *Westminster's* assertion that the critical judgments were "capricious." In a commemorative article after Trollope's death his young friend and neighbor Walter Herries Pollock remarked that it was a good thing that Trollope had never written his projected history of prose fiction, for the *Thackeray* was "perhaps the least satisfactory" of his works, though its discussion of the lucid and easy style described "precisely the masterhood which Trollope himself had obtained."[16] Thoroughly savage was the belated, anonymous review in the *Pall Mall Gazette,* of which newspaper Thackeray's publisher George Smith was proprietor and to which Trollope was himself a frequent contributor. Morley, said the reviewer, could not have made a worse choice than Trollope; even his grammar and style are bad. His praise is conventional and undiscriminating, his criticism unfair and verbose. Trollope short-sightedly faults Thackeray for not going about his writing with Trollope's own regularity, he is in error in some of his "facts," and is entirely incapable of appreciating Thackeray. "It follows that we ought not to blame Mr. Trollope, but rather regret for his own sake that such a task as this was given to him." Trollope's particularity about Thackeray's financial affairs was especially censured: "It must be a source of satisfaction to Thackeray's children to be assured on Mr. Trollope's authority that 'the comfortable income'—the precise figure is stated—which he left behind was 'earned honestly, with the full approval of the world around him.'" FitzGerald thought the article "a little too elaborately hard on him."[17]

This last review was distressing to Trollope, not because of the judgment of his writing and critical ability, but because "there were circumstances in this, connected with Annie, which made me unhappy."[18] What these circumstances were is not clear; did he even suspect that she had a hand in the review? Not until early in 1882 did they meet again; it was at a dinner at George Smith's, and both were glad of the reconciliation. "We smiled at each other, and we had a thorough good talk. I am very glad because my memory of her father was wounded by the feeling of a quarrel," he told Rose. And Annie recorded in her diary that Trollope came over to her, "very big and kind and made it up. . . . I said I'm so sorry I quarrelled with you. He said so am I my dear. I never saw dear Mr. Trollope again."[19] (He died ten months later.)

Trollope's interest in Dickens's posthumous success was not merely aesthetic but financial as well. Chapman and Hall had purchased all Dickens's copyrights outright after his death,[20] and this investment was one of the firm's principal assets. Shortly before that date Trollope had described the firm as "a fine business which has been awfully ill used by want of sufficient work and sufficient capital."[21] It was about this time that he put down £10,000 to purchase a one-third partnership in the firm for his son Henry, a sum repaid to him after Henry withdrew in 1873.[22] But at the same time (late 1870, apparently) he advanced to the company £3,500 on the security of a portion of the Dickens copyrights, his interest being income from a proportionate share of the sales of Dickens's books, reckoned semiannually. By the time the loan was repaid, at the end of 1875, the annual income averaged about £750,—at 21 percent certainly Trollope's most profitable investment. For a time, a Trollope could enjoy the royalties of a Dickens. When the firm repurchased his share, Dickens's copyrights were still bringing in £6,000 a year.[23]

Meanwhile Trollope himself was entering the field of collected editions: in March, 1878, he finally completed arrangements for a project he had had in mind for more than a decade, the publication (in eight volumes) of *The Chronicles of Barsetshire* (of which the copyrights had been owned by Longmans, W. H. Smith, and Smith, Elder); the set was brought out volume by volume by Chapman and Hall from November, 1878, to July, 1879, with new frontispieces by F. A. Fraser, who had illustrated *Ralph the Heir*. As soon as the set was complete he sent a copy to the headmaster of Winchester College for the library there.[24]

≈

Only about a fortnight after finishing the short novel *Cousin Henry* Trollope on December 23 mapped out a new novel nearly three times its length, *Lord Hampstead,* but was interrupted after writing four chapters by the "terrible job" of the *Thackeray*.[25] Then came a pleasant but unexpected invitation to himself and Rose to spend a month in the country at Lowick Rectory while their friend W. Lucas Collins, the incumbent, was traveling in the south of Europe. "That I, who have belittled so many clergymen, should ever come to live in a parsonage!" Heavy April snows kept him indoors,[26] and somewhat playfully, no doubt, he set about writing another short novel, set in that very parsonage (called "Bowick" in the novel); and just as Collins was accustomed to take aristocratic pupils, Trollope's clergyman, Dr. Wortle, conducted a small school to prepare boys for Eton. He wrote the book between April 8 and 29, and sold it in the autumn for publication serially in *Blackwood's* (May–December, 1880) and in two volumes by Chapman and Hall (about January 1, 1881). He was paid £200 and £300 respectively.[27]

It was on the whole a rather lighthearted novel, as Trollope once more turned to the rural rectory and the provincial bishop. Dr. Wortle was much beloved in his parish, open-handed and well-to-do; Dissenters there were none. In nearly twenty years he had seen two bishops depart. The first moved to another diocese, carrying the sting of Wortle's reply when he suggested that Wortle devote himself to his parishioners rather than his school. The second died after long quarreling because, being "one of that large batch of Low Church prelates who were brought forward under Lord Palmerston," he resolutely and persistently tried to teach Wortle his duty. The current bishop also had at first felt obliged to say a word, but learned his lesson quickly, being "a man of the world,—wise, prudent, not given to interference or fault-finding, friendly by nature, one who altogether hated a quarrel, a bishop beyond all things determined to be a friend of his clergymen." "Dr. Wortle knew his man, and was willing enough to be on good terms with his bishop so long as he was allowed to be in all things his own master" (chap. i). For "it was his rule of life to act so entirely on his own will, that he rarely consulted [even his wife] on matters of any importance" (chap. ix).

Dr. Wortle engaged as his chief assistant in the school an intelligent and conscientious former fellow of Trinity College, Oxford, named Peacocke, who had taken orders and emigrated to St. Louis, Missouri, as vice-president of a classical college there (what is now Washington University; Trollope had visited it at the beginning of February, 1862). In St. Louis Peacocke had married an intelligent and charming woman from Louisiana who as young Ella Beaufort had previously married a "Colonel" Ferdinand Lefroy; both had lost their Louisiana properties in the post–Civil War unheavals. Lefroy was a drunkard who beat her and abandoned her, and was now on good authority reported to be dead. With a plot not unlike that of *John Caldigate* in its mystery, Trollope determined this time to risk unpopularity by eschewing all suspense and revealing at the start that Lefroy was not dead; that after Peacocke's marriage he had in fact shown up in St. Louis and threatened to expose the bigamy. Hence Peacocke's determination to return to England with his "wife." Clearly Trollope found it credible that irregular marriages should be common in Australia (as in *Caldigate*) and in the United States; Mrs. Hurtle of *The Way We Live Now* was another American woman of questionable marital status. Rumors spread at Bowick, and Mrs. Stantiloup, mother of a pupil whom Dr. Wortle had sent away, did her best to ruin the school by writing letters to the *Times* on the immorality of the Peacockes' lives: "We might just as well live as pagans, and do without any marriage services, as they do in so many parts of the United States" (chap. xii). She is a splendid comic figure in her indignant troublemaking.

But then Ferdinand Lefroy's brother, "Colonel" Robert Lefroy, appeared at Bowick with the intent of blackmailing the couple. He let slip that Ferdinand was now dead and buried in San Francisco; Peacocke agreed to pay him £1,000 and expenses if he would accompany him there to authenticate the death, and all ended happily.

But there had been tense moments. Just as Cousin Henry had been tormented by the Carmarthen newspaper, so here there was a London weekly called *Everybody's Business* which found in the gossip (before the success of Peacocke's journey was known) material for a lively story against Dr. Wortle.

> It was the purpose of the periodical to amuse its readers, as its name declared, with the private affairs of their neighbours. It went boldly about its work, excusing itself by the assertion that Jones was just as well inclined to be talked about as Smith was to hear whatever could be said about Jones. As both parties were served, what could be the objection? It was in the main good-natured, and probably did most frequently gratify the Joneses, while it afforded considerable amusement to the listless and numerous Smiths of the world. . . . "Everybody's Business" did this for everybody to whom such excitement was agreeable. But in managing everybody's business in that fashion, let a writer be as good-natured as he may and let the principle be ever so well-founded that nobody is to be hurt, still there are dangers. It is not always easy to know what will hurt and what will not. And then sometimes there will come a temptation to be, not spiteful, but specially amusing. There must be danger, and a writer will sometimes be indiscreet. Personalities will lead to libels even when the libeller has been most innocent." (Chap. xiv)

Everybody's Business was of course Edmund Yates's *World,* and Trollope's good-natured handling of it was no doubt a consequence of his recent meeting with Yates at Escott's dinner party.

There are not a few reminiscences of Barchester in the book. One of the most striking is one more echo of the archdeacon's remark to the

Reverend Josiah Crawley near the end of *Last Chronicle,* where Grantly's son was about to marry Crawley's daughter. Here Dr. Wortle's daughter is being courted by Earl Bracy's son; Earl Bracy was quite content with the arrangement because, as Wortle explained to the girl, "A gentleman can do no better than marry a lady. And though it is much to be a nobleman, it is more to be a gentleman" (chap. xx).

૨&

Lord Derby, son of the former Conservative prime minister, became president of the Royal Literary Fund in 1876. At the time he was Disraeli's foreign secretary, and though he resigned in 1878 it was his recent position in government that led to the one bitter moment of Trollope's association with the committee of the fund. By far the most profitable of the anniversary dinners had been that of 1872, when the King of the Belgians took the chair: there were more than three hundred stewards and the profits on the dinner, after all expenses, came to nearly £3,000. Doubtless in the hope of arousing similar public interest, the committee on January 8, 1879, (with Trollope present) voted to ask the twenty-three-year-old Prince Imperial, son of the abdicated and by now deceased Emperor of the French, to take the chair at that year's dinner. Lord Derby was not present, but he quickly informed one of the committee members, Dr. William Smith, that he strongly objected to the invitation (which might indeed, one would think, be embarrassing to the government's relations with the French Republic), and Smith got the consent of the two other registrars of the fund to call a special meeting of the committee on January 15 to reconsider its action. Trollope was present at the special meeting (Lord Derby was not) and seems to have assented to inviting the lord chancellor (Earl Cairns) rather than the Prince Imperial. But the communication of Lord Derby's wishes through the private instrumentality of one member of the committee, who no doubt gave the impression that the matter was too delicate for full discussion, offended Trollope's sense of propriety, and at the next meeting of the committee, on February 12, this time with Derby in the chair, he moved "that no letter shall be read to the committee of the Literary Fund except by the Secretary, and that any letter so read shall be left in the hands of the Secretary." Derby expressed regret that he had behaved improperly and said that he would gladly in future conform to Trollope's wishes. Other members could not understand what the fuss was about, but said they were willing to let him have his way, merely as a concession and to avoid the resignation he threatened. One of them remarked that though Trollope had shown strong feeling in the matter, he had given no reasons. Trollope was not mollified: he wanted assent *on principle.* And so the vote on his resolution was deferred to a special meeting a fortnight hence. During that fortnight the secretary was kept busy with earnest appeals for information on the constitutional issue. Trollope himself made clear the nature of the offense: "It may well be that it should suit [our President] and us to receive his opinion in writing [should he not be at a meeting in person]. But we cannot endure a second President. Such would become the case should it be customary with us to receive at our Board one of ourselves, carrying, as it were, the President in his pocket." A friendly letter from Edward Dicey, a member of the committee who of course had been Trollope's assistant editor on *St. Pauls Magazine,* gives a sense of the esteem in which Trollope was held: "I should . . . I own candidly vote . . . for any resolution not involving a question of principle, which would enable us to retain Mr. Trollope as our colleague. In Mr. Trollope we have a colleague whose name is known & respected throughout the domain of letters, & who, from his long & active professional pursuit of literary labour is almost unequalled. The absence of Mr. Trollope's name, as well as his non-participation in the deliberations of our committee would, in my judgment, not as a friend, but as a literary man, be a loss to the Fund to be avoided by any means in our power." A substitute motion, somewhat more precisely worded than Trollope's but to the same effect, was passed at the special meeting (from which Trollope absented himself), and the crisis was averted.

On the very next day (February 27) the unfortunate Prince Imperial, unaware, of course, of the furor at the Royal Literary Fund's offices at No. 10 John Street, Adelphi, embarked for the Cape of Good Hope, where he lost his life on June 1 fighting on the British side against the Zulus.[28]

As one reads Trollope's long letter to the secretary of the fund, with its firm unwillingness to yield an inch and its equal determination not to break with a group to which he was heartily devoted, one is reminded of Dr. Wortle's long letter to his bishop after the bishop cautioned him about the scandal in "the metropolitan press" (chap. xvii). One might say that when he wrote Wortle's letter Trollope had not "lately seen some Jeffrey Wortle" (to use Trollope's words about Thackeray and Barnes Newcome) but was aware that he had lately *been* a Jeffrey Wortle.

&

There were some subjects Trollope was unwilling to let drop; he worried them as a terrier worries a rat. One of them was fox hunting.* It was nine

---

*Another such subject was male supremacy. In April, 1879, he wrote to an unnamed American correspondent, "You cannot, by Act of Congress or Parliament make the woman's arm as strong as the man's or deprive her of her position as the bearer of children. We may trouble ourselves much by debating a question which superior power has settled

years since the historian Edward A. Freeman condemned the cruelty of the chase in an article on "The Morality of Field Sports" in the *Fortnightly* (October, 1869) and Trollope volunteered a response in the same journal two months later. "There is enterprise in riding to hounds, and skill. Ambition, courage, and persistency are all brought into play. A community is formed in which equality prevails, and the man with small means and no rank holds his own against the lord or the millionaire as he can do nowhere else amidst the scenes of our life. . . . I plead that the end justifies the means, that a minimum of suffering produces a maximum of recreation, and that a fox's life serves as good a purpose as that of any animal which falls that men may live."[30] Certainly his urging that the slaughter of fur-bearing animals to provide fashionable tippets for the ladies is more cruel than fox hunting commands assent, though it may not justify the latter. But he was still full of the subject when in December, 1878, he wrote the second chapter of *Marion Fay* and introduced his hero, Lord Hampstead, who was notably rational and unconventional in his thinking about social distinctions but loved hunting above all else— hunting, that is, as distinguished from shooting, riding after foxes as distinguished from blasting at birds. His argument was exactly what it had been in 1869: the moral judgment must depend on the sufficiency of the gain when weighed against the pain inflicted. "Who can doubt that for a certain maximum of good a certain minimum of suffering may be inflicted without slur to humanity? In hunting, one fox was made to finish his triumphant career, perhaps prematurely, for the great advantage of two hundred sportsmen."

At the same moment Trollope supplied Isbister with an essay for *Good Words* on the recreational value of fox hunting, a lively description of the hunt that did not address its moral implications, though the essay did deny that riding to the hounds was especially dangerous. True, two good friends of his had died on the hunting field, but then Sir Robert Peel and Bishop Samuel Wilberforce had died in falls from their steeds in the ordinary course of life. The essay was first in a series by various hands, and the general topic, "Half Hours in the Fresh Air," seems to have suggested to Trollope yet another piece called "A Walk in the Wood" (completed in mid-May and published in September). This was essentially an account of his method of novel writing.[31]

---

for us, but we cannot alter the law. To avoid, or lessen that trouble, it is I think expedient to explain and make manifest to all, the facts as they have been settled for us by that superior power,—not as doubting what may be the result. The necessity of the supremacy of man is as certain to me as the eternity of the soul. There are other matters on which one fights as subjects which are in doubt,—universal suffrage, ballot, public education, and the like—but not, I think, on these two."[29]

Thinking, he said, is difficult at best, but it "becomes easier out among the woods, with the birds and the air and the leaves and the branches around us, than in the seclusion of any closet." He had spent some two months the preceding summer in Switzerland and Baden as he wrote *Ayala's Angel,* and planned to spend a similar period there in the current year as he wrote *Marion Fay,* so that it is not surprising that he ended his sketch with the statement that "Were I to choose the world all round I should take certain districts in the Duchy of Baden [i.e., the Black Forest] as the hunting ground for my thoughts."

He was entirely unable to plot a whole novel in advance, he said; he did his planning "always out in the open air," but he was never able to plan "so as to know, before the story is begun, how it is to end." He tells us that he had not decided that Lady Mason actually forged her husband's signature to his will until he wrote the chapter of *Orley Farm* immediately before the one in which she confessed. The brilliant stroke of having Lizzie Eustace steal her own diamonds "only struck me when I was writing the page in which the theft is described." And he tells again the story of going home and killing Mrs. Proudie instantly when he overheard someone remarking that she had appeared so often in his pages as to become a bore. The thrust of his essay was that as a novelist his energy "has expended itself on the minute ramifications of tale-telling;—how this young lady should be made to behave herself with that young gentleman;—how this mother or that father would be affected by the ill conduct or the good of a son or a daughter;—how these words or those other would be most appropriate and true to nature if used on some special occasion." There is some confirmation of his statement in the preliminary sketches he made for his novels. In his memoranda for *Marion Fay,* for example, he is uncertain whether Marion should die; he fancies that Lady Kingsbury tried to poison her stepson or that the chaplain tried to shoot him and wounded him, and he plans the death of the Marquis of Kingsbury—none of which events takes place.[32] A remark in a letter to Blackwood shows something of the consequence of this improvisatory procedure: "As to amendments in the telling of the story as between Caldigate & Hester, I tried my hand at it and failed. The task of interpolating new work on a tale is to me so hopeless that I feel that I am sure to destroy the old by the new. My new wine is sure to burst the old bottles. Such as it comes at first it must remain."[33] Trollope's method was by no means unique: early in 1875 Mrs. Margaret Oliphant described to her publisher Alexander Macmillan the characters around whom she was planning her next novel, *The Curate in Charge.* "Exactly what these people are going to do I cannot tell, as the story is not finished and my personages have an unaccountable liking for their own way and never conduct themselves exactly as I intend them to do."[34]

One other remark in Trollope's "Walk in the Wood" seems to have had an interesting sequel. "To think with a barrel organ within hearing is heroic. For myself I own that a brass band altogether incapacitates me. . . . Here, in our quiet square, the beneficent police have done wonders for our tranquility,—not, however, without creating for me personally a separate trouble in having to encounter the stern reproaches of the middle-aged leader of the band when he asks me in mingled German and English accents whether I do not think that he too as well as I,—he with all his comrades,— . . . should not be allowed to earn their bread as well as I." The story is told that during the afternoon preceding his fatal stroke in 1882, Trollope had become overexcited in an altercation with the leader of a German band which played disturbingly under the window of his London hotel.[35]

એ

The quantity of Trollope's writing during the last half-dozen years of his life is so prodigious that one is at first tempted to think that indeed age could not wither him, but in fact his apparent energy is the consequence of his awareness that time was running out. A letter to Cecilia Meetkerke, wife of his distant cousin, expresses with clarity and good humor what most people his age must feel; apologizing for not having acknowledged a piece on Balzac she had sent to him, he said: "When I am written to, I answer like a man, at an interval of a week or so. But in truth, I am growing so old that, though I still do my daily work, I am forced to put off the lighter tasks from day to day: to-morrow will do—and to-morrow! I do not feel like that in the cheery morning; but when I have been cudgelling my overwrought brain for some three or four hours in quest of words, then I fade down, and begin to think it will be nice to go to the club, and have tea, and play whist, and put off my letters till the evening: then there is something else, and the letter is not written." He was haunted by the magnitude of the task of writing his *Life of Cicero,* but determined to complete it. On September 9, 1879, he wrote: "At any rate I am hard at work upon the matter, & have been ever since I came home from Australia last, when there I had my Cicero with me. Since that I have gone through all his works, & have read most of them now for the second, many for the third time. I have done about a quarter. If I live I shall finish the writing by the end of 1880. I shall then take a year for corrections. But what right has a man of 64 to speak of years in that way?"[36] Even his apparently light-hearted essay on "Whist at Our Club" two years earlier is really a lament for the mental losses that accompany old age. "There are perhaps a dozen gentlemen, mostly well stricken in years, who, having not much else to do with their afternoons, meet together and kill the hours between lunch and dinner. I do not know that they could find a wiser expedient for relieving the tedium of their latter years. . . . There comes a time of life when the work of life naturally ceases. . . . At our club the main rules are known. . . . We know how to finesse a queen, and I think we generally count the trumps,—at any rate, early in the afternoon."[37]

Trollope's summer travels in 1879 followed his usual pattern of recent years. Rose crossed to the Continent on July 17, Anthony followed on August 1 and met her at Gerardmer in the Vosges a week later—"a most detestable place to my thinking, as are all these places in France," though he had made the Vosges his setting for *The Golden Lion of Granpere.* "One has to get into Switzerland or South Germany before one finds a pleasant country or a pleasant people."[38] And so they proceeded at once to Felsenegg, in Canton Zug between Zurich and Lucerne. Florence Bland was with them. Tom Trollope was at that moment a patient at the spa of Baden, in the neighboring canton of Aargau, suffering desperately from sciatica; Anthony visited him twice, and wrote a warmly admiring letter to Tom's wife Frances Eleanor, praising her cheerfulness and devoted care of her husband—a letter Tom proudly printed many years later in his autobiography. From September 2 the family was in the Höllenthal, near Freiburg, Baden, and at the end of the month they took the familiar train journey through Luxembourg to reach home on October 1.[39] During the holiday he wrote forty-four chapters of *Marion Fay,* at the rate of nearly a chapter a day. Florence was his amanuensis for about a third of the work on the Continent; their stints were casually distributed and of uneven length. Sometimes when Florence left the desk briefly, for whatever reason, Trollope seized the pen and carried on, if only for a line and a half, until her return.

The book was completed at a more leisurely pace when they reached London—eight chapters in early October, eight more in November. As he wrote, he was of course aware that his last long novel, *Ayala's Angel,* was still unsold. "Nothing really frightens me but the idea of enforced idleness. As long as I can write books, even though they be not published, I think that I can be happy."[40] Indeed, he was quite content that the unpublished manuscripts should be stored up for the future; he told Mrs. Oliphant in March, 1877, that he had more than one novel prepared for posthumous issue.[41]

❧

The September, 1879, number of the *North American Review* (New York) opened with an essay by Trollope on "The Genius of Nathaniel Hawthorne," of which we know nothing as to its arrangements beyond the fact that at some time during the year he sent for copies of *The Blithedale Romance* and the *English Note-books,*[42] neither of which, as it turned out, he was able to crowd into his essay; he exhausted his space when he had dealt with *The Scarlet Letter, The House of the Seven Gables, The Marble Faun,* and the short stories in *Mosses from an Old Manse.* Perhaps G. W. Smalley, head of the European staff of the *New York Tribune* and an occasional dinner guest of Trollope's, had some influence in making the arrangements. (Smalley, in March, 1878, reviewed *South Africa* for the *Tribune:* "I can not tell you how much gratified I was," Trollope wrote to him. The review "was the more agreeable because I am sure you would not be led by any feeling of friendship to speak of any book otherwise than you thought.")[43] Trollope in any case had known Hawthorne on both sides of the Atlantic, and even before meeting him had learned from James T. Fields that Hawthorne admired his novels. The oft-quoted passage in which Hawthorne praised Trollope's realism was published by Fields in 1871–72 from a letter of 1860, and so pleased Trollope that he included it in *An Autobiography,* and now, naturally, in the present article.[44]

Hawthorne in that passage stressed the vast difference in subject and essence between Trollope's novels and his own, and that difference was kept to the fore in Trollope's article. He expressed his affection for the memory of Hawthorne, who had died fifteen years earlier, and recalled him as "a man singularly reticent,—what we generally call shy,—[who] could, when things went well with him, be argumentative, social, and cheery. I have seen him very happy over canvas-back ducks, and have heard him discuss, almost with violence, the superiority of American vegetables. Indeed, he once withered me with a scorn which was anything but mystic or melancholy because I expressed a patriotic preference for English peas" (p. 207).

As a practicing novelist, Trollope felt called upon to explain the superiority of *The Scarlet Letter* to *The House of the Seven Gables.* In writing the former Hawthorne "had the story strongly, lucidly manifest to his own imagination. In composing the other he was driven to search for a plot, and to make a story." Yet Hepzibah Pyncheon is "wonderfully drawn. . . . The reader sees all round her and is sure that she is alive" (p. 215). As for *The Marble Faun,* the inadequacies of plot are even more apparent, and loose ends are left unraveled, but the reader's delight in the characters and scenery of the *Faun* will be extreme: Hawthorne's imagination took the impress of Rome and Italy "and then gave it forth again with that wonderful power of expression which belonged to him" (p. 222). "In the true enjoyment of Hawthorne's work there is required a peculiar mood of mind. The reader should take a delight in looking round corners, and in seeing how places and things may be approached by other than the direct and obvious route" (pp. 216–17).

Hawthorne's son Julian was living in London from 1874 to 1881, presumably not affluently, since he was given a grant of £100 by the Royal Literary Fund in November, 1877.[45] He met Trollope during the winter of 1879, wrote the good-humored review of *Cousin Henry* for the *Spectator* of October 18, 1879, and on the appearance of *An Autobiography* published in the autumn of 1883 an essay on Trollope called "The Maker of Many Books."[46] It contains a lively and admiring sketch of its subject as a social man and a thoughtful account of the style and manner of his novels. Trollope's "touch is eminently civilizing; everything, from the episodes to the sentences, moves without hitch or creak: we never have to read a paragraph twice, and we are seldom sorry to have read it once" (p. 155). And yet there is in this essay the same conflict in taste between Hawthorne the son and Trollope as we have seen between Trollope and the father: "To the view of the present writer, how much good soever Mr. Trollope may have done as a preacher and moralist, he has done great harm to English fictitious literature by his novels," because of his vital sympathy with the commonplace (pp. 160–61). At that encounter in 1879, "a social meeting of literary men at the rooms of a certain eminent publisher," Hawthorne had been struck that almost alone in the gathering Trollope was clad in evening dress (p. 141); such costume in fact was evidence of his continuing strong sense of propriety. When at the end of *The Fixed Period* (written February, 1881) President John Neverbend was forcibly transported from Britannula to England on a British gunboat, his rank required that he be invited to dine at the table of Captain Battleax, and in conveying the invitation Lieutenant Crosstrees remarked that the captain "would resent it as a bitter offence" if Neverbend were to come down to dinner without a white cravat. "He's right, you know; these things do tell," Crosstrees added (chap. xii).

In an abridged edition of the book on *South Africa* published in March, 1879, Trollope included a new chapter on "Zululand," since that region had taken on new significance in England. Then while he was still in Germany in the summer he completed arrangements for two lectures on the Zulus to be given in late October, one at Nottingham and one at Birmingham. By this time the Zulu War was at an end, but was very fresh in the minds of his audience, who crowded the hall in Nottingham "inconveniently" (as the newspaper reported) and applauded him vigorously in his condemnation of the English colonial policy of extermination. A private letter he wrote earlier in the year sums up the view he expressed nearly as bluntly in his lecture: "I can not tell you how much to blame I think we have been in attacking Cetywayo. [Sir Bartle] Frere, for whom personally I have both respect and regard, is a man who thinks that it is England's duty to carry English civilization and English christianity among all Savages. Consequently, having the chance, he has waged war against these unfortunates,—who have lived along side of us in Natal for 25 years without ever having raised a hand against us! The consequence is that we have already slaughtered 10000 of them, and rejoice in having done so. To me it seems like civilization gone mad!"[47]

Henry Trollope was spending much of his time in France, doing translations of current scientific and archaeological books from French into English. He also wrote his short book on *Corneille and Racine* for Blackwood's "Foreign Classics for English Readers," a series like the one for which Trollope had written his *Caesar;* this series, however, was edited by Mrs. Oliphant, who was by no means pleased with either Henry or his work. He "has an extremely *queer* look, and is anything but prepossessing," she told Blackwood when she commissioned the work in 1877, "rather against my will." Henry was somewhat dilatory in completing the task, Mrs. Oliphant in her turn dilatory and arbitrary in dealing with his manuscript. Not unnaturally, Trollope tried to serve as an intermediary both with William Blackwood and with Henry. The book did not come out until 1881; "I daresay the critics will be merciful to his father's son which is the best we can hope for," she wrote to the publisher.[48] At the same time, the affectionate father looked forward eagerly to a long visit in London from Henry: "I am sure it will be better for you to make a tolerably long stop in London," and he could, after all, bring some of his translating work with him.[49]

A dear friend, John Blackwood, died at the end of October; one of his last acts as head of the publishing house had been accepting *Dr. Wortle's School* for his magazine.[50]

ぞ

Early in *An Autobiography* Trollope had described his habit, before and after he entered the Post Office at the age of nineteen, of creating fictions about himself. In these latter days the Post Office years were very much in his mind: "There was a touch of downright love in the depicting of Bagwax [in *John Caldigate*]," he wrote early in 1879. "Was I not once a Bagwax myself?" And in December, 1878, he sketched out a new novel about a clerk in the office of the secretary to the Post Office, George Roden,[51] who, though apparently of humble but respectable origins, does in fact turn out to be an Italian duke. Entirely in keeping with Trollope's affirmation in *An Autobiography* (p. 39) that "there are places in life"— including the Civil Service—"which can hardly be well filled except by 'Gentlemen,'" Roden is indeed a gentleman. Not that it is easy to define the term; to one of Roden's gossipy neighbors in Holloway, a modest quarter in north central London,* the sign of a gentleman is that "his

---

*Not far from Montagu Square, and indeed only a few steps from Trollope's lodgings in Northumberland Street during his Post Office days, there was a disused burial

gloves are clean" (chap. vi). In any case, whatever his birth or family, Roden was a gentleman in his deportment: "there was nothing about him to offend the taste," he was well educated, and "he had more to talk about than others" (chap. iv). The secretary for whom Roden worked was clearly modeled on Trollope's early superior Colonel Maberly, even to having "a little place in the West of Ireland" (Maberly's wife was from Ireland) (chap. lxi). Trollope in the novel retells some of his favorite Post Office stories. But though the office in St. Martin's-le-Grand was the same, Roden was in no way modeled on Trollope; he was a firm believer in Utilitarianism and democratic equality, doctrines which brought him into personal friendship with Lord Hampstead, unorthodox heir to the Marquis of Kingsbury. The principal plot of the novel deals with the young nobleman's love for a bourgeois Quaker's daughter from Holloway and with Roden's love for the sister of Lord Hampstead. ("Anything would be better than a Post Office clerk for a brother-in-law," thought the Marchioness [chap. iv].)

The Quaker's daughter, Marion Fay, is the only survivor of her father's family: her mother and all her brothers and sisters had died of tuberculosis, and she herself, certain that she will soon follow them, declines to marry Hampstead. Before the novel has ended, she is indeed in her grave, though a radiant vision of her comes to reassure the mourning Hampstead of her love. What may seem flagrantly melodramatic in an author's introducing so many deaths was of course simply Trollope's own experience: his brothers Arthur and Henry, his sisters Emily and Cecilia, had died of that disease, and the memory of their fate is revealed in more than one of his novels.*

No novel of Trollope's displays quite the variety of tone or of social range that *Marion Fay* has. The tragedy of Marion is emotionally moving, though it occurs in surroundings of both high and low comedy. As his name suggests, Lord Persiflage† and his family might easily find their way

---

ground on Paddington Street. As recently as June, 1878, he had participated in a move to convert the ground into a garden for the people.[52] In those days the street leading up to the cemetery gates from Marylebone High Street was called "Paradise Street," and perhaps with this name fresh in his mind Trollope invented his "Paradise Row" in Holloway, where Roden lived with his widowed mother. (The former Paradise Street is now Moxon Street, since it no longer leads to a cemetery.)

*Even the settings of parts of the novel call back those events: Hendon, the home of Lord Hampstead, is close to Hadley Cross, where Emily was buried, and Castle Hautboy, where Persiflage lived, was close to Penrith, the first home of Cecilia Trollope and John Tilley.

†In his *Lord Palmerston* Trollope remarked: "[Palmerston, as new home secretary in 1853,] became notorious as a joker. He passed on from the light courteous *persiflage* of the Foreign Minister to the common John Bull fun of an English magistrate, without an apparent effort, but with an evident intention" (p. 148).

into the hilarious society of an Oscar Wilde play: Persiflage himself a man of the world, a secretary of state high in the councils of Her Majesty even though "nobody quite knew of what his great gifts consisted" (chap. xi), his ambitious wife of ducal descent, his daughter Lady Amaldina determined to have a splendid wedding with twenty noble and beautiful bridesmaids, and her fiancé, the Marquis of Llwddythlw, "a young man about forty years of age, of great promise" (chap. xii), who delayed matters so that the bridesmaids gradually drifted away into matrimony themselves. ("When you once know how to pronounce [his name], it is the prettiest word that poetry ever produced!") The low comedy focuses on the gossips of Paradise Row, the chief of whom, Clara Demijohn, also has her matrimonial ambitions. As for Roden, who turns out to be the eldest son of a now-deceased Italian duke, it would be a mistake to take his rank seriously: it is used largely to laugh at the self-satisfaction of his British compatriots who keep pointing out that being an Italian duke is after all not comparable to being an English one. In fact, Trollope initially thought of making him Duke of Cremona—a perfectly possible title— but as the story developed decided to call him Duke of Crinola, a ridiculous name reminiscent of the romantic tale written by Charley Tudor in *The Three Clerks,* "Crinoline and Macassar." Trollope's farcical intentions are made perfectly clear by Lady Amaldina's letter of congratulation to her cousin: "Papa says that the Di Crinolas have always been doing something in Italy in the way of politics, or rebellion, or fighting," and though Roden acquired no money with his title, "Papa says that the young dukes are always as well off at any rate as the young ravens" (chap. xlvi; see Psalm 147:9 and Job 38:41). Even the potentially serious threat of Hampstead's murder by the Slope-like chaplain Thomas Greenwood is dissipated when the man lets "I dare not wait upon I would" (chap. xxxiv) and misses the critical opportunity. His patroness, the Marchioness of Kingsbury, in trying to find a good appointment for him, writes to her brother-in-law, "I don't think Mr. Greenwood would be fit for any duty, because he has been idle all his life, and is now fond of good living; but a deanery would just suit him" (chap. xi).

The manuscript of *Marion Fay* lay in Trollope's desk for nearly a year and a half before he could sell it. He offered the serial rights to Bentley for *Temple Bar,* but Bentley declined. By March 29, 1881, he had made his bargain with the *Graphic,* £400 for initial publication and £50 for the foreign rights.[53] It ran from December 3, 1881, to June 3, 1882, in twenty-six installments, each with a splendid illustration by William Small. Chapman bought the right to the three-volume edition (mid-May, 1882) for perhaps £600, and Chatto and Windus paid £100 for the cheap one-volume edition that followed late in the same year.[54] The publishing world was changing, and Trollope could no longer make a single bargain with one publisher, or even with two. When Chatto's "popular" edition appeared Trollope had just died; writers of his obituaries recalled his earlier, more familiar work, and *Marion Fay* dropped from sight. Yet the reviewer in the *Scotsman* was not very wrong to assert that the novel would "take rank among the best stories that have come from Mr. Trollope's prolific pen."[55]

Chapter XXVII

1880–81

It was a changing world and the novels occasionally reflected the change. As we have seen, Marie Melmotte's elopement was interrupted with the aid of the electric telegraph. One of the issues that divided the political parties in *Marion Fay* was the question of electric lighting for cities. The telephone of the future makes its appearance in *The Fixed Period;* Bell's invention was the subject of a paper at the Royal Society at the beginning of February, 1878, and in 1880 it too became part of the Post Office monopoly.

The world of book publishing was changing also, though the signs of change were not immediately apparent. *The Macdermots,* like nearly all novels in its day, was published in 1847 in three volumes at half a guinea each, and the year after Trollope's death *Mr. Scarborough's Family* and *The Landleaguers* were published in the same form at the same price. There were some fluctuations in the intervening years, but in general the publishing trade was committed to the multivolume novel at half a guinea a volume. The number of volumes was only partially controlled by the actual number of words (*The Way We Live Now* appeared in two half-guinea volumes in 1875, whereas *The Prime Minister,* substantially shorter, came from the same publishers the next year in four half-guinea volumes). The sale, by and large, was not to the reader but to the lending library which in turn rented the books to the reader. In due course, new editions of more convenient size and more modest price were published for sale to individuals. Moreover, as the monopoly of the lending library diminished, the issue of the inexpensive one-volume edition came closer and closer on the heels of the multivolume edition. *Marion Fay* was published in three volumes at a guinea and a half on May 15, 1882, and in one volume at three shillings sixpence in December of the same year.[1] And as with the modern paperback, it was the traveler that demanded the more convenient form.* It had been, then, a shrewd business move for the firm of W. H. Smith, which had newspaper stalls at all the principal railway stations, to contract with Chapman and Hall in 1865 to produce very inexpensive editions in cloth or cardboard covers for distribution at

---

*The library of the University of Michigan has a group of one-volume Trollope novels, each inscribed to Lucy A. Hutton from her husband, and recording the date and destination of the journey on which the book was read.

their bookstalls. A dozen years after Trollope's death the market for the multivolume edition crashed, and by 1897 that form of publication disappeared altogether,[2] but the market had been diminishing much earlier, and it is very likely that Chapman's loss on *The Duke's Children* (which so distressed Trollope in August, 1880) was caused less by the author's fading popularity than by a conservative publisher's failure to perceive the turn the market had taken.

By the end of 1878 Chapman was so short of funds that he was convinced the firm could be saved only by converting it to a limited liability company and selling stock in it; he consulted Trollope and invited him to join the company. At the beginning of 1880 the firm became "Chapman & Hall Ltd.," and in March, 1881, they moved from 193 Piccadilly to 11 Henrietta Street, Covent Garden, premises vacated by a manufacturer of meat essences.[3] Their troubles were not over. On June 14, 1880, Chapman was gazetted under the bankruptcy act and had to resign his membership in the Garrick Club, though he subsequently made arrangements with his creditors that enabled him to avoid actual bankruptcy.[4] The sale of the entire "Select Library of Fiction," chiefly to Ward, Lock, and Co., in July, 1881, was further sign of difficulty.[5]

Fred Chapman became managing director of the new company; the author of the official history of the firm describes his fulfillment of his duties as "a little tired and listless."[6] Trollope was one of the original directors and shareholders, and was loyal to his friend, but found attendance at the directors' meetings arduous and soon resigned. "Nothing more pernicious and damnable ever occurred, or more likely to break a man's heart [than the conversion to a Limited Company]. Twice a week I have to meet my brother directors & sit five hours a day. That I am half ruined is nothing to the trouble and annoyance and shame of such an employment. How could I have avoided it?" Henry Trollope too was a shareholder.[7]

The enterprising young firm of Chatto and Windus, neighbors of Chapman and Hall in Piccadilly, though still publishing some novels in the three-volume format, followed the trend to early publication in cheap single volumes, and purchased from Chapman the right to publish *The Way We Live Now* among their "Piccadilly Novels" in 1875, only a few months after its publication in three volumes; they made the same arrangement as to *Marion Fay,* and became Trollope's regular publisher with *Kept in the Dark, Mr. Scarborough's Family,* and *The Landleaguers.*[8]

❧

"I think that we are going to leave London this summer & go down to live in the country. I only think so,—but I tell you at once."[9] This startling announcement appended as a postscript to a letter to Tom Trollope in the spring of 1880 is our first indication of an apparently not long premeditated move. Indeed only a few months earlier Trollope had purchased two of the ground rents in Montagu Square—a financial investment, to be sure, which he would retain wherever he went, but one which seems to suggest a commitment to his residence there. He recalled that when he moved to London he expected it to be his last move short of the grave, but "it will sometimes take a man more than 5 years to die."[10] (Actually he lived for seven years in Montagu Square.) The only explanations he offered were that the Montagu Square house was not comfortable enough and that "I dislike dinner parties and all going out." Quite simply, "we were tired of London."[11] Once the resolution was taken, they acted quickly; by May 9 they had fixed on a house, "North End," at South Harting, near Petersfield ("in Sussex, but on the borders of Hampshire & close to Surrey") and took a seventeen-year lease.[12] They made the move on July 6. Their nearest railway station (either Rogate, a mile and a half away, or Petersfield, four miles and a half) was a little over two hours from Waterloo Station, London.[13]

Needless to say, the move was arduous, especially as to the books* and the wine, but it was achieved on schedule, and before long he pictured himself "as busy as would be one thirty years younger, in cutting out dead boughs, and putting up a paling here and a little gate there. We go to church and mean to be very good, and have maids to wait on us."[14] The church, indeed, had family associations: a very distant cousin, Arthur William Trollope (who died when Anthony was twelve and whom Anthony probably did not know), had been vicar of Harting from 1792 to 1797. The church dated mainly from the fourteenth century. When Trollope died some two and a half years later, the incumbent wrote that "he rarely, even when his health was failing, missed Sunday morning service, always punctual to the minute—an alert and reverent and audible worshipper, and a steadfast communicant. . . . He was the life of our school manager meetings."[15] Apart from the inconvenience of attending to his regular engagements in town, there was at least one serious flaw in the new arrangement: "I certainly do not play [whist] down at Harting."[16]

A friend describes Trollope's life there:

> At one time two farmhouses, but now joined together, [the house] is among the best and prettiest buildings in the district. Surrounded by an estate of nearly seventy acres, its long line of windows and

---

*Trollope had compiled printed catalogues of his books both at Waltham Cross and at Montagu Square and feared he might have to undertake the task a third time, but apparently he did not do so.

doors opens on a delightful lawn, with a background of copse, studded with Scotch fir and larches. Under these a long walk, worthy of Windsor or Kensington, starting from the garden gate, leads through fields up to a South Down hill. On the lawn itself might have been seen, even since Trollope's day, at one end, the greenhouse, whose flowers he used to tend. . . . Gradually he left his bed later than formerly, and often reduced the number of words forming the diurnal task. Together with this he increased his local hospitalities, as well as enlarged his active interest in all parish concerns whether of business or pleasure. Penny Readings were in those days still popular. Trollope not only patronised and assisted at them, but delighted his rural neighbours by securing on the platform, or in the body of the room, some of his well-known London visitors, notably Sir Henry James and J. E. Millais. [The future poet laureate, Alfred Austin, was another guest.] Not once during his stay at Harting did Trollope see the Goodwood or Hambledon foxhounds "throw off"; and he did not spend more time in the saddle on the South Downs than he would have done during his equestrian constitutionals in Hyde Park.[17]

While the move was still under contemplation, Trollope was a guest at the annual banquet of the Royal Academy (as was Bret Harte, who responded to the toast to "Literature"). One of the principal speakers was Gladstone, whose party had just then won the general election and who had therefore to speak as the new prime minister.[18] Something occurred to hurt Trollope; one can imagine that perhaps Trollope approached Gladstone to speak to him, and at that moment Gladstone turned away. In any case, the man who had carried Gladstone's banner at Beverley wrote to inquire "whether I have in aught offended you? . . . Latterly,— and again yesterday,—I have been made to suppose that you purposely shunned me." Trollope speculated on the cause—offence taken by some friend of Gladstone's, perhaps,—and assured him that "my sympathies are with you in all things." Gladstone replied that he "must have been guilty of a rudeness quite unintentional and due only to the absorption of the present times," and begged forgiveness.[19] A few months later Trollope named the capital city of his fictitious country of "Britannula" in the late twentieth century "Gladstonopolis" and fancied that a Sir William Gladstone, great grandson of the Victorian statesman, was prime minister of England in 1980.

Meanwhile, John Tilley was one of the last to come in for a share of the "pickings" of the outgoing Tory ministry: he retired from his Post Office secretaryship on April 16 and was knighted four days later.[20]

With all his labor of moving, Trollope was also busy with preparing his *Life of Cicero* for the press. "Cicero is nearly completed," he reported on

May 13. "Oh, the work that I have done. The books I have referred to, and the volumes I have read!"[21] He seems to have scanned the reviews much more eagerly than he usually did, and they were varied, from those who warmly praised his "fascinating skill in delineating private life and manners" to those who found it "superfluous, . . . neither thorough nor sustained, nor balanced, nor careful enough to hold its own among a crowd of competitors." His word on the subject was most sensible: "I fancy that we authors owe more to critics than any injustice we receive from them. I am sure that if any critic wanted to spite us, he could better do it by holding his tongue than by speaking evil of us."[22]

                                    ❧

About six weeks after the move to Harting Trollope began his first novel of 1880, *Kept in the Dark,* a short work about the same length as *Cousin Henry* and *Dr. Wortle's School.* Its story bears considerable resemblance to *He Knew He Was Right,* without the moving tragedy of that novel; indeed it even uses the setting in Exeter. A young woman becomes engaged to a scoundrelly baronet and the engagement is announced in the newspapers, but she discovers his true nature in time, breaks off the engagement and goes abroad with her mother. While on their travels in Italy, they meet another Englishman who falls in love with her; the two become engaged and are married on their return to England, without her having found opportunity to disclose the earlier engagement. The baronet, as it turns out, is a neighbor of the new husband, and one he heartily dislikes. Intending to make trouble, the baronet both calls at their home in an unsuccessful attempt to see the wife and writes to the husband explaining that as his home is near to theirs, he "thought it better to call and to offer such courtesies as are generally held to be pleasant in a neighbourhood. . . . It seems but the other day that Cecilia . . . and I were engaged to be married." The husband, "when he came to this passage, felt for a moment as though he had received a bullet in his heart" (chap. xi). Though he is unwilling to believe there was any impropriety in her relation with the baronet (chap. xiv), he is puzzled to understand why he had been kept in the dark about this portion of her life; the thought torments him more and more, until without saying a word he leaves her and their home, intending the separation to be permanent. (The phrase "kept in the dark" occurs with painful frequency in the novel.)

The intellectual heart of the tale is Trollope's presentation of feminine psychology. The husband's sister comes down from Scotland to attempt a reconciliation, and on their first meeting the two women "receive each other with that quick intimacy and immediate loving friendship which it is given only to women to entertain." The older woman explains to Cecilia that men's view of secrecy is different from women's; a man's desires cannot be measured by a woman's, nor a man's sense of honor by what a woman is supposed to feel. "Though a man keep such secrets deep in his bosom through long years of married life, the woman is not supposed to be injured. She may know, or may not know, and may hear the tale at any period of her married life, and no harm will follow. But a man expects to see every thought in the breast of the woman to whose love he trusts, as though it were all written there for him in the clear light, but written in letters which no one else shall read" (chap. viii). Through the agency of the sister, assisted by the news that Cecilia is now pregnant, a joyful reconciliation is effected in the last chapter.

Quite apart from the quarrel between husband and wife, there is a certain amount of other warmed-up Trollope in the novel. An unmarried friend of Cecilia's is altogether devoted to the independence of women and hostile to marriage. She is an Italian woman residing in England, Francesca Altifiorla, whose noble ancestors, well known in Italian history, include a Fiasco and a Disgrazia—names reminiscent of the Duca di Crinola. As in *Marion Fay,* the question is asked by the baronet, "What the devil are they to our old English families?" (chap. xxiii). When, however, she induces the baronet into a laconic proposal of marriage ("Don't you think that you and I know each other well enough to make a match of it?" [chap. xvii]), she reflects that being "Miss Altifiorla" is but small satisfaction. "She had her theories about women's rights, and the decided advantages of remaining single, and the sufficiency of a lady to stand alone in the world. There was probably some vague glimmering of truth in her ideas; some half-formed belief in her own doctrine. But still it had ever been an uncomfortable creed, and one which she was ready to desert at the slightest provocation. Her friends had all deserted it, and had left her as we say high and dry on the barren bank, while they had been carried away by the fertilising stream. She, too, would now swim down the river of matrimony with a beautiful name, and a handle to it, as the owner of a fine family property. Women's rights was an excellent doctrine to preach, but for practice could not stand the strain of such temptation" (chap. xx). But when, true to form, he jilted her, "the idea of a prolonged sojourn in the United States presented itself. In former days there had come upon her a great longing to lecture at Chicago, at Saint Paul's, and at Omaha, on the distinctive duties of the female sex. Now again the idea returned to her. She thought that in one of those large Western Halls, full of gas and intelligence, she could rise to the height of her subject with a tremendous eloquence" (chap. xxiii). "She intended to redress the wrongs of her sex by a great movement, and was devoting herself at present to hard study with that object" (chap. xxiv). And so Dr. Olivia Q. Fleabody's earlier lecture tour of England on behalf of the "Female Disabilities" (*Is He Popenjoy?*) is reciprocated.

Trollope finished the novel on December 16, 1880, and offered it to Isbister for *Good Words* at £200; it was published there monthly from May to December, 1882, and as a book by Chatto and Windus about October 20 of that year. He persuaded Millais to do a drawing, but Millais' heart wasn't in it and he did not get it ready until the second installment: Cecilia at her writing desk in Rome, head in hand, and the dome of St. Peter's visible through the window.[23] The story was not notably suitable for *Good Words,* especially since Trollope let his sporting characters use language Donald Macleod would not have tolerated. *"The expressions shall be softened.* I remember that they are there," he told Isbister. And so more than a dozen mild profanities were removed.[24] The husband's delight in his wife's charms when they were reconciled, however, was not changed; he was still allowed to reflect on "how absolutely symmetrical was the sweet curve of her bust" (chap. xxiv).[25]

Three months after the move to Harting, Trollope wrote to William Blackwood, "I have not seen or heard of G. Eliot. I must write to her."[26] She had married John Cross on May 6 of that year, they had traveled on the Continent, and then prepared for themselves a pleasant house on Cheyne Walk in London, into which they moved on December 3.[27] Then came the news in a letter from her stepson, Charles Lee Lewes, that she had died on December 22. "Your letter has shocked me more than I can say," he wrote to Lewes. "I had no idea that she was ill. Nor indeed, as you say, had any one. I had only been saying on the very morning that she died that I would go and see her, whether she was in the town or country. I did love her very dearly. That I admired her was a matter of course. But my affection for her was thorough and the wound . . . is severe."[28] When Kate Field sought information about her from Trollope, he replied:

> Though I was very intimate with George Eliot, she never spoke to me of her life before I knew her, nor, as far as I am aware did she to her other friends. Nor did he. He was a friendly affectionate man,—but very reticent, especially as to those matters which concerned her. . . . You may say that she had lived down evil tongues before Lewes' death. She was asked to dine with Queen Victoria's daughter, (Crown Princess of Prussia,) when the Princess was in England. I mention this because the English Royal family are awfully particular as to whom they see and do not see. That at any rate is true, because I saw her there. But in truth she was one whose private life should be left in privacy,—as may be said of all who have achieved fame by literary merits.

George Eliot once remarked that had it not been for Trollope she would not have planned *Middlemarch* on so extensive a scale or have persevered with it to its close.[29]

❧

Trollope's letters of this year show an increasing awareness of the physical and mental defects of old age. "I cannot sit down to the reading of any work like a gentleman at ease. . . . I read only by scraps, and take the marrow and pith of my time for my daily work. I also have that to do which, alas, makes me feel the need of working hard towards an expected end, lest the thief should come—" "I have not time for merely promiscuous reading. I am getting old and I prefer going to bed." "How I used to look for the shortening days [of autumn], when I was hunting, and had the first of November as a golden day before me for which my soul could long. I have now [December 21] to look for the time when the green things in the garden may begin to show themselves. But the expectation of green things in another garden prevents me from being sad."[30] And so it is not surprising that one should read, in his next novel, the only partially ironic statement about men who had achieved Trollope's current age: "Let any man look among his friends and see whether men of sixty-five are not in the way of those who are still aspiring to rise in the world. A judge should be deaf on the bench when the younger men below him can hear with accuracy. His voice shall have descended to a poor treble, or his eyesight shall be dim and failing. At any rate, his limbs will have lost all that robust agility which is needed for the adequate performace of the work of the world. It is self-evident that at sixty-five a man has done all that he is fit to do" (*The Fixed Period,* chap. i).

One of Trollope's recent interests had been his subscription to Sir Henry Thompson's Cremation Society of England when it was founded in 1874.[31] Cremation was an almost necessary aspect of euthanasia, and the principal proponent of euthanasia in *The Fixed Period* reflected "how feelings had been allowed in England to stand in the way of the great work of cremation" (chap. i). He and his followers had experimented with the bodies of specially fattened hogs, and if a trapdoor had not been inadvertently left open there would not have been the slightest savor of burnt pork in the atmosphere (chap. vi).[32]

During his career with the Post Office one of Trollope's most persistent concerns had been mistaken notions of "efficiency" in the Civil Service, the characteristic dogmas of the Benthamites, the "political economists." And so he gives to euthanasia's advocate, the president of the new state of Britannula, the same surname he had used for one of the more rigorously doctrinaire of civil servants in *The Three Clerks,* Neverbend (Fidus Neverbend in *The Three Clerks,* John Neverbend in *The Fixed Period*). The younger Neverbend appeals to statistics to support his view of the benefits of relieving the world of all people at the threshold of old age. "We should save on an average £50 for each man and woman who had departed. When our population should have become a million, presuming that only one in fifty would have reached the desired age, the sum actually saved . . . would amount to £1,000,000 a year. It would keep us out of debt, make for us our railways, render all our rivers navigable, construct our bridges, and leave us shortly the richest people on God's earth." In the face of such practical benefits, "tenderness is no better than unpardonable weakness" (chap. i).

Trollope's for him unusual adoption of a fictitious nation and a setting in a future year (1980) was the reflection of a literary current always interesting to the fantasies of readers, and especially so within a decade of the publication of Samuel Butler's very popular *Erewhon* (late March, 1872). About the same time *Blackwood's Magazine* (May, 1871) published "reminiscences" of a fanciful German invasion of England, Sir G. T. Chesney's "The Battle of Dorking," which Trollope actually mentioned in his *Life of Cicero:* "In truth, the great doings of the world do not much affect individual life. We should play our whist at our clubs though the battle of Dorking were being fought" (1: 304n).[33] And so *The Fixed Period* is set in a fictitious South Pacific island colonized by "the *élite* of the selected population of New Zealand," now in the late twentieth century an independent commonwealth framing its laws according to the highest ideals (chap. ii). Like many, or perhaps most, such fanciful tales, it is narrated in the first person by President Neverbend himself, the only novel of Trollope's to employ this technique, though he had used it for several short stories.

The Britannulan law of the "fixed period" provided that on a citizen's sixty-seventh birthday he or she be escorted to a "college," an elegant building in a lovely garden where there would be complete, luxurious happiness and idleness for a year, then a painless euthanasia before the sixty-eighth birthday (chap. i). The first application of the law would be the depositing of the oldest citizen, Gabriel Crasweller, in the college on June 30, 1980.[34] Shortly before that date, however, news of the threatened application of the law was cabled back to England by a British cricket team out for a match with the Britannulans, and the Secretary for Benevolence there despatched a naval vessel, the *John Bright* (named "from a gallant officer who, in the beginning of the century, had seated himself on a barrel of gunpowder, and had, single-handed, quelled a mutiny"). The vessel carried a 250-ton "steam swiveller," the ultimate weapon which could destroy the entire city with one blast. "It is an evil sign of the times,—of the times that are in so many respects hopeful,— that the greatest inventions of the day should always take the shape of engines of destruction" (chap. viii). On board was Sir Ferdinando Brown, former British governor in Ashantee (chap. ix), whose mission, here as there, was to overthrow a government whose principles were un-British, even "murderous" and "cannibalistic." He was a perfect gentleman, like his prototype Sir Bartle Frere, and as "prejudiced" as all educated Englishmen (chap. iv); his arguments had precisely as much reason behind them as the arguments of the British conquerors of the native Africans. Nevertheless, "throughout the world, you will generally find that the highest respect is paid to the greatest battalions" (chap. ix). Neverbend is carried back to England, the independence of Britannula is put to an end, and Neverbend's ambition of being the acknowledged pioneer of a great social discovery ends with the weak consolation that after all, "if you are not able to bear the incidents, you should not undertake the business" (chap. xii); his was the fate of many pioneers. The "college" was converted into a Chamber of Commerce (chap. i). The tale contains strong elements of irony, some good comedy and some rather routine comedy (as when Mrs. Neverbend, taking a loving farewell of her husband, cautions him to wear the flannel drawers she put up for him, the minute he gets out of the tropics). It seems somewhat too long drawn out for its modest substance.

Trollope began the novel on December 17, 1880, immediately after finishing *Kept in the Dark,* and he completed it on February 28. On the same day he offered it to Blackwood, who accepted it enthusiastically for his magazine (where it appeared monthly from October, 1881, to March 1882). Blackwood also published it as a book about March 4. He paid Trollope £450 altogether, and like the publisher of *Kept in the Dark* he begged Trollope to "dispense with the phrases of a religious character." (Trollope's word was, more bluntly, "profanities.")[35]

When Trollope died on December 6, 1882, he had passed his "fixed period" for deposition in the "college" by seven months and a half.

❧

Life in the country had its delights—and its difficulties. Attendance at board meetings of Chapman and Hall, at monthly meetings of the committee of the Royal Literary Fund, and other duties required Trollope's presence in London frequently, but he was further from town than he had been at Waltham Cross and could not now plan to return home every evening. He always stayed at Garland's (or "Garlant's") hotel at the top of Suffolk Street.[36] Very heavy snows in late January prevented his making the journey several times. "I went to day up to the top of the white hill, but to get there was a wonderful undertaking. To get down was worse. There were 3 or 4 feet of snow and a white mist blinding every thing. When will it go away?"[37] In June he had another practical lesson in the inconvenience of country living when Rose's niece Florence "was taken ill, and we had to send for a surgeon up to London. There was one dreadful day during which I thought the poor child would have died. They put her under chloroform and did dreadful things to her. But they saved her life."[38] In similar fashion Mr. Scarborough, in the novel Trollope was at that moment writing, had to send for a surgeon from London to perform an operation; the surgeon stayed three days at a cost of £300.[39]

The April number of the *North American Review* contained a substantial article in which Trollope again paid tribute to one of his American literary friends, this time Henry Wadsworth Longfellow, who was still alive when the article was published. It was primarily a discussion of *Evangeline, Hiawatha, The Courtship of Miles Standish,* and "The Skeleton in Armor," with copious quotations by way of illustration. Trollope modestly claimed that "he might perhaps be allowed to call him my friend," and recalled that a dozen years earlier Longfellow had told him that his poems were read more extensively in England than in America. Almost exactly a year later Longfellow died; Trollope was invited to be a member of a committee to arrange for a bust of the poet in Westminster Abbey and accepted with alacrity, but he did not live to see the bust take its place in March, 1884.[40]

On March 5 Anthony, Rose, and Florence Bland set off to visit Tom and Frances Trollope, who were now living in Rome. There had been some thought that Lucas Collins and his wife would accompany them, but Collins's health was uncertain and they did not go; Anthony had visited him early in January.[41] The party traveled via Monte Carlo, perhaps their first visit there, for Trollope wrote a very glowing chapter in its praise in *Mr. Scarborough's Family,* which he began nine days after leaving London. "I have lately been there," he told his readers, and described the magnificence of the concert hall, where superb music was to be heard at no cost. All was paid for out of the profits of the gaming tables, with money lost by rash gamblers who may for their losses have been moved to put a bullet through their heads. "I was ashamed that I had not put a few napoleons down on the table. Conscience had prevented me, and a wish to keep my money! But should not conscience have kept me away from all that happiness for which I had not paid? I had not thought of it before I went to Monte Carlo, but I am inclined now to advise others to stay away, or else to put down half-a-napoleon at any rate as the price of a ticket" (chap. xi). Word reached Trollope when at Rome that the younger Charles Dickens would like to have another of his novels, and this one was sold to him for £400 for publication in *All the Year Round* from May 27, 1882, to June 16, 1883. It was completed on October 31, long after their return to Harting.[42]

At Tom's house on March 29 Trollope met for the first time E. A. Freeman, the prolific historian who had embarked on the debate with him on "The Morality of Field Sports" a dozen years earlier. "They took to one another in a moment," remarked a witness to their meeting, despite

Trollope's instinct to dislike a man with such contrary ideas on Trollope's favorite sport. They had a good deal of talk on Cicero and together visited the hill of Tusculum, where Cicero's villa had stood. "For Cicero Mr. Trollope had a genuine enthusiasm; one might have thought that his life had been given to Cicero and nothing else." Not surprisingly, his discourse was an echo of his book: "Here, he said, was a Christian before Christianity." Freeman later spoke to two learned friends, one English and one German, on the subject of that book; the former affirmed that Trollope "had the root of the matter in him, that he thoroughly understood the real life of his period and his characters," and the latter "held that it was just Mr. Trollope's own busy life which enabled him really to enter into the true life of Cicero and his contemporaries. . . . It was because Mr. Trollope had seen a good deal of men and things in England and Ireland and other parts of the world that he was able to understand men and things at Rome also."[43]

There was one thing Tom apparently did not mention to Anthony: less than a fortnight after Anthony's return to England he received a bundle of proofs of an anonymous article for the *Cornhill*. "Who has written the 'Roman Penny a liner [in the Eighteenth Century]'?" Trollope asked George Smith, the founder and publisher of the magazine. "Not I. . . . But I would it could have been so! It was 22 years since, or nearly, when I received the first proof for correction. And then, since that, there have been recollections so tender! Think of all the names that crowd upon me. And all the cheques!!! Alas,—that they can never be repeated!"[44] The article was Tom's, and the proofs had been sent to Anthony through a blunder.

ஃ

The journey home began in late April. There were a few days in Florence, where they stumbled into Mrs. Oliphant, and a few hours' visit with Harry at the railway station in Paris. Harry was particularly enjoined to procure for his father four first-rate Havana cigars.[45]

He resumed his regular journeys from the country to London, "one or two nights every week," he told Millais, with whom he exchanged hospitality at their clubs and at Harting. The Trollopes added a porch to their house—or started to add one, but "it takes longer to make a porch than build a house."[46] There were somewhat ominous warning signs, however. A letter to Tom about this time remarks: "For myself I do not know what to say. They tell me my heart is worn out having worked too hard. I cannot, among them, understand anything of it."[47] On the journey, and thereafter, he more than once turned his pen over to Rose or

Florence when he wanted to write a letter; sometimes he was obliged to give up after only four or five words.[48]

One event to which they all looked forward took a tragic turn. On August 16, 1880, the daughter of Tom Trollope and his first wife had been married to Charles Stuart-Wortley at the British embassy in Paris.[49] Beatrice, or "Bice" (and one must give the names their Italian pronunciation) was a lovely and lively young woman, much loved by her father and her uncle. Occasionally, Anthony was called upon to be intermediary in some of her negotiations with her father, especially over money matters.[50] At the time of her marriage she was twenty-seven. Henry James had met her two years earlier when he was visiting London, and thought that she had "more of a certain subtle charm than any English girl I have ever met. . . . How could such a flower have blossomed on that coarse-grained Trollope stem?"[51] She had been especially noted in Florence for her voice; when she was in her late teens Jenny Lind is reported to have said that if she would study and practice professionally she would rival Jenny Lind herself. But practice she would not, nor do anything else seriously. "I remember her uncle Anthony telling me he had offered a five-pound note to each of three nieces of his if they would learn *Lycidas* by heart. Two of them did so; the third, Bice, never gave it another thought," Alfred Austin recalled. (How Anthony loved "Lycidas," and how frequently he quoted it in his novels!) "She won all hearts by her graceful spontaneity."[52]

Anthony, partly because of the move to Harting, did not see much of Bice after her marriage, but the entire family was looking forward to the birth of a child in July. The child, another Beatrice, was born a healthy baby, but Bice developed puerperal fever and died eleven days later. Anthony attended the funeral down at Wortley, near Sheffield in Yorkshire, and later wrote to Lady Pollock, "Poor Bice's child is living, but is a delicate little girl. Is it to be wished that the poor motherless little baby should live?" In fact, she lived until 1973; and her widowed father in 1886 took one of Millais' daughters as his second wife.[53]

≈

Mr. Scarborough's Family is one of the most remarkable of Trollope's novels, a triumph of his old age. The central story has precisely that complexity of plotting that Trollope pretended to despise; in this novel, however (unlike *John Caldigate*) he does not keep his readers ignorant, even though the characters in the story are in the dark. John Scarborough, owner of an entailed estate in Staffordshire that has become exceedingly prosperous because of the value of its clay and water to the manufacture of pottery, has always prided himself on his ability to outwit the law, not from any selfish or criminal motive but because he conceived himself a better judge of particular circumstances than any law promulgated for general application. The entail would leave him no freedom of judgment, and so he planned to defeat it by marrying his English bride twice, both times on the Continent. The first marriage took place in the obscure Prussian village of Rummelsburg in Pomerania; after the birth of a son, he married his wife a second time (with all the formalities of a first marriage) in Nice, and in due course a second son was born. By the time the story begins, the wife is long since dead and Scarborough is an invalid on his estate, his life only prolonged by repeated and painful treatment at the hands of the surgeon brought down from London.*

Both sons were educated at Eton; the elder, Mountjoy, after a year of travel on the Continent, became an officer in the Coldstream Guards, and the younger, Augustus, went to Cambridge, then became a barrister. Mountjoy developed an uncontrollable passion for gambling which even his father's generosity could not keep pace with, and he raised the necessary large sums with post-obits from the moneylenders—notes promising to repay the loans with very substantial premiums over the actual cash advanced, when Mountjoy should come into his inheritance. The rumor of Scarborough's impending demise brought the creditors down on Mountjoy, and the magnitude of the promissory notes threatened to consume the entire value of the entail. At this point Scarborough announced that Mountjoy had been illegitimate, that Augustus was heir to the estate as the oldest legitimate son, and produced evidence of the Nice marriage as if it had been the only one. Since Augustus had not signed the notes the creditors stood to lose everything unless they accepted the offer Scarborough prompted him to make—to repay in full the actual amount borrowed by Mountjoy, but without any premium or interest. They agreed to this arrangement and returned the bonds.

Augustus, however, was thoroughly unpleasant to Mountjoy and could not conceal from Scarborough that he expected the old man to depart this life very promptly. Thereupon Scarborough revealed the Pomeranian marriage that made Mountjoy once more the heir to the entail. On his very deathbed Scarborough asked Mountjoy, "You will do something, I suppose, for poor Gus?" (chap. lviii), and Augustus had to make do with a gift of £25,000. Mountjoy, unable to overcome his passion for gambling, set off for Monte Carlo, "or, as he himself told himself,—for the devil" (chap. lxiv).

Trollope gives special attention to the complex character of Mr. Scarborough—to his cleverness, his willfulness, his unconventional honesty. Perhaps the old man showed himself most distinctly when he said to

---

*The device of the double marriage seems to have been taken from Scott's *St. Ronan's Well*.

Harry Annesley, a friend of both his sons, "You haven't that kind of ingenuity which enables a man to tell a lie and stick to it. I have. It's a very great gift, if a man be enabled to restrain his appetite for lying"—if, that is, the lies are told infrequently and always with a purpose (chap. viii).

But the interest of the novel lies as largely in the range of peripheral characters. There is a niece, Florence Mountjoy, who is clearly Trollope's ideal young woman in appearance and behavior, especially as to her lovely hair, which "was soft and smooth, and ever well dressed, and never redolent of peculiar odours. It was simply Florence Mountjoy's hair, and that made it perfect in the eyes of her male friends generally" (chap. x). It had been Florence's mother's hope that she would marry Mountjoy Scarborough, but Florence fell in love with Harry Annesley, who was nephew and heir to a foolish Hertfordshire squire named Peter Prosper. Prosper's too was an entailed estate, and because Harry had rebelled at listening to Prosper's nightly reading of prayers Prosper determined to circumvent the effects of the entail by marrying the daughter of a village brewer, Matilda Thoroughbung, in order to beget a son. The courtship is splendid comedy; Prosper, however, is so little prepared for Matilda's aggressiveness that he cannot bring himself to go through with the scheme, and Harry remains his heir.

And then there is Scarborough's London solicitor, a very respectable widower of about Scarborough's age, and an old friend, named John Grey. "The light that has guided me through my professional life has been a love of the law. . . . I am sure that the law and justice may be made to run on all fours" (chap. lv). Scarborough's assertion that he had married after Mountjoy's birth shook Grey's confidence, but an investigation of the evidence at Nice convinced him that such was the fact. Then came the reversal, with the revelation of the Pomeranian marriage, and Grey was shattered. "Who would not say that for any attorney to have such a man as Mr. Scarborough of Tretton for his client was not a feather in his cap? But I have found him to be not only fraudulent but too clever for me. In opposition to myself he has carried me into his paths" (chap. lv). And so Grey withdrew from his profession. But, though he was not himself aware of the fact, in the opinion of his younger partner he had indeed grown old and established in routine. Whereas Mr. Barry had always heretofore had the highest respect for Grey's shrewdness and had assented to the proverb "that you cannot twice catch an old bird with chaff," Barry now began to think "that the older the bird became the more often he could be caught with chaff." Grey himself began to see differences in the professional practices of himself and Barry, and to reflect that "old times are changed, old manners gone" (chap. lviii). And then Trollope at sixty-six would not be likely to forget one other question—what would a man who had devoted a life conscientiously to a successful intellectual career do in retirement? read? (to what purpose?) garden? (when it rained, hailed, or was unbearably hot?) eat and drink? (for one who had never been self-indulgent?) work to help others? (would he know how, and would they accept his help?). Grey's daughter told him there were twenty, thirty, fifty things for a man like himself to do, but the problem of an occupation for retirement was not here resolved.

The novel is filled with autobiographical reminiscences. It was set in places Trollope had loved when he was a young man—Cheltenham, Brussels (to which the English flocked "as a place at which education for their children would be cheaper than at home" [chap. x]—so said the author who had once taught at an English school there). Like Thomas Anthony, Harry Annesley had a fellowship at his college which he would have to resign upon marriage, and as with young Harry Trollope "the mind of a young man so circumstanced turns always first to the bar and then to literature" (chap. xxii). Anthony had good reason to have both matters on his mind: only a few months before he began to write the novel he was a guest at the festivities of the New College Gaudy where his father held his fellowship,[54] and one of his current occupations was helping his son, a nonpracticing barrister, with a literary career. Mr. Grey lived at Fulham, as had Anthony's uncle Henry Milton (and as had also the lawyer Sir Thomas Underwood in *Ralph the Heir*). We are told of the bottle of Trollope's favorite claret, Léoville, as a sign that a dinner was elegant (chap. xxxvii). When Anthony died, there was left running in the weekly magazine founded by Charles Dickens and conducted by Charles Dickens junior a novel that gave evidence of his continued greatness.

Chapter XXVIII

1881–82

When William Isbister took over Alexander Strahan's publishing enterprises, including the proprietorship of *Good Words*, he in some sense, as we have seen, inherited Trollope as a contributor to that journal. Following Strahan's example with *Lotta Schmidt* and *An Editor's Tales,* he brought out in book form five short stories Trollope had published three to five years earlier (three of them in *Good Words*) with the title *Why Frau Frohmann Raised Her Prices;* Trollope proposed the volume to him on February 10, 1881, the agreement was dated September 30, and the book appeared about December 10. Trollope received £150. Isbister also had the option of publishing *Kept in the Dark* in book form upon its completion in *Good Words,* but transferred the right to Chatto and Windus. And Isbister became acquainted with young Henry Trollope through his father, and commissioned from him a guide to Normandy, on which Henry was hard at work throughout the autumn and spring of 1881–82.[1] Though Henry's work on Paris for the younger Dickens's series of "Unconventional Handbooks" was published (without Henry's name) in 1882, the Normandy guide for Isbister seems never to have appeared. In giving Henry advice about demands for royalties and travel expenses Anthony provided an interesting evaluation of his two principal publishers that he might not have made except to a member of the family who had business dealings with both: "I think myself that Isbister is a fair dealing man; but that he understands very little of his trade. He knows the paper and printing part of it. But is altogether astray as to whether a book will or will not pay. He is very much like Chapman, only as I think truer and honester."[2] In the course of the next year Trollope again and again had to jog Isbister on the score of punctuality in payments and submission of proofs, though he did so in the gentlest terms. By 1883 Isbister had been forced out of the firm that bore his name.[3]

In early September Trollope agreed to do a short political biography of Lord Palmerston for a series of little books on "English Political Leaders" that Isbister projected, apparently on the model of Macmillan's very successful "English Men of Letters."[4]

 ❧

There were house guests down at Harting, though perhaps less frequently than there had been at Waltham Cross. The head of Blackwood's London office, Joseph Langford, came down early in September to celebrate the completion of proofreading for the first installment of *The Fixed Period.* (He was down again at the very end of the year.) A few weeks later the Tilleys were there, and all went over to Winchester for sightseeing and, no doubt, to revisit the college; "We had a very fine day and enjoyed it very much." The Harting Grange apple trees had a marvelous crop in October.[5]

On October 22 Trollope attended a small dinner in London given in honor of Turgenev by his English translator William R. S. Ralston. Turgenev had already declined to allow a banquet to be staged on this brief visit to England on a partridge-shooting expedition, and now refused to acknowledge the toast in his honor with a formal speech, but, seated at his place, did talk informally about literary life in Russia. What he said is not recorded, but young George Leveson Gower recalled meeting him about this time at the table of the master of Balliol College, Benjamin Jowett. "Asked by the Master . . . what he thought of Dostoieffsky: 'He is no good; all schlimm-schlamm and vish-vash, what you call Brod Church.' "[6] When Turgenev died nine months after Trollope, the *Saturday Review*'s obituary was largely a comparison of the two novelists. "The ease of [Turgenev's] writing is no more a matter of chance than was the case as to that of Anthony Trollope; and in both cases numberless fine details go to make up a singularly living presentment of character, whether in the principal or in the subordinate personages introduced."[7]

Mention must also be made of another great Russian novelist who, though he never met Trollope, admired him greatly. "Trollope kills me, kills me with his mastery," Tolstoy noted in a record of his reading for 1865, referring to *The Bertrams,* which he described as "excellent." In January, 1877, he wrote to his brother that *The Prime Minister* was "splendid." Later in life his evaluation changed; Trollope's heroes, like those of Byron and Maupassant, "would-be generous and noble, are in fact useless wretches, while their women are mere playthings."[8]

In November Trollope spent a few days at Bromley Davenport's, a friend from the Cosmopolitan Club, in Cheshire: "Eating and drinking;—all eating and drinking! But as I dislike eating or drinking more than is usual, the time runs heavy. But alas it has come to that, that all times run more or less heavy with me, unless when I am asleep."[9]

Unexpected business—the need to appoint a clerk to assist Blewitt at the literary fund—took him back to London. His routine there was whist at the Athenaeum from five to seven, then dinner at the Garrick, but he was obliged to decline an invitation from Charles Stuart-Wortley: "To tell the truth I cannot without difficulty climb up to your rooms. Since I saw you last I have become asthmatic,—which is a great misfortune. I fear this place [Harting] does not agree with me." A fragment of an undated letter to his brother Tom gives much the same account: "I drink no wine, I may drink whiskey, thus I sustain myself. All the trouble as to my breath has come upon me in two months. . . . [I fancy] the time has come upon me of which I have often spoken to you, in which I should know that it were better that I were dead."[10] Discontent with the verdict of the Petersfield doctor as to his heart—and with the doctor's fee of five guineas as well—he went to a young doctor in London, William Murrell, who "says that I have not a symptom of A[ngina] P[ectoris] and that [the Petersfield man] is an old idiot."[11] Trollope's cousin's wife, Cecilia Meetkerke, spoke with admiration of Murrell's "first-rate professional skill," given by a man who became "a devoted personal friend." "For more than a year he remained under the same medical care, and got comparatively well. He was enabled to resume his favorite exercise, and his usual animated life, being, however, fairly warned, and that impressively, that he must neither over-work nor over-exert himself. The injunction was perfectly vain. He was extraordinarily impatient and reckless of his own condition; would still dash out of railway carriages before the stopping of the train, would hurry in and out of cabs, and give way in all things to his usual impetuosity."[12] The end was not yet: in the final year of his life he wrote one short novel, four-fifths of a long one, his *Lord Palmerston,* and two short stories. "Superannuated!" he had written more than two decades earlier. "The men who think of superannuation . . . are those whose lives have been idle, not they who have really buckled themselves to work. It is my opinion that nothing seasons the mind for endurance like hard work. Port wine should perhaps be added."[13]

Trollope the father was energetic on behalf of both his sons. He offered to bring to England for education the oldest of Fred Trollope's children, Frank; Fred begged that it might be the second son, Harry, since Frank was not strong enough for the rigors of an English public school. Trollope agreed, and asked that Harry be in England before Easter, 1883.[14] At the same time he was worrying about his older son's election to the Athenaeum Club, and soliciting the support of Millais and other friends there; during the actual balloting on February 13, 1882, he remained in the club, retired to the card room "in a funk" while the ballots were being counted, and rejoiced in the secretary's report that Henry had been elected with an overwhelming majority.[15]

The experienced writer could not help giving advice to his apprentice son on the writing of the guidebook to Normandy: "Your fault always is in being somewhat too long a time,—not thinking quite enough of the days as they run by; and in being a little too timid as to the work as you do it. In this work on which you are now employed you should remember that the time is hardly your own, and that you are bound to make each day go as far as you can. I do not doubt but that you will have done the work well."[16]

And he left the son something to look forward to when he should be called on to act as his father's executor: "I wish you to consider the wine lying in the two further binns as your own. . . . They contain Leoville, in the lower, and Beycheville in the upper binn. . . . I write this note to justify you in claiming them." A very old friend, one of Henry's god-parents indeed, heard of this: "John Merivale says that he will have an action against you for recovery of that claret. I held it on trust for my friends, and had no right to make it over secretly to a son. He said a great deal about your going to him when you were back in London."[17]

&

Trollope was at work on his *Lord Palmerston* by the latter part of August, 1881, when he sent for some pamphlets recently published on the Cri-mean War, and he promised to have the manuscript in Isbister's hands by March.[18] He explained to his brother Tom that he did not intend a biography, but "a small memoir," like his little books on Caesar and Thackeray—"to inform those who wish to know a little by a little easy reading." He finished the task well ahead of his schedule, on February 1, and the manuscript was sent to Isbister on the eighteenth.[19] Isbister's delays were such that Trollope complained, "It will take you longer to print it than it did me to write it." Gradually it occurred to Trollope that the real problem was Isbister's shortage of funds. "I would prefer that it should be published at once, and that I should accept your bill at four months, or even at six if it be necessary," he told the publisher on June 8, and the book appeared in the latter part of the month.[20]

Palmerston was very dear to Trollope, both as a Harrovian and as one who paid great attention to his Irish estate. "I remember having been told on the spot [in County Sligo] nearly forty years ago that that wonderful 'Irishman,' Lord Palmerston, had for the last ten years spent all his income upon the estate. He had just then been over, and the beauty of his presence had probably enhanced the virtue of his operations" (p. 12).* He further endeared himself to Trollope by having taken the chair at the Royal Literary Fund dinner, albeit a year or two before Trollope became

---

*Palmerston was an Englishman, with a family estate at Romsey, some ten miles west of Winchester. His peerage, however, was Irish, and because it was Irish he sat in the House of Commons in Westminster, not in the House of Lords.

associated with the fund. "He made a speech serviceable to the occasion" (i.e., one which stimulated the flow of funds, no doubt) (p. 185).

Though a Whig by party affiliation, Palmerston was at heart a Conservative. "We all know the story of the Tory finding the Whig bathing and running away with his clothes. Of course the Conservative wishes to prevent the Liberal from being successful, and finds he can best do so by carrying out the measures which the Liberal has proposed"—like Disraeli's Reform Bill of 1867 (after Palmerston's death, of course) (p. 83). A good deal of Trollope's representation of parliamentary maneuvering in his novels is based on his observation of Palmerston. E. A. Freeman records that when he and Trollope talked about Palmerston in Somerset soon after the book was finished, "I could see that Mr. Trollope's Liberalism, though very thorough, was more traditional and conventional than mine, and that we looked at things somewhat differently, if only because he was eight years older than I was. . . . [He] measured things by the remembrances of an older time than I did. . . . [He] felt towards Lord Palmerston as a head of the Liberal party, while to me he was simply the long-abiding deceiver of the Liberal party."[21] On one matter only is Trollope severe, that is Palmerston's approval of Louis Napoleon. "To me who write this, even the memory of the Emperor is distasteful" (p. 134).

Trollope's comment on Palmerston's fragmentary autobiography was made no doubt with an eye to what he himself had written and sealed up for posthumous publication: "After nearly forty years [he] has trusted to his memory when his journal failed him," and for better or for worse, future writers of his life will have "the written words, not intentionally false when written" (p. 34). Perhaps one apothegm of Palmerston's may be worth repeating: "Half the wrong conclusions at which mankind arrive are reached by the abuse of metaphors" (p. 64).

"Looking back through all the History of England and her worthies, I do not know the life of any man who has shown such a career of unchequered good fortune and jocund happiness,—or more unblemished honesty and truer courage" (p. 199). Though the technical historians among Trollope's reviewers were inclined to be severe on his blunders, "his judgment of Lord Palmerston's political opinions and temperament is generally sound," and he "describes Lord Palmerston's personal qualities in a heartily sympathetic spirit, and with the dramatic skill of an experienced artist." The little book has "all the lightness and yet strength that he shows in his novels."[22]

In his conclusion Trollope quoted some half-dozen pages from an article Peter Bayne had contributed to *St. Pauls Magazine,* and in return Bayne asked Trollope to recommend to Blackwood a paper he had written on "Shakespeare and George Eliot." "When a man has worked under a master, it is commonly held legitimate on his part to ask for a character," and Bayne was having trouble getting editors to give him a reading.

Blackwood's published the essay.[23] And despite Trollope's disagreement with Sir Theodore Martin's evaluation of the relations between Palmerston and the Queen ("I think," said Trollope, "that the Queen and Prince Albert, and Baron Stockmar behaved badly to Lord Palmerston"), he presented a copy of his book to Martin "with the Authors kind Regards."[24]

࿇

Having finished *Lord Palmerston* so much sooner than he had expected, Trollope used the weeks from February 20 to May 9, 1882, to write a short novel so that he might have something ready should any editor require it for a magazine.[25] He took the occasion to make use of some of his observations in the region of the diamond mines of South Africa.

An Old Man's Love is an uneventful novel with a single, simple plot, set at Alresford in the Hampshire downs, only ten or fifteen miles from Harting. William Whittlestaff, a well-to-do bachelor who had never recovered from being jilted many years ago by his lovely fiancée, "was not a young man, because he was fifty; but he was not quite an old man, because he was only fifty" (chap. ii). When the twenty-five-year-old Mary Lawrie, daughter of his closest friend, was left orphaned and impoverished, he took her into his home, and so came to admire her that he asked her to be his wife. And then a motif from *John Caldigate* was repeated: a young man whom she had known several years earlier and lost her heart to (though there had been no declaration of love between them) returned from a prosperous sojourn in the Kimberley diamond fields in South Africa and sought her out; he found her on the day after she consented to be Whittlestaff's wife. From this point the story is an extended analysis of the dilemma in the minds of both Whittlestaff and Mary; their reflections are rehearsed with considerable repetitiveness. In the end Whittlestaff concludes that the only gentlemanly and decent thing is for him to give her up; he will stand at her wedding as her father, not her husband. There are a few splendid episodes; the scene in which Whittlestaff announces his generous decision to the young man, and yet cannot help being overcome by his own anger and disappointment (chap. xxi), shows Trollope at his best in character analysis. There is an attempt at humor in the person of Whittlestaff's housekeeper, Mrs. Baggett, whose somewhat Dickensian dialect occasionally breaks down in the author's absent-mindedness. And Trollope's affection for the Roman classics is attested by Whittlestaff's love of walking out to a pretty spot among the beech trees and there sitting and reading his Horace, delighting equally in absorbing the poet's wisdom and in fighting against the poet's "pretences" (chaps. xvi–xviii). "Non sum qualis eram bonæ sub regno Cynaræ," he read, and thought of his own circumstances in life; nine years later a young Victorian poet could use that line as title for a poem that now stands for all the decadence of the nineties.* The countryside, "where the downs begin to rise" (chap. xvi), is one of Trollope's favorite haunts at his new home.

The manuscript was locked up in his cabinet until it might be needed, and found a publisher some fifteen months after Trollope's death.

❧

By the end of March Trollope had decided that the current disasters in Ireland were a most appropriate subject for a long novel, and despite his bad health determined to visit the island and see for himself what things were like. Before he left he offered the novel to Bentley for serial publication in *Temple Bar,* but Bentley could not use it.[26] As was usual when Trollope visited an unfamiliar country in search of information, he procured from his London acquaintances letters of introduction.[27] With Florence Bland as companion he set off on May 15, crossed to Dublin and proceeded at once to Cork, where he spent his time talking with the land law judge, John O'Hagan, and with one of the Irish land commissioners, John Edward Vernon. Even from Dublin he wrote, "I have done nothing but talk since I have been here, till I am very tired of it." He also visited one of the court sessions. "It is astonishing how one loses here all sense of rows and riots & how soon one begins to feel that the world is going on the same as ever," he told Rose, and reminded her that when they lived at Clonmel during the great famine they first learned of the people's raids on the bakers' shops there from articles in the *Times* of London. At Limerick on the River Shannon he and Florence drove out with the resident magistrate, an active force against the Land Leaguers, and he was relieved that they were not shot. "You can hardly bring yourself to understand the state of the country here, for among the men who are well-informed & thoroughly loyal there are so many opinions." His own view was that the government should be firm against the "Parnell set" and "the American host at their back." His hostility to Gladstone and home rule was outspoken; as Alfred Austin remarked, "Anthony himself became a 'Unionist,' and denounced Gladstone and all his works in the energetic language that was habitual in his fervid conversation." "Nothing can reconcile me to a man who has behaved so badly about Ireland," he told Rose.[28] This belated shift after a lifetime of party loyalty was a bitter experience to him, especially since he was on such good terms with W. E. Forster.

The work was strenuous, and even a holiday of a few days at Recess in County Galway found him "still . . . in the midst of Irish difficulties and Irish rebels." He was also reliving his early days as a Post Office employee, and recalling old experiences in his letters to Rose. In Dublin he and Florence dined with G. C. Cornwall, still secretary to the Irish

*Ernest Dowson's poem gained an unexpected immortality when an American novelist used one of his lines, "gone with the wind," as the title of her book.

Post Office as he had been since 1850. In Limerick "the Morrisons were [kind] to us just the same as ever,—only he somewhat more stupid." It was near Clonmel that he stayed with Lord Emly in the house of a man they had once known there, who had shot himself in the head shortly after they moved to Mallow; the man's son, Count de la Poer ("Power" when the Trollopes knew the family) was now high sheriff of County Waterford. Nostalgia set in; still, "I will give up being Surveyors clerk as you don't like it," he told Rose, "but in that case must take to being guide at Killarney." They reached home in the middle of June.[29]

Tom and Fanny Trollope were at Harting for a fortnight from the end of July—a fortunate visit in its way, for as Tom wrote to Henry four months later, "It is a great comfort to me that I came to England this year. The last time I saw [your father] was when I went up to his bedroom at Garlants in the morning before we started for Dover. But what will most remain in mind will be the pleasant strolling up and down in the orchard at Harting as we walked and laughed at the dog jumping for apples!" Nevertheless, Anthony told Henry at the time, "I have put up with Harting for the last fortnight so as to [be] here while Tom and Fanny were with me. But the asthma has been very bad quite lately."[30]

A second visit to Ireland with Florence from August 10 to September 11 was spent in the region around Dublin and was intended largely, it seems, for pleasure; Rose at this time was in their favorite holiday haunts in the Black Forest and Switzerland. But the Irish jaunt was a sad failure—the places he most wanted to visit caused him terrible attacks of asthma. They returned to England from Kingstown, where he had first met Rose, and reached London just in time to see Tom and Fanny depart for Italy, and to take the final farewell Tom remembered.[31]

ၜ

In 1881 Trollope received two flattering letters from Henry Howard, the ex-governor of Rhode Island, one of them urging him to bring back once more the Barsetshire characters in a novel. "I cannot hope to do what you propose. . . . Though I still go on writing, the new characters are much less troublesome than the old ones; and can be done without the infinite labour of reading back again and again my old works." Then John Tilley's son Arthur also wrote enthusiastically about *Barchester Towers*. "[It] was written before you were born," Trollope replied with slight exaggeration. "The writer never forgets. And when after 30 years he is told by some one that he has been pathetic, or witty, or even funny, he always feels like lending a five-pound note to that fellow."[32] And so when Donald Macleod in May asked for a longish story for *Good Cheer* (the Christmas supplement to *Good Words*), Trollope turned once more to Barsetshire for "The Two Heroines of Plumplington." "All the world may not know that Plumplington is the second town in Barsetshire, and though it sends no member to Parliament, as does Silverbridge, it has a population of over 20,000 souls, and three separate banks."[33] In fact, except for passing reference to some familiar names—Greshamsbury, Gatherum Castle, Hiram's Hospital, the old Duke of Omnium, old Mr. Gresham—there is nothing familiar to the lovers of old Barchester and Silverbridge, and the story altogether lacks sparkle. It was published just at the time Trollope suffered his fatal stroke.[34]

ठ∿

Life, "a weekly journal of society, literature, the fine arts, and finance," was essentially a gossip sheet like the *World* (founded by Edmund Yates in 1874) and *Truth* (founded by Henry Labouchere in 1877). It was now in its fourth year, and its editor Henry A. Felbermann approached Trollope through an intermediary at the beginning of August to request a very short Christmas story for 1882. The bargain was quickly made, and the pleasant but trivial story, "Not if I Know It," was soon written. Trollope was also now eager to place the new Irish novel on which he was working, *The Landleaguers,* and an agreement was made for that work too.[35] *Life's* publisher regarded the acquisition as something of a coup: the whole back cover of the journal on October 5 announced the coming serial as an inducement to new subscribers, and the announcement was repeated in large type until the novel actually began its run with two chapters on November 16. But by this time Anthony had suffered his stroke; reports on his health were appearing frequently in the daily newspapers, and they did not entirely warrant *Life's* assurance in that issue that "his complete restoration to health is not far distant." When he died as the fourth installment was being published, the editors set aside ten full pages to republish chapters 1–5, and add chapter 6, all in a sober black border and preceded by an obituary essay; the editor assured his public that there was not a bit of truth in the general impression that Trollope had left the novel a mere fragment: "Only an insignificant portion of the novel . . . remains unwritten." Nevertheless, Trollope now joined Mrs. Gaskell and Dickens in the ranks of those who began publication of a novel before the work was completed, and who then did not live to conclude it.[36] The novel ran until October 4, 1883. As part of a bargain for three novels, Chatto and Windus had offered him £600 for the copyright after serialization and Trollope accepted on October 10. The book was published about October 25, 1883; at Henry Trollope's suggestion the publishers paid only £480, since only that proportion of the book had been completed.[37]

Economic depression in Ireland led to strong pressure for reform of land tenure and the Irish National Land League was founded in the summer of 1879, with Parnell as president, and with substantial support from the Irish people in the United States. As the number of tenants evicted for nonpayment of rents increased, so did the number of agrarian outrages against landlords, especially in the western counties of Galway and Mayo. The new Liberal government in 1880, with W. E. Forster as chief secretary for Ireland, followed a policy of coercion and jailed Parnell and two other Irish members of Parliament in the autumn of 1881. (Parnell's mistress, Kitty O'Shea, was the sister of Trollope's long-time correspondent Mrs. Anna Steele, but the liaison was not yet notorious.)[38] The government was slow to take effective steps to alleviate Ireland's agricultural problems, and the rural population began to isolate and cut off from services all landlords who evicted tenants for nonpayment of rents; people who provided such services—trade, transportation, farm and domestic help—were threatened unless they ceased to provide them. (Captain Boycott, one of the earliest of the landlords to be so treated, gave his name to the process.) Murders followed in the wake of such measures as destruction of crops and maiming of cattle. Needing a solution, Gladstone's government in May, 1882, freed Parnell and his associates in the hope of enlisting their support. Forster resigned; his successor, Lord Frederick Cavendish, was murdered in Phoenix Park on May 6, the day of his arrival in Dublin. (This was only eleven days before Anthony and Florence reached Dublin.)* By the end of 1882 the year had seen twenty-six murders and fifty-eight attempted murders. The worst of these occurred at Maamtrasna, in Galway, on August 17, while Anthony and Florence were on their second visit to Ireland; a father, mother, three sons, and a daughter were battered one night in their cottage by ten assailants and only one, a little boy, survived. Trollope's account of the massacre, written as part of his fiction, was among the very last pages he wrote in *The Landleaguers*. His view of it was somewhat justified in the event—that so horrible a state of affairs was intolerable for the poor as well as for the landlords, and by its very extremity would put an end to the atrocities. Five of the Phoenix Park assassins and three of the Maamtrasna murderers were hanged and some measure of order was restored.[39]

Trollope's novel was essentially a political tract, repeating in fiction much of the melodrama of real events. As he had done in *The Three Clerks* on the Civil Service, he included a long chapter (xli) on his view of the state of Ireland. This was essentially an essay on Gladstone's Irish Land Act of 1881, which provided such arbitrary and tiny abatements of rent, in Trollope's view, as to be utterly ineffectual; far better to emigrate to America than to rely on such remedies. He referred to his own experience in the country as far back as 1842, and praised the sagacity and kindness of Judge O'Hagan, whom he had recently interviewed in Cork—but O'Hagan was bound by the irrational laws. "To the liberal statesmen of the day, men in speaking well of whom,—at a

---

*When Trollope wrote his account of the murder in the novel (chap. xxxix) the following October, he mistakenly remembered the event as having occurred in April. He took the opportunity to pay friendly tribute to Cavendish's predecessor.

great distance,—[the present writer] has spent a long life, he is now bound to express himself as opposed."

The principal story in the novel is that of a boycotted landlord near Headford, on Lake Corrib in County Galway. Trollope's customary hunting scene is here modified by making it the occasion of the first sign of the boycott: the tenants killed or drove out the foxes so that the hunt was interrupted and both this season and the next were cut off. The pathos of the story lies principally in the murder of the landlord's eleven-year-old son as he was driving with his father to give testimony in a Galway court (chap. xxx). There is a substantial subplot in the story of a Galway neighbor, Rachel O'Mahony and her father, both American born; he claimed Irish ancestry and had been brought up a Roman Catholic, though he had left the faith. She had been on the stage in a minor way in the United States; at the age of twenty she went to London, climbed to the pinnacle of reputation at Covent Garden Opera House, then lost her voice altogether. "She was very fair, and small and frail to look at. . . . Her beauty was all but perfect, as far as symmetry was concerned, only that there was not enough of it" (chaps. v, vi). She was a warm advocate of women's rights and of earning enough money to stand on her own feet without a husband (chaps. xvii, xviii). Trollope's friend Kate Field was in London from May to the end of July (he began his writing of the novel in June), and Kate was the daughter of a Dublin-born Irishman who had emigrated to the United States. She had been baptized a Roman Catholic, but had left the faith; she was "delicate in physique, . . . very slender and graceful,"[40] and she had achieved some success on the London stage after acting in her native country. As for her view of women's rights, it was a subject Trollope frequently delighted in teasing her about. One might, then, easily suppose that the idea of Rachel was suggested by Kate's visit.

The Landleaguers is interesting as an expression of Trollope's ideas about Ireland; it is insignificant as a novel. One very old friend of his may have been pleased if he read it: Sir Henry Taylor, now eighty-two, would have seen his *Philip van Artevelde* quoted for its wisdom (chap. xxxii).

ε

For the greater part of 1882 Trollope's health was wretched. "I have, alas, been the whole day among the doctors," he wrote to Rose from London on March 20, warning her that a box of medicine was about to arrive at Harting for him.[41] A week later he was proposing to Henry that they might take a small flat in London—"three rooms between us, and some kind of servant for us (to ourselves)"—for the next winter. He told Cecilia Meetkerke that the doctor might order him back to town permanently, but "at my age it will be very mischievous to make another moving; and the more so as this place [Harting] suits my wife."[42] He booked two floors of

Garland's Hotel in Suffolk Street from Monday, October 2, and Henry arrived in England three days earlier. Later in the month he was still looking for more permanent quarters either in Halfmoon Street (off Piccadilly) or in Victoria Street, not far from Tilley's home.[43]

With all his ailments, he was keeping up the pace of his life as well as he could. On October 25 he went out to Somersetshire to spend two days with E. A. Freeman. He regretted having made the commitment, "but still I think it is better to go about." To Freeman he wrote in anticipation of the visit, "I can, with due time, walk up anything,—only I cant sleep, walking or not walking. I cant write, as you see, because my hand is paralyzed. I cant sit easily because of a huge truss I wear, and now has come this damnable asthma! But still I am very good to look at; and as I am not afraid to die, I am as happy as other people."[44] His host took him about the countryside and showed him Wells and Glastonbury. "He enjoyed our scenery, but he did not enjoy either our mud or our stiles, and it was pleasant to see the way in which [our companion, Bishop Clifford of Clifton], more active than I was, helped him over all difficulties." On November 2 Freeman dined with Trollope at the home of the publisher Macmillan in Tooting; "he talked as well and heartily as usual."[45]

Freeman had been unable to attend Trollope's "big dinner" at the Garrick Club the preceding day, but Browning was there. Trollope liked Browning personally, but had mixed feelings about his poetry. In the winter of 1880–81 he read *The Ring and the Book* (!!) aloud to Rose and Florence, but in January, 1882 he described Browning to Henry as "a stodger," who had very few true things in his poetry and whose "phraseology is sometimes fearful."[46]

Lord Emly, having seen Trollope's agony from asthma during the visit to Ireland, had mentioned the fact to Cardinal Newman, and Newman responded by forwarding through Emly's hand an excellent recipe for relieving asthma by fumigation; at the same time he expressed his affection for Trollope's novels. Trollope's last surviving letters are acknowledgments of the favor. "It is when I hear that such men as yourself have been gratified that I feel that I have not worked altogether in vain; but there is no man as to whom I can say that his good opinion would give me such intense gratification as your own." "Many of [your novels] I read again and again. I have just been rereading one for the third time (which I think I first read about 1863)," replied Newman.[47]

ঽ▲

On the evening of November 3 Anthony had dinner in St. George's Square with John Tilley and his daughter Edith, Anthony's niece. As Edith was reading aloud "F. Anstey's" new comic novel *Vice Versa,* at which all were laughing uproariously, Anthony slumped in his chair, the victim of a stroke.[48] He was taken back to Garland's Hotel, and there was looked after for some weeks, attended by Dr. Murrell and by the physician-in-ordinary to the Queen, Sir William Jenner. There were frequent reports on his health in the newspapers, some cautiously optimistic, others less so. Millais wrote to William Howard Russell in Egypt a few weeks later to report that there was little hope. "The whole of one side was paralyzed and his speech gone. . . . I have called frequently and know that he is rarely conscious and has only been able to utter one word since the attack—'No.'"[49] Caring for him at Garland's became increasingly difficult; about November 20 he was moved to a nursing home at No. 34 Welbeck Street, both mind and body shattered, and there he died at six o'clock in the evening on December 6, less than a quarter of a mile from the lodgings in which he lived on Northumberland Street when he was a young clerk in the Post Office. He was buried at Kensal Green Cemetery, where Thackeray lies, on December 9; among the friends at the ceremony were Millais, Browning, Frederic Chapman, the Australian G. W. Rusden, Charles Stuart-Wortley, and Alfred Austin. Tom Trollope did not come over from Rome: "I would have given much to see him once again in his right mind; but I care little for funeral attendances, and would not wish any human being to cross the street to come to mine. . . . Yes! my dear Harry no man as you say ever had a better father; and he was a very loving brother too."[50] In his will, dated October 29, 1878, he left the literary property in trust to Henry and all other properties in trust to Henry and his mother, who was to enjoy the income for her life. After her death the estate was to be divided evenly between Henry and Fred, or their descendants, except for a bequest of £4,000 to Florence Bland. Letters of administration were granted on January 23, 1883, to Rose and Henry, and the estate was valued at £25,892 19s. 3d.[51]

On October 7, 1882, Trollope wrote to the daughter of the deceased barrister James Henry James that he would be at the meeting of the committee of the Royal Literary Fund on November 8 when her application for aid for her mother would be discussed. "I shall be happy if circumstances enable me to do anything on your behalf." For obvious reasons he was not at that meeting. (It would be pleasant to say that Mrs. James nevertheless received the grant, but her husband's writing had been largely technical and the literary claim was held insufficient.)[52] On December 14 the committee officially paid tribute to his eminent services to the fund and to the constancy of his attendance at their meetings. A handsomely engrossed copy of the resolution was forwarded to Rose; Anthony would have deplored the expense. The chairman, Lord John Manners, added his testimonial "to the anxiety [Mr. Trollope] constantly manifested that the relief administered by [the fund] should be efficacious and generous." From April, 1864, until his death he had attended 130 meetings of the general committee and missed 71; he was out of the country on the dates of 29 of the meetings he missed.[53]

Through Millais Rose promptly made known her husband's wish to present to the Athenaeum Club a bust of Milton he had owned, and it was accepted gratefully "in remembrance of one who was loved, & universally esteemed by the members."[54]

❧

Mr. Scarborough's Family was still running in *All the Year Round*, and *The Landleaguers* was just getting started in *Life*. Henry arranged with Blackwood to publish *An Old Man's Love*, which came out in mid-March, 1884. One of Henry's gravest responsibilities was seeing *An Autobiography* through the press; it was published about October 15, 1883.[55] Its frank scorn of the idea of inspiration and its blunt proclamation of Trollope's (pretended) mechanical regularity of compositon moved two American writers to ridicule: "Trollope has amused me for two evenings," wrote Henry Adams. ". . . I mean to do my [autobiography]. After seeing how coolly and neatly a man like Trollope can destroy the last vestige of heroism in his own life, I object to allowing mine to be murdered by any one except myself."[56] And Henry James thought it "one of the most curious and amazing books in all literature for its density, blockishness, and general thickness and soddenness. Not a voice has been lifted to say so. But I must do it, sometime and somewhere."[57] (Both Adams and James later wrote autobiographies.) Contemporary reviewers certainly did not share this opinion: *An Autobiography*, said one of them, was "at least as interesting as any of his novels; and those who love the reality of fact rather than efforts of imagination will be disposed to look upon the book as the author's most valuable contribution to literature."[58] Only three months before *An Autobiography* was published, Henry James, summing up Trollope's literary career, had said, "His great, his inestimable merit was a complete appreciation of the usual. . . . His great distinction is that in resting there his vision took in so much of the field." For all his ambivalence toward Trollope's art, James had clung to that; more than eighteen years earlier he had written, "Mr. Trollope has not the imagination of Mr. Reade, his strong grasp of the possible; but he has a delicate perception of the actual which makes every whit as firm ground to work upon."[59]

❧

Rose survived her husband nearly thirty-five years. She lived for a time in Chelsea, then moved to Minchinhampton, near Stroud, where she died on May 27, 1917, at the age of ninety-six. Charles Stuart-Wortley, husband successively of Bice Trollope and of a daughter of Millais, came down for her funeral. Her granddaughter Muriel Rose, who lived with her at Minchinhampton, remembered her as "not tall, but her pretty figure looked well in the princess dresses she always wore. In early life her wavy hair turned to ivory-cream, and to the end of her days she was very picturesque with *point d'Alençon* lappets on her head, more cream lace on her black velvet 'gown,' and a crimson shawl around her. Her opinion was that because she was elderly she need not be a frump! At ninety-two she had a six-book subscription from the *Times* Book Club in London. . . . I never knew her without embroidery on hand. At eighty-six she worked me a bedspread which I still use."[60] On June 2, 1897, at Alfred Austin's application, A. J. Balfour, first lord of the Treasury in Lord Salisbury's government, granted Rose a Civil List pension of £100 a year "in consideration of the distinguished literary merits of her husband, . . . and of her straitened circumstances."[61] Her will was proved on July 25, 1917, with Henry as executor. Though the estate was valued at only £373 4s. 8d.,[62] it must be remembered that the greater part of her income came from the proceeds of Anthony's bequest, which on her death passed by terms of his trust to Henry and to Fred's survivors. Her obituary in the *Times* began: "A venerable figure, bearing a name which will always be honoured in English literature, has just passed away." She "lived long enough to see [Anthony's] reputation, on the strength of his best work, perhaps even more securely established than at the height of his popularity during his life-time."[63]

In 1884 Henry married Ada Strickland, a schoolmate of Florence Bland's at Aachen and a frequent visitor at Montagu Square.[64] He was, both by inclination and by his father's will, the guardian of Anthony's literary materials, and it is to him that modern scholars owe the preservation of so many of his father's records. He died in 1926; his children Thomas Anthony and Muriel Rose both died unmarried, the one in 1931 and the other in 1953. Muriel continued her father's work in seeing that the scourings of her attic were made available to future scholars. With her death Anthony's line became extinct in England.

Fred, however, was much more prolific than his older brother; he had six sons and two daughters. His oldest son Frank (not his second son Henry, as he had earlier proposed to his father) came to the Wharton Robinson school in Margate in 1883.[65] Fred died before his mother, in 1910. A very distant cousin of Anthony's, Sir John Trollope, bart., had been created Baron Kesteven in 1868. When his grandson, the third Baron, died unmarried in 1913, the peerage, which was restricted to direct male descendants, became extinct, but the baronetcy passed to the nearest male heir, who in course of time was, successively, Fred's third son and then his sixth son. It continues in his line, in the Australia Anthony always loved.[66] The family house there is named "Clavering," after one of Anthony's novels.

Notes

Preface

1. *Ralph the Heir,* chap. xl.
2. Stefan Collini, review of J. S. Mill's *Essays on French History and Historians, Times Literary Supplement* (London), November 8, 1985, p. 1252.
3. Taylor, "The Manuscript of Trollope's *American Senator* Collated with the First Edition," *Papers of the Bibliographical Society of America* 41:123–39 (second quarter, 1947).
4. George Eliot, *Letters,* ed. G. S. Haight (New Haven: Yale University Press, 1955), 7:230; A. Trollope, *Letters,* 2:842.

Chapter I

1. Byron, *Don Juan,* I, xv.
2. T. A. Trollope, *What I Remember* (London, 1887), 1:2–3.
3. *Lady Anna,* chap. xx; *Castle Richmond,* chap. xxv; *The Three Clerks,* chap. xxii.
4. F. E. Trollope, *Frances Trollope* (London, 1895), 1:8–11; T. A. Trollope, *What I Remember,* 1:13, 18–19; Helen Heineman, *Mrs. Trollope* (Athens, Ohio: Ohio University Press, 1972), p. 7; Joseph Foster, *Alumni Oxonienses 1715–1886,* s.v. Milton.
5. Henry Milton, *Letters on the Fine Arts, Written from Paris, in the Year 1815* (London, 1816), pp. 176n, 92n, 239; Anthony Trollope, *Letters,* ed. N. John Hall (Stanford, Calif.: Stanford University Press, 1983), 2:665 (to G. H. Lewes, November 1, 1875); Arthur Lucas, *John Lucas, Portrait Painter* (London, 1910), pp. 3, 6, and pl. III.
6. Mark Napier Trollope, *A Memoir of the Family of Trollope* (London, 1897), p. 92; Foster, *Alumni Oxonienses,* s.v. Trollope; Anthony Trollope, "Address at the Liverpool Institute," *Liverpool Daily Post,* November 14, 1873, p. 6; James Whishaw, *A Synopsis of the Members of the English Bar* (London, 1835), p. 142; *The Records of the Honorable Society of Lincoln's Inn* (London, 1896), 2:[26]; T. A. Trollope, *What I Remember,* 1:47; F. E. Trollope, *Frances Trollope,* 1:18; Anthony Trollope, *An Autobiography,* ed. Frederick Page (London: Oxford University Press, 1950), pp. 2–3. From Winchester Thomas Anthony went first to St. John's College, Cambridge, then migrated to New College, Oxford.—J. A. Venn, *Alumni Cantabrigienses,* pt. 2, vol. 6 (Cambridge, 1954), s.v. Trollope. His chambers were No. 23 in the Old Square. Mr. Furnival's chambers, in *Orley Farm,* were also in Old Square, Lincoln's Inn (chap. xi).

7. Robert Clutterbuck, *The History and Antiquities of the County of Hertford* (London, 1827), 3:521, 572–75; J. E. Cussans, *History of Hertfordshire* (London, 1873), 3:168.

8. Parish registers, Heckfield (marriage), St. George's, Bloomsbury, London, and St. Mary's, Harrow-on-the-Hill (christenings); F. E. Trollope, *Frances Trollope*, 1:42. The inscription on Frances Milton Trollope's tombstone in Florence, composed by her son Tom, tells that she was born in 1780 in Stapleton, Somerset (where her father was incumbent of the parish). Helen Heineman opens her biography of Mrs. Trollope with the statement that she was born March 10, 1779, and cites rather vaguely the authority of the registers of three different parishes in the city of Bristol. Later she seems to accept the birth year of 1780.— *Mrs. Trollope*, pp. 3, 261 n. 6, 255, 297. Heineman gives archival authority for Mrs. Trollope's marriage settlement (p. 262 n. 20).

9. T. A. Trollope, *What I Remember*, 1:5, 21, 4, 16; F. E. Trollope, *Frances Trollope*, 1:47, 2:75.

10. *Orley Farm*, chap. xi.

11. *Dictionary of National Biography (D.N.B.)* Supplement, s.v. Charles Merivale (by James McMullen Rigg). In *An Autobiography* (p. 14) Trollope gives an unhappy account of his lessons at his father's side.

12. *What I Remember*, 2:332.

13. Heineman cites the Poor Rate Books for St. George's parish, Bloomsbury, to establish the date of the move as before the end of 1815, and Lord Northwick's muniments at the Greater London Council for information about Thomas Anthony's dealings with Northwick in Harrow. For the pew rent, correspondence between Thomas Anthony and Lord Northwick in the Vaughan Library, Harrow School.

14. A. Trollope, "Public Schools," *Fortnightly Review* 2:487 (October 1, 1865).

15. M. G. Dauglish and P. K. Stephenson, eds., *The Harrow School Register, 1800–1911,* 3d ed. (London, 1911), under "Entrances, September 1818–Easter 1819"; T. A. Trollope, *What I Remember,* 1:72; E. W. Howson and G. T. Warner, eds., *Harrow School* (London, 1898), p. 80. "I was once told that the surest aid to the writing of a book was a piece of cobbler's wax on my chair. I certainly believe in the cobbler's wax much more than inspiration."—A. Trollope, *An Autobiography,* pp. 121, 323.

16. T. A. Trollope, *What I Remember,* 1:20–21, 63. For date of William Milton's death, see Foster, *Alumni Oxonienses.*

17. Cussans, *History of Hertfordshire,* 3:166; T. A. Trollope, *What I Remember,* 1:62; F. E. Trollope, *Frances Trollope,* 1:46; A. Trollope, *An Autobiography,* p. 3; A. Trollope, *Letters,* 2:848; [Cecilia E. Meetkerke,] "Anthony Trollope," *Blackwood's Edinburgh Magazine* 133:316–20 (February, 1882); [C. E. Meetkerke,] "Last Reminiscences of Anthony Trollope," *Temple Bar* 70:129–34 (January, 1884).

18. T. F. Kirby, *Winchester Scholars* (London, 1885), p. 304; George Butler, *Harrow. A Selection of the Lists of the School* (Peterborough, 1845), p. 133; MS admissions register and copies of school lists in the Vaughan Library, Harrow School; Dauglish and Stephenson, eds., *Harrow School Register, 1800–1911.*

19. F. E. Trollope, *Frances Trollope,* 1:44; Howson and Warner, eds., *Harrow School,* p. 80; letter on "Anthony Trollope's 'Autobiography,' " by An Harrovian, *Spectator* 56:1376–77 (October 27, 1883); *An Autobiography,* p. 4.

20. Trollope's note on his mother's poem about the burial of Byron's daughter Allegra, in *Salmagundi,* ed. N. John Hall, Beta Phi Mu Chapbook no. 11 (Pittsburgh, Pa., 1975), p. 71.

21. *An Autobiography,* pp. 5–6.

22. Dauglish and Stephenson, eds., *Harrow School Register, 1800–1911,* under "Entrances, Easter–Midsummer 1823"; *An Autobiography,* p. 5; information from the Register of Scholars and other archives supplied by Roger Custance, archivist of Winchester College, on June 11, 1979; F. E. Trollope, *Frances Trollope,* 1:95. Anthony was seventeenth out of twenty-nine on the election roll of 1828.

23. *An Autobiography,* p. 5; T. A. Trollope, *What I Remember,* 1:113–18, 121–24, 78, 77.

24. A. Trollope, "Address at the Liverpool Institute," p. 6.

25. A. Trollope, "Public Schools," *Fortnightly Review* 2:477 (October 1, 1865); T. A. Trollope, *What I Remember,* 1:100–106. Anthony's "unequal divisions" (dispars) is in fact a pun; the word was *dispers* (dispertio), for "distribution." The Irish in *The Macdermots* similarly "took the huge lumps of blood-red mutton in their fists, and seemed perfectly independent of such conventional wants as knives and forks, in the ease and enjoyment with which they dispatched their repast."—chap. xii.

26. *An Autobiography,* p. 93; A. Trollope, "Public Schools," p. 478. T. A. Trollope says that the attendance at cathedral services took place only on Sundays, and then only twice; other services were held in the college chapel.—*What I Remember,* 1:137–38. The chaplains were minor canons of the cathedral and also had livings in the city.

27. *Barchester Towers,* chap. xx; *The Landleaguers,* chaps. i, v. Did Tom Trollope ever point out to Anthony the reiterated blunder he makes about Bertram's "double-first degree" at Oxford?

28. "Anthony Trollope: An Appreciation and Reminiscence," *Fortnightly Review* 86:1098 (December, 1906).

29. "Mr. Anthony Trollope on the Civil Service," *Daily News* (London), January 5, 1861, p. 5, col. 5.

30. P. M. Thornton, *Harrow School and Its Surroundings* (London, 1885), pp. 251, 257, 258n.

31. Letter from Thomas Anthony Trollope to Lord Northwick, February 12, 1820 (MS in the Vaughan Library, Harrow School); *An Autobiography,* pp. 3–4.

32. *An Autobiography,* p. 7; F. E. Trollope, *Frances Trollope,* 1:99 (where the Harrow Weald farmhouse is erroneously identified with the one in *Orley Farm*); T. A. Trollope, *What I Remember,* 1:150–51 (where it is erroneously stated that the Reverend J. W. Cunningham at this time took over the house Thomas Anthony had built at Harrow).

33. Heineman, *Mrs. Trollope,* pp. 41, 39.

34. *The Three Clerks,* chap. xliv.

35. Heineman, *Mrs. Trollope,* pp. 28–35, 40–41, 43; see also Celia Morris

Eckhardt, *Fanny Wright: Rebel in America* (Cambridge, Mass.: Harvard University Press, 1984), pp. 63, 73. Frances Wright and her sister Camilla had become close friends of the Trollopes' friends Julia, Harriet, and Fanny Garnett, and she was a member of the Garnett circle in Paris when Thomas Anthony and Frances Trollope visited there in 1823. Her letter attempting to recruit the schoolmaster from New York is printed in a pamphlet called *Fanny Wright Unmasked by Her Own Pen* (New York, 1830), pp. 13–14. It would appear from the date of the letter (February 24, 1828) that he was being asked to fill the post Hervieu abandoned. Mrs. Trollope's handwritten account of the visit to La Grange is now in the library of the University of Illinois, Urbana-Champaign.

36. Heineman, *Mrs. Trollope*, pp. 45–46, 48–49. There is in the Houghton Library, Harvard University, a joint letter from Frances Trollope and Frances Wright to Julia Garnett Pertz dated "Harrow, 7th Oct. 1827." Frances Wright's pamphlet on Nashoba is dated "At Sea, 4th December, 1827" and is printed in *Fanny Wright Unmasked*.

37. Mrs. Trollope first met Dickens at the home of Mrs. George Bartley in March, 1832. "I had a good deal of talk with him."—F. E. Trollope, *Frances Trollope*, 1:295. Dickens first visited America in 1842.

38. Heineman, *Mrs. Trollope*, pp. 49–51.

39. F. E. Trollope, *Frances Trollope*, 1:106, 110–11; Heineman, *Mrs. Trollope*, p. 52.

40. Heineman, *Mrs. Trollope*, pp. 52–57.

41. Heineman, *Mrs. Trollope*, pp. 59–65.

42. T. A. Trollope, *What I Remember*, 1:157–61, 187.

43. *An Autobiography*, p. 9.

44. Foster, *Alumni Oxonienses 1715–1886*, s.v. Trollope; T. A. Trollope, *What I Remember*, 1:191, 211–13.

45. Heineman, *Mrs. Trollope*, pp. 66–69; F. E. Trollope, *Frances Trollope*, 1:125–26, 141; Venn, *Alumni Cantabrigienses*, pt. 2, vol. 6, s.v. Trollope.

46. Heineman, *Mrs. Trollope*, pp. 69–74; F. E. Trollope, *Frances Trollope*, 1:131.

47. *An Autobiography*, pp. 9–10, 15–16, 43; information supplied by Roger Custance of Winchester College; MS records in the archives of Harrow School.

48. *Salmagundi*, ed. Hall, p. 68.

49. Howson and Warner, eds., *Harrow School*, p. 80; and see A. Trollope, *An Autobiography*, p. 13; Sir William Gregory, *An Autobiography*, ed. Augusta, Lady Gregory (London, 1894), p. 35. That young Lewis never returned to Harrow is clear from Dauglish and Stephenson, eds., *The Harrow School Register, 1800–1911*.

50. A. Trollope, *An Autobiography*, p. 19; Thornton, *Harrow School and Its Surroundings*, p. 250n. Anthony "has just got a prize" at Harrow, his mother told Julia Garnett Pertz on November 25, 1831—MS in Houghton Library, Harvard University. Trollope himself asserted that though there were many prizes awarded at Harrow, he never won one.—*An Autobiography*, p. 19.

51. The Harrow names are taken from Dauglish and Stephenson, eds., *The Harrow School Register, 1800–1911;* the Winchester names appear in Kirby, *Winchester Scholars*, and in C. W. Holgate, ed., *Winchester Commoners, 1800–1835*

(Salisbury, 1893). "Vesey" occurs as a given name, as in *Barchester Towers:* John Agmondishan Vesey Kirkland.

52. A. Trollope, "Public Schools," pp. 482–83; preliminary plans for *The Way We Live Now,* Bodleian Library, Oxford, MS. Don. c. 10, fol. 18.

53. MS class lists in the archives of Harrow School; *Salmagundi,* ed. Hall, p. 68; Susan L. Humphreys, "Trollope on the Sublime and Beautiful," *Nineteenth-Century Fiction* 33:198 (September, 1978).

54. F. E. Trollope, *Frances Trollope,* 2:62.

55. Charles Wordsworth, *Annals of My Early Life, 1806–46* (London, 1891), p. 18; *D.N.B.* Supplement, s.v. Merivale.

56. A. Trollope, *An Autobiography,* pp. 12, 17–18. Sir William Gregory also asserted that "the instruction was routine, or worse."—Gregory, *Autobiography,* p. 38.

57. A. Trollope, *Life of Cicero* (London, 1880), 1:270; *An Old Man's Love,* chaps. xvi, xvii.

58. A. Trollope, *Lord Palmerston* (London, 1882), p. 9; *Orley Farm,* chap. ii; *Framley Parsonage,* chap. i.

59. *An Autobiography,* p. 41; *The Small House at Allington,* chap. xiv.

60. *An Autobiography,* p. 42; *Small House,* chap. xiv.

61. F. E. Trollope, *Frances Trollope,* 1:180–83. Mrs. Trollope was also fond of organizing amateur theatrical presentations in her parlor.

62. The book is described and Trollope's notes are published in Humphreys, "Trollope on the Sublime and Beautiful."

63. *Fortnightly Review* 1:477, 479, 486–87 (October 1, 1865).

Chapter II

1. F. E. Trollope, *Frances Trollope,* 1:132, 172; letter from F. M. T. to Julia Garnett Pertz, August 22 (MS in the Houghton Library, Harvard University).

2. F. E. Trollope, *Frances Trollope,* 1:135–36, 142, 151, 153, 157–58.

3. F. E. Trollope, *Frances Trollope,* 1:169.

4. F. E. Trollope, *Frances Trollope,* 1:172; letters from Mrs. Trollope to Julia Pertz in the Houghton Library, Harvard University.

5. Anna W. Merivale, *Family Memorials* (Exeter, 1884), p. 238; F. E. Trollope, *Frances Trollope,* 1:155, 158, 142, 140; T. A. Trollope, *What I Remember,* 1:228, 225–26, 240.

6. T. A. Trollope, *What I Remember,* 1:190, 59; F. E. Trollope, *Frances Trollope,* 1:144–47; A. Trollope, *An Autobiography,* pp. 3, 15, 32.

7. F. E. Trollope, *Frances Trollope,* 1:147–48.

8. F. E. Trollope, *Frances Trollope,* 1:149–50. For young Anthony's project, see N. John Hall, "An Unpublished Trollope Manuscript on a Proposed History of World Literature," *Nineteenth-Century Fiction* 29:206–10 (September, 1974). The MS is in the library of the University of Illinois.

9. F. E. Trollope, *Frances Trollope,* 1:172–80.

10. F. E. Trollope, *Frances Trollope,* 1:184–86; A. Trollope, *Letters,* ed. N. John Hall (Stanford, Calif.: Stanford University Press, 1983), 1:157.

11. F. E. Trollope, *Frances Trollope,* 1:192, 195, 197.

12. F. E. Trollope, *Frances Trollope,* 1:189, 193–95, 205, 199; T. A. Trollope, *What I Remember,* 1:245, 250. The book was *Belgium and Western Germany in 1833.* As early as March 12, 1830, she told Julia Garnett Pertz that she thought of settling "in Germany or France for reasons of economy; the boys' education is very expensive."—MS in Houghton Library, Harvard University.

13. F. E. Trollope, *Frances Trollope,* 1:201–2; *An Autobiography,* p. 26. Anthony's name was entered on the class list at Harrow for March, 1834, then crossed out.—MS list in the archives of Harrow School.

14. F. E. Trollope, *Frances Trollope,* 1:202–4; *An Autobiography,* pp. 26–28, 3.

15. A. Trollope, "The National Gallery," *Saint James's Magazine,* 2:169 (September, 1851).

16. F. E. Trollope, *Frances Trollope,* 1:204; *Salmagundi,* ed. Hall, pp. 21–22, 71. For Louisa Byron Cunningham see the baptismal register for St. Mary's parish church, Harrow-on-the-Hill, August 2, 1817. The name is possibly intended to honor Lady Byron, not Lord Byron, who by this time was separated from her and living permanently abroad.

17. Arthur Pollard, "Trollope and the Evangelicals," *Nineteenth-Century Fiction* 37:329–39 (December, 1982).

18. *The Visitor's Companion to Harrow on the Hill* (London, ca. 1836); *D.N.B.,* s.v. Cunningham (by Leslie Stephen); letter from Cunningham to Northwick (MS in the Vaughan Library, Harrow School); A. Trollope, *Letters,* 1:133–34. It is commonly asserted that Cunningham moved into "Julians" when the Trollopes first gave up that house in the early 1820s, but the date of this letter and the statement that Cunningham had lived for nineteen years in his present house make the earlier date impossible.

19. T. A. Trollope, *What I Remember,* 1:190; *An Autobiography,* p. 17; F. E. Trollope, *Frances Trollope,* 1:203, 205.

20. T. A. Trollope, *What I Remember,* 1:37–38; *He Knew He Was Right,* chap. vii and passim.

21. *An Autobiography,* p. 29; F. E. Trollope, *Frances Trollope,* 1:205–6, 215–16, 221, 228–29; T. A. Trollope, *What I Remember,* 1:250–53.

22. *An Autobiography,* pp. 29–30; *Salmagundi,* ed. Hall, pp. 69–70.

23. At the time of her return from America, Mrs. Trollope told Julia Garnett Pertz that her chief aim in life was to "see my dear boys placed in situations where their talents and good conduct might enable them to gain their bread."—MS in Houghton Library, Harvard University.

24. F. E. Trollope, *Frances Trollope,* 1:224–27; *An Autobiography,* pp. 35–37; Michael Sadleir, *Trollope, a Commentary* (London: Constable, 1927), p. 111. Also: Post Office Records, English Minutes, Post 35, vol. 20, nos. 313V, 400V; Appointments Book, Post 58, vol. 68, no. 558; Establishment Book, Post 59, vol. 37, under "Secretary's Office." The probationary period was three months. Charley Tudor's examination for the Civil Service duplicated Trollope's, even to the copying of a passage from Gibbon.—*The Three Clerks,* chap. ii.

25. *Daily News* (London), January 5, 1861, p. 5, col. 5.

26. T. A. Trollope, *What I Remember,* 1:248–50; *Phineas Finn,* chap. iii.

27. T. A. Trollope, *What I Remember*, 1:253; A. Trollope, *Letters*, 1:2.

28. F. E. Trollope, *Frances Trollope*, 1:141–42.

29. A. Trollope, *Letters*, 1:1; F. E. Trollope, *Frances Trollope*, 1:216; *An Autobiography*, p. 53; *Phineas Redux*, chap. lvi.

30. F. E. Trollope, *Frances Trollope*, 1:231.

31. Post Office Records, uncatalogued, in box of "Secretary's Orders"; dated February 4, 1839.

32. *D.N.B.*, s.v. Freeling and Maberly; *An Autobiography*, pp. 44–45; *Small House*, chap. xxxvi; Yates, *Recollections and Reminiscences* (London, 1884), 1:96–99.

33. A. Trollope, "The Civil Service," *Fortnightly Review* 2:623 (October 15, 1865).

34. *An Autobiography*, pp. 35, 54–57. Awdry (whom Trollope refers to only as "W— A—") is identified in *Letters*, 1:7n.

35. *An Autobiography*, pp. 45–46; *The Three Clerks*, chap. xxvii.

36. *An Autobiography*, pp. 48–49; *The Three Clerks*, chap. xviii. Trollope speaks of the "burden of duns . . . I endured. Sheriffs' officers with uncanny documents, of which I never understood anything, were common attendants on me. And yet I do not remember that I was ever locked up, though I think I was twice a prisoner. In such emergencies some one paid for me." I take this to mean that he was twice unable to venture out of his lodgings until his debt was discharged, for fear of actual arrest. Charley Tudor's luck was not so good: he was taken to a sponging-house in Cursitor Street (the same house in which Rawdon Crawley of *Vanity Fair* had been locked up).—*An Autobiography*, p. 50; *The Three Clerks*, chap. xxviii.

37. *Letters*, 1:1, 3n (the letter dated January 30, 1835); T. A. Trollope, *What I Remember*, 2:1–2, 18.

38. The notebooks are in the Beinecke Library, Yale University, and have been published in *Letters*, 2:1021–28, and in N. John Hall, "Trollope's Commonplace Book, 1835–40," *Nineteenth-Century Fiction* 31:15–25 (June, 1976).

39. The document is in the library of the University of Illinois, Urbana-Champaign, and has been published in *Letters*, 2:1029–32, and in N. John Hall, "An Unpublished Trollope Manuscript on a Proposed History of World Literature," *Nineteenth-Century Fiction* 29:206–10 (September, 1974). Evidence of his voracious reading appears in the marginal notes in books from his library that continue to turn up.

40. *An Autobiography*, pp. 42–43, 52–53.

Chapter III

1. T. A. Trollope, *What I Remember*, 2:256–57.

2. *What I Remember*, 1:258, 262–63, 294–95.

3. A. Trollope, *Thackeray* (London, 1879), p. 3.

4. F. E. Trollope, *Frances Trollope*, 1:254–56, 258–59, 287. In *Trollope in the Post Office* (Ann Arbor: University of Michigan Press, 1981), p. 8, I erroneously dated the move to Hadley as 1837 instead of 1836.

5. *The Bertrams,* chap. xxx. In a less somber vein, he recalled "a pretty woodland lane, running from the back of Hadley church, through the last remnants of what was once Enfield Chase. How many lovers' feet have crushed the leaves that used to lie in autumn along that pretty lane!"—chap. xxviii.

6. T. A. Trollope, *What I Remember,* 1:344, 349.

7. *What I Remember,* 1:257.

8. Post Office Records, English Minutes, Post 35, vol. 27, no. 562CC. It was on an earlier occasion of this sort that, as Trollope tells us, Mrs. Clayton Freeling, "who as I write this, is still living, . . . with tears in her eyes, besought me to think of my mother."—*An Autobiography,* p. 44.

9. Post Office Records, English Minutes, Post 35, vol. 30, nos. 301EE, 470EE.

10. Post Office Records, uncatalogued, i box of "Secretary's Orders."

11. A. Trollope, "The Civil Service," *Dublin University Magazine* 46:421 (October, 1855).

12. *Who Was Who 1897–1916* (London: A. and C. Black, 1919), s.v. Tilley.

13. T. A. Trollope, *What I Remember,* 2:5; marriage register for St. Mary's, Bryanston Square, housed in the Marylebone Public Library.

14. F. E. Trollope, *Frances Trollope,* 1:300; letter to Julia Garnett Pertz, September 26, 1839 (MS in the Houghton Library, Harvard University).

15. Letter from Frances Trollope to Julia Garnett Pertz, Hadley, January 26, 1838 (MS in the Houghton Library, Harvard University); *Times,* July 4, 1838, p. 5, col. 5.

16. T. A. Trollope, *What I Remember,* 1:355, 359.

17. F. E. Trollope, *Frances Trollope,* 1:300, 304; T. A. Trollope, *What I Remember,* 2:18–22, 33.

18. Letter from Frances Trollope to Julia Garnett Pertz, September 26, 1839 (MS in the Houghton Library, Harvard University); Post Office Records, English Minutes, Post 35, vol. 29, no. 31DD.

19. F. E. Trollope, *Frances Trollope,* 1:313–14; T. A. Trollope, *What I Remember,* 2:68; *Lady Anna,* chap. iii.

20. A. Trollope, *Letters,* 1:9.

21. T. A. Trollope, *What I Remember,* 1:366; F. E. Trollope, *Frances Trollope,* 1:303.

22. *What I Remember,* 1:370–74.

23. Post Office Records, English Minutes, Post 35, vol. 36, nos. 442KK, 1025KK, 1044JJ, 260KK; F. E. Trollope, *Frances Trollope,* 1:320.

24. A. Trollope, *Letters,* 1:10; letter from Frances Trollope to Julia Garnett Pertz, May 24, 1840 (MS in the Houghton Library, Harvard University).

25. T. A. Trollope, *What I Remember,* 2:35–36; A. Trollope, *Letters,* 1:9–10; F. E. Trollope, *Frances Trollope,* 2:16.

26. *An Autobiography,* pp. 57–59; Post Office Records, Establishment Books, Post 59, vols. 39–44; English Minutes, Post 35, vol. 42, no. 651QQ.

27. *An Autobiography,* p. 61; F. E. Trollope, *Frances Trollope,* 1:323.

28. Super, *Trollope in the Post Office,* p. 110 (based on Trollope's MS travel accounts and journals in the Parrish Collection, Princeton University Library).

29. Post Office Records, English Minutes, Post 35, vol. 43, nos. 78RR, 174RR, 273RR.

30. Post Office Records, Irish Minutes, Post 36, vol. 12, no. 1002; English Minutes, Post 35, vol. 47, no. 400.

31. *An Autobiography,* pp. 46–47; *Brown, Jones, and Robinson,* chap. xiv.

32. *Prime Minister,* chap. lxxiii; Post Office Records, Irish Minutes, Post 36, vol. 32, no. 1075 and vol. 33, no. 390.

33. *An Autobiography,* pp. 62–63; *Letters,* 1:80. The careful accounts he was obliged to keep in order to claim his travel allowances survive in the Parrish Collection, Princeton University Library, and form a precise and useful record of his movements from day to day. An interesting brief account of the Irish way of life Trollope found in Banagher is given by John Hynes, "Anthony Trollope's Creative 'Culture-Shock': Banagher, 1841," *Éire-Ireland* 21:124–31 (Fall, 1986).

34. *An Autobiography,* pp. 60, 65–66. Trollope does not here specify which postmaster he was dealing with, and the dismissal of an Irish postmaster was very common. Oranmore was in Trollope's district, "in the far west of county Galway," and records show that the postmaster there was dismissed at this time.— Post Office Records, Irish Minutes, Post 36, vol. 12, nos. 952, 1026, 1053, 1063. Trollope's traveling journals show him at Headford, twenty-three miles from Oranmore, on October 1, 6–13, 1841.

35. *Correspondence of Henry Taylor* (London, 1888), pp. 297–98.

36. William White, *General Directory of . . . Sheffield, with Rotherham, Chesterfield, {&c.}* (Sheffield, 1845), pp. 337–42, 346, and s.v. Heseltine; *Reminiscences of Rotherham & District in the Early Part of the Present Century,* by Local Contributors, reprinted from the "Rotherham Advertiser" (Rotherham, 1891), pp. 118–19, 8–9 (written by John Hague, Heseltine's former clerk), 38. For Heseltine's collection of armor, see *Sheffield and Rotherham Independent,* February 22, 1851, p. 8, col. 5.

37. Trollope's traveling journals, 1842, and Post Office Records, Irish Minutes, Post 36, vol. 13, no. 955. For Rose's age, see obituary in the *Times,* May 30, 1917, p. 3, col. 2.

38. *Doctor Thorne,* chap. vii.

39. *The Eustace Diamonds,* chap. ii.

40. T. A. Trollope, *What I Remember,* 2:76–78; A. Trollope, *An Autobiography,* pp. 63–65.

41. Article on Gregory by C. L. Falkiner in *D.N.B.,* Supplement; T. H. S. Escott, *Anthony Trollope: His Public Services, Private Friends, and Literary Originals* (1913; reprint, Port Washington, N.Y.: Kennikat Press, 1967), pp. 49–51. Escott says Gregory "supplied me with much material illustrating Trollope's earlier days in Irish and London society."—p. viii. For Yeats's reading Trollope, see J. I. M. Stewart, *Eight Modern Writers* (Oxford: Clarendon Press, 1963), p. 463; Stewart cites no source.

Chapter IV

1. *An Autobiography,* p. 70; travel diary, September 5–October 4, 1843, Princeton University Library. The ruins are still standing.

2. *An Autobiography,* p. 71.

3. *Letters,* 1:11–12.

4. F. E. Trollope, *Frances Trollope,* 2:29.

5. About a decade earlier, Mrs. Trollope tried to bolster Tom's spirits by recounting her own experience with publishers: "A MS. sent to Colburn, declined; one to Murray returned at the end of six months unopened; another to a man in the Strand, sent back with the assurance that the trade was so bad, no one could publish without loss."—F. E. Trollope, *Frances Trollope,* 1:282.

6. S. M. Ellis, *Wilkie Collins, Le Fanu and Others* (London: Constable and Co., 1931), pp. 272–73.

7. Bodleian, MS. Don. c. 9, fols. 1–6; *Letters,* 1:12–13.

8. M. Sadleir, *Trollope: A Commentary,* rev. ed. (New York: Farrar, Straus and Company, 1947), p. 148n.

9. *Athenaeum,* April 24, 1843, p. 427; May 1, pp. 467–68. The advertisement was correct in other issues of the *Athenaeum,* in the *Spectator,* and in the *Times,* so that the misrepresentation may have been due to a compositor's misreading of slovenly handwriting, as the *Athenaeum* claimed. On the other hand, enough advertisements elsewhere referred to the author as "Mrs. Trollope" to raise the suspicion that the slovenliness was not altogether unintentional: Lance O. Tingay has pointed out five other instances.—"Trollope's First Novel," *Notes and Queries* 195:563–64 (December 23, 1980) and "The Publication of Trollope's First Novel," *Times Literary Supplement* (London) 55:200 (March 30, 1956).

10. Donald Smalley, ed., *Anthony Trollope: The Critical Heritage* (London: Routledge and Kegan Paul, 1969), pp. 546–52.

11. Post Office Records, Irish Minutes, Post 36, vol. 16, no. 512; *Sheffield and Rotherham Independent,* June 15, 1844, p. 5, col. 6. Rose's memoranda are in the library of the University of Illinois, Urbana-Champaign.

12. *Letters,* 1:11–12.

13. F. E. Trollope, *Frances Trollope,* 2:39–40, 52.

14. Post Office Records, Irish Minutes, Post 36, vol. 25, nos. 864, 893, 943; *An Autobiography,* pp. 71–72.

15. Family records now in the library of the University of Illinois, Urbana-Champaign.

16. From his traveling journals, Princeton University Library; *Letters,* 1:15.

17. Post Office Records, Irish Minutes, Post 36, vol. 25, nos. 272, 291, 350a; Rose Trollope's MS memoranda, University of Illinois Library; *Autobiography,* pp. 96–97.

18. *Letters,* 1:13.

19. *Letters,* 1:13–15.

20. Bodleian, MS. Don. c. 9, fols. 9—13*bis.*

21. *Castle Richmond,* chap. xliv.

22. P. 13, col. 5.

23. *Athenaeum,* May 15, 1847, p. 317; July 15, 1848, p. 701. The author is identified in D. Skilton, *Anthony Trollope and His Contemporaries* (London: Longmans, 1972), p. 154.

24. *An Autobiography,* pp. 76–78; *Times,* September 7, 1848, p. 6, col. 2.

25. Bodleian, MS. Don. c. 9, fols. 10–13; *An Autobiography,* pp. 78–79; T. A. Trollope, *What I Remember,* 2:86.

26. Escott, *Trollope,* pp. 50, 52–54; *An Autobiography,* p. 71.

27. *An Autobiography,* p. 70.

28. *An Autobiography,* pp. 70–71.

29. R. C. Terry, "Three Lost Chapters of Trollope's First Novel," *Nineteenth-Century Fiction* 27:71–80 (June, 1972); E. W. Wittig, "Significant Revisions in Trollope's 'The Macdermots of Ballycloran,'" *Notes and Queries* 218:90–91 (March, 1973).

30. *The Journal of Arnold Bennett* (Garden City, N.Y.: Viking Press, 1933), p. 838 (Salzburg, August 2, 1925).

31. T. A. Trollope, *What I Remember,* 1:258–59.

32. Trollope appeared twice as a witness in the case, at a first trial late in March that ended when a juror became ill, and at a second trial on July 26 that ended in a hung jury.—*Tralee Chronicle,* March 31, 1849, and *Kerry Evening Post,* July 28, 1849. Justin McCarthy, who was present in the courtroom in July, gives a somewhat fictionalized account of how Trollope followed the marked coin from post office to post office until, when it disappeared, he seized the guilty postmistress; in fact, Trollope was too well known to postmasters and post-mistresses to have followed the letter incognito. O'Reilly even knew something was up when she heard that Trollope was unexpectedly at Ardfert on the fatal day, but it was too late.—McCarthy, *Reminiscences* (New York, 1899), 1:369–72.

33. *Phineas Redux,* chap. lxi; *Castle Richmond,* chap. xxxv.

34. Post Office Records, Irish Minutes, Post 36, vol. 27, nos. 2311, 105.

35. *An Autobiography,* pp. 66–68.

36. Trollope in the *Examiner,* March 30, 1850, reprinted in Helen Garling-house King, "Trollope's Letters to the *Examiner,*" *Princeton University Library Chronicle* 26:80 (Winter, 1965).

37. *Castle Richmond,* chap. xxxiii.

38. King, "Trollope's Letters," p. 83.

39. *Castle Richmond,* chap. xxxi.

40. Rose Trollope's MS memoranda, University of Illinois Library; King, "Trollope's Letters," p. 99.

41. *Castle Richmond,* chap. xliv.

42. *Letters,* 1:361. It is of course possible that there were earlier contributions by Trollope to the periodicals, but none have been recorded; see Judith Knelman, "Trollope's Journalism," *Library,* 6th ser., 5:140–55 (June, 1983). Trollope describes his review of Charles Merivale as his "first attempt in writing for a magazine."—*An Autobiography,* p. 101.

43. In *An Autobiography,* pp. 81–84, Trollope dates his visit to Forster "in 1848," but S. G. O.'s letters appeared in June and early July, 1849, and Trollope's next visit to London after that date was between February 12 and 19, 1850 (the only period not recorded as occupied by Post Office business in his travel diaries). And so it must be assumed that his first, isolated letter was published before he met Forster.

44. *Castle Richmond,* chap. vii.

45. F. E. Trollope, *Frances Trollope,* 2:91–92, 96, 101, 127–28.

46. Trollope, *Thackeray* (London, 1879), p. 34; Gordon N. Ray, ed., *The Letters and Private Papers of William Makepeace Thackeray* (Cambridge, Mass.:

Harvard University Press, 1946), 2:427–28, 431–33 (Thackeray to Lady Blessington, September–October 1, 1848).

47. Post Office Records, Establishment Book, Post 59, vol. 45, "Secretary's Office."

48. F. E. Trollope, *Frances Trollope,* 2:140, 143 (the words about Cecilia are not Anthony's, but Mrs. Trollope's); Heineman, *Mrs. Trollope,* pp. 237–38; *Times,* April 6, 1849, p. 9, col. 1; A. Trollope, *Letters,* 1:18–19, 19n; Rose Trollope's MS notes, University of Illinois Library. For the dates of Trollope's visit to London, see n. 43, above.

49. Rose Trollope's MS notes; F. E. Trollope, *Frances Trollope,* 2:161, 164, 166, 175, 185.

50. F. E. Trollope, *Frances Trollope,* 2:179.

51. *Times,* January 18, 1850, p. 7, col. 6.

52. *An Autobiography,* p. 79; Bodleian, MS. Don. c. 9, fol. 11.

53. F. E. Trollope, *Frances Trollope,* 2:179; Bodleian, MS. Don. c. 9, fol. 17; *Athenaeum,* May 4, 1850, p. 488; *An Autobiography,* pp. 80–81, 363.

54. "Barère's *Memoirs,*" *Edinburgh Review* 79:276–77 (April, 1844), reprinted in his *Essays,* vol. 5.

55. *Letters,* 2:826 (April 26, 1879).

56. *An Autobiography,* pp. 80–81.

57. Inga-Stina Ekeblad, "Anthony Trollope's Copy of the 1647 Beaumont and Fletcher Folio," *Notes and Queries* 204:153–54 (April, 1959); *Letters,* 1:27. The play was written in a bound, blank-paged notebook that Anthony appropriated from his brother Tom, and is now housed at the Humanities Research Center, University of Texas, Austin. It was published in a limited edition by Michael Sadleir in 1923, unfortunately in a most inaccurate transcription.

58. *The Eustace Diamonds,* chap. lii.

59. F. E. Trollope, *Frances Trollope,* 2:179; *An Autobiography,* pp. 86–87. Mrs. Trollope's similar experience with Murray more than fifteen years earlier has already been mentioned (n. 5 above).

60. *Letters,* 1:23.

61. MS travel diaries, October 18, 1856, Princeton University Library. In *An Autobiography* (p. 102) Trollope asserts that he received no pay for either article on Merivale, but his diary shows otherwise as to the second.

62. F. E. Trollope, *Frances Trollope,* 2:186, 217–19; Post Office Records, Irish Minutes, Post 36, vol. 31, no. 438.

63. F. E. Trollope, *Frances Trollope,* 2:217–18, 223.

Chapter V

1. House of Commons, *Sessional Papers,* 1857 (i), vol. 4:354–60.

2. *Castle Richmond,* chap. xxxvii.

3. Escott, *Trollope,* p. 45; M. O'C. Bianconi and S. J. Watson, *Bianconi, King of the Irish Roads* (Dublin: Alden Figgis, 1962), pp. 118–19.

4. House of Commons, *Sessional Papers,* 1854–55, vol. 11:307, 433.

5. Post Office Records, Establishment Book, Post 59, vol. 45, "Secretary's

Office"; Sir Rowland Hill's (MS) Post Office Journals, Post 100, vol. 11, passim. The conflict between the two was somewhat amusingly carried on in the next generation when Hill's nephew wrote the adulatory article on his uncle for the *Dictionary of National Biography* and was likewise the authority for the disparaging one on Maberly.

6. Post Office Records, Rowland Hill Papers, Post 100, vol. 37, no. 1251; *An Autobiography,* p. 89; Trollope's MS traveling journal, vol. 3. Hill's language in praise of Trollope so much resembles Maberly's a year or so later (Irish Minutes, Post 36, vol. 35, no. 1233, printed in *Letters,* 1:32n) that one may suppose Tilley in fact wrote both memoranda.

7. Post Office Records, Rowland Hill Papers, Post 100, vol. 37, no. 1236a; Irish Minutes, Post 36, vol. 33, no. 2273.

8. Post Office Records, Rural Posts, Post 14, vol. 28, nos. 1189, 1345, 1470, 1472, 1734, 1830, 1844, 2004, 2035. Trollope's long letter on Dawlish and Teignmouth, dated "Exeter 27 October 1851," together with his detailed returns on his proposals, is Post 14, vol. 40, no. 1706.

9. Post Office Records, Rural Posts, Post 14, vol. 28, no. 1206; *An Autobiography,* pp. 88–91.

10. *Is He Popenjoy?* chap. xli.

11. *He Knew He Was Right,* chaps. xviii, lviii; *Small House,* conclusion. I do not know how Trollope arrived at his figure of twopence-farthing a day for his postmistress's stipend. That would amount to one shilling, three pence, three farthings for a seven-day week, or about three pounds, eight shillings, five pence a year. Rural messengers, who walked sixteen miles a day on their delivery routes, were paid twelve to fourteen shillings a week, town supplementary letter carriers about half that amount, a rural subpostmaster about twelve shillings, and the postmaster in a country town £40 to £50 a year. Seven years after Trollope's death a postal employee, probably with an eye to Trollope's account in *Small House,* recorded his recollection of a scene between Anthony and Miss Betsy Trembath, subpostmistress of Mousehole, Cornwall, when he stopped to make inquiries about the local posts; he was in a hurry and impatient, she leisurely and indignant at the bullying, and complained of her "tuppence-farden a day."—J. G. Uren, "My Early Recollections of the Post Office in the West of England," *Blackfriars* 9:158–59 (July–December, 1889). This and very many other first-hand recollections of Trollope are recorded by N. John Hall, "Trollope the Person," in *Trollope Centenary Essays,* ed. John Halperin (New York: St. Martin's Press, 1982), pp. 146–81.

12. Post Office Records, Hill's Post Office Journals, Post 100, vol. 11, pp. 432–33, 435; Trollope, *Letters,* 1:31–33.

13. *An Autobiography,* p. 97; Letter of November 27, 1852 (*Letters,* 1:33); Escott, *Trollope,* pp. 113, 115.

14. Trollope's MS traveling journal, vol. 3; Post Office Records, Post 30, File No. E685 K/1814, Folders 49 B, F. Letters (reports) from Trollope are dated November 21, 1851 (one letter only, not, as Booth's edition says, two) and January 25, 1853. Two recent articles on Trollope's work in the Channel Islands have been published by Philip Stevens, "Anthony Trollope and the Jersey Postal Service," *Bulletin de la Société Jersiane* (1980), pp. 421–33, and "Anthony Trol-

lope and the Guernsey Postal Service," *Transactions of La Société Guernesiaise* (1981), pp. 103–6.

15. For example, "Second Report of the Postmaster General," House of Commons, *Sessional Papers,* 1856, vol. 37:71.

16. Post Office Records, Post 50, File No. E685 K/1814, Folder 49 B.

17. Post Office Records, Tilley's Private Letter Books, Post 101, vol. 8, pp. 13–14.

18. *An Autobiography,* pp. 88, 87.

19. Information about these matters may be found in G. F. A. Best, "The Road to Hiram's Hospital: A Byway of Early Victorian History," *Victorian Studies* 5:135–50 (December, 1961); Ralph Arnold, *The Whiston Matter* (London: Rupert Hart-Davis, 1961); and R. B. Martin, *Enter Rumor: Four Early Victorian Scandals* (London: Faber and Faber, 1962). Both the Rochester and the Winchester cases are alluded to in *The Warden,* chap. ix.

20. *An Autobiography,* pp. 92–93, 95. Trollope's MS travel diaries show that he was in and about Salisbury in late May, 1852, and that he was in Tenbury on Friday, July 29, 1853. Confusion about the year has come about because in the manuscript of *An Autobiography* Trollope gives the latter date as 1852, and by presumption, therefore, the visit to Salisbury was 1851. His son Henry, who saw the book through the press after his father's death, altered the date to 1853, but the Page edition of *An Autobiography* erroneously restored the manuscript reading. Moreover, Henry did not correct his father's dates a few pages later to make them conform to his emendation.

21. Heineman, *Mrs. Trollope,* p. 261; Kirby, *Winchester Scholars,* p. 254.

22. Lionel Stevenson, "Dickens and the Origin of 'The Warden,'" *Trollopian* 2:83–89 (September, 1947).

23. *An Autobiography,* pp. 92–96.

24. *An Autobiography,* pp. 97–98 (again with the years mistaken); *Letters,* 1:38–39; Bodleian, MS. Don. c. 9, fols. 19–20.

25. Advertisements in the *Athenaeum,* December 22, 1854, p. 1547, and the *Times,* December 25, 1854, p. 11, col. 1.

26. Bodleian, MS. Don. c. 10, fols. 178–79; Trollope's MS travel account books, under date of June 29, 1856. (The entry is clearly misplaced here; Longman's accounting is dated June 15, 1855.)

27. On October 25, 1882; Edward A. Freeman, "Anthony Trollope," *Macmillan's Magazine* 47:239 (January, 1881).

28. Chap. xvi.

29. *Letters,* 1:333 (March 8, 1866; the correspondent is not named); Sadleir, *Things Past* (London: Constable, 1944), p. 23.

30. *Letters,* 1:29.

31. T. A. Trollope, *What I Remember,* 1:15–16; *An Autobiography,* p. 93.

Chapter VI

1. Rose Trollope's MS autobiographical memoranda, University of Illinois Library; F. E. Trollope, *Frances Trollope,* 2:244.

2. Post Office Records, Irish Minutes, Post 36, vol. 36, no. 998; vol. 37, no.

1273; English Minutes, Post 35, vol. 137, no. 6123; Establishment Books, Post 59, vols. 53, 56; *Letters,* 1:34–37.

3. Trollope's MS travel diary, beginning of 1855.

4. Post Office Records, Irish Minutes, Post 36, vol. 38, nos. 604–5; vol. 40, no. 40; and 1866, no. 454.

5. *Letters,* 1:34–35, 39; Post Office Records, Irish Minutes, Post 36, vol. 40, no. 69; Rose Trollope's autobiographical reminiscences, 1855.

6. *Belfast News-Letter,* May 17, 1951; *Letters,* 1:53 (illustration).

7. Anonymous, "Mr. Trollope's Father-in-Law," *Three Banks Review* (Edinburgh and London), no. 66:25–38 (June, 1965).

8. F. E. Trollope, *Frances Trollope,* 2:256, 266; William Irvine and Park Honan, *The Book, the Ring, and the Poet* (New York: McGraw-Hill, 1974), p. 348.

9. *An Autobiography,* p. 114; Rose Trollope's autobiographical memoranda; F. E. Trollope, *Frances Trollope,* 2:252–56.

10. Trollope's MS travel diaries; Post Office Records, John Tilley's Private Letter Books, Post 101, vol. 2, pp. 166, 168, 174, 175; House of Commons, *Sessional Papers,* 1854–55, vol. 11:431–532, 598–604.

11. Post Office Records, Tilley's Private Letter Books, Post 101, vol. 2, [p. 183]; Irish Minutes, Post 36, vol. 41, no. 899 (August 16, 1855).

12. Post Office Records, Irish Minutes, Post 36, vol. 42, no. 265.

13. *The New Zealander,* ed. N. John Hall (Oxford: Clarendon Press, 1972).

14. "Here's a Health to them that's awa," item no. 412 in James Johnson's *Scots Musical Museum,* vol. 5 (Edinburgh, 1795); *Barchester Towers,* chaps. xxvii, xlvi. Robert Burns uses this line in his poem of the same title, but not the rest of the stanza as Trollope later quotes it.

15. *Letters,* 1:29.

16. N. John Hall, introduction to *The New Zealander,* p. xxii.

17. *Letters,* 1:42.

18. [R. H. Hutton], *Spectator,* October 27, 1883, p. 1379, citing Greenwood's "Gossip about a Newspaper," *St. James's Gazette,* October 16, 1883, pp. 5–6.

19. *Trollope; a Commentary,* rev. ed. (New York: Farrar, Straus and Company, 1947), p. 178 (first edition published 1927).

20. *Letters,* 1:40. Apart from the manuscript itself, which has some marginal dates of composition on its latter pages (all 1856), our only knowledge of the work comes from two letters formerly in the publisher's files, that from Trollope and that from the publisher's reader. The originals were destroyed during the war, after Sadleir transcribed them, so that we depend only on his copies, in one instance incomplete. He dated Trollope's letter "Dublin, 27 March 1855," but Trollope was in Dublin on that date in 1856, not 1855; the letter mentions his having spoken to Longman about the manuscript "when in London," and this must refer to his visit of January 25–31, 1856 (there was no such visit early in 1855). Trollope himself seems not to have kept Longman's response to the manuscript. The year 1856 corresponds well with the dates of events named in the book. The year of composition must be corrected, then, from 1855 to 1856 in Hall's edition of *The New Zealander,* in *Letters,* 1:40–42, and in my *Trollope in the Post Office,* p. 99. Sadleir's transcripts of the Longman correspondence are in the library of the University of North Carolina, Chapel Hill.

21. *Letters*, 1:40.

22. Bodleian, MS. Don. c. 9, fols. 24–25.

23. *Letters*, 1:44; F. E. Trollope, *Frances Trollope*, 2:15.

24. *An Autobiography*, p. 103.

25. *Letters*, 1:45–47.

26. In chap. vii; *Letters*, 1:52, 54. It was presumably the publisher who had been responsible for the full title of *The Kellys and the O'Kelly's; or Landlords and Tenants. A Tale of Irish Life.*

27. *Letters*, 1:51–52; Michael Sadleir, *Trollope: A Bibliography*, 2d impression (Folkestone, Kent: William Dawson and Sons, 1977), p. 245.

28. Bodleian, MS. Don. c. 10, fols. 190–91, 194–217 passim; advertised in *Athenaeum*, May 2, 1857, p. 555, and March 27, 1858, p. 387.

29. Pamela Hansford Johnson, introduction to *Barchester Towers* (London and Glasgow: Collins, 1952), p. 15.

30. Chap. ix. The recent BBC television production of the Barchester chronicles markedly increased that "six months."

31. Post Office Records, English Minutes, Post 35, vol. 192, no. 4101, par. 7. The quantity of contemporary allusion is made clear in the thoroughly annotated edition by Robin Gilmour (Penguin Books, 1983).

32. *An Autobiography*, p. 103.

33. *An Autobiography*, p. 126.

34. *An Autobiography*, p. 104.

35. *Westminster Review* 68:594–96 (October, 1857); Gordon S. Haight, "George Meredith and the 'Westminster review,'" *Modern Language Review* 53:1–16 (January, 1958).

36. Chap. xxxi.

37. *Letters*, 1:47–51.

38. "The Civil Service," *Dublin University Magazine* 46:409–26 (October, 1855). Trevelyan's list of subjects is given on p. 413.

39. *The Three Clerks*, chap. xxix; *New Zealander*, p. 211.

40. *The Three Clerks*, chap. v; *New Zealander*, pp. 90–91.

41. *The Three Clerks*, chap. xxxi.

42. *The Three Clerks*, chap. xxxii; *New Zealander*, pp. 109–10.

43. *The Three Clerks*, chap. iii.

44. *Letters*, 1:43. Trollope's letter was not published by the *Athenaeum*.

45. *The Three Clerks*, chaps. xxii, xxix, xliv; *Brown, Jones, and Robinson*, chap. viii; *The Three Clerks*, chap. xxviii.

46. Locker-Lampson, *My Confidences*, (London, 1896), p. 336; *An Autobiography*, p. 111.

47. *Letters*, 1:58.

48. Loose leaf in vol. 4 of travel account books, Princeton University Library; Bodleian, MS. Don. c. 9, fol. 205.

49. *The Three Clerks*, chap. xxiv; *Past and Present*, Book III, chap. i.

50. Chap. xx.

51. *The Three Clerks*, chap. vi.

52. Pp. 160–61.

53. Bodleian, MS. Don. c. 9, fols. 29–30; *Letters*, 1:58–59.

54. *Letters*, 1:51; *An Autobiography*, p. 109.

55. *An Autobiography*, pp. 109–11; *Letters*, 1:59–60; F. E. Trollope, *Frances Trollope*, 2:271.

56. Rose Trollope's MS autobiographical memoranda, University of Illinois Library; *Letters*, 1:59; Bodleian, MS. Don. c. 9, fol. 43.

Chapter VII

1. *Letters*, 1:118.

2. *An Autobiography*, p. 117 (where Trollope said that Bentley called on him at the Post Office to withdraw his initial offer; in fact he did so by letter); *Letters*, 1:62, 73, 86.

3. Mrs. Trollope's letter to Julia Pertz, September 24, 1833, in the Houghton Library, Harvard University; Post Office Records, Tilley's Private Letter Books, Post 101, vol. 4, pp. 57, 60; Trollope's traveling journal, vol. 4; *Letters*, 1:63–64.

4. Post Office Records, "Substitution of bags for iron boxes in transmission of mails for Australia," Post 29/126 Packet 256R/1866. Trollope's reports are dated from Alexandria on February 14 and April 3, 1858, from Malta on April 16, and from London on May 22.

5. Escott, *Trollope*, pp. 123–24.

6. Post Office Records, "Indian Mail Service: Conveyance through Egypt," Post 26/86 Packet 1041/1858. Trollope's reports are dated from Cairo, February 16, from Suez, February 23, from Alexandria, March 25, from Glasgow, June 19, and from Dublin, July 1, 1858. See his account in *An Autobiography*, pp. 116, 118, 122–23. Dates of his movements are from his traveling journal. The commendation is in House of Commons, *Sessional Papers*, 1859(i), vol. 8:448.

7. Post Office Records, "Malta—Extension of Money Order System to," Post 29/102 Packet 860M/1861. Trollope's report is dated from Malta, April 16, 1858, and amended by him in London on May 18. He has also drawn up a schedule of the income of the Malta Post Office employees, dated April 15. He wrote a comment, dated September 28, on a letter sent to London by the deputy postmaster general at Malta.

8. *Letters*, 1:64.

9. *The Bertrams*, chap. xxxix.

10. *An Autobiography*, pp. 115–16.

11. "Anthony Trollope," *Century Magazine*, n.s., 4:394 (July, 1883), reprinted in his *Partial Portraits* and in Donald Smalley, ed., *Anthony Trollope: The Critical Heritage* (London: Routledge and Kegan Paul, 1969), p. 544.

12. *Saturday Review* 11:452 (May 4, 1861), reprinted in Smalley, *Critical Heritage*, p. 124.

13. *The Newcomes*, chap. xiii.

14. *National Review* 7:416–35 (October, 1858); *Letters*, 1:74.

15. *An Autobiography*, p. 127.

16. *An Autobiography*, p. 119.

17. The writing schedule for *Doctor Thorne* is Bodleian, MS. Don. c. 9, fols.

43–44; for *The Bertrams,* fols. 53–54. When a week passed that produced no pages of *The Bertrams,* he wrote on his calendar, "Ah me!" When a second week passed, again "Ah me!" When the lapse grew to six weeks, "Ah me! Ah me!!"

18. Rose Trollope's MS notes, University of Illnois Library.

19. *An Autobiography,* pp. 127–28. There is some inconsistency between Trollope's going home to write a love scene at the end of a hard day's work and his oft-repeated (and probably true) boast that he did his writing very early in the morning.

20. Trollope's MS travel diaries, Princeton University.

21. Obituary of Richard Samuel Oldham, *Times* (London), June 26, 1914, p. 10, col. 5.

22. *Letters,* 1:73–74 (June 16, 1858); and see 2:1005.

23. 5:618 (June 12, 1858).

24. Trollope's MS travel diaries, Princeton University.

25. *Letters,* 1:79; Bodleian, MS. Don. c. 9, fols. 51–54.

26. The Geroulds in their *Guide to Trollope* call "Littlebath" "Trollope's pseudonym for Bath." Since many street names in Bath and Cheltenham duplicate each other (for example, "Montpellier," "Paragon"), Trollope's use of these names is not conclusive, but his location of the railway station in Littlebath is suitable only for Cheltenham, and the "Plough," which he describes as "a good inn" (chap. xiii) is the name of a hotel on the High Street in Cheltenham, but not of a hotel in Bath. The older guidebooks describe it as "a comfortable old-fashioned house with an enormous stable-yard." For the Trinity College scholarship, see Edward A. Freeman, "Anthony Trollope," *Macmillan's Magazine* 47:236 (January, 1883), and *An Autobiography,* p. 17.

27. C. S. Dessain, ed., *The Letters and Diaries of John Henry Newman* (London: Thomas Nelson and Sons, 1970), 20:281, 284; *Saturday Review* 7:368 (March 26, 1859); Vsevolod Setschkareff, "Tolstoj und Trollope," in *Festschrift für Max Vasmer* ed. Margarete Woltner and Herbert Bräuer (Wiesbaden: Otto Harrossowitz, 1956), p. 472; *Tauchnitz Edition Centenary Catalogue, 1837–1937* (Leipzig), item 468–69. Twenty-one of Trollope's novels were translated into Russian soon after original publication in English.—K. E. Harper and B. A. Booth, "Russian Translations of Nineteenth-Century English Fiction," *Nineteenth-Century Fiction* 8:191–92 (December, 1953).

28. Trollope's instructions are in Post Office Records, "Instructions to Packet Agents, Colonial Postmasters, &c.," Post 44, vol. 12, pp. 95–101; also Tilley's Private Letter Books, Post 101, vol. 4, pp. 142, 153; Trollope, *The West Indies and the Spanish Main,* p. 7. The instructions from Hill represent a considerable expansion of the mission as first proposed to and accepted by Trollope.—*Letters,* 1:81.

29. *West Indies,* p. 8; Post Office Records, "Transfer of Post Office Control to the local Authorities in Jamaica, &c.," Post 29/96 Packet 531L/1860. Trollope's official letters are dated from Kingston, December 25, 1858, and January 22, 1859; another, February 3, 1859, includes memoranda made in Jamaica on December 28 and January 18.

30. Post Office Records, "West Indies. Next Routes for Mail Services," Post 29/93 Packet 204L/1860 (items 17–19 of Trollope's report of July 16, 1859).

31. *West Indies,* chaps. xi–xiv; letter of instructions dated November 16, 1858, items 10, 12.

32. Letter of instructions dated November 16, 1858, item 17; Post Office Records, "Grenada Postal Convention for the Isthmus of Panama," Post 29/102 Packet 1105M/1861. Trollope's reports are dated from Panama on May 8 and London on July 25, 1859.

33. *West Indies,* pp. 256–58, 334, 338, 345–46, 155.

34. Muriel R. Trollope, "What I Was Told," *Trollopian* 2:233 (March, 1948); *West Indies,* pp. 275–76; Gordon N. Ray, *Thackeray: The Age of Wisdom* (New York: McGraw-Hill, 1958), p. 215; Trollope, *Thackeray,* p. 60; Trollope's letter to Herman Merivale, January 13, 1864 (*Letters,* 1:247–48).

35. *West Indies,* p. 2; Post Office Records, "West Indies. Next Routes for Mail Services," Post 29/93 Packet 204L/1860 (Trollope's letters and reports are dated from London on July 16 and two on September 6); House of Commons, *Sessional Papers,* 1860, vol. 23:337–38; *An Autobiography,* p. 125.

36. *Letters,* 1:80–81; Bodleian, MS. Don. c. 9, fols. 46–48. In *An Autobiography* (p. 129) Trollope somewhat inaccurately says, "As soon as I had learned from the secretary at the General Post Office that this journey would be required, I proposed the book to Messrs. Chapman & Hall."

37. *West Indies,* pp. 252, 23, 132–33, 4–5.

38. *West Indies,* p. 112.

39. *An Autobiography,* p. 129.

40. Travel diaries, Princeton University Library; *West Indies,* pp. 367, 388–95; *Letters,* 1:81; *Times* (London) July 5, 1859, p. 12, col. 5.

41. *Letters,* 1:89, 86, 195.

42. *Letters,* 1:84–85, 98.

43. *West Indies,* p. 231.

44. Bodleian, MS. Don. c. 9, fols. 58–61.

45. Bodleian, MS. Don. c. 10, fols. 173–74.

46. Rose Trollope's MS notes, University of Illinois.

47. *Athenaeum,* October 8, 1859, p. 480.

48. *Letters,* 1:89–91; *Times,* May 23, 1859, p. 12, cols. 4–6 (by E. S. Dallas, but published anonymously).

49. Bodleian, MS. Don. c. 9, fols. 70–73. In *An Autobiography* Trollope says that he began the story "on my journey back to Ireland, in the railway carriage" (p. 142), but unless his writing calendar is in error, his statement must be slightly modified as I have indicated.

50. Leonard Huxley, *The House of Smith, Elder* (London: printed for private circulation, 1923), p. 95.

51. Bodleian, MS. Don. c. 10, fols. 171–72.

52. P. 140.

53. *An Autobiography,* pp. 143–44.

54. March 26, 1859, p. 420.

55. Trollope's MS travel diaries, Princeton University.

56. *An Autobiography,* pp. 110–11. It is curious that Newby added "A Historical Romance" to the title page of the second issue of *The Macdermots* in 1848.

57. *Saturday Review* 9:643–44 (May 19, 1860).

58. *Letters,* 1:100.

Chapter VIII

1. Bodleian, MS. Don. c. 9, fols. 123–26, 142–44. For authoritative circulation figures, see John Sutherland, *"Cornhill's* Sales and Payments: The First Decade," *Victorian Periodicals Review* 19:106–8 (fall, 1986).

2. G. S. Haight, ed., *The George Eliot Letters* (New Haven: Yale University Press, 1955), 4:38.

3. Huxley, *Smith, Elder,* pp. 155–56.

4. *An Autobiography,* p. 147.

5. John Hollingshead, *My Lifetime* (London, 1895), 1:163.

6. Quoted in *An Autobiography,* p. 149, from Sala's *Things I Have Seen* (London, 1894), 1:30.

7. P. 2, col. 1.

8. "Newspaper Gossip," June 23, 1860, pp. 799–800.

9. Huxley, *Smith, Elder,* pp. 104–6.

10. *Letters,* 1:96 (January 20, 1860). Miss Dunstable first appeared in *Doctor Thorne.*

11. *Letters,* 1:97 (February 12, 1860).

12. *Letters,* 1:104 (May 16 and 23, 1860).

13. *Letters,* 1:111.

14. *An Autobiography,* p. 148. A meticulously detailed study of Millais as Trollope's illustrator, based on both published and unpublished evidence, is Michael Mason's "The Way We Look Now: Millais' Illustrations to Trollope," *Art History* 1:309–40 (September, 1978). By his calculation, Millais did eighty-five illustrations and nineteen vignettes for Trollope's works.

15. Huxley, *Smith, Elder,* pp. 112–13; *Letters,* 1:120; see also 1:114. The anonymity of *Framley Parsonage* was in fact a mere token. The editor's "Roundabout Paper" at the end of the first number proclaimed that the two novels in that issue were written under the standard of the author of *Vanity Fair* and under "that fresh and handsome standard which has lately been hoisted on *Barchester Towers*."—1:125 (January, 1860).

16. *Letters,* 1:100.

17. T. A. Trollope, *What I Remember,* 3:359–65.

18. J. A. V. Chapple and Arthur Pollard, eds., *The Letters of Mrs. Gaskell* (Manchester: Manchester University Press, 1966), p. 602 (March 1, 1860).

19. *Letters,* 1:145, 154.

20. *Letters,* 1:157, 219.

21. Post Office Records, "Surveyors' Districts Rearrangement," Post 30/172 E1913/1866; *An Autobiography,* p. 133. Though the Millais illustration of Orley Farm is drawn from the comfortable farmhouse of Julian Hill at Harrow, in which Trollope lived as a young lad, it is transplanted in the novel from Middlesex to one of the eastern counties.

22. Post Office Records, English Minutes, Post 35, vol. 201, nos. 818, 833; vol. 202, no. 1025; vol. 239, no. 1173; vol. 251, nos. 1680, 1693, 1981; vol. 252, nos. 2181, 1360, 2536; vol. 241, nos. 2641, 3224.

23. *Letters*, 1:184, 216, 225, 233, 200, 242.

24. Letters to Merivale (December, 1860), *Letters*, 1:131–33; Royal Literary Fund, Minutes of the General Committee, February 28 and March 14, 1866; Judith Anne Merivale, ed., *Autobiography and Letters of Charles Merivale* (Oxford, 1898), p. 331.

25. This and the next three paragraphs are drawn from Post Office Records, "Committee of Enquiry into Inadequate Payments of Staff & Lack of Accommodation for the Circulation Department," Post 30/148 4801/1861. The confidential printed report with its substantial minutes of evidence before the committee is in this file. See also English Minutes, Post 35, vol. 203, nos. 1716*, 1868.

26. Post Office Records, Hill's Post Office Journals, Post 100, vol. 14, pp. 2–3 and passim, January–June, 1861.

27. "Mr. Anthony Trollope on the Civil Service," *Daily News* (London), January 5, 1861, p. 5, col. 6; *Cornhill Magazine* 3:222 (February, 1861).

28. Post Office Records, Hill's Post Office Journals, Post 100, vol. 14, pp. 2–3; vol. 15, p. 66.

29. Post Office Records, Tilley's Private Letter Books, Post 101, vol. 5, pp. 29, 58–59, 74, 77; "Report of the Select Committee on Civil Service Appointments," House of Commons, *Sessional Papers*, 1860, vol. 9:158–80; Post Office Records, "Promotion Class to Class," Post 30/164 Eng 3849/1863; Trollope, *Letters*, 1:106.

30. *Letters*, 1:216–18.

31. Pollock, *Personal Reminiscences* (London, 1887), 1:149–50. Pollock, a lawyer with long experience in legal documents, astonished Trollope by readily estimating the number of words on a page of his manuscript simply by seeing the size of the sheet and glancing at his handwriting.

32. *Letters*, 1:161 (to Kate Field, November 5, 1861); [W. Lucas Collins], review of *An Autobiography*, *Blackwood's Edinburgh Magazine* 134:591 (November, 1883).

33. Chap. xvii.

34. *Letters*, 1:142.

35. *Letters*, 1:96–97, 103; *An Autobiography*, pp. 144–45; James T. Fields, *Yesterdays with Authors* (Boston, 1872), pp. 63, 87–88.

36. Newton Arvin, ed., *The Heart of Hawthorne's Journals* (Boston: Houghton Mifflin Co., 1929), pp. 303, 329; N. Arvin, *Hawthorne* (Boston: Little, Brown, 1929), p. 256; James C. Austin, *Fields of the Atlantic Monthly* (San Marino, Calif.: Huntington Library, 1953), p. 212.

37. A. M. Terhune, ed., *The Letters of Edward FitzGerald* (Princeton: Princeton University Press, 1980), 2:354 (March 2, 1860).

38. *Letters*, 1:110, 147; G. W. Curtis, ed., *The Correspondence of John Lothrop Motley* (Boston, 1889), 1:227.

39. *Last Chronicle*, chap. lxx; *Popenjoy*, chap. xxvi. The building still stands, but is no longer a hotel.

40. *Letters*, 1:102–3, 106–8.

41. *Letters*, 1:109–12, 118; *George Eliot Letters*, 3:281, 306–8, 326.

42. *Letters*, 1:181–82.

43. *Letters*, 1:134–36. In his article on "Public Schools" in 1865, Trollope

especially praised "St. Andrew's College, established by Mr. Stevens, at Brad-field," for recognizing the need for more masters—one for every thirteen or fourteen boys as against one for twenty-two boys at Harrow, one for twenty at Winchester, and this at a cost of only £130 per annum, everything included.

44. *Letters,* 1:100, 122–23.

45. Paul Landis and R. E. Freeman, eds., *Letters of the Brownings to George Barrett* (Urbana: University of Illinois Press, 1958), pp. 244, 247–48.

46. A. Trollope, *Letters,* 1:125.

47. Kate Field, "Last Days of Walter Savage Landor," *Atlantic Monthly* 17:698 (June, 1866).

48. Lilian Whiting, *Kate Field: A Record* (Boston, 1899), pp. 122–23; Trol-lope, *Letters,* 1:125–27.

49. *Letters,* 1:145 (April 7, 1861).

50. *George Eliot Letters,* 8:279.

51. Chap. ix.

52. *Letters,* 1:114–17.

53. Frederic G. Kenyon, ed., *The Letters of Elizabeth Barrett Browning,* 3d ed. (London, 1898), 2:444–46.

54. Trollope, *Letters,* 1:123, 135–39.

55. *Letters,* 1:140–41.

56. *Letters,* 1:150.

57. Chap. xxii, p. 366.

58. *Framley Parsonage,* chap. xvii.

59. *Letters,* 2:759.

60. Trollope, *Thackeray,* pp. 31–32; Ray, ed., *Letters and Private Papers of William Makepeace Thackeray,* 4:356.

Chapter IX

1. Bodleian, MSS. Don. c. 9, fols. 60–61, 72–73, 82–85; Don. c. 10, fols. 173–74.

2. *Letters,* 1:133–34.

3. *Letters,* 1:134–36; *George Eliot Letters,* 3:378–79; *Athenaeum,* January 26, 1861, p. 123; *Times,* January 1, 1861, p. 7, col. 2; May 23, 1861, p. 12, col. 2.

4. The *Cornhill* version was slightly revised; the lecture as delivered may be read in Morris L. Parrish, ed., *Four Lectures by Anthony Trollope* (London: Consta-ble, 1938), pp. 4–26.

5. On June 1, Trollope sent Millais a pass for a lecture he was soon to deliver, and about which he had spoken to Millais. On June 11 he sent to George Smith a copy of "the lecture—unlectured" for printing, perhaps in the *Cornhill* (where it did not appear). On July 3 he sent "my lecture" on "The National Gallery" to Mrs. S. C. Hall for publication in her *St. James's Magazine,* 2:163–76 (Sep-tember, 1861) and was paid £15 for it. See *Letters,* 1:149–50, 154, 158.

6. *Letters,* 1:153–54.

7. *An Autobiography,* p. 249.

8. T. A. Trollope, *What I Remember,* 2:305.

9. A. Trollope, *An Autobiography*, p. 103; *Letters*, 1:258 (to G. H. Lewes, March 21, 1864).

10. *Letters*, 2:547.

11. Trudy Bliss, ed., *Thomas Carlyle: Letters to His Wife* (London: Victor Gollancz, 1953), p. 394.

12. Joseph Slater, ed., *The Correspondence of Emerson and Carlyle* (New York: Columbia University Press, 1964), p. 545.

13. *Carlyle: Letters to His Wife*, p. 381 (July 27, 1865); see *Fortnightly Review* 1:633–35 (July 15, 1865); Howells, *Heroines of Fiction* (New York, 1901), 2:136. Was Trollope's rather extraordinary attack on Ruskin partly moved by a sense of loyalty to Mrs. Millais, who had been Ruskin's wife and had no reason to love him?

14. *Letters*, 1:304–5. A passage on Carlyle's opinion of novel writing was canceled in the manuscript of *An Autobiography*, chap. xii, and therefore does not appear in most editions of that work. It is printed in the appendix to Frederick Page's edition, pp. 270–71.

15. F. E. Trollope, *Frances Trollope*, 2:83.

16. Five of his seven speeches at anniversary dinners, including this one for 1861, are published by Bradford A. Booth, "Trollope and the Royal Literary Fund," *Nineteenth-Century Fiction* 7:208–16 (December, 1952); the other two may be found in R. H. Super, "Trollope at the Royal Literary Fund," *Nineteenth-Century Fiction* 37:316–28 (December, 1982), which also gives a fuller account of Trollope's association with the fund.

17. *An Autobiography*, pp. 167–68.

18. Bodleian, MS. Don. c. 9, fols. 89–90.

19. Post Office Records, English Minutes, Post 35, vol. 212, no. 1682.

20. Post Office Records, English Minutes, Post 35, vol. 212, no. 1877; Hill's Post Office Journals, Post 100, vol. 15, pp. 66, 50, 52, 57; *An Autobiography*, pp. 160, 162–63; *Athenaeum*, no. 1819:306 (September 6, 1862); Rowland Hill and G. B. Hill, *The Life of Sir Rowland Hill* (London, 1880), 2:361–62.

21. *Letters*, 1:157–58.

22. Trollope's MS travel diaries; Austin, ed., *Fields of the Atlantic Monthly*, p. 215.

23. A. Trollope, *North America*, ed. Donald Smalley and Bradford Allen Booth (New York: Alfred A. Knopf, 1951), pp. 24–29; *Letters*, 1:95n; Trollope's MS travel diaries.

24. Austin, ed., *Fields of the Atlantic Monthly*, pp. 215, 4; H. E. Scudder, *James Russell Lowell* (Boston: Houghton Mifflin, 1901), 2:82–84; *North America*, p. 154.

25. *Our Old Home*, "Leamington Spa," one-third through.

26. Booth, "Trollope and the Royal Literary Fund," pp. 212–13; Trollope, *Marion Fay*, chap. xii.

27. *North America*, pp. 150–52.

28. Frances M. Trollope, *Domestic Manners of the Americans*, ed. Donald Smalley (New York: Vintage Books, 1949), pp. 373–75.

29. *North America*, pp. 164, 171–80, 207; Trollope's MS travel diaries.

30. *North America*, pp. 197, 201; *Nation* (New York), May 8, 1884, pp. 404–

5, reprinted in Matthew Arnold, *Complete Prose Works,* ed. R. H. Super (Ann Arbor: University of Michigan Press, 1974), 10:244–45.

31. *Letters,* 1:161, 164; *North America,* pp. 222–24, 226–28; Slater, ed., *Correspondence of Emerson and Carlyle,* p. 545.

32. *North America,* pp. 229–30.

33. *Letters,* 1:168, 172.

34. *North America,* pp. 233–34.

35. Trollope's MS travel diaries; *Letters,* 1:161, 164; *North America,* p. 312.

36. *North America,* pp. 305, 323–25, 363; *Letters,* 1:164–65, 169, 172.

37. *Letters,* 1:161, 170 and n., 178–81.

38. Trollope, *Lord Palmerston* (London, 1882), p. 195; *An Autobiography,* pp. 165–66; Trollope's MS travel diaries.

39. "The Present Condition of the Northern States of the American Union," in Trollope's *Four Lectures,* p. 54.

40. *North America,* pp. 372–73, 394; F. E. Trollope, *Frances Trollope,* 2:164.

41. *North America,* p. 301.

42. *South Africa,* 2:205.

43. *Letters,* 1:168–72, 174–75; *Orley Farm,* chap. xxxviii; *Dr. Wortle's School,* chap. ii.

44. *North America,* p. 463; Trollope's MS travel diaries.

45. *Letters,* 1:175.

46. Bodleian, MS. Don. c. 9, fols. 89–90; Trollope's MS travel diaries.

47. *An Autobiography,* pp. 164, 166.

48. *North America,* p. 241.

49. When Trollope proposed to sell the American rights to *Orley Farm* to Harpers, and named his price to their London agents (Sampson Low), he was told that he would have to accept whatever figure Harper chose to give, in this case £200. If he did not, they would publish it without payment. Under his contract with Chapman, receipts for American publication were to be divided between Chapman and Trollope; he actually received £93 6s. 8d.—*Letters,* 1:195, 201; Escott, *Trollope,* p. 272; Trollope's MS travel diaries, end of 1862.

50. Bodleian, MS. Don. c. 9, fols. 93–94; *Letters,* 2:1006.

51. Bodleian, MS. Don. c. 9, fols. 95–98.

52. Trollope, "American Literary Piracy," *Athenaeum,* September 6, 1862, pp. 306–7; reply by Fletcher Harper, October 18, p. 496. and rejoinder by Trollope, October 25, pp. 529–30. Trollope's remarks are reprinted in *Letters,* 1:193–98, 200–202.

53. Escott, *Trollope,* pp. 272–73.

54. *Letters,* 1:176.

55. *An Autobiography,* pp. 167, 126.

56. *Saturday Review,* 4:518 (December 5, 1857); *Doctor Thorne,* chaps. xlv, xlvi.

57. Henry S. Drinker, "The Lawyers of Anthony Trollope," in *Two Addresses Delivered to Members of the Grolier Club* (New York: Grolier Club, 1950), p. 33.

58. *Letters of Elizabeth Barrett Browning,* 2:377, 391; *Letters of the Brownings to George Barrett,* p. 247.

59. *Orley Farm,* chap. lix.

Chapter X

1. *Letters,* 1:183 n. 5; *An Autobiography,* pp. 157–58. Trollope was in error as to the year of his election.

2. *The Rules and Regulations of the Garrick Club,* with an Alphabetical List of the Members, corrected to June, 1867 (London, 1867); Guy Boas, *The Garrick Club, 1831–1947* (London: Garrick Club, 1948), pp. 39, 54, 42, 55, 58–59, 60, 62; Percy Fitzgerald, *The Garrick Club* (London: Elliot Stock, 1904), pp. 105–6.

3. Bodleian, MS. Don. c. 9, fols. 121–25.

4. Gordon S. Haight, *George Eliot: A Biography* (Oxford: Clarendon Press, 1968), p. 371; Trollope, *Letters,* 1:186–87.

5. Huxley, *Smith, Elder,* pp. 101–3. Thackeray's conversation is reported in *Disraeli, Derby and the Conservative Party: Journals and Memoirs of Edward Henry, Lord Stanley, 1849–1869,* ed. John Vincent (Hassocks, Sussex: Harvester Press, 1978), p. 156 (February 19, 1863). Because *Romola* was shorter than Smith had originally bargained for, George Eliot received £7,000 instead of £10,000 for it.

6. T. A. Trollope, *What I Remember,* 2:267, 283–85.

7. Donald Macleod, *Memoir of Norman Macleod,* 2d ed. (London, 1877), pp. 291–92.

8. Bodleian, MS. Don. c. 9, fols. 101–5.

9. Bodleian, MS. Don. c. 10*, fols. 15–26.

10. Trollope's MS travel diaries. Rose, in the MS reminiscences she wrote to help him with his *Autobiography* a decade later, placed the journey to Holland with Tilley in 1860, when it was first planned; this entry was then crossed out, and Trollope's own hand wrote "Went to Holland" for 1862. Rose may have remembered that Tilley *made* the trip with Anthony, or she may merely have remembered that he had once *planned* the trip with Anthony.

11. *Cornhill* 6:616–22 (November, 1862); Trollope's MS travel diaries, accounts at end of 1862.

12. *Letters,* 1:192.

13. *Letters,* 1:206. His MS travel diaries for November and December frequently show the letter *H* opposite those days.

14. *Letters,* 1:207, 209–10.

15. The lecture is printed in Parrish, ed., *Four Lectures,* pp. 27–64.

16. *Letters,* 1:232, 234.

17. *Letters,* 1:210–11; 2:606n; Rose Trollope's MS reminiscences for 1863.

18. *Letters,* 1:199, 202, 220.

19. Alexander Strahan, *Norman Macleod, D.D. A Slight Contribution towards his Biography* (London, 1872), pp. 14, 16–17. That the friendship of Trollope and Macleod was established before the *Good Words* episode is affirmed by both men, yet now is the first time Macleod's name has appeared in this biography— evidence of how much the survival of data depends on chance.

20. The publisher's announcement is reproduced in *An Autobiography,* p. 187.

21. Arnold, "The Function of Criticism at the Present Time," two-thirds through.

22. P. 5.

23. D. Macleod, *Memoir of Norman Macleod,* p. 329.

24. *Letters,* 1:223, 225. The seven-and-a-half-page letter in which Macleod had conveyed his unhappy decision to Strahan is printed in Robert Lee Wolff, *Nineteenth-Century Fiction* (New York: Garland Publishing, 1985), 4:205–6. "As far as money is concerned I know you will treat him like a gentleman and make every apology in your power."

25. *Letters,* 1:220. Millais did do a portrait of Rachel as frontispiece for Chapman and Hall's one-volume cheaper edition of October, 1864.—M. Sadleir, *Trollope, a Bibliography,* p. 53; N. John Hall, *Trollope and His Illustrators* (New York: St. Martin's Press, 1983), fig. 43.

26. Bodleian, MS. Don. c. 9, fols. 105–11, 116–17.

27. *An Autobiography,* p. 186; *Memoir of Norman Macleod,* p. 330.

28. *Letters,* 1:336. Strahan did not become a member of the Garrick Club.

29. The manuscript of *Kept in the Dark* is in the Hatcher Library of the University of Michigan.

30. *Letters,* 2:923, about *The Fixed Period.*

31. A. K. H. Boyd, *Twenty-five Years of St. Andrews* (London, 1892), 1:100–101. Edmund Yates responded: "I do not remember ever having heard Trollope swear. He may have [used *damn* occasionally], but he certainly was not an habitual swearer."—*World,* February 24, 1892, p. 19.

32. *Letters,* 2:849; MS correspondence in the University of Illinois Library.

33. *Letters,* 1:132n.

34. *Letters,* 1:215, 226; R. H. Super, "Trollope at the Royal Literary Fund," *Nineteenth-Century Fiction* 37:319–20 (December, 1982); *Marion Fay,* chap. xxxviii. If Trollope had to speak at a day's notice he had six weeks to polish the remarks before they were sent to the printer for the fund's *Annual Report.*

35. June 18, p. 13, col. 4.

36. Rose Trollope's MS reminiscences; *Letters,* 1:226–27, 232, 235.

37. F. E. Trollope, *Frances Trollope,* 2:297–301.

38. Bodleian, MS. Don. c. 9, fols. 127–31.

39. *Letters,* 1:230–32.

40. Robert L. Patten, *Charles Dickens and His Publishers* (Oxford: Clarendon Press, 1978), pp. 270–71; *Letters,* 1:232n.

41. *Letters,* 1:227, 236–39, 243.

42. *An Autobiography,* pp. 174–75, 178–79.

43. *Thackeray,* pp. 124, 129; *An Autobiography,* pp. 178–79.

44. *Thackeray,* p. 9.

45. *Edmund Yates: His Recollections and Experiences* (London, 1884), 1:97; *Small House,* chap. xlvi; *An Autobiography,* p. 179.

46. It should be pointed out that Trollope misdates the beginning of the appearance of *Can You Forgive Her?* in its parts.—*An Autobiography,* p. 173; see p. 393. James Pope-Hennessy suggests that Palliser got his name from "Palliser's Castle," a rock formation near Anthony's home at Clonmel, in southern Ireland.—*Anthony Trollope* (Boston: Little, Brown, 1971), p. 116.

47. H. M. Schueller and R. L. Peters, eds., *The Letters of John Addington Symonds* (Detroit: Wayne State University Press, 1967), 1:268, 443, 451 (letters to A. O. Rutson from Clifton, March 13 and 27, 1864).

Chapter XI

1. *Letters*, 1:244.

2. A. Trollope, *Letters*, 1:129.

3. A. Trollope, *Letters*, 1:125; Thackeray, *Letters and Private Papers*, 4:359.

4. *Letters*, 1:220.

5. *Letters and Private Papers*, 4:236.

6. Ray, *Age of Wisdom*, p. 303; *An Autobiography*, p. 140.

7. Huxley, *Smith, Elder*, p. 109.

8. *Letters and Private Papers*, 4:411; Trollope, *Thackeray*, p. 32.

9. Trollope, *Thackeray*, pp. 59–60; Thackeray, *Letters and Private Papers*, 4:262–63; Trollope, *Letters*, 1:239, 247–48.

10. Ray, *Age of Wisdom*, pp. 425, 419. Anne Thackeray, Lady Ritchie, so quotes Trollope in the biographical introduction to vol. 12 of *The Works of William Makepeace Thackeray* (London, 1903), p. xxi.

11. *Cornhill* 9:129–32 (Dickens), 134–37 (Trollope); *Macmillan's Magazine* 9:356–63 (Kingsley), 363–68 (Masson).

12. February 6, 1864, pp. 148–49.

13. R. W. Emerson, *Journals and Miscellaneous Notebooks* (Cambridge, Mass.: Harvard University Press, 1982), 15:227; Emerson, *Letters and Social Aims*, rev. ed. (Boston: Houghton, Mifflin and Co., 1889). The relevant passage is on p. 300.

14. *Letters*, 1:257.

15. *The Claverings*, chap. i; *Pendennis*, chaps. ii, xv.

16. Mario Praz quotes a number of other passages from Trollope to the same effect. "The abolition of the hero is a salient feature in Trollope, no less—and perhaps even more—than in Thackeray."—*The Hero in Eclipse in Victorian Fiction*, trans. Angus Davidson (London: Oxford University Press, 1956), pp. 267–68. "The age of the hero has passed," is the conclusion of Russell A. Fraser's discussion of this aspect of the two novelists.—"Shooting Niagara in the Novels of Thackeray and Trollope," *Modern Language Quarterly* 19:141–46 (June, 1958). Thackeray and Trollope lived in the world that was beginning to make its appearance in Byron's *Don Juan*.

17. Trollope, *Thackeray*, pp. 184–88, 196–99.

18. Trollope, *Thackeray*, pp. 191–96, 200–201.

19. James, *Partial Portraits* (London, 1888), p. 116; Howells, *Criticism and Fiction* (New York, 1891), end of sec. xv.

20. Henry Kingsley, "Thackeray," *Macmillan's Magazine* 9:359 (February, 1864).

21. *Thackeray*, pp. 191–92. We have seen Trollope making the same remark about "one man's meat" in *An Autobiography*, p. 188. A somewhat fuller statement of parallels between Trollope and Thackeray may be found in my essay, "Trollope's *Vanity Fair*," *Journal of Narrative Technique* 9:12–20 (Winter, 1979). Robert A. Colby, "Trollope as a Thackerayan," *Dickens Studies Newsletter* 11:261–77 (1983), places his principal emphasis on what he takes to be the injustice of Trollope's criticism of Thackeray, especially in the biography. J. Hillis Miller is

far more sympathetic (Colby's word is "uncritical") in "Trollope's Thackeray," *Nineteenth-Century Fiction* 37:350–57 (December, 1982).

22. *Times* (London), December 1, 1883, p. 7, col. 6; Post Office Records, Hill's Post Office Journals, Post 100, vol. 17, pp. 174–75; *An Autobiography,* p. 133; Yates, *Recollections,* 2:223n.

23. Yates, *Recollections,* 2:232.

24. "Tenth Report of the Postmaster General," House of Commons, *Sessional Papers,* 1864, vol. 30:614; Post Office Records, English Minutes, Post 35, vol. 232, nos. 1286, 1339; Establishment Book, Post 59, vol. 56.

25. Post Office Records, English Minutes, Post 35, vol. 143, no. 2497; vol. 191, no. 3181.

26. Post Office Records, Minuted Papers, Post 30/185 E3174/1868; English Minutes, Post 35, vol. 232, no. 1846.

27. Post Office Records, Minuted Papers, Post 30/185 E3174/1868.

28. Post Office Records, Tilley's Private Letter Books, Post 101, vol. 6, p. 184; Minuted Papers, Post 30/185 E3174/1868.

29. *An Autobiography,* p. 134; Barry A. Bartrum, "A Victorian Political Hostess: The Engagement Book of Lady Stanley of Alderley," *Princeton University Library Chronicle* 36:133–46 (Winter, 1975).

30. *Letters,* 1:281.

31. This affirmation is based on the Post Office Records, but Trollope himself also made it in *An Autobiography,* where the pain of the present dispute shows through, though he never mentions it: "During the period of my service in the Post Office I did very much special work for which I never asked any remuneration,—and I never received any, though payments for special services were common in the department at that time."

32. Post Office Records, Tilley's Private Letter Books, Post 101, vol. 6, pp. 270, 274, 278; vol. 8, p. 135.

33. Post Office Records, Hill's Post Office Journals, Post 100, vol. 17, p. 170.

34. T. Humphry Ward, *History of the Athenaeum, 1824–1925* (London: Athenaeum Club, 1926), pp. 115, 145, 151, 154, 175, 179, 182, 187, 191, 199, 208, 53–54, 90; Trollope, *Letters,* 1:183n.

35. Ward, *History of the Athenaeum,* pp. 67–68.

36. Booth, "Trollope and the Royal Literary Fund," pp. 211–12.

Chapter XII

1. *Letters,* 1:232.

2. *Letters,* 1:246–47; Bodleian, MS. Don. c. 9, fol. 130; *Leeds Mercury,* February 19, 1864. Smith printed a few copies of this lecture for Trollope's own use.

3. *Letters,* 1:249, 250–52; *Halstead Times,* February 27, 1864.

4. *Daily Telegraph* (London), May 12, p. 5.

5. *Letters,* 1:250.

6. *Letters,* 1:266–67; Rose Trollope's MS reminiscences, University of Illinois Library.

7. Rose Trollope's MS reminiscences; *Letters,* 1:279, 285.

8. *William Allingham's Diary,* ed. G. Grigson (Fonthill, Sussex: Centaur Press, 1967), pp. 106, 342.

9. Amanda Hopkinson, *Julia Margaret Cameron* (London: Virago Press, 1986), pp. viii–x; Helmut Gernsheim, *Julia Margaret Cameron: Her Life and Photographic Work,* 2d ed. (Millerton, N.Y.: Aperture, 1975), p. 125.

10. J. G. Millais, *The Life and Letters of Sir John Everett Millais* (London, 1899), 1:379; Hall, *Trollope and His Illustrators,* p. 89.

11. *Letters,* 1:235, 244, 249, 258; J. G. Millais, *Life and Letters,* 1:379.

12. *Letters,* 2:1006.

13. *Letters,* 1:282.

14. *Letters,* 1:288, 293.

15. F. G. Kitton, *Dickens and His Illustrators* (London, 1899), p. 113.

16. Bodleian, MS. Don. c. 9, fol. 129; *Can You Forgive Her?* chaps. v–vi.

17. *An Autobiography,* p. 180; review in the *Nation* (New York), 1:409 (September 28, 1865).

18. *An Autobiography,* p. 182. Trollope's letter to this dignitary, addressed merely as "Sir," in reply to his protest is printed in *Letters,* 1:316. The clergyman's complaint was dated September 30, 1865, two months after the complete novel had been published (i.e., after the conclusion was no longer in doubt).

19. Trollope's accounts, in his traveling diaries, Princeton University Library.

20. *An Autobiography,* pp. 173–78. Trollope's language habits are the subject of John W. Clark, *The Language and Style of Anthony Trollope* (London: André Deutsch, 1975).

21. Bodleian, MS. Don. c. 9, vol. 132.

22. For the line of parody see FitzGerald's letter to Hallam Tennyson, April 19, 1883, in the latter's *Alfred Lord Tennyson, a Memoir* (London, 1897), 2:276.

23. *Letters,* 1:264. Trollope two years later attacked "Bazaars for Charity" in the *Pall Mall Gazette* for April 21, 1866, p. 12.

24. Bodleian, MS. Don. c. 9, fols. 152–54.

25. *Letters,* 1:287 (Trollope to Smith, December 13, 1864).

26. *Letters,* 1:321.

27. The book edition somehow omitted the final page of the *Cornhill* version of chap. vi, a defect not remedied in most subsequent reprints prior to the Dover Publications (New York) edition of 1977.

Chapter XIII

1. Matthew Arnold, *Complete Prose Works,* ed. R. H. Super (Ann Arbor: University of Michigan Press, 1962), 3:270–71.

2. *Letters,* 1:288–89, 350–51.

3. C. L. Cline, ed., *The Letters of George Meredith* (Oxford: Clarendon Press, 1970), 1:67n; *Westminster Review* 68:595 (October, 1857).

4. *Letters of Meredith,* 1:288.

5. Prospectus published in the *Athenaeum,* March 25, 1865, p. 436. The *Revue* had regular British distribution though a London agent.

6. *An Autobiography,* pp. 189–94; *Letters,* 1:298. The former gives the capital as £9,000, the latter as £8,000. All shares had been sold by the end of March. Trollope gives a similar account of the founding of the journal in his obituary notice, "George Henry Lewes," *Fortnightly Review* 31:21–22 (January, 1879).

7. *Letters,* 1:288–89; *George Eliot Letters,* 4:169, 172–73, 211. Lewes was not a stockholder.

8. *Letters,* 1:304.

9. *Letters,* 1:350–51; *An Autobiography,* p. 190.

10. *Letters,* 1:290–91.

11. Trollope's contributions to the *Pall Mall Gazette* are discussed in Judith Knelman, "Trollope's Journalism," *Library,* 6th ser., 5:140–55 (June, 1983), along with a "Checklist of Trollope's [nonfiction] Journalism." An earlier discussion, with extensive excerpts from the articles, is Bradford A. Booth's "Trollope and the 'Pall Mall Gazette,'" *Nineteenth-Century Fiction* 4:51–69, 137–58 (June–September, 1949). Booth, however, was not able to trace a number of essays identified by Knelman and by Hall in his edition of the *Letters.*

12. J. W. Robertson Scott, *The Story of the Pall Mall Gazette* (London: Oxford University Press, 1950), pp. 135, 129.

13. Trollope's MS travel diaries, end of 1865 and 1866.

14. *Letters,* 1:301–3 (May 9, 11, 1865).

15. *An Autobiography,* pp. 199, 202–3; *Letters,* 1:300–301.

16. Trollope's Zulu letter is published in Ruth apRoberts's edition of his *Clergymen of the Church of England* (Leicester: Leicester University Press, 1974), pp. 51–60.

17. *An Autobiography,* p. 201; [Alford], "Mr. Anthony Trollope and the English Clergy," *Contemporary Review* 2:240–62 (June, 1866).

18. *Saturday Review* 19:563–64 (May 13, 1865); *Pall Mall Gazette,* May 15, 1865, pp. 9–10.

19. J. W. R. Scott, *Story of the Pall Mall Gazette,* p. 137; Greenwood, "Gossip about a Newspaper," *St. James's Gazette,* October 16, 1883, pp. 5–6.

20. *Letters,* 1:290, 331.

21. *D.N.B.,* s.v. Banting; *George Eliot Letters,* 4:170; *The Fixed Period,* chap. ix (published February, 1882).

22. *Letters,* 1:298.

23. Hester Thackeray Ritchie, ed., *Thackeray and His Daughter* (New York: Harper and Brothers, 1924), pp. 137, 252.

24. *Letters,* 1:300, 306, 313; writing calendar for *The Belton Estate,* Bodleian, MS. Don. c. 9, fol. 139; T. A. Trollope, *What I Remember,* 2:357–58, 378–80; 3:29–30. Tom's narrative here makes no mention of Bice's removal to London, and indeed seems not compatible with it, but Tom was writing more than twenty years after the event.

25. *Letters,* 1:305; Post Office Records, Tilley's Private Letter Books, Post 101, vol. 6, p. 14 (May 27, 1865); *Phineas Finn,* chap. liii.

26. *Letters,* 1:310–11; Mildred Howells, ed., *Life in Letters of William Dean Howells* (Garden City, N.Y.: Doubleday Doran and Co., 1928), 1:93–94; Howells, *My Literary Passions* (New York, 1895), p. 219.

27. Howells, *Criticism and Fiction* (New York, 1891), end of sec. xv; *My Literary Passions,* p. 247.

28. December 2, p. 6, col. 6.

29. *Letters,* 1:318; "The Fourth Commandment" (signed), *Fortnightly Review* 35:529–38 (January 15, 1866); "An Amateur Theologian" (anonymous), *Saturday Review,* February 3, 1866, pp. 131–33; letter to the editor (signed), *Pall Mall Gazette,* February 5, 1866, p. 3.

30. Original in the library of the University of Illinois, Urbana-Champaign.

31. Rose Trollope's reminiscences in the library of the University of Illinois; *An Autobiography,* p. 326; *Letters,* 1:315. Rose calls Pigott only by his last name, but he is presumably the one with whom Trollope frequently corresponded.

32. Bodleian, MS. Don. c. 9, fol. 173.

33. *Letters,* 1:317.

34. *Letters,* 1:313–15, 339–41; Trollope's MS traveling accounts for 1866; Bodleian, MS. Don. c. 10*, fols. 60–61. The £2,000 was paid on October 1.

35. Advertisements in the *Bookseller,* especially those of June 30, 1866, pp. 584, 628; July 31, 1866, p. 644; July 4, 1881, p. 621, and August 4, 1881, p. 738.

36. *Travelling Sketches* (1866), pp. 101–2.

37. *An Autobiography,* p. 196; *Letters,* 1:324.

38. Thomas Carlyle, *Letters and Memorials of Jane Welsh Carlyle,* ed. J. A. Froude (New York, 1883), 2:277; Thurman L. Hood, ed., *Letters of Robert Browning* (New Haven: Yale University Press, 1933), p. 91.

39. *Letters,* 1:320n.

40. *Letters of Meredith,* 1:316.

41. *Letters,* 1:337n.

42. *An Autobiography,* p. 204; *Spectator,* March 23, 1867, p. 329.

43. *Letters,* 1:334–35, 357–58; Bodleian, MS. Don. c. 9, fols. 166–71, 179.

Chapter XIV

1. *Letters,* 1:110, 147, 262, 300, 303, 321. In a footnote on 1:321, Hall quotes Lady Rose Fane's description of the house party from a letter to her mother preserved in the Weigall MSS, Kent County Archives.

2. T. Wemyss Reid, *The Life, Letters, and Friendships of Richard Monckton Milnes, First Lord Houghton* (London, 1890), 2:182; Trollope, *Letters,* 1:319; Augustus J. C. Hare, *The Story of My Life* (London, 1896, 1900), 5:16. Hare's meeting with Rose took place on May 17, 1877.

3. *Letters,* 1:336, 363, 342.

4. Locker-Lampson, *My Confidences* (London, 1896), p. 332. The manuscript of *Small House* is now at the Henry E. Huntington Library, San Marino, California.

5. R. B. Martin, *Tennyson: The Unquiet Heart* (New York: Oxford University Press, 1980), p. 457.

6. *Letters,* 1:334–35; Edward C. McAleer, ed., *Dearest Isa: Robert Browning's*

Letters to Isa Blagden (Austin: University of Texas Press, 1951), p. 231. The story that William Allingham tells in his diary for May 26, 1868, that Browning had offered the plot of the Roman Murder Case (*The Ring and the Book*) "to A. Trollope to turn into a novel, but T. couldn't manage it" has an element of improbability in that Browning knew Tom Trollope much better and much earlier than he knew Anthony, and the plot is closer to the sort of novel Tom wrote than the kind Anthony wrote.

7. Barry A. Bartrum, "A Victorian Political Hostess: The Engagement Book of Lady Stanley of Alderley," *Princeton University Library Chronicle* 36:138–39, 143 (Winter, 1975); Bertrand and Patricia Russell, *The Amberley Papers* (New York: W. W. Norton and Co., 1937), 2:27; A. Trollope, "What It Is to Be a Statesman" (anonymous), *Pall Mall Gazette,* July 18, 1866, pp. 3–4; A. Trollope, *Letters,* 1:343–44. The party described took place on April 8, 1867, but Trollope had also been at the Amberleys' early in July, 1866.

8. *Letters,* 1:326; *Times,* February 10, 1866, p. 12, col. 1.

9. Post Office Records, "Committee of Enquiry into Inadequate Payment of Staff & Lack of Accommodation," Post 30/148 4801/1861.

10. Post Office Records, English Minutes, Post 35, vol. 251, nos. 1619, 1952.

11. Post Office Records, English Minutes, Post 35, vol. 252, nos. 2498, 2796, 2892; vol. 253, no. 3239; Tilley's Private Letter Books, Post 101, vol. 8, pp. 133–35, 137; vol. 9, p. 141.

12. Post Office Records, English Minutes, Post 35, vol. 253, nos. 3242, 3282; vol. 254, no. 4041; Tilley's Private Letter Books, Post 101, vol. 8, pp. 148, 154. There is a printed schedule of salaries dated February 15, 1867, in the bundle of documents on the Reorganization of the London Post Office, Post 30/184 E2987/1868.

13. *Letters,* 1:327–29, 221–32, 364, 382–83; Mary Hamer, "Working Diary for *The Last Chronicle of Barset,*" *Times Literary Supplement* (London), December 24, 1971, p. 1606; Bodleian, MS. Don. c. 9, fols. 149–62.

14. *An Autobiography,* p. 371. The early reviews are quoted in advertisements printed in part 5 of the novel.

15. *Letters,* 1:405, 407.

16. *Letters,* 1:333, 347–48, 350, 352, 355.

17. *An Autobiography,* p. 275.

18. *An Autobiography,* p. 274.

19. The name "Clutterbuck" appears in *The Book of Snobs,* xxv.

20. *An Autobiography,* pp. 178–79.

21. *An Autobiography,* p. 274.

22. *An Autobiography,* p. 276; *Letters,* 1:465, 474. The play was reprinted in 1952 in an edition of 1,000 copies by the Princeton University Library, which owns the earlier printed copy that once belonged to Henry Merivale Trollope. For this edition Robert H. Taylor wrote the introduction.

23. *Letters,* 1:353, 352; Rose Trollope's MS reminiscences; T. A. Trollope, *What I Remember,* 3:41; 2:126; Ada Nisbet, *Dickens and Ellen Ternan* (Berkeley and Los Angeles: University of California Press, 1952), p. 49.

24. Alfred Austin, *Autobiography* (London: Macmillan and Co., 1910), 1:166, 180, 209, 211–12.

25. *Letters,* 1:353.

26. *Letters,* 1:353–54, 359–60, 364, 381; [John Morley and Mrs. Humphry Ward], "Anthony Trollope," *Macmillan's Magazine* 49:56 (November, 1883).

27. *An Autobiography,* pp. 190, 194.

28. *Fortnightly Review* 7:252–55 (February, 1867).

Chapter XV

1. Bodleian, MS. Don. c. 10*, fols. 27a, 27b, 28.

2. Bodleian, MS. Don. c. 9, fols. 175–76.

3. *Letters,* 1:157, 230.

4. Authoritative studies of Virtue's firm have been made by Patricia Thomas Srebrnik, "Trollope, James Virtue, and *Saint Pauls Magazine,*" *Nineteenth-Century Fiction* 37:433–63 (December, 1982), and by Judith Wittosch Malcolm, *Trollope's "Saint Pauls Magazine"* (Ann Arbor: University Microfilms International, 1984). The account given in Michael Sadleir's *Commentary* is entirely fiction ("Virtue . . . had hardly been a book-publisher at all before he started *St. Paul's*. . . . Realising that his publishing ambitions were costing him too dearly to be longer endured, he sold his general business and his magazine to Strahan and, cutting his losses, retired to the old safety of his printing and engraving."— pp. 299–300). Unfortunately, John Sutherland, relying on the only authority then available in print, repeated and elaborated on Sadleir's fictions: "Trollope and *St. Paul's* 1866–70," in *Anthony Trollope,* ed. Tony Bareham (New York: Barnes and Noble, 1980), pp. 116–37.

5. *An Autobiography,* p. 284.

6. Bodleian, MS. Don. c. 10*, fols. 1–2.

7. Bodleian, MSS. Don. c. 10*, fols. 3–4; Don. c. 9, fols. 187–88.

8. Bodleian, MSS. Don. c. 10*, fols. 5–12; Don. c. 9, fols. 183–86.

9. After the letter of April 19; *Letters,* 1:378.

10. *Letters,* 1:368–69; *What I Remember,* 1:71.

11. *Letters,* 1:377.

12. *Letters,* 1:379; Escott, *Trollope,* p. 307.

13. *Letters,* 1:380; Super, "Trollope at the Royal Literary Fund," pp. 318, 323–24.

14. *Letters,* 1:379, 476.

15. Charles Dickens, *Letters,* ed. W. Dexter (London: Nonesuch Press, 1938), 3:100.

16. *Edmund Yates: His Recollections and Experiences* (London: 1884), 2:161.

17. *Letters,* 1:394, 397; [Charles Kent], *The Charles Dickens Dinner* (London, 1867), pp. 3–4, 23–25 (the speech transcribed "from special shorthand notes").

18. *Times,* May 6, 1867, p. 6, col. 5.

19. *Letters,* 1:375, 384–85, 382; Bodleian, MS. Don. c. 9, fols. 179–80.

20. *Letters,* 1:387–90, 406–8.

21. Curtis, ed., *Correspondence of Motley,* 1:265.

22. *Letters,* 1:381–82, 384, 386; Rose Trollope's MS reminiscences; Bodleian, MS. Don. c. 9, fol. 180.

23. Yates, *Recollections,* 2:230–31.

24. Post Office Records, "Surveyors' Districts Rearrangement," Post 30/172 E 1913/1866.

25. *An Autobiography,* pp. 278–79.

26. Post Office Records, English Minutes, Post 35, vol. 263, no. 4206 and vol. 222, no. 3113; Tilley's Private Letter Books, Post 101, vol. 9, pp. 163, 176; *An Autobiography,* pp. 277–81; Bodleian, MS. Don. c. 10*, fols. 7–8 (Trollope to James Virtue, December 14, 1866); Escott, *Trollope,* p. 257, taken in conjunction with the figure mentioned by Sadleir, *Commentary,* p. 272, and Trollope's entry at the end of his travel diary for 1868: "Editing St Pauls £750." Tilley's formal official letter, sent with the Duke's assent, is in the Parrish Collection, Princeton University; *Letters,* 1:392.

27. Photostat in the Post Office Records of a memorandum in Trollope's hand dated October 10, 1867.

28. *World,* no. 921:19 (February 24, 1892).

29. *Times,* November 2, 1867, p. 9, col. 6; *Spectator* 40:1219 (November 2, 1867).

30. *Letters,* 2:773–74 (April 18, 1878); *Who Was Who, 1897–1916,* s.v. Tilley; obituary in *Times,* March 19, 1898, p. 7, col. 6.

31. *Letters,* 1:361–62, 373; *An Autobiography,* p. 317.

32. *Letters,* 1:382–83.

33. *He Knew He Was Right,* ed. P. D. Edwards (St. Lucia: University of Queensland Press, 1974), notes (on p. 31 of appendix) to chaps. lxi and lxii; *Letters,* 1:446–47 (for *The Vicar of Bullhampton*); *An Autobiography,* p. 116n (for *The Eustace Diamonds*); Bodleian, MS. Don. c. 10, fol. 8 (for *Lady Anna*).

34. *An Autobiography,* p. 271; *Letters,* 1:306–7.

35. Reprinted in *Letters,* 1:468.

36. *Fortnightly Review* 4:510–12 (April 1, 1866).

37. *Letters,* 2:692–93 (June 15, 1876). The most satisfying discussion of the problem is by J. W. Dinwiddy, "Who's Who in Trollope's Political Novels," *Nineteenth-Century Fiction* 22:31–46 (June, 1967). Trollope in *An Autobiography* (p. 221) accuses Disraeli of teaching the doctrines of Cagliostro and in *Phineas Redux* lets Monk refer to Daubeny as "a political Cagliostro" (chap. xxxix). Daubeny's character is much more fully developed in *Phineas Redux* than in *Phineas Finn.* A number of critics who attempt to find historical parallels to Trollope's characters take as their focal point the date of publication of *Phineas Finn* as a novel, whereas any historical events subsequent to its date of composition nearly two years earlier must be ruled out.

Chapter XVI

1. *An Autobiography,* p. 284.

2. I include one novel of which this statement is not strictly true: *The Vicar of*

Bullhampton was sold to Bradbury and Evans for *Once a Week,* but they disposed of that journal before the novel began its run. Trollope declined to allow them to publish it in their *Gentleman's Magazine,* and so they brought it out first in parts, then as a book. *Sir Harry Hotspur of Humblethwaite,* published serially in *Macmillan's Magazine,* appeared as a book from Hurst and Blackett; I do not know what their relation to the house of Macmillan was. Tinsley Brothers, who published the book edition of *The Golden Lion* after its serialization in Strahan's *Good Word,* were closely associated financially with both Virtue and Strahan.

3. *The Wellesley Index to Victorian Periodicals 1824–1900* (Toronto: University of Toronto Press, 1966–79), 1:322 and 3:387 n. 8; 3:387; 2:176; *The Life and Adventures of George Augustus Sala,* Written by Himself (New York, 1895), 1:358; John Sutherland, "*Cornhill's* Sales and Payments: the First Decade," *Victorian Periodicals Review* 19:106–8 (fall, 1986).

4. Advertisements in the *Athenaeum* for July 27, 1867, p. 101; August 24, p. 229; September 7, p. 327; *Letters,* 1:358.

5. Arnold's MS diary-notebooks in the Yale University Library, and Matthew Arnold, *Letters,* ed. G. W. E. Russell (London, 1895), 1:195 (June 16, 1863).

6. A. Trollope, *Letters,* 1:424.

7. Her *George Canterbury's Will* was drawing to a close in *Tinsley's Magazine* when her *Bessy Rane* started in *The Argosy.*—advertisements in the *Athenaeum,* February 5, 1870, p. 210 and January 29, 1870, p. 173.

8. W. E. Houghton, after listing five other magazines of the sixties "written . . . for the comfortable, literate, but ill-educated middle-class which read magazines for pure entertainment and easy instruction," went on: "*Temple Bar,* I think, is the best representative of this type of journalism in the sixties. The *Cornhill* and *Saint Pauls* are in another class."—*Wellesley Index to Victorian Periodicals 1824–1900,* 3:387.

9. The author of one essay in the first number was named in the advertisements, but not in the magazine: Henry O'Neil, A.R.A., who contributed an article on "Taste." Of course there was "An Introductory Paper" signed by "the Editor." Thereafter, as Trollope told one contributor, Frederick Locker, "We don't print names, but will print the F.L."—*Letters,* 1:415 (February 24, 1868).

10. *Fortnightly Review* 3:510 (April 1, 1866).

11. Among Trollope's papers in the Bodleian Library, Oxford (MS. Don. c. 10*, fols. 20–21) are two sheets on which he has recorded the names of the contributors and the payments made to them for each number of *St. Pauls* through July, 1869 (when Strahan took over the arrangements). He does not indicate the names of the articles or poems, and so the editors of the *Wellesley Index to Victorian Periodicals* have had to infer who wrote what from the lengths of the articles (with reference to the rate of pay) and from other evidence. The *Wellesley Index* does not list poems. Further identifications of Trollope's contributions are made in Judith Knelman, "Trollope's Journalism," *Library* (London), 6th ser., 5:140–55 (June, 1983).

12. *An Autobiography,* pp. 191–92.

13. *Letters,* 1:371. Virtue's letter, forwarded with this note, has not survived.

14. *Letters,* 1:385, 391, 395.

15. *Letters,* 1:387.

16. March 15, p. 6, col. 6. See also *Letters,* 2:606n.

17. Bodleian, MS. Don. c. 9, fols. 245–46.

18. *Athenaeum,* October 19, 1867, p. 508, col. 3; "Trade and Literary Gossip," *Bookseller,* September 30, 1867, p. 681; *Spectator,* October 5, 1867, pp. 1120–21.

19. *Letters,* 1:212.

20. A careful study of Trollope's editorial relations with Dobson, based on Dobson manuscripts in the Sterling Library, University of London, is Elizabeth R. Epperley, "Trollope and the Young Austin Dobson," *Victorian Periodicals Review* 19:90–99 (fall, 1986).

21. The editors of the *Wellesley Index* used Hutton's and Leakey's applications to the Royal Literary Fund as the means of identifying their authorship of the articles in *Saint Pauls.* For Shew, see R. H. Super, "Trollope at the Royal Literary Fund," p. 323.

22. Bodleian, MS. Don. c. 9, fols. 190–92. The *Publishers' Circular* inferred that Trollope's experiment with sixpenny numbers for *Last Chronicle* must have been successful, or he would not have repeated it; here, however, the publisher hedged by offering monthly parts as well.—31:563–64, 642–43 (October 1 and November 2, 1868).

23. Michael Sadleir has deduced from marginal memoranda in Virtue's own copy of the part issues of *He Knew He Was Right* that Stone received about £500 for his illustrations and that the engraver was paid about £150.—*Trollope: A Bibliography* (Folkestone, Kent: William Dawson and Sons, 1977), p. 293. Virtue, as publisher of the *Art Journal,* was a specialist in printing book illustrations and indeed developed a large secondary market through the sale of used engraved plates.

24. *Letters,* 1:477–78; 2:540–42; 1:488; Bodleian, MS. Don. c. 9, fols. 239–46; *Personal Reminiscences of Sir Frederick Pollock* (London, 1887), 2:151.

25. Cuthbert Bede, "Some Recollections of Mr. Anthony Trollope," *Graphic* 26:707 (December 23, 1882). For the hunting journey and the visit to Sir John Trollope, see *Letters,* 1:411–13, 422. An instance of a very full and sympathetic rejection of a young woman's first novel is Trollope's letter to Sir Henry Taylor on August 10, 1868.—*Letters,* 1:443–44.

26. "Fourteenth Report of the Postmaster General," House of Commons, *Sessional Papers,* 1867–68, vol. 22:733–34; "Postal Conventions (England and America)," *Sessional Papers,* 1868–69, vol. 34:437, 441, etc.; "Reports from the Select Committee on Mail Contracts," *Sessional Papers,* 1868–69, vol. 6:363, 376–77; Post Office Records, Minuted Documents, Post 29/152 Packet 949T/1868. Trollope, *Letters,* 1:416, 425, 427–28, 435–36; there are, also, in Post Office Records, Packet 949T/1868, a formal report from him on May 18, a letter on May 26, a telegram, two letters, and three sheets of memoranda on July 3, a telegram of July 11, and a letter of July 12. His statement of expenses is dated at the General Post Office, July 27, and there is a printed copy of the 1867 agreement with amendments in Trollope's hand, initialed by Randall on July 11.

27. Post Office Records, Tilley's Private Letter Books, Post 101, vol. 10, p. 8; vol. 9, pp. 174–75 for F. Hill's economic doctrine. For the levée, *Times,* March 18, 1868, p. 5, col. 3.

28. Tilley's Private Letter Books, Post 101, vol. 10, pp. 124, 134.

29. *Letters,* 1:432–33; *South Africa* (1878), 1:121. Charles Sumner, Republican senator from Massachusetts, was one of the most vigorous proponents of Johnson's impeachment; hence (and the sound of his name) his coupling with "politics" in Trollope's verse.

30. *Letters,* 1:438, 432.

31. The Duke's remark is among the Post Office Records, Minuted Documents, Post 29/152 Packet 949T/1868.

32. *Letters,* 1:437–38.

33. *An Autobiography,* p. 308.

34. *Transactions of the National Association for the Promotion of Social Science,* Manchester Meeting, 1866 (London, 1867), pp. 119–25; *Times,* October 5, 1866, p. 10, cols. 4–6; *Athenaeum,* October 13, 1866, pp. 467–68; *Publishers' Circular* 30:92 (February 15, 1867). See *Letters,* 1:350, 352.

35. James T. Fields, *Yesterdays with Authors,* p. 186; Lilian Whiting, *Kate Field, a Record* (Boston, 1899), p. 182; Trollope, "Charles Dickens," *Saint Pauls Magazine* 6:371 (July, 1870).

36. Whiting, *Kate Field,* p. 183. Whiting's dates do not fit with the evidence of Trollope's letters, and she refers to "Sunday, May 26," whereas April 26, not May 26, was a Sunday. Whiting also has Kate record a visit from Trollope in New York on June 6, but Trollope's travel diaries show that he left Washington for New York on June 7.

37. *Letters,* 1:426.

38. *Letters,* 1:428, 437; *Evening Transcript,* June 16, 1868.

39. *Letters,* 1:429–31, 432, 438.

40. *Letters,* 1:432–33, 437–39, 449, 509; Whiting, *Kate Field,* p. 183. Kate's eyes must indeed have been striking. In 1868 Isa Blagden wrote to her from Florence: "Is there no chance of your coming this way again? . . . I should like to see your dauntless blue eyes and white throat again. God bless you."— Edward C. McAleer, "Isa Blagden to Kate Field," *Boston Public Library Quarterly* 3:217 (July, 1951). The portrait Trollope requested is published in *Letters,* 1:163.

Chapter XVII

1. *Letters,* 1:440–41, 448.

2. *Letters,* 1:440–41, 445, 410–11, 418–19; C. L. Cline, ed., *The Letters of George Meredith* (Oxford: Clarendon Press, 1970), 1:303.

3. *Letters,* 1:447, 449; *Personal Reminiscences of Sir Frederick Pollock* (London, 1887), 2:164–65.

4. *Letters,* 1:441. If, as seems certain, the expression "among the pictures" alludes to the Royal Academy exhibition, Trollope may have gained admission while the pictures were being taken down, for the exhibition closed on Saturday, July 25, the day of his arrival in Liverpool.

5. A. K. H. Boyd, *Twenty-five Years of St. Andrews* (London, 1892), 1:100–101.

6. He protested vigorously against the deprivation, for example in "The Civil Service as a Profession," *Cornhill Magazine* 3:227–28 (February, 1861).

7. *Letters,* 1:402.

8. *Letters,* 1:454, 415.

9. House of Commons, *Sessional Papers,* 1868–69, vol. 50:13, 109.

10. Detailed accounts of the election, drawn from newspapers and local archives, are given by Lance O. Tingay, "Trollope and the Beverley Election," *Nineteenth-Century Fiction* 5:23–37 (June, 1950); Arthur Pollard, *Trollope's Political Novels* (Hull: University of Hull, 1968), pp. 3–13 and frontispiece; and John Halperin, *Trollope and Politics* (London: Macmillan, 1977), pp. 112–26. See also facsimiles in *An Autobiography,* pp. 303–4, and in Pope-Hennessy, *Trollope,* p. 258.

11. *The Duke's Children,* chap. lv.

12. "In and Out of Society," *Life* (London) 5:1037 (December 14, 1882). I have not been able to establish the precise date of this appearance. For Frances Trollope on the ballot, letter to Julia Pertz, February 18, 1833, in Houghton Library, Harvard University.

13. "Minutes of the Evidence Taken at the Trial of the Beverley Election Petition," House of Commons, *Sessional Papers,* 1868–69, vol. 48:415–523.

14. House of Commons, *Sessional Papers,* 1870, all of vol. 39; vol. 56:175, 177; vol. 1:165–69.

15. House of Commons, *Sessional Papers,* 1870, vol. 29:250–51; 1868–69, vol. 50:13, 60.

16. "It had seemed to me that nothing could be worse, nothing more unpatriotic, nothing more absolutely opposed to the system of representative government, than the time-honoured practices of the borough of Beverley. It had come to pass that political cleanliness was odious to the citizens. . . . To have assisted in putting an end to this, even in one town, was to a certain extent a satisfaction."—*An Autobiography,* p. 306; see also pp. 298–300. Electioneering characters in Trollope's novels received the same warning he said had been given to him. Sir Thomas Underwood was told at Percycross, "You'll spend a thousand pounds in the election. You won't get in, of course, but you'll petition. That'll be another thousand. You'll succeed there, and disfranchise the borough. It will be a great career, and no doubt you'll find it satisfactory. You mustn't show yourself in Percycross afterwards;—that's all."—*Ralph the Heir,* chap. xx. And Phineas Finn was told at Tankerville in Durham, "There isn't a borough in England more sure to return a Liberal than Tankerville if left to itself. And yet that lump of a legislator has sat there as a Tory for the last dozen years by dint of money and brass. . . . He will be elected. You'll petition. He'll lose his seat. There will be a commission. And then the borough will be disfranchised. It's a fine career, but expensive; and then there is no reward beyond the self-satisfaction arising from a good action."—*Phineas Redux,* chap. l.

17. *Letters,* 1:454.

18. T. A. Trollope, *What I Remember,* 2:127–29.

19. *Life of Cicero,* 1:130.

20. James Bryce, *Studies in Contemporary Biography* (New York: Macmillan, 1903), p. 121.

21. Because payments for Mrs. Oliphant's novel were arranged by Virtue, Trollope has left no record of them.

22. *Letters,* 1:456–57.

23. *Letters,* 1:468.

24. Advertisements, *Athenaeum,* June 20, 1868, p. 847; November 28, p. 700; December 26, p. 868; January 2, 1869, p. 4.

25. Bodleian, MS. Don. c. 9, fols. 248–51.

26. William E. Buckler, "E. S. Dallas's Appointment as Editor of 'Once a Week,'" *Notes and Queries* 195:279–80 (June 24, 1950).

27. *Letters,* 1:412, 414, 460–61; Bodleian, MS. Don. c. 9, fols. 209–22.

28. *Letters,* 1:466; *An Autobiography,* pp. 326–28.

29. Advertisement, *Athenaeum,* April 17, 1869, p. 548.

30. *Athenaeum,* July 3, 1869, p. 30; August 7, p. 188; *Bookseller,* August 3, 1869, p. 633.

31. *Athenaeum,* April 9, 1870, p. 484; *Bookseller,* May 2, p. 424.

32. Bodleian, MS. Don. c. 9, fol. 212v records "Reduced by agreement." It has been said that the reduction was made because the *Vicar* turned out "a little short," but in fact the length is precisely that of *The Claverings.* Probably Trollope made the concession as a compromise when the book could not appear in the periodical.—*Letters,* 1:414n, 520; Sadleir, *Bibliography,* p. 295.

33. *Saint Pauls* 4:466–81, attributed in the *Wellesley Index.*

34. *An Autobiography,* p. 322.

35. *An Essay on Comedy,* ed. Lane Cooper (New York: Charles Scribner's Sons, 1918), p. 133 (three-fourths through).

36. P. D. Edwards points out such echoes in the notes to his edition, chaps. xxxviii, lx, xcii.

37. *Letters,* 1:509.

38. Bodleian, MS. Don. c. 9, fol. 221.

39. *Letters,* 1:459.

40. Published in Morris L. Parrish, ed., *Four Lectures by Anthony Trollope* (London: Constable, 1938).

41. *Letters,* 1:456.

42. *Letters,* 1:464–65; Bodleian, MS. Don. c. 9, fols. 227–30. During the negotiations Trollope told Macmillan, "It will be for you to make what arrangements you please in America,—the foreign copyright being yours." Harper and Brothers later claimed to have paid Trollope £700 for this novel; if their statement is true, the net cost to Macmillan was a mere £50.—J. Henry Harper, *The House of Harper* (New York: Harper and Brothers, 1912), p. 114; Trollope, *Letters,* 1:465, and *An Autobiography,* p. 364.

43. *Letters,* 1:532–33.

44. A. O. J. Cockshut, *Anthony Trollope, a Critical Study* (New York: New York University Press, 1968), p. 127.

45. Bradford A. Booth, *Anthony Trollope: Aspects of His Life and Art* (London: Edward Hulton, 1958), p. 216.

46. *Letters,* 1:535, 530.

Chapter XVIII

1. *An Autobiography,* p. 326; Rose Trollope's MS reminiscences; Bodleian, MS. Don. c. 9, fols. 252–53.

2. Joseph Foster, *Men-at-the-Bar* (London, 1885), s.v. Trollope.

3. *Letters,* 1:479–80, 483–84; 2:538–39, 626, 640. A letter of George Meredith's to "My dear Trollope," December 3, 1872, about a manuscript novel, is meant for Henry Trollope, not Anthony as the editor of *The Letters of George Meredith* mistakenly supposes (3:472).

4. Dickens, *Letters,* ed. W. Dexter (London: Nonesuch Press, 1938), 3:716–17; K. J. Fielding, ed., *The Speeches of Charles Dickens* (Oxford: Clarendon Press, 1960), pp. 389–91 (quoting the *Daily Courier*); *Times* (London), April 12, 1869, p. 6, cols. 1–3; Derek Hudson, *Munby: Man of Two Worlds. The Life and Diaries of Arthur J. Munby, 1828–1910* (London: John Murray, 1972), p. 223.

5. Trollope, *Letters,* 1:471.

6. *Pall Mall Gazette,* July 11, 1868, p. 11, quoted by Bradford A. Booth, "Trollope and the 'Pall Mall,'" *Nineteenth-Century Fiction* 4:156–57 (September, 1949).

7. Booth, "Trollope and the Royal Literary Fund," pp. 214–15.

8. *Catalogue of the Library of Louis J. Haber,* pt. 3, December 9–10, 1909 (New York: Anderson Auction Company), item 320; Nigel Cross, *The Common Writer: Life in Nineteenth-Century Grub Street* (Cambridge: Cambridge University Press, 1985), p. 115.

9. My account of the business affairs of Strahan and Virtue depends on Srebrnik's article, "Trollope, James Virtue, and *St. Pauls Magazine.*"

10. Matthew Arnold, *Complete Prose Works* (Ann Arbor: University of Michigan Press, 1972), 8:407.

11. *Letters,* 1:475, 480–81.

12. *Letters,* 1:521–22.

13. Rose Trollope's MS reminiscences.

14. Bodleian, MS. Don. c. 9, fols. 224–25.

15. *Letters,* 1:494–95, 525; Bodleian, MS. Don. c. 10*, fols. 15–18.

16. *Twenty-five Years of St. Andrews,* 1:16.

17. *Spectator,* October 27, 1883, pp. 1373–74.

18. "Anthony Trollope," *Macmillan's Magazine* 49:52 (November, 1883). The article is anonymous, but is authoritatively attributed to Morley and Mrs. Humphry Ward by the *Wellesley Index.*

19. *Edmund Yates: His Recollections and Experiences* (London, 1884), 2:90.

20. *Athenaeum,* February 6, 1869, p. 212.

21. *Wellesley Index,* 2:176; 3:387 n. 8; *Athenaeum,* January 6, 1872, p. 5; *An Autobiography,* p. 288.

22. *Letters,* 1:522, 498.

23. The *Wellesley Index* attributes to him "Mr. Disraeli and the Dukes" (no. 271). "Our Rulers, as Described by One of Themselves" (no. 295) is designated as Trollope's in the advertisements for the November, 1870, number and the attribution can be confirmed on stylistic grounds.

24. Patricia Thomas Srebrnik, *Alexander Strahan* (Ann Arbor: University of Michigan Press, 1986), p. 233.

25. *An Autobiography,* p. 288.

26. For Anthony's birthday in 1879, his son Henry gave him a copy of the Golden Treasury collection (3d ed., 1878) of Bacon's *Essays,* bound in calf, and Anthony at once wrote marginal comments. In general he thought that there was little in Bacon, though he made interesting observations on nos. 10 (on lust and love), 12 (on Disraeli and the ease with which men are taken in), 18 (on why we travel nowadays), 19 (on imperialism and international policy), and 38 (on man's training his nature, not altering it).—M. Sadleir, "Trollope and Bacon's Essays," *Trollopian* 1:21–34 (summer, 1945).

27. Trollope, *Four Lectures,* p. 105.

28. Sadleir, *Bibliography,* pp. 123–29.

29. *Letters,* 1:483, 491–92, 509.

30. *Letters,* 1:496; *An Autobiography,* p. 101.

31. "Occasional Notes" and "As to the Need of Caesars," *Pall Mall Gazette,* February 7, 1865, p. 2, and March 23, 1865, p. 3 (both anonymous).

32. *An Autobiography,* pp. 338–40; *Letters,* 1:507, 510, 522.

33. *An Autobiography,* pp. 338–39; *Letters,* 1:496, 518.

34. *An Autobiography,* pp. 339–40; H. C. Merivale, *Bar, Stage, and Platform: Autobiographical Memoirs* (London: Chatto and Windus, 1902), p. 96. Trollope refers to his critic merely as "one very old and very learned friend"; H. C. Merivale's *Memoirs* identify him.

35. *Letters,* 1:506.

36. *Blackwood's Edinburgh Magazine,* 116:610–11 (November, 1874); Margaret Oliphant, *Autobiography and Letters* (New York, 1899), p. 246.

37. *Letters,* 1:517.

38. George Bentley, *After Business* (bound MS diaries), vol. 6, at the library of the University of Illinois; privately printed as a pamphlet, 1883.

39. Trollope, "Charles Dickens," *Saint Pauls Magazine* 6:370–75 (July, 1870).

40. Trollope, *Four Lectures,* pp. 133–34. For other versions of this inserted leaf, see pp. 127–29, 138.

41. *Letters,* 1:542; Bodleian, MS. Don. c. 9, fols. 236–37.

42. *Letters,* 1:526–35.

Chapter XIX

1. *Letters,* 1:509–10; 2:543–44.

2. *An Autobiography,* p. 345.

3. *Letters,* 2:5; G. S. Haight, ed., *The George Eliot Letters* (New Haven: Yale University Press, 1955), 5:143–44 (Lewes to Charles Lee Lewes, April 26, 1871); Patrick Waddington, "Turgenev and Trollope: Brief Crossings of Paths," *AUMLA,* no. 42:199–201 (November, 1974); Georgiana Burne-Jones, *Memo-*

rials of Edward Burne-Jones (London: Macmillan and Co., 1904), 2:17; George Leveson Gower, *Years of Content* (London: John Murray, 1940), p. 105.

4. Lionel Stevenson, *Dr. Quicksilver: The Life of Charles Lever* (London: Chapman and Hall, 1939), p. 290; Trollope, *Letters,* 2:657.

5. *Letters,* 2:819 (to W. J. Fitzpatrick). His praise of Lever in *An Autobiography,* pp. 151–52, was written in the mid-seventies in the same tone.

6. Edmund Downey, *Charles Lever: His Life in His Letters* (Edinburgh: Blackwood, 1906), 2:227.

7. Escott, *Anthony Trollope,* p. 280.

8. F. E. Trollope, *Frances Trollope,* 1:299.

9. *Saint Pauls Magazine,* 1:419–24 (January, 1868); *Letters,* 2:537.

10. *An Autobiography,* pp. 341–43.

11. *Letters,* 2:545, 548 (to Fields, April 22, and to Alfred Austin, May 5); Bodleian, MS. Don. c. 10, fols. 9–11.

12. Bodleian, MS. Don. c. 10, fols. 7–8; printed in R. D. McMaster, *Trollope and the Law* (London: Macmillan, 1986), pp. 121–22.

13. *Letters,* 1:450n; 2:589–90.

Chapter XX

1. Trollope, *Australia,* ed. P. D. Edwards and R. B. Joyce (St. Lucia: University of Queensland Press, 1967), p. 718. This well-illustrated, painstaking edition is most helpfully annotated as to Australian history, political institutions, and people. It does not include the New Zealand portion of Trollope's book.

2. *Australia,* pp. 586–87.

3. *Australia,* p. 745.

4. Bodleian, MS. Don. c. 9, fols. 257–58.

5. Appendix I of the Edwards and Joyce edition of *Australia* reconstructs his itinerary. A diary Trollope kept on his Australian tour was torn up and the fragments were mounted in copies of the Blackwell–Shakespeare Head Press edition of *An Autobiography* (Oxford, 1929). More than a hundred of the fragments intended for this purpose proved superfluous and found their way into the Houghton Library, Harvard University, bMS Am 1925.4(25).

6. *Australia,* p. 311.

7. October 21, 1871; quoted by Marcie Muir, *Anthony Trollope in Australia* (Adelaide: Wakefield Press, 1949), p. 33.

8. *Letters,* 2:551; *Australia,* p. 347.

9. *Australia,* pp. 682–83, 124.

10. *Australia,* pp. 406–7, 399n.

11. *Australia,* p. 95n.

12. *Australia,* pp. 117, 505–6n.

13. *Australia,* p. 596. This was Gustavus E. C. Hare, half-brother of W. S. Landor's good friends Francis and Julius Hare. See P. D. Edwards, *Anthony Trollope's Son in Australia* (St. Lucia: University of Queensland Press, 1982), p. 45.

14. *Australia,* pp. 645–46n, 673.

15. *New Zealand,* new ed. (London, 1875), pp. 69, 93, 158.

16. Edwards, *Trollope's Son in Australia,* pp. 24–25, 21.

17. *Australia,* pp. 132, 312; diary fragment, Houghton Library, Harvard University.

18. *Australia,* pp. 740, 750.

19. *Australia,* pp. 736–40; Muir, *Trollope in Australia,* pp. 54–55.

20. *Australia,* pp. 323, 322n.

21. Muir, *Trollope in Australia,* pp. 41–44.

22. *Australia,* pp. 386 and n.

23. *Australia,* pp. 383, 374, 739.

24. *Australia,* pp. 392, 524.

25. Muir, *Trollope in Australia,* p. 48, quoting the *Ballarat Courier* of December 29, 1871; *Australia,* pp. 389, 400, 392.

26. *Australia,* p. 536.

27. *Australia,* p. 531; Muir, *Trollope in Australia,* p.59.

28. *Australia,* p. 582.

29. *Australia,* pp. 597–98.

30. R. H. Super, *Walter Savage Landor* (New York: New York University Press, 1954), pp. 278–79.

31. Muir, *Trollope in Australia.* pp. 68 69, quoting Dircksey C. Cowan, "Trollope in Western Australia—a Candid Friend," *Australasian,* June 8, 1929.

32. *Australia,* pp. 752–56, 321, 384; Edwards, *Trollope's Son in Australia,* p. 5; *Letters,* 2:566; diary fragment, Houghton Library, Harvard University.

33. His manuscript, lacking the first seven chapters on New South Wales, is in the National Library of Australia, Canberra; his writing calendar is Bodleian, MS. Don. c. 9, fols. 259–61.

34. *Letters,* 2:567–68.

35. At about 325,000 words, *Australia and New Zealand* is not so long as *Last Chronicle* (346,000), *He Knew He Was Right* (340,000), and *The Way We Live Now* (380,000). Not surprisingly, the copyright brought him much less than he had received for those novels (£1,250).

36. Bradford A. Booth, "Trollope in California," *Huntington Library Quarterly* 3:118 (October, 1939).

37. *New Zealand* (1875), pp. 34–35, 41–42, 102–3; Macaulay, "Barère's Memoirs," *Edinburgh Review* 79:311 (April, 1844), reprinted in his *Essays,* vol. 5.

38. *New Zealand,* pp. 43–45.

39. *New Zealand,* pp. 127–28, 129, 139–40.

40. *New Zealand,* pp. 152–53.

41. *Letters,* 2:569–70; J. P. Corbett, "Two More Trollope Letters," *Notes and Queries* 225:212–15 (June, 1980).

42. *Letters,* 2:569n, 571; Carleton Green, "Trollope in Hawaii," *Trollopian* 3:398–99 (March, 1949).

43. *An Autobiography,* p. 350; *Letters,* 2:571–72.

44. *An Autobiography,* p. 345.

45. Bodleian, MS. Don. c. 9, fols. 262–63; *Letters,* 2:565, 568–69; *An Autobiography,* p. 345.

46. For his title Reade had picked up the phrase in which Neefit urged Ralph Newton to press his suit on Polly: "Don't let's have any shilly-shallying."—chap. ix; also chap. xlii.

47. Hollingshead, *My Lifetime* (London, 1895), 2:44–45.

48. *Letters,* 2:559.

49. *Times,* April 1, 1872, p. 6, col. 5 (and subsequent advertisements); April 2, p. 3, col. 6; February 11, 1873, p. 11, col. 3. The fullest account of the matter is by Bradford A. Booth, "Trollope, Reade, and 'Shilly-Shally,'" *Trollopian* 1:45–54 (March, 1947) and 2:43–51 (June, 1947).

50. *Letters,* 2:558–59, 561–62; *Pall Mall Gazette,* July 16, 1872, p. 5.

51. *Letters,* 2:1012–13.

52. *Daily Telegraph,* August 6, 1872, p. 3; *Letters,* 2:563.

53. Booth, "Trollope, Reade, and 'Shilly-Shally,'" 1:53–54; also Reade to the editor, *Pall Mall Gazette,* July 25, 1872, p. 5.

54. *Letters,* 2:575.

55. *Times,* February 11, 1873, p. 11, cols. 3–4.

56. *An Autobiography,* pp. 253–56; John Coleman, *Charles Reade as I Knew Him* (London: Trübner and Co., 1903), pp. 325–26.

57. *Letters,* 2:1015. The play apparently was not printed, but the manuscript survives in the library of Princeton University. After the London run, it was performed at Liverpool on July 24.

58. R. H. Super, "Trollope at the Royal Literary Fund," *Nineteenth-Century Fiction* 37:325 (December, 1982); *Letters,* 2:1018.

59. *Letters,* 2:583, 587; Hollingshead, *My Lifetime,* 2:48; Booth, "Trollope, Reade, and 'Shilly-Shally,'" 1:51; Percy Fitzgerald, *The Garrick Club* (London: Elliot Stock, 1904), p. 76.

Chapter XXI

1. Royal Literary Fund, Minutes of the General Committee; *Letters,* 2:574. In a footnote Hall quotes an amusing description of Trollope as house guest on the morning of a hunt.

2. *Letters,* 2:579, 582; *An Autobiography,* pp. 350–51.

3. *Letters,* 2:573, 557–58; Gordon S. Haight, *George Eliot: A Biography* (Oxford: Clarendon Press, 1968), p. 493. Edith Simcox had written a disparaging review of *He Knew He Was Right* for the first number of the *Academy* in 1869, but it was not published (Diderik Roll-Hansen, *The Academy 1869–1879* [Copenhagen: Rosenkilde and Bagger, 1957], p. 192). In 1874 she wrote a light-hearted, somewhat ironic account of the story of *Phineas Redux* by way of review (*Academy,* 5:141–43 [February 7, 1874]).

4. *George Eliot Letters,* 5:357; Trollope, *Letters,* 2:575, 580, 626; Edwards, *Trollope's Son in Australia,* p. 10. Shipping lists in the *Sydney Morning Herald* indicate that Henry arrived on board the *Mooltan* on February 21, 1873, and left on July 12. In her MS autobiographical memoranda for 1873, Rose wrote, immediately after recording the six weeks in Ireland, "Henry came back from Australia."

5. *Letters,* 2:576–77, 580; *An Autobiography,* pp. 348–49.

6. *Letters,* 2:578–82; *An Autobiography,* p. 353.

7. Dated 1874; now in the Forster Collection, Victoria and Albert Museum, London. Virtue had also printed for Trollope a catalogue of his library at Waltham House in 1867; a copy of this catalogue was purchased from Muriel Rose Trollope by Gordon N. Ray and is part of his bequest to the Pierpont Morgan Library in New York City. Very useful studies of these catalogues, with their lists of over 5,000 volumes, are: Lance O. Tingay, "Trollope's Library," *Notes and Queries* 195:476–78 (October 28, 1950); Richard H. Grossman and Andrew Wright, "Anthony Trollope's Libraries," *Nineteenth-Century Fiction* 31:48–64 (June, 1976), and Andrew Wright, "Anthony Trollope as a Reader," in *Two English Novelists: Aphra Behn and Anthony Trollope,* Papers Read at a Clark Library Seminar, May 11, 1974 (Los Angeles: William Andrews Clark Memorial Library, UCLA, 1975), pp. 43–68. (Internal evidence, however, weighs heavily against Wright's acceptance of Sadleir's attribution to Trollope of the essay on the "The Migration of a Library.") Eighty-five volumes from Trollope's library are in the Parrish Collection at the Princeton University Library.—"Anthony Trollope," *Princeton University Library Chronicle* 17:106–7 (winter, 1956).

8. *An Autobiography,* p. 83; John Forster, *Life of Dickens* (London, 1872–74), vol. 2, chap. vii. The illustration is Maclise's sketch of Dickens (with a halo) reading *The Chimes* to a dozen friends on December 2, 1844.

9. *Letters,* 2:585.

10. Bodleian, MS. Don. c. 10, fols. 1–3, 13–14; *Letters,* 2:600.

11. G. S. Layard, *A Great "Punch" Editor, . . . Shirley Brooks* (London: Pitman, 1907), p. 568. The illustration was in chap. xvi of the *Graphic* (August 23, 1873, p. 173). In the book it faces 1:147 (chap. xviii).

12. *Letters,* 2:551.

13. P. 6. "Boys who did not grow so fast as he did got above him at school."—*An Autobiography,* p. 326. Edwards and Joyce indicate in detail the parallels between Harry Heathcote and Fred in *Australia,* pp. 762–63.

14. The copy of the book which Anthony presented to Rose is in the library of the University of Michigan.

15. Bodleian, MS. Don. c. 10, fol. 6.

16. Leslie Ward, *Forty Years of 'Spy,'* (London: Chatto and Windus, 1915), pp. 104–6, with a reproduction of the caricature.

17. *Once a Week,* June 1, 1872, p. 499. This cartoon is reproduced in Pope-Hennessy, *Anthony Trollope,* p. 241; the "Spy" cartoon in color is the frontispiece of Pope-Hennessy's book.

18. Yates, *Recollections and Experiences,* 2:232–33; *An Autobiography,* p. 369.

19. *Letters,* 2:589, 591, 588; Lilian Whiting, *Kate Field: A Record* (Boston, 1899), pp. 306, 311, 315.

20. *Letters,* 2:591, 591n; Bernard de Voto, ed., *Mark Twain in Eruption* (New York: Harper and Brothers, 1941), pp. 332–33.

21. *Letters,* 2:592, 598.

22. Rose Trollope's MS autobiographical reminiscences; *Letters,* 2:595–98.

23. "I am at present laid up from a sprained foot, got from a fall"—presumably in the hunting field.—*Letters,* 2:603.

24. Bert G. Hornback, "Anthony Trollope and the Calendar of 1872: The Chronology of 'The Way We Live Now,'" *Notes and Queries* 208:454–57 (December, 1963) and P. D. Edwards, "The Chronology of 'The Way We Live Now,'" *Notes and Queries* 214:214–16 (June, 1969). It might be noted parenthetically that when Trollope wrote a novel, he always had a calendar of the current year before him in the form of the record of his writing progress: his writing calendar showed both day of the week and date.

25. The memoranda in the Bodleian Library, MS. Don. c. 10, fols. 12–22, and the manuscript of the book in the Pierpont Morgan Library have been analyzed by John A. Sutherland, "Trollope at Work on *The Way We Live Now,*" *Nineteenth-Century Fiction* 37:472–93 (December, 1982), a study which significantly corrects details in Sutherland's preface and appendix to the World's Classics edition of the novel (Oxford, 1982). What I have called the "final list" consists of a hundred chapter titles in the published order, grouped into twenty parts; three of these titles were changed in the printed version, but the alteration implied no change in content.

26. *Letters,* 2:602; *Athenaeum,* December 6, 1873, p. 743; December 27, p. 884.

27. *Letters,* 2:592, 598 and n.

28. *Letters,* 2:613.

29. The annotations and the introductory matter in Robert Tracy's edition of *The Way We Live Now* (Indianapolis: Bobbs-Merrill, 1974) provide a wealth of information that enriches the reader's understanding of the novel.

30. *Letters,* 2:766.

31. *Latter-Day Pamphlets,* no. 7, "Hudson's Statue" (July 1, 1850). N. John Hall, in his edition of Trollope's *The New Zealander* (Oxford: Clarendon Press, 1972) calls attention to the way in which Trollope's comments on the society which produced Sadleir foreshadow those in *The Way We Live Now:* "It is not of swindlers and liars that we need live in fear, but of the fact that swindling and lying are gradually becoming not abhorrent to our minds. These vile offences are allowed to assume pseudonyms under which their ugliness is hidden; and thus they show their faces to the world unabashed, and are even proud of their position. Could the career of that wretched man who has lately perished have been possible, had falsehood, dishonesty, pretences, and subterfuges been odious in the eyes of those who came daily in contact with his doings?"—pp. xxxviii, 211.

32. *Times,* March 23, 1872, p. 8, col. 2.

33. Once again Tracy's edition of the novel, with its interesting introduction, deserves praise. An account of Hudson's career may be found in Robert Bernard Martin, *Enter Rumour: Four Early Victorian Scandals* (London: Faber and Faber, 1962), pp. 185–241.

34. *Liverpool Daily Post,* Friday, November 14, 1873, p. 6, col. 3; Frederick G. Blair, "Trollope on Education: An Unpublished Address," *Trollopian* 1:2 (March, 1947). Blair publishes Trollope's lecture from a manuscript in the Athenaeum Library, Liverpool, but it should be noted that this manuscript contains none of Trollope's remarks on novel reading as reported in the *Liverpool Daily Post* and *Daily Courier.* Indeed that aspect of the talk so impressed the *Courier* that it entitled a leading article "Mr. Trollope's Defence of Novels."

35. *An Autobiography,* pp. 110–11. Trollope had not yet begun to write his autobiography when he wrote *The Way We Live Now.*

36. *Letters,* 2:645; see 2:623 and 1:473n.

37. *Times,* August 11, 1875, p. 9, cols. 1–2.

38. *Times,* August 24, 1875, p. 4, col. 4. For attribution, see David Skilton, *Anthony Trollope and His Contemporaries* (London: Longman, 1972), p. 162.

Chapter XXII

1. Layard, *A Great "Punch" Editor,* p. 526.

2. *Letters,* 2:599.

3. *Letters,* 1:525; *Punch* 62:119 (March 23, 1872).

4. *Letters,* 2:620–21.

5. *Letters,* 2:610–12, 614–20; *D.N.B.,* s.v. Brooks. Trollope reported the subscription as about £1,000; Hall says it raised £2,000.—*Letters,* 2:618n, 620.

6. *Punch* 60:103 (March 11, 1871); 66:258 (June 20, 1874); 69:86 (August 28, 1874).

7. Muriel Rose Trollope, "What I Was Told," *Trollopian* 2:233 (MARCH 1948). Her date for the cartoon, 1871, is certainly wrong, however, and I have not found such a cartoon.

8. *Letters,* 1:409n.

9. Bodleian, MS. Don. c. 10, fols. 23–25; *Letters,* 2:633.

10. *Times,* July 8, 1874, p. 5, col. 6; July 22, p. 9, cols. 5–6; Mrs. Oliphant, *Autobiography,* p. 245.

11. *Letters,* 2:611–12, 624–26; Rose Trollope's MS autobiographical notes.

12. R. H. Dana 3d, *Hospitable England in the Seventies: The Diary of a Young American, 1875–76* (Boston: Houghton Mifflin, 1921), pp. 46, 329. The earlier of the two meetings recorded by young Dana cannot have occurred at the Cosmopolitan Club on July 28, 1875, as Dana records, since Trollope was then in Australia.

13. *The New Zealander,* ed. N. John Hall (Oxford: Clarendon Press, 1972), pp. 48–49.

14. *Times,* September 24, 1874, p. 4, col. 5; September 28, p. 5, col. 3; November 27, p. 6, col. 6; December 10, p. 7, col. 6 (all reprinted in *Letters,* 2:627–29, 637, 638–39); *Saturday Review,* September 25, pp. 406–7.

15. *An Autobiography,* p. 294.

16. *An Autobiography,* p. 306.

17. E. C. McAleer, ed., *Learned Lady: Letters from Robert Browning to Mrs. Thomas FitzGerald* (Cambridge, Mass.: Harvard University Press, 1966), p. 32; A. H. and A. B. Terhune, eds., *The Letters of Edward FitzGerald* (Princeton: Princeton University Press, 1980), 4:144. Anthony told the story correctly, with the fox, in *The Life of Cicero* (1880), 1:395. The source is Plutarch's life of Lycurgus, three-fifths through.

18. *An Autobiography,* p. 560n. As the parts issue of the novel was drawing to a close, he wrote to Mary Holmes: "Though I myself am prepared to stand up for the character of the Prime Minister, and for all his surroundings, I acknowledge the story of the soi-disant hero, Lopez, and all that has to do with him, to be

bad," and "The Palliser people . . . [are] (as I think) the best I ever made. The Lopez part of the book has only been to me a shoehorn for the other."—*Letters*, 2:687, 693.

19. Edwards, *Trollope's Son in Australia*, p. 10; *Letters*, 2:642.

20. *Letters*, 2:630–31.

21. *Letters*, 1:434; 2:632; *An Autobiography*, p. 258.

22. *Letters*, 2:642–44, 644n, with a reference to an eye-witness account of the hunting mishap in R. F. Ball and T. Gilbey, *The Essex Foxhounds* (London, 1896), p. 162.

23. *Letters*, 2:647, 676, 689, 946.

24. Rose Trollope's MS autobiographical memoranda; *Letters*, 2:653–54, 642.

25. *Letters*, 2:649. She was author of a practical book on the kindergarten system and (under the *nom de plume* of "Leigh Tempest") of some popular fiction written to make money.

26. *Letters*, 2:650.

27. *Letters*, 2:644–47.

28. Trollope, *The Tireless Traveler*, ed. B. A. Booth (Berkeley: University of California Press, 1941), p. 33.

29. "Popjoy," recorded as late as the eighteenth century, is one of many variants of "Popinjay" that were used as English surnames.

30. *Letters*, 2:623.

31. *Sheffield and Rotherham Independent*, November 27, 1847, p. 6, col. 6.

32. It is tempting to speculate how Trollope hit upon the name of a well-known eighteenth-century military man and politician for his hero, Lord George Germain. There is in Lowick Church (which Trollope and his wife first visited in 1870 as guests of the Reverend W. Lucas Collins) an eighteenth-century tomb with the effigy of Lady Mary Germain (d. 1708), first wife of Sir John Germain, about whom there had been enough scandal to afford Collins's company a good deal of conversation. Sir John's second wife, then widow, Lady Betty Germain, subsequently bequeathed her property to Lord George Sackville on condition that he take the surname of Germain.

33. T.C.D., "Victorian Editors and Victorian Delicacy," *Notes and Queries* 187:251–53 (December 2, 1944), based on a comparison of the version in *All the Year Round* and the (presumably restored) text of the volume edition. Since only two of Trollope's novels have been edited with any attempt at collating the manuscripts and the substantive editions, we must rely on the chance curiosity of antiquarians for observations such as this. But the manuscript of *Is He Popenjoy?* apparently has not survived in any case.

34. Bodleian, MS. Don. c. 10*, fols. 79–82 (with Trollope's record of the dates on which he sent the letters, fols. 83–84); *Letters*, 2:639–40, 649–50, 653, 662.

35. Letter xi. The twenty letters have been collected and published by Bradford A. Booth as *The Tireless Traveler*.

36. *Tireless Traveler*, pp. 195–99.

37. *Letters*, 2:651–53; *Tireless Traveler*, pp. 27–32.

38. *Tireless Traveler*, p. 38; and see I Kings 10:22.

39. *Tireless Traveler*, pp. 70, 68; *Letters*, 2:659.

40. *Tireless Traveler,* pp. 89–90; Muir, *Trollope in Australia,* pp. 93–96.
41. *Letters,* 2:659.
42. Edwards, *Trollope's Son in Australia,* pp. 11–17; Bodleian, MS. Don. c. 10, fol. 32.
43. Muir, *Trollope in Australia,* pp. 96–100.
44. *Tireless Traveler,* p. 221.
45. *Letters,* 2:662–63, 665–67 and nn.
46. *Letters,* 2:608n, 606; "Never, Never,—Never, Never," *Sheets for the Cradle* (Boston), December 6, 8, 10, 1875. A copy is preserved in the Rare Book Department of the Boston Public Library.

Chapter XXIII

1. *Letters,* 2:647, 673, 694; *Athenaeum,* May 6, 1876, p. 634.
2. *Sheffield and Rotherham Independent,* January 3, 1845, p. 5, col. 5.
3. *An Autobiography,* p. 194.
4. *Letters,* 2:701–2.
5. *An Autobiography,* pp. 11–13.
6. *Letters,* 2:667, 673–74, 679–81.
7. He expressed the same idea four months earlier to the same correspondent, G. W. Rusden.—*Letters,* 2:691, 696.
8. *An Autobiography,* p. xxiii. Henry refers to his father's memorandum preserved with the manuscript in the British Library: "An Autobiography — Begun 1 Jany 1876 Finished 11 April 1876."
9. *Letters,* 2:598 and n.
10. Trollope wrote to Rusden about this time: "That doctrine which I broached before you and others at the Garrick as to the expediency of an artist working for money, I have always found it difficult to explain as I would have it explained. You ask me whether I would have willingly written for money any thing which would have been prejudicial to a reader. The same test may be given to a shoemaker. His primary object is a living. But if he be an honest man he will prefer a poor living by good shoes, to a good living by bad shoes. It is the same with the author, and with the lawyer, and the divine—But in each case bread and meat should be the rewards of work."—*Letters,* 2:692.
11. *Letters* 2:551; Alexander Welsh, *From Copyright to Copperfield: The Identity of Dickens* (Cambridge, Mass.: Harvard University Press, 1987), pp. 2–7.
12. *Times,* March 4, 1876, p. 11, col. 3; November 29, p. 6, col. 5. The Quebec Institute was an affiliate of the Society of Arts and of the Science and Art Department, South Kensington.
13. A. Trollope, *The Life of Cicero* (London, 1880), 1:195–96.
14. *Letters,* 2:645–46, 660–61, 689. In July Browning "saw yesterday, in the course of my walks, . . . A. Trollope, who confided to me his profound dislike of 'Deronda.' "—Edward C. McAleer, ed., *Learned Lady: Letters from Robert Browning to Mrs. Thomas FitzGerald, 1876–89* (Cambridge, Mass.: Harvard University Press, 1966), p. 32.
15. G. S. Haight, *George Eliot: A Biography* (Oxford: Clarendon Press, 1968), p. 473.

16. As long ago as 1905 Gamaliel Bradford pointed out the parallels in plot between *The Fixed Period* and *The Old Law*.—"Trollope and the Osler Treatment," *Nation* (New York) 80:458 (June 8, 1905). Most of Trollope's annotated copies of the old plays are now housed in the Folger Library, Washington, D.C., and have been listed in the order in which Trollope read them (with the dates of reading, from November 26, 1866, to August, 1882) by Elizabeth Epperley, "Trollope's Notes on Drama," *Notes and Queries* 229:491–97 (December, 1984). The plays of Beaumont and Fletcher which Trollope read from December 1, 1850, to December 19, 1853, are similarly listed from his copy now in the library of the Shakespeare Institute, Stratford-on-Avon, by Inga-Stina Ekeblad, "Anthony Trollope's Copy of the 1647 Beaumont and Fletcher Folio," *Notes and Queries* 204:153–55 (April, 1959). In 1958, Bradford A. Booth introduced some of these notes into his book on Trollope's art, and announced as forthcoming a collaborative study, with Hugh G. Dick, of Trollope's dramatic criticism.— *Anthony Trollope: Aspects of His Life and Art* (Bloomington: Indiana University Press, 1958), p. xi. Unfortunately both Booth and Dick died prematurely and their work on the dramatic criticism never appeared. Robert Tracy, in his study of *Trollope's Later Novels* (Berkeley, Calif.: University of California Press, 1978), also made appropriate, but brief, use of Trollope's notes. A year later Geoffrey Harvey faced the problem squarely in "Trollope's Debt to the Renaissance Drama" (*Yearbook of English Studies* 9:256–69), tracing five of the novels directly to individual plays. Unfortunately, a reading of the plays with the novels leaves one unconvinced, as Christopher Herbert remarks in *Trollope and Comic Pleasure* (Chicago: University of Chicago Press, 1987), and all Harvey's examples antedate *An Autobiography*. Herbert's own book is very sharp-minded and illuminating, and he too has gone back to Trollope's copies of the plays to see what they reveal. But even his rigorous common sense cannot resist temptation: he finds in a passage about fifty words long in *The Belton Estate* a "nearly verbatim" quotation from *The Taming of the Shrew* (p. 68), though in fact the two passages have scarcely a word in common. Perhaps the subject is altogether intractable; as Booth says, "Scholarship, in its persistent and perhaps wrongheaded attempt to trace sources, often finds influences where only like-mindedness exists" (p. 138).

In January, 1876, Trollope sent his Montagu Square neighbor, young Walter Pollock, some books as a wedding present, including "a great many Elizabethan Plays."—*Letters*, 2:677. After Trollope's death, Pollock wrote a warmly affectionate tribute that is worth reading as showing how attractive Trollope could be to his friends.—"Anthony Trollope," *Harper's New Monthly Magazine* 66:907–12 (May, 1883).

17. *Letters*, 2:691.

18. *An Autobiography*, pp. xxii–xxiii; *Letters*, 2:685–86; N. John Hall, "Letters of Thomas Adolphus Trollope to Henry Merivale Trollope, 1882–92," *Library Chronicle* (University of Pennsylvania) 39:121 (Spring, 1973). The MS is in the library of the University of Illinois.

19. Eleanor C. Smyth, *Sir Rowland Hill: The Story of a Great Reform* (London: T. Fisher Unwin, 1907), p. 278.

20. *An Autobiography*, p. 325.

21. Leveson Gower, *Years of Content, 1858–1886* (London: John Murray, 1940), p. 70; *Letters,* 2:760 (March 6, 1878), 684.

22. *Letters,* 2:659.

23. *Letters,* 2:696, 659n.

24. *Letters,* 2:685; *Times,* May 8, 1876, p. 8, cols. 5–6. It is not clear in what order the names of distinguished guests are listed, but these five names occur together.

25. Lilian Whiting, *Kate Field: A Record* (London, 1899), pp. 339–40; *Athenaeum,* April 29, 1876, pp. 609–10. "In the part of *Volante* [in John Tobin's comedy *The Honeymoon* at the Gaiety Theatre], Miss Mary Keemle [i.e., Kate Field] made her first appearance on the London stage. She is an actress of much intelligence and vivacity, and her performance evinced a genuine feeling for comedy."

26. *Letters,* 1:374n; 2:698. The woman was Frances Minto Elliot, wife of the dean of Bristol and a contributor to Trollope's *St. Pauls Magazine.* "Of all the expressions ever made regarding Kate Field, in life or in death, this sentence of Mr. Trollope . . . most perfectly suggests her brilliant, vivid, yet delicate personality," remarked Kate's biographer.—Whiting, *Kate Field,* p. 573.

27. Hollingshead, *My Lifetime* (London, 1895), 2:54.

28. *An Autobiography,* pp. 312–13.

29. Bodleian, MS. Don. c. 10, fols. 81–82.

30. *Last Chronicle,* chap. lxxxiii.

31. *Letters,* 2:682–83.

32. Bodleian, MS. Don. c. 10, fols. 81–82; *An Autobiography,* p. 161n. See also Chauncey B. Tinker's introduction to the World's Classics edition of the novel (London: Oxford University Press, 1971), pp. v–vi, and Andrew Wright, "Trollope Revises Trollope," in John Halperin, ed., *Trollope Centenary Essays* (London: Macmillan, 1982), pp. 121–29. The manuscript of the novel is in the library of Yale University.

33. *An Autobiography,* pp. 197, 363–64.

34. A. M. and A. B. Terhune, eds., *The Letters of Edward FitzGerald* (Princeton: Princeton University Press, 1980), 4:8.

35. *The Duke's Children,* chap. xxi.

36. *Letters,* 2:696.

37. *Times,* Saturday, December 9, 1876, p. 7, col. 3; Florence E. Hardy, *The Early Life of Thomas Hardy, 1840–1891* (New York: Macmillan Company, 1928), p. 148; Eastern Question Association, *Report of the Proceedings of the National Conference at St. James's Hall, London, December 8, 1876,* pp. 19–21.

38. Henry James, *Letters,* ed. Leon Edel (Cambridge, Mass.: Harvard University Press, 1975), 2:101.

39. Bryce, *Studies in Contemporary Biography* (New York: Macmillan, 1903), pp. 120, 118.

Chapter XXIV

1. *Letters,* 2:705, 707–8, 711; R. H. Super, "Trollope at the Royal Literary Fund," *Nineteenth-Century Fiction* 37:322, 327 (December, 1982).

2. Super, "Trollope at the Royal Literary Fund," p. 327; *Letters*, 2:720–21, 723–35. In the letter of May 18, "engaging" is an editor's misreading for "engrossing."

3. *Times*, February 12, 1877, p. 9, col. 6.

4. Mary Blackwood Porter, *Annals of a Publishing House: John Blackwood* (Edinburgh and London, 1898), p. 409.

5. *Times*, July 13, 1877, p. 11, col. 4, quoting *Athenaeum* of July 7.

6. Henry James, *Letters*, ed. Leon Edel (Cambridge, Mass.: Harvard University Press, 1975), 2:101, 114, 221.

7. *Letters*, 2:725.

8. Bodleian, MS. Don. c. 10, fols. 49–50; *Letters*, 2:719.

9. *Australia*, ed. Edwards and Joyce, pp. 124, 299.

10. Appendix 3 of *Australia* is a very useful discussion by Edwards and Joyce of Trollope's Australian novels.

11. J. B. Seymour, *The Stamps of Great Britain* (London: Royal Philatelic Society, 1934), pt. 1, pp. 31–32.

12. *Letters*, 2:783.

13. Bodleian, MS. Don. c. 10, fol. 49.

14. *Life of Cicero*, 1:270. Ruth apRoberts points to Edith Hamilton's statement that "the gentleman, the English gentleman, who has meant much to many generations, may well have had his beginning in, certainly he was fostered by, the English schoolboys' strenuous drilling in Cicero."—*The Roman Way* (New York: W. W. Norton and Co., 1932), pp. 79–80. Though Cicero was one of Hamilton's principal figures, and though she at least twice mentions Trollope for the "incomparabl[e] . . . view of what mid-Victorian England was like" (pp. viii–ix, 118), she does not mention his *Life of Cicero*. Professor apRoberts's *Trollope: Artist and Moralist* (London: Chatto and Windus, 1971)—a book published by one of Trollope's own publishers—explores with extraordinary sensitivity Trollope's dept to Cicero's view of human nature. Appropriately, she has written the introduction to the 1981 reprint of *The Life of Cicero* (New York: Arno Press).

15. *The Life of Cicero* (1880), 1:1–2.

16. *Dublin University Magazine* 48:30–31 (July, 1856).

17. C. L. Cline, ed., *The Letters of George Meredith* (Oxford: Clarendon Press, 1970), 1:538.

18. 1:24; see also 1:82–83 and 1:130. Trollope made the same remark in *The Duke's Children*.

19. *Letters*, 2:702. He read *The Faerie Queene* aloud at the same time. The set of Latin authors is the *Bibliothèque Latine-Française*, ed. C. L. F. Panckoucke, recently discovered and offered for sale by Bernard Quaritch, Ltd. of London, catalogue no. 1083, item 45 (1987). Mary Ridley of that firm has kindly furnished me with a generous sampling of Trollope's comments and a full record of his dates of reading.

20. *Letters*, 2:869.

21. A letter to his Australian friend, G. W. Rusden, explains his view of his task: "I do not know whether I have ever told you that I also have an opus magnum for my old age. I am writing a Life of Cicero. Middleton is antiquated—Forsyth is dull & written with no feeling as to the great man—A score

of men have taken upon themselves of late to belittle the great patriot: Merivale, Mommsen, Beesley & now Froude."—*Letters,* 2:842.

22. *Letters,* 2:871, 874.

23. *Saturday Review,* February 26, 1881, pp. 279–80; *Athenaeum,* August 6, 1881, pp. 170–71; *St. James's Gazette,* January 7, 1881, pp. 12–13; *Blackwood's Edinburgh Magazine* 129:212 (February, 1881).

24. *Good Words* 18:377–84 (June, 1877); *Good Cheer,* December 25, 1877, reprinted in *Why Frau Frohmann Raised Her Prices and Other Stories.*

25. *Letters,* 2:723.

26. *Letters,* 2:730n, 735, 739, 744, 746. Bianconi's daughter, Mrs. Morgan John O'Connell, not only did not place Henry Trollope's name on the title page, she made no acknowledgment whatsoever of his help, and claimed in her preface that "save where the text will show the interposition of another hand, I have worked out and written all this book myself."—*Charles Bianconi: A Biography, 1786–1873* (London, 1878), p. vi. Nevertheless the publisher paid Henry £50 or £60 for his services. When Mrs. O'Connell, whose husband had been a fellow member of the Garrick Club, asked Trollope if she might properly in her book refer to the Bianconi cars by their popular name, he replied: "Certainly call the cars 'Bians' ['By-anns']. The name became too well known to be slang."— M. O'C. Bianconi and S. J. Watson, *Bianconi, King of the Irish Roads* (Dublin: Allen Figgis, 1962), p. 60.

27. *Letters,* 2:721, 724.

28. *South Africa* (London, 1878), 2:55, 3.

29. *Proceedings of the Royal Colonial Institute* (London) 8:405–7 (1876–77).

30. *Letters,* 2:726. He left the Colonial Institute early in order to meet General Grant, who was celebrating his relief from the American presidency by touring England; "but I did not meet him after all."

31. *Letters,* 2:727–28; Escott, *Trollope,* p. 288; Trollope, *South Africa,* ed. J. B. Davidson (Cape Town: A. A. Balkema, 1973), p. 38. The diary is now in the Parrish Collection, Princeton University Library.

32. Monday, June 18, p. 11, col. 6.

33. *Letters,* 2:734, 779; Robert H. Taylor, "The Trollopes Write to Bentley," *Trollopian* 2:212 (December, 1948).

34. *Letters,* 2:732; *South Africa* (1878), 1:77.

35. *South Africa,* 1:185, 182–83, 198–200; *Letters,* 2:734–35.

36. *South Africa,* 1:16–18, 60–61; 2:186, 332; 1:59, 92–93.

37. Matthew Arnold had his sport with Colenso's literal-minded soberness; see "The Bishop and the Philosopher" (January, 1863), in *Complete Prose Works,* ed. R. H. Super (Ann Arbor: University of Michigan Press, 1963), 3:40–55 and nn. Colenso was a year older than Trollope.

38. Peter Hinchliff, *John William Colenso, Bishop of Natal* (London: Thomas Nelson and Sons, 1964), pp. 29, 140–41; *South Africa,* 1:284–85, 256–59.

39. *Colenso Letters from Natal,* ed. Wyn Rees (Pietermaritzburg: Shuter and Shooter, 1958), pp. 337–38; *South Africa,* 1:290, 292. For Mrs. Colenso's comment on *South Africa* when it was published, see *Colenso Letters,* loc. cit.: "He looks through a pair of government spectacles."

40. *South Africa,* 1:339–40, 165, 298, 74.

41. *South Africa,* 1:342–43, 351–52; 2:4–5.

42. *Letters,* 2:738–39.

43. Haggard, *The Days of My Life* (London: Longmans, Green and Co., 1926), 1:136–37.

44. *South Africa,* 2:112, 116, 119, 129.

45. *South Africa,* 2:125–26, 128–29.

46. *South Africa,* 2:161, 168, 169–81.

47. *South Africa,* 2:188–89.

48. *South Africa,* 2:190. See *North America,* ed. Smalley and Booth, pp. 402–12.

49. *South Africa,* 1:6, 292. See David Skilton, *Anthony Trollope and His Contemporaries* (London: Longman, 1972), p. 162.

50. *South Africa,* 2:328–29.

51. *Letters,* 2:732–33n.

52. *Times* (London), January 4, 1878, p. 7, col. 5.

53. *South Africa,* 2:327; *Letters,* 2:741.

54. *Times,* January 16, 1878, p. 6, col. 5; see also January 17, p. 10, col. 2.

55. *South Africa,* 1:307, 313.

56. *Saturday Review* 45:241–43 (February 23, 1878) (anonymous); *Times,* April 18, 1878, p. 7 (anonymous).

Chapter XXV

1. Mary Blackwood Porter, *Annals of a Publishing House: John Blackwood* (Edinburgh and London, 1898), p. 317; *Letters,* 2:759.

2. House of Commons, *Sessional Papers,* 1878, vol. 24:178, 221–22; *Times,* January 12, 1878, p. 4, col. 6 and January 23, p. 9, col. 6.

3. MS Minutes of the General Committee of the Royal Literary Fund. Arnold referred to Morell a few years later as "that poor Morell who was dismissed," and reviewed a book of his in order to help him: "A 'Friend of God,'" in *Complete Prose Works,* ed. R. H. Super (Ann Arbor: University of Michigan Press, 1977), 11:180–89 and nn.

4. *Letters,* 2:752–53.

5. *Letters,* 2:765, 767–68.

6. R. H. Super, "Trollope at the Royal Literary Fund," *Nineteenth-Century Fiction* 37:322 (December, 1982).

7. Super, "Trollope at the Royal Literary Fund," pp. 324–25; *Letters,* 2:774–76; archives of the Royal Literary Fund.

8. *Letters of Robert Louis Stevenson to His Family and Friends,* ed. Sidney Colvin (London: Methuen and Co., 1901), 1:126; A. M. and A. B. Terhune, eds., *The Letters of Edward FitzGerald* (Princeton: Princeton University Press, 1980), 4:133 (June, 1878).

9. T. H. S. Escott, *Anthony Trollope* (London: John Lane, the Bodley Head, 1913), pp. 150, 158; Yates, *Recollections and Experiences,* p. 232.

10. *Letters,* 2:769–70.

11. A few months later, as Trollope described a young man's wavering between two young women, the waverer reflected, "With Alice how sweet would it be to sit by some brook side and listen to the waters!"—"Alice Dugdale," chap. ii.

12. Bodleian, MS. Don. c. 10, fols. 93–98, 100; Sadleir, *Bibliography,* p. 183.

13. *Letters,* 2:737, 871, 844, 988, 906, 880. Trollope actually repaid £104 17*s.*—Bodleian, MS. Don. c. 10*, fol. 79. His agreement with Charles Dickens junior for publication in *All the Year Round* is in the Houghton Library, Harvard University, bMS. Am 1925.4(26).

14. Bodleian, MS. Don. c. 10*, fols. 40–42; *Waterloo Directory of Victorian Periodicals,* phase I, s.v. "Light."

15. Patricia Thomas Srebrnik, *Alexander Strahan, Victorian Publisher* (Ann Arbor: University of Michigan Press, 1986), pp. 28, 47, 120–21.

16. Bodleian, MS. Don. c. 10*, fols. 36b–37, 34–36a. Sadleir's *Bibliography* is in error in saying that the story appeared in one installment in December, 1877.—p. 185.

17. April 18, 1878.

18. Bodleian, MS. Don. c. 10*, fols. 29–33; *Letters,* 2:793.

19. *Letters,* 2:778; G. S. Haight, ed., *The George Eliot Letters* (New Haven: Yale University Press, 1955), 7:28–29.

20. The will is preserved at Somerset House, London.

21. *Letters,* 2:781n.

22. *Letters,* 2:782–83.

23. *Letters,* 2:852. A copy in the University of Michigan Library carries the bookplate of Edmund Yates, but with no indication whether he procured it from Trollope.

24. *Letters,* 2:779–80.

25. Bodleian, MS. Don. c. 10, fols. 63–67; *Letters,* 2:800.

26. Trollope consulted a lawyer friend on the legal consequences of this lack of provision.—*Letters,* 2:799.

Chapter XXVI

1. *Letters,* 1:285–86.

2. *Letters,* 2:798.

3. Printed in Morris L. Parrish, ed., *Four Lectures by Anthony Trollope* (London: Constable, 1938).

4. *Letters,* 2:761–62, 784, 1018; A. Trollope, *Thackeray* (London, 1879), p. 56.

5. *Letters,* 2:812.

6. A. Trollope, *Thackeray,* pp. 10n, 27. See *Letters,* 2:671, 691.

7. Bodleian, MS. Don. c. 10, fols. 71–73. Trollope has been criticized for inaccuracies in his account—for dating Thackeray's marriage in 1837 instead of 1836, for example (p. 20); the error here, however, was Annie's. An interesting study by Robert A. Colby inclines to be severe whenever Trollope is at all critical of Thackeray, though Trollope's first-hand experience with events may make the critical comments more justifiable than Colby is willing to admit. — "Trollope as Thackerayan," *Dickens Studies Annual* 22:261–77 (1983).

8. *Letters,* 2:813.

9. A. M. and A. B. Terhune, eds., *The Letters of Edward FitzGerald* (Prince-

ton: Princeton University Press, 1980), 4:4; A. Trollope, *Letters,* 2:819; see 2:816, 820, and FitzGerald, *Letters,* 4:491.

10. FitzGerald, *Letters,* 4:182–83, 188; A. Trollope, *Letters,* 2:813.

11. This is the thrust of an article by J. Hillis Miller, "Trollope's *Thackeray,*" *Nineteenth-Century Fiction* 37:350–57 (December, 1982).

12. Such "confidences" are one of the resemblances between Thackeray and Trollope with which I deal in "Trollope's *Vanity Fair,*" *Journal of Narrative Technique* 9:12–20 (Winter, 1979).

13. *Letters,* 2:814. The dinner was Saturday, February 15, 1879, and the poem is Harte's "Plain Language from Truthful James."

14. *Letters,* 2:831.

15. FitzGerald, *Letters,* 4:236. FitzGerald's objection was essentially to what he presumed was the editorial policy of the series: he wanted more about the man, less about the writer.

16. *Literary World* (Boston) 10:279 (August 30, 1879); *Westminster Review* 112:258 (July, 1879; by J. R. Wise); W. H. Pollock, "Anthony Trollope," *Harper's New Monthly Magazine* 66:911–12 (May, 1883).

17. *Pall Mall Gazette,* October 18, 1879, p. 12, quoting Trollope, *Thackeray,* pp. 45, 59; FitzGerald, *Letters,* 4:268.

18. *Letters,* 2:854–55.

19. *Letters,* 2:947; Winifred Gérin, *Anne Thackeray Ritchie, a Biography* (Oxford: Oxford University Press, 1981), p. 193.

20. Arthur Waugh, *A Hundred Years of Publishing, Being the Story of Chapman & Hall, Ltd.* (London: Chapman and Hall, 1930), p. 178.

21. *Letters,* 1:479 (August 13, 1869).

22. *Letters,* 2:626, 640.

23. *Letters,* 2:551, and letters from Frederic Chapman to Trollope, December 28 and 30, 1875, with memorandum of Trollope's dated December 30, 1875, in the library of the University of Illinois.

24. *Letters,* 1:405, 407; 2:760, 763, 770, 835.

25. *Letters,* 2:815.

26. *Letters,* 2:822; see 2:828.

27. Bodleian, MS. Don. c. 10, fols. 104–6.

28. Super, "Trollope at the Royal Literary Fund," pp. 325–27; *Letters,* 2:811, 816–18. The King of the Belgians had been invited to take the chair after Longfellow was unable to do so.—Minutes of the General Committee, July 12 and November 8, 1871.

29. *Letters,* 2:821.

30. "Mr. Freeman on the Morality of Hunting," *Fortnightly Review* 12:618, 625 (December, 1869). Dr. David Arnett has called my attention to Freeman's response to Trollope in the *Daily Telegraph,* December 18, 1869, p. 5, cols. 5–6 and December 29, p. 3, cols. 2–4—a response that occupies more than four full columns. Mill's stepdaughter Helen Taylor entered the debate on Freeman's side in the *Fortnightly* of January 1, 1870 (13:63–68).

31. *Letters,* 2:809, 827, 829; *Good Words,* February, 1879, pp. 98–105, and September, 1879, pp. 595–600.

32. *Marion Fay,* ed. R. H. Super (Ann Arbor: University of Michigan Press, 1982), pp. xxi–xxiii.

33. *Letters,* 2:815.

34. Vineta and Robert A. Colby, *The Equivocal Virtue: Mrs. Oliphant and the Victorian Literary Market* (New York: Archon Books, 1966), p. 123.

35. M. Sadleir, *Trollope: A Commentary,* rev. ed. (New York: Farrar, Straus and Company, 1947), p. 331; C. P. Snow, *Trollope: His Life and Art* (New York: Charles Scribner's Sons, 1975), p. 173.

36. *Letters,* 2:813, 842.

37. "Whist at Our Club," *Blackwood's Edinburgh Magazine* 121:597, 600–601 (May, 1877).

38. *Letters,* 2:834, 836.

39. *Letters,* 2:837, 843.

40. *Marion Fay,* ed. Super, pp. xviii, xxv; *Letters,* 2:886 (December 21, 1880).

41. V. and R. A. Colby, *The Equivocal Virtue,* p. 232.

42. *North American Review* 129:203–22 (September, 1879); *Letters,* 2:852.

43. *Letters,* 2:763.

44. *An Autobiography,* pp. 144–45; *Letters,* 1:96–97n.

45. MS Minutes, General Committee of the Royal Literary Fund, meeting of November 14, 1877; Nigel Cross, ed., *Archives of the Royal Literary Fund* (microfilm), case file no. 2036. See Maurice Bassan, *Hawthorne's Son* (Columbus: Ohio State University Press, 1970), pp. 121–22.

46. *Manhattan* (New York) 2:573–78 (December, 1883); reprinted in J. Hawthorne, *Confessions and Criticisms* (Boston, 1887), pp. 140–62.

47. *Letters,* 2:839, 826; *Nottingham and Midland Counties Daily Express,* October 24, 1879, p. 3, col. 5 (a very full report of the lecture); *Birmingham Daily Post* (October 30, 1879) (a brief account).

48. *Letters,* 2:735, 838, 840, 856–57, 861, 868; V. and R. A. Colby, *The Equivocal Virtue,* pp. 160–161.

49. *Letters,* 2:838 (from Felsenegg, August 29, 1879).

50. *Letters,* 2:846.

51. *An Autobiography,* pp. 42–43; *Letters,* 2:815; Bodleian, MS. Don. c. 10, fols. 133–34.

52. *Letters,* 2:779.

53. *Letters,* 2:872, 906, 914–15n; Bodleian, MS. Don. c. 10, fol. 133.

54. *Letters,* 2:988. See n. 1 to chap. XXVII, below.

55. Quoted from the publisher's advertisement. In 1982 the University of Michigan Press brought out an edition of the novel with its text based on the manuscript in the library of Princeton University, with illustrations from the *Graphic* and a preface by R. H. Super.

Chapter XXVII

1. The price of the cheaper edition, that is, was one-ninth that of the three-volume edition. In the preface to my edition of the novel (1982) I mistakenly dated the first one-volume edition as 1884 (pp. xviii, xxvi); the 1884 and subsequent editions were printed from the same setting of type as the one-volume edition advertised in December, 1882.

2. Guinevere L. Griest, *Mudie's Circulating Library* (Bloomington: Indiana University Press, 1970), p. 208.

3. *Bookseller,* January 3, 1880, p. 4, and April 4, 1881, pp. 349, 319; *Letters,* 2:889, 900; Arthur Waugh, *A Hundred Years of Publishing* (London: Chapman and Hall, 1930), pp. 181–82.

4. *Bookseller,* June 3, 1880, p. 530; *Letters,* 2:905.

5. *Bookseller,* August 3, 1881, p. 683.

6. Waugh, *A Hundred Years of Publishing,* p. 186.

7. *Letters,* 2:867. Waugh (p. 180) says that Trollope "resigned from the Board after one year's service," but Trollope speaks of himself as a director of the company as late as June 12, 1881.—*Letters,* 2:910.

8. The business records of Chapman and Hall have not survived, but John Sutherland draws on those of Chatto and Windus in "The Commercial Success of *The Way We Live Now:* Some New Evidence," *Nineteenth-Century Fiction* 40:460–67 (March, 1986).

9. He made the same announcement to his son Henry—clearly the first intimation of his plan—on April 13.—*Letters,* 2:864, 861.

10. *Letters,* 2:870.

11. *Letters,* 2:870, 874, 888.

12. *Letters,* 2:865, 867, 870, 887–88.

13. *Letters,* 2:870, 875, 878.

14. *Letters,* 2:888.

15. *Guide to the Church of St. Mary and St. Gabriel, Harting* (Harting, 1970); Henry Doddridge Gordon in *Publisher's Circular,* December 18, 1882, pp. 1515–16; *Letters,* 2:888.

16. *Letters,* 2:888.

17. Escott, *Trollope,* pp. 299–301.

18. *Times,* May 3, 1880, pp. 9–10.

19. *Letters,* 2:864–65.

20. *Letters,* 2:863.

21. *Letters,* 2:867.

22. *Letters,* 2:911, 895; *Critic* (New York), January 29, 1881, pp. 3–4; *Saturday Review,* February 26, 1881, pp. 279–80.

23. Bodleian, MS. Don. c. 10; *Letters,* 2:886, 904, 906–7, 910, 971, 949, 952–53, 956.

24. *Letters,* 2:910. The manuscript of the novel with its original language is in the library of the University of Michigan.

25. Trollope's admiration for such curves is the subject of Philip Collins's essay, "Business and Bosoms: Some Trollopian Concerns," *Nineteenth-Century Fiction* 37:293–315 (December, 1982).

26. *Letters,* 2:881.

27. Gordon S. Haight, *George Eliot: A Biography* (Oxford: Clarendon Press, 1968), pp. 537, 546.

28. *Letters,* 2:887.

29. *Letters,* 2:892; Escott, *Trollope,* p. 185. Kate, on the very evening of George Eliot's death, wrote a long essay of reminiscences of her on the invitation of Whitelaw Reid of the *New York Tribune.*—Whiting, *Kate Field,* pp. 395–401.

30. *Letters,* 2:858, 862, 886. See Matthew 24:43–44.

31. *Letters,* 1:409n.

32. An excellent discussion of the novel in the context of its time is David Skilton, *"The Fixed Period:* Anthony Trollope's Novel of 1980," *Studies in the Literary Imagination* 6, no. 2:39–50 (Fall, 1973).

33. My colleague Professor Cecil Eby called my attention to the allusion. Trollope also referred to the "Battle of Dorking" in his life of Palmerston (1882), p. 190.

34. The first time the date is mentioned it is printed as "13th of June," but even here it is "30th of June" in the manuscript in the library of the University of Michigan. Elsewhere the date is uniformly the 30th.

35. *Letters,* 2:886, 908, 923.

36. *Letters,* 2:935. There is a picture of the hotel in C. P. Snow, *Trollope: His Life and Art* (New York: Charles Scribner's Sons, 1975), p. 172.

37. *Letters,* 2:894–95.

38. *Letters,* 2:911.

39. *Mr. Scarborough's Family,* chap. vii.

40. Trollope, "Henry Wadsworth Longfellow," *North American Review* 132:383–406 (April, 1881); correspondence between Trollope and W. C. Bennett in the library of the University of Illinois; *Letters,* 2:981.

41. *Letters,* 2:888–89.

42. *Letters,* 2:906; Bodleian, MS. Don. c. 10, fols. 144–45.

43. Freeman, "Anthony Trollope," *Macmillan's Magazine* 47:236–38 (January, 1883).

44. *Letters,* 2:909.

45. *Letters,* 2:906–8.

46. *Letters,* 2:916.

47. *Letters,* 2:912. Since only this fragment of the letter survives, the date is uncertain.

48. *Letters,* 2:907, 920–22.

49. *Times,* August 19, 1880, p. 1, col. 3.

50. *Letters,* 2:797–98, 853.

51. Henry James, *Letters,* ed. Leon Edel (Cambridge, Mass.: Harvard University Press, 1975), 2:246.

52. Alfred Austin, *Autobiography* (London: Macmillan and Co., 1911), 1:211.

53. *Letters,* 2:888, 917–19.

54. *Letters,* 2:881.

Chapter XXVIII

1. *Letters,* 2:897–98, 922, 930, 910, 923; Bodleian, MS. Don. c. 10*, fol. 43a and Don. c. 10, fols. 113–14.

2. *Letters,* 2:928 (October 5, 1881).

3. Srebrnik, *Alexander Strahan* (Ann Arbor: University of Michigan Press, 1986), pp. 201, 246.

4. *Letters,* 2:922.

5. *Letters,* 2:923, 932, 924, 927.

6. Ralston, "Ivan Sergueyevitch Tourguenief," *Athenaeum,* September 15, 1883, p. 338; Patrick Waddington, "Turgenev and Trollope: Brief Crossings of Paths," *AUMLA,* no. 42:200–204 (November, 1974); Leveson Gower, *Years of Content, 1858–1886* (London: John Murray, 1940), p. 105.

7. *Saturday Review* 56:306 (September 8, 1883).

8. N. John Hall, review of C. P. Snow's *Trollope: His Life and Art, Nineteenth-Century Fiction* 31:214–15 (September, 1976).

9. *Letters,* 2:931.

10. *Letters,* 2:937, 936.

11. *Letters,* 2:938–39.

12. [Cecilia E. Meetkerke], "Anthony Trollope," *Blackwood's Edinburgh Magazine* 133:320 (February, 1883) and "Last Reminiscences of Anthony Trollope," *Temple Bar* 70:134 (January, 1884).

13. *Castle Richmond,* chap. xli.

14. *Letters,* 2:929–30.

15. *Letters,* 2:932, 945–48.

16. *Letters,* 2:930.

17. *Letters,* 2:938, 941.

18. *Letters,* 2:921–22.

19. *Letters,* 2:935, 944–45, 949.

20. *Letters,* 2:961, 969, 973.

21. Freeman, "Anthony Trollope," *Macmillan's Magazine* 47:239 (January, 1883). W. L. Burn, professor of modern history at the University of Durham, in a discussion of "Anthony Trollope's Politics," finds his utterances explicitly parallel to those of Palmerston. Trollope "was a Liberal primarily because he was an optimist."—*Nineteenth Century and After* 143:169 (March, 1948).

22. *Saturday Review* 54:182–83 (August 5, 1882); sentence from the *Scotsman* quoted in Isbister's advertisement in the *Bookseller,* Christmas number, 1882, p. 90.

23. *Letters,* 2:940.

24. *Letters,* 2:935; presentation copy in the library of the University of Michigan. Martin was Prince Albert's biographer.

25. Bodleian, MS. Don. c. 10, fols. 150–51.

26. *Letters,* 2:957.

27. *Letters,* 2:958 (to the O'Conor Don, April 5, 1882).

28. *Letters,* 2:962–63, 978; Alfred Austin, *Autobiography* (London: Macmillan and Co., 1911), 1:180.

29. *Letters,* 2:962–67.

30. *Letters,* 2:1037, 977.

31. *Letters,* 2:976–82.

32. *Letters,* 2:901, 920, 933.

33. *Letters,* 2:961, 973; "Two Heroines," chap. i.

34. Advertisement in the *Bookseller,* November 6, 1882, p. 1126.

35. Bodleian, MSS. Don. c. 10*, fols. 23–24 and Don. c. 10, fol. 155; *Letters,* 2:957.

36. *Life,* November 16, 1882, p. 958; December 14, pp. 1037, 1044. Though Felbermann did not know Trollope personally, he had invited Anthony to dine at his house with some common friends, including Rusden from Australia and an acquaintance from South Africa, but Trollope's illness prevented his keeping the engagement.

37. *Letters,* 2:983–84n, 988.

38. *Letters,* 1:398n.

39. R. C. K. Ensor, *England, 1870–1914* (Oxford: Clarendon Press, 1936), pp. 53–57, 72–76.

40. Lilian Whiting, *Kate Field: A Record* (Boston, 1899), pp. 410, 11, 37–39. There is no mention of her seeing Trollope on this visit, but it is inconceivable that they did not meet.

41. *Letters,* 2:955.

42. *Letters,* 2:957, 959.

43. *Letters,* 2:985–86, 991.

44. *Letters,* 2:990–91.

45. Freeman, "Anthony Trollope," *Macmillan's Magazine* 47:239–40 (January, 1883).

46. *Letters,* 2:989, 1034, 941. The exclamation points are Trollope's.

47. *Letters,* 2:991–94; C. S. Dessain and Thomas Gornall, eds., *The Letters and Diaries of John Henry Newman* (Oxford: Clarendon Press, 1976), 30:154–55; 31:97*–98*.

48. Sir John A. C. Tilley, *London to Tokyo* (London: Hutchinson and Co., [1942]), p. 8.

49. J. B. Atkins, ed., *The Life of Sir William Howard Russell* (London: John Murray, 1911), 1:316–17.

50. *Letters,* 2:1039, 1036; *Times,* December 8, 1882, p. 1, col. 1 and p. 3, col. 6; Escott, *Trollope,* pp. 307–8.

51. Somerset House, Calendar of Probate, 1883, no. 86, and the will.

52. *Letters,* 2:987; R. H. Super, "Trollope at the Royal Literary Fund," *Nineteenth-Century Fiction* 37:326, 321 (December, 1982).

53. MS in the library of the University of Illinois; Minutes of the General Committee of the Royal Literary Fund, London.

54. Millais to Rose Trollope, Christmas Day, 1882; MS in the library of the University of Illinois.

55. For Henry's difficulties, see N. John Hall, "Seeing Trollope's *An Autobiography* through the Press," *Princeton University Library Chronicle* 47:189–223 (Winter, 1986).

56. Newton Arvin, ed., *Selected Letters of Henry Adams* (New York: Farrar, Straus and Young, 1951), p. 84 (dated "Washington, 23 January, 1883"—clearly an error).

57. Henry James, *Letters,* ed. Leon Edel (Cambridge, Mass.: Harvard University Press, 1980), 3:14.

58. *Christian World,* October 18, 1883, pp. 720–21. N. John Hall, in his study of the editing and publishing of the book, has assembled overwhelming evidence of the general public admiration of it.

59. "Anthony Trollope," *Partial Portraits,* pp. 100–101; review of Harriet

Elizabeth Prescott's *Azarian: an Episode, North American Review* 100:277 (January, 1865). James singled out for praise the very quality Julian Hawthorne held up as reprehensible.

60. Muriel Rose Trollope, "What I Was Told," *Trollopian* 2:235, 266 (March, 1948).

61. House of Commons, *Sessional Papers,* 1897, vol. 52:130; letter from Bernard Mallet to Austin in the library of the University of Illinois. At the same time the widow of the younger Charles Dickens was granted an identical pension on the same grounds.

62. Somerset House, Calendar of Probate and Letters of Administration, 1917.

63. *Times,* May 30, 1917, p. 3, col. 2.

64. Muriel Trollope, "What I Was Told," p. 230.

65. Letters (1977) from Katharine M. Longley of Holme on Spalding Moor, Yorkshire, to Mary Ceibert, Rare Book Room, University of Illinois Library; preserved there.

66. *Burke's Peerage,* 1967. The terms under which a title is passed on are set forth in the royal patent that bestows the title.

Index

GENERAL INDEX

A reference to a page of text may include the notes to that page.

ANTHONY TROLLOPE

Separately Published Works

Short Stories, Journalism, Lectures, Reports, Reviews, Dramas

Appearance, Character, Opinions, Writing Habits, etc.